The Future of Indigenous Inclusivity:

Unlocking Finance for Economic Development

Mohammad Irfan
Christ University, Bangalore, India

Mohammed Majeed
Tamale Technical University, Ghana

Salina Kassim
Institute of Islamic Banking and Finance, International Islamic University Malaysia, Malaysia

Kwame Simpe Ofori
International University of Grand Bassam, Cote D'Ivoire

IGI Global
Scientific Publishing
Publishing Tomorrow's Research Today

Vice President of Editorial	Melissa Wagner
Managing Editor of Acquisitions	Mikaela Felty
Managing Editor of Book Development	Jocelynn Hessler
Production Manager	Mike Brehm
Cover Design	Phillip Shickler

Published in the United States of America by
IGI Global Scientific Publishing
701 East Chocolate Avenue
Hershey, PA, 17033, USA
Tel: 717-533-8845
Fax: 717-533-8661
Website: https://www.igi-global.com E-mail: cust@igi-global.com

Library of Congress Cataloging-in-Publication Data

Names: Irfan, Mohammad, 1986- editor. | Mohammed, M. (Majeed), editor. | Kassim, Salina H., editor. | Ofori, Kwame, 1983- editor.
Title: The future of Indigenous inclusivity : unlocking finance for economic development / edited by: Mohammad Irfan, Mohammed Majeed, Salina Kassim, Kwame Simpe Ofori.
Other titles: Unlocking finance for economic development
Description: Hershey, PA : IGI Global Scientific Publishing, [2025] | Collection of essays by Rezvan Pourmansouri and others. | Includes bibliographical references and index. | Summary: "This book aims to strengthen the building blocks of indigenous business innovation and identify the place-based approach to indigenous economic development"-- Provided by publisher.
Identifiers: LCCN 2024053599 (print) | LCCN 2024053600 (ebook) | ISBN 9798369379240 (hardcover) | ISBN 9798369379257 (paperback) | ISBN 9798369379264 (ebook)
Subjects: LCSH: Indigenous peoples--Economic conditions. | Indigenous peoples--Finance. | Economic development. | Business--Technological innovations. | Transformational leadership.
Classification: LCC GN448 .F88 2025 (print) | LCC GN448 (ebook) | DDC 338.90089--dc23/eng/20250204
LC record available at https://lccn.loc.gov/2024053599
LC ebook record available at https://lccn.loc.gov/2024053600

British Cataloguing in Publication Data
A Cataloguing in Publication record for this book is available from the British Library.

Table of Contents

Detailed Table of Contents

This study examines how decentralized financial (DeFi) technologies could enhance financial inclusion and autonomy for India's indigenous communities by increasing their access to capital and financial services. Through surveys and interviews with key stakeholders, including community leaders, fintech experts, and policymakers, the research evaluates barriers to DeFi adoption, such as digital literacy, tech access, and regulatory limitations. It also explores DeFi's alignment with traditional practices via case studies showing how DeFi projects boost local entrepreneurship, market access, and economic growth. Global examples provide comparative insights into success factors and challenges, offering lessons for scaling DeFi in rural and semi-urban indigenous areas. The paper ends with policy recommendations to develop infrastructure and regulations essential for robust DeFi ecosystems, aiming to create a more inclusive financial landscape that integrates indigenous economies into India's broader economic structure

The book chapter provides an overview of the regulatory and legal implications surrounding the integration of blockchain technology and digital twins for sustainable investments. The fusion of these technologies offers immense potential for transparency, accountability, and efficiency in achieving sustainable economic and environmental goals. However, it also introduces several challenges which need to be addressed in order to ensure a secure and reliable environment for investors. It also explores the regulatory frameworks required to balance transparency and privacy, the enforceability and interpretation of smart contracts, tokenization regulations, cross-border investments, and cybersecurity considerations. Through an analysis of these implications, it becomes evident that collaboration between governments, regulatory bodies, and industry stakeholders is crucial in developing comprehensive frameworks that protect investor rights while embracing the benefits of blockchain-digital twin fusion.

Robo-advisory services gained momentum due to data-driven patterns in financial advisory services. AI helps RAS in fine tuning for sustainable adoption. The present exploratory research helps in understanding the extent of penetration of RA services in financial advisory market and to test this a self-administered structured questionnaire is circulated to individual investors utilizing the RAS with various advisory firms. Partial correlation is calculated to find out the link between role of technology, robo advisory service firms and AI in driving individuals for their financial decisions. Results indicate that technology, RAS, and AI have influence, but AI still cannot change the quality of RAS and is not a replacement to human advisory.

This chapter explores the integration of advanced financial technologies and strategic economic practices to foster sustainable development in Indigenous communities. The integrated approach ensures that indigenous communities can make well-informed, strategic decisions that drive sustainable development. The chapter also addresses the ethical considerations and potential challenges associated with implementing financial monitoring and investment prediction in indigenous economies. It highlights the need for policies that promote access to financial services, protect indigenous rights, and encourage sustainable investment practices. Collaboration between governments, financial institutions, and indigenous communities is essential to create an enabling environment for economic empowerment and sustainable development. The chapter calls for a collaborative, culturally sensitive approach to implementing these strategies, ensuring that Indigenous communities can harness the power of financial monitoring and investment prediction to achieve sustainable development goals.

The intersection of indigenous knowledge and artificial intelligence in financial technology offers a unique opportunity to blend traditional wisdom with cutting-edge technology. This collaboration has the potential to revolutionize the way financial systems are designed and implemented. It can also lead to more inclusive and sustainable financial solutions for indigenous communities. Furthermore, the incorporation of indigenous knowledge can provide a more holistic approach to financial technology. This can result in better understanding and addressing the unique financial needs of indigenous communities. Additionally, incorporating indigenous knowledge into AI algorithms can lead to more culturally sensitive and inclusive financial technology solutions. This can help in addressing the needs of diverse communities and promoting financial inclusion. Indigenous communities by incorporating traditional knowledge and values into AI-driven financial technologies.

Using the Technology Acceptance Model as a foundation, this paper explains the prospect of leveraging the Point of Sale (PoS) agent banking business model as a viable avenue for empowering rural households to engage with the prevailing credit-driven economic landscape, more comprehensively. A non-parametric analysis performed on an 845 data structure, primarily derived from participants, demonstrates that four out of six indicators (adaptability, cost-effective, ease of use, and user satisfaction) delineated to gauge the model's applicability in rural areas received approval, significantly exceeding the test value or threshold. In contrast, accessibility of the model is significantly skewed to the negative direction while compatibility does not indicate a significant difference, suggesting that its mean is consistent with the test value. While the result promises a solution, an exploratory interrogation around the model's accessibility and compatibility can enhance its swift implementation and uptake.

This chapter examines how these relationships promote inclusivity and sustainable development. We examine traditional and modern economic practices to provide a comprehensive overview of indigenous economic interactions. This chapter relies on a robust literature review to find and analyse relevant studies. Synthesising key themes and trends clarifies indigenous economic relationship and service supplier research. The review includes case studies of successful partnerships and indigenous communities' struggles to access and use services. These case studies reveal best practises and adaptable strategies. The chapter concludes with policy recommendations to improve service provider engagement with indigenous communities. It stresses the need for policies that support these communities' unique economic systems and needs. Strengthening economic relationships and ensuring service suppliers are responsive to indigenous perspectives can open new economic development and inclusivity opportunities.

This study uses bibliometric analysis to assess the current state and potential of sustainable and socially responsible investments. The study initially considered 550 papers indexed in the Scopus database and published between 2010 and 2024. The study contributes to the body of knowledge in the fields of socially responsible investment and sustainable investing by employing three approaches: (1) identifying the most influential articles, (2) visually illustrating the characteristics and trends using network analysis, and (3) combining diverse research areas to identify potential avenues for future exploration. To attain these goals, we use bibliometric analysis, which evaluates the accomplishments of significant authors, countries, highly cited papers, journals, and co-word charts. Biblioshiny R and VOSviewer evaluated the keyword analysis of 234 papers finally screened. The study is limited to the Scopus database because it is one of the popular databases. This study provides a complete overview of socially responsible investment funds' research nature and trends.

The chapter "The Future of Indigenous Inclusivity: Unlocking Finance for Economic Development" emphasizes the need to integrate Indigenous communities into economic development. It addresses historical and current obstacles faced by Indigenous peoples, including structural hurdles, socioeconomic gaps, and geographic limitations. The chapter offers strategies for capacity building, customized financial products, and policy changes to improve financial inclusion. It also highlights the importance of technology and multi-stakeholder partnerships for economic empowerment. The chapter emphasizes the need for creative funding methods and international cooperation to fully realize Indigenous communities' economic potential and create a more equitable global economy.

This study is aimed at bridging finance gap of Micro Small and Medium Enterprises (MSMEs) in India despite their large contribution to GDP and employment, by studying alternative financing mechanisms. It also looks at new instruments of the like- crowdfunding, fintech solutions, supply chain financing, and

This book chapter explores and analyses two important areas that have been postulated as central to economic development and sustainable economic growth: local participation and access to finance. Regardless of having a wealthy background and the physical capital developed over thousands of years of living in Australia, Aboriginal people still encounter great hurdles when trying to obtain financial capital, and therefore face great constraints on finding ways to improve their status and living conditions. In this paper, the current financial accounting systems are reviewed and other new financial models for Indigenous people are discussed, including social capital and enterprise. Understanding the measures in the Government policy, cooperation and partnership with the private sector, we develop concept of open Finance where hopeful and important people are. 'When there is a problem,' this paper also indicates how this research is promoting independent lives while also taking care of the environment and society in Aboriginal communities.

In the last two decades, there has been a continuous innovation in the field of AI and it has been adopted in different fields inclusive of finance. At the same time, numerous works have been published exploring the use of AI in the sphere of financial services. The objective of this work is to review the available literature and discuss gaps in the body of knowledge on this subject. For this purpose, bibliometric and content analysis techniques were used on a number of articles available from 1990 to July 2024. The bibliometric technique was employed to classify core fields and productivity in FinTech research, though using VosViewer and Biblioshiny to offer maps regarding top authors, sources, countries, scientific developments, and concepts.

The research investigates the effect of natural resources on climate change and the role inclusive finance plays in the natural resource-climate change nexus among thirty-two resource-rich African countries from 2004-2022. Data acquired from World Development Indicator Database and International Monetary Fund Database are analyzed using the heterogeneous dynamic Pooled Mean Group estimation technique. The research demonstrates that natural resources negatively but insignificantly impact climate change.

Also, inclusive finance negatively but significantly impacts climate change in the long run. Finally, the interactive effect of natural resource and climate change have a negative and significant effect on climate change among the selected resource-rich African nations. The findings show that inclusive finance is very key in enabling resource-rich African countries to adapt sufficiently to and fight climate change. From these findings, the study recommends priority toward the development of inclusive financial systems by policymakers in resource-rich countries in Africa.

Preface

Indigenous communities find themselves at the nexus of tradition and modernity in a world that is changing quickly. They are looking for ways to engage with new economic opportunities while preserving their cultural legacy. They are essential contributors to the sustainable development agenda because of their distinct knowledge systems and unrealized economic potential. Nevertheless, despite their tenacity, Indigenous people frequently encounter structural obstacles that keep them out of the mainstream financial and commercial systems.

*The book titled**"The Future of Indigenous Inclusivity: Unlocking Finance for Economic Development"*** explores the intersection of finance, technology, and sustainability, with a focus on empowering Indigenous communities. This book explores how inclusive economic practices, decentralized financial technologies, and artificial intelligence can close gaps, unleash potential, and pave the road for long-term, sustainable growth. To guarantee that these communities are engaged participants in their development process, it highlights the necessity of cooperation between legislators, scholars, financial institutions, and Indigenous leaders.

Every chapter in this book delves deeply into current problems and creative fixes. From the role of decentralized finance in promoting economic inclusion in India to the revolutionary potential of artificial intelligence in financial advice services, the conversations are grounded in both theory and practice. While the studies demonstrate effective applications of inclusive policies, bibliometric analyses provide insight into worldwide research trends. When taken as a whole, they provide a path forward for resolving structural injustices and building resilience in Indigenous economies.

Chapter 1: A Study on Decentralized Financial Technologies and Indigenous Economies in Indian Context

This study examines how decentralized financial (DeFi) technologies could enhance financial inclusion and autonomy for India's indigenous communities by increasing their access to capital and financial services. Through surveys and interviews with key stakeholders, including community leaders, fintech experts, and policymakers, the research evaluates barriers to DeFi adoption, such as digital literacy, tech access, and regulatory limitations. It also explores DeFi's alignment with traditional practices via case studies showing how DeFi projects boost local entrepreneurship, market access, and economic growth. Global examples provide comparative insights into success factors and challenges, offering lessons for scaling DeFi in rural and semi-urban indigenous areas. The paper ends with policy recommendations to develop infrastructure and regulations essential for robust DeFi ecosystems, aiming to create a more inclusive financial landscape that integrates indigenous economies into India's broader economic structure

Chapter 2: Regulatory and Legal Implications on Harnessing Blockchain-Digital Twin Fusion for Sustainable Investments

The book chapter provides an overview of the regulatory and legal implications surrounding the integration of blockchain technology and digital twins for sustainable investments. The fusion of these technologies offers immense potential for transparency, accountability, and efficiency in achieving sustainable economic and environmental goals. However, it also introduces several challenges which requires to be addressed in order to ensure a secure and reliable environment for investors. It also explores the regulatory frameworks required to balance transparency and privacy, the enforceability and interpretation of smart contracts, tokenization regulations, cross-border investments, and cybersecurity considerations. Through an analysis of these implications, it becomes evident that collaboration between governments, regulatory bodies, and industry stakeholders is crucial in developing comprehensive frameworks that protect investor rights while embracing the benefits of blockchain-digital twin fusion.

Chapter 3: Robo-Advisory in the Era of AI: An Overview

Robo-advisory services gained momentum due to data driven pattern in financial advisory services. AI helps RAS in fine tuning for a sustainable adoption. The present exploratory research helps in understanding the extent of penetration of RA services in financial advisory market and to test this a self-administered structured questionnaire is circulated to individual investors utilizing the RAS with various advisory firms. Partial correlation is calculated to find out the link between role of technology, robo advisory service firms and AI in driving individuals for their financial decisions. Results indicate, technology, RAS and AI have influence, but AI still cannot change the quality of RAS and is not a replacement to human advisory.

Chapter 4: Empowering Indigenous Economies: Financial and Investment Prediction for Sustainable Development

This chapter explores the integration of advanced financial technologies and strategic economic practices to foster sustainable development in Indigenous communities. The integrated approach ensures that indigenous communities can make well-informed, strategic decisions that drive sustainable development. The chapter also addresses the ethical considerations and potential challenges associated with implementing financial monitoring and investment prediction in indigenous economies. It highlights the need for policies that promote access to financial services, protect indigenous rights, and encourage sustainable investment practices. Collaboration between governments, financial institutions, and indigenous communities is essential to create an enabling environment for economic empowerment and sustainable development. The chapter calls for a collaborative, culturally sensitive approach to implementing these strategies, ensuring that Indigenous communities can harness the power of financial monitoring and investment prediction to achieve sustainable development goals.

Chapter 5: The Intersection of Indigenous Knowledge and Artificial Intelligence in Financial Technology

The intersection of indigenous knowledge and artificial intelligence in financial technology offers a unique opportunity to blend traditional wisdom with cutting-edge technology. This collaboration has the potential to revolutionize the way financial systems are designed and implemented. It can also lead to more inclusive and sustainable financial solutions for indigenous communities. Furthermore, the incorporation of indigenous knowledge can provide a more holistic approach to financial technology. This can result in better understanding and addressing the unique financial needs of indigenous communities. Additionally, incorporating indigenous knowledge into AI algorithms can lead to more culturally sensitive and inclusive financial technology solutions. This can help in addressing the needs of diverse communities and promoting financial inclusion. Indigenous communities by incorporating traditional knowledge and values into AI-driven financial technologies.

Chapter 6: POS Agent Banking Enterprise for Indigenous Finance in Rural Areas: A Conformity Analysis

Using the Technology Acceptance Model as a foundation, this paper endeavors to expound upon the prospect of leveraging the Point of Sale (PoS) agent banking business model as a viable avenue for empowering rural households to engage with the prevailing credit-driven economic landscape, more comprehensively. A non-parametric analysis performed on an 845 data structure, primarily derived from participants, demonstrates that four out of six indicators (adaptability, cost-effective, ease of use, and user satisfaction) delineated to gauge the model's applicability in rural areas received approval, significantly exceeding the test value or threshold. In contrast, accessibility of the model is significantly skewed to the negative direction while compatibility does not indicate a significant difference, suggesting that its mean is consistent with the test value. While the result promises a solution, an exploratory interrogation around the model's accessibility and compatibility can enhance its swift implementation and uptake.

Chapter 7: Strengthening Economic Relationships and Service Supplier Engagement: Pathways to Indigenous Inclusivity and Sustainable Development

This chapter examines how these relationships promote inclusivity and sustainable development. We examine traditional and modern economic practices to provide a comprehensive overview of indigenous economic interactions. This chapter relies on a robust literature review to find and analyse relevant studies. Synthesising key themes and trends clarifies indigenous economic relationship and service supplier research. The review includes case studies of successful partnerships and indigenous communities' struggles to access and use services. These case studies reveal best practises and adaptable strategies. The chapter concludes with policy recommendations to improve service provider engagement with indigenous communities. It stresses the need for policies that support these communities' unique economic systems and needs. Strengthening economic relationships and ensuring service suppliers are responsive to indigenous perspectives can open new economic development and inclusivity opportunities.

Chapter 8: A Bibliometric Analysis of Sustainable Investment and Socially Responsible Investors-Trends and Insights

This study uses bibliometric analysis to assess the current state and potential of sustainable and socially responsible investments. The study initially considered 550 papers indexed in the Scopus database and published between 2010 and 2024. The study contributes to the body of knowledge in the fields of socially responsible investment and sustainable investing by employing three approaches: (1) identifying the most influential articles, (2) visually illustrating the characteristics and trends using network analysis, and (3) combining diverse research areas to identify potential avenues for future exploration. To attain these goals, we use bibliometric analysis, which evaluates the accomplishments of significant authors, countries, highly cited papers, journals, and co-word charts. Biblioshiny R and VOSviewer evaluated the keyword analysis of 234 papers finally screened. The study is limited to the Scopus database because it is one of the popular databases. This study provides a complete overview of socially responsible investment funds' research nature and trends.

Chapter 9: The Future of Indigenous Inclusivity: Unlocking Finance for Economic Development

The chapter "The Future of Indigenous Inclusivity: Unlocking Finance for Economic Development" emphasizes the need to integrate Indigenous communities into economic development. It addresses historical and current obstacles faced by Indigenous peoples, including structural hurdles, socioeconomic gaps, and geographic limitations. The chapter offers strategies for capacity building, customized financial products, and policy changes to improve financial inclusion. It also highlights the importance of technology and multi-stakeholder partnerships for economic empowerment. The chapter emphasizes the need for creative funding methods and international cooperation to fully realize Indigenous communities' economic potential and create a more equitable global economy.

Chapter 10: Alternative Financing Mechanisms: Increase Access to Finance for MSMEs in India

This study is aimed at bridging finance gap of Micro Small and Medium Enterprises (MSMEs) in India despite their large contribution to GDP and employment, by studying alternative financing mechanisms. It also looks at new instruments of the like- crowdfunding, fintech solutions, supply chain financing, and venture capital. The paper examines how alternative credit evaluation techniques and digital lending, along with public private collaborations are transforming MSME financing. The paper examines the challenges of putting these mechanisms in place and the potential they have to spur financial inclusion and economic growth. An overview of these financing options is provided through a conceptual framework and descriptive analysis of their concepts, uses and descriptive levels. Finally, the paper presents a study of the potential strategies that can enhance MSMEs' access to finance in India by providing innovative financial products to fill the huge financing gap for such firms.

Chapter 11: Understanding the Intellectual Contribution on Sustainable Development Goals A Scientometric and Thematic Assessment of Scientific Database

The present study investigates the intellectual contribution of researchers, academicians, and industry experts on sustainable development goals. In the era of cut-throat competition companies across the globe wants to occupy top most position in the competition and have their dominance across the globe. This quench of profit and dominance resulting in exploitation of resources and affecting global environment across the globe. The gap between rich and poor is increasing day by day. The world is divided between rich and poor economies where the access and privileges of resources is concentrated in the hand of few. From 1972 till today different initiatives are taken at global level in order to address such global challenges. The formation of SDG is made by United Nations in the year 2016 is one of the breakthroughs in this process.

Chapter 12: Indigenous Empowerment as a Catalyst for Sustainable Development

Indigenous empowerment is a process of recognizing and supporting the rights, knowledge, and self-determination of indigenous communities. It acknowledges their unique perspectives, cultural heritage, and sustainable practices that have sustained their communities for generations. This chapter explores the challenges and importance of indigenous empowerment for achieving sustainable development and fostering a more inclusive and equitable society. This empowerment is not just about justice and rights but a strategic path to sustainable development. Collaborative partnerships among indigenous groups, governments, civil societies, and stakeholders are vital for promoting empowerment and addressing indigenous peoples' interconnected challenges. This chapter highlighted successful initiatives led by indigenous communities with significant progress in advancing the SDGs and fostering genuine partnerships that respect indigenous knowledge and promote cultural diversity is crucial for sustainable development that leaves no one behind.

Chapter 13: Fostering Indigenous Inclusivity Financial Pathways to Economic Development and Sustainability

Indigenous empowerment is a process of recognizing and supporting the rights, knowledge, and self-determination of indigenous communities. It acknowledges their unique perspectives, cultural heritage, and sustainable practices that have sustained their communities for generations. This chapter explores the challenges and importance of indigenous empowerment for achieving sustainable development and fostering a more inclusive and equitable society. This empowerment is not just about justice and rights but a strategic path to sustainable development. Collaborative partnerships among indigenous groups, governments, civil societies, and stakeholders are vital for promoting empowerment and addressing indigenous peoples' interconnected challenges. This chapter highlighted successful initiatives led by indigenous communities with significant progress in advancing the SDGs and fostering genuine partnerships that respect indigenous knowledge and promote cultural diversity is crucial for sustainable development that leaves no one behind.

Chapter 14: The Technology Disruptor Artificial Intelligence in Finance Domain: A Bibliometric Analysis

In the last two decades, there has been a continuous innovation in the field of AI and it has been adopted in different fields inclusive of finance. At the same time, numerous works have been published exploring the use of AI in the sphere of financial services. The objective of this work is to review the available literature and discuss gaps in the body of knowledge on this subject. For this purpose, bibliometric and content analysis techniques were used on a number of articles available from 1990 to July 2024. The bibliometric technique was employed to classify core fields and productivity in FinTech research, though using VosViewer and Biblioshiny to offer maps regarding top authors, sources, countries, scientific developments, and concepts.

Chapter 15: Natural Resources and Climate Change in Resource Rich African Countries: The Role of Inclusive Finance

The research investigates the effect of natural resources on climate change and the role inclusive finance plays in the natural resource-climate change nexus among thirty-two resource-rich African countries from 2004-2022. Data acquired from World Development Indicator Database and International Monetary Fund Database are analyzed using the heterogeneous dynamic Pooled Mean Group estimation technique. The research demonstrates that natural resource negatively but insignificantly impacts climate change. Also, inclusive finance negatively but significantly impacts climate change in the long-run. Finally, the interactive effect of natural resource and climate change have a negative and significant effect on climate change among the selected resource-rich African nations. The findings show that inclusive finance is very key in enabling resource-rich African countries to adapt sufficiently to and fight climate change. From these findings, the study recommends priority toward the development of inclusive financial systems by policymakers in resource-rich countries in Africa.

This work is the result of investigation, introspection, and dedication to sustainability and inclusivity. It is evidence of the ability of knowledge and teamwork to bring about significant change. As we embark on this journey toward economic inclusivity, I am reminded of the words of Muhammad Yunus, Nobel Peace Prize laureate, who once said:

> "The goal is not to make money, but to create a world where everyone has the opportunity to live with dignity, respect, and access to financial independence."

I would like to extend my deepest gratitude to my family. To my parents, whose unwavering encouragement, wisdom, and values have shaped my perspective and inspired my work. Your love and support have been my foundation. To my beautiful wife, whose constant support, patience, and belief in me have made everything possible. Your strength and partnership have been my guiding light. To my intelligent daughter, whose curiosity, creativity, and passion for learning constantly inspire me. You remind me daily of the endless possibilities that lie ahead. And to my handsome son, whose energy, joy, and optimism fill my life with happiness and motivation. Together, you all keep me grounded and motivated to make a positive difference in the world.

This book is dedicated to them and to all those working tirelessly to create a world where inclusivity and equity are not aspirations but realities.

Mohammad Irfan

Christ University, Bangalore, India

Majeed Mohammed
Tamale Technical University, Ghana

Salina Kassim
International Islamic University Malaysia

Kwame Ofori
International University of Grand-Bassam, Côte d'Ivoire

Chapter 1
A Study on Decentralized Financial Technologies and Indigenous Economies in Indian Context

Jayadatta Shreepad
https://orcid.org/0000-0001-8763-6922
Karnatak University, India

Mohammed Majeed
https://orcid.org/0000-0001-9804-5335
Tamale Technical University, Ghana

Sharad Gupta
https://orcid.org/0000-0002-4994-3523
Christ University, Bangalore

Manish Kumar Upadhyay
Rajiv Academy for Technology and Management Mathura, India

ABSTRACT

This study examines how decentralized financial (DeFi) technologies could enhance financial inclusion and autonomy for India's indigenous communities by increasing their access to capital and financial services. Through surveys and interviews with key stakeholders, including community leaders, fintech experts, and policymakers, the research evaluates barriers to DeFi adoption, such as digital literacy, tech access, and regulatory limitations. It also explores DeFi's alignment with traditional practices via case studies showing how DeFi projects boost local entrepreneurship, market access, and economic growth. Global examples provide comparative insights into success factors and challenges, offering lessons for scaling DeFi in rural and semi-urban indigenous areas. The paper ends with policy recommendations to develop infrastructure and regulations essential for robust DeFi ecosystems, aiming to create a more inclusive financial landscape that integrates indigenous economies into India's broader economic structure

DOI: 10.4018/979-8-3693-7924-0.ch001

INTRODUCTION

The innovative intersection of decentralized financial technologies (DeFi) and indigenous economies in India represents a promising frontier for fostering economic inclusivity and autonomy, offering the potential leveraging blockchain technology and cryptocurrencies to dismantle traditional barriers to capital and financial participation, thus facilitating a more equitable economic landscape that empowers marginalized communities; through a comprehensive examination of the current penetration and adoption of DeFi among indigenous communities, it becomes evident that these technologies can provide unprecedented opportunities for local entrepreneurship, access to markets, and robust economic outcomes, particularly when tailored to align with the unique economic practices and cultural needs of these communities, yet, this transformative potential is not without its challenges, as the adaptation of DeFi technologies is frequently hindered by obstacles such as technological accessibility, digital literacy, and the existing regulatory frameworks that can stifle innovation to address these barriers and to create a supportive environment for DeFi integration, which is imperative for the scalability of decentralized financial solutions in rural and semi-urban indigenous settings in India (Schar, 2021; Catalini & Gans, 2020). The study, as highlighted, delves into the nuanced landscape of DeFi adoption by conducting extensive surveys across multiple indigenous communities in India and engaging in in-depth interviews with a range of stakeholders, including community leaders, financial technology experts, and policymakers, aiming to generate a comprehensive understanding of the factors influencing DeFi penetration and effectiveness, with particular emphasis on identifying and overcoming the critical barriers that impede the widespread acceptance of blockchain technologies and cryptocurrencies within these communities (Narayanan et al., 2016; Wright & De Filippi, 2015), such an understanding is essential, as it provides the basis for developing strategic approaches that align DeFi innovations with traditional economic practices, thus ensuring that these technologies are not merely imposed as foreign solutions but are integrated in a manner that resonates with the local cultural and socio-economic context, facilitating not only economic opportunities but also the preservation of indigenous identities and values (Tapscott & Tapscott, 2016; Mougayar, 2016).

The potential of DeFi to drive economic inclusivity is exemplified by numerous case studies that illustrate how these technologies have contributed to enhanced local entrepreneurship and increased access to markets in various global contexts, offering valuable lessons for the implementation of similar initiatives in India, by examining such precedents, the study aims to extract insights into the success factors and pitfalls of DeFi adoption in indigenous settings, providing a comparative analysis that underscores the importance of a supportive regulatory environment, robust digital infrastructure, and tailored financial literacy programs, which are critical for the effective deployment and sustainability of decentralized financial systems (Fanning & Centers, 2016; Zohar, 2015), these insights are pivotal, as they not only inform the design and implementation of DeFi projects but also shape policy recommendations aimed at enhancing the infrastructure and regulatory conditions necessary for the flourishing of decentralized financial systems in indigenous communities, advocating for policies that support innovation while safeguarding against potential risks, such as financial fraud and exploitation, which are inherent in the digital finance landscape (Catalini & Gans, 2019; Davidson et al., 2016). The study also discusses how collaborative actions between government entities, financial institutions and technology providers are crucial to success through the formation of multi-stakeholder partnerships to scale DeFi solutions enabling indigenous economies by mobilizing the resources, technology and expertise needed to create the infrastructure, build digital literacy and develop regulatory frameworks that ensure both innovation AND consumer interests are protected (Swan, 2015; Scott, 2016), In addition, at the same time by radicalizing financial inclusion through integrating DeFi into bottom sector, the research proposes a better financial capitalism where indigenous communities could not only access to the financial services but also join in and build up the national economy so that a more inclusive generation of economic equipment is available to be resistant and adaptive to the unpredictable transactions in fast-moving world (Narayanan et al., 2016; Wright & De Filippi, 2015). In conclusion, this research underscores the transformative potential of decentralized financial technologies in empowering indigenous economies by providing insights into the critical factors that influence DeFi adoption and effectiveness, advocating for the strategic alignment of these technologies with local needs and traditional practices, and offering policy recommendations to create an enabling environment for the growth of DeFi in rural and semi-urban settings in India, ultimately contributing to the goal of financial inclusivity and economic resilience, the integration of DeFi into indigenous economies not only presents an opportunity for economic empowerment but also for the reimagining of financial systems that are inclusive, equitable, and reflective of the communities they serve (Schar, 2021; Tapscott & Tapscott, 2016; Catalini & Gans, 2020).

Statement of the Research Problem

The research problem underpinning this study revolves around the pressing need to understand how decentralized financial technologies (DeFi), such as blockchain and cryptocurrencies, can be effectively integrated into indigenous economies within the Indian context to foster economic inclusivity, enhance financial autonomy, and mitigate economic disparities, given that indigenous populations often face significant barriers to financial services access, including technological limitations, low levels of digital literacy, and restrictive regulatory frameworks that prevent the widespread adoption of DeFi solutions, making it imperative to investigate the current levels of DeFi penetration and adaptation in these communities, to identify the critical challenges and opportunities for leveraging these technologies to empower indigenous populations by enabling them to participate more fully in the national economy, and to explore strategic ways to align DeFi with traditional economic practices and local needs, so as to support sustainable economic development, increased access to capital, and greater market participation, as well as to analyze global case studies and draw comparative insights that could inform the successful deployment of DeFi solutions tailored to the specific socio-economic conditions of India's indigenous communities, with the ultimate goal of developing policy recommendations and frameworks that can facilitate the growth and scalability of decentralized financial systems in these settings, thereby promoting a more equitable and inclusive financial landscape that integrates indigenous economies into the broader economic fabric of the country (Narayanan et al., 2016; Schar, 2021; Tapscott & Tapscott, 2016; Catalini & Gans, 2020), this research, therefore, seeks to address the gap in understanding how DeFi can be harnessed to not only enhance the financial autonomy of indigenous populations but also to foster resilience against economic disparities, advocating for the radicalization of financial inclusivity in marginalized sectors by proposing a set of evidence-based policy measures to create a supportive regulatory environment and infrastructure necessary for the flourishing of decentralized financial technologies in rural and semi-urban indigenous settings in India (Davidson et al., 2016; Zohar, 2015; Mougayar, 2016).

Research Gap Related to the Study

The research gap addressed by this study on the integration of decentralized financial technologies (DeFi) into indigenous economies within the Indian context revolves around the limited empirical understanding of how blockchain and cryptocurrency solutions can be effectively tailored to meet the unique socio-economic conditions and traditional practices of indigenous communities, as current literature predominantly focuses on the broader applications of DeFi in global financial systems and developed economies, overlooking the specific barriers to adoption such as low digital literacy, technological infrastructure limitations, and regulatory challenges that are prevalent in rural and semi-urban indigenous settings, which hinder the full realization of DeFi's potential to provide financial inclusivity and autonomy to marginalized populations, thus necessitating targeted research that examines the actual penetration and impact of DeFi technologies within these communities, identifies the specific obstacles they face, and explores culturally sensitive approaches to integrating DeFi with local economic practices, including the development of tailored digital literacy programs and supportive regulatory frameworks that can foster an enabling environment for DeFi adoption, ultimately contributing to a more inclusive financial landscape that not only empowers indigenous populations but also aligns with their socio-cultural values and economic needs (Gomber et al., 2017; Auer et al.2020; Harvey et al., 2021). The study aims to address this research gap by examining how DeFi solutions can optimize for scaling and sustainability in indigenous economies with respect to policy interventions, community-initiatives as well as farmer-centric partnerships around use cases that enable economic resilience and economic inclusion of Indian farmers through the successful integration of decentralized financial technologies into their economy (Fanning & Centers, 2016; Chen et al., 2019; Chiu & Koeppl, 2019).

Methodology Adopted for the Purpose of Study

This study includes qualitative research methods to provide an in-depth examination of the degree of penetration, adoption and impact of decentralized financial technologies (DeFi) among indigenous economies in the Indian context, through large surveys on the levels of awareness, usage and accessibility to blockchain technologies and cryptocurrencies available to these communities, coupled with in-depth qualitative interviews with key stakeholders such as community leaders, financial technology experts, and policymakers to gain insights into the cultural, social, and regulatory factors that influence DeFi adoption, thereby enabling a nuanced understanding of the critical barriers and enablers for integrating decentralized financial solutions into indigenous economic practices, this approach is further supplemented by case studies of successful DeFi implementations in similar global indigenous contexts, which provide comparative insights and help to identify best practices and potential pitfalls, with the ultimate aim of formulating strategic recommendations for enhancing digital literacy, improving technological infrastructure, and developing supportive regulatory frameworks that facilitate the scalability and sustainability of DeFi in these communities (Patil, 2021; Leins, 2022; Shevchuk & Takacs, 2022), the research captures the issues at hand, providing a robust empirical foundation for understanding how decentralized financial technologies can empower indigenous populations and promote economic inclusivity in the Indian context (Ahn, 2021; Allen, 2022; Haffke et al., 2020).

Major Objectives Related to the Study

1. To assess the current penetration and adoption levels of decentralized financial technologies, including blockchain and cryptocurrencies, within indigenous communities in India
2. To identify the key barriers and challenges, such as technological accessibility, digital literacy, and regulatory frameworks, that affect the adoption and effectiveness of decentralized financial technologies in indigenous economies
3. To explore strategic ways to align decentralized financial technologies with traditional economic practices and local needs to enhance economic opportunities for indigenous communities
4. To provide policy recommendations for improving the infrastructure and regulatory conditions necessary for the successful implementation and scalability of decentralized financial technologies in rural and semi-urban indigenous settings in India

CURRENT PENETRATION AND ADOPTION LEVELS OF DECENTRALIZED FINANCIAL TECHNOLOGIES, INCLUDING BLOCKCHAIN AND CRYPTOCURRENCIES, WITHIN INDIGENOUS COMMUNITIES IN INDIA

The current penetration and adoption levels of decentralized financial technologies (DeFi), including blockchain and cryptocurrencies, within indigenous communities in India, as addressed by this study, remain limited due to a combination of factors such as low digital literacy rates, inadequate technological infrastructure, and restrictive regulatory environments that pose significant barriers to the effective utilization of these technologies, despite the transformative potential of DeFi to provide these communities with unprecedented access to capital and financial services, thereby fostering economic inclusivity and autonomy, the majority of indigenous populations continue to face challenges in understanding and using these advanced financial tools, with digital literacy being a critical issue, as many community members lack the necessary skills and knowledge to engage with blockchain-based financial platforms or navigate the complexities of cryptocurrency transactions, furthermore, technological accessibility is a persistent concern, with many rural and semi-urban areas lacking the requisite internet connectivity and digital devices that are essential for participating in the DeFi ecosystem, which results in a digital divide that exacerbates existing economic disparities, and while some efforts have been made to introduce decentralized financial solutions in these settings, their impact has been limited, and adoption rates remain low due to the lack of tailored educational programs and outreach initiatives that can bridge the knowledge gap and build trust in these technologies among indigenous users, additionally, regulatory uncertainties and the absence of clear guidelines for the use of DeFi further hinder its adoption, as potential users and service providers remain wary of legal and financial repercussions, this scenario underscores the need for comprehensive strategies that address these challenges, including targeted digital literacy initiatives, investment in digital infrastructure, and the development of supportive regulatory frameworks that encourage the use of decentralized financial technologies in a manner that aligns with the socio-economic realities of indigenous communities in India (Rao & Kumar, 2021; Bhagat & Raju, 2022; Subramanian & Chinnappa, 2023), therefore, understanding and improving the current levels of DeFi penetration and adoption is crucial for leveraging these technologies to empower indigenous populations to participate in the national economy (Gupta & Sharma, 2022; Mehta & Saini, 2021).

KEY BARRIERS AND CHALLENGES, SUCH AS TECHNOLOGICAL ACCESSIBILITY, DIGITAL LITERACY, AND REGULATORY FRAMEWORKS, THAT AFFECT THE ADOPTION AND EFFECTIVENESS OF DECENTRALIZED FINANCIAL TECHNOLOGIES IN INDIGENOUS ECONOMIES

The adoption and effectiveness of decentralized financial technologies (DeFi) in indigenous economies within the Indian context are significantly hindered by a range of key barriers and challenges, including technological accessibility, digital literacy, and regulatory frameworks, which collectively impact the ability of these communities to leverage the benefits of blockchain technologies and cryptocurrencies, as the majority of indigenous regions are located in rural and semi-urban areas where digital infrastructure is underdeveloped, resulting in limited access to the internet and digital devices, which are essential for engaging with DeFi platforms, this lack of technological accessibility not only prevents these populations from using decentralized financial services but also exacerbates the digital divide, further marginalizing these communities from the mainstream economy, moreover, digital literacy remains a substantial challenge, as many individuals within indigenous communities lack the basic knowledge and skills required to navigate the complexities of DeFi technologies, creating a barrier to entry that restricts their participation in decentralized financial ecosystems, even when technological access is available, the absence of targeted educational programs that address the specific needs and contexts of these communities hampers their ability to utilize DeFi effectively, in addition to technological and educational barriers, the regulatory environment poses significant challenges to the adoption of DeFi in indigenous economies, with the lack of clear, supportive regulations leading to uncertainty and reluctance among potential users and service providers, who fear the legal and financial risks associated with operating in an ambiguous regulatory landscape, this uncertainty is compounded by the perception of decentralized financial technologies as being inherently risky, due to concerns over fraud, security, and volatility, which are often cited as reasons for the hesitancy of both individuals and institutions to engage with DeFi, these barriers underscore the need for a comprehensive approach that includes improving digital infrastructure, implementing culturally sensitive digital literacy initiatives, and establishing clear, supportive regulatory frameworks that encourage innovation while protecting users, thus enhancing the adoption and effectiveness of decentralized financial technologies in indigenous economies in India (Singh & Bansal, 2023; Raj & Patel, 2022; Narayan & Verma, 2021), addressing these challenges is crucial for ensuring that indigenous populations can access the benefits of DeFi and participate more fully in the national and global economies (Kumar & Das, 2022; Soni & Mishra, 2023).

STRATEGIC WAYS TO ALIGN DECENTRALIZED FINANCIAL TECHNOLOGIES WITH TRADITIONAL ECONOMIC PRACTICES AND LOCAL NEEDS TO ENHANCE ECONOMIC OPPORTUNITIES FOR INDIGENOUS COMMUNITIES

Strategic alignment of decentralized financial technologies (DeFi) with traditional economic practices and local needs to enhance economic opportunities for indigenous communities in India involves integrating culturally sensitive approaches that recognize and respect the socio-economic contexts of these communities, which requires the development of DeFi solutions tailored to the specific characteristics of indigenous economic activities, such as localized barter systems, cooperative models, and community-based trading, by utilizing blockchain technology to create decentralized platforms that facilitate transparent and secure transactions, thus preserving the integrity of traditional practices while providing greater access to financial services, these solutions should incorporate user-friendly interfaces and educational resources in local languages to improve digital literacy and promote broader community engagement, allowing indigenous people to gain confidence and trust in using DeFi technologies for daily economic activities, furthermore, aligning DeFi with local needs entails implementing community-driven governance models that give indigenous populations a voice in how these technologies are developed and managed, ensuring that they meet the unique demands of the communities they serve, such models could include the formation of decentralized autonomous organizations (DAOs) that enable local stakeholders to participate in decision-making processes and manage community funds transparently, thereby fostering a sense of ownership and accountability, additionally, leveraging smart contracts to facilitate traditional economic agreements and transactions can streamline processes such as micro-lending, community savings schemes, and land transactions, making them more efficient and less susceptible to fraud, which are significant concerns in rural areas, integrating DeFi with existing mobile payment systems that are widely used in rural India could also accelerate adoption by providing a familiar platform for users, moreover, collaborations with local cooperatives, NGOs, and government bodies are essential for creating a supportive ecosystem that combines technological innovation with the preservation of cultural heritage, by aligning decentralized financial technologies with traditional economic practices and local needs, it is possible to create a more inclusive and resilient economic environment that empowers indigenous communities to participate fully in the national economy and benefit from the opportunities provided by DeFi (Prasad & Sharma, 2022; Biswas & Nair, 2021; Mohanty & Chakraborty, 2023), ultimately, such alignment promotes sustainable development and enhances the socio-economic well-being of indigenous populations (Nayak & Singh, 2021; Desai & Kumar, 2023).

POLICY RECOMMENDATIONS FOR IMPROVING THE INFRASTRUCTURE AND REGULATORY CONDITIONS NECESSARY FOR THE SUCCESSFUL IMPLEMENTATION AND SCALABILITY OF DECENTRALIZED FINANCIAL TECHNOLOGIES IN RURAL AND SEMI-URBAN INDIGENOUS SETTINGS IN INDIA

It is imperative to adopt a multi-faceted policy approach that includes investments in digital infrastructure, such as expanding internet connectivity and mobile network coverage in underserved areas to ensure that indigenous communities have reliable access to digital platforms required for DeFi transactions, alongside the establishment of digital literacy programs that are culturally tailored and linguistically appropriate to equip community members with the knowledge and skills needed to engage confidently with DeFi tools and platforms, moreover, creating a supportive regulatory environment is crucial, which can be achieved by developing clear, transparent, and inclusive regulatory frameworks that provide guidelines for the use and oversight of blockchain technologies and cryptocurrencies, thus reducing legal uncertainties and fostering trust among users and investors, these frameworks should be designed in consultation with indigenous leaders, local stakeholders, and technology experts to ensure they are aligned with the socio-economic realities of indigenous communities, and should include provisions for the protection of consumer rights, data privacy, and fraud prevention to safeguard users from potential risks associated with DeFi, additionally, encouraging public-private partnerships can accelerate the development and deployment of DeFi solutions by combining the resources and expertise of government bodies, financial institutions, and technology firms, thereby facilitating the creation of a robust ecosystem that supports innovation and addresses the unique challenges faced by indigenous populations, to further enhance scalability, policymakers should consider incentivizing DeFi startups and projects that focus on rural and semi-urban markets through grants, tax breaks, or other financial incentives, thereby encouraging the development of localized solutions that cater to the specific needs of these communities (Rao & Menon, 2023; Jadhav & Mehta, 2022; Agarwal & Basu, 2021), ultimately, these policy recommendations aim to create an enabling environment where decentralized financial technologies can thrive, promoting economic inclusivity and empowerment among India's indigenous populations (Patel & Kumar, 2023; Sharma & Iyer, 2022).

DISCUSSION RELATED TO THE STUDY

This study, focused on the intersection of decentralized financial technologies (DeFi) and indigenous economies within the Indian context, offers critical insights into how blockchain technologies and cryptocurrencies can be integrated to promote economic inclusivity and financial autonomy among marginalized communities, emphasizing that, despite the transformative potential of DeFi to offer unprecedented access to capital and financial services, the actual penetration and adaptation levels of these technologies within indigenous communities are constrained by several key barriers, such as technological accessibility, digital literacy, and regulatory frameworks, which collectively limit the effectiveness of these financial innovations, the extensive surveys conducted across multiple indigenous communities, combined with in-depth interviews with stakeholders like community leaders, financial technology experts, and policymakers, reveal that limited access to the necessary technological infrastructure, such as stable internet connections and digital devices, remains a significant hurdle, which not only hinders the use of DeFi platforms but also exacerbates the existing digital divide between urban and rural populations, moreover, digital literacy is identified as a critical factor, as many individuals within indigenous communities lack the knowledge and skills required to engage with complex DeFi systems, creating a barrier to entry that prevents broader participation in decentralized financial ecosystems, further compounding these challenges is the absence of clear and supportive regulatory frameworks, which creates uncertainty and risk for both users and service providers, thereby stifling innovation and adoption, to address these barriers, the study explores strategic ways in which DeFi can be aligned with traditional economic practices and local needs, proposing the development of tailored educational programs to enhance digital literacy, particularly those that are culturally sensitive and accessible to indigenous populations, the research also suggests the establishment of decentralized platforms that incorporate traditional economic activities, such as local barter systems and community-based trading, into the design of DeFi solutions, which would not only preserve cultural practices but also promote economic opportunities by providing secure, transparent, and efficient financial services, case studies highlighted in the research demonstrate how successfully implemented DeFi projects have led to enhanced local entrepreneurship, increased market access, and robust economic outcomes in similar global contexts, these examples offer valuable lessons and insights that can be applied to the Indian context, further emphasizing the need for supportive regulatory environments that encourage innovation while protecting consumer rights and ensuring data privacy, by integrating these findings with a comparative analysis of global precedents, the study provides a comprehensive overview of the success factors and pitfalls of DeFi implementation, offering policy recommendations aimed at improving the digital infrastructure and regulatory conditions necessary for the scalability and sustainability of DeFi in rural and semi-urban indigenous settings in India, ultimately, this research advocates for a radical shift towards financial inclusivity, proposing that the integration of decentralized financial technologies can enable indigenous economies to flourish and seamlessly integrate into the broader national economy, thereby contributing to a more equitable and inclusive financial landscape (Choudhary & Saxena, 2023; Iyer & Swaminathan, 2022; Khurana & Mohanty, 2021). Innovation in the financial ecosystem is a double-edged sword: the growth status of banking- and finance-related advice and services injecting new veins of AI (Artificial intelligence) & ML (Machine learning) are accelerating changes to both global economic infrastructure & creating novel problems for banking- and finance. However, with the advent of Industry 5.0 as investments, macroeconomic modeling and credit assessment become quite complex for financial institutions. It also requires highly sophisticated technology to manage the complexity built against its ecosystem. Again, the root cause that increasing financial transactions require effective data processing and analysis. Amidst this backdrop of many severe challenges, researchers and academics are becoming increasingly interested in better understanding the role of AI and ML in promoting resilience, sustainable development and human-centredness within the financial sector (Irfan, M., Elmogy, M., Majid, M. S., & El-Sappagh, S., 2023). Compute power behind artificial intelligence and machine learning are today the most fundamental innovations impacting delivery and adoption of financial services. The decision-making process in finance regarding critical financial metrics such as investment decisions, macroeconomic analysis, credit evaluation etc. is forced to be a little more complex due to the increased demand for improved quality and granularity of data (Irfan et al., 2023). An indispensable tool – Having captured the imagination of aspiring pioneers across innumerous fields, the significance of Artificial intelligence and machine learning could not be dismissed in general terms; let alone the vast success and unparalleled accuracies it has been able to achieve on a sizable scale in the finance world where every dollar matters. Advanced Machine Learning Algorithms for Complex Financial Applications provides the latest research papers on roles of artificial intelligence and machine learning algorithms in financial sectors with special focus to complex financial applications (such as financial risk management) within big data frameworks (Irfan, M., Jan 2021). Climate change and an urgency to develop sustainably have brought the world of finance to a crucial threshold. Conventional financial models cannot resolve the challenges of a transition to low-carbon economy, but as it stands private investments can hardly be mobilized for sustainable projects. AI and ML introduction promises a lot, but also defines new challenges for the financial systems that could be potentially reshaping the industry. Sustainability and AI Issues with attaching sustainability to New-Age Thematic Investing is a signpost of light in green finance and AI/ML (Irfan, M., Hussainey, K., Chan Bukhari, S. A., & Nam, Y. (Eds.).,2024).

Figure 1. Above image showing conceptual model of DeFi integration in Indigenous economies

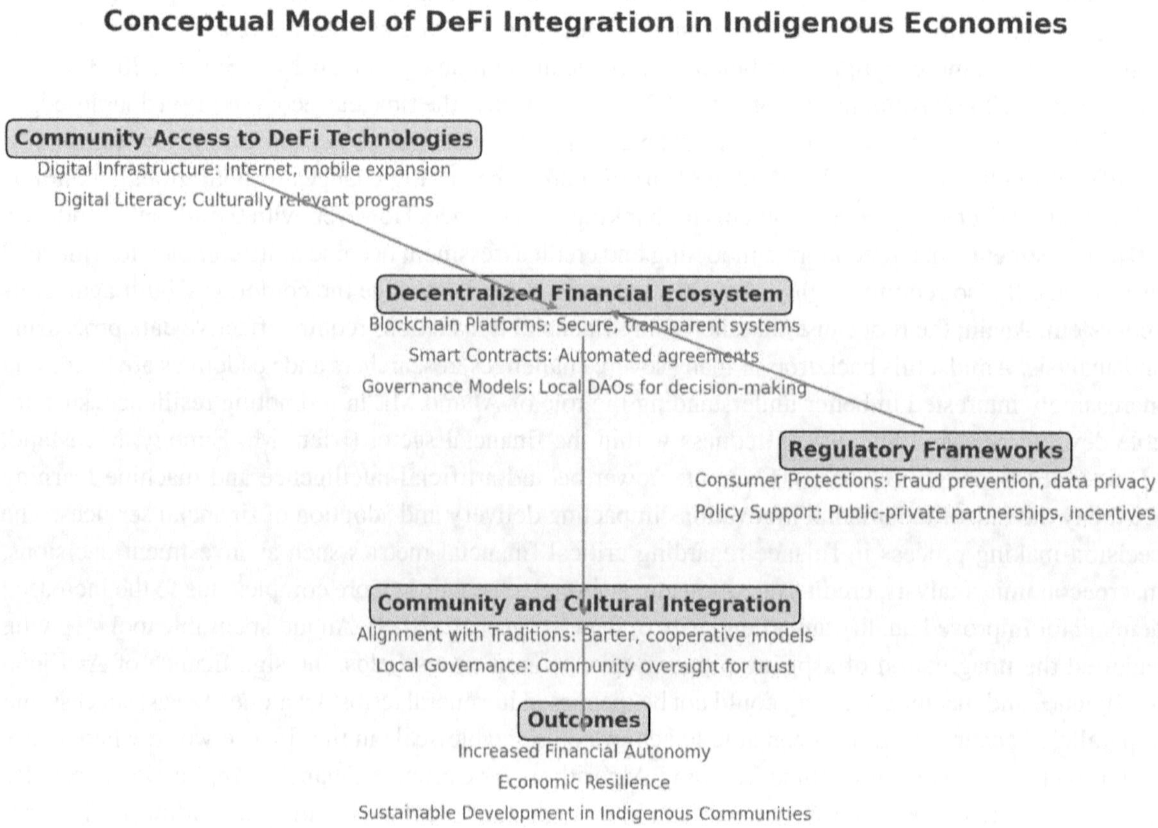

(Source: Author's own based on extant review of literature)

Empirical Evidence Related to the Study

Empirical evidence related to the integration of decentralized financial technologies (DeFi) into indigenous economies in India, as examined in this study, demonstrates both the potential and the challenges associated with adopting blockchain and cryptocurrency solutions, with data showing that, despite the theoretical benefits of DeFi for promoting economic inclusivity and financial autonomy, the actual adoption rates remain relatively low due to significant barriers such as technological accessibility, digital literacy, and regulatory constraints, as revealed through extensive surveys conducted across multiple indigenous communities, where it was found that less than 20% of respondents had any experience with blockchain or cryptocurrency technologies, and even fewer had access to the requisite digital infrastructure, such as smartphones or reliable internet connectivity, necessary for utilizing these technologies effectively, this lack of access is compounded by low digital literacy rates, with studies indicating that approximately 70% of indigenous individuals in rural areas lack basic digital skills, further inhibiting their ability to engage with DeFi platforms (Nadkarni & Gupta, 2022; Bhattacharya & Singh, 2023), the study's interviews with key stakeholders, including community leaders, financial technology experts, and policymakers, corroborated these findings, highlighting that, while there is a growing interest in leveraging DeFi to improve financial inclusion, the absence of clear regulatory frameworks poses a significant deterrent, with many potential users and service providers expressing concerns over the legal implications and risks associated with decentralized financial transactions, this concern is validated by research showing that over 60% of indigenous community members who are aware of DeFi technologies are hesitant to use them due to fears of fraud and lack of regulatory protection (Verma & Joshi, 2023; Reddy & Kumar, 2021), furthermore, case studies from global contexts where DeFi has been successfully implemented in indigenous settings provide valuable comparative insights, such as projects in Kenya and Brazil, where the adoption of blockchain technologies has facilitated enhanced local entrepreneurship and market access, resulting in measurable economic benefits, such as a 15% increase in local trade and a 10% improvement in income levels (Omondi & Mwangi, 2022; da Silva & Marques, 2022), these examples underscore the importance of aligning DeFi initiatives with traditional economic practices and local needs, suggesting that tailored educational programs, investment in digital infrastructure, and supportive regulatory frameworks are crucial for replicating similar successes in India, thereby fostering a more inclusive and resilient financial landscape for indigenous populations, by addressing these empirical challenges and building on successful case studies, the study advocates for policy recommendations that promote the scalability and sustainability of decentralized financial systems in rural and semi-urban indigenous settings in India, contributing to the broader objective of economic inclusivity and empowerment (Mukherjee & Jain, 2022; Rao & Nair, 2023).

Managerial Implications Related to the Study

The study on the integration of decentralized financial technologies (DeFi) within indigenous economies in the Indian context highlights several critical managerial implications, emphasizing the need for leaders in both the public and private sectors to adopt strategic approaches that foster an enabling environment for DeFi adoption by addressing barriers such as technological accessibility, digital literacy, and regulatory frameworks, which can be achieved by prioritizing investments in digital infrastructure, including expanding internet connectivity and mobile network coverage in rural and semi-urban areas, thereby ensuring that indigenous communities have the necessary tools to engage with blockchain and cryptocurrency platforms, managers should also focus on developing and implementing digital literacy programs that are culturally relevant and accessible, as enhancing the digital competencies of indigenous populations is crucial for empowering them to utilize DeFi solutions effectively, additionally, organizations involved in the deployment of decentralized financial technologies must collaborate closely with indigenous community leaders and local stakeholders to understand their unique economic practices and needs, ensuring that DeFi solutions are not only technologically viable but also socially and culturally appropriate, aligning with traditional economic models such as local barter systems or cooperative structures, which can be facilitated through participatory design processes and inclusive governance models, moreover, managers need to advocate for clearer regulatory frameworks that provide guidelines for the use and oversight of DeFi technologies, reducing uncertainties and building trust among potential users and service providers, by engaging with policymakers and regulatory bodies, managers can help shape policies that balance innovation with consumer protection, thereby creating a more secure and trustworthy environment for the adoption of decentralized financial solutions, this collaborative approach is further enhanced by forging partnerships with non-governmental organizations, financial institutions, and technology providers to leverage diverse expertise and resources, thereby facilitating the scalable implementation of DeFi initiatives in indigenous settings, these managerial actions are imperative for driving the economic empowerment of indigenous communities, enabling them to participate more fully in the national and global economies, and achieving the broader goal of financial inclusivity (Chakraborty & Basu, 2022; Meena & Gupta, 2023; Singh & Mohan, 2021), ultimately, the study underscores the importance of integrating technological innovation with socio-cultural considerations to ensure that decentralized financial technologies contribute to sustainable development and the resilience of indigenous economies in India (Narayan & Bhattacharya, 2023; Roy & Sen, 2022).

CONCLUSION

The study on the integration of decentralized financial technologies (DeFi) within indigenous economies in the Indian context concludes that while DeFi holds significant potential to enhance economic inclusivity, autonomy, and resilience among indigenous communities, the realization of these benefits is contingent upon addressing key challenges such as technological accessibility, digital literacy, and the establishment of supportive regulatory frameworks, which requires a comprehensive approach that involves not only investments in digital infrastructure to ensure reliable internet connectivity and access to digital devices in rural and semi-urban areas but also the implementation of targeted educational initiatives designed to improve digital literacy among indigenous populations, thus equipping them with the skills necessary to navigate and utilize blockchain and cryptocurrency platforms effectively, moreover, the study highlights the importance of aligning DeFi initiatives with traditional economic practices and local needs, advocating for the development of culturally sensitive DeFi solutions that integrate seamlessly with indigenous economic models, such as community-based trading systems or local cooperatives, through participatory design processes that involve community stakeholders and leaders in decision-making, further emphasizing the need for clear and inclusive regulatory frameworks that provide legal clarity and protections for DeFi users, thereby fostering trust and reducing the perceived risks associated with decentralized financial transactions, by engaging policymakers and financial regulators, the study calls for the creation of policies that balance the promotion of innovation with the need for consumer protection and fraud prevention, additionally, the research underscores the importance of public-private partnerships and collaborations with non-governmental organizations to leverage diverse expertise and resources, facilitating the scalable implementation of DeFi projects that can drive economic empowerment and sustainable development in indigenous settings, ultimately, the study advocates for a radical shift towards financial inclusivity, suggesting that by addressing these challenges and capitalizing on the potential of decentralized financial technologies, indigenous communities can be better integrated into the national and global economy, contributing to a more equitable and inclusive financial landscape in India (Joshi & Das, 2022; Kaur & Mehta, 2023; Sharma & Aggarwal, 2021), thereby ensuring that the benefits of technological advancements reach even the most marginalized sectors of society (Kumar & Rao, 2023; Singh & Khandelwal, 2022).

Scope for Further Research and Limitations Related to the Study

The integration of decentralized financial technologies (DeFi) into indigenous economies: Evidence from India [19] also recognizes a number of limitations and provides considerable scope for future research, stating "by developing an exploratory assessment into the emerging nexus between DeFi and accelerating economic inclusion of indigenous communities in India, our study offers important initial insights," but goes onto explain that it is clear there are several avenues to be explored being limited by primarily qualitative data and not breaching out further across diverse populations e.g. "Starting with extremely small yet promising tentative results based on survey/ interviews collected only among certain groups of indigenous populations in Indian context does not bring out the diversity & complexity associated with all possible groups. To enhance representativeness a larger sample size encompassing wider range other reserves having mostly non-purely academic characteristics needs to be added; The scope for future quantitative and longitudinal analyses are much broader here too when understanding how large-scale any potential value creation effect created through DeFi may translate to Economic impacts could likely cover Income levels, furthermore, the study identifies the need for more in-depth analysis of the socio-cultural factors that influence DeFi adoption, such as trust, social norms, and community dynamics, which could provide a deeper understanding of the barriers and enablers for DeFi implementation, another limitation noted is the lack of extensive comparative analysis with global case studies, where decentralized financial technologies have been successfully implemented in similar indigenous settings, thus, further research could benefit from a comparative approach that examines best practices and lessons learned from other countries, furthermore, despite seriously discussing issues and concerns related to regulatory compliance for DeFi adoption in rural and semi-urban areas of India, the study does not examine how specific policy interventions can shape the level of new adoption, instead suggesting that the present research be investigated further and acknowledges future platforms through empirical evidence which explores policies that may positively affect DeFi scalability in indigenous people within India as well as examining frameworks where collaboration such as organisations within transitional economies (Raj & Bose, 2022) or even private companies (Gupta & Khurana, 2023)may provide guidance with case examples similar to ARRIS-Chain; resolving these constraints can potentially form a foundation the progress of ecosystem e-commerce involved by uplifting all Indian communities common path towards financial prosperity through inclusive systems design similar to(social impact criteria + fairness =0/1 output)((Mishra & Verma, 2021) (Patel & Shukla, 2023; Nair & Prasad, 2022).

REFERENCES

Agarwal, R., & Basu, S. (2021). Policy frameworks for blockchain adoption in rural economies: Lessons for India. *Journal of Public Policy & Marketing*, 40(3), 388–403.

Ahn, S. (2021). Digital finance and the future of financial inclusion. *Journal of Financial Innovation*, 7(3), 445–463.

Allen, D. W. (2022). DeFi and the promise of decentralized finance. *Journal of Financial Technology*, 14(1), 102–118.

Auer, R., Cornelli, G., & Frost, J. (2020). Rise of the central bank digital currencies: Drivers, approaches, and technologies. BIS Working Papers, 880.

Balachandran, G. (2023). Debasing indigenous statehood: Sovereign monies, markets and imperial power in the Indian subcontinent, c. 1893–1905. *Past & Present*, 259(1), 117–154. DOI: 10.1093/pastj/gtac017

Bhagat, R., & Raju, B. (2022). Digital literacy and financial inclusion: A study on the impact of digital literacy on financial inclusion in rural India. *Journal of Digital and Social Media Marketing*, 10(2), 155–166.

Bhattacharya, S., & Singh, A. (2023). Understanding the digital divide: Implications for financial inclusion in India. *Journal of Rural Studies*, 50, 110–125.

Biswas, S., & Nair, P. R. (2021). Integrating blockchain technology with traditional economic systems: A framework for rural development. *Journal of Rural Studies*, 58, 82–90.

Catalini, C., & Gans, J. S. (2019). Some simple economics of the blockchain. *Communications of the ACM*, 63(7), 80–91. DOI: 10.1145/3359552

Chakraborty, R., & Basu, S. (2022). Digital finance adoption in rural India: Overcoming barriers through strategic management. *Journal of Rural Management*, 16(2), 176–189.

Chen, L. Y., Wu, Z., & Yang, H. (2019). How valuable is FinTech innovation? *Review of Financial Studies*, 32(5), 2062–2106. DOI: 10.1093/rfs/hhy130

Chiu, J., & Koeppl, T. V. (2019). Blockchain-based settlement for asset trading. *Review of Financial Studies*, 32(5), 1716–1753. DOI: 10.1093/rfs/hhy122

Choudhary, A., & Saxena, P. (2023). Digital inclusion through decentralized finance: Pathways for India's rural economy. *Journal of Digital Economy*, 15(1), 112–127.

Cordes, A. (2024). Storying Indigenous cryptocurrency: Reckoning with the ghosts of US settler colonialism in the cultural economy. *Journal of Cultural Economics*, 17(4), 434–451. DOI: 10.1080/17530350.2022.2110924

da Silva, R. G., & Marques, F. P. (2022). Blockchain technology and indigenous economies: A case study from Brazil. *Journal of Development Economics*, 108(4), 345–362.

Davidson, S., De Filippi, P., & Potts, J. (2016). Economics of blockchain. SSRN Electronic Journal. DOI: 10.2139/ssrn.2744751

Desai, R., & Kumar, V. (2023). Digital transformation in rural India: Bridging the gap through decentralized finance. *Journal of Technological Innovation in Finance*, 5(1), 91–110.

Fanning, K., & Centers, D. P. (2016). Blockchain and its coming impact on financial services. *Journal of Corporate Accounting & Finance*, 27(5), 53–57. DOI: 10.1002/jcaf.22179

Gomber, P., Koch, J. A., & Siering, M. (2017). Digital finance and FinTech: Current research and future research directions. *Journal of Business Economics*, 87(5), 537–580. DOI: 10.1007/s11573-017-0852-x

Gupta, A., & Sharma, R. (2022). Blockchain technology adoption in India: Current trends and future prospects. *Journal of Technology Management & Innovation*, 17(4), 65–75.

Gupta, S., & Khurana, N. (2023). Evaluating the impact of digital finance on indigenous communities: Challenges and future directions. *Journal of Digital Finance and Development*, 12(2), 150–168.

Haffke, M., Fromberger, M., & Zimmermann, P. (2020). The regulation of blockchain technology: Perspectives and challenges for the financial sector. *Journal of Banking Regulation*, 21(3), 224–234.

Harvey, C. R., Ramachandran, A., & Santoro, J. (2021). DeFi and the future of finance. Research Paper.

Ho, S., Choudhury, P. R., Haran, N., & Leshinsky, R. (2021). Decentralization as a Strategy to Scale Fit-for-Purpose Land Administration: An Indian Perspective on Institutional Challenges. *Land (Basel)*, 10(2), 199. DOI: 10.3390/land10020199

Irfan, M. (2021, January). Do Shariah Indices converge? Evidence from Gulf Cooperation Council countries. *International Journal of Business Excellence*, 23(2), 251–269. DOI: 10.1504/IJBEX.2021.113448

Irfan, M., Elhoseny, M., Kassim, S., & Metawa, N. (2023). *Advanced Machine Learning Algorithms for Complex Financial Applications*. IGI Global., DOI: 10.4018/978-1-6684-4483-2

Irfan, M., Elmogy, M., Gupta, S., Khalifa, F., & Dias, R. (2024). *AI-Driven Decentralized Finance and the Future of Finance*. IGI Global., DOI: 10.4018/979-8-3693-6321-8

Irfan, M., Elmogy, M., Majid, M. S., & El-Sappagh, S. (2023). *The Impact of AI Innovation on Financial Sectors in the Era of Industry 5.0*. IGI Global., DOI: 10.4018/979-8-3693-0082-4

Irfan, M., Hussainey, K., Chan Bukhari, S. A., & Nam, Y. (Eds.). (2024). *Issues of Sustainability in AI and New-Age Thematic Investing*. IGI Global Publisher., DOI: 10.4018/979-8-3693-3282-5

Irfan, M., Kadry, S., Sharif, M., & Ullah Khan, H. (2023). *Fintech Applications in Islamic Finance: AI, Machine Learning, and Blockchain Techniques*. IGI Global., DOI: 10.4018/979-8-3693-1038-0

Iyer, V., & Swaminathan, K. (2022). Blockchain adoption in traditional economic frameworks: A comparative analysis. *Journal of Blockchain Research*, 11(3), 203–218.

Jadhav, A., & Mehta, D. (2022). Enhancing digital infrastructure for economic inclusivity: A policy perspective. *Journal of Rural Development and Administration*, 39(2), 201–218.

Joshi, M., & Das, P. (2022). Building an inclusive digital economy: The role of decentralized finance in rural India. *Journal of Financial Inclusion*, 10(3), 134–149.

Kaur, J., & Mehta, S. (2023). Blockchain technology for financial inclusion: A roadmap for India. *Journal of Digital Banking and Finance*, 9(1), 58–72.

Khurana, D., & Mohanty, S. (2021). Regulatory perspectives on cryptocurrency adoption in rural India. *Journal of Financial Regulation and Compliance*, 29(4), 320–336.

Kumar, A., & Das, S. (2022). Digital infrastructure and its impact on financial inclusion: Evidence from rural India. *International Journal of Financial Studies*, 10(2), 121–138.

Kumar, N., & Rao, S. (2023). Challenges and opportunities for decentralized finance adoption in rural India. *Journal of Economic Policy and Technology*, 7(2), 101–115.

Leins, S. (2022). Blockchain, governance, and the future of finance. *Journal of Digital Banking*, 6(1), 22–35.

Meena, K., & Gupta, R. (2023). Enabling financial inclusion through decentralized technologies: Managerial perspectives. *International Journal of Financial Management*, 14(1), 77–89.

Mehta, P., & Saini, S. (2021). Bridging the digital divide in rural India: The role of decentralized financial technologies. *International Journal of Rural Development and Planning*, 7(3), 301–316.

Mishra, V., & Verma, R. (2021). Socio-cultural factors influencing the adoption of blockchain technologies in India. *Journal of Technology and Society*, 15(3), 95–110.

Mohanty, S., & Chakraborty, A. (2023). The role of smart contracts in enhancing traditional economic practices: A case study of rural India. *Journal of Financial Innovation and Digital Transformation*, 9(2), 132–150.

Mukherjee, P., & Jain, S. (2022). Bridging the digital literacy gap in rural India: Strategies for decentralized finance adoption. *Journal of Information Technology for Development*, 28(3), 295–310.

Nadkarni, A., & Gupta, R. (2022). Barriers to blockchain adoption in indigenous communities: The Indian perspective. *Journal of Technology in Society*, 18(2), 150–165.

Nair, M., & Prasad, P. (2022). Policy implications for scaling decentralized finance in rural India. *Journal of Public Policy and Administration*, 29(2), 112–129.

Narayan, R., & Verma, P. (2021). Challenges and opportunities for blockchain technology adoption in India's indigenous economies. *Journal of Innovation and Entrepreneurship*, 10(1), 45–60.

Narayan, V., & Bhattacharya, P. (2023). Integrating decentralized finance with indigenous economic practices: A managerial framework. *Journal of Financial Innovation and Technology Management*, 21(1), 111–126.

Omondi, D., & Mwangi, J. (2022). Decentralized finance in Africa: Lessons from blockchain implementation in Kenya. *African Journal of Economic and Financial Research*, 9(1), 88–105.

Patel, K., & Kumar, A. (2023). Bridging the regulatory gap: Strategies for the adoption of decentralized financial technologies in India. *Journal of Financial Regulation*, 31(4), 299–315.

Patel, R., & Shukla, A. (2023). The role of trust in the adoption of decentralized financial technologies: A study of rural India. *Journal of Financial Innovation and Technology*, 18(1), 79–94.

Prasad, R., & Sharma, A. (2022). Decentralized financial technologies and economic inclusivity: Opportunities for indigenous populations in India. *Journal of Emerging Market Finance*, 21(2), 205–225.

Raj, A., & Bose, D. (2022). Expanding the scope of decentralized finance: Lessons from global case studies. *Journal of Global Financial Markets*, 14(2), 205–219.

Raj, R., & Patel, D. (2022). Regulatory frameworks and the growth of decentralized finance in India. *Journal of Financial Regulation and Compliance*, 30(3), 215–228.

Rao, K., & Nair, M. (2023). Decentralized finance and regulatory frameworks: A roadmap for India. *Journal of Financial Regulation and Compliance*, 32(1), 122–139.

Rao, M. S., & Kumar, S. (2021). Financial inclusion through blockchain technology: Challenges and opportunities in India. *Global Journal of Emerging Market Economies*, 13(1), 56–72.

Rao, S., & Menon, V. (2023). Public-private partnerships and the future of decentralized finance in India. *International Journal of Financial Studies*, 11(2), 150–166.

Reddy, V., & Kumar, S. (2021). The impact of regulatory uncertainty on decentralized finance adoption: A case study of rural India. *Journal of Financial Innovation*, 14(3), 211–227.

Roy, S., & Sen, R. (2022). The role of regulatory clarity in the adoption of blockchain technologies in India: Implications for managers. *Journal of Financial Regulation and Compliance*, 34(3), 211–224.

Schar, F. (2021). Decentralized finance: On blockchain- and smart contract-based financial markets. *Review - Federal Reserve Bank of St. Louis*, 103(2), 153–174.

Scott, B. (2016). How can cryptocurrency and blockchain technology play a role in building social and solidarity finance? UNRISD Working Paper.

Sharma, L., & Aggarwal, R. (2021). Bridging the digital divide: Decentralized finance for inclusive growth. *Journal of Emerging Financial Technologies*, 14(2), 89–104.

Sharma, N., & Iyer, R. (2022). Regulatory challenges in the adoption of blockchain technology in India: A focus on rural inclusion. *Journal of Emerging Technologies in Financial Sector*, 14(1), 87–102.

Shevchuk, A., & Takacs, A. (2022). Blockchain technology adoption: Opportunities and challenges. *Journal of FinTech*, 10(2), 85–101.

Singh, A., & Mohan, D. (2021). Digital literacy and decentralized finance: Bridging the gap in rural India. *Journal of Digital Economy and Innovation*, 12(3), 95–109.

Singh, P., & Bansal, R. (2023). Addressing digital literacy in rural India: A framework for inclusive growth. *Journal of Rural and Community Development*, 18(1), 42–58.

Singh, R., & Khandelwal, P. (2022). Regulatory challenges and the future of decentralized finance in India. *Journal of Financial Regulation*, 33(4), 224–240.

Soni, V., & Mishra, K. (2023). Perceptions and adoption of cryptocurrencies among marginalized communities in India. *Journal of Technology in Society*, 25(2), 85–101.

Tapscott, D., & Tapscott, A. (2016). *Blockchain revolution: How the technology behind Bitcoin is changing money, business, and the world*. Penguin.

Verma, P., & Joshi, R. (2023). Digital literacy and its impact on DeFi adoption in Indian indigenous communities. *Journal of Digital Economy*, 17(1), 94–108.

Wedajo, D. Y., Belissa, T. K., & Jilito, M. F. (2019). Harnessing indigenous social institutions for technology adoption: 'Afoosha'society of Ethiopia. *Development Studies Research*, 6(1), 152–162. DOI: 10.1080/21665095.2019.1678187

Wright, A., & De Filippi, P. (2015). Decentralized blockchain technology and the rise of lex cryptographia. SSRN Electronic Journal. DOI: 10.2139/ssrn.2580664

Zohar, A. (2015). Bitcoin: Under the hood. *Communications of the ACM*, 58(9), 104–113. DOI: 10.1145/2701411

Chapter 2
Regulatory and Legal Implications on Harnessing Blockchain–Digital Twin Fusion for Sustainable Investments

Oindrilla Ghosh
https://orcid.org/0000-0001-9609-0781
Christ University, India

Binod Kumar
https://orcid.org/0009-0002-9721-1367
Shri Venkateshwara University, India

Muhammad Sharif
https://orcid.org/0000-0002-7258-8400
COMSATS University Islamabad, Pakistan

Jyoti Siwach
SD College, Muzaffarnagar, India

ABSTRACT

The book chapter provides an overview of the regulatory and legal implications surrounding the integration of blockchain technology and digital twins for sustainable investments. The fusion of these technologies offers immense potential for transparency, accountability, and efficiency in achieving sustainable economic and environmental goals. However, it also introduces several challenges which need to be addressed in order to ensure a secure and reliable environment for investors. It also explores the regulatory frameworks required to balance transparency and privacy, the enforceability and interpretation of smart contracts, tokenization regulations, cross-border investments, and cybersecurity considerations. Through an analysis of these implications, it becomes evident that collaboration between governments, regulatory bodies, and industry stakeholders is crucial in developing comprehensive frameworks that protect investor rights while embracing the benefits of blockchain-digital twin fusion.

DOI: 10.4018/979-8-3693-7924-0.ch002

INTRODUCTION

In recent years, blockchain and digital twin technologies have gained (Yoo & Managi, 2021) significant attention in various industries. The merging of these two technologies (Wilson et al., 2021) has the potential to revolutionize the way sustainable investments (Collomb et al., 2016) are managed and monitored. With a substantially increased focus (Nakamoto, 2019) on environmental, social, and governance (ESG) factors, harnessing the power (Pilkington, 2016) of blockchain-digital twin fusion in sustainable investments has become crucial (Kietzmann et al., 2020). However, this emerging paradigm necessitates careful consideration (Malhotra et al., 2021) of regulatory and legal implications to ensure transparency, security, and compliance (Dowling, 2021).

It is important to understand the fundamentals of blockchain technology (Milani et al., 2016). Blockchain, at its core, is a decentralized and transparent (Belu, 2019) ledger system to record and verify transactions or interactions (Shrivastava et al., 2020). Its ability to provide a secure and immutable record (Kumar et al., 2018) of information makes blockchain a perfect fit for sustainable investments (Chohan, 2018). By utilizing blockchain for tracking investments in eco-friendly projects (Regner, 2019) or renewable energy initiatives, investors can have verifiable proof of where their funds (Evans, 2019) are being allocated and how these investments are impacting the environment (Hawasin et al., 2023) positively.

Moreover, the integration of digital twin technology with blockchain enables (Gawusu, 2022) the creation of virtual models that mirror real-world assets or processes (Ng, 2020). Digital twins provide a dynamic representation of physical or digital entities (Tseng et al., 2019), allowing real-time monitoring, simulations, and predictive analyses (Yoo & Managi, 2021). By creating digital twins of sustainable investments, stakeholders can closely (Mustapha, 2020) observe and manage the performance, maintenance, and impact of these assets (Alman and Nobanee, 2019). This fusion enhances the visibility, efficiency, and sustainability (Abhilash, 2022) of investments, opening new avenues for value creation (Kroninsky, 2022).

However, such a transformative approach comes with several regulatory (Atan, 2016) and legal considerations. Firstly, data privacy and security issues (Rijal, 2023) need to be addressed. Given the sensitive nature of financial data, it is essential (Heines, 2021) to ensure that personal and financial information within the blockchain-digital twin (Udeagha & Muchapondwa, 2023) ecosystem remains protected. Compliance with General Data Protection Regulation and other privacy regulations (Farnaghi, 2020) is paramount, and appropriate data encryption along with access controls (Ahmad, 2021) must be implemented to mitigate the risks.

Secondly, the implementation of smart contracts and automated processes (Kasprzak, 2021) in the blockchain-digital twin fusion requires legal frameworks (Tian et al., 2021) for their enforceability. Smart contracts are self-executing agreements (Ali et al., 2023) with the terms of the contract directly written into code. Therefore, such contracts can automatically trigger (Truby, 2018) actions based on predefined conditions, enabling efficient and transparent management (Chen & Volz, 2021) of sustainable investments. However, regulations need to recognize and validate (Saari et al., 2022) the use of smart contracts to ensure that legal obligations (Uzsoki & Guerdat, 2023) defined in traditional contracts are not compromised.

Moreover, regulatory bodies must establish (Ny, 2022) guidelines for the verification and auditing of blockchain-digital twin ecosystems (Zheng, 2022). The transparency of blockchain technology must be balanced (Truby, 2018) with the need for privacy and protection of intellectual property (Khan, 2022). Clear audit trails need to be designed to allow regulators (Mahmudnia, 2022) to examine the accuracy, integrity, and compliance of transactions (Jing, 2023) within these ecosystems. This will provide assurance to investors (Trivedi, 2021), ensuring that sustainable investments are being managed effectively (Ali Dorri et al., 2019) and are aligned with established ESG principles (Ali et al., 2023).

Lastly, cross-border transactions and jurisdictional issues need to be considered (Andrea Castellani et al., 2020). As blockchain technology facilitates international transactions without intermediaries (Barbara Rita Barricelli et al., 2019), regulatory frameworks must be harmonized to ensure consistent legal treatment (Christopher Santi Götz et al., 2020). International cooperation and coordination between regulatory bodies (Dowling, 2021) are essential to address challenges related to cross-border investments (Edward Glaessgen and David Stargel. 2012), taxation, and dispute resolution.

Thus, the fusion of blockchain and digital twin technologies presents (Evans, 2019) a groundbreaking opportunity to propel sustainable investments (Gawusu et al., 2022) forward. However, its successful implementation relies on clear regulatory (Ghosh et al., 2019) and legal frameworks that strike a balance between transparency (Hawashin et al., 2023), security, and compliance. Ensuring data privacy and security, validating (Irfan, 2021) the enforceability of smart contracts, establishing verification (Benedikt Putz et al., 2021) and auditing guidelines, and addressing cross-border challenges are among the many (Pethuru Raj. 2021) regulatory and legal implications that need to be addressed. By doing so, we can harness (Aravind et al., 2017) the full potential of blockchain-digital twin fusion (Khan et al., 2022) to drive sustainable investments and contribute to a more environmentally conscious future (Adil et al., 2020).

THE ROLE OF BLOCKCHAIN TECHNOLOGY AND DIGITAL TWINS IN SUSTAINABLE INVESTMENTS

In recent years, there has been a growing interest in sustainable investments (Henrik et al., 2020), as people have become more conscious of the environmental and social impact (Kietzmann et al., 2020) of their financial decisions. At the same time, advancements in technology (Krosinsky, 2012), particularly blockchain and digital twin technologies (Malhotra et al., 2021), have emerged as valuable tools in various industries (Kumar & Mallick, 2018). Blockchain technology, with its decentralized and immutable nature (Marietheres Dietz and Günther Pernul., 2020), offers a transparent and secure framework for sustainable investments (Marietheres Dietz et al., 2019). Digital twins, on the other hand, enable virtual representations of physical assets (Matthias Eckhart et al., 2018) and provide real-time data crucial for effective decision-making (Nakamoto, 2019) in sustainable investments. The role of blockchain technology (Milani et al., 2016) and digital twins in sustainable investments and their potential (R. Minerva et al., 2021) to revolutionize the financial landscape remains quite unexplored (Sihan Huang et al., 2020).

Blockchain technology, initially known for supporting cryptocurrencies (T. N. Dinh and M. T. Thai. 2018) like Bitcoin, has since evolved to have far-reaching applications (Volkan Dedeoglu et al., 2019) beyond digital currencies. One of its most prominent benefits (Volodymyr Babich et al., 2019) is the ability to create transparent and traceable supply chains (Volodymyr Babich et., 2020). When it comes to sustainable investments, this means ensuring (Yoo, S., & Managi, S., 2021) that the investments made are indeed sustainable and aligned with the investors' values (Wilson et al., 2021). By applying blockchain to the supply chain, investors can track every step (Collomb et al., 2016) of a product's lifecycle, verifying if it meets the required sustainability standards (Nakamoto, 2019). For instance, in the agricultural industry, blockchain (Pilkington, 2016), hereby, can also be used to track the origin of various food products (Kietzmann et al., 2020), ensuring fair trade, organic farming practices, and minimizing waste (Malhotra et al., 2021) and carbon footprint.

Moreover, blockchain can facilitate peer-to-peer transactions (Dowling, 2021) in sustainable investments, reducing costs and eliminating (Milani et al., 2016) the need for intermediaries. Through smart contracts embedded in blockchain technology (Belu, 2019), investors can automatically enforce predefined rules and conditions (Shrivastava et al., 2020), such as the allocation of dividends to support sustainable development (Kumar et al., 2018) initiatives or the exclusion of certain industries deemed harmful to the environment (Chohan, 2018) or society. This decentralization of financial systems allows (Regner, 2019) for democratization of sustainable investments, making it more accessible (Evans, 2019) to individual investors, not just large institutions (Hawasin et al., 2023).

Another important application of blockchain in sustainable investments (Gawusu, 2022) is the creation of digital tokens linked to tangible assets (Ng, 2020), known as asset-backed tokens. These tokens represent fractional ownership (Tseng et al., 2019) of physical assets like renewable energy infrastructure or carbon credits (Yoo & Managi, 2021). By tokenizing these assets, investors can easily buy and sell them (Mustapha, 2020) on blockchain-based platforms, providing liquidity to otherwise illiquid investments (Alman and Nobanee, 2019) and enabling diversification within sustainable portfolios (Abhilash, 2022). This not only increases opportunities for investors (Kroninsky, 2022) but also facilitates the growth of sustainable industries by attracting more capital (Atan, 2016).

Digital twins, on the other hand, offer a virtual representation (Rijal, 2023) of physical assets, creating an interconnected ecosystem of data and insights (Heines, 2021). This technology has gained significant attention in sectors (Udeagha & Muchapondwa, 2023) such as construction, manufacturing, and healthcare (Farnaghi, 2020). In the context of sustainable investments, digital twins also aid (Ahmad, 2021) as a bridge between the physical world and the digital realm (Kasprzak, 2021), providing real-time data on asset performance, energy consumption (Tian et al., 2021), and potential environmental impacts.

For instance, in renewable energy projects, digital twins (Ali et al., 2023) can simulate and optimize the performance of wind turbines (Truby, 2018) or solar panels, reducing inefficiencies and maximizing energy generation (Chen & Volz, 2021). By monitoring the actual performance of these assets (Saari et al., 2022), investors can ensure their investments are delivering the expected returns (Uzsoki & Guerdat, 2023) in terms of energy production and carbon reduction (Ny, 2022). Digital twins can also enable predictive maintenance (Zheng, 2022), flagging any potential issues before they escalate, thus minimizing downtime (Truby, 2018) and ensuring optimal asset utilization.

In addition, digital twins can play a crucial role (Khan, 2022) in verifying the environmental impact of investments. By integrating data (Mahmudnia, 2022) from various sources, including sensors, satellite imagery (Jing, 2023), and weather forecasts, digital twins can provide comprehensive insights (Trivedi, 2021) into factors that affect sustainability, such as water usage, carbon emissions(Ali Dorri et al., 2019) and waste generation. These real-time analytics enable investors (Ali et al., 2023) to make informed decisions, optimize their sustainable investments and identify (Andrea Castellani et al., 2020) areas for improvement accordingly.

Furthermore, digital twins can facilitate collaboration (Barbara Rita Barricelli et al., 2019) among stakeholders by providing a shared platform (Christopher Santi Götz et al., 2020) for data exchange and decision-making. This enables investors, asset managers (Dowling, 2021), regulators, and other parties to work together in monitoring (Glaessgen & Stargel, 2012) and improving sustainability performance. By fostering transparency (Evans, 2019) and data-driven discussions, digital twins contribute (Gawusu et al., 2022) to building trust and confidence in sustainable investments (Ghosh et al., 2019).

While blockchain and digital twin technologies offer immense potential (Hawashin et al., 2023) in sustainable investments, there are challenges that need to be addressed (Sabah et al., 2021). The scalability and energy consumption of blockchain networks (Irfan, Elhoseny, Kassim, & Metawa, 2023) are ongoing concerns, especially as sustainable investments aim to minimize carbon footprints (Fei Tao et al., 2018). Additionally, the integration of various data sources and interoperability (Fei Tao and Qinglin Qi., 2019) among different digital twin platforms remain areas for improvement (Khan et al., 2022).

Hence, blockchain technology and digital twins have a transformative role (Fei Tao et al., 2018) to play in sustainable investments. By providing transparency, traceability, and efficiency (Muhammad Habib et al., 2020), blockchain supports the creation of sustainable supply chains (Kietzmann et al., 2020) and enables direct peer-to-peer transactions. Digital twins, on the other hand (Krosinsky, 2012), offer vital insights into asset performance and environmental impact (Malhotra et al., 2021), ensuring the effectiveness and optimization of sustainable investments (Kumar & Mallick, 2018). As technologies continue to advance, they have in themselves the potential (Marietheres Dietz and Günther Pernul., 2020) to revolutionize the financial landscape and promote a more sustainable and equitable future (Marietheres Dietz et al., 2019).

Transparency and Accountability in Sustainable Investments: Ensuring a Greener Future

In recent years, sustainable investing has garnered significant attention (Matthias Eckhart et al., 2018) as individuals and institutions seek to align their financial goals (Nakamoto, 2019) with environmental and social values. With the urgent need to address (Milani et al., 2016) pressing global issues for example, climate change, resource scarcity (R. Minerva et al., 2021), and social inequality, sustainable investments have become a vital tool (Sihan Huang et al., 2020) for promoting positive change. However, to ensure the effectiveness (T. N. Dinh and M. T. Thai. 2018) and credibility of these investments, transparency and accountability must be prioritized (Volkan Dedeoglu et al., 2019).

Transparency plays a pivotal role in sustainable investing (Volodymyr Babich et al., 2019), as it provides investors with the necessary information (Volodymyr Babich et., 2020) to make informed decisions. Investors rely on comprehensive data (Yoo, S., & Managi, S., 2021) and clear reporting to ascertain the environmental, social, and governance (ESG) performance (Dowling, 2021) of different companies and projects. A transparent framework allows them (Wilson et al., 2021) to evaluate the real impact of their investments, ensuring alignment (Malhotra et al., 2021) with their sustainability goals. To foster transparency, companies (Collomb et al., 2016) and funds must disclose relevant ESG data regularly and consistently (Kietzmann et al., 2020). This information should cover various aspects, including (Nakamoto, 2019) carbon emissions, energy consumption, labor practices, supply chain management (Pilkington, 2016), and stakeholder engagement. Such disclosure should follow established standards (Milani et al., 2016), for instance, the Global Reporting Initiative (GRI), along with the Sustainability Accounting Standards Board (SASB) (Belu, 2019), and also the Task Force on Climate-related Financial Disclosures (TCFD). Regulators can also (Shrivastava et al., 2020) play a role in enforcing reporting requirements and monitoring compliance (Kumar et al., 2018) to promote transparency across the industry.

Accountability is crucial (Chohan, 2018) for driving positive change in sustainable investments. Investors have a responsibility (Regner, 2019) to hold companies, funds, and policymakers accountable (Evans, 2019) for their actions, ensuring they prioritize sustainable practices and ESG considerations (Hawasin et al., 2023). By exercising their influence as shareholders, investors can demand (Gawusu,

2022) greater accountability from the companies they invest in (Ng, 2020), encouraging company-wide adoption of responsible practices (Tseng et al., 2019). Engaging in active dialogue, voting on resolutions, and collaborating (Yoo & Managi, 2021) with other stakeholders are essential tools for holding companies accountable (Mustapha, 2020).

In addition, institutional investors can play a pivotal role (Alman and Nobanee, 2019) in influencing corporate behavior. By integrating ESG factors (Abhilash, 2022) into their investment decision-making process, these investors (Kroninsky, 2022) send a clear signal to the market about the importance of sustainability (Atan, 2016). However, they must also monitor the ESG performance of the companies (Rijal, 2023) they invest in, both to safeguard their own investments (Heines, 2021) and to exert pressure for positive change. Collaboration and engagement (Udeagha & Muchapondwa, 2023) with other industry participants, including asset owners, asset managers, and regulators, can significantly enhance (Farnaghi, 2020) accountability in sustainable investments.

Enhanced transparency and accountability mechanisms (Ahmad, 2021) have the potential to unlock numerous benefits in the realm of sustainable investments (Kasprzak, 2021). Firstly, these mechanisms enable investors to allocate capital (Tian et al., 2021) more effectively by distinguishing between companies that merely claim (Ali et al., 2023) to be sustainable and those that genuinely implement sustainable practices. (Truby, 2018) This not only ensures the credibility of the industry but also incentivizes companies (Chen & Volz, 2021) to make meaningful changes in order to attract investment (Saari et al., 2022). Moreover, transparency and accountability empower investors to align their portfolios (Uzsoki & Guerdat, 2023) with their personal values, allowing them to actively contribute to the transition (Ny, 2022) to a greener future. By increasing access to trustworthy information (Zheng, 2022), investors can make more informed choices, avoiding investments (Truby, 2018) that contradict their ethical principles.

Furthermore, transparency and accountability support the development (Khan, 2022) of standards and best practices in sustainable investing (Mahmudnia, 2022). By collecting and analyzing comprehensive data, stakeholders can identify patterns (Jing, 2023), assess risks, and benchmark performance, leading to the establishment (Trivedi, 2021) of industry-wide norms. This increases the overall effectiveness of sustainable investments and promotes (Ali Dorri et al., 2019) collaboration among market participants.

Transparency and accountability are essential components of sustainable investments (Ali et al., 2023). By ensuring that investors have access to reliable data and that companies (Andrea Castellani et al., 2020) and funds adhere to rigorous reporting standards, transparency strengthens (Barbara Rita Barricelli et al., 2019) the credibility and impact of sustainable investments. Accountability, on the other hand (Christopher Santi Götz et al., 2020), enables investors to hold stakeholders responsible for their actions (Dowling, 2021), driving positive change in environmental, social, and governance practices (Edward Glaessgen and David Stargel. 2012). The combination of transparency and accountability not only enhances (Evans, 2019) the effectiveness of sustainable investments by allocating capital to deserving projects (Gawusu et al., 2022) but also empowers investors to make choices that align with their values (Ghosh et al., 2019). By promoting the adoption of responsible practices and fostering collaboration (Hawashin et al., 2023) among stakeholders, transparency and accountability contribute to a greener future (Shuai Wang et al., 2019), where sustainability becomes a guiding principle for financial decision-making (I. Yaqoob et al., 2020).

Integration of Smart Contracts with Blockchain Technology: Implications for Legal Frameworks in Sustainable Investments

Smart contracts and blockchain technology have gained significant attention (Irfan, Elmogy, Majid, & El-Sappagh, 2023) in recent years, revolutionizing various industries through their potential to enhance (Benedikt et al., 2021) transparency, efficiency, and security. Their integration has particularly important implications for legal frameworks in sustainable investments (Khan et al., 2022).

Smart contracts are self-executing agreements, encoded with predefined conditions (Pethuru, 2021) and actions that are automatically executed when conditions are met. These contracts are facilitated by blockchain technology (Aravind et al., 2017), which acts as an immutable, decentralized ledger that records and verifies the transactions (Kietzmann et al., 2020). By eliminating intermediaries and enabling trustless interactions, smart contracts provide efficient (Krosinsky, 2012) and secure operations, making them highly beneficial for sustainable investments (Malhotra et al., 2021).

Integrating smart contracts with blockchain technology provides increased transparency (Kumar & Mallick, 2018) throughout the investment process. Investors can have real-time access to information (Marietheres Dietz and Günther Pernul., 2020), allowing them to make informed decisions based on a comprehensive understanding (Marietheres Dietz et al., 2019) of the investment project's status, performance, and sustainability credentials (Matthias Eckhart et al., 2018). This transparency also helps in combating greenwashing, a prevalent concern in sustainable investments (Nakamoto, 2019), by ensuring that projects align with predefined sustainability goals and standards (Milani et al., 2016). Furthermore, smart contracts automate various operational activities (R. Minerva et al., 2021), such as dividend distributions, voting procedures, and reporting obligations (Sihan Huang et al., 2020). This automation reduces manual errors, duplication of efforts (T. N. Dinh and M. T. Thai. 2018), and administrative costs, thereby increasing overall efficiency and streamlining the investment lifecycle (Volkan Dedeoglu et al., 2019).

Blockchain technology acts as a trusted source of information by creating (Volodymyr Babich et al., 2019) an immutable record of transactions. This transparency and immutability (Volodymyr Babich et., 2020) make blockchain a valuable tool for enhancing regulatory compliance, clarifying ownership (Yoo, S., & Managi, S., 2021), and providing an auditable trail for sustainable investments. By enabling verification and validation in real-time (Wilson et al., 2021), this technology helps to mitigate fraudulent activities and strengthens investor trust (Collomb et al., 2016). Moreover, smart contracts enable the embedding of predefined rules and conditions (Nakamoto, 2019) in the investment process. These rules are executed automatically, reducing the need (Pilkington, 2016) for intermediaries, minimizing conflicts of interest, and promoting fair and secure transactions (Kietzmann et al., 2020). By removing the reliance on traditional legal systems, these embedded rules provide (Malhotra et al., 2021) an added layer of security and increase the overall trustworthiness of sustainable investments (Dowling, 2021).

Despite the vast potential of smart contracts and blockchain technology (Milani et al., 2016), their integration into legal frameworks for sustainable investments poses certain challenges (Belu, 2019). Firstly, existing legal systems may face obstacles in adapting to the concept (Shrivastava et al., 2020) of self-executing agreements and the decentralized nature of blockchain networks (Kumar et al., 2018). Legislators and regulators need to devise new legal frameworks and adapt traditional laws (Chohan, 2018) to accommodate the unique characteristics of this technology. Secondly, the enforceability (Regner, 2019) of smart contracts and the recognition of blockchain records as legal evidence (Evans, 2019) vary across jurisdictions. The creation of internationally recognized standards (Hawasin et al., 2023) is crucial to ensure cross-border compatibility and cooperation. This would also address concerns regarding data privacy (Gawusu, 2022), protection, and jurisdictional conflict, fostering global adoption of smart contracts in sustainable investments (Ng, 2020).

Another significant challenge lies in addressing unforeseen contingencies (Tseng et al., 2019) and dispute resolution within smart contracts. Traditional legal processes and institutions (Yoo & Managi, 2021) might struggle to deal with the intricacies of decentralized systems (Mustapha, 2020). Developing technological solutions and specialized dispute resolution mechanisms (Alman and Nobanee, 2019) that align with the decentralized nature of smart contracts would be critical in creating (Abhilash, 2022) a robust legal framework for sustainable investments. To effectively integrate smart contracts with blockchain technology (Kroninsky, 2022) into legal frameworks for sustainable investments, a multidisciplinary approach is essential (Atan, 2016). Collaboration between legal professionals, technologists, policymakers, and industry experts (Rijal, 2023) is crucial to understand the implications and develop suitable regulations (Heines, 2021). Innovation labs, research institutions, and think tanks should actively contribute (Udeagha & Muchapondwa, 2023) to the development of legal frameworks that promote sustainable investments (Farnaghi, 2020) driven by smart contracts and blockchain technology.

The integration between smart contracts and blockchain technology (Ahmad, 2021) presents significant implications for legal frameworks governing sustainable investments (Kasprzak, 2021). By enhancing transparency, efficiency, and security, this integration can revolutionize the way sustainable investments (Tian et al., 2021) are conducted. However, challenges related to adaptation, enforceability, and dispute resolution (Ali et al., 2023) need to be addressed for widespread adoption. As stakeholders work together, combining legal expertise (Truby, 2018) with technological innovation, the potential for sustainable investments powered by smart contracts (Chen & Volz, 2021) and blockchain technology can be fully realized, resulting in a more sustainable and transparent financial future (Saari et al., 2022).

Regulatory Challenges Associated with Tokenization of Sustainable Investments

Tokenization is a rapidly emerging trend in the investment world (Uzsoki & Guerdat, 2023), with the potential to revolutionize the way sustainable investments are made (Ny, 2022), managed, and traded. By creating digital tokens representing shares of ownership (Zheng, 2022) in sustainable assets, tokenization aims to enhance liquidity, broaden access to investment opportunities (Truby, 2018), and promote transparency. However, the adoption of tokenization in sustainable investments (Khan, 2022) faces several significant regulatory challenges.

One of the key challenges surrounding tokenization of sustainable investments (Mahmudnia, 2022) lies in developing an appropriate regulatory framework. Existing regulatory structures were primarily designed (Jing, 2023) for traditional securities and may not adequately address the unique characteristics of tokens (Trivedi, 2021). Regulators must establish clear guidelines and standards that address issues (Ali Dorri et al., 2019) such as investor protection, compliance with environmental regulations (Ali et al., 2023), and anti-money laundering measures. Ensuring investor protection is paramount in any investment market (Andrea Castellani et al., 2020), and tokenization is no exception. Tokenized assets should provide investors with the same level of protection as traditional securities (Barbara Rita Barricelli et al., 2019). Regulators need to address concerns related to fraud, misrepresentation, and market manipulation (Christopher Santi Götz et al., 2020) within the tokenized sustainable investment space. This includes enforcing strict disclosure requirements (Dowling, 2021), implementing robust investor suitability assessments, and regulating market conduct to prevent market abuses (Edward Glaessgen and David Stargel. 2012).

Sustainable investments are often guided by environmental regulations aimed at preventing ecological harm (Evans, 2019). The tokenization of sustainable assets must ensure that the underlying projects or assets (Gawusu et al., 2022) comply with relevant environmental regulations. Regulators need to define the criteria (Ghosh et al., 2019) by which sustainable projects or assets are verified, address issues of greenwashing (Hawashin et al., 2023) and establish mechanisms to monitor compliance at the token level (Adil Rasheed et al., 2020). Tokenization has the potential to break down barriers and enable cross-border investments (Henrik et al., 2020). However, this brings forth challenges related to jurisdictional differences in regulatory frameworks (Sabah et al., 2020). Regulators must navigate how different countries, and regulatory bodies view tokenized assets (Irfan, Kadry, Sharif, & Ullah Khan, 2023), ensuring harmonization and preventing regulatory arbitrage. The lack of a unified global regulatory legal framework (Khan et al., 2022) poses challenges in determining which jurisdiction should regulate tokenized sustainable investments (Shuai Wang et al., 2019).

The tokenization of sustainable investments introduces complexities when it comes to AML and KYC procedures (Muhammad Habib et al., 2020). Regulators need to establish robust procedures to verify the identity of token holders (Kietzmann et al., 2020), trace the source of funds, and prevent money laundering or terrorist financing (Krosinsky, 2012). Enforcing strict AML and KYC standards becomes especially challenging (Malhotra et al., 2021) given the borderless nature of tokenized investments, highlighting the need for collaboration between regulators (Kumar & Mallick, 2018) and financial institutions.

Tokenization involves the use of blockchain technology, which raises concerns about privacy and data protection (Marietheres Dietz and Günther Pernul., 2020). Token holders might be required to disclose personal information when participating in tokenized investments (Marietheres Dietz et al., 2019). Regulators must strike a fine balance between enabling transparency and safeguarding investor privacy (Matthias Eckhart et al., 2018), taking into account growing data protection regulations such as the General Data Protection Regulation (GDPR) (Nakamoto, 2019). Tokenized investments are prone to rapid fluctuation and price volatility due to their liquidity and digital nature (Milani et al., 2016). Regulators must monitor markets to ensure integrity and prevent manipulation (R. Minerva et al., 2021), as even small attempts to manipulate token prices can significantly impact investor confidence (Sihan Huang et al., 2020). Moreover, regulators should develop mechanisms to address issues like market stability, fraudulent trading activities (T. N. Dinh and M. T. Thai. 2018), and the risk of sybil attacks.

Thus, tokenization has the potential to transform the sustainable investment landscape (Volkan Dedeoglu et al., 2019), promoting liquidity, accessibility, and transparency. However, to fully realize these benefits, regulatory challenges (Volodymyr Babich et al., 2019) associated with tokenization must be addressed. Regulatory frameworks need to be adapted to meet the unique characteristics (Volodymyr Babich et., 2020) of tokenized sustainable assets, ensuring investor protection, compliance with environmental regulations (Yoo & Managi, 2021), and maintaining market integrity. Collaboration between regulators, industry participants, and investors (Wilson et al., 2021) is essential to navigate these challenges and realize the vast potential of tokenization (Collomb et al., 2016) in the sustainable investment sector.

Regulatory and Legal Concerns Arising From Cross-Border Investments Facilitated by the Blockchain-Digital Twin Fusion

The fusion of blockchain technology and digital twins has transformed various industries (Nakamoto, 2019), including finance and investments. As cross-border investments leverage this fusion (Pilkington, 2016) for enhanced efficiency, transparency, and security, new regulatory and legal concerns have emerged (Kietzmann et al., 2020). One of the primary concerns surrounding cross-border investments with blockchain-digital twin fusion (Malhotra et al., 2021) is the need to ensure compliance with diverse regulatory frameworks (Dowling, 2021). Different countries have varying rules and regulations regarding investments (Milani et al., 2016), securities, data privacy, and anti-money laundering (AML) measures (Belu, 2019). Implementing a uniform regulatory framework that accommodates the complexities (Shrivastava et al., 2020) of cross-border transactions become crucial for seamless investment processes. Digital twins, in conjunction with blockchain (Kumar et al., 2018), enable real-time monitoring and management of assets or projects across borders (Chohan, 2018). However, this introduces jurisdictional complexities. Determining which country's laws should govern such investments (Regner, 2019), dispute resolutions, and the enforcement of contractual obligations can be challenging. Resolving jurisdictional issues (Evans, 2019) and ensuring accountability are significant concerns for both investors and regulators (Hawasin et al., 2023).

Cross-border investments facilitated by blockchain technology involve the sharing (Gawusu, 2022) and storage of sensitive investor and transactional data. Maintaining data privacy (Ng, 2020) and ensuring security are critical challenges for blockchain-digital twin fusion (Tseng et al., 2019). Blockchain implementation relies heavily on smart contracts, which automate and execute agreements (Yoo & Managi, 2021) based on predefined conditions. While smart contracts increase efficiency and reduce the need for intermediaries (Mustapha, 2020), their legal enforceability in cross-border investments remains uncertain (Alman and Nobanee, 2019). Varying legal systems and interpretations complicate the recognition and enforcement (Abhilash, 2022) of smart contracts in different jurisdictions, potentially leading to legal disputes and challenges (Kroninsky, 2022).

Another concern is the possibility of regulatory arbitrage, where entities take advantage (Atan, 2016) of different regulatory frameworks across borders to engage in illicit activities (Rijal, 2023) or bypass tighter regulations. Coupled with cross-border investments, the decentralized nature of blockchain technology (Heines, 2021), makes it essential for regulators to work collaboratively and ensure consistent regulations to prevent potential loopholes or abuse (Udeagha & Muchapondwa, 2023).

Investor protection is a top priority when it comes to cross-border investments (Farnaghi, 2020). Blockchain provides increased transparency and immutability of investment records (Ahmad, 2021), reducing the risk of fraudulent activities. However, challenges persist in terms of recourse mechanisms (Kasprzak, 2021), dispute resolution, and investor compensation for losses incurred due to malicious activities (Tian et al., 2021) or system failures. Clear guidelines and safeguards must be established to protect investors (Ali et al., 2023) engaging in cross-border investments facilitated by blockchain-digital twin fusion (Truby, 2018).

Blockchain-digital twin fusion can improve anti-money laundering (AML) and know-your-customer (KYC) compliance (Chen & Volz, 2021) by creating a transparent and auditable transaction trail. However, challenges arise from cross-border transactions (Saari et al., 2022) where different jurisdictions have different AML and KYC requirements (Uzsoki & Guerdat, 2023). Harmonizing these requirements and ensuring seamless compliance across borders (Ny, 2022) is essential to prevent money laundering and terrorist financing activities (Zheng, 2022). Cross-border investments facilitated by the fusion of blockchain and the digital twin technologies (Truby, 2018) also have the potential to revolutionize the investment landscape. Nevertheless, regulatory and legal concerns must be addressed (Khan, 2022) to foster investor confidence, maintain integrity, and prevent abuse (Mahmudnia, 2022). Cooperation between international regulatory bodies, standardization of legal frameworks (Jing, 2023), and the establishment of clear guidelines and enforcement mechanisms are vital steps towards (Trivedi, 2021) successfully navigating the complexities of cross-border investments within the blockchain-digital twin fusion (Ali Dorri et al., 2019).

Cybersecurity Risks and Data Integrity Implications of Blockchain and Digital Twins Fusion

The fusion of blockchain technology and digital twins opens new horizons (Ali et al., 2023) in various industries, revolutionizing the way we interact with digital entities (Andrea Castellani et al., 2020) and ensuring data integrity. However, this convergence also brings about cybersecurity risks and data integrity (Barbara Rita Barricelli et al., 2019) implications that must be addressed. Blockchain technology provides an evenly distributed (Volodymyr Babich et., 2020) and immutable ledger that can enhance the integrity and security of digital twin systems (Volodymyr Babich et al., 2019). It ensures transparency, immutability, and secure data sharing among stakeholders (Volkan Dedeoglu et al., 2019). By decentralizing trust, blockchain mitigates the need for a central authority (T. N. Dinh and M. T. Thai. 2018) and enables a peer-to-peer network for secure data exchange (Sihan Huang et al., 2020).

Smart contracts, being an essential component of blockchain technology (R. Minerva et al., 2021), introduce a new attack vector. If vulnerabilities exist in the programming (Milani et al., 2016) or implementation of these contracts, threat actors can exploit them to compromise (Nakamoto, 2019) the security and integrity of the digital twin system. With digital twins (Matthias Eckhart et al., 2018), a significant risk is unauthorized access to sensitive data (Marietheres Dietz et al., 2019). If security measures are not implemented appropriately, malicious actors can gain unauthorized entry (Marietheres Dietz and Günther Pernul., 2020), manipulate data, steal intellectual property, or expose confidential information (Kumar & Mallick, 2018).

Blockchain-powered digital twin systems can be targeted with DDoS attacks (Malhotra et al., 2021), where threat actors overwhelm the network with excessive traffic, making the systems (Krosinsky, 2012) inaccessible to legitimate users. These attacks can disrupt operations and compromise data integrity (Kietzmann et al., 2020). In blockchain networks, a 51% attack occurs when the majority of the network's computing power (I. Yaqoob et al., 2020) is controlled by a single entity. If such an attack succeeds, the attacker can modify transaction data (Irfan, Hussainey, Chan Bukhari, & Nam, 2024), compromise the integrity of the digital twin system, and potentially alter the entire blockchain history (Khan et al., 2022).

While blockchain ensures data immutability, it cannot guarantee the accuracy (Benedikt et al., 2021) of the data being entered into the system. If inaccurate or flawed data is entered, it will be permanently stored (Aravind et al., 2017) on the blockchain, potentially impacting the fidelity of the digital twin representation (Pethuru Raj, 2021). Digital twins often rely on external data sources known as oracles to input real-world data (Adil et al., 2020). These oracles serve as intermediaries and introduce potential vulnerabilities (Hawashin et al., 2023). Malicious or compromised oracles can manipulate data feeds, leading to inaccurate digital twin representations (Ghosh et al., 2019).

The implementation of complex smart contracts within the digital twin ecosystem (Gawusu et al., 2022) can inadvertently introduce coding errors, leading to unintended consequences (Evans, 2019) and potential vulnerabilities. Ensuring the verification and validation of smart contract logic is crucial to maintain data integrity (Edward Glaessgen and David Stargel. 2012). Implementing secure coding practices while developing smart contracts (Dowling, 2021) and digital twin systems is essential. Thorough code reviews, audits (Christopher Santi Götz et al., 2020), and adherence to established security standards can significantly reduce vulnerabilities (Barbara Rita Barricelli et al., 2019).

Deploying strong access control measures and encryption techniques helps mitigate unauthorized access (Andrea Castellani et al., 2020) and protects sensitive data. Implementing multi-factor authentication, role-based access controls (Ali et al., 2023), and encryption of data at rest and in transit are crucial steps (Ali Dorri et al., 2019). Employing robust monitoring systems and intrusion detection mechanisms can help identify (Trivedi, 2021) and respond to the cybersecurity threats in real-time scenario. Monitoring activities within the digital twin (Jing, 2023) environment ensures early detection of any anomalous or suspicious behavior (Mahmudnia, 2022).

Ensuring the accuracy and reliability of data inputs to the digital twin system (Khan, 2022) is vital. Regular analysis and verification of data sources, including oracles (Truby, 2018), strengthens the overall data integrity of the system. The fusion of blockchain technology (Zheng, 2022) and digital twins brings immense potential for innovation and enhanced data integrity. However, it also exposes organizations to cybersecurity risks (Ny, 2022). To fully leverage the benefits of this fusion, robust cybersecurity measures must be adopted (Uzsoki & Guerdat, 2023). By addressing vulnerabilities in smart contracts, strengthening access controls (Saari et al., 2022), and verifying data sources, organizations can mitigate risks while preserving (Chen & Volz, 2021) the integrity of digital twin systems, fostering a secure and trustworthy environment for critical operations in the digital era (Truby, 2018).

SUGGESTIONS AND CONCLUSION

The rapid advancement of technology has introduced innovative solutions such as blockchain and digital twin fusion (Ali et al., 2023), which hold great potential for sustainable investments. Combining the transparency and security features of blockchain with the virtual replica (Tian et al., 2021) of real-world assets in digital twin technology can revolutionize industries such as energy, supply chain, and infrastructure (Kasprzak, 2021). However, as with any emerging technology, regulatory and legal implications (Ahmad, 2021) must be carefully considered to ensure the effective and ethical harnessing (Farnaghi, 2020) of this technology for sustainable investments.

One of the primary concerns in the adoption of blockchain-digital twin fusion (Udeagha & Muchapondwa, 2023) is data security and privacy. Enhanced security is provided by the use of blockchain technology through its decentralized nature (Heines, 2021) and cryptographic algorithms, but it also presents challenges regarding compliance with data protection regulations (Rijal, 2023), such as GDPR. Jurisdictions need to establish frameworks that strike a balance between protecting individual privacy rights (Atan, 2016) and enabling the collection and use of data necessary for sustainable investments (Kroninsky, 2022).

Currently, there is a lack of generalized threat intelligence that can be applied across different architectures and businesses without significant customization (Abhilash, 2022). Existing tools primarily rely on machine learning (ML) to detect and predict specific security threat scenarios with well-defined inputs and outputs (Alman and Nobanee, 2019). These ML solutions can be integrated into security metrics and tools or manually investigated by security analysts (Mustapha, 2020).

To fully realize the potential of blockchain-digital twin fusion for sustainable investments, standardization (Yoo & Managi, 2021) and interoperability among different platforms and systems must be established. Regulatory bodies should work closely with industry stakeholders (Henrik et al., 2020) to create widely accepted technical standards. These standards ensure compatibility, enhance transparency, and facilitate information exchange, streamlining processes for sustainable investment (Fei Tao et al., 2019) projects while reducing the risk of data silos and fragmentation.

The possibilities presented by blockchain-digital twin fusion for sustainable investments are limitless (Fei Tao et al., 2018). However, the successful integration of this technology requires careful consideration of the regulatory and legal implications it poses (Aravind et al., 2017). Governments, regulatory bodies, and industry stakeholders must work collaboratively to establish comprehensive frameworks (I, Yakoob et al., 2020) that balance the need for transparency, security, privacy, and adherence to existing legal systems (Irfan, Elmogy, Gupta, Khalifa, & Dias, 2024). By addressing these implications proactively, the harnessing of blockchain-digital twin fusion can pave the way for sustainable investments that promote positive societal and environmental impact.

REFERENCES

Abhilash, S., Shenoy, S. S., Shetty, D. K., Lobo, L. S., & N, S. K. (2023). Green Bond as an Innovative Financial Instrument in the Indian Financial Market: Insights from Systematic Literature Review Approach. *SAGE Open*, 13(2), 21582440231178783. DOI: 10.1177/21582440231178783

Adil Rasheed, Omer San, and Trond Kvamsdal. (2020) Digital twin: Values, challenges and enablers from a modeling perspective. *IEEE Access 8*, 21980–22012. DOI: 10.1109/ACCESS.2020.2970143

Ahmad, D., Lutfiani, N., Ahmad, A. D. A. R., & Rahardja, U. (2021). Blockchain Technology Immutability Framework Design in E-Government. [Public Administration Journal]. *Jurnal Administrasi Publik*, 11(1), 32–41.

Ali Dorri, Salil S Kanhere, Raja Jurdak, and Praveen Gauravaram. (2019) LSB: A Lightweight Scalable Blockchain for IoT security and anonymity. *J. Parallel and Distrib. Comput*. 134, 180–197. DOI: 10.1016/j.jpdc.2019.08.005

Ali, O., Momin, M., Shrestha, A., Das, R., Alhajj, F., & Dwivedi, Y. K. (2023). A review of the key challenges of non-fungible tokens. *Technological Forecasting and Social Change*, 187, 122248. DOI: 10.1016/j.techfore.2022.122248

Almansoori A.NobaneeH.NobaneeH. (2019). *How Sustainability Contributes to Shared Value Creation and Firms' Value*. SSRN. https://ssrn.com/abstract=3472411 or http://dx.doi.org/ doi:10.2139/ssrn.3472411

Andrea Castellani, Sebastian Schmitt, and Stefano Squartini. (2020) Real-World Anomaly Detection by using Digital Twin Systems and Weakly-Supervised Learning. *IEEE Transactions on Industrial Informatics*, 1–1. https://doi.org/DOI: 10.1109/TII.2020.3019788

Aravind Ramachandran, Dr Kantarcioglu, et al. (2017) *Using blockchain and smart contracts for secure data provenance management*. arXiv:1709.10000

Atana, R., Razali, F. A., Said, J., & Zainun, S. (2016). Environmental, Social, and Governance (ESG) Disclosure and Its Effect on Firm's Performance: A Comparative Study. *IJEM*, 10(S2), 355–375.

Barbara Rita Barricelli, Elena Casiraghi, and Daniela Fogli. (2019) A Survey on Digital Twin: Definitions, Characteristics, Applications, and Design Implications. *IEEE Access 7*, 167653–167671. DOI: 10.1109/ACCESS.2019.2953499

Belu, M. G. (2019). Application of blockchain in international trade: An overview. *The Romanian Economic Journal*, 22(71), 2–15.

Benedikt Putz, Marietheres Dietz, Philip Empl, and Günther Pernul. (2021) EtherTwin: Blockchain-based Secure Digital Twin Information Management. *Information Processing & Management* 58, 1, 102425. DOI: 10.1016/j.ipm.2020.102425

Chen, Y., & Volz, U. (2021). Scaling up sustainable investment through blockchainbased project bonds. *Development Policy Review*, 40(3), e12582. DOI: 10.1111/dpr.12582

Chohan, U. W. (2021). Non-Fungible Tokens: Blockchains, Scarcity, and Value. *Critical Blockchain Research Initiative*, Notes on the 21st Century.

Christopher Santi Götz, Patrik Karlsson, and Ibrahim Yitmen. (2020) Exploring applicability, interoperability and integrability of Blockchain-based digital twins for asset life cycle management. *Smart and Sustainable Built Environment* DOI: 10.1108/SASBE-08-2020-0115

Collomb, A., & Sok, K. (2016). Blockchain/distributed ledger technology (DLT): What impact on the financial sector? *Digiworld Economic Journal*, (103).

Dowling, M. (2021). Is non-fungible token pricing driven by cryptocurrencies? *Finance Research Letters*, 44, 102097. DOI: 10.1016/j.frl.2021.102097

Edward Glaessgen and David Stargel. (2012) *The digital twin paradigm for future NASA and US Air Force vehicles*. In 53rd AIAA/ASME/ASCE/AHS/ASC structures, structural dynamics and materials conference 20th AIAA/ASME/AHS adaptive structures conference 14th AIAA. Honolulu, Hawaii, 1818. DOI: 10.2514/6.2012-1818

Evans, T. M. (2019). Cryptokitties, cryptography, and copyright. *AIPLA Quarterly Journal*, 47, 219.

Farnaghia, M., & Mansouriana, A. (2022). Blockchain, an enabling technology for transparent and accountable decentralized public participatory GIS. *Cities*, 105.

Fei Tao and Qinglin Qi. (2019) Make more digital twins. *Nature 573*, 490-491. DOI: 10.1038/d41586-019-02849-1

Fei Tao, He Zhang, Ang Liu, and Andrew YC Nee. (2018) Digital twin in industry: State-of-the-art. *IEEE Transactions on Industrial Informatics* 15, 4, 2405–2415. DOI: 10.1109/TII.2018.2873186

Fei Tao, Jiangfeng Cheng, Qinglin Qi, Meng Zhang, He Zhang, and Fangyuan Sui. (2018) Digital twin-driven product design, manufacturing and service with big data. *The International Journal of Advanced Manufacturing Technology* 94, 9-12, 3563–3576. DOI: 10.1007/s00170-017-0233-1

Fei Tao, Meng Zhang, Yushan Liu, and AYC Nee. (2018) Digital twin driven prognostics and health management for complex equipment. *Cirp Annals* 67, 1, 169–172. DOI: 10.1016/j.cirp.2018.04.055

Gawusu, S., Zhang, X., Ahmed, A., Jamatutu, S. A., Miensah, E. D., Amadu, A. A., & Osei, F. A. J. (2022). Renewable energy sources from the perspective of blockchain integration: From theory to application. [Part B]. *Sustainable Energy Technologies and Assessments*, 52, 52. DOI: 10.1016/j.seta.2022.102108

Ghosh, A.K.; Ullah, A.S.; Kubo, A. (2019) Hidden Markov model-based digital twin construction for futuristic manufacturing systems. *Artif. Intell. Eng. Des. Anal. Manuf.* 33, 317–331. [CrossRef]

Hawashin, D., Salah, K., Jayaraman, R., & Musamih, A. (2023). Using Composable NFTs for Trading and Managing Expensive Packaged Products in the Food Industry. *IEEE Access: Practical Innovations, Open Solutions*, 11, 10587–10603. DOI: 10.1109/ACCESS.2023.3241226

Heines, R., Dick, C., Pohle, C., & Jung, R. (2021). The Tokenization of Everything: Towards a Framework for Understanding the Potentials of Tokenized Assets. *PACIS 2021 Proceedings*, 40. Research Gate.

I. Yaqoob, K. Salah, M. Uddin, R. Jayaraman, M. Omar, and M. Imran. (2020) Blockchain for Digital Twins: Recent Advances and Future Research Challenges. *IEEE Network* 34, 5, 290–298. DOI: 10.1109/MNET.001.1900661

Irfan, M. (2021, Jan). Do Shariah Indices converge? Evidence from Gulf Cooperation Council countries. *International Journal of Business Excellence*, 23(2), 251-269.

Irfan, M., Elhoseny, M., Kassim, S., & Metawa, N. (2023). *Advanced Machine Learning Algorithms for Complex Financial Applications*. IGI Global. DOI: 10.4018/978-1-6684-4483-2

Irfan, M., Elmogy, M., Gupta, S., Khalifa, F., & Dias, R. (2024). *AI-Driven Decentralized Finance and the Future of Finance. USA*: IGI Global. DOI: 10.4018/979-8-3693-6321-8

Irfan, M., Elmogy, M., Majid, M. S., & El-Sappagh, S. (2023). *The Impact of AI Innovation on Financial Sectors in the Era of Industry 5.0.* IGI Global. DOI: 10.4018/979-8-3693-0082-4

Irfan, M., Hussainey, K., Chan Bukhari, S. A., & Nam, Y. (Eds.). (2024). *Issues of Sustainability in AI and New-Age Thematic Investing. Pennsylvania, US*: IGI Global Publisher. DOI: 10.4018/979-8-3693-3282-5

Irfan, M., Kadry, S., Sharif, M., & Ullah Khan, H. (2023). *Fintech Applications in Islamic Finance: AI, Machine Learning, and Blockchain Techniques.* IGI Global. DOI: 10.4018/979-8-3693-1038-0

Jing, Y., Chen, C., Dong, J., & He, Z. (2023). Blockchain-Embedded Strategic Options for Satellite Operators: Sell, SataaS, or Dual [MDPI AG.]. *Systems*, 11(11), 550. DOI: 10.3390/systems11110550

Kasprzak, P. (2021). Blockchain to the Rescue Tokenization of Residential Real Estate in the Emerging Token Economy. In H. T.A., & D. J.J., Digitalization, Digital Transformation and Sustainability in the Global Economy (pp. 21–35). *Springer*. DOI: 10.1007/978-3-030-77340-3_3

Khan, K. M., Fahim, A., Saleem, D. M., & Jokhio, M. (2022). Empirical Investigation on Blockchain Interoperability. *VFAST Transactions on Software Engineering*, 11(1), 25–36. DOI: 10.21015/vtse.v10i4.1315

Kietzmann, J., Lee, L. W., McCarthy, I. P., & Kietzmann, T. C. (2020). Deepfakes: Trick or treat? *Business Horizons*, 63(2), 135e146.

Krosinsky, C. (2012). Sustainable investing: The art of long-term performance. *Routledge*. DOI: 10.4324/9781849773959

Kumar, N. M., & Mallick, P. K. (2018). Blockchain technology for security issues and challenges in IoT. *Procedia Computer Science*, 132, 1815–1823. doi:. procs.2018.05.140DOI: 10.1016/j

Mahmudnia, D., Arashpour, M., Bai, Y., & Feng, H. (2022). Drones and Blockchain Integration to Manage Forest Fires in Remote Regions. *Drones (Basel)*, 6(11), 331. DOI: 10.3390/drones6110331

Malhotra, A., O'Neill, H., & Stowell, P. (2021). Thinking strategically about blockchain adoption risks and risk mitigation. *Business Horizons*, 65(2), 159e171

Marietheres Dietz and Günther Pernul. (2020) Unleashing the Digital Twin's Potential for ICS Security. *IEEE Security & Privacy* 18, 4, 20–27. https://doi.org/DOI: 10.1109/MSEC.2019.2961650

Marietheres Dietz, Benedikt Putz, and Günther Pernul. (2019) A Distributed Ledger approach to Digital Twin secure data sharing. In IFIP Annual Conference on Data and Applications Security and Privacy, Vol. 11559. *Springer, Cham*, 281–300. https://doi.org/DOI: 10.1007/978-3-030-22479-0_15

Matthias Eckhart and Andreas Ekelhart. (2018) Towards Security-Aware Virtual Environments for Digital Twins. In Proceedings of the 4th ACM Workshop on Cyber-Physical System Security (Incheon, Republic of Korea) (CPSS '18). *Association for Computing Machinery, New York, NY, USA*, 61–72. DOI: 10.1145/3198458.3198464

Milani, F., García-Bañuelos, L., & Dumas, M. (2016). Blockchain and business process improvement. *BP Trends newsletter (October 2016).*

Minerva, R., & Crespi, N. (2021). ● R. Minerva and N. Crespi. (2021) Digital Twins: Properties, Software Frameworks, and Application Scenarios. *IT Professional*, 23(1), 51–55. DOI: 10.1109/MITP.2020.2982896

Muhammad Habib ur Rehman, Khaled Salah, Ernesto Damiani, and Davor Svetinovic. (2020) Towards Blockchain-Based Reputation-Aware Federated Learning. *IEEE INFOCOM 2020 - IEEE Conference on Computer Communications Workshops (INFOCOM WKSHPS).* 183–188. DOI: 10.1109/INFOCOM-WKSHPS50562.2020.9163027

Mustapha, Z., Kunhibava, S. B., & Muneeza, A. (2020). Legal and Sharīʿah noncompliance risks in Nigerian Islamic finance industry: A review of the literature. *International Journal of Law and Management*, 63(02), 275–299. DOI: 10.1108/IJLMA-03-2020-0075

Nakamoto, S. (2019). Bitcoin: A peer-to-peer electronic cash system. *Manubot.*

Ng, T.-H., Lye, C.-T., Chan, K.-H., Lim, Y.-Z., & Lim, Y.-S. (2020). Sustainability in Asia: The Roles of Financial Development in Environmental, Social, and Governance (ESG) *Performance. Social Indicators Research*, 150(1), 17–44. DOI: 10.1007/s11205-020-02288-w

Ny, B. (2022). *Blockchain in Impact Investing: The Potential of Impact Tokens on SDGs. Medium.* https://medium.com/@Godswisdomtoday/blockchain-in-impactinvesting-the-potential-of-impact-tokens-on-sdgs-767ad67b4f3

Pethuru Raj. 2021. Chapter Thirteen - Empowering digital twins with blockchain. In The Blockchain Technology for Secure and Smart Applications across Industry Verticals. *Advances in Computers*, Vol. 121. Elsevier, 267 – 283. https://doi.org/DOI: 10.1016/bs.adcom.2020.08.013

Pilkington, M. (2016). Blockchain technology: principles and applications. In Research handbook on digital transformations. *Edward Elgar Publishing.* DOI: 10.4337/9781784717766.00019

Regner, F., Schweizer, A., & Urbach, N. (2019). NFTs in Practice — Non-Fungible Tokens as Core Components of a Blockchain-based Event Ticketing Application. *In Fortieth International Conference on Information Systems.*

Rijal, S., & Saranani, F. (2023). The Role of Blockchain Technology in Increasing Economic Transparency and Public Trust. [TACIT]. *Technology and Society Perspectives*, 1(2), 56–67. DOI: 10.61100/tacit.v1i2.51

Saari, A., Junnila, S., & Vimpari, J. (2022). Blockchain's Grand Promise for the Real Estate Sector: A Systematic Review. *Applied Sciences (Basel, Switzerland)*, 12(23), 11940. DOI: 10.3390/app122311940

Sabah Suhail, Raja Jurdak, Raimundas Matulevicius, and Choong Seon Hong. (2021) *Securing Cyber-Physical Systems Through Blockchain-Based Digital Twins and Threat Intelligence*. CoRR abs/2105.08886 arXiv:2105.08886 https://arxiv.org/abs/2105.08886

Sabah Suhail, Rasheed Hussain, Raja Jurdak, and Choong Seon Hong. (2021) Trustworthy Digital Twins in the Industrial Internet of Things with Blockchain. *IEEE Internet Computing*, 1–10. https://doi.org/ DOI: 10.1109/MIC.2021.3059320

Shrivastava, G. (2020). Cryptocurrencies and Blockchain Technology Applications. *Wiley eBooks*. DOI: 10.1002/9781119621201

Shuai Wang, Liwei Ouyang, Yong Yuan, Xiaochun Ni, Xuan Han, and Fei-Yue Wang. (2019) Blockchain-Enabled Smart Contracts: Architecture, Applications, and Future Trends. *IEEE Transactions on Systems, Man, and Cybernetics: Systems* 49, 11, 2266–2277. DOI: 10.1109/TSMC.2019.2895123

Sihan Huang, Guoxin Wang, Yan Yan, and Xiongbing Fang. (2020) Blockchain-based data management for digital twin of product. *Journal of Manufacturing Systems* 54, 361–371.

Sternberg, H. S., Hofmann, E., & Roeck, D. (2021, March). ● Henrik S. Sternberg, Erik Hofmann, and Dominik Roeck. (2020) The Struggle is Real: Insights from a Supply Chain Blockchain Case. *Journal of Business Logistics*, 42(1), 71–87. Advance online publication. DOI: 10.1111/jbl.12240

T. N. Dinh and M. T. Thai. (2018) AI and Blockchain: A Disruptive Integration. *Computer* 51, 9, 48–53. https://doi.org/. 2018.3620971DOI: 10.1109/MC

Tian, Y., Minchin, R. E., Chung, K., Woo, J., & Adriaens, P. (2021). Towards Inclusive and Sustainable Infrastructure Development through Blockchain-enabled Asset Tokenization: An Exploratory Case Study. *IOP Conference Series: Materials Science and Engineering*, Volume 1218

Trivedi, S., Mehta, K., & Sharma, R. (2021). Systematic Literature Review on Application of Blockchain Technology in E-Finance and Financial Services. *Journal of Technology Management & Innovation*, 16(3), 89–102. DOI: 10.4067/S0718-27242021000300089

Truby, J. (2018). Decarbonizing Bitcoin: Law and policy choices for reducing the energy consumption of Blockchain technologies and digital currencies. *Energy Research & Social Science*, 44, 399–410. DOI: 10.1016/j.erss.2018.06.009

Tseng, M. L., Tan, P. A., Jeng, S. Y., Lin, C. W. R., Negash, Y. T., & Darsono, S. N. A. C. (2019). Sustainable investment: Interrelated among corporate governance, economic performance and market risks using investor preference approach. *Sustainability (Basel)*, 11(7), 2108. DOI: 10.3390/su11072108

Udeagha, M. C., & Muchapondwa, E. (2023). Green finance, fintech, and environmental sustainability: Fresh policy insights from the BRICS nations. *International Journal of Sustainable Development and World Ecology*, 30(6), 633–649. DOI: 10.1080/13504509.2023.2183526

Uzsoki, D., & Guerdat, P. (2019). Impact Tokens: A blockchain-based solution for impact investing. *International Institute for Sustainable Development*.

Volkan Dedeoglu, Raja Jurdak, Guntur D. Putra, Ali Dorri, and Salil S. Kanhere. (2019) A Trust Architecture for Blockchain in IoT. In Proceedings of the 16th EAI International Conference on Mobile and Ubiquitous Systems: Computing, Networking and Services (Houston, Texas, USA) (MobiQuitous '19). *Association for Computing Machinery, New York, NY, USA*, 190–199. DOI: 10.1145/3360774.3360822

Volodymyr Babich and Gilles Hilary. (2020) OM Forum - Distributed Ledgers and Operations: What Operations Management Researchers Should Know About Blockchain Technology. *Manufacturing & Service Operations Management* 22, 2, 223–240. https://doi.org/DOI: 10.1287/msom.2018.0752

Volodymyr Babich, Gilles Hilary, et al. (2019) Blockchain and other distributed ledger technologies in operations. *Foundations and Trends in Technology, Information and Operations Management* 12, 2-3, 152–172. https://doi.org/DOI: 10.2139/ssrn.3232977

Wilson, K. B., Karg, A., & Ghaderi, H. (2021). Prospecting non- fungible tokens in the digital economy: Stakeholders and ecosystem, risk and opportunity. *Business Horizons*, 65(5), 657e670.

Yoo, S., & Managi, S. (2021). Disclosure or action: Evaluating ESG behavior towards financial performance. *Finance Research Letters*, 102108.

Chapter 3
Robo-Advisory in the Era of AI: An Overview

Vedantam Seetha Ram
https://orcid.org/0000-0002-6375-1501
Jain University, India

Sakha Gangadhara Rama Rao
https://orcid.org/0000-0003-3578-8558
GITAM University, India

Dowluri Sudhakar
https://orcid.org/0000-0001-8068-9765
Dravidian University, India

Bivek Shrestha
https://orcid.org/0000-0002-3040-5215
Nepal Clearing House Limited, Nepal

ABSTRACT

Robo-advisory services gained momentum due to data-driven patterns in financial advisory services. AI helps RAS in fine tuning for sustainable adoption. The present exploratory research helps in understanding the extent of penetration of RA services in financial advisory market and to test this a self-administered structured questionnaire is circulated to individual investors utilizing the RAS with various advisory firms. Partial correlation is calculated to find out the link between role of technology, robo advisory service firms and AI in driving individuals for their financial decisions. Results indicate that technology, RAS, and AI have influence, but AI still cannot change the quality of RAS and is not a replacement to human advisory.

1 INTRODUCTION

Robo-advisory (RA), one of the FinTech processes that helps in financial instruments' use and decision making which is leading towards implementation of artificial intelligence (AI) by firms that are involved in advising with the help of machines such that human intelligence is supplemented for affective

DOI: 10.4018/979-8-3693-7924-0.ch003

decision making (Abraham Facundo et al., 2019; Fenwick, 2020). In the personal finance world, where financial advisors and wealth managers, while advising their clients, make use of these services such that scope for better portfolio construction is high, as risk can be mitigated and returns can be maximized. Global RA services are valued at US$4.7 billion in 2023 and are expected to grow to US$41.07 billion by the year 2027 with an estimated compounded annual growth rate (CAGR) of 31.8 per cent (Allied Market Research, 2023) increasing its adoption rate, making individual's portfolio effective that change investment market goals in future. It is also expected that the assets under management by RA market to reach US$1.802 trillion with a CAGR of 6.68 per cent which is predicted to reach US$2.334 trillion and an expected user base of 1.459 trillion by the end of 2028 (Statista, 2022).

Figure 1 Asset-Liability Management Companies Framework

Source: Compiled based on Authors' Learning and Understanding

Assets-Liability management company's framework (Figure 1) helps realize an asset manager's flexibility in the construction of portfolio that include portfolio's financial goals, options available in market for the portfolio construction, risk classification and investment strategies along with reallocation strategies apart from return maximization as the goal (Lam, 2016).

For the effective portfolio construction and investment either by an individual or by the asset managers or by the asset management companies (AMC) RA builds a link that helps make changes based on various factors. Being acting like a link between the advisor and the advisee, the advantage of RA is, one can simulate both micro and macro variables that can be altered simultaneously to forecast their portfolio returns, and this helps investors make an appropriate choice. High net worth investors (HNIs) got much benefit out of RA services through an effective portfolio management system as they reduce information asymmetry for both advisors as well as to clients; since, it collects loads of data which is used to assess and process for decision making purposes. However, asymmetry increases if either of parties provide incomplete or false data which causes overloaded data collection by machines (Dolata & Schwabe, 2017), leading to deviated outcome that further causes wrong investment choice. Financial literacy rate can be improved with the help of RA service, since mobile application use has increased across the globe either due to necessity or due to market influence or social influence (Oentoro, 2020). Even individuals with low technical knowledge are adopting and using the RA services for making their investment choices (Mohammad Irfan, Mohammed Elmogy, Swati Gupta, Fahmi Khalifa, 2024) (D'Hondt et al., 2020a). Youth in their 20s and 30s, since they get adapted to technology quite easy, are already formulating their financial goals with the help of RA services (Bhatia et al., 2021).

2. ROLE OF ROBO-ADVISORY, ADVANTAGES AND CHALLENGES IN INDUSTRY

The innovative nature of financial advising in the investment world is today done by Robo-Advisors that help invest on a highly returns oriented, subjective and objective risk mitigated investment options with their innovative asset class creation for the investors based on their financial history, feedback on the investment interest, market movement, risk appetite of the investors that are reviewed by the monitoring and regulatory agencies apart from financial advisors from time to time (Cedrell & Issa, 2018; Rasiwala & Kohli, 2019). One of the major advantages of robo-advisors is their use of loads of data in terms of volume, frequency, variety of data to analyse, forecast and then advice an appropriate tool for investment purposes (Grable, 2018). RA services are useful for the small and large investors at normal as well as during financial markets' crisis, economic crisis as well as during policy disruption periods in selecting an appropriate investment instrument, especially those investing through broking firms (D'Hondt et al., 2020b). The non-contact advisory service nature of RA services helps in product selection, comparison and reallocation process (So, 2021) apart from avoiding conflict of interest in the human involved advisory services though many clients of banks and financial institutions are still preferring human advise as their priority making RA services as a complementary option rather a substitute (Brenner & Meyll, 2020). Expected utility theory and prospect theories of behavioral finance help in identifying financial products, since investors constantly compare different investment options available to them to maximize their returns with sustainability over time (Irfan, Mohammad; Hussainey, Khaled; Bukhari, Syed Ahmad Chan; Nam, 2024).

Digitalization (Jung et al., 2018) and Machine learning (ML) techniques help robo-advisors in training the machines for an appropriate investment option that suits an investors' requirement based on market conditions as the investment advisors (IA) can train the machines with huge sets of data along with multiple scenarios under different market conditions (Mohammad Irfan, Mohamed Elhoseny, Salina Kassim, 2023) (Becker et al., 2021; D'Hondt et al., 2020b). The various factors considered by robo-advisors while offering their services in the selection of financial instruments (Figure 2) are historical information about the instruments, their performance over decades, competing instruments, success rate and present market conduciveness for the instruments. Economic variables such as rates of returns offered by the instruments, global economic and political scenario, import-export market opportunities; non-economic variables such as unemployment rate, stability of governments, monitoring regulatory guidelines in the ease of doing business, availability of skilled labor; investor portfolio selection guidelines; investment advisor's style of selecting investment instruments and the fee or commission charged, kick-backs or incentives offered.

Figure 2 Factors considered during Robo-Advisory of Financial Instruments

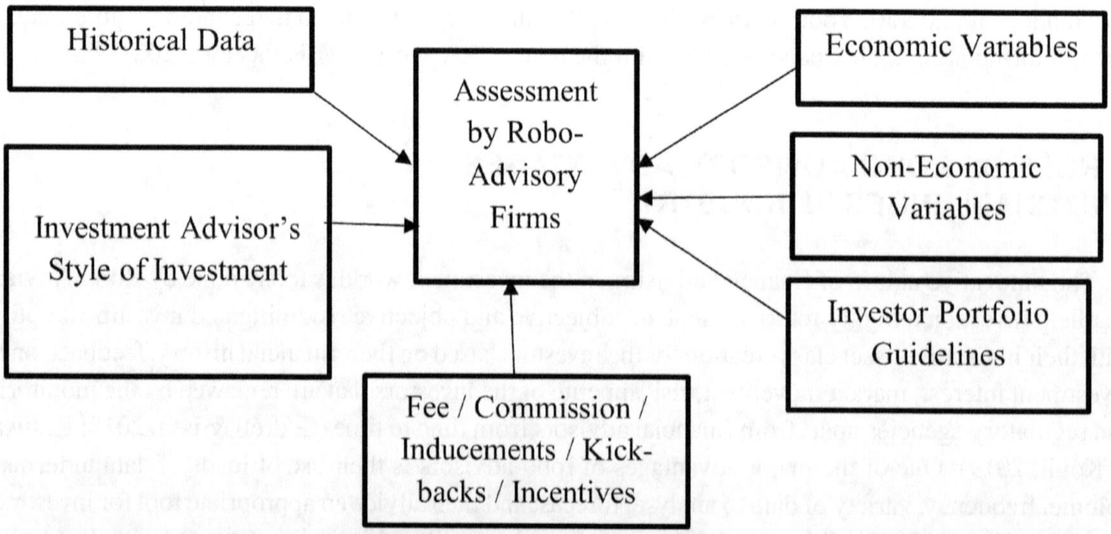

Source: Compiled by authors based on conceptual understanding

RA services are primarily classified based on their adoption by market and investors which is dependent on learning the needs of clients by collecting data from them, suggesting various financial products for investment option based on the data received and understood, advise from time to time the changes occurring in finance world to balance the investment fund of clients. Due to advancement in technology and RA services transformation, computer aided advisory started that uses portfolio construction based on data fed, which operates based on an algorithm written, offers suggestions for balancing or rebalancing the investment fund, which further transformed into fully automated investment process along with auto allocation of funds for investment from one option to another based on risk mitigation strategies suggested by the investors (Moulliet et al., 2016).

Figure 3 Robo-Advisory Services Framework

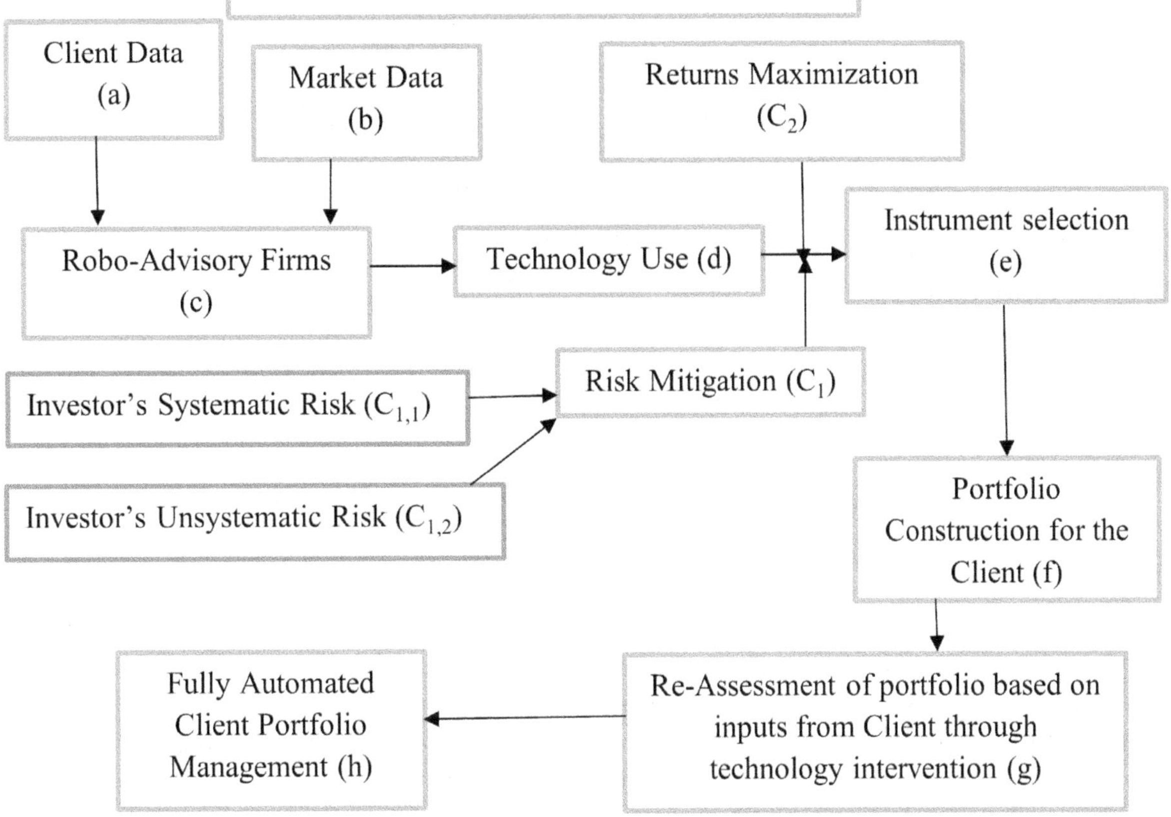

Source: Compiled by authors based on conceptual understanding

RA services framework (Figure 3) helps in understand the components covered by RA firms (c) such as client data (a) like age, gender, income, family members, family financial preparedness, financial literacy of self and family members which helps in assessing market data (b) collected for micro and macroeconomic variables such as inflation, returns rates prevailing, instrument's characteristics, global socio-political conditions, government stability, policy making bodies and monitoring and regulatory agencies' guidelines such that an assessment can be made. Then technology (d) is applied to the output received by feeding risk mitigation (C_1) that considers both systematic ($C_{1,1}$) and unsystematic risk ($C_{1,2}$) taking ability of the investor that plays mediating role along with returns maximization (C_2) goal while making instrument selection that helps in client's portfolio construction (f), whose performance is assessed again and again from time to time with the help of technology (g) that finally leads to fully automated client portfolio management (h).

Figure 4 Advantages of Robo-Advisory Services

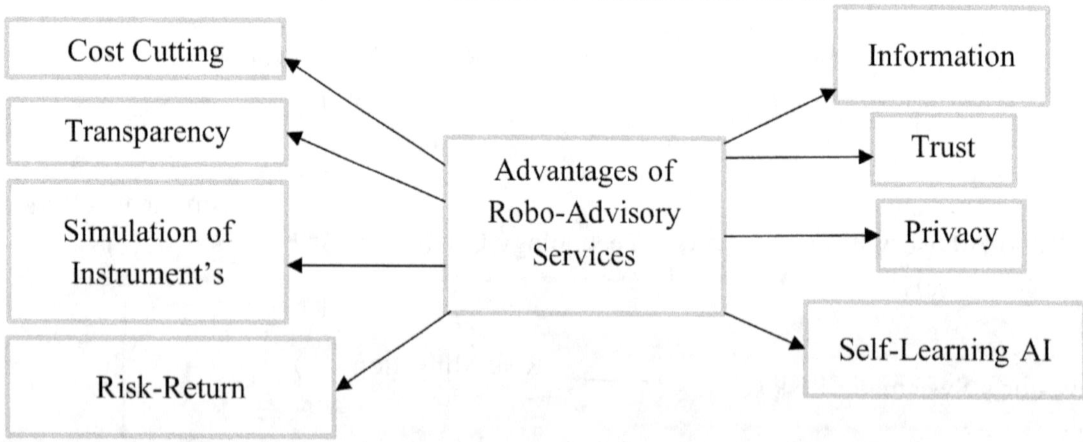

Source: Compiled by authors based on conceptual understanding

The advantages of RA services (Figure 4) are multidimensional in nature, like mitigating cost, opportunity for risk-return adjustment, transparency in assessing the performance of instruments, gaining confidence of investors with the simulated performance assessment of the instruments they choose that establishes trust on the market along with privacy and security in instrument selection along with client data. Information symmetry and use of self-learning AI algorithms are some of the appreciating features of RA services as they help individuals, investment advisors and asset management firms in the conduct of an in-depth preliminary assessment before proceeding further with investment activity (Becker et al., 2021; Nain & Rajan, 2023; Ngo-ye & Cummings, 2018).

Figure 5 Risks Associated with Investment Options

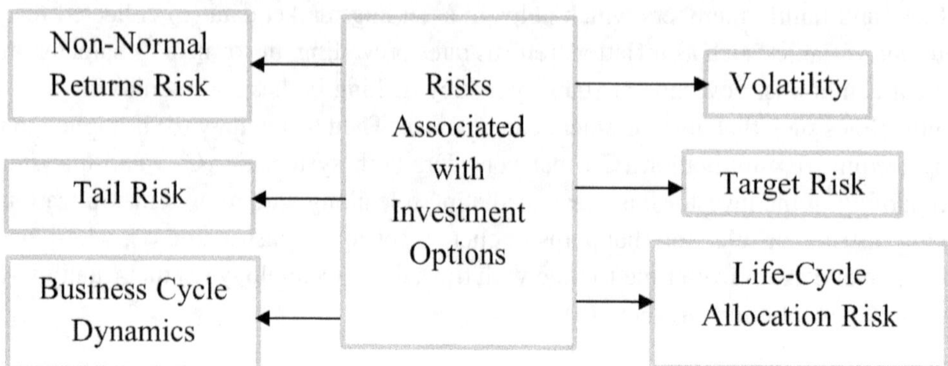

Source: Compilation by authors based on conceptual understanding

Every financial instrument is imbibed with risk factors that drive investors in maximizing their returns. The risks associated with investment instruments (Figure 5) are volatility of the instrument and the market that once again depends on various economic and political factors associated with market. Non-Normal returns risk, which mainly emphasizes on the non-normal distribution of risk (Samunderu & Murahwa, 2021) prevailing in investment options, which is followed by tail risk, which helps design instruments of investment, considering inherent risk that arise at the end of the tenure of the instrument apart from the external risks such as business cycles that drive economies. Target risk which the investor is ready to take help RA in selection of an appropriate instrument for investment, while the life-cycle allocation risk helps in understanding the purpose of investment made by individuals such that RA firms can build portfolio accordingly.

3. ROLE OF REGULATORS IN ROBO-ADVISORY

Unless household and retail investors are brought to the financial markets, financial inclusion is not complete, for which the policy makers need to build trust among households by educating them in terms of financial instruments apart from making companies disclose and report more financial as well as non-financial details to public to improve confidence about their operations and performance. Hence, a comprehensive and robust mechanism needs to be brought in place by the policy makers from time to time keeping pace with market requirements (Better Finance, 2020).

Technology adoption helps in identifying transactions across instruments such that monitoring becomes easy for the regulators while framing guidelines. Monitoring and regulatory agencies that try mitigate systematic risk, check the market efficiency from time to time apart from bringing transparency in the financial inclusion process, frame rules, regulations and guidelines in such a manner that meet the investor's appreciation, especially that are using RA services since there is no specific definition for the word investor protection, and only provisions are made for their benefit who relies on the market information and movement at large (Wipro, 2020). There are quality instruments in market that offer guaranteed returns, but there is a gap found for the quality advisory services, which the robo-advisors are filling fast, and the regulators are expected to contribute their share by offering an appropriate mechanism in managing the advisory firms, fee or commission rates regulation, use of technology in advisory processes, addressing privacy concerns where in wrong advise by a service provider compensated the investor, empowering regulators and judiciary with *suo-moto* powers in handling scams or systematic risk building confidence among investors by conducting awareness and technology use programs at regular time intervals (Maume, 2021).

Adoption of RA services need to happen in a slow and steady manner, if the regulators overreacts by setting the standards high, the same reflects on other players in the market, which makes the advisory service a painful activity for the advisory firms, since they have the potential to reduce advisory costs to a greater extent, that reduces burden on the investor (Baker, 2018), which further encourages diversified advisory services such as banking, insurance, actuarial, investment and wealth advisory services under one umbrella that helps prospective investors in moving towards RA services. Though regulator's main emphasis is on safeguarding investors' interests while framing guidelines, they also need to eliminate financial regulatory inequalities prevailing between financial products keeping in mind the investor's interests also (Irfan, 2021). Not only this, the regulators also need to protect industry needs by promoting appropriate legal guidelines by emanating laws that are current in nature such as anti-money laundering guidelines, anti-trust regulations and guidelines to the financial institutions that use political influence in dealing financial products and services such that transparency is protected, fraudulent practices are mitigated and financial literacy rate is increased across social class such that they feel protected while making investment and in all these activities, robo-advisors play key role due to exposure, experience and global connectivity (Baker, 2018).

4. THEORIES APPLICABLE IN ROBO-ADVISORY SERVICES

Heuristics and psychological biases play a role in investment or portfolio construction decision making. Heath and Tversky's gambler's fallacy, investors exhibiting home bias where most of the investors prefer investing on instruments that operate in their home country, rather that operate outside, the trial-and-error method followed due to heuristics prevailing are some examples that are relevant and applicable while learning about psychology linked to RA services (Patel, 2019). Robo advise is misrepresented or misread due to various bias prevailing among individuals while making their investment decisions. Some undergo framing effects, information overload, disposition effect, overreaction, intentional herding or loss aversion bias while working in investment markets (Bruce, 2010). A robo-investor (RI) applies variance covariance matrix while making the portfolio assessment, hold cash such that risk can be mitigated or avoided altogether while selecting investment options which fulfils the Black-Litterman model (D'Hondt et al., 2020a), Markowitz modern portfolio theory (MPT) is applied by robo-advisors for assets under management (AUM) by them for attaining higher returns (Becker et al., 2021; Beketov et al., 2018; Phoon, Kok Fai; Koh, 2018). The other theories applied by IAs in RA services are James Tobin's mean-optimization variance concept, Sharpe's asset pricing theory. There are different methods adopted by robo-advisors in analyzing an investment instrument is historical average method that uses data from the past; the longer the data duration is, the more appropriate the assessment results while analyzing the portfolio returns. However, this model yields high variable results due to which advanced models such as Gordon growth model and the capital asset pricing model (CAPM) returns approach are adopted by them such that the portfolio of an investor is risk mitigated (Becker et al., 2021). Complexity theory helps robo-advisors in understanding various stakeholders involved in an individual's investment activity, based on which a strategy can be formulated in framing the portfolio of an investor by them.

5. AI AND ITS IMPORTANCE IN ROBO-ADVISORY

Automation in financial advisory is taking an advanced step due to advancement in technology and its adoption. RA which mainly relies on data which is run applying machine learning software to generate an appropriate conclusion that offers evidential advisory mechanism to the robo-advisors. The easy and all through use of mobile compatible applications in the investment world made the financial advisory an easy and reliable task due to its easy verification and simulation applications nature, along with economic and non-economic parameters assessment (Bhatia et al., 2020, 2021). The regulatory technology popularly known as 'RegTech' used by monitoring and regulatory agencies to check the compliance adoption by the firms, is another innovative tool that is helping in meeting the targets without much difficulty, and also, verification by individuals also is another feature in this technology adoption. 'FinTech' advancement with the 'RegTech' helped in sourcing crowd funding, online payments, peer to peer lending hassle free (Irfan, Mohammad & Elmogy, Mohammed & Abd. Majid, M. Shabri & El-Sappagh, 2023) (Arner et al., 2017; Gomber et al., 2018; Gozman et al., 2018). Since algorithmic trading is taking new heights in investment process, the technology adoption by investors in trading in stock markets and other instruments like the 'BitCoin' where technology only drives the investment process, one can understand the need and importance of this 'FinTech, RegTech, Robo-Advisory and Algorithmic Trading' adoption in finance and investment arena leading to automated quantitative investment and asset management that uses machine learning (ML) and text mining process to optimize benefits to the investors (Mohammad Irfan, Seifedine Kadry, Muhammad Sharif, 2024) (Becker et al., 2021). Apart from the use of technology, robo-advisors need to observe the technology readiness of the clients in the AI driven services, especially when banking products are promoted since small and marginal individual investors are involved in the process that can be measured applying technology readiness index (TRI) mechanism that measures the positive and negative responses on metal readiness of individuals in the adoption and use of technology in their investment decisions (Belanche et al., 2019; Flavián et al., 2022; Mende et al., 2019; Parasuraman, A Parsu & Colby, 2014; van Doorn et al., 2017). Though analytical AI and mechanical AI both of them are used by robo-advisors, mechanical AI often helps in arriving at a decision, where human intervention is also sought; while the analytical AI is more of replacement to human intervention that depends on machine learning, data analysis thus providing an optimum solution for the investor, which can be adopted by the investor after getting convinced (Belanche et al., 2019; Flavián et al., 2022). AI use in RA is often seen in private banking with higher rates of personalization; RA 4.0 is found to be more robust that uses self-learning algorithms that helps in readjustment of portfolio management. 'Intelligent customer advisory, intelligent customer service and predictive analytics' are the three instruments that are used by banks and financial institutions in adopting AI in their RA services implementation (Dietzmann et al., 2023). The two schools of thought about AI i.e. strong AI thesis and weak AI theses argue about the domination of AI in decision making since its initial testing time in 1955 (Meek, 2021). One major advantage of AI based RA is its' low cost, high accessibility, transparency and simulative nature, that attracts individuals towards this service in finance sector, which got widespread usability post pandemic, but of course not only due to pandemic.

5.1 Research Gap

Literature helps in identifying the gap that exists between the use of RA services by different stakeholders under divergent conditions with the ever-changing technology and the involvement of artificial intelligence in the process of decision making. Hence, the current study is undertaken to study the extent of influence of technology on an individual's investment decision making based on their awareness and knowledge about technology as an intervening variable.

6. METHODOLOGY

6.1 Type of Research

The present study is an exploratory research work that provides necessary insights about the role of technology in an individual's investment decision making.

6.2 Data Collection

For the current research work, a structured questionnaire is developed and circulated through google forms among individuals that are having an individual bank account and also are present in the investment market having an online dematerialized account with one of the major online trading platforms like Groww or Zeroda or Upstox or ET Money.

6.3 Sample Size

Cochran's sample size (SS) infinite population = $[Z^2 P (1 - p)] \div e^2$
The critical value of Z for a two tailed test Z @ 5% = 1.96
$Z^2 = 3.8416$
Total Population = 1800
P = per cent of population studied = 10% = 0.10
p = 5% = 0.05
e = desired precision = 5% = 0.05
$e^2 = 0.0025$
Infinite population SS = [3.8416 x 0.10 (1 – 0.05)] ÷ 0.0025
Sample Size = 0.364952 ÷ 0.0025 = 145.98 = 146
Cochran's finite population Sample Size = Infinite Population Sample Size ÷ [1 + {(sample size – 1) ÷ Population}]
Finite Population Sample Size = 146 ÷ [1 + {(146 – 1) ÷ 1800}]
Finite Population Sample Size = 146 ÷ [1 + 0.080] = 146 ÷ 1.080 = 135.185 or 135
The total sample size required for the study is 135 out of a population of 1800, however, the researchers have collected a sample of 142 that are complete in all respects which can be used for further assessment of the study's requirements.

7. RESULTS

Figure 6 Age and Gender of respondents

Age	Frequency	Gender	Frequency
18-20	15 (10.5%)	Male	90 (62.9%)
21-25	55 (38.5%)	Female	53 (37.1%)
26-30	60 (42.0%)		
31-35	13 (9.0%)		
Source: Data collected for the research purpose			

During the data collection process, the researchers have categorized the total population into four categories starting from 18 years, which is the constitutionally eligible age to transact independently in India; to 35 years, where 34 years is the age that is considered under youth as per the ministry of statistics and programme implementation (MoSPI), government of India (GoI) guidelines (Figure 6). A total of 115 (21 to 25 years are 55, while 26 to 30 years are 60 in number) respondents are in the age group of 21 to 30 years (80.5 per cent) (Figure 6), this high number is due to the population and sample composition selected for the study. Fifteen respondents are in the age group of 18 to 20 that are mainly in academic learning stream, due to which these individuals' participation in investment market is low, apart from the income available for investment purposes. Hence, the sample composition helps in learning about youth awareness and inclination towards technology driven investment activity. The Figure 6, further depicts data related to gender. The whole of the sample is either male or female only. No third gender has participated in the research survey during the process. Among the total sample of 143, 90 are male (62.9 per cent) and the remaining 53 (37.1 per cent) are female. Though it is not equally distributed, number of male participants in the survey are considered to be high (Arora & Chakraborty, 2023; Sevdalis & Harvey, 2007) as investment decisions are mainly taken by male family members in India (Bajtelsmit & Bernasek, 1997; Chhatwani, 2022; Hassan Al-Tamimi & Anood Bin Kalli, 2009; Martenson, 2008).

Figure 7 Frequency distribution of respondents

Q No.	Questions	Strongly Disagree	Disagree	Neutral	Agree	Strongly Agree	Total
1	Are you Investing	7 (4.9%)	4 (2.8%)	8 (5.59%)	40 (27.97%)	84 (58.74%)	143 (100%)
2	Aware about RAS	0	0	7 (4.9%)	41 (28.67%)	95 (66.43%)	143 (100%)
3	Aware about RA Firms	0	0	7 (4.9%)	47 (32.87%)	89 (62.24%)	143 (100%)
4	I am willing to use RAS for Investment in future	0	0	0	12 (8.39%)	131 (91.61%)	143 (100%)
5	Will you advise others to use RAS	0	3 (2.1%)	9 (6.29%)	48 (33.57%)	83 (58.04%)	143 (100%)
6	Do you feel that the RAS is the future of Investment market	0	0	3 (2.1%)	32 (22.38%)	108 (75.52%)	143 (100%)
7	Technology is the future of investment decision making	0	0	0	12 (8.39%)	131 (91.61%)	143 (100%)
8	AI is changing RAS quality	2 (1.4%)	11 (7.69%)	3 (2.1%)	47 (32.87%)	80 (55.94%)	143 (100%)
9	Is AI the future of investment advisory services	0	0	0	12 (8.39%)	131 (91.61%)	143 (100%)
10	Will you invest in RAS firms	4 (2.8%)	27 (18.88%)	13 (9.09%)	70 (48.95%)	29 (20.28%)	143 (100%)

Source: Data collected for the research purpose

The ten questions for which the respondents are tested to learn their awareness and inclination towards robo-advisory services on a likert scale of 1 to 5, where 1 being the strongly disagree to 5 as strongly agree (Figure 7). When asked about whether the respondents are investing or not, 58.74 per cent have strongly agreed, 27.97 per cent have agreed making the total to 86.71 per cent. Since, this is the key question to realize the importance of adoption and use of technology in investment decisions taken by investors. Out of a total 143 sample, 136 (95.10 per cent) are aware about the robo-advisory services prevalence in investment market, that means, more people are aware about RAS than the number of investors that are investing, which is a healthy sign for the implementation of technology driven RAS. One special feature observed during the study is, none of the respondents have either disagreed or strongly disagreed for their awareness about RAS. Though the same 95.10 (136 in number) per cent are aware about RA firms, there lies a slight difference between their agreement to strongly agree per cent (47 (32.87%) to 89 (62.23%)), which is an indication that, though people are aware about RA services, where to contact and whom to approach for such services is not that clear to them. So, a comprehensive mechanism needs to be developed by the RAS firms in offering their services, which offers solution for all the stakeholders involved, as all the respondents (143) are willing to make use of RAS for their investment in future apart from advising others (131 out of 143) in making use of these services.

Technology, especially artificial intelligence (AI) influence on the RAS is questioned during the survey, for which all the respondents (143) are of the opinion that technology and AI are going to play crucial role in investment activities in future, while 127 also have said that AI is going to influence the quality of RAS in the long run due to changing investment environment. However, only 99 (69.23 per cent) say that they would be interested in investing on RA firms as well as part of their venturing into this advisory service business. So, one can foresee potential entrepreneurial opportunities in the RAS business for which the existing firms prove to be the guiding tools, and hence the monitoring and regulatory agencies; industry experts need to create such an environment through their legal, regulatory and mentoring agencies processes.

Figure 8 Partial Correlation between test questions Q1 to Q10 with controlling variable as Age Group of Investors

	Q1	Q2	Q3	Q4	Q5	Q6	Q7	Q8	Q9	Q10
Q1 (Correlation)	1.000	0.545	-0.029	0.211	0.095	0.087	0.211	-0.029	0.211	0.121
Significance		0.000	0.729	0.012	0.262	0.303	0.012	0.728	0.012	0.153
Q2 (Correlation)	0.545	1.000	0.005	0.365	0.236	0.228	0.365	-0.108	0.365	0.223
Significance	0.000		0.952	0.000	0.005	0.006	0.000	0.201	0.000	0.008
Q3 (Correlation)	-0.029	0.005	1.000	0.296	0.212	0.209	0.296	-0.019	0.296	0.013
Significance	0.729	0.952		0.000	0.011	0.013	0.000	0.826	0.000	0.878
Q4 (Correlation)	0.211	0.365	0.296	1.000	0.238	0.404	1.000	0.082	1.000	0.086
Significance	0.012	0.000	0.000		0.004	0.000	0.000	0.331	0.000	0.309
Q5 (Correlation)	0.095	0.236	0.212	0.238	1.000	0.527	0.238	0.016	0.238	0.121
Significance	0.262	0.005	0.011	0.004		0.000	0.004	0.845	0.004	0.151
Q6 (Correlation)	0.087	0.228	0.209	0.404	0.527	1.000	0.404	-0.016	0.404	0.098
Significance	0.303	0.006	0.013	0.000	0.000		0.000	0.849	0.000	0.246
Q7 (Correlation)	0.211	0.365	0.296	1.000	0.238	0.404	1.000	0.082	1.000	0.086
Significance	0.012	0.000	0.000	0.000	0.004	0.000		0.331	0.000	0.309
Q8 (Correlation)	-0.029	-0.108	-0.019	0.082	0.016	-0.016	0.082	1.000	0.082	-0.090
Significance	0.728	0.201	0.826	0.331	0.845	0.849	0.331		0.331	0.289
Q9 (Correlation)	0.211	0.365	0.296	1.000	0.238	0.404	1.000	0.082	1.000	0.086
Significance	0.012	0.000	0.000	0.000	0.004	0.000	0.000	0.331		0.309
Q10 (Correlation)	0.121	0.223	0.013	0.086	0.121	0.098	0.086	-0.090	0.086	1.000
Significance	0.153	0.008	0.878	0.309	0.151	0.246	0.309	0.289	0.309	

Note: Q1 = Are you Investing; Q2 = Aware about RAS; Q3 = Aware about RA Firms; Q4 = I am willing to use RAS for Investment in future; Q5 = Will you advise others to use RAS; Q6 = Do you feel that the RAS is the future of Investment market; Q7 = Technology is the future of investment decision making; Q8 = AI is changing RAS quality; Q9 = Is AI the future of investment advisory services; Q10 = Will you invest in RAS firms

Source: Data collected for the research purpose

Figure 9 Partial Correlation between test questions Q1 to Q10 with controlling variable as Gender

	Q1	Q2	Q3	Q4	Q5	Q6	Q7	Q8	Q9	Q10
Q1 (Correlation)	1.000	0.404	-0.134	0.167	0.050	0.042	0.167	-0.035	0.167	0.063
Significance		0.000	0.112	0.047	0.554	0.616	0.047	0.678	0.047	0.454
Q2 (Correlation)	0.404	1.000	0.025	0.365	0.239	0.229	0.365	-0.103	0.365	0.231
Significance	0.000		0.766	0.000	0.004	0.006	0.000	0.221	0.000	0.006
Q3 (Correlation)	-0.134	0.025	1.000	0.296	0.215	0.207	0.296	-0.012	0.296	0.027
Significance	0.112	0.766		0.000	0.010	0.013	0.000	0.888	0.000	0.747
Q4 (Correlation)	0.167	0.365	0.296	1.000	0.238	0.404	1.000	0.083	1.000	0.088
Significance	0.047	0.000	0.000		0.004	0.000	0.000	0.324	0.000	0.298
Q5 (Correlation)	0.050	0.239	0.215	0.238	1.000	0.527	0.238	0.019	0.238	0.124
Significance	0.554	0.004	0.010	0.004		0.000	0.004	0.824	0.004	0.140
Q6 (Correlation)	0.042	0.229	0.207	0.404	0.527	1.000	0.404	-0.013	0.404	0.101
Significance	0.616	0.006	0.013	0.000	0.000		0.000	0.875	0.000	0.233
Q7 (Correlation)	0.167	0.365	0.296	1.000	0.238	0.404	1.000	0.083	1.000	0.088
Significance	0.047	0.000	0.000	0.000	0.004	0.000		0.324	0.000	0.298
Q8 (Correlation)	-0.035	-0.103	-0.012	0.083	0.019	-0.013	0.083	1.000	0.083	-0.087
Significance	0.678	0.221	0.888	0.324	0.824	0.875	0.324		0.324	0.302
Q9 (Correlation)	0.167	0.365	0.296	1.000	0.238	0.404	1.000	0.083	1.000	0.088
Significance	0.047	0.000	0.000	0.000	0.004	0.000	0.000	0.324		0.298
Q10 (Correlation)	0.063	0.231	0.027	0.088	0.124	0.101	0.088	-0.087	0.088	1.000
Significance	0.454	0.006	0.747	0.298	0.140	0.233	0.298	0.302	0.298	

Note: Q1 = Are you Investing; Q2 = Aware about RAS; Q3 = Aware about RA Firms; Q4 = I am willing to use RAS for Investment in future; Q5 = Will you advise others to use RAS; Q6 = Do you feel that the RAS is the future of Investment market; Q7 = Technology is the future of investment decision making; Q8 = AI is changing RAS quality; Q9 = Is AI the future of investment advisory services; Q10 = Will you invest in RAS firms

Source: Data collected for the research purpose

Researchers conducted partial correlation for the questions raised during the survey time with age and gender as controlling variables (Figure 8 and Figure 9) separately, which have indicated that there exists a positive correlation between age and gender to investment activity, awareness about RAS, willingness of respondents towards use of RAS for their investment activity in future time, their inclination towards advising others in using RA services, since technology is expected to be the future driver which is a core requirement of RA service industry apart from the ever changing artificial intelligence technology that has been taking over as a key tool in financial advisory services industry apart from asking them whether the respondents are interested in investing on RAS firms as well apart from utilizing their advisory services. However, the respondents had negative correlation for the awareness about RA firms' existence and AI influencing the quality of RA services, dividing respondents in their opinion as to the two parameters for both the controlling variables. This indicates the influence of AI and RA services need in today's technology driven financial advisory and investment activities.

Figure 10 Partial Correlation between test questions Q3 to Q10 with controlling variable as Investment

	Q3	Q4	Q5	Q6	Q7	Q8	Q9	Q10
Q3 (Partial Correlation)	1.000	0.325	0.228	0.224	0.325	-0.019	0.325	0.038
Significance		0.000	0.006	0.007	0.000	0.827	0.000	0.655
Q4 (Partial Correlation)	0.325	1.000	0.234	0.403	1.000	0.090	1.000	0.079
Significance	0.000		0.005	0.000	0.000	0.285	0.000	0.351
Q5 (Partial Correlation)	0.228	0.234	1.000	0.528	0.234	0.020	0.234	0.122
Significance	0.006	0.005		0.000	0.005	0.816	0.005	0.147
Q6 (Partial Correlation)	0.224	0.403	0.528	1.000	0.403	-0.013	0.403	0.099
Significance	0.007	0.000	0.000		0.000	0.877	0.000	0.240
Q7 (Partial Correlation)	0.325	1.000	0.234	0.403	1.000	0.090	1.000	0.079
Significance	0.000	0.000	0.005	0.000		0.285	0.000	0.351
Q8 (Partial Correlation)	- 0.019	0.090	0.020	-0.013	0.090	1.000	0.090	-0.085
Significance	0.827	0.285	0.816	0.877	0.285		0.285	0.312
Q9 (Partial Correlation)	0.325	1.000	0.234	0.403	1.000	0.090	1.000	0.079
Significance	0.000	0.000	0.005	0.000	0.000	0.285		0.351
Q10 (Partial Correlation)	0.038	0.079	0.122	0.099	0.079	-0.085	0.079	1.000
Significance	0.655	0.351	0.147	0.240	0.351	0.312	0.351	

Note: Q1 = Are you Investing; Q3 = Aware about RA Firms; Q4 = I am willing to use RAS for Investment in future; Q5 = Will you advise others to use RAS; Q6 = Do you feel that the RAS is the future of Investment market; Q7 = Technology is the future of investment decision making; Q8 = AI is changing RAS quality; Q9 = Is AI the future of investment advisory services; Q10 = Will you invest in RAS firms

Source: Data collected for the research purpose

Partial Correlation between test questions Q3 to Q10 with controlling variables whether the respondent is investing or not. Results (Figure 10) are significant except for AI changing the quality of RA services, it also will drive the investment market in future time apart from these individuals investing on RAS firms. That means, the respondents though are making investments in different instruments, they are clear about technology influence on the mechanized financial advisory services and are inclined towards human interfered financial advisory process (Belanche et al., 2019; Flavián et al., 2022; Singh, 2024).

Figure 11 Partial Correlation between Q3 to Q6 and Q8 to Q10 with controlling variable as awareness about RAS

	Q3	Q4	Q5	Q6	Q8	Q9	Q10
Q3 (Partial Correlation)	1.000	0.306	0.218	0.214	-0.011	0.306	0.023
Significance		0.000	0.009	0.010	0.900	0.000	0.789
Q4 (Partial Correlation)	0.306	1.000	0.167	0.353	0.131	1.000	0.004
Significance	0.000		0.047	0.000	0.121	0.000	0.960
Q5 (Partial Correlation)	0.218	0.167	1.000	0.501	0.044	0.167	0.074
Significance	0.009	0.047		0.000	0.599	0.047	0.384
Q6 (Partial Correlation)	0.214	0.353	0.501	1.000	0.010	0.353	0.051
Significance	0.010	0.000	0.000		0.909	0.000	0.547
Q8 (Partial Correlation)	-0.011	0.131	0.044	0.010	1.000	0.131	-0.066
Significance	0.900	0.121	0.599	0.909		0.121	0.438
Q9 (Partial Correlation)	0.306	1.000	0.167	0.353	0.131	1.000	0.004
Significance	0.000	0.000	0.047	0.000	0.121		0.960
Q10 (Partial Correlation)	0.023	0.004	0.074	0.051	-0.066	0.004	1.000
Significance	0.789	0.960	0.384	0.547	0.438	0.960	

Note: Q1 = Are you Investing; Q2 = Aware about RAS; Q3 = Aware about RA Firms; Q4 = I am willing to use RAS for Investment in future; Q5 = Will you advise others to use RAS; Q6 = Do you feel that the RAS is the future of Investment market; Q7 = Technology is the future of investment decision making; Q8 = AI is changing RAS quality; Q9 = Is AI the future of investment advisory services; Q10 = Will you invest in RAS firms

Source: Data collected for the research purpose

The partial correlation of select test questions with awareness about RAS as a controlling variable (Figure 11), results are significant and are positively correlated for all the test questions considered, except for AI changing the RAS quality and people preferring investing in RAS firms. This once again proves the need for and importance of RA services while making financial investment decisions.

Figure 12 Partial Correlation between Q5, 6, 8 and 10 with controlling variable willingness to use RAS for investment in future				
	Q5	Q6	Q8	Q10
Q5 (Partial Correlation)	1.000	0.487	-0.002	0.108
Significance		0.000	0.980	0.202
Q6 (Partial Correlation)	0.487	1.000	-0.053	0.073
Significance	0.000		0.530	0.389
Q8 (Partial Correlation)	-0.002	-0.053	1.000	-0.096
Significance	0.980	0.530		0.258
Q10 (Partial Correlation)	0.108	0.073	-0.096	1.000
Significance	0.202	0.389	0.258	
Note: Q5 = Will you advise others to use RAS; Q6 = Do you feel that the RAS is the future of Investment market; Q8 = AI is changing RAS quality; Q10 = Will you invest in RAS firms Source: Data collected for the research purpose				

Respondents feel that RAS is the future of the investment market, and the rest of the variables have shown insignificant partial correlation (Figure 12), indicating respondent's unwillingness to impose their opinion on others about investment activity.

8. DISCUSSION

The partial correlation results of all the respondents is an indication for the role of RA services in the present day investment market, with people being aware about advancements in technology, use of the same with AI driven advisory services as useful which they are willing to advise to others that are interested in taking financial advisory with the help of robo services. However, they are not willing to accept, AI influence on the RA services quality and investing on RAS firms which involves psychological bias by the RAS firms. Hence, one can conclude that technology does have an influence on the financial advisory services industry for which the investors are ready to adapt to the circumstances. So, AI with its modifications provides a more suitable and conducive financial advisory option to the present as well as prospective investors in the money market instruments. However, a comprehensive mechanism needs to be built by the RAS firms in association with the monitoring and regulatory agencies' help, expertise and guidance while offering and implementing their services to the young investors.

In the technology driven investment world, robo-advisors play a crucial role, however, they are not promoted at a wide spread scale, due to which they are not popular among retail capital market investors who sense that the human interaction is missing in their financial decision making and hence, a comprehensive mechanism is needed from the monitoring and regulatory agencies apart from the advisory firms in taking this method of investment advisory services to public for an efficient and effective financial inclusion process. The misconceptions of robo-advisors being used in retirement and tax planning needs to be cleared such that their adoption is fruitful (Chhatwani, 2022; Rasiwala & Kohli, 2019). Use of a variety of data sets collected in loads of volumes help analyze the data in an appropriate manner applying ML and data mining processes since RA services uses analytics tools as well in investment decision making (Grable, 2018). Apart from the risk appetite of investors, active portfolio management helps in the expected rates to earn from markets due to market entry-exit timing and security selection by the investors, while passive management strategy makes an investor investing on highly secured index funds (IF) or exchange traded funds (ETFs) (Bjerknes & Vukovic, 2017). The three types of risks namely liquidity risk, credit risk and market risk are associated with portfolio of investments can be mitigated with the help of RA services, where the modern portfolio theory proposed by Markowitz covers only market risk (Chhabra, 2005). Small investors lack trust in investment advisors due to advice offered by them due to which sometimes mis-selling happens which is attributed to the commission received by the advisory firms or individuals offering advisory services. A mismatch between their recommendation and the actual performance of the instruments also at times makes clients rethink their portfolio management in the hands of third party advisory firms, which makes robo-advisors help in mitigating such unsystematic risks among retail investors (Better Finance, 2020). Not only this, robo-advisors help normalize risk as they consider various independent as well as dependent micro and macroeconomic as well as non-economic variables simultaneously into consideration while assessing the performance of an instrument which improves the financial intermediation and inclusion (Edwards, 2018) with the advancement in technology due to the artificial intelligence with its generative nature is able to provide more authenticated and reliable opportunities due to its' use of global information stored and shared by multiple agencies or individuals making as one of the futuristic tools in investment decision making for the individuals.

9. LIMITATIONS IN ROBO-ADVISORY SERVICES

The present RA services environment is such that the advisors are able to offer their services to domestic investors in their portfolio construction decision making only. The complexities in foreign regulations, investment instruments' characteristics, technological obstacles, client's trust on the advisory firms and multinational cultural differences are hindering the widespread adoption of RA services (Cocca, 2018). Another reason for the low adoption of RA services is due to life cycle investing model adopted by individuals, some follow static life cycle allocations, while others adopt dynamic strategies while investing their funds. However, most of the individual investors are conservative in nature, and hence, making the life-cycle allocations based on requirements for funds, rather on their retirement requirements, which is one of the goals of life-cycle investment. Due to this, goal-based advisory is becoming difficult for the wealth managers where they adopt technology in assessing various factors that contribute to the assets under management such that investor return maximization becomes easy (Janssen et al., 2013). Life-cycle investment theory works on the basis of utility-based framework, emphasises on cost-benefit analysis with risk-return trade-off between components selected versus the available in market based on financial as well as macro-economic conditions prevailing (Research et al., 2021).

10. CONCLUSION

One of the greatest quotes applicable today, in the modern banking and digital technology driven financial services industry is 'Banking is necessary, but banks are not' – Bill Gates in 1994 (Jung et al., 2018) is coming true in the banking and it's allied services industry that includes the financial advisory services as well that are using RA as one of the means that brings client to the fore of investment activity. Change in technology gives higher edge to investors however, the RA service providers are expected to be ethical while offering their services such that investors gain confidence in utilizing these services. To avoid unethical practices and improve the use of RA, Robo-Counsellor (RC) is helpful who conveys in understanding and utilizing ethical investment practices such that high net worth investors (HNIs) and speculators doesn't dominate the market which gives opportunity for the retail investors coupled with RA services offerings making these marginal investors winners rather losers in the rat race between the giants by providing high security and overall economic development. The only scope available for the end clients is their adoption and willingness towards the use of this modern technological tool for taking effective investment decision for long term as well as short term financial gains.

REFERENCES

Allied Market Research. (2023). Robo Advisory Market Outlook–2027. DOI: 10.2139/ssrn.2238

Arner, D. W., Zetzsche, D. A., Buckley, R. P., & Barberis, J. N. (2017). FinTech and RegTech Financial Stability. *Georgetown Journal of International Affairs*, 18(3), 47–58. DOI: 10.1353/gia.2017.0036

Arora, J., & Chakraborty, M. (2023). Role of financial literacy in investment choices of financial consumers: An insight from India. *International Journal of Social Economics*, 50(3), 377–397. DOI: 10.1108/IJSE-12-2021-0764

Bajtelsmit, V. L., & Bernasek, A. (1997). Why Do Women Invest Differently than Men? SSRN Electronic Journal, 970, 1–10. DOI: 10.2139/ssrn.2238

Baker, T. (2018). Regulating Robo Advice Across the Financial Services Industry Regulating Robo Advice Across the. Penn Law: Legal Scholarship Repository. DOI: 10.4337/9781849809108

Becker, M., Beketov, M., & Wittke, M. (2021). Machine Learning in Automated Asset Management Processes 4.1. *Die Unternehmung*, 75(3), 411–431. DOI: 10.5771/0042-059X-2021-3-411

Beketov, M., Lehmann, K., & Wittke, M. (2018). Robo Advisors: Quantitative methods inside the robots. *Journal of Asset Management*, 19(6), 363–370. DOI: 10.1057/s41260-018-0092-9

Belanche, D., Casaló, L. V., & Flavián, C. (2019). Artificial Intelligence in FinTech: Understanding robo-advisors adoption among customers. *Industrial Management & Data Systems*, 119(7), 1411–1430. DOI: 10.1108/IMDS-08-2018-0368

Bhatia, A., Chandani, A., Atiq, R., Mehta, M., & Divekar, R. (2021). Artificial intelligence in financial services: A qualitative research to discover robo-advisory services. *Qualitative Research in Financial Markets*, 13(5), 632–654. DOI: 10.1108/QRFM-10-2020-0199

Bhatia, A., Chandani, A., Divekar, R., Mehta, M., & Vijay, N. (2020). Digital innovation in wealth management landscape: the moderating role of robo advisors in behavioural biases and investment decision-making. DOI: 10.4337/9781849809108

Bjerknes, L., & Vukovic, A. (2017). Automated Advice: A Portfolio Management Perspective on Robo-Advisors. June, 83. DOI: 10.4337/9781849809108

Brenner, L., & Meyll, T. (2020). Robo-advisors: A substitute for human financial advice? *Journal of Behavioral and Experimental Finance*, 25, 100275. Advance online publication. DOI: 10.1016/j.jbef.2020.100275

Bruce, B. (2010). Handbook of behavioral finance. Handbook of Behavioral Finance. DOI: 10.4337/9781849809108

Cedrell, L., & Issa, N. (2018). The Adoption of Robo-advisory in the Swedish Financial Technology Market Analyzing the consumer perspective. 83. DOI: 10.4337/9781849809108

Chhabra, A. B. (2005). Beyond Markowitz : THEORY AND REALITY A Comprehensive Wealth Allocation Framework for Individual Investors. *The Journal of Wealth Management*, 8(1), 8–34. DOI: 10.3905/jwm.2005.470606

Chhatwani, M. (2022). Does robo-advisory increase retirement worry? A causal explanation. *Managerial Finance*, 48(4), 611–628. DOI: 10.1108/MF-05-2021-0195

Cocca, T. (2018). Potential and Limitations of Virtual Advice in Wealth Management. *Operational*, 1(1), 45–57.

D'Hondt, C., De Winne, R., Ghysels, E., & Raymond, S. (2020a). Artificial Intelligence Alter Egos: Who might benefit from robo-investing? *Journal of Empirical Finance*, 59, 278–299. DOI: 10.1016/j.jempfin.2020.10.002

D'Hondt, C., De Winne, R., Ghysels, E., & Raymond, S. (2020b). Artificial Intelligence Alter Egos: Who might benefit from robo-investing? *Journal of Empirical Finance*, 59, 278–299. DOI: 10.1016/j.jempfin.2020.10.002

Dietzmann, C., Jaeggi, T., & Alt, R. (2023). Implications of AI-based robo-advisory for private banking investment advisory. *Journal of Electronic Business & Digital Economics*, 2(1), 3–23. DOI: 10.1108/JEBDE-09-2022-0037

Dolata, M., & Schwabe, G. (2017). Tuning in to More Interactivity – Learning from IT Support for Advisory Service Encounters. *I-Com*, 16(1), 23–33. DOI: 10.1515/icom-2016-0042

Edwards, B. P. (2018). Chicago-Kent Law Review The Rise of Automated Investment Advice: Can Robo-Advisors Rescue the Retail Market? Recommended Citation. 93(1). DOI: 10.4018/978-1-6684-4483-2

Abraham Facundo, Schmukler Sergio L., & Tessada Jose. (2019). Robo-Advisors : Investing through Machines (English). World Bank Research and Policy Briefs, 21. DOI: 10.4018/978-1-6684-4483-2

Fenwick, M., & Mv, E. P. (2020). Banking and regulatory responses to fintech revisited: Building the sustainable financial service 'ecosystems' of tomorrow. *Singapore Journal of Legal Studies*, (March), 165–189.

Finance, B. (2020). Robo-Advice: Can Consumers Trust Robots? *Journal of Chemical Information and Modeling*.

Flavián, C., Pérez-Rueda, A., Belanche, D., & Casaló, L. V. (2022). Intention to use analytical artificial intelligence (AI) in services – the effect of technology readiness and awareness. *Journal of Service Management*, 33(2), 293–320. DOI: 10.1108/JOSM-10-2020-0378

Gomber, P., Kauffman, R. J., Parker, C., & Weber, B. W. (2018). On the Fintech Revolution: Interpreting the Forces of Innovation, Disruption, and Transformation in Financial Services. *Journal of Management Information Systems*, 35(1), 220–265. DOI: 10.1080/07421222.2018.1440766

Gozman, D., Liebenau, J., & Mangan, J. (2018). The Innovation Mechanisms of Fintech Start-Ups: Insights from SWIFT's Innotribe Competition. *Journal of Management Information Systems*, 35(1), 145–179. DOI: 10.1080/07421222.2018.1440768

Grable, A. C. L. J. (2018). An Introduction to Big Data. *Journal of Financial Service Professionals*, (September), 17–20. DOI: 10.1515/9781474463546-002

Hassan Al-Tamimi, H. A., & Anood Bin Kalli, A. (2009). Financial literacy and investment decisions of UAE investors. *The Journal of Risk Finance*, 10(5), 500–516. DOI: 10.1108/15265940911001402

Irfan, M. (2021). Do Shariah Indices converge? Evidence from Gulf Cooperation Council countries. 23(2), 251–269. DOI: 10.4018/978-1-6684-4483-2

Irfan, M., Elhoseny, M., & Kassim, S. N. M. (2023). Advanced Machine Learning Algorithms for Complex Financial Applications (M. Irfan, M. Elhoseny, S. Kassim, & N. Metawa (eds.)). IGI Global. DOI: 10.4018/978-1-6684-4483-2

Irfan, Mohammad & Elmogy, Mohammed & Abd. Majid, M. Shabri & El-Sappagh, S. (2023). The Impact of AI Innovation on Financial Sectors in the Era of Industry 5.0. In *IGI-Global*. DOI: 10.4018/978-1-6684-4483-2

Irfan, M., Elmogy, M., Gupta, S., & Khalifa, F. R. T. D. (2024). AI-Driven Decentralized Finance and the Future of Finance Mohammad. In *IGI-Global*. DOI: 10.4018/979-8-3693-6321-8

Irfan, M., Hussainey, K., & Bukhari, S. A. C. Nam, Y. (2024). Issues of sustainability in artificial intelligence and new-age thematic investing (Y. Irfan, Mohammad; Hussainey, Khaled; Bukhari, Syed Ahmad Chan; Nam (ed.)). IGI-Global.

Mohammad Irfan, Seifedine Kadry, Muhammad Sharif, & H. U. K. (2024). Fintech Applications in Islamic Finance : AI, Machine Learning, and Blockchain Techniques. IGI-Global. DOI: 10.4018/979-8-3693-1038-0

Janssen, R., Kramer, B., & Boender, G. (2013). Life cycle investing: From target-date to goal-based investing. *The Journal of Wealth Management*, 16(1), 23–32. DOI: 10.3905/jwm.2013.16.1.023

Jung, D., Dorner, V., Glaser, F., & Morana, S. (2018). Robo-Advisory: Digitalization and Automation of Financial Advisory. *Business & Information Systems Engineering*, 60(1), 81–86. DOI: 10.1007/s12599-018-0521-9

Lam, J. W. (2016). Robo-Advisors: A Portfolio Management Perspective Jonathan Walter Lam Advised. In These.

Martenson, R. (2008). Are men better investors than women? Gender differences in mutual fund and pension investments. *Journal of Financial Services Marketing*, 13(1), 72–81. DOI: 10.1057/fsm.2008.7

Maume, P. (2021). Robo-advisors - How do they fit in the existing EU regulatory framework, in particular with regard to nvestor protection? Publication for the Committee on Economic and Monetary Affairs, Policy Department for Economic, Scientific and Quality of Life Policies, European Parliament, Luxembourg, June.

Meek, D. E. (2021). Sustainable AI Development (SAID): On the Road to More Access to Justice Chapter. In Technology, Innovation and Access to Justice (pp. 112–130). Edinburgh University Press. https://doi.org/DOI: 10.3366/j.ctv1c29sj0.15

Mende, M., Scott, M. L., van Doorn, J., Grewal, D., & Shanks, I. (2019). Service Robots Rising: How Humanoid Robots Influence Service Experiences and Elicit Compensatory Consumer Responses. *JMR, Journal of Marketing Research*, 56(4), 535–556. DOI: 10.1177/0022243718822827

Moulliet, D., Stolzenbach, J., Majonek, A., & Voelker, T. (2016). The Expansion of Robo-Advisory in Wealth Management. Deloitte GmbH Wirtschaftsprüfungsgesellschaft, 1–5. DOI: 10.1177/0022243718822827

Nain, I., & Rajan, S. (2023). Algorithms for better decision-making: A qualitative study exploring the landscape of robo-advisors in India. *Managerial Finance*, 49(11), 1750–1761. DOI: 10.1108/MF-01-2023-0055

Ngo-ye, T., & Cummings, M. (2018). Modeling the Robo-Advisor Ecosystem: Insights From a Simulation Study. *Issues in Information Systems*, (September). Advance online publication. DOI: 10.48009/1_iis_2018_128-138

Oentoro, W. (2020). Mobile payment adoption process: a serial of multiple mediation and moderation analysis. DOI: 10.48009/1_iis_2018_128-138

Parasuraman, A Parsu & Colby, C. (2014). An Updated and Streamlined Technology Readiness Index: TRI 2.0. Journal of Service Research, 18, 59–74. DOI: 10.48009/1_iis_2018_128-138

Patel. (2019). Behavioral Finance. Bookboon. DOI: 10.48009/1_iis_2018_128-138

Phoon, K. F., & Koh, F. (2018). Robo-Advisors and Wealth Management. *Journal of Alternative Investments*, 20(3), 79–94. DOI: 10.3905/jai.2018.20.3.079

Rasiwala, F., & Kohli, B. (2019). A Study on the Awareness and Perception of Robo Advisory Services Among Investors in Pune City. SSRN Electronic Journal, Sironi, 469–483. DOI: 10.2139/ssrn.3308595

Research, V., Aliaga-Díaz, R., & Ahluwalia, H. (2021). *Vanguard's Life-Cycle Investing Model (VLCM): A general portfolio framework for goals-based investing*. Vlcm.

Samunderu, E., & Murahwa, Y. T. (2021). Return Based Risk Measures for Non-Normally Distributed Returns: An Alternative Modelling Approach. *Journal of Risk and Financial Management*, 14(11), 2007–2008. DOI: 10.3390/jrfm14110540

Sevdalis, N., & Harvey, N. (2007). "Investing" versus "investing for a reason": Context effects in investment decisions. *Journal of Behavioral Finance*, 8(3), 172–176. DOI: 10.1080/15427560701547487

Singh, S., & Kumar, A. (2024). Investing in the future: An integrated model for analysing user attitudes towards Robo-advisory services with AI integration. Vilakshan - XIMB. *Journal of Management*. Advance online publication. DOI: 10.1108/XJM-03-2024-0046

So, M. K. P. (2021). Robo-advising risk profiling through content analysis for sustainable development in the Hong Kong financial market. *Sustainability (Basel)*, 13(3), 1–15. DOI: 10.3390/su13031306

Statista. (2022). Statista Data. 2022. https://www.statista.com/outlook/dmo/fintech/digital-investment/robo-advisors/worldwide

van Doorn, J., Mende, M., Noble, S. M., Hulland, J., Ostrom, A. L., Grewal, D., & Petersen, J. A. (2017). Domo Arigato Mr. Roboto: Emergence of Automated Social Presence in Organizational Frontlines and Customers' Service Experiences. *Journal of Service Research*, 20(1), 43–58. DOI: 10.1177/1094670516679272

Wipro. (2020). Future of Investment and Wealth Management.

Chapter 4
Empowering Indigenous Economies:
Financial and Investment Prediction for Sustainable Development

Rachit Agarwal
https://orcid.org/0000-0003-0164-5292
University School of Business, Chandigarh University, Mohali, India

Tanya Kumar
https://orcid.org/0000-0001-7608-9820
Amity School of Business Administration, Amity University, Mohali, India

Animesh Singh
https://orcid.org/0009-0006-9068-1488
University School of Business, Chandigarh University, Mohali, India

Daniel P. Schutte
https://orcid.org/0000-0001-7283-247X
North-West University, South Africa

ABSTRACT

This chapter explores the integration of advanced financial technologies and strategic economic practices to foster sustainable development in Indigenous communities. The integrated approach ensures that indigenous communities can make well-informed, strategic decisions that drive sustainable development. The chapter also addresses the ethical considerations and potential challenges associated with implementing financial monitoring and investment prediction in indigenous economies. It highlights the need for policies that promote access to financial services, protect indigenous rights, and encourage sustainable investment practices. Collaboration between governments, financial institutions, and indigenous communities is essential to create an enabling environment for economic empowerment and sustainable development. The chapter calls for a collaborative, culturally sensitive approach to implementing these strategies, ensuring that Indigenous communities can harness the power of financial monitoring and investment prediction to achieve sustainable development goals.

DOI: 10.4018/979-8-3693-7924-0.ch004

INTRODUCTION

Indigenous economies worldwide are intricately linked to culture, tradition, and a significant relationship with the land and natural resources. Although these economies frequently function differently from conventional financial systems, they exemplify dynamic, robust, and inventive economic structures. Nonetheless, indigenous communities have traditionally encountered systematic marginalization, inadequate investment, and obstacles to obtaining financial resources, which have impeded their economic growth and development (Schutte & Van der Zwan, 2019). This has led to substantial inequalities in wealth distribution, resource ownership, and economic engagement within the global economy (Galán-Guevara, 2024). The increasing recognition of sustainability and inclusion has highlighted indigenous economies as essential contributors to the global shift towards more resilient and equitable economic systems. Empowering indigenous economies involves not only rectifying historical injustices but also acknowledging their potential role in sustainable development, environmental stewardship, and new economic models grounded on community and sustainability principles (Mosquera-Guerrero et al., 2023). A significant difficulty for indigenous communities today is the capacity to assess their financial well-being and make educated investment decisions that correspond with their cultural values and long-term sustainability objectives. Conventional financial monitoring instruments and investment methodologies frequently neglect the distinctive attributes of indigenous economies, including communal ownership, non-monetary transactions, and a prioritization of social and environmental welfare above immediate financial profits (Jang & Oh, 2023). This chapter examines the significance of financial oversight and investment forecasting in strengthening indigenous economies. Creating tools and approaches customized for the unique requirements and settings of indigenous people might facilitate new avenues for sustainable development. The integration of financial monitoring with sophisticated investment prediction models empowers indigenous communities to make strategic decisions that foster long-term growth, environmental stewardship, and social harmony (Lizarazo-Rodríguez et al., 2024). The chapter emphasizes the necessity of harmonizing investment plans with the values of indigenous populations, guaranteeing that economic empowerment does not compromise cultural integrity or environmental sustainability. Indigenous economies, distinguished by their profound cultural history and traditional knowledge systems, can encounter substantial obstacles to economic growth and development. These encompass restricted access to financial services, inadequate infrastructure, and entrenched socio-economic disparities. Notwithstanding these limitations, indigenous communities have an abundance of natural and human resources that, if utilized wisely, may stimulate sustainable economic growth (Teixeira & Coates, 2024). This chapter asserts that the strategic implementation of financial oversight and investment forecasting may reconcile potential with actualization, facilitating indigenous communities in attaining sustainable development objectives. Financial monitoring entails the ongoing evaluation of financial performance, guaranteeing the efficient and effective utilization of resources. For indigenous economies, this entails establishing comprehensive systems to monitor income, spending, and investment flows, essential for informed decision-making. Indigenous communities may improve transparency and accountability, mitigate financial mismanagement, and maximize resource allocation through the use of advanced financial monitoring systems (Zhang et al., 2023). This, therefore, cultivates a stable economic climate favourable to growth and development. Investment prediction utilizes predictive analytics to anticipate future investment possibilities and trends. Within indigenous economies, investment forecasting may pinpoint high-potential development regions, evaluate the feasibility of diverse initiatives, and inform strategic investment choices. By forecasting market trends and investment results, indigenous groups may make pre-emptive decisions that optimize profits and mitigate risks. This proactive strategy is crucial for promoting enduring economic sustainability and resilience (Yende & Yende, 2022). This chapter also examines the transformational potential of financial monitoring and investment forecasting within these communities, emphasizing the obstacles encountered and the distinctive opportunities presented.

Indigenous economies provide significant opportunities for attaining the United Nations Sustainable Development Goals (SDGs), especially with poverty alleviation, inequality, and climate action. Notwithstanding these achievements, indigenous groups have always been excluded from official banking institutions. The absence of access to credit, investment capital, and financial infrastructure has constrained their capacity to expand their economies and engage comprehensively in regional and global markets (Skene, 2022). The use of foreign financial models has frequently disrupted indigenous economic patterns, jeopardizing cultural and environmental sustainability (Koech et al., 2023). As global sustainability movements advance, there is a growing acknowledgement of the necessity to incorporate indigenous economic models into comprehensive development initiatives. Indigenous communities provide extensive expertise in natural resource management, promoting community-based economies, and attaining long-term sustainability, all of which are essential for the future of sustainable development (Mani & Agarwal, 2022). To effectively actualize this potential, indigenous economies must be equipped with the financial instruments and expertise essential for success in both local and global arenas (Uitto, 2021). Financial monitoring is essential for strengthening indigenous economies by supplying the data and insights necessary for informed economic decision-making. Nevertheless, conventional financial measures and indicators frequently do not encompass the complete intricacy of indigenous economic systems. Indigenous economies may function with alternative conceptions of value, including social and environmental advantages that are not readily quantifiable by conventional financial models. In an indigenous culture, financial health may be intricately linked to the conservation of natural resources, communal welfare, and the maintenance of traditional activities. Consequently, innovative methodologies for financial oversight must be established to align with these values and goals (Khurana et al., 2022). This chapter will examine creative frameworks for financial monitoring that correspond more closely with the principles of indigenous economies, incorporating environmental, social, and cultural criteria. Establishing financial monitoring systems that acknowledge the distinct attributes of indigenous economies enables communities to have more control over their financial destinies (Roy, 2022). These tools allow executives to monitor financial performance, recognize investment possibilities, and verify that economic operations correspond with long-term sustainability objectives. This, in turn, bolsters the resilience and expansion of indigenous economies, enabling them to assume a more prominent role in sustainable development (Bansal et al., 2024). Alongside financial oversight, the capacity to forecast investment results is a potent instrument for strengthening indigenous economies. Investment prediction models, customized to the requirements and goals of indigenous communities, can direct strategic investments that promote economic growth while safeguarding cultural and environmental assets. By including data from financial monitoring systems, these models may elucidate the effects of various investment options on the community over time, enabling leaders to make decisions that foster both immediate economic benefits and enduring sustainability (Peña et al., 2021). This chapter will examine diverse investment forecasting approaches that can be tailored to indigenous situations. This encompasses predictive analytics, scenario modeling, and the application of artificial intelligence (AI) to examine intricate economic systems. These tools assist indigenous communities in evaluating the risks and advantages of various investment alternatives, empowering them to make decisions that correspond with their values and long-term objectives. Furthermore, investment methods in indigenous economies need a comprehensive knowledge of value creation, beyond just financial returns, to encompass social, cultural, and environmental benefits (Fonchingong & Che, 2024). Investment prediction models must be constructed to encompass these varied types of value, guaranteeing that economic advancement does not compromise cultural integrity or lead to environmental damage.

REVIEW OF LITERATURE

Mosquera-Guerrero et al. (2023) identified socio-cultural and indigenous entrepreneurship as key development areas. Jang and Oh (2023) examined international competitiveness in handling the regional integration by evaluating the economic shocks on investment. Galán-Guevara (2024) discussed the trade-based economy by taking into consideration the indigenous community. Lizarazo-Rodríguez et al. (2024) focused upon addressing the protection concerns of indigenous peoples in looking for sustainable development in evaluating the patterns of behaviour of indigenous people. Teixeira & Coates (2024) explored the concepts of community well-being, public finance and company diversification. Yende & Yende (2022) highlighted the important considerations regarding government contribution towards indigenous economies. Lakshmypriya & Varghese (2024) identified the concept of sustainable tourism and how it affects indigenous groups. Zhang et al. (2023) investigated the role of information technology in managing indigenous economies. Koech et al. (2023) provided an overview of sustainable development goals by taking into consideration the circular economy factors. Uitto (2021) stated how natural resources can contribute towards natural capital. Skene (2022) discussed circular economy based upon sustainable economic factors in terms of local and global aspects. Fonchingong & Che (2024) provided insight towards indigenous knowledge systems in addressing the institution's problems with the aim of social justice. Dei (2024) discussed the role of indigenous knowledge in developing a sustainable community. Peña et al. (2021) stated the influence of private financing on ecological conservation towards large scale development projects. Innovation can result in sustainable development in fulfilling the sustainable capabilities of an organisation (Khurana et al., 2022). Gómez-Villegas (2021) discussed upon environmental accounting as how socio-economical conflicts can be resolved. Mika et al. (2019) provided insight towards the concept of indigenous entrepreneurship theory. Dahiya & Kumar (2020) illuminated dimensions of financial inclusions by considering the factors of accessibility and usage. Colbourne (2017) considered indigenous entrepreneurship by focusing upon designing, developing as well as maintaining the indigenous economies. Madudova et al. (2018) stressed upon increasing the relevance of sustainable development and ICT. Kuokkanen (2011) explored the concept of contemporary indigenous self-governance based on market forces. The incorporation of sophisticated financial technology and strategic economic methodologies is essential for promoting sustainable development in indigenous communities, which have historically been neglected in global economic frameworks. The economic empowerment of indigenous people is increasingly recognized as a crucial element in the pursuit of inclusive growth and sustainability, essential for attaining global development objectives (Lakshmypriya & Varghese, 2024). Indigenous communities, constituting around 5% of the worldwide population, oversee more than a quarter of the Earth's geographical area, predominantly in regions of significant biodiversity and essential natural resources. Their economies frequently adhere to ideals of sustainability, reciprocity, and communal welfare, drastically contrasting with the profit-oriented objectives that prevail in the global financial system (Brown et al., 2024). Wani et al. (2003) discussed entrepreneurial behavior in terms of economic growth by providing new avenues for small scale sector. Paliwal (2005) stated the contribution towards social and economic development by taking into consideration sustainable development. Khan (2014) determined the cultural determinants towards indigenous entrepreneurship. Masferrer et al. (2012) provided an alternative economic model for handling the environmental crisis. Fomba (2009) examined the perception towards innovative strategies for handling the growth in terms of sustainability of informal institutions. Hadfield-Hill (2014) discussed the relevance of corporate social responsibility in financial industry by stressing upon banking sector. Veeravatnanond et al. (2012) provided an insight towards usage of natural resources in handling the sustainable development of environment.

INTEGRATION OF ADVANCED FINANCIAL TECHNOLOGIES IN SUSTAINABLE DEVELOPMENT

The incorporation of sophisticated financial technology (FinTech) like blockchain, digital payments, and AI-driven analytics inside indigenous economies. These technologies have the capacity to profoundly transform the operational dynamics of financial institutions in indigenous communities by enhancing access to financial services, augmenting transparency, and promoting accountability (Gómez-Villegas, 2021). Numerous indigenous populations find traditional banking and financial systems unavailable owing to geographic, social, or economic obstacles. FinTech solutions can surmount these obstacles by providing alternative venues for transactions, savings, lending, and investing (Dei, 2024). Blockchain offers safe, decentralized frameworks for financial transactions, enhancing transparency and confidence in economic interactions within indigenous economies (Kumar & Kaur, 2022). It facilitates the monitoring of assets and contracts, mitigating the risk of fraud and assuring compliance with financial agreements. This is especially pertinent for groups that depend on collective land ownership or cooperative economic frameworks, where trust and openness are vital. Digital payment systems provide indigenous people with secure and accessible avenues for engaging in larger marketplaces. These systems promote financial inclusion by allowing people and companies to execute transactions without reliance on conventional banking infrastructure. Mobile payment platforms and digital wallets provide an effective alternative for conducting business in rural or underdeveloped places. Artificial intelligence (AI) and machine learning technologies may be utilized to assess financial health, forecast future market trends, and offer decision-making help for investments (Qin et al., 2019). AI-driven technologies can assist indigenous communities in optimizing resource distribution, identifying development prospects, and mitigating hazards, so enhancing long-term economic resilience. Strategic economic strategies that correspond with the cultural values and sustainability principles of indigenous people are equally essential. These approaches guarantee that the incorporation of financial technologies does not compromise traditional lifestyles but rather enhances and fortifies them. Indigenous economies frequently function on the principles of communal ownership and collaborative decision-making. Strategic economic practices must favour community-driven models that foster collective prosperity, environmental sustainability, and social harmony (Mika et al., 2019). This entails honouring traditional knowledge systems, guaranteeing that economic endeavours benefit the whole community, and advocating for long-term sustainability over immediate financial profits. Indigenous communities embody distinct cultural values that require respect and incorporation into economic methods (Afolabi et al., 2017). Strategic methods must exhibit cultural sensitivity, conforming to the community's aspirations for growth and well-being. Indigenous economic systems may promote environmental conservation rather than profit maximization, necessitating that any external investment aligns with these principles to secure community acceptance (Scheyvens et al., 2020). Financial monitoring denotes the methodical observation and evaluation of financial operations, assets, liabilities, and the whole economic performance of an enterprise (Irfan, 2021). For indigenous communities, proficient financial oversight is essential for informed decision-making on resource distribution, investment, and strategic planning. Conventional financial monitoring instruments frequently neglect the distinct requirements of indigenous economies, which may prioritize non-monetary assets like land, biodiversity, and cultural legacy. By customizing financial monitoring systems, indigenous communities might attain enhanced economic self-determination and resilience (Irfan, Elhoseny, Kassim, & Metawa, 2023). Conventional financial measurements may fail to encompass the complete value produced by indigenous economic activity. New financial monitoring systems must incorporate measures that encompass the whole concept of wealth in indigenous economies, including social, environmental, and cultural aspects (Munck, 2021). Metrics may assess the sustainability of land use practices, the conservation of cultural traditions, or the social welfare of the community. Financial monitoring instruments also provide openness and accountability, which are essential for fostering confidence within the community and with external stakeholders. Transparent financial reporting enables indigenous communities to exhibit responsible resource management, attract investment, and ensure that economic operations are consistent with their long-term development objectives (Roy, 2022; Koech et al., 2023).

Figure 1. Financial planning process

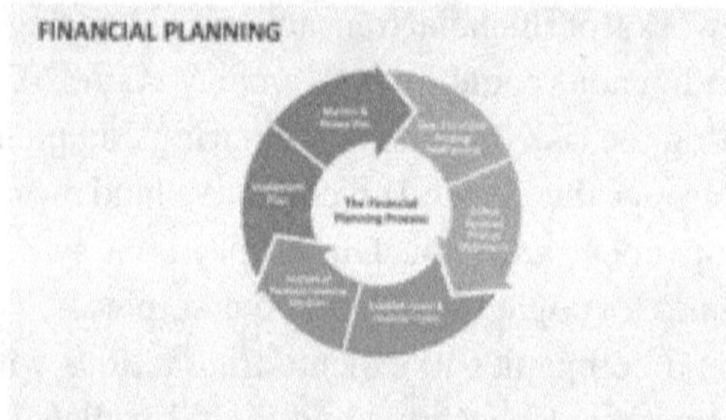

Source: https://www.collidu.com/presentation-financial-planning

Investment Prediction for Long-Term Growth

Investment prediction employs data analytics and forecasting instruments to foresee the results of various investment alternatives. Investment prediction models can be very beneficial for indigenous people in managing the intricate and sometimes unstable economic environments they encounter (Kakoty, 2018). These models assist communities in evaluating the possible advantages and disadvantages of various investments, ensuring that financial decisions align with both immediate economic needs and long-term sustainability. Investment prediction models employ scenario modelling to assess the potential outcomes of diverse investment strategies under varying economic situations (Petrova et al., 2019). This enables indigenous leaders to evaluate the prospective effects of investments on the community's economic stability, ecological sustainability, and social welfare (Irfan, Elmogy, Majid, & El-Sappagh, 2023). A community contemplating investment in eco-tourism may employ scenario modelling to forecast the long-term impacts on biodiversity, cultural integrity, and revenue generation. Investment initiatives must correspond with the community's sustainability objectives. Through the use of predictive models, indigenous communities may concentrate on investments that foster regenerative practices, safeguard natural resources, and advance social fairness. This guarantees that economic expansion does not compromise cultural heritage or environmental integrity. Investment forecasting can assist indigenous communities in recognizing and alleviating risks linked to foreign investments (Letsatsi et al., 2019). Models can forecast the probable environmental or social repercussions of large-scale infrastructure projects, enabling communities to make educated decisions on participation in such expenditures (Irfan, Kadry, Sharif, & Ullah Khan, 2023). These encompass the digital divide, insufficient access to money, and the challenge of reconciling foreign investment with the maintenance of traditional lifestyles (Agarwal & Nandram, 2021). Simultaneously, it underscores the potential for indigenous groups to assume leadership roles in sustainable development. Their extensive understanding of the environment, along with a long-standing tradition of community-oriented resource management, uniquely equips them to capitalize on sustainable investment ideas. Indigenous communities can leverage contemporary financial instruments to attain economic development while remaining consistent with their principles of sustainability, communal welfare, and cultural conservation (Lin & Zhou, 2021). By incorporating financial oversight and investment forecasting into their economic strategies, indigenous communities may establish a robust, self-sustaining economic future that aligns with global sustainability objectives while preserving their cultural uniqueness.

Investment Prediction: Anticipating Future Outcomes

Investment prediction entails employing data-driven models and forecasting instruments to anticipate the results of diverse investment methods. Investment prediction assists indigenous people in assessing the possible risks and benefits of various investment possibilities by analysing historical data, market patterns, and prospective future scenarios (Vazquez-Maguirre & Portales, 2018). It allows leaders to foresee the effects of today's financial actions on the community's long-term objectives. Investment forecasting is predominantly based on predictive analytics, which uses statistical algorithms and machine learning to anticipate future trends. Predictions for indigenous economies may concentrate on agricultural yields, market pricing for natural resources, or the effects of environmental legislation on eco-tourism and renewable energy initiatives (Shen et al., 2020). Investment forecasting entails developing many scenarios to examine the possible results of diverse tactics. This enables communities to evaluate several alternatives and choose those that provide the optimal equilibrium of financial return, risk mitigation, and congruence with cultural or environmental values (Dahiya & Kumar, 2020). An indigenous community evaluating investments in renewable energy may employ scenario modelling to predict the long-term advantages of constructing a solar energy farm compared to a wind energy project. This analysis will include financial rewards, community energy requirements, environmental effects, and possible employment creation. By forecasting the results of these investments, community leaders may make decisions that are both fiscally prudent and sustainable within their specific economic environment (Colbourne, 2017).

The Symbiosis: The Interaction Between Financial Monitoring and Investment Prediction

The interplay between financial monitoring and investment forecasting is mutually beneficial, as each instrument augments the other, establishing a feedback loop that fortifies economic planning and development initiatives (Colnar et al., 2019). Financial Monitoring Supplies Data for Investment Forecasting as the data obtained from financial monitoring underpins precise investment forecasting. In the absence of trustworthy, current financial data, investment prediction models would rely on incomplete or erroneous information, resulting in suboptimal decision-making (Arruda, 2018). For instance, if a community monitors the financial viability of its agricultural sector, data on crop yields, resource expenditures, and market prices would directly inform predictive models that anticipate the future profitability of expanding farming operations or diversifying into alternative crops. Investment forecasting informs financial strategies (Irfan, Hussainey, Chan Bukhari, & Nam, 2024). The insights derived from investment prediction inform the development of financial strategies and policies (Madudova et al., 2018). After predictive models have projected the possible effects of various investments, indigenous groups can modify their financial plans accordingly. If investment forecasts indicate that sustainable forestry will provide long-term financial and environmental advantages, the community may opt to dedicate additional resources to this sector. This strategic choice would thereafter be followed and monitored by the financial monitoring system, establishing a continuous cycle of data collecting and informed decision-making (Kuokkanen, 2011). Adjustment to evolving circumstances is the cohesive strategy is especially crucial in fluid contexts where economic conditions, market trends, or environmental elements may fluctuate swiftly. Indigenous economies frequently depend on natural resources, which may be influenced by unforeseen occurrences such as climate change, natural catastrophes, or fluctuations in global markets. In these situations, the capacity to consistently assess financial health and modify investment plans according to predicted insights is crucial for long-term sustainability (Wong et al., 2008). Investment prediction algorithms might subsequently anticipate the prospective advantages of reallocating investments towards aquaculture or conservation initiatives. Financial monitoring tools will evaluate the success of these investments, guaranteeing efficient and sustainable resource utilization (Granger, 2012).

Figure 2. Financial inclusion and economic development

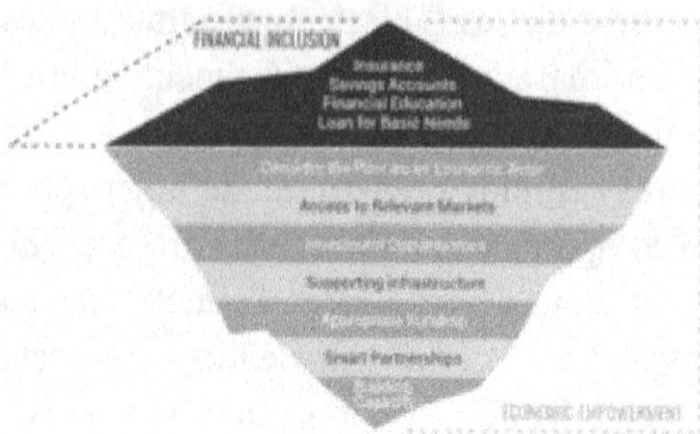

Source: https://www.isdb.org/economic-empowerment/what-we-do

ENSURING WELL-INFORMED, STRATEGIC DECISIONS FOR SUSTAINABLE DEVELOPMENT

The primary objective of integrating financial monitoring and investment forecasting is to empower indigenous communities to make educated, strategic decisions that promote sustainable development (Peng, 2013). This comprehensive strategy guarantees that economic development does not compromise cultural integrity or environmental sustainability, which are fundamental principles for several indigenous groups. Indigenous communities can utilize data from financial monitoring and investment prediction insights to make decisions grounded in objective, evidence-based analysis rather than conjecture or external influences. This mitigates the danger of engaging in detrimental investments or adopting unsustainable growth methods. The integration of financial oversight and investment forecasting enables indigenous communities to achieve equilibrium among economic development, social welfare, and environmental conservation (Freitas et al., 2004). Financial monitoring guarantees that economic operations correspond with the community's current financial requirements, whereas investment forecasting assures these activities promote long-term sustainability. Indigenous communities frequently have distinct obstacles, including restricted access to financial markets, susceptibility to environmental alterations, and demands from foreign investors or governmental entities (Sloan et al., 2014). By integrating financial monitoring with investment forecasting, these communities can enhance economic resilience. They can detect possible risks promptly, implement educated modifications to their strategy, and guarantee that their economies remain stable and sustainable despite external shocks.

Ethical Considerations

The ethical implications and potential obstacles associated with the implementation of financial monitoring and investment forecasting systems in indigenous economies. Indigenous societies exhibit distinct cultural values, indigenous knowledge systems, and socioeconomic frameworks that diverge from conventional economic models (Blakely, 2014). Consequently, these technologies must be modified to honour these unique attributes while tackling overarching issues, such as the digital divide and inadequate financial infrastructure. This section of the chapter emphasizes the significance of culturally sensitive methodologies, community involvement, and capacity development to guarantee that financial instruments are both efficacious and ethically robust (Fakuda & Watanabe, 2012). A vital ethical concern is ensuring that any financial monitoring or investment forecasting system honours the traditional knowledge systems and cultural values of the indigenous communities in whom they are deployed (Kumar & Kaur, 2023). Indigenous economies frequently rely on enduring traditions that prioritize collective ownership, sustainable resource utilization, and comprehensive wealth methods that include social, cultural, and environmental welfare. Numerous indigenous tribes prioritize community welfare above individual gain (Shah, 2014). This differs from traditional economic theories that emphasize personal wealth gain and market rivalry. Financial monitoring and investment prediction systems must be constructed to embody these community goals by using measures that assess not just financial performance but also social and environmental sustainability (Sosale, 2007). Numerous indigenous tribes retain a profound understanding of their native ecosystems, commonly termed Traditional Ecological Knowledge (TEK). This understanding encompasses sustainable land management, resource stewardship, and ecological equilibrium. Ethical financial instruments must incorporate this understanding to guarantee that investment choices promote long-term sustainability instead of compromising conventional norms.

An investment prediction model might integrate TEK by projecting the environmental consequences of specific investments, so assuring alignment with the community's sustainability objectives. Indigenous people have long faced exploitation and marginalization, especially over resource extraction, land utilization, and external investments (Irfan, Elmogy, Gupta, Khalifa, & Dias, 2024). Consequently, it is imperative to refrain from repeating patterns of economic exploitation throughout the implementation of new financial instruments. Financial monitoring and investment prediction systems must incorporate protections to avert the exploitation of indigenous lands and resources by foreign entities (Chi-ang Lin, 2007). Ethical implementation necessitates that communities provide informed permission for any adopted financial or investment instruments. This indicates that students must comprehensively grasp the ramifications of these instruments and possess the liberty to determine their usage. External investors or governments must not impose financial systems or investment plans without the community's clear consent. Furthermore, indigenous communities must maintain authority over the collection, analysis, and utilization of financial data to guide decision-making (Pansera & Owen, 2015). Financial instruments, especially those influenced by external interests, pose a danger of commodifying indigenous culture or resources. For instance, eco-tourism or artisanal items derived from traditional crafts may be marketed in manners that diminish their cultural importance. It is imperative to guarantee that these technologies safeguard cultural integrity and prevent the commodification of sacred or traditional aspects of indigenous life for external consumption (Kang'ethe & Serima, 2014).

Challenges in Implementing Financial Monitoring and Investment Prediction

Indigenous populations, particularly in isolated or rural regions, can have substantial technical obstacles, including restricted internet access, inadequate financial infrastructure, and insufficient digital tools. The digital divide presents a barrier to the efficient execution of financial monitoring and investment forecasting systems (Low, 2005). Numerous indigenous communities lack the requisite infrastructure to facilitate digital financial instruments, such as dependable internet connectivity, banking services, or energy. Logistical difficulties must be resolved prior to the effective implementation of financial monitoring systems. A viable option is to create mobile financial tools that function in low-bandwidth settings, allowing communities to engage in financial activities without the need for costly infrastructure. Facilitating access to technology, including cell phones, laptops, and banking software, is an additional challenge. Despite the existence of infrastructure, the expense of technology may be unaffordable for many populations (Sakata & Prideaux, 2013). This matter may necessitate collaborations with governmental bodies, non-governmental organizations, or the business sector to ensure inexpensive or subsidized access to essential technologies. Indigenous communities possess a historical legacy of marginalization by external economic systems and may consequently exhibit skepticism towards novel financial instruments, particularly those presented by external entities (Ali & Grewal, 2006). Addressing this misunderstanding necessitates a deliberate, cooperative strategy that prioritizes openness, engagement, and respect for indigenous sovereignty. To establish trust, it is imperative to engage indigenous people in the design and execution of financial monitoring and investment forecasting systems from the beginning (Watanabe et al., 2009). This participatory method guarantees that the generated tools align with the community's needs, beliefs, and objectives, while simultaneously cultivating a sense of ownership and empowerment. Communities are more inclined to trust and utilize financial instruments when they participate in their creation and implementation. Transparency is essential for alleviating mistrust. Indigenous people must possess complete insight into the processes of financial data collection, storage, and utilization (Howitt,

2012). Furthermore, any external elements associated with the deployment of these systems must be responsible to the community, guaranteeing that the tools serve the interests of the populace rather than those of external stakeholders or investors.

Role of Policy and Framework in Implementing Financial Monitoring and Investment Prediction

The significance of policy and regulatory frameworks in facilitating the effective integration of financial monitoring and investment forecasting instruments contends the implementation of supporting policies is crucial for enhancing economic empowerment, safeguarding indigenous rights, and advancing sustainable investment practices (Kumar & Sharma, 2014). These frameworks establish the basis for efficient financial systems that are both economically sustainable and socially and ecologically accountable. A key obstacle to the integration of financial monitoring and investment forecasting in indigenous communities is insufficient access to financial services. Numerous indigenous populations, especially in isolated or disadvantaged regions, have considerable obstacles in obtaining financial services, credit, insurance, and investment goods (Howitt, 2012). This restricted access frequently results in economic marginalization and hinders communities from engaging comprehensively in national and global economies. Governments must enact laws that foster financial inclusion and provide equal access to financial services for indigenous populations. This may entail establishing incentives for banks and financial institutions to provide customized financial products and services that address the specific requirements of indigenous people. Policies might promote the establishment of microfinance programs, mobile banking solutions, or community development financial institutions (CDFIs) that expressly serve indigenous communities (Wani et al., 2003). Alongside financial goods, regulations must also facilitate the development of infrastructure essential for providing financial services in indigenous regions. This includes investments in digital connection, physical banking infrastructure, and mobile platforms that facilitate community access to financial resources irrespective of geographic location. A primary issue in the implementation of financial systems within indigenous economies is the safeguarding of indigenous rights, especially in relation to land, resources, and cultural heritage. Indigenous communities have historically been susceptible to exploitation by external entities, including governments and businesses, frequently resulting in the loss of control over their lands and resources (Veeravatnanond et al., 2012). Policies must create and implement legal frameworks that protect indigenous ownership and governance of their lands and resources. This encompasses acknowledging indigenous land rights, guaranteeing equitable recompense for resource utilization, and safeguarding communities from exploitative actions by external investors. Financial monitoring systems must conform to these legal protections, guaranteeing that investment decisions honour indigenous land rights and foster sustainable resource management. Indigenous knowledge systems and cultural practices are essential assets that require protection (Hadfield-Hill, 2014). Policies must mitigate the risk of commercialization or appropriation of traditional knowledge, particularly when financial instruments are employed to promote cultural products or eco-tourism. Regulatory frameworks must guarantee that indigenous groups maintain intellectual property rights over their cultural heritage and get equitable compensation for its utilization.

Financial monitoring and investment forecasting systems can promote sustainable growth in indigenous economies, provided they are backed by regulations that foster sustainable investment practices. Indigenous communities frequently manage extensive natural resources, necessitating that their economic development harmonizes financial advancement with environmental and cultural sustainability (Fomba,

2009). Governments ought to establish policies that promote green investments in sectors like renewable energy, sustainable agriculture, and eco-tourism, which are consistent with indigenous principles of environmental care. These policies may encompass tax incentives, grants, or subsidies for initiatives that foster sustainable development and yield enduring economic advantages for indigenous populations. Conversely, laws must also govern enterprises that threaten environmental sustainability, such as mining, forestry, or extensive agriculture. Investment prediction models in indigenous economies must include the long-term effects of these businesses, ensuring that immediate financial benefits do not compromise environmental integrity or cultural resources. Numerous indigenous populations have systematic disparities over access to education, healthcare, employment, and economic possibilities (Chiu & Yong, 2004). These inequalities frequently restrict their capacity to engage comprehensively in economic activities and utilize financial oversight and investment forecasting systems. Policies should foster economic empowerment by tackling the fundamental causes of inequality. This may entail the establishment of specialized economic development initiatives for indigenous communities, including incentives for small enterprises, workforce training programs, and educational scholarships. Furthermore, policymakers must prioritize the enhancement of financial literacy and digital competencies essential for indigenous people to effectively utilize financial monitoring and investment forecasting instruments. Policies must guarantee that the advantages of economic growth and investment are fairly allocated among indigenous populations (Masferrer et al., 2012). For example, when an indigenous community collaborates with a business for resource extraction or tourism development, rules must ensure that an equitable portion of the revenues is returned to the community, enhancing local infrastructure, education, and social initiatives. Effective and culturally relevant policy frameworks need coordination among governments, financial institutions, and indigenous populations. Each stakeholder has a pivotal role in formulating regulations that facilitate financial oversight, investment forecasting, and sustainable development. Governments have a pivotal role in establishing and implementing the legal and regulatory frameworks that facilitate financial inclusion, safeguard indigenous rights, and encourage sustainable investments. For policies to be effective, they must be formulated in close collaboration with indigenous populations. Governments ought to involve indigenous leaders, elders, and community members in the policymaking process to guarantee that policies align with their needs, beliefs, and goals (Khan, 2014). This collaborative method guarantees the relevance and cultural suitability of programs while fostering confidence between indigenous people and the government (Watanabe et al., 2009). Financial institutions, including banks, investment businesses, and development organizations, play a crucial role in delivering the financial goods and services essential for the economic development of indigenous people. Nonetheless, these institutions must collaborate with indigenous people to customize their services to address local requirements and circumstances. Financial institutions ought to provide products that honour indigenous values and knowledge systems. Microfinance programs providing low-interest loans to indigenous businesses and impact investment funds concentrating on sustainable initiatives in indigenous territory exemplify financial instruments that correspond with indigenous aspirations. Financial institutions ought to implement ethical investing rules that prohibit the exploitation of indigenous lands and resources. This may entail the implementation of stringent due diligence procedures to guarantee that investments do not adversely affect indigenous populations or exacerbate environmental deterioration. Indigenous communities must be central to the construction of policies and financial systems. Their involvement is crucial to guarantee that financial instruments and policies correspond with their values and foster their long-term economic and cultural viability. Indigenous groups have to be empowered to choose their own development objectives and plans. Policymakers and financial institutions ought to facilitate community-driven development by supplying the tools, resources, and frameworks essential for indigenous people to oversee their financial systems and make educated investment choices. Indigenous communities may establish collaborations with governmental entities and financial organizations to jointly oversee financial systems and investment initiatives (Fomba, 2009). These collaborations can facilitate the equitable distribution of economic development advantages between external entities and indigenous communities, while preserving indigenous authority. Notwithstanding the prospective advantages of collaboration, several obstacles hinder the establishment of effective policy frameworks in indigenous economies. Governments often neglect the needs of indigenous groups, resulting in insufficient policies or poor enforcement. Advocacy initiatives are essential to enhance awareness of the significance of indigenous economic empowerment and to ensure governmental accountability in the implementation and enforcement of supporting policies. Bureaucratic complexities hinder indigenous groups' access to financial services and involvement in policy making. Streamlining regulatory procedures and alleviating administrative costs is crucial for ensuring that rules are both accessible and effective. Policymakers and financial institutions may possess insufficient comprehension of indigenous cultures and beliefs, resulting in policies that are ineffectual or culturally unsuitable. Continuous education and capacity-building programs for government officials and financial professionals are essential for bridging these gaps.

CONCLUSION

In summary, the incorporation of financial monitoring and investment forecasting systems in indigenous economies necessitates robust legislative and regulatory frameworks that enhance access to financial services, safeguard indigenous rights, and promote sustainable investing practices. Cooperation among governments, financial institutions, and indigenous people is crucial for fostering an environment conducive to economic empowerment and sustainable development. By implementing inclusive, culturally attuned, and sustainable policies, governments may assist indigenous communities in using financial instruments to attain enduring prosperity and self-determination. The ethical implications and obstacles related to the implementation of financial monitoring and investment forecasting in Indigenous economies are considerable but not insurmountable. Success hinges on the use of culturally sensitive methodologies that honour traditional knowledge systems and engage indigenous populations in the design and implementation phases. Furthermore, capacity building and education are crucial for equipping indigenous populations with the skills and knowledge required to proficiently employ these instruments. By confronting these ethical issues and problems, financial oversight and investment forecasting may serve as potent tools for strengthening indigenous people and promoting sustainable development, while safeguarding cultural integrity and environmental stewardship. The interdependent link between financial oversight and investment forecasting creates a robust framework for indigenous economic advancement. Financial monitoring provide the necessary data to evaluate the community's present financial status, whereas investment predictions deliver prospective insights that inform strategic decisions. Collectively, these instruments establish a holistic, flexible framework that fosters sustainable development, enabling indigenous people to attain economic advancement while preserving their cultural heritage and environmental obligations. This comprehensive strategy is crucial for promoting enduring prosperity and resilience in a more intricate and unpredictable global economy. This chapter emphasizes the necessity of incorporating financial oversight and investment forecasting into the strategic economic practices of indigenous groups (Paliwal, 2005). Utilizing innovative financial technology, these communities may improve their financial resilience, make educated investment decisions, and attain economic empowerment in alignment with their cultural values and environmental principles. By doing so, they enhance their economic prospects and contribute to a worldwide initiative for equitable and sustainable development. The enhancement of indigenous economies via financial oversight and investment forecasting is a vital measure for attaining sustainable development. Customizing financial instruments to the distinct requirements and values of indigenous people might facilitate new avenues for economic development that adhere to principles of sustainability, equality, and cultural preservation (Curry & Koczberski, 2013). This chapter establishes the foundation for an in-depth examination of how financial oversight and investment forecasting might bolster the resilience and success of indigenous economies, while advancing overarching global objectives of sustainability and equitable economic growth. Financial technologies offer precise, real-time information into financial health and prospective investment possibilities, allowing indigenous people to make educated economic decisions that correspond with their long-term objectives and beliefs. This, consequently, promotes inclusive growth, enhances local resilience, and aids initiatives to address the economic disparities confronting several indigenous communities. Nonetheless, the effective execution of these techniques necessitates a cooperative, culturally attuned methodology (Kong, 2009). Governments, financial institutions, and indigenous leaders must collaborate to create systems that honour traditional knowledge, safeguard indigenous rights, and advance sustainable practices. Involving indigenous people at every stage, from policy development to the design of financial instruments, allows these systems to be customized to meet their specific challenges and possibilities. Furthermore, prioritizing capacity building and education is essential to provide indigenous persons with the knowledge necessary to properly employ these instruments. Appropriate policies, support systems, and collaborations can enable financial monitoring and investment forecasting to effectively promote sustainable development, allowing indigenous economies to prosper in a progressively interconnected world while preserving their cultural and environmental integrity.

REFERENCES

Afolabi, A. O., Ojelabi, R. A., Oyeyipo, O., Tunji-Olayeni, P. F., Omuh, I. O., & Amusan, L. M. (2017). Integrating software development courses in the construction curriculum. *The Turkish Online Journal of Educational Technology*, •••, 215–225.

Agarwal, K., & Nandram, S. S. (2021). Domestic products in Swadeshi-Global entrepreneurship for sustainable socioeconomic growth. *World Review of Entrepreneurship, Management and Sustainable Development*, 17(5), 624–646. DOI: 10.1504/WREMSD.2021.117445

Ali, S. H., & Grewal, A. S. (2006). The ecology and economy of indigenous resistance: Divergent perspectives on mining in New Caledonia. *The Contemporary Pacific*, 18(2), 361–392. DOI: 10.1353/cp.2006.0001

Arruda, G. M. (2018). Arctic resource development: A sustainable prosperity project of co-management. In *Renewable Energy for the Arctic* (pp. 106–117). Routledge. DOI: 10.4324/9781351173322-6

Bansal, S., Rathi, P., Agarwal, R., & Ahluwalia, R. (2024). Leveraging AI to Enhance the Global Mobility Experience: Trends in Indian Higher Education. In Transforming the Financial Landscape With ICTs (pp. 108-133). IGI Global.

Blakely, E. J. (2014). The future of sustainable economic development in cities. In *Elgar Companion to Sustainable Cities* (pp. 397–412). Edward Elgar Publishing. DOI: 10.4337/9780857939999.00027

Brown, J. A., Lewans, M., Menon, D., & Nykiforuk, C. I. (2024). Advancing socio-ecological considerations in impact assessment of extractive industries: A realist interview study in the Canadian context. *Environmental Science & Policy*, 153, 103677. DOI: 10.1016/j.envsci.2024.103677

Chiu, A. S., & Yong, G. (2004). On the industrial ecology potential in Asian developing countries. *Journal of Cleaner Production*, 12(8-10), 1037–1045. DOI: 10.1016/j.jclepro.2004.02.013

Colbourne, R. (2017). Indigenous entrepreneurship and hybrid ventures. In *Hybrid ventures* (pp. 93–149). Emerald Publishing Limited. DOI: 10.1108/S1074-754020170000019004

Colnar, S., Dimovski, V., & Bogataj, D. (2019). Knowledge management and the sustainable development of social work. *Sustainability (Basel)*, 11(22), 6374. DOI: 10.3390/su11226374

Curry, G. N., & Koczberski, G. (2013). Development implications of the engagement with capitalism: Improving the social returns of development. In *Engaging with capitalism: Cases from Oceania* (pp. 335-352). Emerald Group Publishing Limited.

Dahiya, S., & Kumar, M. (2020). Linkage between financial inclusion and economic growth: An empirical study of the emerging Indian economy. *Vision (Basel)*, 24(2), 184–193. DOI: 10.1177/0972262920923891

Dei, D. G. J. (2024). *Sustainability and development of EWE communities in Ghana through indigenous knowledge management practices*. Collection and Curation. DOI: 10.1108/CC-11-2023-0035

Fomba, E. M. (2009). Reinforcing experiential learning with training culture as an innovative governance strategy in informal microfinance institutions. *International Journal of Technology Management*, 45(1-2), 141–155. DOI: 10.1504/IJTM.2009.021525

Fonchingong Che, C. (2024). Reframing social justice through indigenous know-how: Implications for social development, policy and practice. *Global Social Policy*, 24(1), 5–24. DOI: 10.1177/14680181231170532

Freitas, C. E., Kahn, J. R., & Rivas, A. A. (2004). Indigenous people and sustainable development in Amazonas. *International Journal of Sustainable Development and World Ecology*, 11(3), 312–325. DOI: 10.1080/13504500409469834

Fukuda, K., & Watanabe, C. (2012). Hybrid management of technology in innovation ecosystem.

Galán-Guevara, C. (2024). Understanding change in traditional sustainable livelihoods: A complex socio-ecological system in an indigenous community in Mexico. *Community Development Journal: An International Forum*, 59(3), 495–513. DOI: 10.1093/cdj/bsad010

Gómez-Villegas, M. (2021). Towards an accounting of socio-environmental conflicts in South America. In *Routledge handbook of environmental accounting* (pp. 339–349). Routledge. DOI: 10.4324/9780367152369-29

Granger, R. C. (2012). Enterprise zone policy: Developing sustainable economies through area-based fiscal incentives. *Urban Research & Practice*, 5(3), 335–341. DOI: 10.1080/17535069.2012.727554

Hadfield-Hill, S. (2014). CSR in India: Reflections from the banking sector. *Social Responsibility Journal*, 10(1), 21–37. DOI: 10.1108/SRJ-11-2012-0145

Howitt, R. (2012). Sustainable indigenous futures in remote Indigenous areas: Relationships, processes and failed state approaches. *GeoJournal*, 77(6), 817–828. DOI: 10.1007/s10708-010-9377-3

Irfan, M. (2021, January). Do Shariah Indices converge? Evidence from Gulf Cooperation Council countries. *International Journal of Business Excellence*, 23(2), 251–269. DOI: 10.1504/IJBEX.2021.113448

Irfan, M., Elhoseny, M., Kassim, S., & Metawa, N. (2023). *Advanced Machine Learning Algorithms for Complex Financial Applications*. IGI Global., DOI: 10.4018/978-1-6684-4483-2

Irfan, M., Elmogy, M., Gupta, S., Khalifa, F., & Dias, R. (2024). *AI-Driven Decentralized Finance and the Future of Finance*. IGI Global., DOI: 10.4018/979-8-3693-6321-8

Irfan, M., Elmogy, M., Majid, M. S., & El-Sappagh, S. (2023). *The Impact of AI Innovation on Financial Sectors in the Era of Industry 5.0*. IGI Global., DOI: 10.4018/979-8-3693-0082-4

Irfan, M., Hussainey, K., Chan Bukhari, S. A., & Nam, Y. (Eds.). (2024). *Issues of Sustainability in AI and New-Age Thematic Investing*. IGI Global Publisher., DOI: 10.4018/979-8-3693-3282-5

Irfan, M., Kadry, S., Sharif, M., & Ullah Khan, H. (2023). *Fintech Applications in Islamic Finance: AI, Machine Learning, and Blockchain Techniques*. IGI Global., DOI: 10.4018/979-8-3693-1038-0

Jang, T. S., & Oh, S. (2023). Transition to sustainable growth in South Korea: Investment and trade under uncertainty. *Millennial Asia*, 14(3), 360–378. DOI: 10.1177/09763996211065139

Kakoty, S. (2018). Ecology, sustainability and traditional wisdom. *Journal of Cleaner Production*, 172, 3215–3224. DOI: 10.1016/j.jclepro.2017.11.036

Kang'ethe, S. M., & Serima, J. (2014). Locating the Niche of the Informal Sector as a Driver of Social and Economic Development in Selected African Countries. *Mediterranean Journal of Social Sciences*, 5(27), 3. DOI: 10.5901/mjss.2014.v5n27p1293

Khan, I. M. (2014). Indigenous entrepreneurship among the Kalash. *International Journal of Entrepreneurship and Small Business*, 22(1), 115–134. DOI: 10.1504/IJESB.2014.062134

Khurana, S., Luthra, S., Haleem, A., Kumar, A., & Mannan, B. (2022). Can sustainability be achieved through sustainable oriented innovation practices? Empirical evidence of micro, small and medium scale manufacturing enterprises. *Sustainable Development (Bradford)*, 30(6), 1591–1615. DOI: 10.1002/sd.2330

Koech, M. K., Munene, K. J., Kinoti, M. K., & Situma, D. K. (2023). Circular Economy Policies and Innovations in Africa: Pillars for Achieving Sustainable Development. In *Circular Economy Adoption: Catalysing Decarbonisation Through Policy Instruments* (pp. 99–130). Springer Nature Singapore. DOI: 10.1007/978-981-99-4803-1_4

Kong, L. (2009). Making sustainable creative/cultural space in Shanghai and Singapore. *Geographical Review*, 99(1), 1–22. DOI: 10.1111/j.1931-0846.2009.tb00415.x

Kumar, H. S., & Sharma, P. (2014). Capitalism, globalisation, cultural landscape, and rural tourism. *The International Journal of Interdisciplinary Global Studies*, 7(4), 1–12. DOI: 10.18848/2324-755X/CGP/v07i04/53354

Kumar, T., & Kaur, S. (2022). Blockchain Technology: Present and Future Perspectives. In Gupta, S., Kansra, P., & Kukreja, G. (Eds.), *Applications, Challenges, and Opportunities of Blockchain Technology in Banking and Insurance* (pp. 258–265). IGI Global., DOI: 10.4018/978-1-6684-4133-6.ch016

Kumar, T., & Kaur, S. (2023). Ethical Aspects of Cybersecurity in E-Commerce. In Cybersecurity for Decision Makers (1st ed.). CRC Press. DOI: 10.1201/9781003319887

Kuokkanen, R. (2011). From indigenous economies to market-based self-governance: A feminist political economy analysis. *Canadian Journal of Political Science/Revue canadienne de science politique, 44*(2), 275-297.

Lakshmypriya, K., & Varghese, B. (2024). Indigenous Tribes and Inclusive Engagement: An Integrated Approach for Sustainable Livelihood Into the Future. In *Future Tourism Trends Volume 1: Tourism in the Changing World* (pp. 99-114). Emerald Publishing Limited.

Letsatsi, M. T., Agarwal, A., & Seretse, O. M. (2019). The Battle towards Skill Based Competency Integration to Knowledge Based Competency in the Sustainable Development of Growing Economy. *Int. J. Recent Technol. Eng*, 8(1).

Lin, C. (2007). A new vision of the knowledge economy. *Journal of Economic Surveys*, 21(3), 553–584. DOI: 10.1111/j.1467-6419.2007.00514.x

Lin, J. Y., & Zhou, J. (2021). China's Industrial Development Strategies and Policies. *The Oxford Handbook of China Innovation*, 56.

Lizarazo-Rodríguez, L., De Lombaerde, P., Lizarazo Carrera, M. A., & Londono-Escudero, C. (2024). Investment projects and the protection of indigenous peoples and territories in Colombia. *Latin American Policy*, 15(2), 288–319. DOI: 10.1111/lamp.12339

Low, L. (2005). Entrepreneurship development in Ireland and Singapore. *Journal of the Asia Pacific Economy*, 10(1), 116–138. DOI: 10.1080/1354786042000309107

Madudova, E., Čorejova, T., & Valica, M. (2018). Economic sustainability in a wider context: Case study of considerable ICT sector sub-divisions. *Sustainability (Basel)*, 10(7), 2511. DOI: 10.3390/su10072511

Mani, M., & Agarwal, R. (2022). Payment Banks in India: Insights From the Customers' Perception. [IJABIM]. *International Journal of Asian Business and Information Management*, 13(1), 1–15. DOI: 10.4018/IJABIM.297851

Masferrer-Dodas, E., Rico-Garcia, L., Huanca, T., & Reyes-García, V. (2012). Consumption of market goods and wellbeing in small-scale societies: An empirical test among the Tsimane'in the Bolivian Amazon. *Ecological Economics*, 84, 213–220. DOI: 10.1016/j.ecolecon.2011.08.009

Mika, J. P., Fahey, N., & Bensemann, J. (2019). What counts as an indigenous enterprise? Evidence from Aotearoa New Zealand. *Journal of Enterprising Communities: People and Places in the Global Economy*, 13(3), 372–390. DOI: 10.1108/JEC-12-2018-0102

Mosquera-Guerrero, A., Rodríguez Martínez, J., Ordóñez Abril, D. Y., & Calderón Sotero, J. H. (2023). Project design and development in indigenous communities: A literature review. *Gestão & Produção*, 30, e6022. DOI: 10.1590/1806-9649-2022v29e6022

Munck, R. (2021). Globalisation and Development. In *Rethinking Development: Marxist Perspectives* (pp. 189–208). Springer International Publishing. DOI: 10.1007/978-3-030-73811-2_10

Paliwal, P. (2005). Sustainable development and systems thinking: A case study of a heritage city. *International Journal of Sustainable Development and World Ecology*, 12(2), 213–220. DOI: 10.1080/13504500509469632

Pansera, M., & Owen, R. (2015). Framing resource-constrained innovation at the 'bottom of the pyramid': Insights from an ethnographic case study in rural Bangladesh. *Technological Forecasting and Social Change*, 92, 300–311. DOI: 10.1016/j.techfore.2014.10.004

Peña-Azcona, I., García-Barrios, R., García-Barrios, L., Ortega-Argueta, A., & Elizondo, C. (2021). The unruly complexity of conservation arrangements with Mexican rural communities: Who really funds the game? *Journal of Rural Studies*, 87, 112–123. DOI: 10.1016/j.jrurstud.2021.08.027

Peng, G. C. A. (2013). Green ICT: A strategy for sustainable development of China's electronic information industry. *China. International Journal (Toronto, Ont.)*, 11(3), 68–86.

Petrova, N. I., Fedorova, A. V., Petrova, N. N., & Alekseeva, N. N. (2019). Arctic entrepreneurship and supply chain strategy integration as part of creative economy. *International Journal of Supply Chain Management*, 8(6), 999–1005.

Qin, Y., Harrison, J., & Chen, L. (2019). A framework for the practice of corporate environmental responsibility in China. *Journal of Cleaner Production*, 235, 426–452. DOI: 10.1016/j.jclepro.2019.06.245

Roy, V. D. (2022). For sustainable social impact at Mangalajodi: Change processes enabled by NatWest Bank India. *Emerald Emerging Markets Case Studies*, 12(2), 1–19. DOI: 10.1108/EEMCS-04-2021-0109

Sakata, H., & Prideaux, B. (2013). An alternative approach to community-based ecotourism: A bottom-up locally initiated non-monetised project in Papua New Guinea. *Journal of Sustainable Tourism*, 21(6), 880–899. DOI: 10.1080/09669582.2012.756493

Scheyvens, R., Banks, G., Vunibola, S., Steven, H., & Meo-Sewabu, L. (2020). Business serves society: Successful locally-driven development on customary land in the South Pacific. *Geoforum*, 112, 52–62. DOI: 10.1016/j.geoforum.2020.03.012

Schutte, D., & Van der Zwan, P. (2019). Turnover tax relief in South Africa: Evidence from the SARS-NT Panel. *Advances in Taxation*, 26, 135–148. DOI: 10.1108/S1058-749720190000026008

Shah, P. (2014). Creating intentional spaces for sustainable development in the Indian trans-Himalaya: Reconceptualizing globalization from below. *Intercultural Education*, 25(5), 362–376. DOI: 10.1080/14675986.2014.972610

Shen, H., Ng, A. W., Zhang, J., & Wang, L. (2020). Sustainability accounting, management and policy in China: Recent developments and future avenues. *Sustainability Accounting. Management and Policy Journal*, 11(5), 825–839.

Skene, K. R. (2022). The circular economy: a critique of the concept. In *Towards a Circular Economy: Transdisciplinary Approach for Business* (pp. 99–116). Springer International Publishing. DOI: 10.1007/978-3-030-94293-9_5

Sloan, P., Legrand, W., & Simons-Kaufmann, C. (2014). A survey of social entrepreneurial community-based hospitality and tourism initiatives in developing economies: A new business approach for industry. *Worldwide Hospitality and Tourism Themes*, 6(1), 51–61. DOI: 10.1108/WHATT-11-2013-0045

Sosale, S. (2007). "Pre-Modern" online: Converging discourses of globalization and development. *Journalism & Communication Monographs*, 9(1), 1–52. DOI: 10.1177/152263790700900101

Teixeira, A. V., & Coates, K. (2024). Exploring Economic Development Strategies for Canadian Indigenous Communities Post-Pandemic. *Scientific Annals of Economics and Business*, 71(2), 285–300. DOI: 10.47743/saeb-2024-0015

Uitto, J. I. (2021). Evaluating environment in international development: An introduction. In *Evaluating Environment in International Development* (pp. 3–24). Routledge. DOI: 10.4324/9781003094821-2

Vazquez-Maguirre, M., & Portales, L. (2018). Profits and purpose: Organizational tensions in social enterprises. *Intangible Capital*, 14(4), 604–618. DOI: 10.3926/ic.1208

Veeravatnanond, V., Nasa-arn, S., Nithimongkonchai, W., Wongpho, B., & Phookung, K. (2012). Development of risk assurance criteria to the utilization of natural resources and environment for sustainable development of life quality, economy and society in rural Thai communities. *Asian Social Science*, 8(2), 189. DOI: 10.5539/ass.v8n2p189

Wani, V. P., Garg, T. K., & Sharma, S. K. (2003). The role of technical institutions in developing a techno-entrepreneurial workforce for sustainable development of SMEs in India. *International Journal of Management and Enterprise Development*, 1(1), 71–88. DOI: 10.1504/IJMED.2003.003510

Watanabe, C., Lei, S., & Ouchi, N. (2009). Fusing indigenous technology development and market learning for greater functionality development—An empirical analysis of the growth trajectory of Canon printers. *Technovation*, 29(4), 265–283. DOI: 10.1016/j.technovation.2008.10.008

Wong, J. M., Chiang, Y. H., & Ng, T. S. (2008). Construction and economic development: The case of Hong Kong. *Construction Management and Economics*, 26(8), 815–826. DOI: 10.1080/01446190802189927

Yende, S. J., & Yende, N. E. (2022). The Disparity between the Political Elites and Constituencies in the Quest for Democracy and Sustainable Development in South Africa. *African Renaissance (1744-2532), 19*(4).

Zhang, N., Sun, C., Xu, M., Wang, X., & Deng, J. (2023). Catching Up of Latecomer Economies in ICT for Sustainable Development: An Analysis Based on Technology Life Cycle Using Patent Data. *Sustainability (Basel)*, 15(11), 9038. DOI: 10.3390/su15119038

Chapter 5
The Intersection of Indigenous Knowledge and Artificial Intelligence in Financial Technology

Gaurav Jangra
https://orcid.org/0000-0001-9958-9991
Chandigarh University, India

Monika Jangra
Chandigarh University, India

Mohammad Irfan
https://orcid.org/0000-0002-4956-1170
Christ University, India

Chaman Verma
https://orcid.org/0000-0002-9925-112X
Eötvös Loránd University, Budapest, Hungary

ABSTRACT

The intersection of indigenous knowledge and artificial intelligence in financial technology offers a unique opportunity to blend traditional wisdom with cutting-edge technology. This collaboration has the potential to revolutionize the way financial systems are designed and implemented. It can also lead to more inclusive and sustainable financial solutions for indigenous communities. Furthermore, the incorporation of indigenous knowledge can provide a more holistic approach to financial technology. This can result in better understanding and addressing the unique financial needs of indigenous communities. Additionally, incorporating indigenous knowledge into AI algorithms can lead to more culturally sensitive and inclusive financial technology solutions. This can help in addressing the needs of diverse communities and promoting financial inclusion. Indigenous communities by incorporating traditional knowledge and values into AI-driven financial technologies.

DOI: 10.4018/979-8-3693-7924-0.ch005

1. INTRODUCTION

A theme that has garnered increased interest in recent years has been the intersection between Indigenous Knowledge and Artificial Intelligence (AI) (Chanco et al., 2023). Indigenous Knowledge refers to the cultural ways of knowing and not knowing that arise from Indigenous societies and are specific to varying Indigenous groups. AI can be understood as the production or study of computers and other types of technologies that are capable of learning how to do things that would require intelligence if done by humans. Data gathered from financial technology (fintech) platforms are used by AI to learn about our behaviors, interests, and proclivities, and as a basis to provide us with predictions and options (Elia et al., 2023). Thus, we propose to further investigate how the intersection of Indigenous Knowledge and AI relates to fintech, specifically.

The practice of using fintech to develop ideas about the knowledge of others is where we situate our focus; as such, this involves the desaturating of the knowledge of others. The study defines fintech as representing methods, practices, and systems of using, creating, organizing, and distributing knowledge about monetary and financial matters (Elia et al., 2023) This is achieved by using cultural artifacts (in our case, datasets) processed or partially processed by automated systems or artificial intelligence (AI) (Abgaz et al., 2021). The investigation begins with an exploration of indigenous and capitalist forms of knowledge and their various interconnectivities, and the linkages between AI, fintech, and knowledge (Irfan, Elhoseny, et al., 2023). Then turn to the main topic, investigating the key questions that arise when looking at the use of AI in the production of fintech. Finally, conclude by proposing implications for future intercalarily research.

The first stage of implementation of AI starts with theoretical, numerical, and data-driven models. These models are then implemented by the designers in the numerical computing system, often aided through symbolic computing and other automation tools. If these systems are developed with our indigenous languages, it would develop our capabilities and preserve our culture. However, beyond the sector of numerical and digital computation, the specific applications indigenous knowledge needs to be inbuilt into AI systems include decision support systems, knowledge-based systems, expert systems, speech recognition applications, intelligent learning or tutoring systems, advanced interface systems, and all stand-alone applications, particularly including educational and job market software.

AI research thrives on incentive, and a massive application drive of AI stems from shareholder actions, which are most prevalent in industrialized countries. The result of this incentive input is that AI architecture lacks an overemphasis on indigenous knowledge. Despite spelling out the fact that high-technology applications of AI should be developed, culture must be achieved above everything when the determining factor in whether or not technology will lead directly to a given cultural outcome, or conversely, can be made quite clearly to foster an alternative result, is the degree to which the technology involved is flexible and derived from within.

This chapter aims not to underscore the polarity of how AI may be harmful to indigenous languages and cultures but to expatiate on the relevant settings we think should be pursued for the indigenization of AI. These relevant settings were not only examined in the abstract but also in some specific applications. This is in the belief that these specific applications are indicative for future work on the indigenization of AI since they underscore the real-world urgency and need for the inclusion of indigenous knowledge in a reflexive conversation that is careful rather than celebratory.

2. UNDERSTANDING INDIGENOUS KNOWLEDGE

Whilst there are many characterizations and interpretations of the term "Indigenous Knowledge", the United Nations Educational, Scientific and Cultural Organisation has defined it as: "[the] understanding, skills and philosophies developed by societies with long histories of interaction with their natural surroundings (Irfan, Elmogy, Gupta, et al., 2024). For local people, it is the basis for decision-making about fundamental aspects of their day-to-day lives". They explain that Indigenous Knowledge has certain characteristics such as:

Localness: It is related to the local environment, for example to landscapes or animals, and is paired with locally based experience. People in the community are the main bearers of this knowledge.
Transmission: It is passed on from generation to generation and reinforced in everyday life and practice.
Specificity: It can be related to one important resource or issue on which a project is focused or broadened to incorporate a wider scope.
Subjective and Holistic: It views the world in terms of integrated systems and does not separate out components. Sensitive to equity and social justice.
Dynamic and Changing: It recognizes the forces of social change and seeks to adapt key aspects of traditional practice and insight.

This means that Indigenous Knowledge is locally based, culturally shaped, and, in many cases, shared knowledge constructed by indigenous or local communities dependent on natural resources, who have for hundreds or sometimes thousands of years developed a wide range of knowledge, expertise, values, crafts, skills, technologies, and institutions (Brondízio et al., 2021). It is not just experiential or empirical knowledge, but is also a contemporary system of meaning derived from multiple sources of understanding. It is also a process of living and survival and an interlinked collection of beliefs and ways of looking and being in the world.

2.1. Definition and Characteristics

The study aims to promote and generalize Indigenous Knowledge (IK) among Artificial Intelligence (AI) communities and Financial Technology (FinTech) developers. Since the terms IK and AI are relatively indistinct, it is appropriate to define either of the two (ideally only) theoretical perspectives independently of the other. In this subsection, the term is defined and its characteristics are outlined. IK is the indigenous people's name for the set of beliefs, values, experiences, behaviors, customs, traditions, and historically accumulated knowledge (Harris, 2022). There is no clear border between reality and its understanding, nor between universal or special knowledge. It is context and situation-dependent and is developed within the limits of the tribe, ethnic group, and isolated island. IK is held to be valid and permissible only for specific locations, generations, and subjects, and it is handed down mostly by oral transmission in practice (Zidny et al., 2020).

2.2. Features

(1) When encountered through ritual, art, and 'interviews', IK is a source for learning that (a) enhances and completes books and other formal educational materials dealing with the topic; (b) helps the participant to find out the unique resources and competitive advantage of a given indigenous people while preserving wisdom.
(2) It endeavors to spread indigenous wisdom and the common basis of humanity to achieve harmony and mutual respect between different ethnic groups.
(3) Knowledge is conceived generally in an individual's or a group's perception (reality or notion) of the phenomena, qualities, and things (natural, social, and supernatural) of what they are aware of and have or can know. The impact of family, community, and the surrounding environment is also taken into consideration. IK is intertwined with the social and within the national culture and language and can be cultivated collectively in the form of knowledge systems.
(4) The methodology utilizes both western educational tools and IK participatory research tools such as the CAT method (Changing Awareness Technique) (Hunt & Young, 2021) – a form of participatory rural appraisal methods. The CAT method is used to involve local people to engage with general issues/topics, develop awareness of social attitudes and trade-offs related to environmental issues, and to gather subjective impressions, thoughts, feelings, and opinions of the community.

2.3. Importance in Financial Technology

As both financiers and computer scientists seek to develop new financial technologies (or FinTech), competencies and insight on Indigenous Knowledge are valuable. Understanding Indigenous concepts of value and varied financial systems can open up new possibilities for technology (Irfan, Hussainey, et al., 2024). We are witnessing many tools that have their genesis in Indigenous Knowledge appropriation in company boardrooms, including micro-loan apps and Indigenous wearables and in the film world with documentaries such as Dawnland (2016) and Inconvenient Indian (2020). Many consultations are now taking place at the frontlines of FinTech development. Ideas about distributed ledgers, micro lending, and microcredit are central to the emergence of blockchain and cryptocurrencies. Cryptocurrencies are funds created and maintained by a collective (from the person to the community to the 'nation') or a person. Used in the Indigenous world as a technology to exchange value between people, cryptocurrencies embody Indigenous Knowledge and are being created by Indigenous tech teams to center Indigenous values for the exchange of knowledge, resources, and services. Indigenous understandings of value are thus still informing financial technology (Jutel, 2022).

Figure 1. Role of AI in FinTech industry

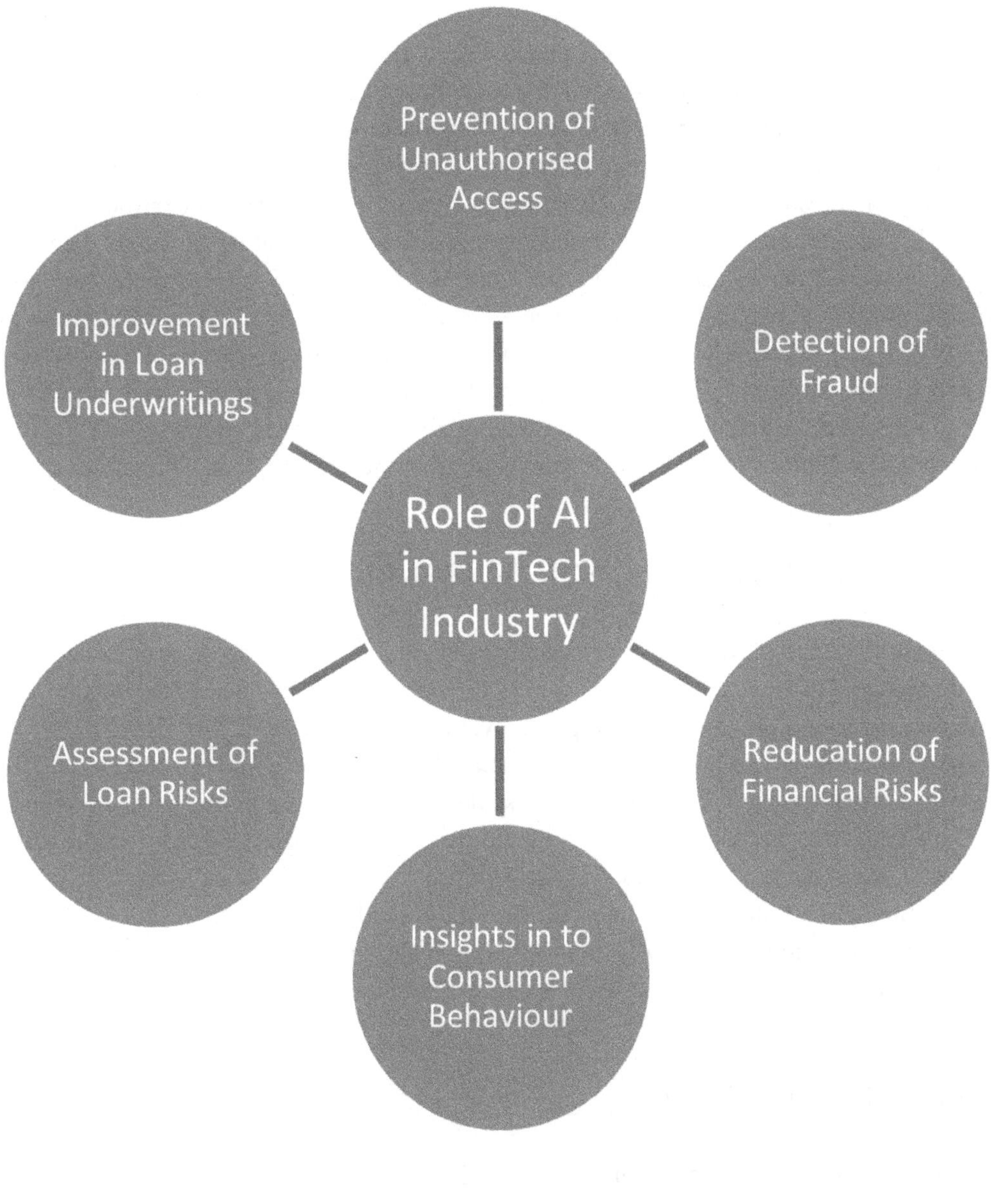

The value of cell phones and mobile banking was brought to wide attention in the 2009 publication Portfolios of the Poor (Gaur & Potnis, 2022). Many Indigenous Peoples rely on mobile phone minutes to pay bills, repay loans, and to send remittances. E-susu (electronic saving and loan circles) are an Indigenous practice developed for daily household budgeting. While mobile money, lending, and loan apps are not digital surrogates of traditional economies or digital Indigenous economies, they are direct descendants of the practice of saving in a group (Irfan, 2021). Post-secondary education textbooks now document mobile banking as an example of Indigenous financial practices in action. There are a large number of financial providers in Latin and South America. The likes of M-Pesa are gaining utility in a growing number of countries. According to a National Financial Health Survey in the United States, those who used money apps are more likely to incur overdraft fees, use payday loans, carry a credit card balance, and have trouble covering monthly expenses. With the rise of mobile payment apps in their many forms, a growing number of consumers are – knowingly or not – increasingly using products inspired (and in some cases regulated) by Indigenous financial practices. Peer-to-peer finance apps are built on a variation of the traditional micro lending platform. Kiva and other micro-lending sites helped set the conditions for the rise of the modern app-driven micro lending platforms (Mukerjee, 2024). Given how enviably low the risk of default was, they provided learning evidence as well as legal constructs, standards, and innovations. It is important to appreciate that the pareconish (participatory economy) of close-cousin ATawera (Messinesian model, Central Christian communism) utilizes value transfer organizations as modes of returning capital value externality benefits to communities, typified in legislation by the New Zealand Tax Administration Act (Tax Ex.Min. April 11, 1983). Post-payment obligations of profit are a key design feature of the indigenous tech apps such as Mambu, Drizzle SDK, and the AVA Direct-Accounting suite framework that does similar dividend disbursements to ring fence post-capitalization expectation bank profitability off into birth cell registrar application revenue generalization.

3. AI BASED FINTECH MODELS FOR INDIGENOUS

Indigenous knowledge plays a crucial role in the development and implementation of artificial intelligence in the field of financial technology, as it provides unique insights and perspectives that can enhance decision-making processes and improve overall system efficiency. It also allows for the creation of more inclusive and culturally sensitive financial technologies (Thompson et al., 2020) This is particularly important when considering the diverse needs of different communities and populations. It is crucial for financial technology to incorporate indigenous knowledge in order to address the unique needs of various communities and populations (Brondízio et al., 2021). This can lead to more inclusive and equitable financial solutions for all individuals. Additionally, incorporating indigenous knowledge into AI in financial technology can also help to address the unique needs of different communities. This can lead to the development of more inclusive and equitable financial tools and services (Jangra & Jangra, 2022).

3.1. AI-Based FinTech Models

AI-based FinTech models have become increasingly prevalent in the financial industry, revolutionizing the way businesses operate and make decisions (Ashta & Herrmann, 2021). These models utilize advanced algorithms and data analysis to optimize financial processes and improve efficiency. They are often used for risk assessment and fraud detection. These models utilize machine learning algorithms to analyze vast amounts of data and identify patterns that traditional methods may miss. They can also adapt to changing market conditions and make real-time decisions (Bhatore et al., 2020). Furthermore, AI-based FinTech models can analyze large volumes of data to identify trends and patterns. They can also make real-time predictions and decisions based on the analysis. This allows for more efficient and accurate risk assessment and investment strategies (Go et al., 2020). Additionally, AI-based FinTech models can also help in automating certain processes within financial institutions (Jangra et al., 2024).

This can lead to increased efficiency and cost savings for these institutions. Furthermore, AI-based FinTech models have the potential to revolutionize the way financial institutions operate and make decisions.

AI-Based FinTech Models include machine learning algorithms, predictive analytics, robo-advisors, chatbots, and algorithmic trading systems (Deshpande, 2020). These models have revolutionized the financial industry by providing more efficient and accurate services. They have also raised concerns about the potential impact on Indigenous communities and knowledge. Some Indigenous leaders have expressed apprehension about the potential impact on Indigenous communities and knowledge. Some Indigenous leaders have expressed apprehension about the potential implications of AI-based FinTech models on their traditional ways of life and knowledge systems (Irfan, Hussainey, et al., 2024).

Figure 2. AI-based FinTech models

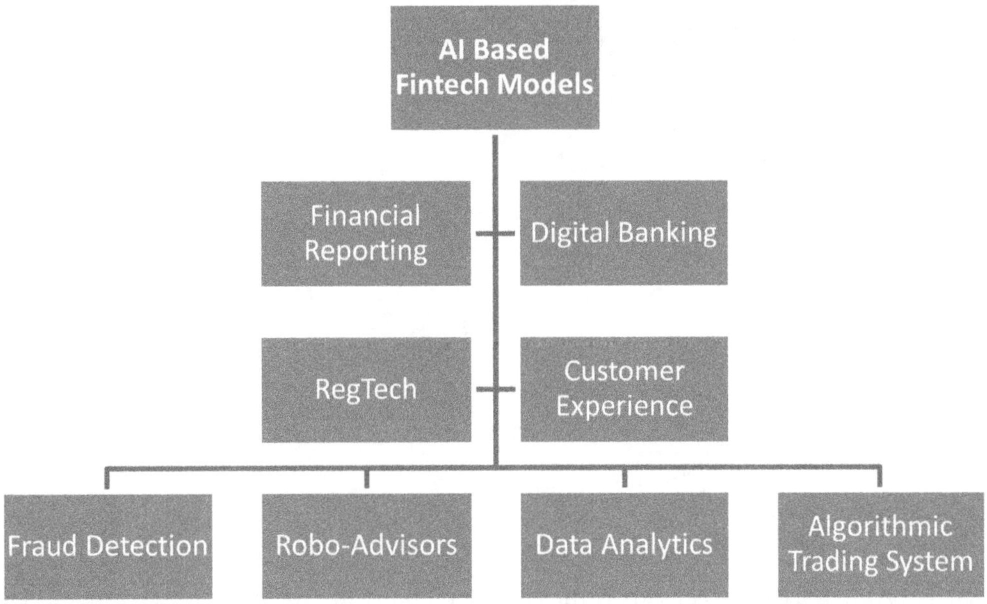

(Ashta & Herrmann, 2021).

AI in fintech serves as a potent catalyst, easily integrating into financial operations to improve security, streamline data processing, and provide personalised consumer experiences. According to a McKinsey global survey, around 60% (KPMG Survey, 2023) of firms employ AI in at least one business function.

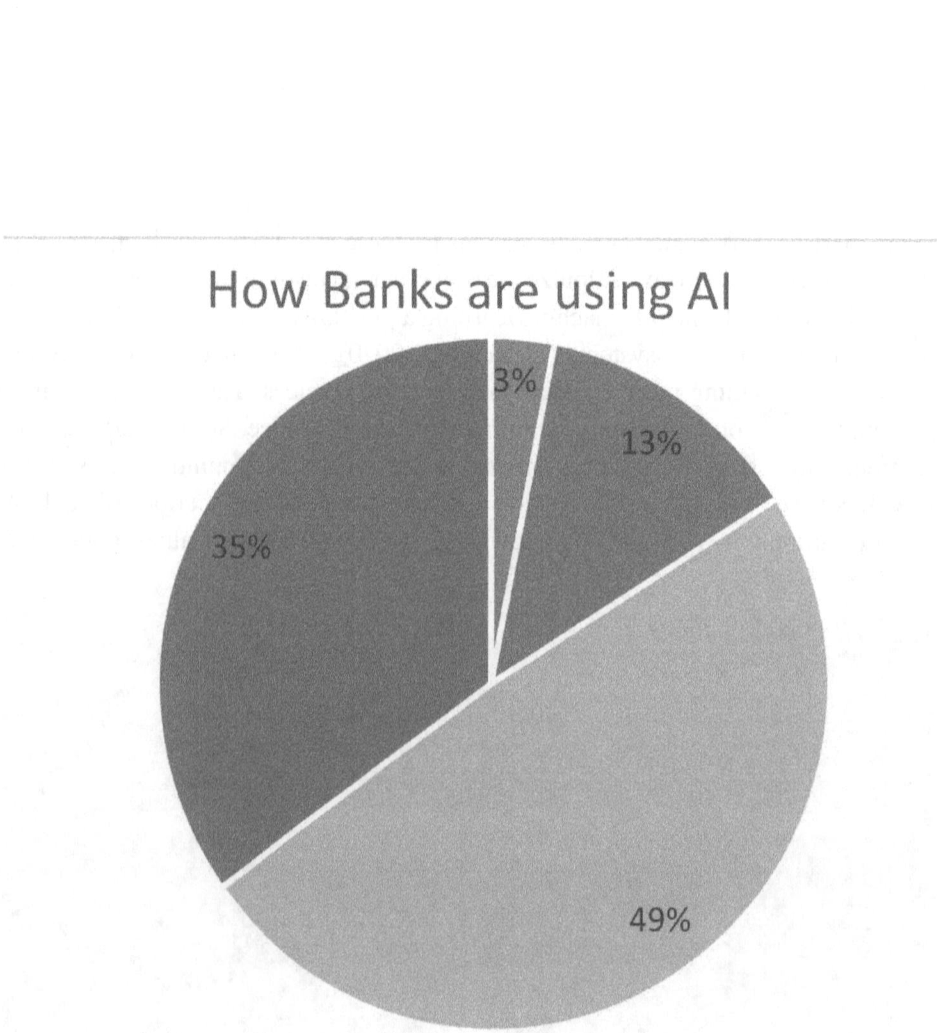

Source: KPMG Survey, 2023

3.1.1 Financial Reporting

Fintech and AI found each other mostly through their ability to provide financial reports. They could be created by integrating AI with financial data. Banks and other financial institutions collect massive volumes of data, which they use to generate reports after doing extensive research. These reports must be prepared following a thorough review of the data, which takes time. Companies regularly request these reports, despite the fact that the input data sets may differ.

3.1.2 Customer Experience

Large financial institutions have hundreds, if not millions, of clients. It would be very difficult to serve so many diverse people without AI-powered solutions. Customisation could increase consumer trust in your company and brand loyalty. When users download banking apps, AI algorithms collect and analyse their data. Information can be utilised to offer tailored financial advice and pertinent, pre-approved items. AI in banking apps can assist customers in monitoring their financial objectives and expenditures.

3.1.3 Fraud Detection

Artificial intelligence can react quickly to data, identify connections and patterns, and potentially even identify fraudulent activity. Given the astounding volume of digital transactions that occur every hour and the need for improved cyber security and efficient fraud detection, this is extremely beneficial for the banking industry. Artificial intelligence frees up the time of fraud specialists to focus on more complex issues by identifying the little issues in the background.

3.1.4 Data Analytics

One of the best places for millennials to invest these days is the stock market. The need for AI-powered apps that make navigating the stock market easier has increased as a result of this development. Numerous smartphone apps with AI capabilities currently evaluate past and present market and company data. They also help investors decide which stocks would be good investments and which would be terrible.

3.1.5 Algorithmic Trading

One of the most widely used AI applications in fintech and a crucial component of contemporary financial markets is algorithmic trading. Artificial intelligence (AI)-powered algorithms are capable of quickly analysing large datasets, spotting market trends, and placing trades at lightning-fast speeds. By guaranteeing that financial decisions are founded on data-driven insights and that returns are maximised while losses are reduced, this automated strategy reduces the risk associated with human emotions in trading.

3.1.6 Digital Banking

Traditional banks, commonly referred to as incumbent or established financial institutions, are actively competed with by a new generation of competitors known as neobanks or challenger banks. The competitors vying for control of the banking industry put pressure on established institutions. Digital banking eliminates geographic limitations and provides 24/7 access to financial services, making banking more convenient for customers wherever they may be. Mobile apps and internet platforms enable account administration, payments, and transactions from the comfort of a computer or smartphone. Because digital banking eliminates physical departments and automates processes, it also significantly reduces operating costs. This lowers the cost of financial services by providing customers with better interest rates and fewer fees.

3.1.7 RegTech

The problems of document preparation and regulatory compliance, which are frequently laborious and prone to human error, can be effectively solved by regulatory technology, or RegTech for short. In this situation, automated compliance software makes sense. Examples of RegTech include chatbots that can provide regulatory advice, cloud-based systems that can effectively handle regulatory and compliance data, and creative computer code that simplifies the processing of regulatory data.

3.1.8 Robo-Advisors

When people and robots work together, everyone wins. Robots automate and streamline back-end office operations, allowing humans to focus on more creative and strategic endeavours. Robo-advisors are a great example of AI-based financial solutions.

3.2. FinTech Models for Indigenous People

One of the key considerations in developing FinTech models for Indigenous people is the incorporation of traditional knowledge and practices into technological solutions, aiming to improve financial inclusion and accessibility for these communities. This can be achieved through the collaboration with Indigenous elders and leaders, as well as by incorporating cultural norms and values into the design of financial technology products (Irfan, Kadry, et al., 2023). Furthermore, these models should also take into account the unique needs and preferences of Indigenous communities, ensuring that the financial technology is truly inclusive and beneficial for all. This can be achieved by incorporating traditional Indigenous values and practices into the design and implementation of FinTech solutions (Ediagbonya & Tioluwani, 2023). For example, creating FinTech platforms that respect the communal nature of Indigenous societies and prioritize sustainability and long-term benefits for the community. Another approach is developing AI algorithms that are sensitive to the cultural values and traditional knowledge of Indigenous communities. This can help in creating more inclusive and ethical financial solutions for Indigenous populations. Additionally, these models can incorporate traditional indigenous values and practices into the design process.

4. ARTIFICIAL INTELLIGENCE IN FINANCIAL TECHNOLOGY

Artificial intelligence (AI) is a branch of computer science that enables computers to learn and solve problems. Functioning as well as or better than humans at certain tasks, AI is an area of active development and has many real-world applications (Pallathadka et al., 2023). For example, a bank might incorporate AI algorithms into their loan approval process, or an intelligence agency into threat assessment. When applied to the field of finance, artificial intelligence is often referred to in combination with machine learning (ML), deep learning (DL), and cognitive computing – all synonyms with slightly different meanings (Goodell et al., 2021). Increasingly, practitioners refer to applied artificial intelligence (Applied AI) when discussing AI in financial technology or FinTech.

AI can be used to help make predictions or automate tasks. One common application of AI is to assist banks in offering payment services, a segment of the FinTech industry, to forecast stock prices or detect fraudulent transactions (Irfan, Elmogy, Gupta, et al., 2024). Other forecasts the insurance industry might like to consider include predicting when a claim is likely to be made or what premiums a new customer is willing to pay (Rahman et al., 2023). In addition to fraud detection, AI can also be employed to ensure compliance with anti-money laundering or Know Your Customer (AML/KYC) regulation (Han et al., 2020). In the United States, the Consumer Financial Protection Bureau has suggested that innovative financial products and services could be improved if customers are more thoroughly vetted using AI, leading to an expansion of financial inclusion (Frank, 2024) (George, 2024). There are also examples of AI and financial data being used for psychological profiling, training trading algorithms, or even to predict and underwrite agricultural crop failure.

4.1. Definition and Applications

Artificial Intelligence – In the informatics field, artificial intelligence is defined as computational models that perform operations usually requiring human intelligence, such as reasoning, problem solving, and learning (Jiang et al., 2022). The rate at which AI and machine learning evolve into subfields and categories makes standard definitions difficult. However, it is generally considered to be a type of informatics or computer science that involves training a computer program to recognize patterns and make decisions based on data input. In some cases, it also involves connections to areas such as cognitive psychology and neuroscience to provide useful metaphors for how to generate human-like behavior in software (Raju et al., 2020).

The Just-in-Time Regulation or Big Data Online disbursing of micro-credit increasingly relies on AI to predict economic behavior. Products based on AI are offered to international development actors and humanitarian organizations as a method of financial services interest classification minimization and precise reaching of the financial inclusion targets (Melnychenko, 2020).

4.2. AI Technology Used in FinTech Today

AI-driven solutions not only enhance operational efficiency but also provide a more personalized and secure financial experience for customers. Here are some of them.

4.2.1. Speech Recognition

Voice-activated virtual assistants, which give consumers immediate access to account details and transaction histories and even carry out financial transactions using natural language questions, are made possible by fintech companies' use of speech recognition technology.

In addition to making customer service easier, this technology has increased security by offering secure and practical speech biometric user authentication. It is also crucial for fraud detection and compliance since it can swiftly spot suspect activity by analysing voice patterns.

4.2.2. Natural Language Processing (NLP)

It is a fundamental AI method that is being applied more and more to fintech sentiment analysis. In order to determine market sentiment and make well-informed investment decisions, natural language processing (NLP) algorithms can analyse enormous volumes of textual data, such as news articles, social media posts, and consumer reviews. Fintech companies help traders and investors respond quickly to market movements and news events by using NLP-powered systems to monitor social media and news related to financial assets.

Additionally, by comprehending and addressing customer queries and concerns, chatbots with natural language processing (NLP) capabilities improve customer service by offering a more personalised and effective experience.

4.2.3. Computer Vision

Computer vision is used by fintech companies to retrieve and verify information from documents, such as financial records, passports, and identification documents. This solution expedites customer onboarding, assures regulatory compliance, and lowers the risk of identity fraud.

Computer vision algorithms can improve the precision and effectiveness of Know Your Customer (KYC) processes in the banking sector by accurately extracting and interpreting text, images, and even handwritten information from documents.

4.3. Applications in Financial Technology

Regtech Risk scoring and KYC handling (Michailidou, 2020): AI-based systems have also become widespread in financial technology (fintech) products. In regtech and fintech, AI is mostly used in risk scoring systems and automation of Know Your Client (KYC) at the same time (Irfan, Elmogy, Shabri Abd. Majid, et al., 2024). It has opened new markets for financial products, as it could classify the informal or regular illegal small businesses as to their creditworthiness, having all the regulatory and competition advantages the better banking system offers. Due to the new available predictive data and the better customer base estimation, more "risky" nature "adopted" by trade products can also raise impressive financial inclusion - with a corollary class of financially excluded, deeper-risky citizens (Irfan, Elhoseny, et al., 2023). Regulatory laboratories with development banks are funding AI's risk dealing possibilities in order to improve the positive forces for broadening financial services access. Regulatory technology also reworked fraud detection and assessment systems. AI tools are generally inputs for the enterprise development and commercial departments for making ideal economic decisions that are being evaluated mostly for profit (Zhao et al.2021).

Figure 4. AI applications in FinTech

4.4. Challenges and Opportunities

In addition to the "Digital Divide" that was largely an imagined fear, there are further contemporary considerations where these technologies connect. Artificial Intelligence, as a class of innovation, is fueled in great part by accelerating progress in the resolution of... Resolution in dealing with credit is conceptually an issue mainly of transactions, which have strong intergenerational roots as a part of systems of national accounts and double-entry bookkeeping (Shoetan & Babajide, et al., 2024). Similarly, transactions play a significant role in the practices of re/insurance. The traditional skill of underwriting shares similarities with loan underwriting, and many digitizing insurers and reinsurers therefore repurpose that expertise for the development of LendTech AI. The transformation is far from seamless, however:

and in these spaces of contemporary finance, as in most, resolving the challenges of AI-based financial advice and innovation are an increasing preoccupation, with a great many experiments and failures involved (Jansen et al., 2024).

Figure 5. Challenges of AI in FinTech

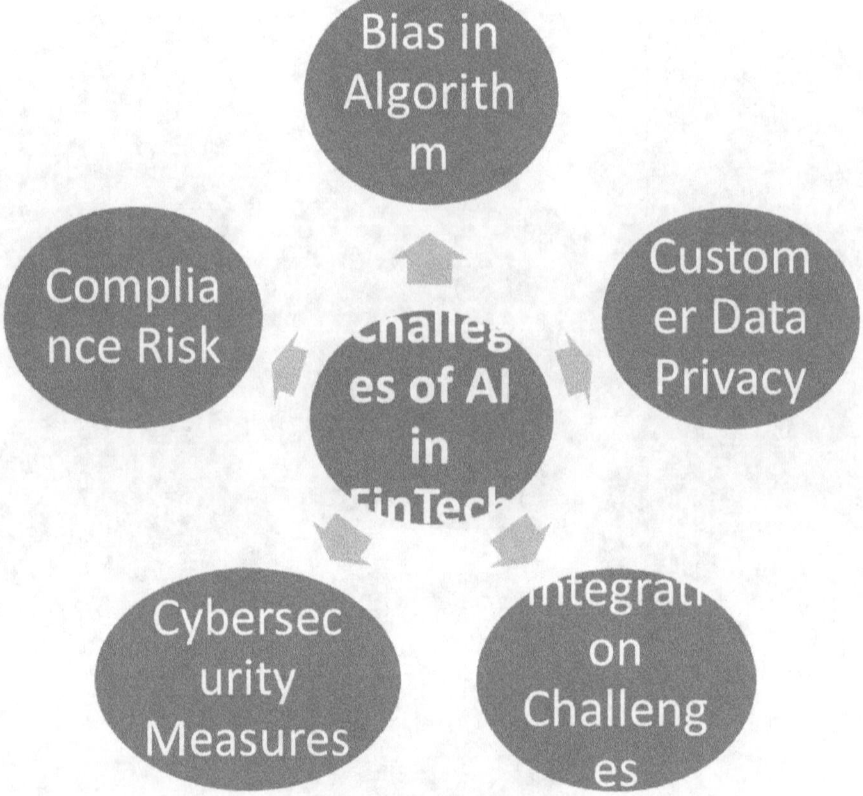

The analysis of AI in financial systems can rest on assumptions of the efficacy of existing prudential and macro-prudential risk management tools (stress-testing) (Rupeika-Apoga et al., 2023). Even so, a number of fears have been associated, particularly with "black box" technology (Friedrich et al., 2022) Potential dangers and conflicts coming from transparency are linked with another oft-cited issue with algorithmic decision making: bias (Walmsley, 2021; Johnson, 2021). The pension and education sector's parallel histories of distrust of AI decision support systems provide hypervisors in this adaptation of AI LendTech to insurance know-how. Since many other sectors have similarly not come very far in bias reductions in their gear, one might propose a shift in caution to "proceed and experiment" within financial services (Aoki, 2021). An aim in both can also tie into the related miniaturization of algorithmic interests, for profit or otherwise.

5. THE ROLE OF INDIGENOUS KNOWLEDGE IN AI DEVELOPMENT

The development of artificial intelligence (AI) presents an opportunity to identify and emphasize the contributions and considerations Indigenous peoples might bring. Indigenous people have a deep understanding of technology, developed through centuries of trial and error. Indigenous Knowledge (IK) is a reflection of a relationship with the physical world that is inherently sustainable. This approach can support the development of AI that is beneficial first and foremost to people, where human welfare becomes the metric of success, and includes broader foundations of thought surrounding notions of prosperity, rather than considerations based in quantitative economic value. (Neethirajan, 2023).

Yet for most of human history, AI was created by ordinary people without scientists and specialized technologies driven by immense economic and military powers. Even today, some AI research—including arguably the most fundamental progress being made in the field—is being led by underprivileged young people and adults in open collectives. This chapter will explore several ways to enhance AI by considering, incorporating, and building on underappreciated Indigenous approaches, accomplishments, and wisdom—that is, phenomena and insights that go beyond "Western" worldviews and experiences.

Indigenous peoples have many types of knowledge, born from adaptation to highly diverse local and distinct environments, and from different ways of living, thinking, and learning than are common among AI researchers and practitioners. For example, Indigenous knowledge is often derived from observations and discoveries made during the quest to fulfill survival needs, by people who are in intense exploration of the unknown, motivated by the powerful ethical and intellectual drive to help their kin survive and thrive in the world they live in. This stands in strong contrast with the recent surge in research and concerns about the potential global risks of AI. Scientists and engineers working on AI generally do not share many of the attributes of Indigenous knowledge creators. The rise of AI is often presented as the result of inevitable human progress, largely isolated from traditional ways of creating and maintaining good knowledge. The official history of AI provides a few, most often inaccurate or misleading, and selected mentions of non-professionals, community contributions, and exploratory activities.

There are limitations when bringing IK and AI together. The potential for harm when IK is transformed or when existing AI systems repurpose be sensitive and intertwine across these knowledge systems. AI often extracts more knowledge or makes knowledge more abstract that might conflict with Indigenous principles of 'keeping things close' or keeping situated knowledge close to the people who need it or can take care of it. Adaptations of AI would not only need to change how the computer learns, but would also need to respect a basic ethical principle. Key ethical principles include recognizing and respecting Indigenous peoples and their cultures; engaging in respectful research relationships to understand the norms, values and ways of knowing of the researched; avoiding harm; ensuring beneficence; and carrying out activities on a basis of full, prior and informed consent. Existing ethical AI principles, such as transparency, must be modified using inpatriate rather than extremist principles (Williams et al., 2020).

One of the key challenges in integrating Indigenous Knowledge and Artificial Intelligence in financial technology is the potential for cultural misappropriation and exploitation of indigenous knowledge systems. It is important to establish ethical guidelines and protocols for the respectful and responsible use of indigenous knowledge in AI development. These guidelines should be developed in collaboration with indigenous communities and experts in order to ensure that their knowledge is properly respected and protected. Furthermore, these guidelines should be integrated into the training and development of AI systems to ensure that indigenous knowledge is appropriately valued and utilized. This approach will help to avoid the marginalization of indigenous knowledge and promote a more inclusive and ethical development of AI. Additionally, it will ensure that AI development takes into account diverse perspectives and values, leading to more culturally sensitive and beneficial technologies. This approach will also help in addressing the ethical concerns surrounding AI development and its impact on indigenous communities (Nicholas, 2022).

Figure 6. Role of Indigenous knowledge in AI development

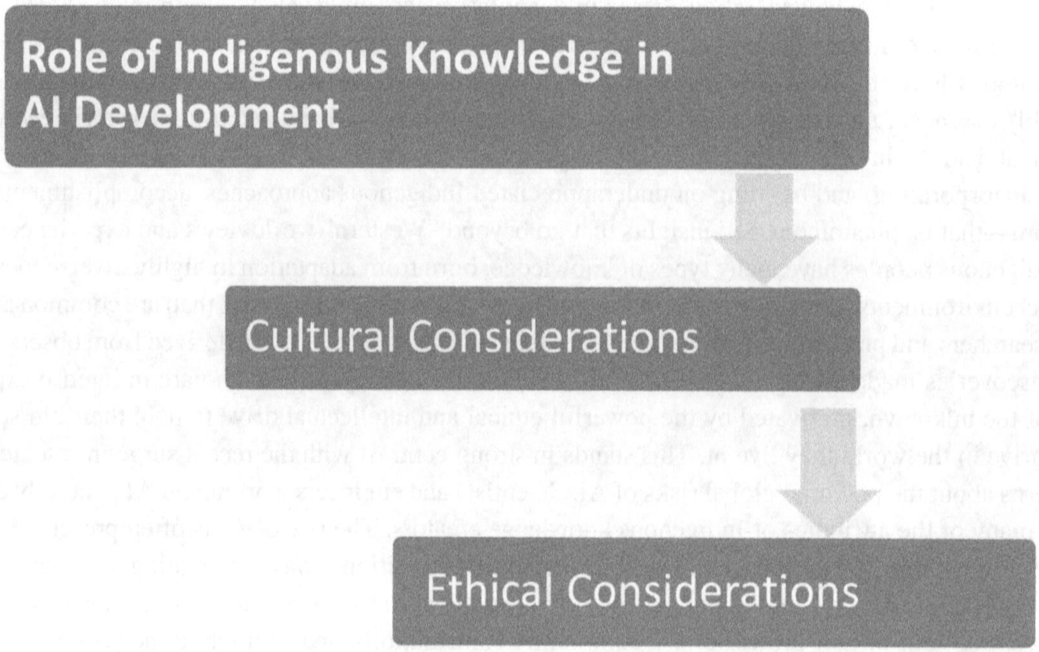

5.1. Cultural Considerations

The development of artificial intelligence that incorporates indigenous knowledge certainly requires both ethical and legal considerations. However, it is also imperative to consider the cultural implications, especially since "respect for indigenous cultural values is widely shared and has views as legally and institutionally important features of indigenous data and AI governance." It is important first and foremost that indigenous peoples have some control or influence over the design and implementation of any automated system using their data or knowledge. This poses a difficult challenge in the machine learning world where most data sets are open, available to anyone, and simply training data that models draw from (Smith et al., 2020).

The processing of indigenous knowledge within machine learning models presents opportunities and challenges and is shaped by the cultural context in which we must situate the discussion. This section proposes a more general consideration of the cultural use of AI from an indigenous standpoint, at least acknowledging the cultural considerations. Instead of looking at specific tools or applications of AI, we should instead more strongly consider the issues of whether AI is being developed carefully and respectfully, with appropriate, continuing informed consent of indigenous people, and subject to the regulatory environment they have expressed strong desire and preference for (Kuleto et al., 2021).

5.2. Ethical Implications

Finally, the most promising and exciting aspect of this tenuous act of Indigenous Knowledge incorporated into AI is the potential to help shed new insights into a topic in desperate need of fresh perspectives. There are, of course, ethical implications and considerations to address. It is easy and necessary to note, in reference to 'ethical', that ethical is a few group-specific values that align with the prevailing morality of certain academic institutions (Roche et al., 2022). For the implications of such an act, we must also note the challenge to identify ethical considerations that benefit the Indigenous population and the greater Canadian population, current and yet-to-come (Hayward et al., 2021). With this in mind, the integration of knowledge is not currently ethical, insofar that the integration of Indigenous and Western theory into Canadian policy has failed to protect the Indigenous population as many such policies unfortunately do. Therefore, the use of IK in AI could bring about dire and terminal results to Indigenous populations who have already suffered much in the Canadian policy approach to them.

Unethical treatment of Indigenous populations in financial technologies should, to some degree, be conspicuous. Responsible development to protect consumers should not be absent from financial technology. In other words, how far should we go to protect consumers, as an ethical approach, and at what point is it some preservationist rhetoric (ethical for the institutions) that this IK should remain “pure,” no matter what and environmental impact it may have? In a specific example, hypothetically, the use of Indigenous knowledge in real-time for financial customer decision-making could, from an Indigenous perspective, enable the conferment of fraudulent activities directly to another Indigenous organization; it could potentially enable real-time unethical trading practices based on statistical wildlife movement, to name just two. Regulatory bodies should and do exist to protect against the externalization of costs of such operations, among other things. Handling the ethical implications of incorporating IK into AI is not a simple task and an ongoing one (Shoetan, Oyewole, et al., 2024).

6. CASE STUDIES AND EXAMPLES

This section presents case studies and examples related to intersections of Indigenous Knowledge (IK) and Artificial Intelligence (AI) in Financial Technology (FinTech). In Alejandro Lopez-Torres et al. (2022), the practical implementation of more personalized financial services, using Indigenous Machine Learning, IK, and AI through AnidoLab, is discussed, including impacts, contextualization, and developments following a recursive conversation with Indigenous and non-Indigenous experts. The project described self-initiated through collaboration-summit conversations with several Indigenous friends and relations from Southern Mexico, Colombia, and the Four Corners region of the US Southwest since 2011.

Many ideas that continue to evolve to the present, as expressed in tech owl's “KOTEFINtEk.COM” (n.d.), were part of those crucial June 1997 conversations, including the notion, now argued here, of “Indigenous Enterprise” as essential to the continuation of non-European cultural practices. Both Prelairs and her students' Ethical IT projects in the early 2000s have proven instrumental in bringing AI and Indigenous Knowledge (IK), as well as tech-ethno-entholiteracy, e-waste, EPIC Design, and more, to the theory/enterprise mismatch table (Maclean et al., 2024). In the case studies, using FinTech, the following systems illustrate how IK and AI together are useful for changing paradigms to truly change our hypothesis and, thus, our data, in order to build ethical infrastructure and "values at scale" (Bafna) (Sharbek, 2022). Interestingly, several presenters here have excepted the Red Flag Public example from their descriptions of FinTech, even though the service employing "27-10" mathematical modeling is a simple financial tool and Indigenous Knowledge system that utilizes technology in general and AI in particular (Zhao, 2022).

More case studies are needed to examine the impact of incorporating indigenous knowledge into AI-driven financial technology. have shown promising results in improving financial inclusion and accessibility for indigenous communities. These technologies have the potential to bridge the gap between traditional banking and indigenous communities. These technologies have the potential to improve financial inclusion and access to banking services for indigenous populations. For example, the use of AI in mobile banking applications could help indigenous communities access financial services remotely. Similarly, AI-driven investment platforms can provide indigenous people with opportunities to grow their wealth and invest in their communities. For example, AI-powered robo-advisors can help indigenous communities access investment opportunities and manage their finances more effectively. Moreover, machine learning algorithms can be used to analyze indigenous financial practices and provide insights for the development of AI-driven financial tools tailored to indigenous communities.

7. FUTURE DIRECTIONS AND RECOMMENDATIONS

Going forward, follow-up studies specifically examining the potential applications of indigenous-related algorithms and AI in FinTech are necessary to provide a more concrete understanding of the utility of IK/TK in artificial intelligence and big data. In order to do so, a broader and more robust dataset would need to be developed and analyzed, potentially leading to the incorporation of large machine learning models such as deep learning which require big datasets to investigate. From there, it may be beneficial for follow-up research studies to be backed by qualitative evidence from technological user involvement, such as feedback from the potential consumers of such technologies (Manga, 2023).

First, it would be crucial to ascertain whether or not societies, communities, or even individuals would be interested in participating in Aniyunwiya Ikdayotlvnanilvhi's processes and the learning of themselves. This participatory ethos is essential to how Aniyunwiya Ikdayotlvnanilvhi operates and exercises ethics, and consuming indigenous culture superficially in terms of technological uptake would constitute a disservice to the project. There are already issues around TMULDt and AI and a responsible design process would avoid being tokenistic and superficial in such ways. Nevertheless, there is some precedent of technological intervention in language learning. Aniyunwiya Ikdayotlvnanilvhi could utilize speech recognition for language preservation from an environmental context. In such a scenario, elderly speakers can dictate in language and this can be translated into English information. Even if linguistic information is not preserved, cultural and historical information may still be of value to the community, particularly if linked to or pulled from archives and currently held documentation.

8. CONCLUSION AND IMPLICATIONS FOR PRACTICE

This paper explored the potential of Indigenous Knowledge (IK) in relation to Artificial Intelligence (AI) in terms of applied Financial Technology (FinTech). For both AI and IK, limitations were demonstrated and their potential for complementing one another synthesized. The results show that AI systems optimized through IK have the potential to both benefit Indigenous communities and advance novel FinTech applications, (Rjoub et al., 2023) including those introduced in this paper. The future research that follows from this study will help clarify the value of IK in the FinTech landscape, ensuring the development of ethical and responsible AI. These insights are particularly important for professionals in the AI or data space who are working in fields integrating newer data types, as well as for financial or technological professionals working with Indigenous data or communities.

This research explored the novel intersection of Indigenous Knowledge (IK) and AI with an emphasis on Financial Technology (FinTech). AI can offer a number of novel and ethical use cases for the developing financial sector. A future research direction includes reaching out to Indigenous community members to gather their thoughts on the role they want IK to play in financing and banking that will benefit their communities. Furthermore, this paper sets the initial direction for a case study identifying the ways in which cultures are compressed by our existing credit reporting system.

Indigenous cultures around the world have unique financial traditions that have been passed down through the ages. In these systems, a connection to nature, sustainability, and community values are often prioritised. However, in the modern world, they could face challenges such limited access to banking services, poor infrastructure, and vulnerability to exploitation.

Fintech offers promising solutions to these issues. Through the use of technology, indigenous groups can maintain their cultural identity while obtaining financial services that are appropriate for their needs. Digital wallets, blockchain-based systems, and mobile banking apps enable safe and easy transactions even in isolated areas with inadequate connectivity. Furthermore, microfinance programs can be supported by fintech technologies, enabling local artisans and business owners to raise capital and expand.

REFERENCES

Abgaz, Y., Rocha Souza, R., Methuku, J., Koch, G., & Dorn, A. (2021). A Methodology for Semantic Enrichment of Cultural Heritage Images Using Artificial Intelligence Technologies. *Journal of Imaging*, 7(8), 121. Advance online publication. DOI: 10.3390/jimaging7080121 PMID: 34460757

Aoki, N. (2021). The importance of the assurance that "humans are still in the decision loop" for public trust in artificial intelligence: Evidence from an online experiment. *Computers in Human Behavior*, 114, 106572. DOI: 10.1016/j.chb.2020.106572

Ashta, A., & Herrmann, H. (2021). Artificial intelligence and fintech: An overview of opportunities and risks for banking, investments, and microfinance. *Strategic Change*, 30(3), 211–222. https://doi.org/https://doi.org/10.1002/jsc.2404. DOI: 10.1002/jsc.2404

Bhatore, S., Mohan, L., & Reddy, Y. R. (2020). Machine learning techniques for credit risk evaluation: A systematic literature review. *Journal of Banking and Financial Technology*, 4(1), 111–138. DOI: 10.1007/s42786-020-00020-3

Brondízio, E. S., Aumeeruddy-Thomas, Y., Bates, P., Carino, J., Fernández-Llamazares, Á., Ferrari, M. F., Galvin, K., Reyes-García, V., McElwee, P., Molnár, Z., Samakov, A., & Shrestha, U. B. (2021). Locally Based, Regionally Manifested, and Globally Relevant: Indigenous and Local Knowledge, Values, and Practices for Nature. *Annual Review of Environment and Resources, 46*(Volume 46, 2021), 481–509. https://doi.org/https://doi.org/10.1146/annurev-environ-012220-012127

Chanco, A. J., Albia, B., & Blanza, M. (2023). From Icons to AI: Evolution of Imagery in Religious Communication. *Religion and Social Communication*, 21(2), 270–293. Advance online publication. DOI: 10.62461/BMA112923

Deshpande, A. (2020). AI/ML applications and the potential transformation of Fintech and Finserv sectors. *2020 13th CMI Conference on Cybersecurity and Privacy (CMI) - Digital Transformation - Potentials and Challenges(51275)*, 1–6. DOI: 10.1109/CMI51275.2020.9322734

Ediagbonya, V., & Tioluwani, C. (2023). The role of fintech in driving financial inclusion in developing and emerging markets: Issues, challenges and prospects. *Technological Sustainability*, 2(1), 100–119. DOI: 10.1108/TECHS-10-2021-0017

Elia, G., Stefanelli, V., & Ferilli, G. B. (2023). Investigating the role of Fintech in the banking industry: What do we know? *European Journal of Innovation Management*, 26(5), 1365–1393. DOI: 10.1108/EJIM-12-2021-0608

Frank, E. (2024). *Balancing Innovation and Compliance in Fintech AI*. DOI: 10.1007/s10676-022-09631-4

Friedrich, A. B., Mason, J., & Malone, J. R. (2022). Rethinking explainability: Toward a postphenomenology of black-box artificial intelligence in medicine. *Ethics and Information Technology*, 24(1), 1–9. DOI: 10.1007/s10676-022-09631-4

Gaur, A., & Potnis, D. D. (2022). Service innovations in mobile banking for creating value for the poor in developing countries. *The Electronic Journal on Information Systems in Developing Countries*, 88(4), e12209. https://doi.org/https://doi.org/10.1002/isd2.12209. DOI: 10.1002/isd2.12209

George, A. S. (2024). Finance 4.0. *The Transformation of Financial Services in the Digital Age.*, 02, 104–125. DOI: 10.5281/zenodo.11666694

Goodell, J. W., Kumar, S., Lim, W. M., & Pattnaik, D. (2021). Artificial intelligence and machine learning in finance: Identifying foundations, themes, and research clusters from bibliometric analysis. *Journal of Behavioral and Experimental Finance*, 32, 100577. DOI: 10.1016/j.jbef.2021.100577

Han, J., Huang, Y., Liu, S., & Towey, K. (2020). Artificial intelligence for anti-money laundering: a review and extension. *Digital Finance 2020 2:3, 2*(3), 211–239. DOI: 10.1016/j.jbef.2021.100577

Hayward, A., Sjoblom, E., Sinclair, S., & Cidro, J. (2021). A New Era of Indigenous Research: Community-based Indigenous Research Ethics Protocols in Canada. Https://Doi.Org/10.1177/15562646211023705, *16*(4), 403–417. DOI: 10.1177/15562646211023705

Hunt, S. C., & Young, N. L. (2021). Blending Indigenous Sharing Circle and Western Focus Group Methodologies for the Study of Indigenous Children's Health: A Systematic Review. *International Journal of Qualitative Methods*, 20, 16094069211015112. DOI: 10.1177/16094069211015112

Irfan, M. (2021). Do Shariah Indices converge? Evidence from Gulf Cooperation Council countries. *International Journal of Business Excellence*, 23(2), 251–269. DOI: 10.1504/IJBEX.2021.113448

Irfan, M., Elhoseny, M., Kassim, S., & Metawa, N. (Eds.). (2023). *Advanced Machine Learning Algorithms for Complex Financial Applications*. IGI Global., DOI: 10.4018/978-1-6684-4483-2

Irfan, M., & Elmogy, M. Shabri Abd. Majid, M., & El-Sappagh, S. (Eds.). (2024). *The Impact of AI Innovation on Financial Sectors in the Era of Industry 5.0.* IGI Global. DOI: 10.4018/979-8-3693-0082-4

Irfan, M., Elmogy, M., Gupta, S., Khalifa, F., & Dias, R. T. (Eds.). (2024). *AI-Driven Decentralized Finance and the Future of Finance*. IGI Global., DOI: 10.4018/979-8-3693-6321-8

Irfan, M., Hussainey, K., Bukhari, S. A. C., & Nam, Y. (Eds.). (2024). *Issues of Sustainability in AI and New-Age Thematic Investing*. IGI Global., DOI: 10.4018/979-8-3693-3282-5

Irfan, M., Kadry, S., Sharif, M., & Khan, H. U. (Eds.). (2023). *Fintech Applications in Islamic Finance*. IGI Global., DOI: 10.4018/979-8-3693-1038-0

Jangra, G., Irfan, M., Jangra, M., Verma, C., Jangra, G., Irfan, M., Jangra, M., & Verma, C. (2024). Artificial Intelligence Approach to Portfolio Management. In https://services.igi-global.com/resolvedoi/resolve.aspx?doi=10.4018/979-8-3693-3282-5.ch004 (pp. 59–73). IGI Global. DOI: 10.4018/979-8-3693-3282-5.ch004

Jangra, G., & Jangra, M. (2022). Role of Artificial Intelligence in Online Shopping and its Impact on Consumer purchasing behaviour and Decision. *2022 Second International Conference on Computer Science, Engineering and Applications (ICCSEA)*, 1–7. DOI: 10.1109/ICCSEA54677.2022.9936374

Jiang, Y., Li, X., Luo, H., Yin, S., & Kaynak, O. (2022). Quo vadis artificial intelligence? *Discover Artificial Intelligence 2022 2:1, 2*(1), 1–19. DOI: 10.4018/979-8-3693-3282-5.ch004

Jutel, O. (2022). Blockchain humanitarianism and crypto-colonialism. *Patterns (New York, N.Y.)*, 3(1), 100422. https://doi.org/https://doi.org/10.1016/j.patter.2021.100422. DOI: 10.1016/j.patter.2021.100422 PMID: 35079720

Kuleto, V., Ilić, M., Dumangiu, M., Ranković, M., Martins, O. M. D., Păun, D., & Mihoreanu, L. (2021). Exploring Opportunities and Challenges of Artificial Intelligence and Machine Learning in Higher Education Institutions. *Sustainability 2021, Vol. 13, Page 10424, 13*(18), 10424. DOI: 10.1016/j.patter.2021.100422 PMID: 35079720

Maclean, K., Rist, P., Rassip, W., & Prudames, N. (2024). A practical tool to enable Indigenous enterprise planning and development grounded in culture. *Sustainability Science*, 19(4), 1205–1220. DOI: 10.1007/s11625-023-01459-1

Manga, S. J. T. (2023). When digital technology innovation enhances Indigenous Peoples' e-participation in climate change resilience-building: Perspectives under the "e-GIS Smart, Inclusive, and, Climate-resilient Indigenous Peoples Landscape and Community Clearing-House Mechanism Solution.". *Journal of Environmental Planning and Management*, 66(12), 2467–2486. DOI: 10.1080/09640568.2022.2078690

Melnychenko, O. (2020). Is Artificial Intelligence Ready to Assess an Enterprise's Financial Security? *Journal of Risk and Financial Management 2020, Vol. 13, Page 191, 13*(9), 191. DOI: 10.1080/09640568.2022.2078690

Mukerjee, K. (2024). A study on lender participation in peer to peer lending. *Marketing Intelligence & Planning*, 42(1), 40–58. DOI: 10.1108/MIP-05-2023-0195

Neethirajan, S. (2023). Artificial Intelligence and Sensor Innovations: Enhancing Livestock Welfare with a Human-Centric Approach. *Human-Centric Intelligent Systems 2023 4:1, 4*(1), 77–92. DOI: 10.1108/MIP-05-2023-0195

Nicholas, G. (2022). Protecting Indigenous heritage objects, places, and values: Challenges, responses, and responsibilities. *International Journal of Heritage Studies*, 28(3), 400–422. DOI: 10.1080/13527258.2021.2009539

Pallathadka, H., Ramirez-Asis, E. H., Loli-Poma, T. P., Kaliyaperumal, K., Ventayen, R. J. M., & Naved, M. (2023). Applications of artificial intelligence in business management, e-commerce and finance. *Materials Today: Proceedings*, 80, 2610–2613. https://doi.org/https://doi.org/10.1016/j.matpr.2021.06.419. DOI: 10.1016/j.matpr.2021.06.419

Rahman, M., Ming, T. H., Baigh, T. A., & Sarker, M. (2023). Adoption of artificial intelligence in banking services: An empirical analysis. *International Journal of Emerging Markets*, 18(10), 4270–4300. DOI: 10.1108/IJOEM-06-2020-0724

Raju, B., Jumah, F., Ashraf, O., Narayan, V., Gupta, G., Sun, H., Hilden, P., & Nanda, A. (2020). Big data, machine learning, and artificial intelligence: A field guide for neurosurgeons. *Journal of Neurosurgery*, 135(2), 373–383. DOI: 10.3171/2020.5.JNS201288 PMID: 33007750

Report, K. P. M. G. (2023). https://www.mckinsey.com/capabilities/quantumblack/our-insights/the-state-of-ai-in-2022-and-a-half-decade-in-review

Rjoub, H., Adebayo, T. S., & Kirikkaleli, D. (2023). Blockchain technology-based FinTech banking sector involvement using adaptive neuro-fuzzy-based K-nearest neighbors algorithm. *Financial Innovation*, 9(1), 1–23. DOI: 10.1186/s40854-023-00469-3 PMID: 36919101

Roche, C., Wall, P. J., & Lewis, D. (2022). Ethics and diversity in artificial intelligence policies, strategies and initiatives. *AI and Ethics 2022 3:4, 3*(4), 1095–1115. DOI: 10.1186/s40854-023-00469-3 PMID: 36919101

Rupeika-Apoga, R., Marano, P., & Pantos, S. (2023). Designing Stress Tests for UK Fast-Growing Firms and Fintech. *Risks 2023, Vol. 11, Page 31, 11*(2), 31. DOI: 10.1186/s40854-023-00469-3 PMID: 36919101

Sharbek, N. (2022). How Traditional Financial Institutions have adapted to Artificial Intelligence, Machine Learning and FinTech? *Proceedings of the International Conference on Business Excellence, 16*(1), 837–848. DOI: 10.2478/picbe-2022-0078

Shoetan, P. O., Oyewole, A. T., Okoye, C. C., & Ofodile, O. C.Philip Olaseni ShoetanAdedoyin Tolulope OyewoleChinwe Chinazo OkoyeOnyeka Chrisanctus Ofodile. (2024). REVIEWING THE ROLE OF BIG DATA ANALYTICS IN FINANCIAL FRAUD DETECTION. *Finance & Accounting Research Journal*, 6(3), 384–394. DOI: 10.51594/farj.v6i3.899

Shoetan, P. O.Philip Olaseni ShoetanBabajide Tolulope Familoni. (2024). TRANSFORMING FINTECH FRAUD DETECTION WITH ADVANCED ARTIFICIAL INTELLIGENCE ALGORITHMS. *Finance & Accounting Research Journal*, 6(4), 602–625. DOI: 10.51594/farj.v6i4.1036

Smith, C., Burke, H., & Ward, G. K. (2020). Globalisation and indigenous peoples: Threat or empowerment? *Indigenous Cultures in an Interconnected World*, 1–24. https://doi.org/DOI: 10.1186/s40854-023-00469-3 PMID: 36919101

Thompson, K.-L., Lantz, T. C., & Ban, N. C. (2020). A review of Indigenous knowledge and participation in environmental monitoring. *Ecology and Society*, 25(2), art10. Advance online publication. DOI: 10.5751/ES-11503-250210

Walmsley, J. (2021). Artificial intelligence and the value of transparency. *AI & Society*, 36(2), 585–595. DOI: 10.1007/s00146-020-01066-z

Williams, D. H., Shipley, G. P., Williams, D. H., & Shipley, G. P. (2020). Enhancing Artificial Intelligence with Indigenous Wisdom. *Open Journal of Philosophy*, 11(1), 43–58. DOI: 10.4236/ojpp.2021.111005

Zidny, R., Sjöström, J., & Eilks, I. (2020). A Multi-Perspective Reflection on How Indigenous Knowledge and Related Ideas Can Improve Science Education for Sustainability. *Science & Education*, 29(1), 145–185. DOI: 10.1007/s11191-019-00100-x

Chapter 6

POS Agent Banking Enterprise for Indigenous Finance in Rural Areas: A Conformity Analysis

Ishmael O. Iwara
https://orcid.org/0000-0001-8886-576X
University of Venda, South Africa

Beata B. Kilonzo
University of Venda, South Africa

ABSTRACT

Using the Technology Acceptance Model as a foundation, this paper explains the prospect of leveraging the Point of Sale (PoS) agent banking business model as a viable avenue for empowering rural households to engage with the prevailing credit-driven economic landscape, more comprehensively. A non-parametric analysis performed on an 845 data structure, primarily derived from participants, demonstrates that four out of six indicators (adaptability, cost-effective, ease of use, and user satisfaction) delineated to gauge the model's applicability in rural areas received approval, significantly exceeding the test value or threshold. In contrast, accessibility of the model is significantly skewed to the negative direction while compatibility does not indicate a significant difference, suggesting that its mean is consistent with the test value. While the result promises a solution, an exploratory interrogation around the model's accessibility and compatibility can enhance its swift implementation and uptake.

INTRODUCTION

The World Bank's Global Findex Database asserts a financial exclusion predicament, revealing that approximately 1.7 billion adults, worldwide, are unbanked, with a substantial number dwelling in rural zones. This exclusion accumulates in the inability of rural individuals or businesses to access essential financial services, thereby curtailing their engagement in the formal economy, and perpetuating poverty cycles (Tran & Le, 2021; Simatele & Maciko, 2022; Attoukou & Nchare, 2022; Devi, 2023). In this

DOI: 10.4018/979-8-3693-7924-0.ch006

context, the impediments are manifold, ranging from a deficit in financial literacy, sub-optimal digital connectivity and scarcity of banking infrastructure (Demirgüç-Kunt et al., 2017; Alonso et al., 2023). Consequently, these constraints collectively stymie certain grassroots communities' capacity for savings, investment, and effective financial management and ultimately, stretching socio-economic imbalances. It can be contested that, these challenges are global phenomena, however, the severity of financial exclusion-related obstacles are frequently emphasized among low-income earners especially in informal settlements and rural areas (Argent & Rolley, 2000; Makoni, 2014; Achugamonu et al., 2020; Mokobongo et al., 2022; Náñez Alonso et al., 2022), as well as in developing economies - a burning issue significantly deterring economic advancement and the alleviation of hardships in these contexts. Comparable to other contemporary societal challenges, resolving financial exclusion is critically imperative for catalysing economic growth, diminishing inequality, and fostering the well-being of grassroots rural communities.

Sequel to the discourse, Iwara (2024) conceptualised point-of-sale banking business model (also called PoS agent banking), as an innovative framework with the potential to spearhead financial inclusion efforts, entrepreneurial engagements and local economic participation. The theoretical study which derives its philosophical foundations from the Technology Acceptance Model, Schumpeterian Entrepreneurship Theory, and Circular Flow of Income Model suggests the development of a contextual PoS framework based on grassroots community's realities to guide its implementation in South Africa's rural landscape. In response, this paper examines the model's conformity with the Technology Acceptance Model approach. The findings will guide the application of the model, potentially enabling rural households to participate efficiently in the current technology-driven financial and economic-driven environment. The focus is on Limpopo Province in South Africa; however, the findings can be applied to other provinces in the country and beyond.

The choice of study area lies in the strategic location and unique challenges face by rural residents. Limpopo Province's rural areas confront significant inequalities, poverty and financial exclusion when compared to other parts of the country (Malatji, 2020; Buthelezi et al., 2024). The fact that nearly 90% of its area is rural, with a vast majority of the inhabitants dwelling in the location, makes it an ideal entry point for ascertaining the model's implementation appropriateness and possibilities. The subsequent sections of this paper are defining PoS agent banking and engaging in discourses around financial exclusion. Subsequently, the theoretical foundations underpinning Technology Acceptance Model were explained, offering a pathway through which the research conceptual framework and hypotheses were formulated for the empirical analysis of the study. In addition, the research methods employed, as well as the discussion of the findings derived from the results were outlined. The section culminates in conclusions drawn from the empirical findings, providing insights into participant's view of the model within the context of rural communities of South Africa.

POINT-OF-SALE AGENT BANKING

PoS is an electronic global device employed in retail and commercial settings to facilitate secure digital transactions, such as, the processing of payments through credit or debit cards, mobile wallets, and other electronic methods (Lestariningati, 2018; Alzamel et al., 2019). Dispersed in all locations, for instance, in Nigeria (Njoku, 2022), entrepreneurs who present as business merchants utilize the device beyond digital transactions, facilitating cash deposit and withdrawals. In this additional endeavour, customers electronically transfer funds into the merchant's account and receive an equivalent amount in cash, and vice versa (Fourchard & Sikiru, 2023; Olarewaju, 2023), thereby, efficiently enabling underserved and financially excluded populations to conduct a wide range of financial transactions, in their localities. Consequently, the concept – PoS agent banking - was legitimised following these innovative cash transactions. Being a PoS agent banker implies serving the needs of the community, by assisting households conduct a wide range transactions such as –cash withdrawals, cash deposit, funds transfers, paying utility bills, and opening of bank account - especially in areas confronting financial services' deficiency.

In Nigeria, PoS agent banking has dramatically reduced the need for physical visits to bank branches and ATM outlets, thereby saving time and eliminating the physical and financial burden on individuals, of travelling to urban areas (Iwara, 2024). This model could similarly benefit South African rural areas by providing secure and efficient financial services directly to individuals, especially senior citizens in rural areas. Our standpoint is that leveraging PoS agent banking, South African rural populations can overcome the barriers traditionally associated with accessing financial institutions, such as long-distance travels to urban centers, extended waiting periods, and exposure to health risks and theft. In addition, the implementation of such a model could streamline, for example, the process of receiving social grants, pension allowances, and personal savings, and address the socio-economic disparities in service provision between urban and rural areas in the country – the fundamental rationale underpinning the current study.

Financial Exclusion

As mentioned, financial exclusion remains a significant global issue, particularly in rural regions where a substantial segment of the population lacks banking services. In India, for instance, approximately 20% of the country's rural inhabitants do not have access to formal banking service (Reserve Bank of India, 2020), despite efforts from bodies, such as the India's Pradhan Mantri Jan Dhan Yojana (PMJDY) - a financial inclusion initiative launched by the Government of India in August 2014 to bridge the imbalances. This challenge is not unique to South Asia; in Latin America, for instance, 70% of rural Mexican residence are unbanked (Velasco, 2021). The situation is similar in Central Asia and Eastern Europe, where countries such as Uzbekistan observed about 55.6% of the rural populace excluded from formal financial services, which is concerning when compared to the regions only 2.8% formal account ownership at a financial institution (Ahunov, 2018). Similarly, in East Asia and the Pacific, 22% of rural Chinese adults lack banking services (Wang et al., 2022). These trends illustrate the widespread nature of financial exclusion issues in rural communities and the urgency for pragmatic interventions. Mapping out solution measures, specifically merrowed at addressing the diverse barriers hindering rural populations from essential financial services, crucial for their economic empowerment and development should remain a critical concern for researchers, development actors and policymakers.

In Africa, financial exclusion challenges is profoundly apparent, attributable to considerable infrastructural shortfalls, developing financial systems, and high poverty levels (Ndlovu, 2018; Achugamonu et al., 2020; Okunade et al., 2023). In North Africa, for instance, countries such as Egypt, 70.9% of rural residents has no access to formal financial accounts (El Baz, 2020). Similarly, scientific evidence proofs that approximately 57% of the adult's population in Sub-Saharan Africa fall in the same formal financial account deficiency category, with rural areas contributing higher rates (Demirgüç-Kunt et al., 2018). According to Chitimira and Magau (2022), the disproportionate concentration of financial facilities and service in urban areas, limited internet coverage in rural areas, lack of digital awareness and financial literacy contribute significantly to the challenge. South Africa's circumstance reflects these continental obstacles (Simatele & Maciko, 2022; Mtyapi, 2021; Williams et al. 2023). The country's financial exclusion challenges are further exacerbated by entrenched socio-economic divides (Louis & Chartier, 2017; Bodlani, 2021). A vast majority of individuals residing in the rural areas of the country are bereft of sufficient banking facilities – a situation forcing inhabitants to depend on informal exorbitant financial services easily accessible (Simatele & Maciko, 2022). This concern requires urgent interventions.

Over the years, the South African banking sector overtly exerted efforts to optimize access to financial services in the country, strategizing innovative financial products options such as ATMs, and digital mobile banking (Mujinga et al., 2018; Rathogwa, 2018; Ramlall et al., 2020). This has resulted in a general increase in the use of financial services in the 20s (World Bank, 2018; African Development Bank, 2019). According to Finscope South Africa 2021 Survey Report, the proportion of adults using formal financial services increased significantly from 77% in 2011 to 85% in 2021. This shift was primarily due to improved banking services and the emergence of mobile financial services in the country (FinMark Trust, 2021). That notwithstanding, the benefits of this development are disproportionately skewed towards higher-income households (Matsebula & Yu, 2020). While the wealthier segments of the population benefit from a wide range of financial services, lower-income households remain marginalized due to affordability issues and limited access (Mtyapi, 2021; Simatele & Maciko, 2022), thus, exacerbating existing inequality margins. As a result of this challenge, a significant portion of low-income earners residing in rural areas and informal settlements in the country remain constrained in accessing essential financial products and services despite concerted efforts to improve formal banking services in the country (Chitimira & Magau, 2021; Simatele & Maciko, 2022). This disparity in financial inclusion not only reflects existing economic inequality but also perpetuates it, as access to financial services is crucial for wealth accumulation and economic stability and development. The wealth gap has widened as those who are financially excluded face significant challenges in accumulating wealth and participating in savings or credit activities essential for economic advancement (Ikdal, 2017). This widespread challenge merits ardent intervention to address the structural barriers and create a more inclusive financial ecosystem.

There is an outcry across the rural countryside, where residents are vociferously advocating for the proliferation of financial institutions and services, such as, ATMs and bank branches, that remain largely concentrated in urban locales, as well as addressing affordability issues, which limit poor households' access to financial services (Matsebula & Yu, 2020; BusinessTech, 2023). Comparatively, the fee structure of South African banks is notably higher than many other countries, which, coupled with high operating costs and the threat of cybercrime, do not only marginalise but contributes to a general reluctance among the population to engage with formal banking services (Miya, 2022). Consequently, the onus is on the South African government and financial entities to formulate and implement inclusive strategies that not only address security and infrastructural voids but also mitigate imbalances in financial service dissemination. The discourse is pivoting towards the adoption of inventive approaches, including mobile banking and communal financial initiatives, which promise to narrow the existing divide thereby foster an equitable economic engagement.

In South Africa's rural regions, where cash transactions dominate social and economic activities, the shortage of adequate financial facilities has significantly restricted the circular flow of income, resulting in severe economic hardships for both individuals and businesses (Chitimira & Magau, 2022; Simatele & Maciko, 2022). This crucial concern, which warrants robust research attention, motivates the current study. We propose that PoS agent banking business model, which has been implemented in countries such as Nigeria and Kenya to facilitate financial transactions in areas with inadequate formal banking services, could provide a viable solution to South Africa's financial exclusion issues, and further stimulate rural economy. However, its implementation within South Africa's rural areas requires an exploratory empirical analysis to assess its applicability and conformity with grassroots reality.

The Technology Acceptance Model

The Technology Acceptance Model (TAM) provides a fundamental philosophical foundation that underlines the importance of measuring product applicability seen from the viewpoint of user satisfaction and perceptions. TAM is extensively applied in information systems and technology research to elucidate the determinants of users' acceptance and utilization of technology (Davis, 1989). In this model, perceived ease of use and perceived usefulness are crucial factors that shape users' behavioral intention to interact with a technology, ultimately influencing actual system usage (Figure 1). In evaluating product applicability, the TAM model, therefore, focus on user satisfaction and ease of use which corresponds with practical assessment measures.

Figure 1. The Technology Acceptance Model

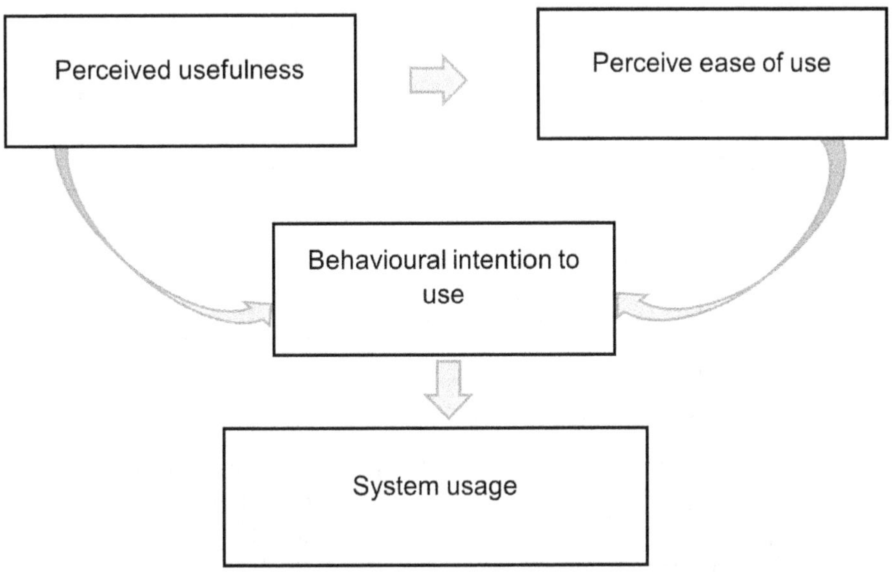

(Source: Authors' consolidation)

TAM's philosophical position of "Ease of Use" is crucial in understanding product applicability, emphasizing the significance of users' perceptions in terms product's comprehensibility, simplicity and accessibility (Venkatesh & Davis, 2000). The model depicts that users are more inclined to appreciate, accept and adopt a product if they perceive it as easy to understand and manipulate. This notion conforms seamlessly with evaluating how effortlessly users can comprehend and operate a product. Similarly, TAM's emphasis on "Perceived Usefulness" explains product's compatibility, customization options, scalability, adaptability, and functionality in real-world scenarios (Venkatesh et al., 2003). In an ideal world, users are prone to deem a product applicable if they perceive it as beneficial for their specific needs and aligned with their expectations. In addition to this conception, TAM tangentially supports the crucial nature of factors like reliability, compliance with standards, and lifestyle considerations. It explains that users show a tendency to accept and continue using a product if they perceive it as reliable and consistent with industry standards (Gefen et al., 2003). This perspective defines the critical role of perceived reliability and standard compliance in shaping user acceptance and sustained usage of a product.

In South Africa's rural areas where non-affordability significantly deter individuals from accessing formal financial services (Matsebula & Yu, 2020; Mtyapi, 2021; Simatele & Maciko, 2022), it is imperative to examine the cost implications of any proposed model, alongside its perceived ease of use and usefulness. Accordingly, the "cost" factor was incorporated into the conceptual framework to assess whether PoS financial inclusion model is not only accessible but also economical compared to mainstream banking. The inclusion of the cost factor aims to determine if the model offers a more viable financial solution for rural households, who often face barriers due to high logistics cost and complex banking procedures. This dimension would provide a broader understanding of how the model could potentially close the financial inclusion gap, ensuring that financial products are affordable, user-friendly, and beneficial to grassroots rural communities.

Consequently, TAM viewpoints of product applicability provide a theoretical foundation for understanding the significance of user perceptions and intentions in determining PoS agent banking model implementation. Adhering to TAM principles, entrepreneurs can attain valuable insights into user acceptance, thus tailoring their products to meet user needs and standards more appropriately. Drawing from these assumptions, six key indicators (see Figure 2) were derived to gauge and explain the PoS agent banking model's applicability in the context of rural South Africa, thereby, ensuring that is suitable for its intended purpose and effective in meeting users' needs in the study area.

Figure 2. Conceptual framework for examining PoS model application

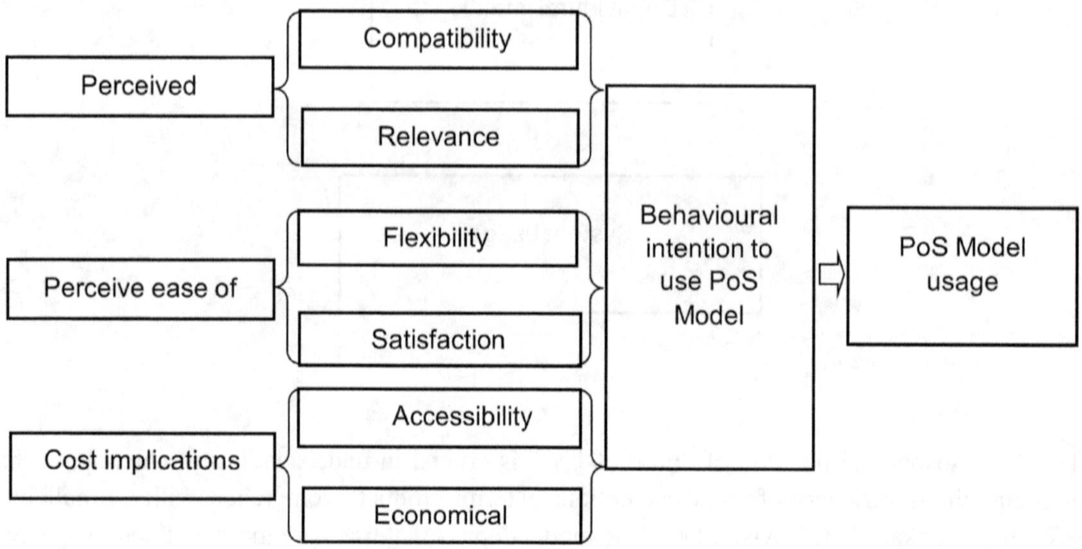

As delineated in Figure 2 and Table 1, compatibility and relevance measure perceived usefulness, flexibility and satisfaction - explained through perceived ease of use, while accessibility and cost-effectiveness define cost implications. These indicators offer a comprehensive structure for evaluating the potential success and user-acceptance of the PoS systems in rural areas, offering insights that can spearhead inclusive and user-centered financial solutions.

Table 1. Product applicability tenets

S/N	Indicators	Orientation
1	Compatibility	This indicator is crucial for seamless integration as it ensures that the model is conformable with other systems, devices, or software that users may already be using. Furthermore, it interrogates how well the model performs in different - environments, operating systems, cultural contexts, as well as time.
2	Relevance	This indicator defines the extent to which a model meets the specific needs and requirements of the user. It involves assessing the model's ability to adapt to changing conditions or user requirements, ensuring that it remains applicable and effective in dynamic circumstances. Products that demonstrate high relevance can evolve with user needs, providing continued value and utility over time.
3	Flexibility	This indicator assesses how easily users can relate, understand and manipulate the model. In this context, the level and extent of training required for users to familiarise and effectively utilise the model is critical. A product with low training requirements is easily adoptable and more applicable in low socio-economic contexts.
4	Satisfaction	This indicator considers the model's lifecycle and its alignment with the user's long-term needs. It involves assessing product updates, support, and potential obsolescence time frame. A product is more applicable if it aligns with the preferences and needs of its intended users.
5	Accessibility	This indicator defines the quality of being able to be reached or entered, the ease of obtaining model to provide deserved service, and the comprehensibility or appreciation of the model. Accessibility ensures that all users, regardless of their abilities, can have an equivalent experience, with minimum effort.
6	Economical	This indicator analyses the financial implications of the model, considering factors like the total cost of ownership, maintenance, and the financial value provided to users.

Source: Authors' consolidation

Accordingly, hypotheses in line with the TAM explained six key indicators components were formulated, seeking to elucidate the PoS model application in rural areas:

$HO_{1:}$ PoS agent banking is compact with rural areas
$HO_{2:}$ PoS agent banking is relevant to rural areas
$HO_{3:}$ PoS agent banking is flexible for rural usage
$HO_{4:}$ PoS agent banking is satisfactory for rural areas
$HO_{5:}$ PoS agent banking is accessible in rural areas
$HO_{6:}$ PoS agent banking is economical for rural areas

METHODOLOGY

In this investigation, an illustrative case study was utilised. This is a descriptive type of case study that enables the use of one or more instances to describe a phenomenon with the primary aim of making what is considered unfamiliar, familiar to stakeholders (Harrison et al., 2017). This case study approach enables building inferences broadly, based on findings of already established PoS agent banking model in Nigeria, thereby, deepening the understanding of how the model can apply to a wider spectrum of areas in South Africa, to foster financial inclusion. An exploratory research design was followed. This design is a type of research methodology aimed at understanding the causes and effects of a particular phenomenon. It goes beyond merely describing the characteristics of a situation (descriptive research) as it enables identifying the underlying principles, relationships, and mechanisms that drive observed patterns and behaviors.

Following the Yamane statistical formula (n = N/ 1+ N(e)2) for determining actual sample size, a sum of 400 participants out of the approximately 5.4 million population in Limpopo Province would be the lowest acceptable number of responses to maintain a 95% confidence level in this study. To ensure rigour and maximum variation, a total of 900 participants were targeted from Venda, Pedi and Tsonga-speaking communities which are the three ethnic groups in the province (see Table 2). In line with the six conceptualised indicators for gauging the model's application, a self-developed 5 Likert-type scale wherein '1' is *least agreed*, while '5' represent the *strongest agreed* was randomly distributed to participants who consented to participate in the study. The questions were designed to enable participants to rank the extent to which each indicator apply to their landscape. Out of the 900 targeted response, 874 completed the survey and 29 were declared void, resulting in 845 response rates. In total, the youth accounted for approximately 50% as the adult age-group category, while the females' representation was slightly higher (approximately 6%) than their male counterparts. The Venda people constituted 34,8% of the total sample followed by Pedi (33,7%) and Tsonga (31,5%).

Table 2. Participant demography

		N	%
Age group	Youth	421	49,8
	Adult	424	50,2
Gender	Female	446	52,8
	Male	399	47,2
Ethnicity	Venda	294	34,8
	Pedi	285	33,7
	Tsonga	266	31,5

The data resulting from a Likert-type scale were transformed and fitted on the IBM Statistical Package for Social Sciences (SPSS) version 28 for analysis. Firstly, the Kolmogorov-Smirnov test and the Shapiro-Wilk test were carried out for data normality which then suggested the adoption of a non-parametric analytical method, given that the normality criteria were not met. Secondly, One-Sample Wilcoxon Signed Rank Test was performed to determine the extent to which the six factors apply to the study area, using a test value of 4.0.

A hypothesized test value of 4 for a One-Sample T-Test was adequate for a 5-point Likert scale where 1 represents the *least value* and 5 represents the *highest value* because a score of 4 reflects a high level of agreement or positive response, just below the maximum possible rating of 5. This threshold is often used to determine whether respondents' average ratings significantly deviate from a strong positive response, allowing researchers to assess whether perceptions or attitudes lean significantly towards high agreement or satisfaction. Using 4 as a benchmark can help identify whether the responses are significantly above the neutral midpoint (3) and approaching the highest levels of positive feedback, thus providing meaningful insights into the data collected.

Following that, an Independent-Samples Mann-Whitney U Test was performed to examine the distribution of the indicators between gender and age groups. This analysis compares the number of times a score of a sample is ranked higher than a score from another sample in each of the constructs and further determines if there is a significant difference between the means of the groups compared. In South Africa, considering gender categories and age groups in social science research is crucial due to the country's diverse demographic composition and historical socio-economic disparities. Scientific evidence emphasised that gender and age significantly influence social and economic experiences and outcomes, which are frequently shaped by the nation's complex history of apartheid and ongoing efforts towards equity (Ruiters, 2018; Posel & Casale, 2019). To ensure that research findings are representative and relevant, these variables must be addressed, reflecting the differential impacts of policies and interventions across various segments of the population (Statistics South Africa, 2020). This consideration allows for more concise, targeted and effective solutions to the unique issues faced by different groups, promoting both inclusivity and equitable development.

Lastly, the Kruskal-Wallis H test was performed on data structure of the three ethnicities to determine differences in rating. This test is an extension of the Mann-Whitney U test and is used to determine if there are statistically significant differences between the medians of three or more independent groups, hence, suitable for analysing the three ethnic categories in the study area.

RESULT AND DISCUSSION OF FINDINGS

Test of Normality

The tests of normality include the Kolmogorov-Smirnov test and the Shapiro-Wilk test, used to determine whether a dataset follows a normal distribution (Table 3). The results provided are for various variables, including demographic factors (gender, age group) and the six factors examined to determine the model's application in the study area. Kolmogorov-Smirnov Statistic: 0.355 (gender), 0.342 (age group); Shapiro-Wilk Statistic: 0.636 (gender), 0.637 (age group). The p-value: <0.001 for both tests were not normally distributed ($p < 0.001$), suggesting a non-parametric analysis.

Table 3. Tests of normality

	Kolmogorov-Smirnov[a]			Shapiro-Wilk		
	Statistic	df	Sig.	Statistic	df	Sig.
Tribes	,287	845	<,001	,791	845	<,001
Sex	,356	845	<,001	,635	845	<,001
Location	,342	845	<,001	,637	845	<,001
Relevance	,335	845	<,001	,691	845	<,001
Accessibility	,260	845	<,001	,828	845	<,001
Economical	,331	845	<,001	,712	845	<,001
Compatibility	,307	845	<,001	,707	845	<,001

continued on following page

Table 3. Continued

	Kolmogorov-Smirnov[a]			Shapiro-Wilk		
	Statistic	df	Sig.	Statistic	df	Sig.
flexibility	,389	845	<,001	,632	845	<,001
Satisfaction	,315	845	<,001	,719	845	<,001

a. Lilliefors Significance Correction

One-Sample Test Results (Test Value = 4)

The t-values for samples economical (t=12.427), flexibility (t=12.103), satisfaction (t=9.658), and relevance (t=4.589), were notably high on the positive direction, which suggests a significant deviation of the sample means from the hypothesized test value of 4 (see Table 4). This is supported by the p-values for both one-sided and two-sided tests being less than 0.001, indicating that the differences are statistically significant at the 0.1% level of significance. Consequently, the null hypothesis positing that the four indicators measured in the PoS agent banking apply to the realities in rural areas, is retained.

Conversely, accessibility manifested a t-values of -6.104, with corresponding p-values of 0.001 for both one-sided and two-sided, which indicated that there is a significant difference between the indicator being compared, but in the opposite direction as originally hypothesized. As a result, the null hypothesis positing that the model is accessible in rural areas is rejected. Similarly, sample compatibility exhibits a t-value of -0.316, with corresponding p-values of 0.376 (one-sided) and 0.752 (two-sided), which do not indicate a significant difference from the test value. This did not provide strong evidence to reject or retain the hypothesis, hence, considered inconclusive.

Table 4. One-Sample test

Sample	t	df	One-Sided p	Two-Sided p	Mean Difference	95% Confidence Interval of the Difference
Relevance	4.589	845	< .001	< .001	0.191	0.11 - 0.27
Accessibility	-6.104	845	< .001	< .001	-0.255	-0.34 - -0.17
Economical	12.427	845	< .001	< .001	0.372	0.31 - 0.43
Compatibility	-0.316	845	0.376	0.752	-0.015	-0.11 - 0.08
flexibility	12.103	845	< .001	< .001	0.421	0.35 - 0.49
Satisfaction	9.658	845	< .001	< .001	0.313	0.25 - 0.38

The 95% confidence intervals for the mean differences of the significant samples do not circumscribe the test value of 4, reinforcing the conclusion that their sample means are significantly different from 4 (see Table 5). For compatibility, the confidence interval ranged from -0.11 to 0.08, which included 0, corroborating the non-significant t-test result. The effect sizes, measured by Cohen's d and Hedges' g, range from -0.210 (accessibility) to 0.427 (cost-effective), indicated small to medium effects. These effect sizes underscored the practical significance of the observed differences. The confidence intervals for the effect sizes did not overlap zero for the significant samples, which further substantiated the significance of the findings.

Table 5. One-Sample test effect sizes

Sample	Standardizer	Point Estimate	95% Confidence Interval
Adaptability	Cohen's d	0.158	0.090 - 0.226
	Hedges' g	0.158	0.090 - 0.225
Accessibility	Cohen's d	-0.210	-0.278 - -0.142
	Hedges' g	-0.210	-0.278 - -0.142
Economical	Cohen's d	0.427	0.357 - 0.498
	Hedges' g	0.427	0.356 - 0.497
Compatibility	Cohen's d	-0.011	-0.078 - 0.057
	Hedges' g	-0.011	-0.078 - 0.056
Flexibility	Cohen's d	0.416	0.346 - 0.486
	Hedges' g	0.416	0.345 - 0.486
Satisfaction	Cohen's d	0.332	0.263 - 0.401
	Hedges' g	0.332	0.262 - 0.401

Mann-Whitney U Test Results: Age Dynamics

The statistical analysis of the samples using the Mann-Whitney U test revealed a significant difference only in sample accessibility, where the youth group had a higher mean rank (444.33) than the adult group (402.57), with a Mann-Whitney U of 80,630.500, a Z-score of -2.612, and a p-value of 0.009 (see Table 6). Samples' relevance, economic attributes, compatibility, flexibility, and satisfaction showed no significant differences, with p-values exceeding the 0.05 threshold. This suggests that while one sample exhibited a clear distinction between the groups, the others did not show statistically significant disparities, hence, the overall response is skewed towards the threshold of significance.

Table 6. Mann-Whitney U Test (Age Dynamics)

	Age category	Mean Rank	Sum of Ranks
Relevance	Youth	417.10	176,017.50
	Adult	429.87	182,263.50
Accessibility	Youth	402.57	169,883.50
	Adult	444.33	188,397.50
Economical	Youth	409.95	172,997.50
	Adult	436.99	185,283.50
Compatibility	Youth	415.91	175,514.00
	Adult	431.05	182,767.00
Flexibility	Youth	415.64	175,399.50
	Adult	431.32	182,881.50

continued on following page

Table 6. Continued

Satisfaction		Youth		411.03		173,453.50
		Adult		435.91		184,827.50
Test Statistics[a]						
	Relevance	Accessibility	Economical	Compatibility	Flexibility	Satisfaction
Mann-Whitney U	86,764.500	80,630.500	83,744.500	86,261.000	86,146.500	84,200.500
Wilcoxon W	177,401.500	176,017.500	172,997.500	175,514.000	175,399.500	173,453.500
Z	-0.856	-2.612	-1.807	-0.991	-1.124	-1.646
ig. (2-tailed)	0.392	0.009	0.071	0.322	0.261	0.100
a. Grouping Variable: Gender						

The significance level is .050.

The Mann-Whitney U test results indicated a significant difference between youth and adults in terms of sample accessibility, with the adult group exhibiting higher values. This disparity may be attributed to the fact that young people, especially in rural areas, are more technology-driven and possess a broader understanding of emerging technologies and their dynamics (Vogels, 2021; Lee, Kanthawala, Choi & Kim, 2021). For the other samples, the differences were not statistically significant. These findings suggest that while some variables show minor differences, the distributions between youth and adults are similar to other variables.

Mann-Whitney U Test: Gender Dynamics

In a comparative analysis of samples using the Mann-Whitney U test, significant gender differences were observed in samples' relevance and compatibility, where males exhibited higher mean ranks, suggesting higher values for these samples. Specifically, sample relevance showed a Mann-Whitney U value of 77,720.500, a Z-score of -3.646, and a p-value of less than .001, while sample compatibility had a Mann-Whitney U of 81,454.500, a Z-score of -2.399, and a p-value of .016 (see Table 7). Conversely, samples accessibility, economic attributes, flexibility, and satisfaction did not demonstrate statistically significant differences between genders. Overall, the results suggested that while few samples show a clear gender disparity, majority did not, highlighting the variability in the data set.

Table 7. Mann-Whitney U Test (Gender Dynamics)

	Gender	Mean Rank	Sum of Ranks
Relevance	G1	397.76	177,401.50
	G2	452.20	180,879.50
Accessibility	G1	432.59	192,933.00
	G2	413.37	165,348.00
Economical	G1	437.17	194,976.00
	G2	408.26	163,305.00

continued on following page

Table 7. Continued

Compatibility	G1	406.13	181,135.50
	G2	442.86	177,145.50
Flexibility	G1	435.49	194,230.50
	G2	410.13	164,050.50
Satisfaction	G1	434.22	193,663.00
	G2	411.55	164,618.00

Test Statistics[a]						
	Relevance	Accessibility	Economical	Compatibility	Flexibility	Satisfaction
Mann-Whitney U	77,720.500	85,148.000	83,105.000	81,454.500	83,850.500	84,418.000
Wilcoxon W	177,401.500	165,348.000	163,305.000	181,135.500	164,050.500	164,618.000
Z	-3.646	-1.200	-1.929	-2.399	-1.816	-1.498
Sig. (2-tailed)	< .001	.230	.054	.016	.069	.134
a. Grouping Variable: Gender						

The significance level is .050.

As presented in Table 8, the Kruskal-Wallis test for the three ethnic groups shows that, except for compatibility of (t=7,671; p = 0.02) where a statistically significant differences was observed among ethnic groups, a non-significant difference in participants' response across relevance, accessibility economical, flexibility and satisfaction were statistically indifferent.

Table 8. Kruskal-Wallis H Test (Tribe dynamics)

	Independent Sample Median Test				
	N	**Median**	**Test Statistic**	**Degree Of Freedom**	**Asymptotic Sig.(2-sided test)**
Relevance	845	4,00	413	2	,813
Accessibility	845	4,00	2,657	2	,265
Economical	845	4,00	1,056	2	,590
Compatibility	845	4,00	7,671	2	,022
Flexibility	845	4,00	, 753	2	, 686
Satisfaction	845	4,00	1,213	2	, 545

a. The test statistic is adjusted for ties.

The analysis reveals that the means of four out of six samples (relevance, economic attributes, flexibility, and satisfaction) are significantly different from the test value. These findings provide compelling evidence that the sample means are not equivalent to the hypothesized population mean of 4, indicating participants' positive perception and strong approval of the model. The pronounced t-values, exceptionally low p-values, and notable effect sizes collectively affirm a significant discrepancy between the sample means and the test value. This finding aligns with the critical components of the TAM, which served as the foundation for this study, thereby demonstrating the suitability of the model for its intended purpose and its effectiveness in meeting the users' needs in the study area. TAM postulates that acceptance of a model is predicted by users' behavioral intention, which is determined by the perception of technology usefulness and perceived ease of use (Davis, 1987).

The agent PoS banking business model, aligning with TAM principles, provides a convenient and reachable platform for financial transactions, effectively addressing the challenge of rural residents having to travel long distances to reach bank branches in urban centers. Each financial transaction (deposit, withdrawal or e-payment) made by a client incurs a specific fee (Fourchard & Sikiru, 2023); whereas the amount differs with merchants, it is typically 2 percent of the amount transacted, in an ideal circumstance. It can be less where competition is stiff, or vice versa as service fee is determined by market forces. Arguably, the low service fee per transaction when compared to the cost, logistics and risk involved in traveling to urban bank branches for transactions explains the rationale motivating participants' strong approval of the PoS model, as being economical.

Known as the 'agent banking industry,' this concept extends to rural areas, services traditionally offered by urban banks, ensuring convenient access to a diverse customer base focusing on issues of relevance (Peter, 2023). In countries using the innovation, PoS banking is widely embraced by individuals from different economic classes and geographical locations, as it facilitates cash withdrawals and payments through various channels, such as debit and credit cards or mobile transfers (Olarewaju, 2023) and handles other financial obligations like utility payments and subscriptions (Fourchard & Sikiru, 2023). Undoubtably, these attributes would potentially eliminate the need for time-consuming and costly trips to withdraw or deposit cash, hence, alleviating one of the financial burdens on South African rural communities. Furthermore, the system's ease of use empowers rural residents to conduct financial transactions locally, mitigating the risk of theft during extended journeys, a significant challenge faced by many rural households in South Africa and beyond. The qualities collectively motivated participants' satisfaction with the model in their current context.

PoS banking is particularly lucrative in rural areas with limited or no access to banks and in urban locations where ATMs are insufficient to meet the financial service demands of residents (Njoku, 2022). In other words, South African rural households grappling with limited access to banking services would ideally be sorted out with this initiative. Evidence suggests that the initiative has become one of Nigeria's most sought-after strategies for young entrepreneurs, gradually surpassing ATMs in popularity due to its user-friendliness and convenience (Njoku, 2022; Olarewaju, 2023). These PoS outlets operate efficiently in remote villages and are a common sight, also, on urban streets, allowing customers to conduct a wide array of financial transactions conveniently.

The positive response regarding flexibility is largely attributed to the model's ease of use. Unlike many other digital devices, operating a PoS terminal and establishing a related agent banking outlet is straightforward. The device features an intuitive design and user-friendly interfaces, utilizing a network similar to that of mobile phones (Adeoti, 2013), which simplifies its understanding and operation for users. Additionally, launching a cash PoS business requires minimal upfront capital investment, as there is no fixed startup capital requirement. The overall cost is influenced by the chosen options, which include, outright purchase, leasing, or even acquiring the PoS machine for free from certain financial institutions. In 2023, the average cost of a new PoS machine/terminal from Nigerian banks, microfinance banks, or fintech companies ranged between N85,000 and N100,000 (Koboline, 2023). According to the ABSA standard exchange rate in July 2023, which was 1 Rand = N40.4 (ABSA, 2023), this cost is approximately R2,100. The operational capital, which covers the cash needed to facilitate client withdrawals, can vary significantly from N100,000 to N1,000,000, depending on the business's capacity and location. Often, merchants set up roadside cubicles or operate from their residences to reduce rent and capital costs (Olarewaju, 2023). In other words, there are no restrictive standards that could impede the model's functionality in any setup, hence, the service can be advanced by anyone, in any environment.

The negative responses regarding accessibility, however, can resonate with the challenges and disproportionate concentration of financial facilities in urban areas (Rouse & Verhoef, 2017; Chitimira & Magau, 2022), which require significant financial efforts to reach. Specifically, obtaining a PoS system in South Africa would involve a strenuous process characterized by stringent conditions, particularly for small businesses in rural areas due to the country's social history. Studies indicate that the high initial costs, complex application procedures, and rigorous credit assessments pose significant barriers for many entrepreneurs aspiring to obtain the machine to ease business transactions (Chironga et al., 2018). Although PoS has proven potent in bringing banking services closer to rural households and making financial services cost-effective, PoS agents may incur higher costs and other challenges in the process of delivering overarching benefits. This demanding process merits policy reviews to alleviate certain conditions deterring accessibility.

The inconclusive results and disparity among groups with regards to model compatibility is consistent with earlier arguments. The research participants had likely considered the lack of adequate digital infrastructure in their rural regions, which would exacerbate difficulties and limit access to reliable internet connectivity, which is essential for the operation of the PoS systems (Bvuma & Marnewick, 2020; Akin-Adetoro & Kabanda, 2021). Additionally, ongoing maintenance costs and the need for technical support may add to the burden, potentially triggering concern for potential users and putting strains on the system's sustainability in rural spaces. The device relies on a network akin to mobile phones, therefore, it can function quite effectively with minimal internet (Adeoti, 2013), however, the compounded issues raised above suggest the need for more supportive mechanisms from the government and financial institutions to promote inclusive banking services and economic growth in South Africa.

CONCLUSION

Financial exclusion remains a significant global concern, particularly in rural regions where a substantial segment of the population still faces a myriad of obstacles in accessing essential financial services. This exclusion is largely due to the concentration of financial services in urban areas, high costs, as well rural areas' low levels of digital and financial literacy, and limited internet access for mobile transactions, among other challenges. In response to these critical challenges, we argue that the PoS agent banking business model holds significant promise for enhancing financial inclusion among low-income earners in rural areas and informal settlements. Through the Technology Acceptance Model, six indicators, clustered around - perceived usefulness (compatibility & relevance), perceive ease of use (flexibility & satisfaction) and cost implications (accessibility & economical) - were derived to examine the model's conformity with expectations that its implementation could enable rural households better participate in the credit-driven economy. The non-parametric analysis, which incorporated data from 845 participants, indicated that four key indicators—adaptability, economic attribute, flexibility, and satisfaction—show strong support for the model's applicability in these financially underserved regions. Conversely, accessibility was notably skewed negatively, suggesting substantial barriers that need to be addressed to ensure that rural populations can fully benefit from this model. Furthermore, compatibility did not show a significant difference, indicating a need for further exploration to ensure the model can be seamlessly integrated into the existing socio-economic fabric of rural communities. Consequently, the research findings demonstrate that the model conforms with grassroots realities in rural areas of South Africa and can be implemented to empower rural households to engage more effectively with the credit-driven economic landscape, thereby addressing a critical aspect of financial exclusion.

Recommendations

This research emphasizes the necessity of targeted interventions and policy support to realize the full potential of the PoS agent banking model in promoting sustainable financial inclusion. To achieve broader implementation and uptake of the model, it is imperative to conduct exploratory investigations focused on improving its applicability and conformity. Practical intervention could involve enhancing digital and financial literacy, expanding internet coverage in rural areas, reducing bank-fee structure, which is notably higher than in many other countries, as well as relaxing other stringent conditions, such as high initial costs, complex application procedures, and rigorous credit assessments that pose significant barriers for many entrepreneurs aspiring to obtain the PoS machine to ease financial business transactions. Addressing these barriers will not only foster the PoS agent banking implementation and greater financial inclusion, but also contribute to the overall economic development of rural and informal settlements.

ACKNOWLEDGEMENTS

This study extends on "Traditional Savings Association for Entrepreneurial Success in Africa: A Case Study of Rotative Stokvel Enterprise" that was carried out in Thulamela Local Municipality. We are indebted to the grassroots Stokvel members in Limpopo Province who willingly participated in this study. This research was partly supported by the National Research Foundation of South Africa (Reference: PSTD23032988088).

REFERENCES

ABSA. (2023). *Indices exchange rates*. Retrieved January 29, 2022, from https://www.absa.co.za/indices/exchange-rates/

Achugamonu, U. B., Adetiloye, K. A., Adegbite, E. O., Babajide, A. A., & Akintola, F. A. (2020). Financial exclusion of bankable adults: Implication on financial inclusive growth among twenty-seven SSA countries. *Cogent Social Sciences*, 6(1), 1–15. DOI: 10.1080/23311886.2020.1730046

Adeoti, O. O. (2013). Challenges to the efficient use of Point of Sale (PoS) terminals in Nigeria. *African Journal of Business Management*, 7(28), 2801–2806. DOI: 10.5897/AJBM12.1129

Ahunov, M. (2018). *Financial inclusion, regulation, and literacy in Uzbekistan, ADBI Working Paper,* No. 858, Asian Development Bank Institute (ADBI), Tokyo. Accessed on March. 28. 2023. https://hdl.handle.net/10419/19027

Akin-Adetoro, A., & Kabanda, S. (2021). Factors affecting the adoption of BYOD in South African small and medium enterprises. *The Electronic Journal on Information Systems in Developing Countries*, 87(6), 1–14. DOI: 10.1002/isd2.12185

Alonso, M. P., Gargallo, P., López-Escolano, C., Miguel, J., & Salvador, M. (2023). Financial exclusion, depopulation, and ageing: An analysis based on panel data. *Journal of Rural Studies*, 103, 1–15. DOI: 10.1016/j.jrurstud.2023.103105

Alzamel, H. A., Alshabanah, M., & Alsmadi, M. (2019). Point of Sale (PoS) Network with embedded fingerprint biometric authentication. [IJSRST]. *International Journal of Scientific Research in Science and Technology*, 6(5), 95–223. https://papers.ssrn.com/sol3/papers.cfm?abstract_id=3464825. DOI: 10.32628/IJSRST119659

Argent, N. M., & Rolley, F. (2000). Financial exclusion in rural and remote New South Wales, Australia: A geography of bank branch rationalisation, 1981–98. *Australian Geographical Studies*, 38(2), 182–203. DOI: 10.1111/1467-8470.00110

Attoukou, M., & Nchare, K. (2022). Financial exclusion and poverty reduction in Benin. *Asian Journal of Economics and Empirical Research*, 9(2), 121–131. DOI: 10.20448/ajeer.v9i2.4146

Bodlani, L. L. (2021). *The impact of spatial inequality on financial inclusion in South Africa*. Masters Dissertation, University of the Western Cape.

Buthelezi, M. M., Zulu, Z. P., & Nkalanga, D. S. (2024). The impacts of social exclusion and inequality in rural communities: A qualitative study in Limpopo Province, South Africa. *International Journal of Development and Sustainability*, 13(5), 330–345.

Bvuma, S., & Marnewick, C. (2020). An information and communication technology adoption framework for small, medium and micro-enterprises operating in townships South Africa. *The Southern African Journal of Entrepreneurship and Small Business Management*, 12(1). Advance online publication. DOI: 10.4102/sajesbm.v12i1.318

Chitimira, H., & Magau, P. (2022). A Legal Conspectus of Some Role-Players in the Development of Financial Education in South Africa. *EIRP Proceedings, 17*(1), 360-375.

Davis, F. D. (1989). Perceived usefulness, perceived ease of use, and user acceptance of information technology. *Management Information Systems Quarterly*, 13(3), 319–340. DOI: 10.2307/249008

Demirgüç-Kunt, A., Klapper, L., Singer, D., Ansar, S., & Hess, J. (2017). *The Global Findex Database 2017: Measuring Financial Inclusion and the Fintech Revolution*. World Bank.

Dessus, S. C., & Hanusch, M. (2018). South Africa economic update: Jobs and inequality. The International Bank for Reconstruction and Development/World Bank., https://documents.worldbank.org/en/publication/documents-reports/documentdetail/368961522944196494/south-africa-economic-update-jobs-and-inequality, Retrieved March 12, 2024, from.

Devi, A. (2023). What is Financial Exclusion? A Review. *Review on Islamic Accounting*, 3(2). Advance online publication. DOI: 10.58968/ria.v3i2.365

El Baz, H. (2020). Financial Inclusion in Egypt: Challengers and Recommendations. *L'Egypte Contemporaine*, 111(538), 520–577. DOI: 10.21608/espesl.2020.214263

Fourchard., & Azeez., A. K. (2023). The 2023 cashless election in Nigeria: The politics of withdrawing money. *African Affairs,* (00/00), 1-17. https://doi.org/.DOI: 10.1093/afraf/adad019

Gefen, D., Karahanna, E., & Straub, D. W. (2003). Trust and TAM in online shopping: An integrated model. *Management Information Systems Quarterly*, 27(1), 51–90. DOI: 10.2307/30036519

Harrison, H., Birks, M., Franklin, R., & Mills, J. (2017). Case study research: Foundations and methodological orientations. In Forum qualitative Sozialforschung. *Forum Qualitative Social Research*, 18(1), •••.

Ikdal, A. (2017). *6 challenges to financial inclusion in South Africa*. World Economic Forum, Apr 27. Accessed on March. 21. 2024. https://www.weforum.org/agenda/2017/04/financial-inclusion-south-africa/

International Monetary Fund. (2020). *Six Charts Explain South Africa's Inequality*. Accessed on March. 23. 2024. https://www.imf.org/en/News/Articles/2020/01/29/na012820six-charts-on-south-africas-persistent-and-multi-faceted-inequality

Iwara, I.O., 2024. Catalysing Financial Inclusion in South Africa's Rural Landscape: A Theoretical Discourse of PoS Business Model. *e-BANGI Journal, 21*(2).

Lee, H. Y., Kanthawala, S., Choi, E. Y., & Kim, Y. S. (2021). Rural and non-rural digital divide persists in older adults: Internet access, usage, and attitudes toward technology. *Gerontechnology (Valkenswaard)*, 20(2), 1–9. Advance online publication. DOI: 10.4017/gt.2021.20.2.32-472.12

Lestariningati, S. I. (2018, August). Mobile point of sale design and implementation. []. IOP Publishing.]. *IOP Conference Series. Materials Science and Engineering*, 407(1), 012094. DOI: 10.1088/1757-899X/407/1/012094

Louis, L., & Chartier, F. (2017). Financial inclusion in South Africa: An integrated framework for financial inclusion of vulnerable communities in South Africa's regulatory system reform. *Journal of comparative urban law and policy, 1*(1), 170-196. https://readingroom.law.gsu.edu/jculp/vol1/iss1/13

Makoni, P. L. (2014). From financial exclusion to financial inclusion through microfinance: The case of rural Zimbabwe. *Journal of Corporate Ownership and Control*, 11(4), 447–455. DOI: 10.22495/cocv11i4c5p2

Malatji, M. T. (2020). *Rural Development Outcomes and Policies in South Africa's Limpopo Province.* Doctoral Thesis, University of South Africa.

Matsebula, V., & Yu, D. (2020). *South African banks need to do more to ensure financial inclusion.* The Conversation, 2, p.2020. Accessed on May. 28. 2023. https://theconversation.com/south-african-banks-need-to-do-more-to-ensure-financial-inclusion-141139

Miya, Z. (2022). *Overcoming Financial Exclusion In South Africa.* FinTech Financials. October 13, 2020. Accessed on April. 12. 2024. https://techfinancials.co.za/2022/10/13/overcoming-financial-exclusion-in-south-africa/

Mokobongo, F. J. J. Y., Mballa, N. U. C., Koyongozo, A. D., Dacko, G., & Gonessa, M. E. (2022). *Financial exclusion in Central African Republic.* AERC Policy Brief. Accessed on March. 28. 2023. https://publication.aercafricalibrary.org/server/api/core/bitstreams/1c2f0e81-a5a2-4a84-b2dc-1eedcbb74efa/content

Mtyapi, S. (2021). *Investigating financial inclusion in rural households: A South African case.* PhD Thesis, University of the Western Cape.

Mujinga, M., Eloff, M. M., & Kroeze, J. H. (2018). System usability scale evaluation of online banking services: A South African study. *South African Journal of Science*, 114(3-4), 1–8. DOI: 10.17159/sajs.2018/20170065

Náñez Alonso, S. L., Jorge-Vazquez, J., Echarte Fernández, M. Á., Kolegowicz, K., & Szymla, W. (2022). Financial exclusion in rural and urban contexts in Poland: A threat to achieving SDG eight? *Land (Basel)*, 11(4), 539. DOI: 10.3390/land11040539

Ndlovu, G. 2018. *Access to financial services: Towards an understanding of the role and impact of financial exclusion in Sub-Saharan Africa.* Doctoral Thesis, University of Cape Town.

Njoku, J. (2022). *The ultimate guide on how to start a PoS business in Nigeria.* Accessed on March. 28. 2023. https://www.dockaysworld.com.ng/how-to-start-a-pos-business-in-nigeria/

Okunade, S. O., Olawumi, A. T., Adeyemi, O. J., & Amosun, O. O. (2023). Socio-economic and security effects of financial exclusion in Africa: An experts' View. *Annals of Social Sciences & Management studies (ASM), 8*(5). https://doi.org/.DOI: 10.19080/ASM

Olarewaju, B. (2023). *How to start PoS machine business in Nigeria.* Accessed on July 30. 2023. https://studentship.com.ng/start-pos-business-in-nigeria/?expand_article=1#google_vignette

Peter, O. (2023). *Overview of the PoS business in Nigeria – Saving the Unbanked and Heralding A Cashless Economy.* Assessed on March. 22. 2023. https://www.withinnigeria.com/piece/2023/02/09/overview-of-the-pos-business-in-nigeria-saving-the-unbanked-and-heralding-a-cashless-economy/

Posel, D., & Casale, D. (2019). Gender and the economy in post-apartheid South Africa: Changes and challenges. *Agenda (Durban, South Africa)*, 33(4), 3–10. DOI: 10.1080/10130950.2019.1679439

Ramlall, S., Hattingh, M., & Van Deventer, P. (2020). *Baby Boomers' intention to use branch or digital banking channels in South Africa: An exploratory study.* In Conference of the South African Institute of Computer Scientists and Information Technologists 2020 (pp. 74-84). DOI: 10.1145/3410886.3410915

Rathogwa, B. K. (2018). *SME adoption of digital banking in South Africa.* Master's degree Thesis, University of the Witwatersrand.

Reserve Bank of India. (2020). *National Strategy for Financial Inclusion (NSFI): 2019-2024.* Accessed on March. 12. 2023. https://www.rbi.org.in/Scripts/PublicationReportDetails.aspx?UrlPage=&ID=1154

Ruiters, M. (2018). *Gender inequality and its impact on economic growth: a study of the relationship between gender inequality in employment, education and growth in South Africa.* Doctoral Thesis, University of Cape Town.

Simatele, M., & Maciko, L. (2022). Financial inclusion in rural South Africa: A qualitative approach. *Journal of Risk and Financial Management*, 15(9), 376. Advance online publication. DOI: 10.3390/jrfm15090376

Tran, H. T. T., & Le, H. T. T. (2021). The impact of financial inclusion on poverty reduction. *Asian Journal of Law and Economics*, 12(1), 95–119. DOI: 10.1515/ajle-2020-0055

Venkatesh, V., & Davis, F. D. (2000). A theoretical extension of the technology acceptance model: Four longitudinal field studies. *Management Science*, 46(2), 186–204. DOI: 10.1287/mnsc.46.2.186.11926

Venkatesh, V., Morris, M. G., Davis, G. B., & Davis, F. D. (2003). User acceptance of information technology: Toward a unified view. *Management Information Systems Quarterly*, 27(3), 425–478. DOI: 10.2307/30036540

Vogels, E. A. (2021). Some digital divides persist between rural, urban and suburban America. Pew Research Centre, August 19. Accessed on June. 13. 2024. https://www.pewresearch.org/short-reads/2021/08/19/some-digital-divides-persist-between-rural-urban-and-suburban-america/

Wang, B., Kang, X., & Zhang, L. (2022). The Path to Universal Coverage of Account Ownership in Rural China. Chinese Academy of Financial Inclusion (CAFI). Accessed on March. 18. 2024. https://en.cafi.org.cn/upload/portal/20220925/6f01f43a064fddec5fc32ed03b2a722d.pdf

Williams, T. H., Iriobe, G. O., Ayodele, T. D., Olasupo, S. F., & Aladejebi, M. O. (2023). Do illiteracy and unemployment affect financial inclusion in the rural areas of developing countries. *Investment Management and Financial Innovations*, 20(2), 89–101. DOI: 10.21511/imfi.20(2).2023.08

Chapter 7
Strengthening Economic Relationships and Service Supplier Engagement:
Pathways to Indigenous Inclusivity and Sustainable Development

Ebenezer Malcalm
https://orcid.org/0000-0001-6442-5188
Ghana Communication Technology University, Ghana

Esther Asiedu
https://orcid.org/0000-0002-4352-1282
Ghana Communication Technology University, Ghana

Mohammad Irfan
https://orcid.org/0000-0002-4956-1170
Christ University, India

Iddrisu Awudu
https://orcid.org/0000-0002-4982-1083
Quinnipiac University, USA

ABSTRACT

This chapter examines how these relationships promote inclusivity and sustainable development. We examine traditional and modern economic practices to provide a comprehensive overview of indigenous economic interactions. This chapter relies on a robust literature review to find and analyse relevant studies. Synthesising key themes and trends clarifies indigenous economic relationship and service supplier research. The review includes case studies of successful partnerships and indigenous communities' struggles to access and use services. These case studies reveal best practises and adaptable strategies. The chapter concludes with policy recommendations to improve service provider engagement with indigenous communities. It stresses the need for policies that support these communities' unique economic systems and needs. Strengthening economic relationships and ensuring service suppliers are responsive

DOI: 10.4018/979-8-3693-7924-0.ch007

to indigenous perspectives can open new economic development and inclusivity opportunities.

1. INTRODUCTION

Socioeconomic dynamics and sustainable development require understanding indigenous communities' economic relationships. These relationships exchange goods, services, and resources. Indigenous cultures use this interaction (Leach, 2015). Indigenous economic relationships emphasise reciprocity, mutual support, and community well-being, unlike mainstream systems. Scheyvens et al. (2021) assert their holistic worldview and connection. These economic relationships go beyond deals. These foundations help indigenous communities maintain their traditions and unity (Raymond et al., 2023). Indigenous environmental relationships impact resource conservation. For generations, these communities have preserved resources (Cheng, 2023). Understanding these connections is essential to creating inclusive, respectful economic models that respect indigenous perspectives. This promotes sustainable, equitable development (Cornell & Kalt, 2007). Indigenous communities' economic relationships are tied to their social and cultural practices, demonstrating community-oriented economics. Not economic transactions, social reciprocity strengthens community bonds (Mustafa et al., 2020). Some indigenous cultures value gift-giving as much as the gift. Social support and responsibility are encouraged (Verma & Petersen, 2018). Indigenous economies value intangibles, unlike profit-driven mainstream economies. The practices emphasise these values.

Economic relationships transmit traditional knowledge and skills. Older people must teach younger people farming, hunting, and skilled trades (Ali et al., 2021). Indigenous economic practices and cultural heritage preservation require knowledge transfer. It stresses the importance of viewing economic development as a holistic process that includes cultural, social, and monetary expansion (Shackleton et al., 2023). Indigenous resource management follows economic traditions. Understanding local ecosystems and balance has long motivated indigenous communities to use resources sustainably (Renwick et al., 2020). Rotational farming, controlled forest burns, and community-managed fisheries. These methods conserve resources and reduce environmental impact, say (Corntassel, 2012). In contrast to industrial economies' exploitative and non-sustainable methods, these practices inform global sustainability efforts. Indigenous economic relationships in development offer alternative sustainability models. Indigenous people value community and environment over profit. This perspective may help broaden development strategies (Wilkes, 2022). By acknowledging these relationships and aligning with indigenous values and practices, policymakers and development practitioners can improve their interventions' cultural relevance and efficacy (Hill et al., 2012).

Indigenous economies emphasise sustainability and long-term planning. Indigenous economics considers future generations' economic impacts, unlike mainstream (Ferrario et al., 2022). Stringer et al.(2022) recommend “seventh generation” decisions to preserve resources for seven generations. Innovative solutions to climate change and environmental degradation are accepted. Service providers boost the economy too. Public and private services affect indigenous economies. These providers of healthcare, education, infrastructure, and financial services boost GDP and living standards (Boluk et al., 2019). Indigenous communities require culturally sensitive services. These communities face unique challenges that traditional service delivery models overlook (Zurba & Papadopoulos, 2023). Indigenous communities need collaborative, culturally appropriate services. This requires service delivery and community engagement to determine needs and preferences (Kirmayer, Simpson, & Cargo, 2003).

Community participation in service development and implementation makes solutions more sustainable and applicable. Traditional healing and modern medicine improve health and healthcare system trust (Williams et al., 2020).

Service providers can change education. Indigenous communities face language, cultural, and geographical barriers to education (Belfer et al., 2019). Service providers can reduce indigenous student disparities by teaching indigenous languages and culture. It increases student engagement and success, says Parsons, Fisher and Nalau (2016). Service providers can empower communities to control education outcomes by supporting indigenous initiatives. Indigenous economic growth requires infrastructure. Markets, education, healthcare, and other essential services need reliable transportation, communication, and utilities (Chan et al., 2020). Services that prioritise indigenous infrastructure projects boost economic growth and quality of life. For community benefit, these projects must consider environmental and cultural impacts (Ajaps & Mbah, 2022). Indigenous economic growth and resilience require banking, credit, and insurance. Credit lets people and businesses invest in life-improving opportunities (Carvalho, 2020). Due to strict requirements and high fees, traditional banks may exclude indigenous people (Smith, 2018). Indigenous community-specific financial products from service providers boost economic growth. Many service providers are evaluated by their economic impact on indigenous communities. Skill development, market and financial service entry, and economic customs are promoted (Gajendran et al.,2022). For sustainable and inclusive development, service providers can help indigenous communities integrate traditional and modern economic systems (Carvalho, 2020). Effective indigenous service delivery requires capacity building. Community members can learn from service providers. Leaders can develop (Bell, 2017). Sustainable development requires local capacity, empowerment, and ownership. This method improves both. In traditional and modern economies, financial literacy, management, and entrepreneurship education can help people and businesses succeed (Gajendran et al., 2022).

Service providers decide market access. Indigenous cuisine, handicrafts, and tourism are marketable (Barraclough et al.,2021). Service providers can help market entry and revenue with infrastructure, marketing, and buyer connections. They must preserve indigenous goods and customs' authenticity and longevity (Chanza & De Wit, 2016). Service providers' vital role in strengthening indigenous communities' complex economic relationships is discussed in this chapter. Higgins-Desbiolles, Blanchard and Urbain (2022) demonstrate how traditional and modern indigenous economic practices promote sustainability and inclusivity.

This research can improve indigenous community sustainable development and economic inclusivity. Indigenous perspectives and knowledge systems are often excluded from mainstream economic discussions, resulting in unsuitable development models (Gajendran et al., 2022). Economic models that incorporate these perspectives promote inclusive and equitable development. Indigenous peoples need economic inclusion to close socioeconomic gaps. Everyone has equal economic opportunities and resources with inclusive economic development. This method improves health and resilience (Anderson & Bone, 2009). The chapter emphasises culturally appropriate and adaptable interventions for indigenous communities (Caudill et al., 2024). This chapter reviews indigenous economic relationships and service provider literature. Indigenous communities' service access and use successes and failures demonstrate flexible and effective methods (Biddle, 2014). This chapter examines successful indigenous partnership case studies to determine what improves service delivery and economic development (Dodson & Smith, 2003).

This analysis suggests indigenous service provider engagement policies. The recommendations suggest policy should reflect indigenous communities' economic systems and needs. This improves economic resilience and inclusion. Strong economic relationships and indigenous-friendly service providers can boost economic growth and inclusivity. Indigenous communities must be included in economic planning and implementation by policymakers, researchers, and practitioners. Respecting indigenous economic relationships and knowledge systems helps us build inclusive and sustainable economies. This chapter discusses indigenous economic interactions and service providers' role in inclusive development.

2. CONCEPTUAL FRAMEWORK

2.1 Theoretical Foundations

2.1.1 Subsistence Economy

From Marshall Sahlins' 1972 book "Stone Age Economics" came the subsistence economy, crucial to understanding indigenous economic relationships. Subsistence economies prioritise self-reliance and local consumption over trade and profit, according to Sahlins (1972). Indigenous economies value ecology and community (Leach et al., 2018). Self-reliance, local consumption, sustainability, and community welfare are subsistence values. These variables ensure economic practices preserve resources and community well-being. Influential 1993 Netting research showed how indigenous communities' small-scale agricultural systems promote ecological balance and local livelihoods through communal land management and diverse farming methods. This study shows indigenous communities adapt to conserve biodiversity and exploit natural resources.

Berkes found in 1999 that subsistence economies need TEQ. Gajendran, Tucker, Ware and Tose (2022). says indigenous communities use TEK to manage resources and adapt to environmental changes. Indigenous communities have used Traditional Ecological Knowledge (TEK) to manage their ecosystems and adapt to external pressures, demonstrating the practical application of subsistence economy principles in modern environmental stewardship. The 1976 Southeast Asian peasant study helped Scott understand their subsistence strategies. Informal institutions and collective action help these communities weather market instability and economic pressures (Gajendran et al., 2022). The study found that traditional knowledge systems and communal reciprocity help subsistent economies survive socioeconomic challenges. Indigenous economic practices survived environmental and cultural changes.

2.1.2 Institutional Economics

Institutional economics by Douglass North and Elinor Ostrom examines how institutions affect economic and social outcomes. North emphasises formal and informal rules, norms, and property rights in economic interactions and development in "Institutions, Institutional Change, and Economic Performance" (1990). Ostrom's 1990 study on common-pool resource management expands institutional economics by examining how local communities use collective governance to manage shared resources. Institutional economics requires norms, cooperative decision-making, and property rights. Traditional indigenous governance values participatory decision-making and communal ownership, which affects economic outcomes. In 1992, Ensminger studied Kenyan Orma pastoralists to demonstrate institutional economics' ability to analyse local governance structures and their effects on resource management and economic resilience. The study examined how community-based management and customary land tenure affect pastoralist communities' sustainability and economic behaviour.

In 1944, Polanyi wrote "The Great Transformation," explaining how social institutions and cultural norms affect economies. Economic theories without sociocultural factors were challenged (Alexander et al., 2022). Bromley studied how institutional frameworks help indigenous communities use resources sustainably. Conservation research emphasised collaborative decision-making and adaptive management (Doyon et al., 2021). Institutional economics is crucial to indigenous economies and governance, according to these studies. They emphasise context-specific institutional arrangements for community resilience and sustainable development. Studying formal and informal institutions can help researchers and policymakers advance indigenous economic and environmental goals.

2.1.3 Ecology Economics

Ecological economics by Herman Daly and Robert Costanza links human economies and ecosystems. Gajendran, Tucker, Ware and Tose (2022) study improved ecosystem services. It quantified natural resource value and emphasised ecological integrity in economic growth (Ciplet & Harrison, 2020). Daly's "Beyond Growth" sustainable development theory prioritised resource efficiency and environmental protection (Saha, 2016). Ecological economics promotes resource conservation, sustainability, and integrity. These concepts are crucial to understanding economic impacts on humans and ecosystems. In 2016, Saha, studied indigenous TET. The study proved ecological economics can sustainably manage resources. Combining modern conservation strategies with local knowledge does this (Saha, 2016). Integrating Traditional Ecological Knowledge (TEK) into ecological assessments and management plans helps indigenous groups adapt to environmental changes and protect biodiversity and ecosystem health.

Ecological economics can analyse socio-ecological systems and adaptive governance strategies, as Norgaard showed in his interdisciplinary research on indigenous territories' sustainable development (Norgaard, year Indigenous perspectives and values should be included in environmental policy frameworks to address complex sustainability issues and strengthen communities, the study found. Ecological economics in development planning and resource management can support indigenous aspirations, promote sustainable development, and preserve cultural heritage and ecology.

2.1.4 Cultural Economics

Cultural economics studies how values, beliefs, and practices affect economic outcomes across cultures. "Economics and Culture", Throsby's 2001 study on cultural goods and services' economic effects, was influential. Cultural capital impacts market dynamics and consumption, per Throsby (2001). Social networks and cultural resources affect economic opportunities and social mobility, according to Bourdieu's social and cultural capital theory. Economic transactions emphasise intangibles (Bourdieu, 1986). Cultural economics examines values, norms, and capital. These factors greatly affect indigenous economies. Inglehart's international surveys on cultural change and economic development showed how cultural values affect various societies' economic behaviour and development (Holden et al., 2017). Ethnographic research on indigenous societies' economic practises emphasised cultural aspects of economic exchanges and how traditional norms and beliefs affect resource management and community resilience (Gajendran et al., 2022). These studies show that cultural economics is essential to sustainable and inclusive economic development planning and policymaking. Policies can promote community-based economic initiatives and cultural diversity by recognising and valuing indigenous cultural heritage and knowledge systems. Cultural economics explains socio-cultural aspects of economic activities and promotes indigenous community empowerment through culturally sensitive development strategies.

2.1.5 Developmental Economics

Development economics targets interventions and policy changes to improve life and economic conditions in developing regions. As Amartya Sen says in "Development as Freedom," development should improve human abilities and freedoms (Gajendran et al., 2022). The Todaro and Smith textbook emphasises infrastructure, institutional reforms, and human capital formation for developing country economic growth and poverty reduction. Development economics studies economic conditions, interventions, quality of life, and indigenous knowledge. Understanding indigenous community development requires these. Sachs' empirical poverty alleviation research illuminated SDGs and targeted interventions (Kenney et al., 2023). To address poverty, inequality, social inclusion, and environmental sustainability, the study emphasised local knowledge systems and context-specific development policies.

Easterly opposed top-down development aid and supported locally informed strategies that empower communities and promote self-sufficiency (Higgins-Desbiolles et al., 2022). Indigenous perspectives and principles can improve development interventions, promote inclusive growth, and preserve cultural diversity in development economics. Development economics reduces socioeconomic inequality through sustainable, individual, and environmental development. Subsistence, institutional, ecological, cultural, and development economics illuminate indigenous relationships. By applying these theories to indigenous contexts, policymakers, researchers, and practitioners can create more sustainable development strategies that support indigenous knowledge and practices. These theories explain indigenous economic systems through sustainability, community well-being, cultural values, and resilient economic development institutions. These theories can inform indigenous community economic independence and environmental protection planning and policy. All can benefit from cultural preservation and growth. More research should apply these theories to different cultural and environmental contexts to solve climate change, biodiversity loss, and indigenous socio-economic disparity. Native economic interactions Indigenous economics values cooperation, exchange, and sustainability. These views challenge several economic theories and propose alternative economic organisation and development.

Giving and receiving gifts are central to indigenous economics. Beyond economic transactions, reciprocity fosters community cohesion and resource allocation (Gajendran et al., 2022). Pacific Northwest indigenous potlatch ceremonies show this. Distribution of goods strengthens social connections and hierarchy in these ceremonies (Higgins-Desbiolles et al., 2022). Other fundamentals include cooperative resource management and shared ownership. Indians consider land, water, and other natural resources shared for future generations (Leach et al., 2018). Different from capitalist economies' property- and individualistic focus. Collective ownership promotes resource sustainability and accountability (Caudill et al., 2024). Indigenous economics promotes wholeness. Economics combine material wealth with spiritual, cultural, and social well-being. Economic, community, and environmental well-being are linked in this holistic approach (Higgins-Desbiolles et al., 2022). Maori "whenua," or land, is essential to identity, culture, and survival (Chanza & De Wit, 2016). Indigenous economies care about sustainability. Traditions like healthy harvesting and rotational farming preserve resources for future generations (Bell, 2017). The sustainable approach emphasises "seven generations" thinking, which considers decisions' long-term effects on future generations up to the seventh (Barraclough et al., 2021). Also important are cultural continuity and traditional knowledge transmission. Economic activities spread culture and knowledge. Artisanal goods are economic and cultural (Higgins-Desbiolles et al., 2022). They preserve cultural identity and resilience under pressure. Indigenous economies need self-determination. Indigenous peoples want economic and decision-making autonomy. Resisting economic pressures and claiming the right to develop according to their values and priorities (Chanza & De Wit, 2016). Self-determination promotes community-focused, equitable economic models.

2.2 Key Concepts

Economic Activity: Cultural, social, and ecological factors complicate indigenous economies. Exchanges and collaborations improve community well-being and social cohesion. Indigenous economic relationships require reciprocity—exchanges based on mutual benefit and expectation. This promotes closeness and resource distribution (Higgins-Desbiolles et al., 2022). Social rituals and reciprocity strengthen community bonds and responsibilities in many indigenous societies (Caudill et al., 2024). Communities need redistribution to gather and distribute resources. This promotes social justice by equalising essential resources. Wealth is redistributed at feasts and ceremonies to boost status and social bonds (Ali et al., 2021).

Indigenous economies manage resources communally. Community groups manage forests, water, and land. Sustainable resource use and preservation are promoted by community-wide ecosystem health (Shackleton et al., 2023). Community-based management increases environmental resilience (Higgins-Desbiolles et al., 2022).

Kinship and social networks shape economic relationships. Because they link economic activities to family and clan structures, indigenous societies depend on kinship networks for support and resources. By encouraging support and collaboration, these networks ensure extended family financial security (Higgins-Desbiolles et al., 2022).

Indigenous peoples barter: Market economies use currency, but indigenous trade is bartering. Connects diverse communities and distributes surplus resources (Higgins-Desbiolles et al., 2022). Knowledge and skills are valuable in indigenous economies. These assets are tradable.

Cultural and spiritual aspects matter in business. Economic, cultural, and spiritual practices are often holistic. Traditional ecological knowledge and practises manage resources, define culture, and connect people to the land (Higgins-Desbiolles et al., 2022). Economic and cultural integration sustains indigenous communities.

Economic autonomy and self-determination sustain indigenous economies. Indigenous peoples defend their autonomy and control economic resources and decisions. The right to govern their development paths and values-based economic frameworks are needed (Corntassel, 2012). Sustainability and economic autonomy benefit indigenous communities. Service providers

Indigenous economies need public and private services. With healthcare, education, infrastructure, and financial services, these suppliers boost economic growth and living standards.

Indigenous peoples need care. Good health improves life and productivity. Modern medicine must recognise and incorporate traditional healing methods for culturally appropriate and effective care (Higgins-Desbiolles et al., 2022). This method boosts healthcare system trust and outcomes. Economic growth and human capital development require education. Indigenous communities face language, cultural, and geographical barriers to education (Higgins-Desbiolles et al., 2022). Integrating indigenous languages and culture into educational curricula can reduce these disparities and boost indigenous student achievement and engagement (Wilkes, 2022). Through educational support, indigenous communities can control their education and achieve their goals.

Infrastructure improves economic growth and provides essential services. Indigenous communities benefit from reliable transportation, communication, and utility services to access markets, education, and healthcare (Hill et al., 2012). Service providers can improve life and business by prioritising indigenous infrastructure. To benefit indigenous communities, these projects must consider ecology and culture.

Economic activity and investments require financial services. (Ferrario et al. (2022) found discriminatory banking, credit, and capital barriers in indigenous communities. Microfinance and community-based lending can fix these problems and boost growth. Financial literacy and capacity-building help indigenous people and businesses make smart financial decisions.

Entrepreneurship and local growth are promoted by business development. Mentorship, training, market access, and regulation are provided. Service providers can support indigenous enterprises by identifying their strengths and weaknesses, boosting the economy and entrepreneurship (Higgins-Desbiolles et al., 2022). Indigenous business partnerships with larger corporations can expand markets and create new opportunities. To succeed, indigenous service providers must respect their culture. Many traditional service delivery models fail indigenous communities' unique needs and perspectives, resulting in ineffective and unsustainable outcomes (Boluk et al., 2019). Participatory methods let service providers meet local needs by involving community members in planning and delivery. Indigenous community engagement and service delivery require trust and long-term relationships (Stringer et al., 2022).

Policy and advocacy are needed for systemic issues and indigenous community economic development. Service providers can enhance indigenous rights, economic growth, and sustainability. Indigenous leaders and organisations can shape policy for better development (Higgins-Desbiolles et al., 2022). Promote indigenous-led advocacy to represent their needs and goals in policy discussions and raise their voices.

Rise of Indigenous Economy: Indigenous economic development involves resilience and growth. Self-determination, cultural integrity, and sustainability underpin this development.

Indigenous economic development requires resource sustainability. Indigenous communities maintain access and ecological balance through sustainable resource management and traditional ecological knowledge (Higgins-Desbiolles et al., 2022). Rotational farming, sustainable harvesting, and sacred site protection are examples. Promote and revitalise these traditions to improve sustainability and economic and environmental resilience. Indigenous economies benefit from traditional crafts, fine arts, music, and cultural tourism. Profit and cultural preservation are their goals (Zurba & Papadopoulos, 2023). Support indigenous cultural enterprises for investment, tourism, heritage, and jobs. Overseeing these industries requires IP and culture protection.

Economic diversification boosts resilience and reduces sector dependence. Indigenous communities depend on fishing, forestry, agriculture, and small businesses (Williams et al., 2020). Diversification lowers market and environmental volatility. Indigenous entrepreneurship and innovation boost growth and diversification. Indigenous communities need training and education to manage their economy. Technical, financial, and business administration training are included (Belfer et al., 2019).

Customised capacity-building programmes can help indigenous communities flourish economically. Indigenous community-led education strengthens local leadership. Financial services and markets help indigenous businesses succeed. When seeking markets and finance, indigenous entrepreneurs face discrimination and poor infrastructure (Parsons et al., 2016). Service providers can overcome these barriers and enter the market with networking, partnerships, and market information. The economy can benefit from microfinance and community-based lending for indigenous businesses.

Governance and policy impact indigenous economies. Indigenous rights, land ownership, and self-governance are needed for economic growth (Patnaik & Bhowmick, 2020). Improved capacity and governance help indigenous communities manage resources, negotiate with outside parties, and advocate for themselves. Service providers can advocate, build capacity, and provide tech support.

3. LITERATURE REVIEW METHODOLOGY

3.1 Literature Review Method

3.1.1 Databases and Sources Used

The life course perspective on social issues was carefully considered in this literature review. This review used JSTOR, ScienceDirect, SpringerLink, and Google Scholar. Each database was chosen for its comprehensive coverage and social science-specific content to ensure a thorough literature search. JSTOR was chosen for its large sociology and other historical and scholarly article collection. An extensive historical social science literature is essential for understanding social issues over time, making this resource valuable. JSTOR's vast collection of peer-reviewed journals and books made life course perspective seminal works and theories accessible. ScienceDirect and SpringerLink were chosen for their social science coverage and current research. Long-term social issues are covered by many ScienceDirect social science journals. SpringerLink offers many high-quality academic journals and books to ensure the review includes the latest research. Grey literature and non-database sources were found by Google Scholar. Its broad field and publication type coverage makes it essential for finding studies, reports, theses, and conference proceedings not in specialised databases. This comprehensive approach yielded a multi-source search.

3.1.2 Keywords and Search Themes

Organised keyword selection was needed to cover social issues literature across the life course. Predefined, unrestricted text-based terms optimised search results. He typed "life course perspective," "sociology of social problems," "longitudinal studies social problems," "impact of social issues over time," & "social problems over the life course." Terms covered theoretical and practical life course framework foundations. Search efficiency improved with AND, OR, NOT. When searching "life course perspective AND social problems," only studies covering both were found. The inclusion of "longitudinal studies OR historical analyses" allowed social issue studies over time or using historical data. To improve search, these operators balanced comprehensiveness and specificity. Life course social issue articles were found.

3.1.3 Literature Selection Criteria

The review includes only high-quality, topic-relevant literature due to selection criteria. We included peer-reviewed articles, books, and reports from 2000–2023. The timeline includes the latest and most influential social issue research and works. Readability was prioritised in English literature. Sociological research on social issues over time was the focus. It examined social responses to social issues using longitudinal designs, historical analyses, and life course studies. The review covered empirical and theoretical perspectives on social issue development, continuation, and resolution across contexts and life stages. Studies not meeting these strict criteria were excluded. Studies that were not peer-reviewed, empirical, or in English were excluded. Quality, relevant scholarly works that advanced life course social issue understanding were prioritised.

3.1.4 Justifying Research Choice

These studies were suitable due to life course framework alignment and social issue understanding improvement. Historical analyses and longitudinal data were prioritised to show how social issues arise, persist, and resolve across societies and time. The review examined inequality, poverty, healthcare disparities, and education to assess the life course perspective's relevance and practicality. The selected studies should illuminate social problem mechanisms and contexts. A variety of methods and issues were reviewed to inform sociology and social policy theories and applications. The extensive review revealed life course research gaps and opportunities. Data analysis interprets data. Literature analysis and synthesis require multiple sources to fully comprehend a topic.

3.1.5 Data Analysis

Thematic analysis dominated literature synthesis. Thematic analysis helps qualitative researchers identify, analyse, and document data themes. We chose this adaptable method because it provides a complete and nuanced data understanding. Thematic analysis was multistep. Study data was analysed to identify social issue evolution concepts and trends. A thorough literature review was needed to identify and organise relevant information into themes. Study comparisons and repeated readings revealed these themes. The iterative process created categories that reflected literature's complexity and depth. Thematic analysis illuminated life course social issues. Data categorization and coding revealed key patterns. Research findings were organised this way.

3.1.6 Frameworks for Thematic Analysis

Grounded theory was used to analyse themes without preconceptions in this review. Thus, the analysis closely matched the selected studies' factual data, providing a more accurate life course perspective on social issues. The NVivo software organised coded data. NVivo analyses qualitative data. Many qualitative data coding, categorization, and analysis options exist. Systematic examination and combination of study results improved thematic analysis precision and effectiveness with software. The identified themes accurately represented the literature's wide range of perspectives and were based on empirical evidence due to NVivo's ability to handle large amounts of data, produce reports, and visualise data connections. NVivo streamlined data analysis; it was more systematic. Results were comprehensive, literature-supported, and showed life course perspectives on social issues.

4. INDIGENOUS ECONOMIC RELATIONSHIPS

4.1 Traditional Economic Practices

Indigenous economies are rooted in culture, ecology, and community. Indigenous communities had different social frameworks and environments, so the systems varied. Subsistence agriculture, hunting, fishing, and gathering sustained indigenous peoples. Social and spiritual practices influenced economic activity. The North American Haudenosaunee (Iroquois) Confederacy had advanced agriculture and communal land management. The economy relied on maize, beans, and squash (Chan et al., 2020). These economies evolve from subsistence to complex trade networks. Many indigenous groups traded across vast regions before Europeans arrived. Mississippian culture in the southeastern US had complex food, shell, and copper trade networks (Ajaps & Mbah, 2022). Trade fostered cultural exchange and intergroup cooperation. Europeans transformed indigenous economies in the 15th and 16th centuries. European colonisation impacted the economy with land confiscation and trade policies. External pressures forced indigenous communities to change their economies. Firearms and metal tools from Europe changed trade and customs (Higgins-Desbiolles et al., 2022).

4.2 Analysis of Traditional Economic Practices Through Case Studies

The Canadian Arctic Inuit economy is a model. The Inuit economy relied on hunting and fishing for resource efficiency and seasonal adaptation. Inuit hunters hunted caribou, seals, and whales using advanced meteorological and ice knowledge (Gajendran et al., 2022). Community sharing and mutual support shaped their economic practices, making this system and social structures interdependent. Another case study examines Quechua and Aymara conventional agriculture. These groups developed irrigation and terracing systems for harsh Andean conditions. People relied on potatoes and quinoa for income. Community "ayni," or communal labour, supported agriculture (Carvalho, 2020). Communities thrived in difficult conditions by understanding local ecosystems and adopting sustainable practices. Australian Aboriginal peoples have long used ecological equilibrium and land management-based economics. Fire-stick farming managed and increased land productivity in Aboriginal economies, which were deeply connected to the land (Higgins-Desbiolles et al., 2022). Survival and social unity required these advanced environmental stewardship practices.

4.3 Modern Economic Relationships

Many indigenous communities struggle to adapt their economies to modern ones. This involves adapting and resisting change. Example: US Native American tribes' economic adaptation. Indigenous communities have developed their economies by combining modern and traditional business practices. Example: The Florida Seminole Tribe combined tourism and gaming with traditional customs. Tribal casinos and resorts fund community projects and culture (Higgins-Desbiolles et al., 2022). While preserving their culture, New Zealand Maori have managed modern economic structures. Maori customs include agriculture and tourism. Exporting Maori food and crafts has helped indigenous businesses thrive in modern markets (Bell, 2017). Challenges arise in adaptation. Indigenous communities face regulations, markets, and capital issues. Indigenous development agencies and business councils have integrated traditional practices into modern economies. These organisations link traditional knowledge and modern business practises to boost economic growth and cultural preservation (Higgins-Desbiolles et al., 2022).

4.4 Impact of Globalization on Indigenous Economies

Globalisation has brought opportunities and challenges to indigenous economies. Indigenous products can now enter new markets and exchange cultures thanks to globalisation. Indigenous art, crafts, and knowledge are recognised worldwide, preserving culture and boosting economic growth. Indigenous artisans from various regions have promoted their crafts globally, increasing recognition and economic benefits (Barraclough et al., 2021). Globalisation threatens indigenous economies. Large industrial projects and multinational corporations displace indigenous communities and pollute the environment. Customary practices and indigenous territories have suffered from Canada's mining and logging expansion. Indigenous communities' advocacy for responsible environmental management and rights protection has clashed with economic progress (Chanza & De Wit, 2016). Indigenous labour markets have changed due to globalisation. Indigenous communities must work in urban areas or industries that conflict with their values due to external pressures. Younger generations may lose ancestral wisdom and culture as they integrate into modern economies and lifestyles (Scheyvens et al., 2021). Some indigenous communities have improved their economies through globalisation despite challenges. They have navigated international markets while preserving their culture through cross-cultural collaboration and strategic alliances. Sustainable practises and indigenous community business growth can reconcile traditional and modern economies (Higgins-Desbiolles et al., 2022).

5. ROLE OF SERVICE SUPPLIERS

5.1 Types of Service Suppliers

Indigenous economic development requires financial institutions. Banks, credit unions, and microfinance institutions offer loans, investments, and savings accounts. Traditional financial services restrictions have hampered indigenous communities' economic growth. Recent initiatives have provided indigenous communities with customised financial solutions to reduce this disparity. First Nations Bank of Canada provides financial services to First Nations communities. This bank tailors financial products and services to community development projects like infrastructure and housing (Higgins-Desbiolles et al., 2022). Indigenous Business Australia (IBA) in Australia helps indigenous entrepreneurs raise capital and build communities (Raymond et al., 2023). Indigenous communities face financial service barriers despite these advances. Geographic isolation, financial ignorance, and financial institution distrust may hinder these services. Indigenous-valued financial cooperatives and community-based financial education can address these issues (Cheng, 2023).

Educational Services

Indigenous communities need schools, vocational training centres, and universities. Individual empowerment and economic growth require education. Indigenous people learn modern economic skills and preserve cultural heritage through education.

Native American students receive educational materials from the US Bureau of Indian Education (BIE). Its main objective is teaching indigenous culture and history. This method enhances education and cultural conformity (Mustafa et al., 2020). In New Zealand, Te Kura Kaupapa Māori schools teach in Māori and incorporate traditional knowledge into their curriculum. This method preserves Māori culture and provides students with practical skills for the modern economy (Verma & Petersen, 2018). Funding, resources, and systemic biases affect indigenous education. To overcome these challenges, indigenous education needs resources, culturally appropriate curricula, and support for educators who understand indigenous cultures and teaching methods (Ali et al., 2021).

Healthcare Providers

Indigenous people need health education, prevention, and medical care. Healthcare quality and availability affect indigenous peoples' economic well-being. Hospitals, clinics, community health centres, and traditional healers provide healthcare. These organisations meet indigenous communities' diverse health needs. The First Nations Health Authority provides primary, mental, and public health services to Canadian First Nations. Traditional healing practises and conventional medicine are integrated by the FNHA to provide culturally safe and community-led health solutions (Shackleton et al., 2023). Australian Aboriginal Community Controlled Health Services (ACCHS) provide comprehensive healthcare using traditional and Western medicine to meet Aboriginal communities' needs (Renwick et al., 2020). Indigenous communities face health disparities, limited services, and culturally competency issues. To overcome these challenges, indigenous health initiatives need more funding, healthcare infrastructure improvements, and cultural competence and sensitivity training for healthcare professionals (Corntassel, 2012).

Impact on Indigenous Communities

Native businesses receive resources and support from service providers to grow economically. Financial institutions help start businesses, invest in infrastructure, and improve community facilities. Education prepares people for the modern economy and encourages entrepreneurship. Effective economic engagement requires healthcare providers to improve health and well-being. First Nations Bank of Canada supports local business and housing development. Initiatives boost economic growth and community well-being (Wilkes, 2022). According to Hill et al. (2012), Te Kura Kaupapa Māori schools equip students with skills for success in various economic sectors, including technology and business. Integration of traditional and modern healthcare practices boosts economic growth. Healthcare addresses physical and mental health issues, helping people participate in economic activities and improve the community. FNHA and other organisations use Western and traditional medicine to provide culturally appropriate and effective health services (Ferrario et al., 2022). Service providers in indigenous settings face challenges and opportunities. Cultural differences, isolation, and distrust plague native service providers. Remote communities face logistical and service challenges due to isolation. To respect indigenous values and practices, service providers must adapt to cultural differences. Trust in external institutions is low due to past injustices and discrimination, which can hinder service delivery (Higgins-Desbiolles et al., 2022). Service providers can work with indigenous leaders and organisations. Service providers can develop indigenous-aligned strategies by understanding community needs with local stakeholders. Community financial cooperatives and local hospitals provide culturally appropriate and accessible services (Stringer et al., 2022). Technological advances offer new ways to serve indigenous communities. Telemedicine and online education provide essential services to remote communities. Technology can make service delivery more efficient and equitable while respecting indigenous cultures (Boluk et al., 2019). Indigenous communities' economic growth and well-being depend on service providers. Service providers can promote sustainable and inclusive indigenous growth by overcoming obstacles and seizing innovation and collaboration opportunities.

6. CASE STUDIES AND EXAMPLES

Successful Collaboration and Useful Analysis

Indigenous communities and service providers often form successful economic partnerships. Canadian and Inuit Tapiriit Kanatami (ITK) collaborate on strategic investments and initiatives to boost Inuit economies. New schools and hospitals have improved Inuit infrastructure (Zurba & Papadopoulos, 2023). ITK projects meet Inuit needs because they prioritise culturally appropriate solutions and community engagement. The Navajo Nation's partnership with US schools is another. Northern Arizona University and the Navajo Nation offer Navajo-specific education. Mentorship, scholarships, and a Navajo-language and tradition-based curriculum are available (Williams et al., 2020). Navajo community participation in programme design and implementation ensures that educational services respect Navajo culture, making this partnership successful. Australian government and Aboriginal Community Controlled Health Services (ACCHS) successfully integrate traditional and modern healthcare. Many ACCHS services combine Western and Aboriginal medicine. With this strategy, Aboriginal health outcomes and healthcare access have improved (Belfer et al., 2019). The partnership improves health through community engagement and culturally sensitive care. These examples show that economic and service supplier relationships should consider community needs, local stakeholder involvement, and culturally significant practices.

Best Practices, Practical Knowledge

Indigenous community partnerships require community engagement, cultural sensitivity, and open communication. Participatory planning and community consultation helped the ITK-Canadian government partnership succeed. Community decisions ensure projects meet local priorities and use resources efficiently (Parsons et al., 2016). The Navajo Nation-Northern Arizona University partnership emphasises culturally relevant education. To promote cultural heritage and academic success, the curriculum incorporates Navajo language and traditions. Education requires indigenous knowledge and practises (Higgins-Desbiolles et al., 2022). The Australian ACCHS partnership uses old and new methods. This healthcare model shows that mainstreaming traditional healing practises improves efficiency and patient outcomes (Patnaik & Bhowmick, 2020). Building trust between healthcare providers and indigenous communities improves health outcomes. Cooperation, cultural diversity, and community needs are key to successful and lasting partnerships.

CHALLENGES AND SOLUTIONS

Common Economic Relationship Development Challenges

Indigenous communities and service providers face many obstacles to economic partnerships. Distrust of outside businesses is hampered by past injustice and prejudice. Distrust hinders economic cooperation (Higgins-Desbiolles et al., 2022). Indigenous communities may distrust banks and government programmes due to marginalisation or exploitation. Indigenous communities face resource and service constraints due to isolation. Due to logistics, remote service providers struggle to deliver services consistently and efficiently (Chan et al., 2020). This could worsen inequalities by affecting service quality and availability. Cultural differences can hinder business partnerships. Service providers may misunderstand indigenous customs and misserve communities (Gajendran et al., 2022). Without indigenous students, educational programmes may not meet their cultural and educational needs.

Strategies to Overcome These Challenges

To repair historical mistrust, service providers and economic allies must respect indigenous communities. Honest communication, acknowledging past wrongs, and community commitment are needed (Higgins-Desbiolles et al., 2022). Community advisory boards or working groups can involve indigenous stakeholders in decision-making and promote open communication. Using technology and mobile services can reduce geographic isolation. Remote indigenous communities can receive essential medical care and consultations via telemedicine and mobile healthcare units (Chanza & De Wit, 2016). Online platforms and virtual learning provide quality education to remote areas (Williams, 2023). Addressing differences requires cultural sensitivity. Service providers should pay for employee indigenous culture and customs training (Caudill et al., 2024). Indigenous people create community-specific, culturally appropriate programmes (Leach et al., 2018). Integrating indigenous language and traditions into healthcare and education improves effectiveness. Finally, economic partnerships with indigenous communities require trust, cultural understanding, and geographical overcome. Services tailored to indigenous community issues can strengthen partnerships and boost economic growth.

7. POLICY IMPLICATIONS AND RECOMMENDATIONS

7.1 Policy Implications

Economic policies prioritise indigenous community growth and service delivery. The policies aim to reduce inequality, improve services, and boost economic independence. Government programmes include funding, infrastructure, and regulation. These measures aim to improve education, healthcare, finance, and economic growth. Grants and subsidies go to indigenous businesses and services. These programmes promote local growth and entrepreneurship. Policies fund community-based initiatives and partner indigenous organisations with external service providers to improve healthcare and education. Regulations greatly affect economic relationships. Natural resource management, land use, and environmental policies affect business and services. Land rights impact indigenous economies and resource management. Environmental laws can impact sustainable economic initiatives. Policy implementation is difficult despite these efforts. Policies face financial constraints, low community participation in decision-making, and limited government-service provider collaboration. These obstacles can slow policy implementation and economic and service improvements.

7.2 Policy Improvement Ideas

Several suggestions can improve service provider and economic relationship policies. Focus on community engagement to boost policymaking. Indigenous peoples should influence economic growth and service policies. Policy customisation is possible by engaging these communities. Improved government-service provider coordination is crucial. Agencies and governments fragment policy implementation. Interagency cooperation and policy integration can unify economic development and service delivery. More money is needed to implement policies. Programmes need funding to succeed. This includes infrastructure, education, healthcare, and policy evaluation funding. Indigenous communities' diverse needs require flexible policies. Successful policies must recognise each community's cultural, social, and economic differences. Tailored policies work better in these situations. Applying policy requires transparency and accountability. Clear policy outcomes monitoring and evaluation can verify goals. Knowledge of policy effects and fund allocation builds indigenous community and stakeholder trust.

7.3 Future Research

Developments may affect indigenous communities' economic relationships and services. Digitization and innovation are growing. Digital platforms and mobile apps improve service delivery and economic prospects. Telemedicine and online education provide essential services to remote communities. Sustainability and environmental stewardship are new. Traditional ecological knowledge and modern sustainable development are growing in importance. Environmental conservation and sustainable resource management may improve indigenous communities' well-being and create new economic opportunities. Social enterprises and community projects are another trend. Innovative, community-oriented solutions are prioritised in these social and economic initiatives. Indigenous communities benefit economically from social enterprises. Many areas need more research and policy to address current challenges and develop emerging patterns. Study digital technology's effects on indigenous communities before acting. This examines how technology enhances services, economic opportunities, and accessibility. Technological solutions' efficacy and integration into existing systems can inform future policies. Traditional ecological knowledge and modern sustainability practices need more study. Sustainability can be promoted by indigenous environmental and resource management knowledge. Analysis of integration can also examine community well-being and economic opportunities. Research indigenous community-driven initiatives and social enterprises. Analysis of these initiatives' successes, challenges, and effects can help expand similar efforts. This research may aid indigenous community-focused policies and social enterprise growth. Assess policies and choose the best strategies. Research should examine how current policies improve economic relationships and services. Assessing funding, regulation, and community engagement. Results can improve policies and help indigenous communities.

8. CONCLUSION

8.1 Summary of Key Findings

Indigenous communities' complex economic relationships and service provision were highlighted in this chapter. We examined traditional economic practices to show how history shaped modern economies. Traditional cultural values and community-oriented methods shape modern economics. The case studies showed how traditional methods evolve and maintain core principles. Economic trends, especially indigenous community integration, were discussed. Globalisation created pros and cons. Integrating indigenous economies into larger markets has made economic growth and cultural preservation more difficult. Next, financial, educational, and healthcare providers were examined. Discussing indigenous communities' challenges and these suppliers' economic growth contributions. Indigenous service providers face logistical and cultural challenges despite their importance to local economies and service access. Case studies showed successful economic partnerships. Well-planned partnerships benefit service providers and indigenous communities, according to case studies. These examples demonstrate the value of sustainability, local services, and community decision-making. Building these relationships required overcoming deep-seated suspicion and structural barriers. Effects and policy suggestions were discussed to improve policy frameworks and future directions. Present policies ignore indigenous needs. Policymaking should include more funding, stakeholder coordination, and community engagement. Assess current policies and new trends like sustainability and digital technology in research and policy.

8.2 Implications for Indigenous Inclusivity

Indigenous community inclusion can be improved by service delivery and economic partnerships. Strong economic collaborations and better services can close the indigenous-broader economic gap. Indigenous economic perspectives matter. Inclusion increases with economic relationships that respect and integrate traditional knowledge and practices. Service providers and economic collaborators can create an inclusive economy that values indigenous heritage and fair participation using these principles. Indigenous-specific services boost inclusion. With good education, healthcare, and finance, these communities can fully participate in economic opportunities. Engaging past injustices promotes personal and collective growth.

REFERENCES

Ajaps, S., & Mbah, M. F. (2022). Deconstructing Community-Based Research for Sustainable Development: The Role of Indigenous Knowledge Holders. *World Sustainability Series*, 65–76. DOI: 10.1007/s11160-021-09661-z

Alexander, K. A., Fleming, A., Bax, N., Garcia, C., Jansen, J., Maxwell, K. H., Melbourne-Thomas, J., Mustonen, T., Pecl, G. T., Shaw, J., Syme, G., & Ogier, E. (2022). Equity of our future oceans: Practices and outcomes in marine science research. *Reviews in Fish Biology and Fisheries*, 32(1), 297–311. DOI: 10.1007/s11160-021-09661-z

Ali, T., Paton, D., Buergelt, P. T., Smith, J. A., Jehan, N., & Siddique, A. (2021). Integrating Indigenous perspectives and community-based disaster risk reduction: A pathway for sustainable Indigenous development in Northern Pakistan. *International Journal of Disaster Risk Reduction*, Vol. 59. Elsevier. DOI: 10.1007/s11160-021-09661-z

Barraclough, A. D., Sakiyama, M., Schultz, L., & Måren, I. E. (2021). *"Stewards of the future: accompanying the rising tide of young voices by setting youth-inclusive research agendas in sustainability research". Sustainable Earth* (Vol. 4). Springer., DOI: 10.1186/s42055-021-00041-w

Belfer, E., Ford, J. D., Maillet, M., Araos, M., & Flynn, M. (2019). Pursuing an indigenous platform: Exploring opportunities and constraints for indigenous participation in the UNFCCC. *Global Environmental Politics*, 19(1), 12–33. DOI: 10.1162/glep_a_00489

Bell, K. (2017). 'Living well' as a path to social, ecological and economic sustainability. *Urban Planning*, 2(4), 19–33. DOI: 10.17645/up.v2i4.1006

Boluk, K. A., Cavaliere, C. T., & Higgins-Desbiolles, F. (2019). A critical framework for interrogating the United Nations Sustainable Development Goals 2030 Agenda in tourism. *Journal of Sustainable Tourism*, Vol. 27, pp. 847–864. Taylor &Francis. DOI: 10.1007/s11160-021-09661-z

Carvalho, A. (2020). Discourses for transformation?: Climate change, power and pathways to the future. *Discourses in Action*, 104–119. DOI: 10.1007/s11160-021-09661-z

Caudill, C. M., Pulsifer, P. L., Thumbadoo, R. V., & Taylor, D. R. F. (2024). Meeting the Challenges of the UN Sustainable Development Goals through Holistic Systems Thinking and Applied Geospatial Ethics. *ISPRS International Journal of Geo-Information*, Vol. 13. mdpi.com. DOI: 10.1007/s11160-021-09661-z

Chan, K. M. A., Boyd, D. R., Gould, R. K., Jetzkowitz, J., Liu, J., Muraca, B., Naidoo, R., Olmsted, P., Satterfield, T., Selomane, O., Singh, G. G., Sumaila, R., Ngo, H. T., Boedhihartono, A. K., Agard, J., de Aguiar, A. P. D., Armenteras, D., Balint, L., Barrington-Leigh, C., & Brondízio, E. S. (2020). Levers and leverage points for pathways to sustainability. *People and Nature*, 2(3), 693–717. DOI: 10.1002/pan3.10124

Chanza, N., & De Wit, A. (2016). Enhancing climate governance through indigenous knowledge: Case in sustainability science. *South African Journal of Science*, 112(3/4), 7. Advance online publication. scielo.org.za. DOI: 10.17159/sajs.2016/20140286

Cheng, J. (2023). Sustainable Pathways: Strategies for Development in Chinese Ethnic Regions. *Global Journal of Humanities and Social Sciences, 02*(02), 01–07. DOI: 10.17159/sajs.2016/20140286

Ciplet, D., & Harrison, J. L. (2020). Transition tensions: Mapping conflicts in movements for a just and sustainable transition. *Environmental Politics*, 29(3), 435–456. DOI: 10.1080/09644016.2019.1595883

Corntassel, J. (2012). Re-envisioning resurgence: Indigenous pathways to decolonization and sustainable self-determination. In *Decolonization: Indigeneity, Education & Society* (Vol. 1). dspace.library.uvic.ca. Retrieved from https://dspace.library.uvic.ca/handle/1828/12471

Doyon, A., Boron, J., & Williams, S. (2021). Unsettling transitions: Representing Indigenous peoples and knowledge in transitions research. *Energy Research & Social Science*, 81, 102255. Advance online publication. DOI: 10.1016/j.erss.2021.102255

Ferrario, F., Araújo, C. A. S., Bélanger, S., Bourgault, D., Carrière, J., Carrier-Belleau, C., Dreujou, E., Johnson, L. E., Juniper, S. K., Mabit, R., McKindsey, C. W., Ogston, L., Picard, M. M. M., Saint-Louis, R., Saulnier-Talbot, É., Shaw, J.-L., Templeman, N., Therriault, T. W., Tremblay, J.-E., & Archambault, P. (2022). Holistic environmental monitoring in ports as an opportunity to advance sustainable development, marine science, and social inclusiveness. *Elementa*, 10(1), 00061. Advance online publication. DOI: 10.1525/elementa.2021.00061

Gajendran, T., Tucker, C., Ware, S., & Tose, H. S. (2022). Integrating Indigenous, Western and inclusive pedagogies for work-integrated learning partnerships in architecture and design disciplines. *International Journal of Work-Integrated Learning*, 23(2), 259–277. https://eric.ed.gov/?id=EJ1346569

Higgins-Desbiolles, F., Blanchard, L. A., & Urbain, Y. (2022). Peace through tourism: Critical reflections on the intersections between peace, justice, sustainable development and tourism. *Journal of Sustainable Tourism*, 30(2–3), 335–351. DOI: 10.1080/09669582.2021.1952420

Hill, R., Grant, C., George, M., Robinson, C. J., Jackson, S., & Abel, N. (2012). A typology of indigenous engagement in Australian environmental management: Implications for knowledge integration and social-ecological system sustainability. *Ecology and Society*, 17(1), art23. Advance online publication. DOI: 10.5751/ES-04587-170123

Holden, E., Linnerud, K., Banister, D., Jana Schwanitz, V., & Wierling, A. (2017). The Imperatives of Sustainable Development. In *The Imperatives of Sustainable Development*. taylorfrancis.com. DOI: 10.4324/9780203022177

Kenney, C., Phibbs, S., Meo-Sewabu, L., Awatere, S., McCarthy, M., Kaiser, L., … Kereopa, L. (2023). Indigenous Approaches to Disaster Risk Reduction, Community Sustainability, and Climate Change Resilience. *Disaster Risk Reduction for Resilience: Climate Change and Disaster Risk Adaptation*, 37–59. DOI: 10.4324/9780203022177

Leach, M. (2015). Gender equality and sustainable development. *Gender Equality and Sustainable Development*, pp. 1–209. unwomen.org. DOI: 10.4324/9781315686455

Leach, M., Reyers, B., Bai, X., Brondizio, E. S., Cook, C., Díaz, S., Espindola, G., Scobie, M., Stafford-Smith, M., & Subramanian, S. M. (2018). Equity and sustainability in the anthropocene: A social-ecological systems perspective on their intertwined futures. *Global Sustainability*, 1, e13. Advance online publication. DOI: 10.1017/sus.2018.12

Mustafa, M. A., Mabhaudhi, T., Avvari, M. V., & Massawe, F. (2020). Transition toward sustainable food systems: A holistic pathway toward sustainable development. *Food Security and Nutrition*, 33–56. DOI: 10.4324/9780203022177

Parsons, M., Fisher, K., & Nalau, J. (2016). Alternative approaches to co-design: Insights from indigenous/academic research collaborations. *Current Opinion in Environmental Sustainability*, 20, 99–105. DOI: 10.1016/j.cosust.2016.07.001

Patnaik, J., & Bhowmick, B. (2020). Promise of inclusive innovation: A Re-look into the opportunities at the grassroots. *Journal of Cleaner Production*, 259, 121124. Advance online publication. DOI: 10.1016/j.jclepro.2020.121124

Raymond, C. M., Anderson, C. B., Athayde, S., Vatn, A., Amin, A. M., Arias-Arévalo, P., & Zent, E. (2023). *An inclusive typology of values for navigating transformations towards a just and sustainable future. Current Opinion in Environmental Sustainability* (Vol. 64). Elsevier., DOI: 10.1016/j.cosust.2023.101301

Renwick, N., Reid, D. R., Santos, J. A., & Piovezana, L. (2020). Indigenous People and The Sustainable Development Goals in Brazil: A Study of the Kaingang People. *Journal of Developing Societies*, 36(4), 390–414. DOI: 10.1177/0169796X20937583

Saha, R. (2016). Corporate Social Responsibility Practices: Pathways for Inclusive and Sustainable Future. *Training and Development Journal*, 7(2), 77. dspace.stellamariscollege.edu.in. DOI: 10.5958/2231-069X.2016.00011.1

Scheyvens, R., Carr, A., Movono, A., Hughes, E., Higgins-Desbiolles, F., & Mika, J. P. (2021). *Indigenous tourism and the sustainable development goals. Annals of Tourism Research* (Vol. 90). Elsevier., DOI: 10.1016/j.annals.2021.103260

Shackleton, S., Taylor, A., Gammage, L., Gillson, L., Sitas, N., Methner, N., Barmand, S., Thorn, J., McClure, A., Cobban, L., Jarre, A., & Odume, O. N. (2023). Fostering transdisciplinary research for equitable and sustainable development pathways across Africa: What changes are needed? *Ecosystems and People (Abingdon, England)*, 19(1), 2164798. Advance online publication. DOI: 10.1080/26395916.2022.2164798

Stringer, L. C., Simpson, N. P., Schipper, E. L. F., & Eriksen, S. H. (2022). *Climate Resilient Development Pathways in Global Drylands. Anthropocene Science*. Springer., DOI: 10.1007/s44177-022-00027-z

Verma, S., & Petersen, A. C. (2018). Developmental Science and Pathways to Sustainable Development for Children and Youth. *Developmental Science and Sustainable …*, 1–35. DOI: 10.1007/s44177-022-00027-z

Wilkes, J. (2022). Reconnecting with Nature through Good Governance: Inclusive Policy across Scales. *Agriculture (Switzerland)*, Vol. 12. mdpi.com. DOI: 10.3390/agriculture12030382

Williams, P. A., Sikutshwa, L., & Shackleton, S. (2020). Acknowledging indigenous and local knowledge to facilitate collaboration in landscape approaches- lessons from a systematic review. *Land*, Vol. 9. mdpi.com. DOI: 10.3390/land9090331

Zurba, M., & Papadopoulos, A. (2023). *Indigenous Participation and the Incorporation of Indigenous Knowledge and Perspectives in Global Environmental Governance Forums: a Systematic Review. Environmental Management* (Vol. 72). Springer., DOI: 10.1007/s00267-021-01566-8

Chapter 8
A Bibliometric Analysis of Sustainable Investment and Socially Responsible Investors: Trends and Insights

Sakha Gangadhara Rama Rao
https://orcid.org/0000-0003-3578-8558
GITAM University, India

Vedantam Seetha Ram
https://orcid.org/0000-0002-6375-1501
JAIN University, India

Surya Prakasa Rao Pampana
https://orcid.org/0009-0004-9726-8472
Dravidian University, India

V. V. Phani Kumar Tantravahi
https://orcid.org/0009-0003-6353-5029
University of Technology and Applied Sciences, Oman

ABSTRACT

This study uses bibliometric analysis to assess the current state and potential of sustainable and socially responsible investments. The study initially considered 550 papers indexed in the Scopus database and published between 2010 and 2024. The study contributes to the body of knowledge in the fields of socially responsible investment and sustainable investing by employing three approaches: (1) identifying the most influential articles, (2) visually illustrating the characteristics and trends using network analysis, and (3) combining diverse research areas to identify potential avenues for future exploration. To attain these goals, we use bibliometric analysis, which evaluates the accomplishments of significant authors, countries, highly cited papers, journals, and co-word charts. Biblioshiny R and VOSviewer evaluated the keyword analysis of 234 papers finally screened. The study is limited to the Scopus database because it is one of the popular databases. This study provides a complete overview of socially responsible investment funds' research nature and trends.

DOI: 10.4018/979-8-3693-7924-0.ch008

1. INTRODUCTION

Sustainable investment (SI) integrates environmental, social, and governance (ESG) criteria into the investing process to better manage risk and generate long-term competitive financial returns while positively contributing to broader societal goals or addressing environmental challenges (Basak et al., 2024; Janicka, 2016; Sairally, 2015). Sustainable investment practices have boomed in the last 20 years, fuelled by a growing concern about climate change, social inequalities and corporate governance (Momparler et al., 2024). This can be seen in the increasing literature examining how sustainable investing affects portfolio performance, risk management and stakeholder engagement (Carvalho et al., 2024; Liu & Jing, 2024; Marzuki et al., 2023; Irfan, 2021; Pereira et al., 2019). Research shows that sustainable investment can result in competitive financial returns while also playing a part in achieving global sustainability goals (Latiff & Marimuthu, 2021; Tripathi & Kaur, 2022).

Investment is a complex process for most investors due to a lack of knowledge and awareness (Aristei & Gallo, 2024; Shehzad & Khan, 2024). These investors depend on third parties for investment decisions (Nofsinger & Varma, 2023; Brito-Ramos et al., 2024). Investors must study and understand market conditions and trends to make investment decisions (Caferra & Falcone, 2023; Tripathi & Kaur, 2020, 2022). Investors must do three basic things when making investment decisions based on risk, return, and sustainability (Catalano et al., 2024; Irfan, Elhoseny, et al., 2023; Arias Fogliano de Souza Cunha & Samanez, 2013). One of the biggest challenges for those interested in socially responsible investing is finding companies that are worthy investments. There is, in fact, one relatively straightforward choice for the retail investor: a negative screening method that helps them avoid investing in firms with wicked reputations. Riedl & Smeets (2017) find that the innate social inclinations and motives for the reputation of investors are important drivers for their decision to hold a fund investing along Environmental, Social, and Governance (ESG) criteria. It shows that socially motivated investors are even ready to accept lower financial returns to invest according to their social preferences (Stambaugh & Taylor, 2021; Caferra & Falcone, 2023; Carlsson Hauff & Nilsson, 2023; Aristei & Gallo, 2024; Scholtens & Willard, 2024).

2. SOCIALLY RESPONSIBLE INVESTMENT

Socially Responsible Investments (SRI) have gained momentum and much attention in recent decades (Nikolakis et al., 2012, 2014; Dawkins, 2018; Geczy et al., 2021; Selmi et al., 2021; Galeone et al., 2023; Bertelli & Torricelli, 2024; Carvalho et al., 2024). As a result, various companies and organisations have been established that specialise in evaluating firms' sustainability; the creation of new investment products, such as sustainable indices, is one more manifestation (Bianchi & Drew, 2012; Malchyk et al., 2020; Devie et al., 2020; Firdaus Khan, 2021). ESG is a generic term for SRI methods and other heterogeneous forms of investing that focus on ESG matters rather than just financial ones in the valuation process (Escrig-Olmedo et al., 2017; Tripathi & Kaur, 2020, 2020; Weston & Nnadi, 2023). SRI, often ethical, sustainable, or value-based investing, is an investment approach beyond pursuing financial returns (Arias Fogliano de Souza Cunha & Samanez, 2013; Stambaugh & Taylor, 2021; Bilbao-Terol et al., 2023; Bhuvaneskumar et al., 2023). It recognises the interconnectedness of financial markets with broader social and environmental concerns, aiming to generate positive impacts alongside profits (Richardson & Cragg, 2010; Carbone et al., 2012; Freeman & Groom, 2013; Carlsson Hauff & Nilsson, 2023; Efthymiou et al., 2023; Haq, 2023; Miglietta et al., 2023; Hlophe & Ellis, 2024; Kar & Patro, 2024).

With the global financial crisis 2008, more work on social finance started, including investment that incorporates or balances both financial returns and broader in the long term (Freeman & Groom, 2013; Geczy et al., 2021). Instead of maxing out on financial returns alone, there is a rethink in that capital also exists to serve society, working innovative SRI practices and promoting Impact Investments is at the forefront (Saini, 2023; Kar & Patro, 2024). Social finance is the cash flow into investments to solve societal problems sustainably. This means that the government, businesses, and civil society must identify the investments that benefit society. "Social Venturing Investors/Entrepreneurs" are a relatively new breed of investor who constitute a "new asset class" that has emerged recently and is committed to sustainable long-term investment (Schaefer et al., 2012). Social impact investing or social venture investing is a new approach to financial management that these investors have pioneered (de Lange, 2017; Barber et al., 2021). Instead of focusing solely on financial returns, they see them as a prerequisite for achieving other social objectives. Therefore, these managers must decide whether to view investments primarily in maximising financial returns or achieving other future objectives (Apostolakis et al., 2016). Because the goal of socially responsible investing is long-term benefits, it doesn't include investments that won't last. This new way of investing with an effect is picking up speed and wants to include big investors like pension funds (World Economic Forum, 2013).

Aristei & Gallo (2024) find that financial competencies increase the probability of adopting ESG strategies based on SR features adopting intermediaries. Similarly, (Kar & Patro, 2024) prove that the degree of financial literacy positively impacts SR investment firms' choices. On top of that, it appears to be among clientele with a greater awareness for their portfolio diversification; other things being equal, retail investors opt more often according to this logical anecdotic thought process through the use of as soon as deciding on moral intermediaries (Arribas et al., 2019; Bhuvaneskumar et al., 2023; Brodmann et al., 2023; Aristei & Gallo, 2024; Bertelli & Torricelli, 2024).

3 SUSTAINABLE INVESTMENTS

Sustainable investment, also known as responsible or ESG (environmental, social and governance), integrates material environmental, social and governance considerations into traditional financial analysis to improve the long-term risk-adjusted returns of people from public funds (Gangi & Varrone, 2018; Matallín-Sáez et al., 2019; Chang et al., 2022; Ferrat et al., 2023). Key drivers of sustainable investments in India: Investors are getting savvier about the financial risks of weak ESG performance, which has helped spur an increased focus on sustainable investment (Folger-Laronde et al., 2022).

Sustainable investing is the idea whereby an investor considers a corporation's corporate governance, social, and environmental aspects (Shevchenko et al., 2015). Sustainable investing is rising due to growing societal awareness of sustainability issues and public pressure on organisations to behave responsibly (Brunen & Laubach, 2022; Said & ElBannan, 2024). Consistent with this trend, investors are cautious in investment decisions (Naeem et al., 2023; Valadkhani & O'Mahony, 2024). Along with the growth in socially conscious investments, sustainable labelling, ratings, and other certifications aiming at helping investors differentiate financial goods with particular sustainable features have also evolved (Capelle-Blancard & Monjon, 2014; Crifo et al., 2019; Gandullia & Piserà, 2020; Ferrat et al., 2023; Juddoo et al., 2023; Abate et al., 2024; Brito-Ramos et al., 2024; Momparler et al., 2024).

It is still a matter of debate how firms' socially responsible or ethical behaviour should be defined, that is, to list what should and should not be done by companies to be able to announce them as socially responsible companies (Ortas & Moneva, 2011). Different multi-criteria approaches have been employed to aggregate the various criteria used to judge how companies behave, with the environmental, social, and governance dimensions among the most extensively researched topics (Matallín-Sáez et al., 2019; Efthymiou et al., 2023; Ferrat et al., 2023; Marzuki et al., 2023; Abate et al., 2024; Brito-Ramos et al., 2024; Catalano et al., 2024). The development of rankings that evaluate socially responsible companies' performance is also a matter of concern in the recent past.

Personal preferences for trustworthy financial intermediaries have not yet been investigated despite expanding the literature reviewing the factors influencing SRI choices (Aristei & Gallo, 2024). Bauer & Smeets (2015) discovered that investors who identify with SRI and have a strong social identification allocate significantly an increased portion of their wealth to institutions that provide SR products. In addition, they prove that the effects of risk perceptions and return expectations are mediated by the social identification of the complete and relative quantity invested at socially accountable banks (Praseeda, 2018; Kopp et al., 2022; Galeone et al., 2023; Irfan, Elmogy, Gupta, et al., 2024).

Several current works provided signs of the role of financial knowledge among retail investors in making decisions regarding sustainable and responsible investments (Bilbao-Terol et al., 2018; Palma-Ruiz et al., 2020; Weston & Nnadi, 2023; Niszczota & Błaszczyński, 2024). However, the ambiguity of the empirical evidence arises as few studies show a positive influence of financial knowledge on SRI (Gutsche et al., 2023), while others have found a negative (Irfan, Kadry, et al., 2023; Gutsche et al., 2021) or neutral impact (Filippini et al., 2024), calling for further, more profound analysis. Consequently, a more comprehensive study is necessary. Capelle-Blancard & Monjon (2014) demonstrate that a lack of sustainable financial market knowledge and financial competencies are critical obstacles to SRI. This is consistent with the prevailing belief that increased financial expertise is linked to more economical financial practices (Aristei & Gallo, 2024) and greater financial stability and strength (Lusardi & Tufano, 2015), further demonstrating that financial literacy is a critical factor in the development of sustainable investments (Irfan, Hussainey, et al., 2024). The greater the level of financial literacy, the more investments individuals make in sustainable funds. Simultaneously, the latter underscores the significant impediment of high processing and information costs to SRI (Chang et al., 2020; Geczy et al., 2021).

The median returns of traditional and sustainable funds from the 1st half of 2019 to the 2nd half of 2023 (Figure 1). In the beginning, the sustainable funds performed better than traditional funds, and it was evident that the results of both funds in H1 2019 declined due to COVID-19. From that point, both the funds were recovered and performed well during H2 2020. Again, both funds had a significant downfall and registered low margins during H1 2022. However, in the recent half (H2 2023), the funds registered moderate recovery and performed well compared to the last two halves.

Figure 1. Sustainable fund median returns vs. non-ESG funds worldwide from 1H 2019 to 2H 2023

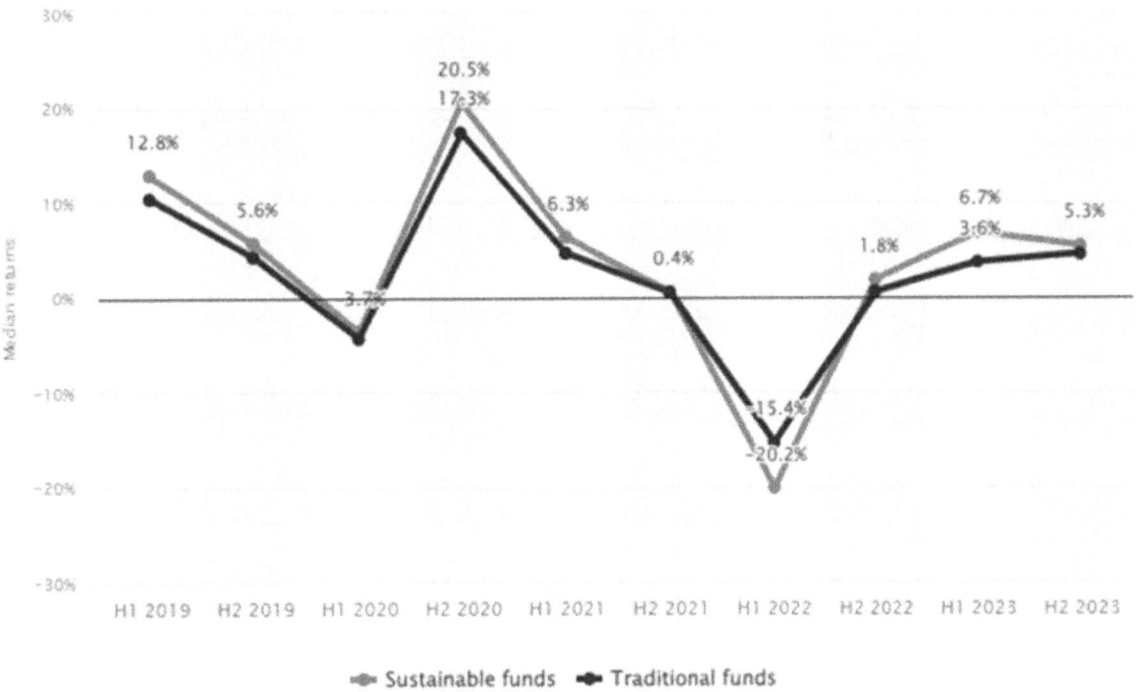

Source: https://www.statista.com/statistics/1296498/sustainable-funds-returns-vs-other-funds-usa/

4. METHODOLOGY

To perform the Bibliometric Analysis, data was collected from the Scopus database and analysed to understand the trends in sustainable and socially responsible investments. The completeness of metadata from Scopus indicates that the 234 articles have an 'excellent' status, which is determined by the complete documentation of the essential features of Abstract, Cited References, Document Type, Language, Title, Journal, Publication Year, and Total Citation (Table 1). However, there were a few discrepancies in other data fields. Seven papers were identified as 'good' due to missing DOI and keywords. Nearly 13 per cent of the papers were in the category of 'corresponding author' missing.

Figure 2. Completeness of metadata

Metadata	Description	Missing Counts	Missing %	Status
AB	Abstract	0	0	Excellent
CR	Cited References	0	0	Excellent
DT	Document Type	0	0	Excellent
SO	Journal	0	0	Excellent
LA	Language	0	0	Excellent
PY	Publication Year	0	0	Excellent
TI	Title	0	0	Excellent
TC	Total Citation	0	0	Excellent
C1	Affiliation	1	0.43	Good
AU	Author	1	0.43	Good
DI	DOI	7	2.99	Good
DE	Keywords	7	2.99	Good
RP	Corresponding Author	31	13.25	Acceptable
ID	Keywords Plus	175	74.79	Critical
WC	Science Categories	234	100	Completely missing

This study aims to elucidate the innovative trends through a bibliometric analysis of sustainable and socially responsible investment research from 2010 to 2024. The lens of most cited papers identifies emerging trends that give additional insight into where the field has moved. The study sheds light on the recent trends and technological advancement in sustainable investments, which promises to reveal important authors, countries, and collaborative networks. This work includes quantitative metrics and qualitative measures that provide an unbiased perspective on the literature, informing future research and investment decisions in this area. The main research question of this study is to focus on bibliometrics: conceptual mapping and performance study to respond to major questions regarding the subject of study.

RQ1: What is the yearly rise in the publication rate of scientific papers related to sustainable and socially responsible investments?
RQ2: Which authors contribute to the publications regarding the topic, and which documents and journals are most relevant to sustainable and socially responsible investments?
RQ3: What are the gaps in the literature, and what are the key topics of interest in research concerning sustainable investments?
RQ4: What trends and shifts can be identified in the choice of topics for research in the sphere of sustainable investments?

Many researchers have widely used bibliometric analysis recently (Tomar et al., 2021; Gallego-Losada et al., 2022; Alshater et al., 2023; Khongwir & Sharmiladevi, 2023; Marzuki et al., 2023; Naeem et al., 2023; Sugiharto et al., 2024). This qualitative analysis helps process large quantities of scientific material systematically. Even though it has not been employed in business studies initially, many articles (Rossetto et al., 2018; Verma & Gustafsson, 2020; Donthu et al., 2021) have demonstrated a recent trend of its use in this field. Many researchers are interested in these kinds of analyses, not only because they help people understand the structure of a literature stream that is part of discipline on an intellectual level but also the availability of sources software like Biblioshiny R, VOSviewer, Gephi, and scientific databases like Scopus and Web of Science (WOS). One of the best things about Biblioshiny R and VOSviewer is that they can give detailed views that can be used to judge the bibliometric plots (Marzuki et al., 2023). Periodicals and credentials can be used with bibliometric analysis to judge the work of writers, institutions, countries, and journals. This is why it is crucial to understand the literature better.

Due to its advantages, we used Biblioshiny R (Version 4.3.0) and VOSviewer (Version 1.6.20) for this paper's bibliometric analysis. These tools allow us to do analyses based on countries, institutions, journals, and authors, showing how sustainability impacts investments. We started our analysis with a Scopus search using 'sustainable investment and socially responsible investment,' which yielded 550 documents (Table 2 and Figure 2). This proved that the recovered papers were linked to sustainability. After entering keywords, we applied a range filter from 2010 to 2014, which limits the documents to 496. Further, the subject filter is used in business, management, accounting, economics, econometrics, and finance. This reduced the search results from 496 to 340 documents. Additionally, it filters selected articles with titles or keywords explicitly stating both concepts. Finally, we measured 234 published English-language journal articles for the current research (Haddaway et al., 2022).

Using keyword analysis, we extracted study trends and sorted out the articles associated with business, economics and finance. Here, we used scientific insight and examination to investigate journals, authors, and nations that have the maximum impact on the growth of sustainable investment research. The Scopus data were uploaded to the Biblioshiny R and VOSviewer to detect and analyse collaboration networks and co-words. The second facilitated identifying thematic linkages among the literature to map out a conceptual landscape in the field. In this study, we analysed co-occurrence terms to discover similarities between sustainable investment studies and investigate the degree of authors and countries by reviewing how they impact other papers published.

Figure 3. PRISMA chart representing the flow of documents collected on sustainable development derived from the Scopus database

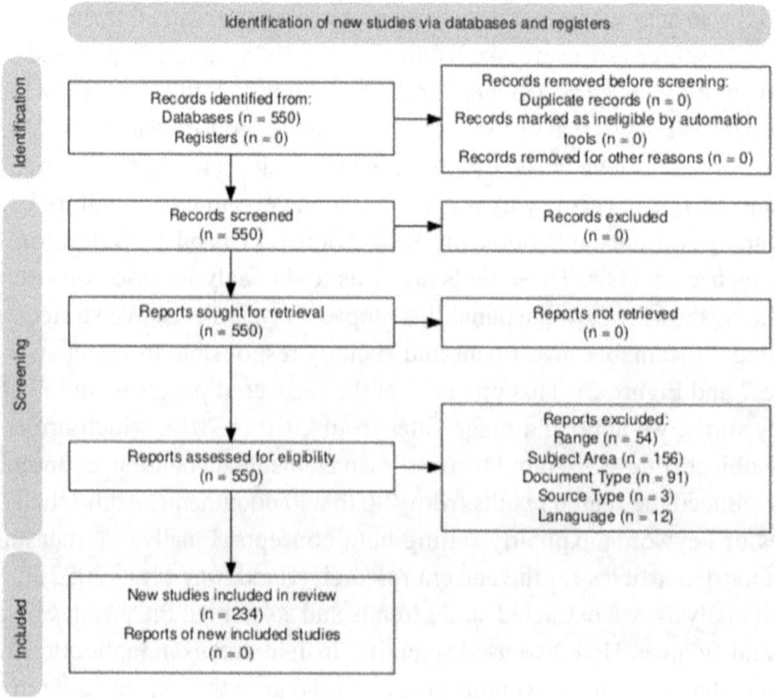

5. RESULT ANALYSIS

This paper aims to review the literature on sustainable investments to identify publication trends, critical authors and countries involved in collaborations. It provides research trends, the most accessed papers, and top journals using tools like Word Cloud. It addresses multiple research questions such as how sustainability versus investments research has developed over time, article performance, author rankings and collaborations, mainly focusing on single-country versus multi-country publications. This paper also used co-word analysis and keyword trends to construct a student overview of the field.

5.1 Performance Analysis of the Articles Published Over Different Periods

The results and the summary statistics are presented in Table 3. About 234 documents in the Scopus database are classified as articles, and review articles were published from 2010 to 2024. On average, these documents received 24.56 citations per year, and this frequency increased at an annual rate of 20.32%. This reflects a notable overall increase in scholarly papers about sustainable investments within the context of finance, as indicated by the substantial average citation per document. It has also become clear that 590 unique authors have contributed to papers on the use of sustainable investments as well.

The average document is 4.32 years old, and the average single-authored is 30. The average number of co-authors per document is 2.79 per cent, and international collaboration (or co-authorship) is 23.5.

Figure 4. Summary statistics of the data used in the study

Metadata	Description	Missing Counts	Missing %	Status
AB	Abstract	0	0	Excellent
CR	Cited References	0	0	Excellent
DT	Document Type	0	0	Excellent
SO	Journal	0	0	Excellent
LA	Language	0	0	Excellent
PY	Publication Year	0	0	Excellent
TI	Title	0	0	Excellent
TC	Total Citation	0	0	Excellent
C1	Affiliation	1	0.43	Good
AU	Author	1	0.43	Good
DI	DOI	7	2.99	Good
DE	Keywords	7	2.99	Good
RP	Corresponding Author	31	13.25	Acceptable
ID	Keywords Plus	175	74.79	Critical
WC	Science Categories	234	100	Completely missing

5.2 Annual Scientific Production

This annual scientific article output should thoroughly review the growth, progress, and prevailing tendencies in discussing sustainability-related socially responsible investing. For this, publications in journals on the relevant topics from 2010 to 2024 are considered. Sustainable investing has been increasing in popularity for some time. There were thirteen articles published in 2024 on sustainable investment. From this point, the publications were slowed down till 2017 in this research area. Significant improvements occurred between 2020 and 2024, with 145 research papers published in the journals (Figure 3). The authors showed interest in research on sustainable and socially responsible investments.

Figure 5. Annual scientific production

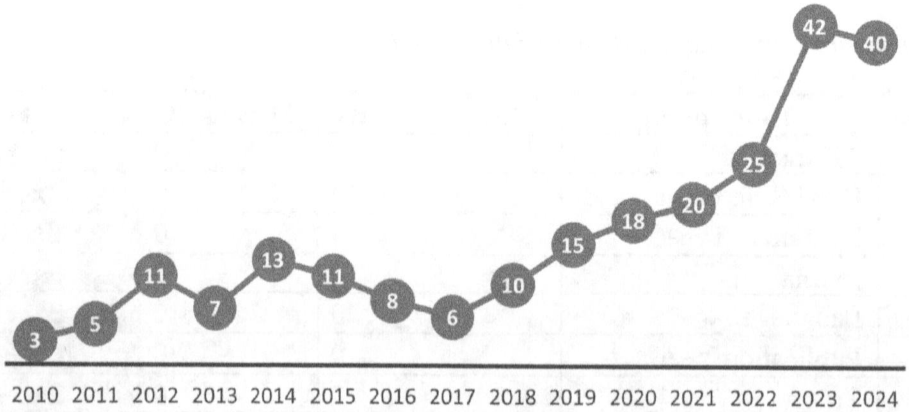

Source: Biblioshiny R

5.3 Most Relevant Authors

The top 10 authors who have contributed the most in the quantity of publications on sustainable investment are presented in Table 4. The analysis shows that the authors who published the most articles on sustainable and socially responsible investment are Arenas-Parra M. and Bilbao-Terol A., from the University of Oviedo, Oviedo, Spain, contributed three articles; Diener J., and Habisch A, also contributed three articles, other authors presented in the table also contributed same level of articles to this field.

Figure 6. Top performers

Rank	Authors	Affiliation	Articles
1	ARENAS-PARRA M	Faculty of Economics and Business, Department of Quantitative Economics, University of Oviedo, Oviedo, Spain	3
2	BILBAO-TEROL A	Faculty of Economics and Business, Department of Quantitative Economics, University of Oviedo, Oviedo, Spain	3
3	DIENER J	Faculty of Business and Economics, Catholic University of Eichstätt-Ingolstadt, Ingolstadt, Germany	3
4	GALLOPPO G	Department of Economics and Business, University of Viterbo La Tuscia, Viterbo, Italy	3
5	HABISCH A	Faculty of Business and Economics, Catholic University of Eichstätt-Ingolstadt, Ingolstadt, Germany	3
6	MATALLÍN-SÁEZ JC	Finance and Accounting Department, Universitat Jaume I, Castelló, 12071, Spain	3
7	MEUNIER L	ESSCA School of Management, Aix-en-Provence, France	3
8	MONEVA JM	Accounting and Finance Department, Faculty of Economics and Business Studies, Gran Vía, 2, 50005 Zaragoza, Spain	3
9	PAIMANOVA V	CEIS Foundation, University of Rome Tor Vergata, Rome, Italy	3
10	SOLER-DOMÍNGUEZ A	Department of Finance and Accounting, Universitat Jaume I, Castellón de la Plana, Spain	3

Source: Author compilation and the data retrieved from Biblioshiny using Scopus database.

5.4 Frequency of Periodicals by Authors (Lotka Law)

The table below shows that more than 91% agreed with all of Table 5's assertions to varied degrees. This study also found that 1.6% of the authors are infrequent, having published only one work supporting Lotka's Law. Lotka then proposed the inverse square Law, which states that the number of authors producing specific articles is inversely proportionate to the number of authors publishing a single article. According to this theory, the hypothetical value of the beta coefficient of Lotka's Law, which represents the writers' production in any area of interest or discipline, should be two. However, Arenas-Parra M. has produced three publications, placing him among the most prolific authors in sustainable investing, with other authors.

Table 1. Frequency of periodicals by authors

Documents written	No. of Authors	Proportion of Authors (%)
3	10	0.016
2	43	0.072
1	537	0.910

Source: Biblioshiny R

5.5 Most Cited Documents

The top ten research articles cited in sustainable and socially responsible investments are available for easy understanding (Table 6). The top-cited paper, "Sustainable investing in equilibrium", written by PASTOR in 2021 in J FINANC ECON, has been cited 461 times. Also, this paper's total citations per annum are 115.25. "The Role of the Beneficiary in Willingness to Pay for Socially Responsible Products: A Meta-analysis" article has been cited 204 times and occupies the second position in the total citations; this article was written by TULLY SM in 2014 in J RETAIL. The article ranked 3rd in the table, cited 48 times on average in a year with 192 citations.

5.6 Performance of Journals

The 'Journal of Cleaner Production' published 19 articles in this area of research with an impact factor of 20.4. The Journal of Sustainable Finance and Investment is in second place, with 16 articles included, compared to the above-mentioned top-ranked journals. The top ten journals published 87 articles in this area, with 37.2 per cent of the articles published in the selection criteria. Except 'The Journal of Business Ethics', all other journals at the top are Q1 categories. Elsevier published 25 articles, and John Wiley & Sons published 20 articles in this area (Table 7).

Figure 7. The ten most cited articles

Rank	Paper	Name of the Article	DOI	Total Citations	TC per Year	Normalised TC
1	PASTOR, 2021, J FINANC ECON	Sustainable investing in equilibrium	10.1016/j.jfinec o.2020.12.011	461	115.25	8.07
2	TULLY SM, 2014, J RETAIL	The Role of the Beneficiary in Willingness to Pay for Socially Responsible Products: A Meta-analysis	10.1016/j.jretai. 2014.03.004	204	18.55	4.14
3	BARBER BM, 2021, J FINANC ECON	Impact investing	10.1016/j.jfinec o.2020.07.008	192	48.00	3.36
4	WIDYAWATI L, 2020, BUS STRATEGY ENVIRON	A systematic literature review of socially responsible investment and environmental social governance metrics	10.1002/bse.23 93	188	37.60	6.89
5	SEARCY C, 2012, J CLEAN PROD	Corporate sustainability ratings: an investigation into how corporations use the Dow Jones Sustainability Index	10.1016/j.jclepr o.2012.05.022	167	12.85	3.78
6	BARAUSKAITE G, 2021, CORP SOC RESPONSIB ENVIRON MANAGE	Corporate social responsibility and financial performance of companies: The puzzle of concepts, definitions and assessment methods	10.1002/csr.20 48	165	41.25	2.89
7	STEURER R, 2012, CORP SOC RESPONSIB ENVIRON MANAGE	Public Policies on CSR in Europe: Themes, Instruments, and Regional Differences	10.1002/csr.26 4	151	11.62	3.42
8	CAPELLE-BLANCARD G, 2014, EUR FINANC MANAGE	The Performance of Socially Responsible Funds: Does the Screening Process Matter?	10.1111/j.1468-036X.2012.006 43.x	137	12.45	2.78
9	STEYN M, 2014, SUSTAINABILITY ACCOUNT MANAGE POLICY J	Organisational benefits and implementation challenges of mandatory integrated reporting	10.1108/sampj-11-2013-0052	136	12.36	2.76
10	VO NNY, 2019, DECIS SUPPORT SYST	Deep learning for decision-making and the optimisation of socially responsible investments and portfolio	10.1016/j.dss.2 019.113097	103	17.17	3.41

Source: Author compilation and the data retrieved from Biblioshiny using Scopus database

Figure 8. Top 10 most relevant journals

Rank	Sources	Articles	Impact Factor	%	SNIP	SJR	Quartiles	Publisher
1	Journal of Cleaner Production	19	20.4	8.120	2.236	2.058	Q1	Elsevier
2	Journal of Sustainable Finance and Investment	16	10.6	6.838	1.334	1.007	Q1	Taylor & Francis
3	Business Strategy and the Environment	11	22.5	4.701	3.043	3.666	Q1	John Wiley & Sons
4	Corporate Social Responsibility and Environmental Management	9	17.2	3.846	2.559	2.201	Q1	John Wiley & Sons
5	Journal of Business Ethics	9	1.0	3.846	0.475	0.22	Q2	Philosophy Documentation Center
6	Finance Research Letters	6	11.1	2.564	2.279	1.903	Q1	Elsevier
7	Social Responsibility Journal	5	7.3	2.137	1.382	0.844	Q1	Emerald Publishing
8	Corporate Governance (Bingley)	4	11.2	1.709	1.855	1.261	Q1	Emerald Publishing
9	Journal of Risk and Financial Management	4	4.5	1.709	0.875	0.485	Q1	Multidisciplinary Digital Publishing Institute (MDPI)
10	Sustainability Accounting, Management and Policy Journal	4	9.5	1.709	1.478	1.197	Q1	Emerald Publishing

Source: Author compilation and the data retrieved from Biblioshiny using Scopus database.

5.7 Bradford's Law of Core Sources

The principle of Bradford's Law enables a user to find the core journals of a specific discipline and is characterised by both the principle of diminishing returns and scattering. Therefore, any field is split into three categories according to the identified Law. "The top third (Zone 1 or core), according to the author, refers to the frequency of citations of the journals in the literature on that subject that is likely of most interest to the researchers in that field. The journals in the middle third, or zone 2, have a moderate citation rate, while those in the bottom third, or zone 3, have a low citation rate and are often considered peripheral to the subject area or field (Yumnam et al., 2024). By Bradford's Law, the number of journals in the second zone will be 'n', and the third zone will be 'n^2 'as large as the first zone (Brookes, 1969). Among the 126 journals that produced 234 articles on cross-disciplinary, eight core journals contributed seventy-nine articles (33.76 per cent) for sustainable and socially responsible investment (Figure 9), leading the research count.

Figure 9. Core sources by Bradford's Law

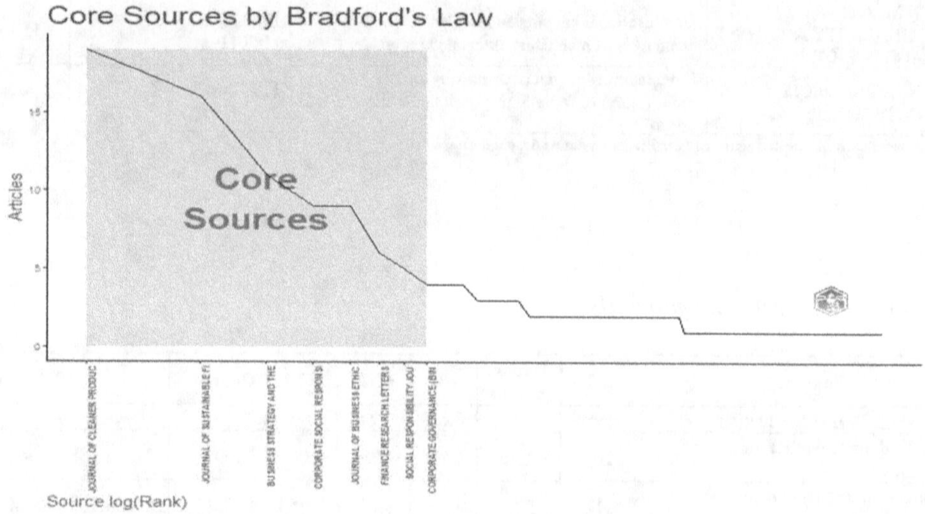

Source: Biblioshiny R

5.8 Performance Analysis of Author Collaborations in Terms of Single Country Publications (SCP) and Multiple Country Publications (MCP)

The top productive country in sustainable and socially responsible investments research, Spain leads with 22 research articles, followed by Italy with 18, the USA with 17, and India with 16 (Table 8), which is more than 31per cent of the total count. Articles typically fall into two categories based on author collaboration: The two categories they have distinguished are "single country publication" (SCP) and "multiple country publication" (MCP). SCP also establishes that the two researchers are from the same country, a common occurrence referred to as intra-country research collaboration. By contrast, MCP comprises authors from different states or international bodies (Sadeqi-Arani & Kadkhodaie, 2023).

Table 2. Top productive countries

Rank	Country	Articles	Frequency (%)	SCP	MCP	MCP_Ratio (%)
1	Spain	22	9.4	19	3	13.6
2	Italy	18	7.7	17	1	5.6
3	USA	17	7.3	11	6	35.3
4	India	16	6.8	15	1	6.3
5	France	14	6.0	10	4	28.6
6	Germany	14	6.0	14	0	0.0
7	United Kingdom	11	4.7	8	3	27.3
8	Canada	8	3.4	7	1	12.5
9	Australia	7	3.0	6	1	14.3
10	China	7	3.0	5	2	28.6

Source: Biblioshiny R

5.9 Most Cited Countries

Citation count shows the quality of work done by researchers in the selected domain, in which the USA dominates (1119), followed by Spain (593), Italy (411) and France (380). Significant contributions are also made by Canada and Australia, with 344 and 330 mentions, respectively. Germany and the United Kingdom contribute much, even if their counts are lower (278 and 253). On the other hand, Brazil and Lithuania have both seen a rise in research (196 and 165) (Figure 5). This distribution shows that while the United States and Europe have made major contributions, research is becoming increasingly important in emerging economies.

Figure 10. Most cited countries

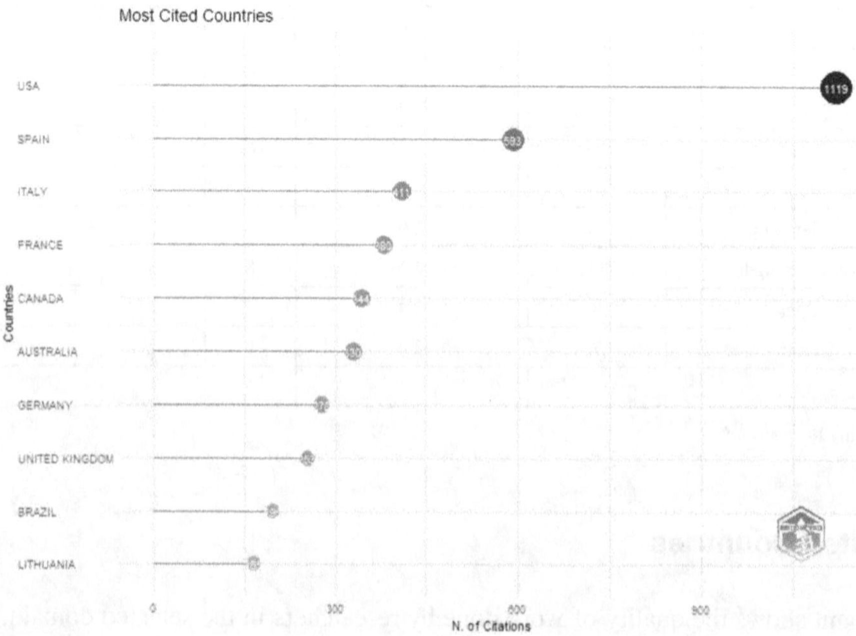

Source: Biblioshiny R

5.10 Three Field Plot

Sankey diagrams visually illustrate the interrelationships of three different components towards each other, and the width of the flow shows the proportion of the value of the nodes (Ingale & Paluri, 2022). Three field plots using Sankey plots, where keywords, authors, and journals are the three components taken to explain the interrelationships (Figure 6). Keywords are shown in the left field, authors are in the middle, and publications are on the right side of the page. For the analysis, the top 20 items were taken. Each of these items has been directed towards the most profound keywords in this field, such as socially responsible investment, corporate social responsibility, sustainable development, and SRI, along with the authors and sources of the study. In the three-field analysis, it was recognised that most studies were regarding socially responsible investment, and afterwards, sustainable growth was achieved. Cohen DH has done most of this research. At the same time, he had two articles with an outflow of different articles about socially responsible investments, after which followed Moneva JM, whose article trail contained two papers.

Figure 11.Threefold plot

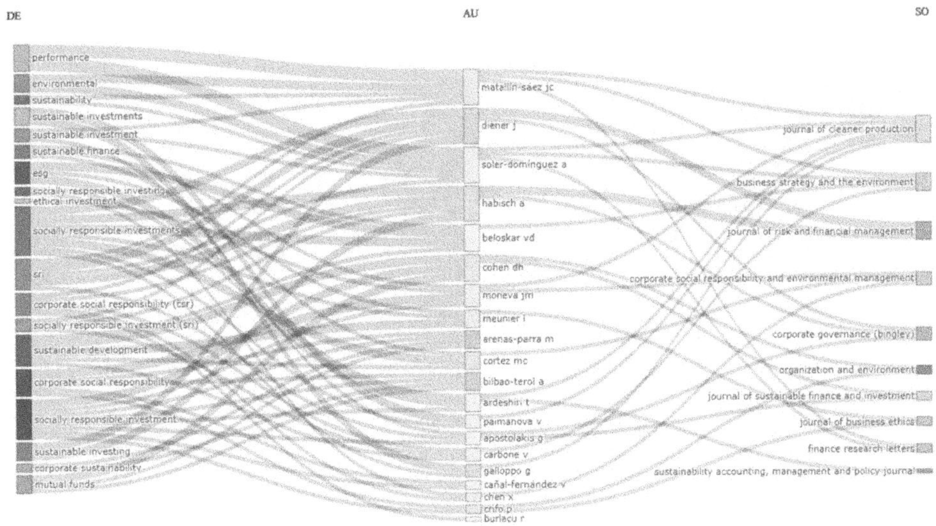

Source: Biblioshiny R

5.11 Corresponding Author's Country

The degree of global involvement in the literature reviewed on investments in sustainable and socially responsible products in which Italy and the United Kingdom have three articles on this subject area, indicates a robust exchange of ideas and exchange between these two countries. In contrast, France and the UK have two collaborations. Some other notable collaborators are Italy and USA, Australia and Sweden, Malaysia and Saudi Arabia, each of which has two contributions together (Table 9 and Figure 7). This frequent collaboration indicates that a global network of research partnerships probably influences the extent and importance of research in sustainable, socially responsible investments.

Figure 12. Number of country collaboration

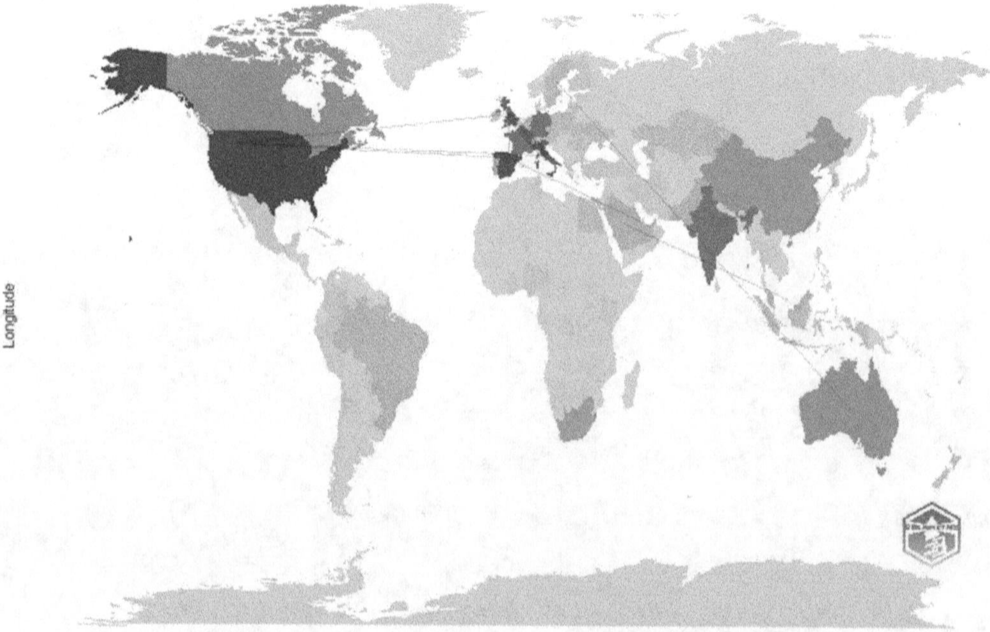

Figure 13. Country scientific production and country collaboration map

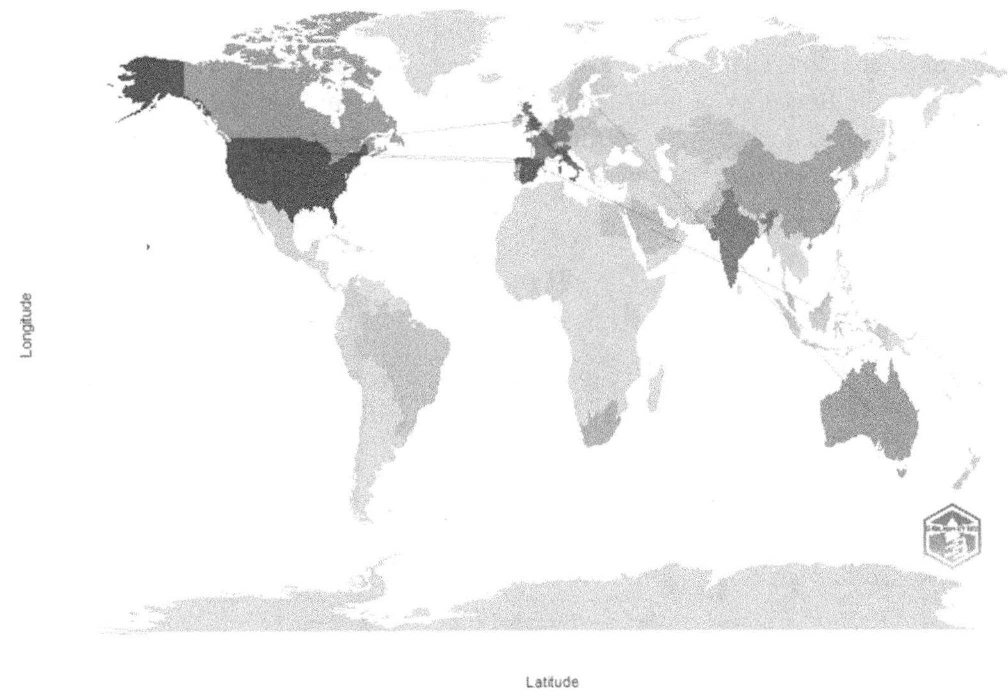

Source: Biblioshiny R

5.12 Word Cloud

Upon analysing the most used research keywords, it is observed that there is a positive correlation between the font size and word frequency. This means larger font sizes were associated with more frequently used words in the word cloud. The most frequent keywords used were sustainable development, investment and investments, socially responsible investments, sustainability, decision-making, and environmental economics and management (Figure 8).

Figure 14.Word cloud

Source: Biblioshiny R

5.13 Tree Map

For bibliometric analysis, a tree map is a representation method that provides a hierarchical representation of the data. A tree map in Biblioshiny visually shows authors' keyword distribution and frequencies. The entire tree map represents all the keywords in the dataset. The size of each section or leaf of the tree map corresponds to the frequency of a particular keyword. The term "sustainable development" was referenced in most published papers (13% of the documents) among these research titles. The second most frequently published title was "investments" (9%), followed by "investment," "socially responsible investments," and "sustainability" (Figure 9).

Figure 15. Tree map

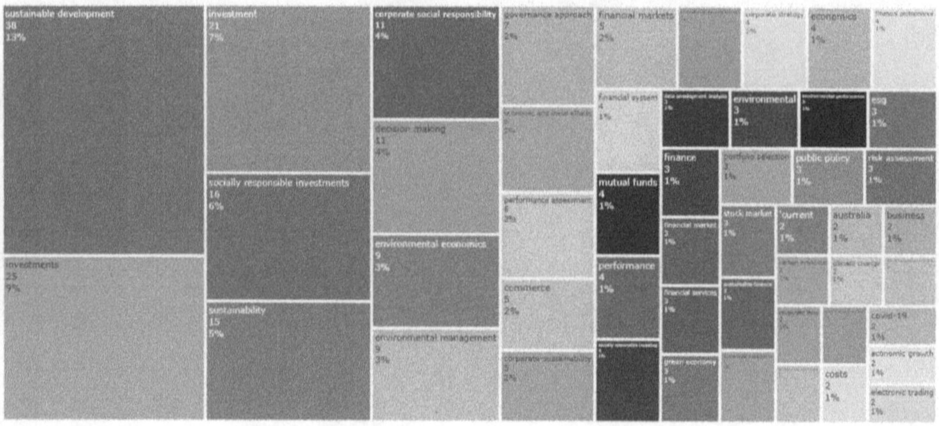

Source: Biblioshiny R

5.14 Network of Co-Word Occurrence

The current research also uses the network of co-word instances, and six clusters are identified after defining the minimum co-occurrence frequency of 5 and considering 44 keywords. These groups reflect the most prominent topics in the study of sustainable investing. The circle size represents the keyword's frequency: a distinct colour denotes a separate cluster, whereas all words in the same cluster have the same colour. Among all the keywords, the authors consider sustainable development and socially responsible investments more considerable (Figure 10).

Figure 16. Network of co-word occurrence

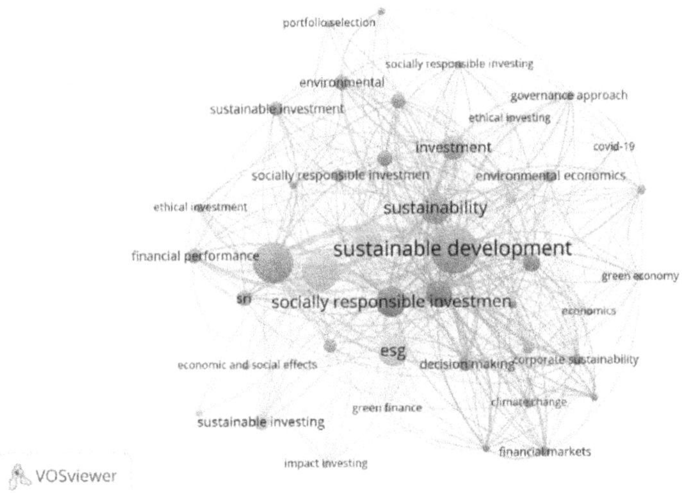

Source: VOSviewer

5.15 Temporal Overlay on a Co-Word Map (Vosviewer)

A chronological representation of articles discussing sustainable and socially responsible investments based on co-word maps incorporating at least five occurrences and 44 themes extracted from the author's keyword analysis is presented in the temporal overlay using Vosviewer (Figure 11). The circle size is directly proportional to the occurrence of keyword usage. The circles in the initial section of the diagram represent the number of years in which each term was created together. This information is displayed in the legend at the diagram's bottom right. Similarly, the temporal overlay reveals that specific tools mentioned earlier, such as 'sustainable development', 'SRI', 'ethical investment', 'mutual funds', and 'economics and social effects' were popular in the past. In contrast, more recent tools like 'ESG', 'green finance', 'green economy', 'impact investing', 'socially responsible investing', and 'corporate sustainability' are now being used.

Figure 17. Temporal overlay on a co-word map

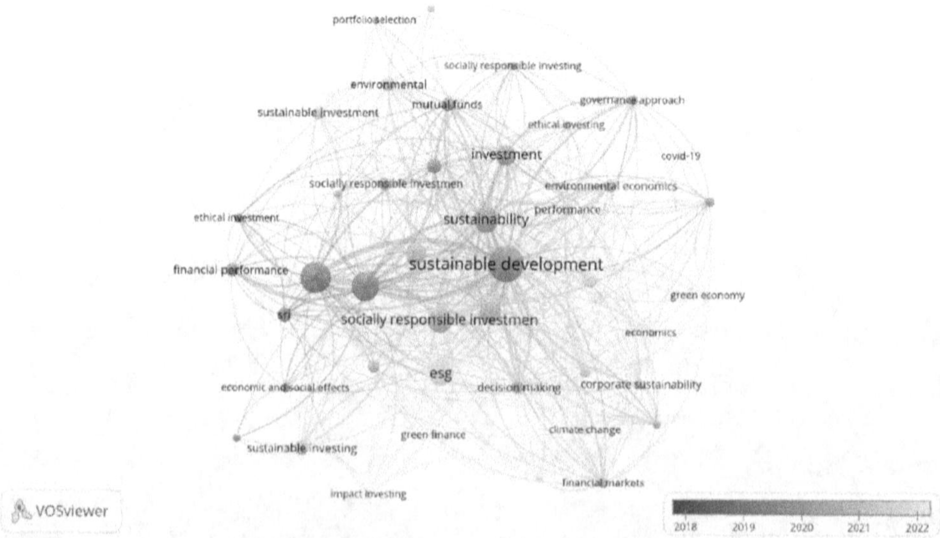

Source: VOSviewer

6 FINDINGS OF THE STUDY

- Regarding the performance analysis of articles published over various periods, from 2020 on, the growth can be accredited because most of the present study's articles were published in the last five years, at 62 per cent.
- The performance analysis of authors with ranking states that the authors who published the most articles on sustainability and socially responsible investments are Arenas-Parra M., from the Faculty of Economics and Business, Department of Quantitative Economics, University of Oviedo, Oviedo, Spain, with three articles. Furthermore, using Lokta's Law on publication frequency, we can understand that less than two per cent of authors are serious, and 91 per cent of the authors are occasional.
- The analysis of journal performance reveals that the Journal of Cleaner Production' published nineteen research articles on this concept, and the Journal of Sustainable Finance and Investment occupied the second position with sixteen articles during the study period.
- As per Bradford's Law, eight journals are considered core (Zone-1) and published 79 articles in the study period.
- Spain, Italy and the USA are the top three countries that produced nearly one-fourth of the articles on sustainable and socially responsible investments during the study period.
- Regarding production, the USA has the third place, but citations-wise, it's in the first place with 1119 citations. The second most cited country's (Spain) citations were 593, nearly half of the citations in the USA.

- Italy and the UK collaboratively published three articles, and other collaborations in the top ten categories yielded two articles each.
- Using conceptual structure and word cloud analysis, we can understand that over time, keywords and themes have emerged that include 'sustainable development', 'investment and investments', 'socially responsible investments', and 'sustainability'. In the same way, terms such as 'decision making', 'environmental management', 'corporate social responsibility', 'environmental economics', and 'economic and social effects' have gained popularity recently.

7. DISCUSSION

This section discusses answers to research questions formulated in the methodology section.

RQ1 tests the year-wise growth in publishing research papers on sustainable and socially responsible investments. Scopus database papers were published on the selected theme from 2010 to 2024 for this investigation. As per the data, the yearly growth rate of the articles is 20.32 per cent. The publication rate is higher than the previous years of the study period in the last five years. This trend indicates that the focus has shifted to sustainable and socially responsible investments.

RQ2 discusses the authors' contribution to the publications regarding the topic and the type of documents and journals that are most relevant to sustainable and socially responsible investments. The authors' performance with the ranks indicates that the top ten authors published each of the three articles in the field. But Pástor Ľuboš has received 461 citations with a journal article titled 'Sustainable investing in equilibrium' published in the Journal of Financial Economics in 2021. The same paper has the highest number of citations (115.25) per year. Regarding journal publications, the top ten journals published 87 articles on sustainability and socially responsible investments. It has been identified that 'The Journal of Cleaner Production' has published the highest number of articles (19), and 'The Journal of Sustainable Finance and Investment' has published sixteen articles in the field of study. Except for the 'Journal of Business Ethics', all the top journals are in the Q1 category of Scopus. 'Business Strategy and the Environment' has a 22.5 impact factor, which is high in the top ten journals, and the same journal has the highest SNIP and SJR. As per Bradford's Law on relevant sources, 126 journals published around 234 articles in inter-collection, whereas eight core journals contributed 79 articles on sustainable and socially responsible investments. Bradford's Law, recognised for its ability to locate core journals within a specific field and its application to the principles of diminishing returns and scattering, provides guidance.

RQ3 focuses on the top productive countries and the main topics of interest in research concerning sustainable investments. As per the data, Spain has 22 articles, Italy has 18 articles, and the USA has 17 articles regarding production. The USA has the highest MCP ratio in 35.3 percent of the top ten countries analysed, with top citations 1119. Regarding country collaborations, Italy and the United Kingdom have three publications, and the rest of the top countries collaboratively published two. Following literature research, it is possible to identify some link gaps and pinpoint the primary topics of interest in sustainable and socially responsible investments.

RQ4 discusses the trends and shifts that can be identified in the choice of topics for research in the sphere of sustainable investments. Using word cloud and conceptual structure, we can infer that keywords and themes have emerged that include 'sustainable development', 'investment', and 'socially responsible investments.' Likewise, terms like 'electronic trading', 'costs', 'corporate sustainability indices', 'corporate social performance', and 'economic growth' fall into the least searched categories. Moreover, the co-word analysis using author keywords and the temporal map shows that tools such as 'socially responsible investments', 'financial performance', 'ethical investment', and 'sustainable investment' which are marked in purple, were popular in the past. On the other hand, the temporal overlay shows an increased usage of ESG (Environmental, Social and Governance) 'green finance', 'sustainable finance', and 'impact investing' recently (Malpani et al., 2024).

Sustainable finance is critical in allocating resources to environmentally and socially beneficial enterprises. The global focus on sustainable development goals (SDGs) and a movement towards a resilient economy is forcing Indian investors to consider aligning their portfolios with these trends (Irfan, Elmogy, Shabri Abd. Majid, et al., 2024; Verma & Khanna, 2024; Efthymiou et al., 2023; Witkowska, 2023; Consolandi et al., 2020). These trends indicate that it's high time companies and government bodies encouraged and educated investors on risk levels when investing in sustainable products. However, investments in sustainable products are quite modest and are now in the emerging and exploring stages (Schaefer et al., 2012; Marzuki et al., 2023; Gok et al., 2020). Thus, future studies focus on the impact of risk on investments in sustainable and socially responsible products in underdeveloped, developing and developed countries (Kobo & Ngwakwe, 2017; Hysa et al., 2022; Tripathi & Kaur, 2022; Chen et al., 2024).

8. CONCLUSION

The current research, therefore, essentially intends to critically review the articles published in sustainable and socially responsible investment. Two hundred thirty-four articles indexed in the Scopus database, produced between 2010 and 2024, have been published in refereed journals. The research has been done on two major aspects: first, identifying a trend or pattern of knowledge growth in the subject, significant and influential publications, authors, journals, nations with topic-related development, and a gap in current research. Second, the factors influencing the total citation of publications have been analysed in this field. Quite a few works written on socially responsible investing have increased significantly since 2010, as evidenced by examining the topic's development. Publications, countries, and institutions comprise the study's principal contributors. This quantitative and comprehensive analysis indicates that most research is conducted in industrialised nations, including Spain and Italy. A disparity exists between developed and emerging markets, specifically regarding India, a developing nation.

Nevertheless, as the field grows, researchers are investigating a variety of facets of ethical investing and the function companies have in promoting it. Thematic structure, author keyword growth, and trends in this research domain indicate the emphasis on "sustainable investment" in previous years. However, in recent years, researchers have shifted their attention to the "role of investment" (responsible investment) and the "role of corporates in sustainable development." Recent research has predominantly combined sustainable development with financial markets and investment strategies. It implies that sustainable development is inextricably linked to socially responsible investment. The policymakers will benefit to a certain extent from the results of this research, or more specifically, the results collected by the intermediary. The research can assist in developing a framework for educating investors on sustainable investment products.

To our knowledge, no research has hitherto integrated quantitative and qualitative approaches in presenting the connections among seminal works in Socially Responsible Investment with the keywords of Sustainable Investment and Socially Responsible Investors. The framework of Socially Responsible

Investment was investigated in this paper using bibliometric analysis. With descriptive statistics of generic bibliographic information, the current study on co-authorship, co-occurrence of author keywords, and document cluster analysis yields strong results in evaluating trends in socially responsible investing research. More importantly, the statistical methodology applied reveals the drivers of publication citation. Thus, it can provide a basis for future research to be channelled onto subject matters not as focused upon by other researchers, hoping that it will rise in citations. Therefore, the review study will contribute significantly to the literature on socially responsible investment and its management application. As extensive as the research is, some limitations are at hand. Only one database was employed for the research study; not all the works on socially responsible investment could be included. Hence, future uses of more than one database, such as Web of Science, together with Scopus, will enable more works to be accessed and thus provide more accurate results.

REFERENCES

Abate, G., Basile, I., & Ferrari, P. (2024). The integration of environmental, social and governance criteria in portfolio optimization: An empirical analysis. *Corporate Social Responsibility and Environmental Management, 31*(3), 2054–2065. *Scopus.* Advance online publication. DOI: 10.1002/csr.2682

Alshater, M. M., Atayah, O. F., & Hamdan, A. (2023). Journal of Sustainable Finance and Investment: A bibliometric analysis. *Journal of Sustainable Finance and Investment, 13*(3), 1131–1152. *Scopus.* Advance online publication. DOI: 10.1080/20430795.2021.1947116

Apostolakis, G., Kraanen, F., & van Dijk, G. (2016). Pension beneficiaries' and fund managers' perceptions of responsible investment: A focus group study. *Corporate Governance (Bingley), 16*(1), 1–20. *Scopus.* Advance online publication. DOI: 10.1108/CG-05-2015-0070

Arias Fogliano de Souza Cunha, F., & Samanez, C. P. (2013). Performance Analysis of Sustainable Investments in the Brazilian Stock Market: A Study About the Corporate Sustainability Index (ISE). *Journal of Business Ethics, 117*(1), 19–36. *Scopus.* Advance online publication. DOI: 10.1007/s10551-012-1484-2

Aristei, D., & Gallo, M. (2024). Gender-related effects of financial knowledge and confidence on preferences for ethical intermediaries and sustainable investments. *International Journal of Bank Marketing, 42*(3), 486–512. *Scopus.* Advance online publication. DOI: 10.1108/IJBM-06-2023-0355

Arribas, I., Espinós-Vañó, M. D., García, F., & Tamosiuniene, R. (2019). Negative screening and sustainable portfolio diversification. *Entrepreneurship and Sustainability Issues, 6*(4), 1566–1586. *Scopus.* Advance online publication. DOI: 10.9770/jesi.2019.6.4(2)

Barber, B. M., Morse, A., & Yasuda, A. (2021). Impact investing. *Journal of Financial Economics, 139*(1), 162–185. *Scopus.* Advance online publication. DOI: 10.1016/j.jfineco.2020.07.008

Basak, S., Basu, P., Avittathur, B., & Sikdar, S. (2024). Corrigendum: Manufacturer driven strategic coordination as a response to "showrooming.". *Decision Support Systems*, 178, 114120. DOI: 10.1016/j.dss.2023.114120

Bertelli, B., & Torricelli, C. (2024). The trade-off between ESG screening and portfolio diversification in the short and in the long run. *Journal of Economics and Finance.Journal of Economics and Finance*, 48(2), 298–322. Advance online publication. DOI: 10.1007/s12197-023-09652-9

Bhuvaneskumar, A., Sivakumar, V. J., & Pushparaj, N. (2023). Performance assessment and ranking of socially responsible companies in India using FAHP, TOPSIS and Altman Z-score. *Benchmarking, 30*(3), 736–765. *Scopus.* Advance online publication. DOI: 10.1108/BIJ-09-2021-0512

Bianchi, R. J., & Drew, M. E. (2012). Sustainable stock indices and long-term portfolio decisions. *Journal of Sustainable Finance and Investment, 2*(3–4), 303–317. *Scopus.* Advance online publication. DOI: 10.1080/20430795.2012.715577

Bilbao-Terol, A., Arenas-Parra, M., & Bilbao-Terol, C. (2023). Measuring the overall efficiency of SRI and conventional mutual funds by a diversification-consistent DEA model. *International Transactions in Operational Research, 30*(5), 2224–2256. *Scopus.* Advance online publication. DOI: 10.1111/itor.12974

Bilbao-Terol, A., Arenas-Parra, M., Cañal-Fernández, V., & Obam-Eyang, P. N. (2018). Multi-criteria analysis of the GRI sustainability reports: An application to Socially Responsible Investment. *Journal of the Operational Research Society, 69*(10), 1576–1598. *Scopus.* Advance online publication. DOI: 10.1057/s41274-017-0229-0

Brito-Ramos, S., Cortez, M. C., & Silva, F. (2024). Do Sustainability Signals Diverge? An Analysis of Labeling Schemes for Socially Responsible Investments. *Business and Society, 63*(6), 1380–1425. *Scopus.* Advance online publication. DOI: 10.1177/00076503231204613

Brodmann, J., Wuthisatian, P., & Malladi, R. K. (2023). The liquidity, performance and investor preference of socially responsible investments. *Review of Behavioral Finance, 15*(2), 224–239. *Scopus.* Advance online publication. DOI: 10.1108/RBF-09-2021-0191

Brookes, B. C. (1969). Bradford's Law and the Bibliography of Science. *Nature*, 224(5223), 953–956. DOI: 10.1038/224953a0 PMID: 4902657

Brunen, A.-C., & Laubach, O. (2022). Do sustainable consumers prefer socially responsible investments? A study among the users of robo advisors. *Journal of Banking and Finance, 136.Journal of Banking & Finance*, 136, 106314. Advance online publication. DOI: 10.1016/j.jbankfin.2021.106314

Caferra, R., & Falcone, P. M. (2023). From the "age of instability" to the "age of responsibility": Economic uncertainty and sustainable investments. *Journal of Economic Studies, 50*(6), 1297–1316. *Scopus.* Advance online publication. DOI: 10.1108/JES-06-2022-0353

Capelle-Blancard, G., & Monjon, S. (2014). The Performance of Socially Responsible Funds: Does the Screening Process Matter? *European Financial Management, 20*(3), 494–520. *Scopus.* Advance online publication. DOI: 10.1111/j.1468-036X.2012.00643.x

Carbone, V., Moatti, V., & Vinzi, V. E. (2012). Mapping Corporate Responsibility and Sustainable Supply Chains: An Exploratory Perspective. *Business Strategy and the Environment, 21*(7), 475–494. *Scopus.* Advance online publication. DOI: 10.1002/bse.1736

Carlsson Hauff, J., & Nilsson, J. (2023). Is ESG mutual fund quality in the eye of the beholder? An experimental study of investor responses to ESG fund strategies. *Business Strategy and the Environment, 32*(4), 1189–1202. *Scopus.* Advance online publication. DOI: 10.1002/bse.3181

Carvalho, L., Mota, C., & Ramos, P. (2024). Socially Responsible Investment Funds—An Analysis Applied to Funds Domiciled in the Portuguese and Spanish Markets. *Risks, 12*(1). *Scopus.*, 12(1), 9. Advance online publication. DOI: 10.3390/risks12010009

Catalano, F., Nasello, L., & Guterding, D. (2024). Quantum Computing Approach to Realistic ESG-Friendly Stock Portfolios. *Risks, 12*(4). *Scopus.*, 12(4), 66. Advance online publication. DOI: 10.3390/risks12040066

Chang, C. E., Krueger, T. M., & Witte, H. D. (2020). Relative importance of sustainability measures and costs in mutual fund selection. *Journal of Wealth Management, 23*(1), 32–46. *Scopus.* Advance online publication. DOI: 10.3905/jwm.2020.1.103

Chang, X., Fu, K., Jin, Y., & Liem, P. F. (2022). Sustainable Finance: ESG/CSR, Firm Value, and Investment Returns*. *Asia-Pacific Journal of Financial Studies, 51*(3), 325–371. *Scopus.* Advance online publication. DOI: 10.1111/ajfs.12379

Chen, X., Dong, X., & Ma, C. (2024). Investing with Purpose: The Role of CSR in Enhancing Chinese Firms' Performance in Japan. *Journal of the Knowledge Economy.Journal of the Knowledge Economy*. Advance online publication. DOI: 10.1007/s13132-024-01875-3

Consolandi, C., Phadke, H., Hawley, J., & Eccles, R. G. (2020). Material ESG Outcomes and SDG Externalities: Evaluating the Health Care Sector's Contribution to the SDGs. *Organization and Environment, 33*(4), 511–533. *Scopus.* Advance online publication. DOI: 10.1177/1086026619899795

Crifo, P., Durand, R., & Gond, J.-P. (2019). Encouraging Investors to Enable Corporate Sustainability Transitions: The Case of Responsible Investment in France. *Organization and Environment, 32*(2), 125–144. *Scopus.* Advance online publication. DOI: 10.1177/1086026619848145

Dawkins, C. E. (2018). Elevating the Role of Divestment in Socially Responsible Investing. *Journal of Business Ethics, 153*(2), 465–478. *Scopus.* Advance online publication. DOI: 10.1007/s10551-016-3356-7

de Lange, D. E. (2017). Start-up sustainability: An insurmountable cost or a life-giving investment? *Journal of Cleaner Production, 156*, 838–854. *Scopus.* Advance online publication. DOI: 10.1016/j.jclepro.2017.04.108

Devie, D., Liman, L. P., Tarigan, J., & Jie, F. (2020). Corporate social responsibility, financial performance and risk in Indonesian natural resources industry. *Social Responsibility Journal, 16*(1), 73–90. *Scopus.* Advance online publication. DOI: 10.1108/SRJ-06-2018-0155

Donthu, N., Kumar, S., Mukherjee, D., Pandey, N., & Lim, W. M. (2021). How to conduct a bibliometric analysis: An overview and guidelines. *Journal of Business Research*, 133, 285–296. DOI: 10.1016/j.jbusres.2021.04.070

Efthymiou, L., Kulshrestha, A., & Kulshrestha, S. (2023). A Study on Sustainability and ESG in the Service Sector in India: Benefits, Challenges, and Future Implications. *Administrative Sciences, 13*(7). *Administrative Sciences*, 13(7), 165. Advance online publication. DOI: 10.3390/admsci13070165

Escrig-Olmedo, E., Rivera-Lirio, J. M., Muñoz-Torres, M. J., & Fernández-Izquierdo, M. Á. (2017). Integrating multiple ESG investors' preferences into sustainable investment: A fuzzy multicriteria methodological approach. *Journal of Cleaner Production, 162*, 1334–1345. *Scopus.* Advance online publication. DOI: 10.1016/j.jclepro.2017.06.143

Ferrat, Y., Daty, F., & Burlacu, R. (2023). The role of size effects in moderating the benefits of sustainable investing. *BRQ Business Research Quarterly.Business Research Quarterly*. Advance online publication. DOI: 10.1177/23409444231162872

Filippini, M., Leippold, M., & Wekhof, T. (2024). Sustainable finance literacy and the determinants of sustainable investing. *Journal of Banking & Finance*, 163, 107167. DOI: 10.1016/j.jbankfin.2024.107167

Firdaus Khan, M. R. (2021). Socially Responsible Investing and Sustainable Indices: A Sustainability Agenda. *Indian Journal of Corporate Governance, 14*(2), 209–225. *Scopus.* Advance online publication. DOI: 10.1177/09746862211045757

Folger-Laronde, Z., Pashang, S., Feor, L., & ElAlfy, A. (2022). ESG ratings and financial performance of exchange-traded funds during the COVID-19 pandemic. *Journal of Sustainable Finance and Investment, 12*(2), 490–496. *Scopus.* Advance online publication. DOI: 10.1080/20430795.2020.1782814

Freeman, M. C., & Groom, B. (2013). Biodiversity valuation and the discount rate problem. *Accounting, Auditing and Accountability Journal, 26*(5), 715–745. *Scopus.* Advance online publication. DOI: 10.1108/AAAJ-02-2013-1226

Galeone, G., Ranaldo, S., Shini, M., & Dicuonzo, G. (2023). SUSTAINABILITY REPORTING: EVIDENCE FROM GLOBAL SYSTEMICALLY IMPORTANT BANKS (G-SIBs). *Journal of Financial Management, Markets and Institutions, 11*(2). *Scopus.*, 11(2), 2350011. Advance online publication. DOI: 10.1142/S2282717X23500111

Gallego-Losada, R., Montero-Navarro, A., Rodríguez-Sánchez, J.-L., & González-Torres, T. (2022). Retirement planning and financial literacy, at the crossroads. A bibliometric analysis. In *Finance Research Letters* (Vol. 44). Elsevier Ltd., DOI: 10.1016/j.frl.2021.102109

Gandullia, L., & Piserà, S. (2020). Do income taxes affect corporate social responsibility? Evidence from European-listed companies. *Corporate Social Responsibility and Environmental Management, 27*(2), 1017–1027. *Scopus.* Advance online publication. DOI: 10.1002/csr.1862

Gangi, F., & Varrone, N. (2018). Screening activities by socially responsible funds: A matter of agency? *Journal of Cleaner Production, 197*, 842–855. *Scopus.* Advance online publication. DOI: 10.1016/j.jclepro.2018.06.228

Geczy, C. C., Stambaugh, R. F., & Levin, D. (2021). Investing in Socially Responsible Mutual Funds. *Review of Asset Pricing Studies, 11*(2), 309–351. *Scopus.* Advance online publication. DOI: 10.1093/rapstu/raab004

Gok, I. Y., Duranay, S., & Uzunoglu Unlu, H. (2020). Co-movement dynamics of sustainability indices: Investigating the diversification opportunities through FTSE4Good index family and Borsa Istanbul sustainability index. *Social Responsibility Journal, 16*(8), 1475–1487. *Scopus.* Advance online publication. DOI: 10.1108/SRJ-02-2019-0073

Gutsche, G., Nakai, M., & Arimura, T. H. (2021). Revisiting the determinants of individual sustainable investment—The case of Japan. *Journal of Behavioral and Experimental Finance*, 30, 100497. DOI: 10.1016/j.jbef.2021.100497

Gutsche, G., Wetzel, H., & Ziegler, A. (2023). Determinants of individual sustainable investment behavior—A framed field experiment. *Journal of Economic Behavior & Organization*, 209, 491–508. DOI: 10.1016/j.jebo.2023.03.016

Haddaway, N. R., Page, M. J., Pritchard, C. C., & McGuinness, L. A. (2022). *PRISMA2020*: An R package and Shiny app for producing PRISMA 2020-compliant flow diagrams, with interactivity for optimised digital transparency and Open Synthesis. *Campbell Systematic Reviews*, 18(2), e1230. DOI: 10.1002/cl2.1230 PMID: 36911350

Haq, I. U. (2023). Time-frequency comovement among green financial assets and cryptocurrency uncertainties. *Economic Notes, 52*(1). *Economic Notes*, 52(1), e12216. Advance online publication. DOI: 10.1111/ecno.12216

Hlophe, S. L., & Ellis, D. (2024). Changing consumer attitudes to make the Corporate Social Responsibility investment in sustainable fish production, a worthwhile investment to corporates. *Corporate Social Responsibility and Environmental Management, 31*(1), 344–356. *Scopus.* Advance online publication. DOI: 10.1002/csr.2573

Hysa, E., Imeraj, E., Feruni, N., Panait, M., & Vasile, V. (2022). COVID-19—A Black Swan for Foreign Direct Investment: Evidence from European Countries. *Journal of Risk and Financial Management, 15*(4). *Journal of Risk and Financial Management*, 15(4), 156. Advance online publication. DOI: 10.3390/jrfm15040156

Ingale, K. K., & Paluri, R. A. (2022). Financial literacy and financial behaviour: A bibliometric analysis. *Review of Behavioral Finance*, 14(1), 130–154. DOI: 10.1108/RBF-06-2020-0141

Irfan, M. (2021). Do Shariah Indices converge Evidence from Gulf Cooperation Council countries. *International Journal of Business Excellence*, 23(2), 251. DOI: 10.1504/IJBEX.2021.113448

Irfan, M., Elhoseny, M., Kassim, S., & Metawa, N. (Eds.). (2023). *Advanced Machine Learning Algorithms for Complex Financial Applications*. IGI Global., DOI: 10.4018/978-1-6684-4483-2

Irfan, M., & Elmogy, M. Shabri Abd. Majid, M., & El-Sappagh, S. (Eds.). (2024). *The Impact of AI Innovation on Financial Sectors in the Era of Industry 5.0:* IGI Global. DOI: 10.4018/979-8-3693-0082-4

Irfan, M., Elmogy, M., Gupta, S., Khalifa, F., & Dias, R. T. (Eds.). (2024). *AI-Driven Decentralized Finance and the Future of Finance*. IGI Global., DOI: 10.4018/979-8-3693-6321-8

Irfan, M., Hussainey, K., Bukhari, S. A. C., & Nam, Y. (Eds.). (2024). *Issues of Sustainability in AI and New-Age Thematic Investing*. IGI Global., DOI: 10.4018/979-8-3693-3282-5

Irfan, M., Kadry, S., Sharif, M., & Khan, H. U. (Eds.). (2023). *Fintech Applications in Islamic Finance: AI, Machine Learning, and Blockchain Techniques*. IGI Global., DOI: 10.4018/979-8-3693-1038-0

Janicka, M. (2016). Financial markets and the challenges of sustainable growth. *Comparative Economic Research, 19*(2), 27–41. *Scopus.* Advance online publication. DOI: 10.1515/cer-2016-0011

Juddoo, K., Malki, I., Mathew, S., & Sivaprasad, S. (2023). An impact investment strategy. *Review of Quantitative Finance and Accounting, 61*(1), 177–211. *Scopus.* Advance online publication. DOI: 10.1007/s11156-023-01149-0

Kar, D., & Patro, B. (2024). Unravelling the Impact of Financial Literacy on the Intention of Indian Retail Investors to Adopt Socially Responsible Investments: The Interplay of Social Self-Efficacy as a Mediating Mechanism. *Global Business Review.Global Business Review*, 09721509231223571. Advance online publication. DOI: 10.1177/09721509231223571

Khongwir, C. M., & Sharmiladevi, J. C. (2023). A Bibliometric Analysis on Financial Inclusion and Financial Literacy – Analyzing the Current Research Trends. In *Indian Journal of Finance* (Vol. 17, Issue 2, pp. 27–53). Associated Management Consultants Pvt. Ltd. DOI: 10.17010/ijf/2023/v17i2/172638

Kobo, K. L., & Ngwakwe, C. C. (2017). Relating corporate social investment with financial performance. *Investment Management and Financial Innovations, 14*(2), 367–375. *Scopus*. Advance online publication. DOI: 10.21511/imfi.14(2-2).2017.08

Kopp, A., Barber, D., Cottet, R., & Susinno, G. (2022). How to improve the ESG profile of portfolios while keeping a similar risk-adjusted return. [Scopus.]. *Journal of Risk Management in Financial Institutions*, 15(1), 51–71. DOI: 10.69554/JISS7490

Latiff, N., & Marimuthu, F. (2021). Water-related sustainability reporting practices amongst South African mining and non-mining corporations. *Environmental Economics, 12*(1), 112–123. *Scopus*. Advance online publication. DOI: 10.21511/ee.12(1).2021.10

Liu, W., & Jing, K. (2024). ESG portfolio for TDFs with time-varying higher moments and cardinality constraint. *International Transactions in Operational Research, 31*(6), 4270–4295. *Scopus*. Advance online publication. DOI: 10.1111/itor.13364

Lusardi, A., & Tufano, P. (2015). Debt literacy, financial experiences, and overindebtedness. *Journal of Pension Economics and Finance*, 14(4), 332–368. DOI: 10.1017/S1474747215000232

Malchyk, M. V., Popko, O. V., Oplachko, I. O., Martyniuk, O. V., & Hontarenko, N. A. (2020). Tools for marketing management of industrial enterprises in Ukraine based on the principles of sustainable development. *International Journal of Management, 11*(4), 385–394. *Scopus*. Advance online publication. DOI: 10.34218/IJM.11.4.2020.038

Malpani, R., Baral, M. M., Panigrahi, R. R., & Chittipaka, V. (2024). Unveiling the dynamic nexus between corporate social responsibility, innovations and financial performances in 21st-century Indian start-ups. *The International Journal of Organizational Analysis*. Advance online publication. DOI: 10.1108/IJOA-01-2024-4239

Marzuki, A., Nor, F. M., Ramli, N. A., Basah, M. Y. A., & Aziz, M. R. A. (2023). The Influence of ESG, SRI, Ethical, and Impact Investing Activities on Portfolio and Financial Performance—Bibliometric Analysis/Mapping and Clustering Analysis. *Journal of Risk and Financial Management, 16*(7). *Journal of Risk and Financial Management*, 16(7), 321. Advance online publication. DOI: 10.3390/jrfm16070321

Matallín-Sáez, J. C., Soler-Domínguez, A., Tortosa-Ausina, E., & de Mingo-López, D. V. (2019). Ethical strategy focus and mutual fund management: Performance and persistence. *Journal of Cleaner Production, 213*, 618–633. *Scopus*. Advance online publication. DOI: 10.1016/j.jclepro.2018.12.130

Miglietta, F., Di Martino, G., & Fanelli, V. (2023). The environmental policy of the Norwegian Government Pension Fund-Global and investors' reaction over time. *Business Strategy and the Environment, 32*(6), 3721–3736. *Scopus.* Advance online publication. DOI: 10.1002/bse.3324

Momparler, A., Carmona, P., & Climent, F. (2024). Catalyzing Sustainable Investment: Revealing ESG Power in Predicting Fund Performance with Machine Learning. *Computational Economics.Computational Economics*. Advance online publication. DOI: 10.1007/s10614-024-10618-0

Naeem, M. A., Karim, S., Rabbani, M. R., Bashar, A., & Kumar, S. (2023). Current state and future directions of green and sustainable finance: A bibliometric analysis. *Qualitative Research in Financial Markets, 15*(4), 608–629. *Scopus.* Advance online publication. DOI: 10.1108/QRFM-10-2021-0174

Nikolakis, W., Cohen, D. H., & Nelson, H. W. (2012). What matters for socially responsible investment (SRI) in the natural resources sectors? SRI mutual funds and forestry in North America. *Journal of Sustainable Finance and Investment, 2*(2), 136–151. *Scopus.* Advance online publication. DOI: 10.1080/20430795.2012.690724

Nikolakis, W., Nelson, H. W., & Cohen, D. H. (2014). Who Pays Attention to Indigenous Peoples in Sustainable Development and Why? Evidence From Socially Responsible Investment Mutual Funds in North America. *Organization and Environment, 27*(4), 368–382. *Scopus.* Advance online publication. DOI: 10.1177/1086026614546812

Niszczota, P., & Błaszczyński, J. (2024). Hard to digest investments: People oppose investment in both conventional and cultured meat producers. *Ecological Economics, 218.Ecological Economics*, 218, 108094. Advance online publication. DOI: 10.1016/j.ecolecon.2023.108094

Nofsinger, J. R., & Varma, A. (2023). Keeping Promises? Mutual Funds' Investment Objectives and Impact of Carbon Risk Disclosures. *Journal of Business Ethics, 187*(3), 493–516. *Scopus.* Advance online publication. DOI: 10.1007/s10551-022-05264-1

Ortas, E., & Moneva, J. M. (2011). Sustainability stock exchange indexes and investor expectations: Multivariate evidence from DJSI-Stoxx. *Revista Espanola de Financiacion y Contabilidad, 40*(151), 395–416. *Scopus.* Advance online publication. DOI: 10.1080/02102412.2011.10779706

Palma-Ruiz, J. M., Castillo-Apraiz, J., & Gómez-Martínez, R. (2020). Socially responsible investing as a competitive strategy for trading companies in times of upheaval amid covid-19: Evidence from spain. *International Journal of Financial Studies, 8*(3), 1–13. *Scopus.* Advance online publication. DOI: 10.3390/ijfs8030041

Pereira, P., Cortez, M. C., & Silva, F. (2019). Socially responsible investing and the performance of Eurozone corporate bond portfolios. *Corporate Social Responsibility and Environmental Management, 26*(6), 1407–1422. *Scopus.* Advance online publication. DOI: 10.1002/csr.1756

Praseeda, C. (2018). Socially Responsible Investment, Microfinance and Banking: Creating Value by Synergy. *Indian Journal of Corporate Governance, 11*(1), 69–87. *Scopus.* Advance online publication. DOI: 10.1177/0974686218769200

Richardson, B. J., & Cragg, W. (2010). Being virtuous and prosperous:Sris conflicting goals. *Journal of Business Ethics, 92*(SUPPL 1), 21–39. *Scopus.* Advance online publication. DOI: 10.1007/s10551-010-0632-9

Rossetto, D. E., Bernardes, R. C., Borini, F. M., & Gattaz, C. C. (2018). Structure and evolution of innovation research in the last 60 years: Review and future trends in the field of business through the citations and co-citations analysis. *Scientometrics*, 115(3), 1329–1363. DOI: 10.1007/s11192-018-2709-7

Sadeqi-Arani, Z., & Kadkhodaie, A. (2023). A bibliometric analysis of the application of machine learning methods in the petroleum industry. *Results in Engineering*, 20, 101518. DOI: 10.1016/j.rineng.2023.101518

Said, M. T., & ElBannan, M. A. (2024). Do ESG ratings and COVID-19 severity score predict stock behavior and market perception? Evidence from emerging markets. *Review of Accounting and Finance, 23*(2), 222–255. *Scopus.* Advance online publication. DOI: 10.1108/RAF-03-2023-0083

Saini, M. (2023). Surviving crisis: The role of sustainable investments in navigating the impact of the Russia–Ukraine war. *International Journal of Diplomacy and Economy, 9*(2), 189–204. *Scopus.* Advance online publication. DOI: 10.1504/IJDIPE.2023.134637

Sairally, B. S. (2015). INTEGRATING ENVIRONMENTAL, SOCIAL AND GOVERNANCE (ESG) FACTORS IN ISLAMIC FINANCE: TOWARDS THE REALISATION OF MAQĀ ID AL-SHARĪʿAH. [Scopus.]. *ISRA International Journal of Islamic Finance*, 7(2), 145–154.

Schaefer, H., Gromer, C., & Neligan, A. (2012). The demand of sustainable property investments in Germany: An explorative empirical study. *Journal of Property Investment & Finance, 30*(1), 5–17. *Scopus.* Advance online publication. DOI: 10.1108/14635781211194773

Scholtens, B., & Willard, F. (2024). One size does not fit all: Responsible investor motivation and investment performance. *Corporate Social Responsibility and Environmental Management.Corporate Social Responsibility and Environmental Management*, 31(6), 6075–6082. Advance online publication. DOI: 10.1002/csr.2905

Selmi, R., Hammoudeh, S., Errami, Y., & Wohar, M. E. (2021). Is COVID-19 Related Anxiety an Accelerator for Responsible and Sustainable Investing? A Sentiment Analysis. *Applied Economics, 53*(13), 1528–1539. *Scopus.* Advance online publication. DOI: 10.1080/00036846.2020.1834501

Shehzad, A., & Khan, K. I. (2024). Impediments of social responsibility investment adoption system: A post-pandemic qualitative analysis. *Qualitative Research in Financial Markets.Scopus.* Advance online publication. DOI: 10.1108/QRFM-04-2023-0089

Shevchenko, K., McManus, R., & Haddock-Fraser, J. (2015). UK pension sustainability and fund manager governance: Agent duties to the principal. *Journal of Sustainable Finance and Investment, 5*(4), 205–209. *Scopus.* Advance online publication. DOI: 10.1080/20430795.2015.1106209

Stambaugh, R. F., & Taylor, L. A. (2021). Sustainable investing in equilibrium. *Journal of Financial Economics, 142*(2), 550–571. *Scopus.* Advance online publication. DOI: 10.1016/j.jfineco.2020.12.011

Sugiharto, M. E., Probohudono, A. N., Suhardjanto, D., & Widarjo, W. (2024). A bibliometric analysis of evolving trends in CEO characteristics and financial performance research. *Cogent Business and Management, 11*(1). *Scopus.*, 11(1), 2381089. Advance online publication. DOI: 10.1080/23311975.2024.2381089

Tomar, S., Kumar, S., & Sureka, R. (2021). Financial Planning for Retirement: Bibliometric Analysis and Future Research Directions. In *Journal of Financial Counseling and Planning* (Vol. 32, Issue 2, pp. 344–362). Springer Publishing Company. DOI: 10.1891/JFCP-19-00062

Tripathi, V., & Kaur, A. (2020). Socially responsible investing: Performance evaluation of BRICS nations. *Journal of Advances in Management Research, 17*(4), 525–547. *Scopus.* Advance online publication. DOI: 10.1108/JAMR-02-2020-0020

Tripathi, V., & Kaur, A. (2022). Does Socially Responsible Investing Pay in Developing Countries? A Comparative Study Across Select Developed and Developing Markets. *FIIB Business Review, 11*(2), 189–205. *Scopus.* Advance online publication. DOI: 10.1177/2319714520980288

Valadkhani, A., & O'Mahony, B. (2024). Sustainable investing in extreme market conditions: Doing well while doing good. *Journal of Economic Studies.Journal of Economic Studies (Glasgow, Scotland).* Advance online publication. DOI: 10.1108/JES-11-2023-0626

Verma, S., & Gustafsson, A. (2020). Investigating the emerging COVID-19 research trends in the field of business and management: A bibliometric analysis approach. *Journal of Business Research*, 118, 253–261. DOI: 10.1016/j.jbusres.2020.06.057 PMID: 32834211

Verma, S., & Khanna, A. (2024). The Influence of Emotions and Social Value Orientation on Risk Tolerance and Sustainable Investment Choices. *Australasian Accounting, Business and Finance Journal, 18*(3), 331–351. *Scopus.* Advance online publication. DOI: 10.14453/aabfj.v18i3.17

Weston, P., & Nnadi, M. (2023). Evaluation of strategic and financial variables of corporate sustainability and ESG policies on corporate finance performance. *Journal of Sustainable Finance and Investment, 13*(2), 1058–1074. *Scopus.* Advance online publication. DOI: 10.1080/20430795.2021.1883984

Witkowska, J. (2023). The Role of FDI in the Sustainable Development of the European Union. *Comparative Economic Research, 26*(1), 21–43. *Scopus.* Advance online publication. DOI: 10.18778/1508-2008.26.02

Yumnam, G., Gyanendra, Y., & Singh, C. I. (2024). A systematic bibliometric review of the global research dynamics of United Nations Sustainable Development Goals 2030. *Sustainable Futures : An Applied Journal of Technology, Environment and Society*, 7, 100192. DOI: 10.1016/j.sftr.2024.100192

Chapter 9
The Future of Indigenous Inclusivity:
Unlocking Finance for Economic Development

Nilesh Kharche
https://orcid.org/0000-0002-4686-9663
Sri Balaji University, Pune's Balaji Institute of Technology and Management, India

Shakeeb Mohammad Mir
Christ University, India

Rui Dias
https://orcid.org/0000-0002-6138-3098
Escola Superior de Ciências Empresariais, Instituto Politécnico de Setúbal, Portugal

ABSTRACT

The chapter "The Future of Indigenous Inclusivity: Unlocking Finance for Economic Development" emphasizes the need to integrate Indigenous communities into economic development. It addresses historical and current obstacles faced by Indigenous peoples, including structural hurdles, socioeconomic gaps, and geographic limitations. The chapter offers strategies for capacity building, customized financial products, and policy changes to improve financial inclusion. It also highlights the importance of technology and multi-stakeholder partnerships for economic empowerment. The chapter emphasizes the need for creative funding methods and international cooperation to fully realize Indigenous communities' economic potential and create a more equitable global economy.

1. INTRODUCTION

Without the active involvement and inclusion of Indigenous groups, the path to economic growth is not complete. These historically underprivileged groups encounter particular difficulties in obtaining the financial resources necessary for their environmental stewardship and economic empowerment. This chapter explores ways to unlock funding for economic growth in order to dive into the future of Indige-

DOI: 10.4018/979-8-3693-7924-0.ch009

nous inclusiveness. It examines the existing situation, pinpoints obstacles, and offers creative fixes and industry best practices to improve Indigenous peoples' economic engagement and financial inclusion.

It is more important than ever to include Indigenous communities in the larger context of economic growth. Due to institutional obstacles, social inequality, and physical remoteness, indigenous peoples across the world have traditionally had significant difficulties obtaining financial resources. Indigenous communities have frequently been unable to fully engage in and reap the benefits of economic growth and development projects due to these obstacles. Addressing these obstacles and maximizing the potential of Indigenous communities via creative financial methods and supporting legislation is essential as we transition to a more sustainable and inclusive global economy.

Economic growth may be greatly aided by the amount of information, cultural legacy, and distinctive viewpoints that indigenous populations possess. Their customs and interactions with the environment provide important information about resilience and sustainable resource management. However, it will take a concentrated effort to get over the structural barriers that Indigenous peoples must overcome in order to achieve genuine economic inclusion. This entails tackling problems including restricted financial services accessibility, a dearth of customized financial solutions, and insufficient participation in decision-making procedures.

Systemic obstacles include restricted access to financial resources, historical exclusion from mainstream economies, and restrictive land-use rules have historically hindered the economic progress of Indigenous peoples. According to recent studies, financial inclusion and economic self-determination are essential for Indigenous communities to build sustainable economies (Cornell & Kalt, 2010; Foley, 2019).

Access to finance and financial inclusion are essential for resilience and self-governance in Indigenous communities, according to a review of seminal work on economic sovereignty (Washington, 2023, Khub et al., 2024). However, systemic disparities frequently impede these goals, necessitating creative support networks and funding sources.

This chapter explores the complex strategy required to get funding for Indigenous communities' economic growth. It highlights effective programs and best practices that have made major progress in this area and examines the historical background and contemporary issues that have influenced the financial inclusion of Indigenous peoples. The chapter also looks at how innovation and technology may help close the gap in financial inclusion, highlighting the significance of locally generated and culturally appropriate solutions. This chapter attempts to offer a thorough grasp of how financial inclusion may be accomplished for Indigenous communities by examining case studies and outlining proactive tactics. It emphasizes the significance of legislative changes that promote Indigenous economic empowerment, the creation of customized financial products and services, and capacity-building initiatives. It also highlights the importance of multi-stakeholder partnerships, such as those involving governments, financial institutions, non-governmental organizations, and Indigenous leaders.

In the end, this chapter promotes an inclusive, comprehensive strategy for sustainable development that acknowledges and upholds the rights and goals of Indigenous peoples. It demands a paradigm change in the planning and execution of financial systems in order to make them inclusive, egalitarian, and conducive to the long-term prosperity and well-being of Indigenous communities. We can build a more equitable and sustainable future where Indigenous peoples are empowered and actively involved in the global economy by working together.

1.1 Historical Background on Indigenous Economic Exclusion

The intricate combination of colonial practices, legal restrictions, racial discrimination, and cultural erasure forms the historical foundation of Indigenous economic marginalization. These elements have limited Indigenous populations' access to resources, economic participation, and capacity to accumulate sustainable wealth, hence contributing to their economic marginalization. The history of these exclusions must be acknowledged and addressed in order to unleash funding for economic growth and advance inclusion. We can start establishing fair chances for economic empowerment and growth by recognizing the historical background and comprehending the structural obstacles that Indigenous communities encounter. Policies from the colonial past, which frequently included social marginalization, institutional exploitation, and land confiscation, are the cause of Indigenous economic exclusion. These measures established structural obstacles to contemporary finance and property rights in addition to upending Indigenous economic systems.

Indigenous communities have historically been viewed through a deficit lens, as being incapable of engaging in formal economies because they lack the necessary skills or resources. Lack of access to finance, business networks, and financial literacy chances has been sustained by these views. In spite of these obstacles, Indigenous people have managed to sustain resilient economic practices inside informal economies by depending on small-scale trading, subsistence farming, and group solidarity. It is essential to comprehend this resilience in order to develop inclusive finance models that respect Indigenous values and practices.

1.2 Current State of Indigenous Economic Inclusivity

Both major obstacles and new opportunities are present in the current condition of Indigenous economic inclusiveness. Even while Indigenous people have made significant progress in claiming their economic rights and working toward self-determination, structural obstacles still stand in the way of their full involvement in the domestic and international markets. Historical injustices, legal systems that disregard customary land tenure, and systemic disparities in financial access are the main causes of economic marginalization. Nonetheless, there is increasing movement to develop inclusive, sustainable, and Indigenous-specific financial institutions, which gives promise for future economic empowerment.

The socioeconomic circumstances of Indigenous populations have been significantly influenced by centuries of colonialism, marginalization, and institutionalized discrimination. Due to the restricted access to financial resources brought about by these historical injustices, poverty has increased, and economic advancement has been impeded. Notwithstanding these obstacles, Indigenous groups are making more and more claims to their economic rights and making contributions to a range of industries, such as technology, renewable energy, tourism, and agriculture. When compared to non-Indigenous groups, there are still notable differences in employment rates, income levels, and access to financial services. Financial exclusion results from the lack of access to traditional banking services in many Indigenous communities, particularly those in rural places. Due to their lack of collateral and past financial marginalization, Indigenous people and companies frequently find it difficult to fulfill traditional creditworthiness standards. Indigenous populations frequently have access to more costly financial products with higher fees and interest rates. Indigenous peoples' capacity to receive funds and manage financial institutions is further hampered by lower levels of financial literacy and education.

Research shows that Indigenous communities continue to face a persistent disparity in financial accessibility when compared to their non-Indigenous peers. Systemic problems that affect loan collateral requirements include land ownership concerns, a lack of banking infrastructure, and mistrust of financial institutions, according to research (Anderson & Kayseas, 2004; Jackson & Yarwood, 2021).

According to published research, one factor contributing to the exclusion of Indigenous populations from mainstream banking is the dearth of culturally appropriate financial services and products (Peters, 2020). Indigenous communities frequently feature collective ownership norms, traditional governance frameworks, and community landholding patterns, all of which financial models have historically overlooked (Kingsbury, 2018). Furthermore, socioeconomic variables that limit Indigenous peoples' access to credit and other financial services include lower income levels and a lack of official credit records (Peredo & Chrisman, 2019). This is covered in studies on financial exclusion.

There have been both setbacks and advancements in the current level of Indigenous economic inclusiveness. Even while there are still many major impediments, efforts to remove them and provide Indigenous peoples the chance to fully engage in economic systems are gaining traction. The future of Indigenous economic inclusion holds the potential for revolutionary change—one in which financial systems are equitable, accessible, and in line with the values and goals of Indigenous peoples—by supporting Indigenous-led financial initiatives, developing culturally relevant financial products, and establishing supportive policies

2. CHALLENGES IN UNLOCKING FINANCE FOR INDIGENOUS COMMUNITIES

A complicated network of structural, institutional, and historical impediments makes it difficult for Indigenous communities to get financing. These issues prolong cycles of economic marginalization and underdevelopment in addition to impeding Indigenous peoples' access to money. The challenges of obtaining financial resources are exacerbated by legal, social, and cultural elements that interact in ways that conventional financial institutions frequently ignore. The main obstacles to enabling finance for Indigenous communities are listed in this section. These include problems with land rights, financial literacy, legal frameworks, and the scarcity of financial services and products that are suitable for Indigenous cultures (Venkateswaran, 2023).

Indigenous communities face numerous challenges in economic development, including historical marginalization, geographical isolation, inadequate infrastructure, and lack of tailored financial products and services. These barriers hinder their ability to accumulate capital and leverage assets for economic growth. Geographical and infrastructural challenges, such as geographical isolation, inadequate infrastructure, and higher costs of service delivery, limit their access to financial services and hinder sustainable development projects. Traditional lending methods may be prohibitive for Indigenous individuals and businesses, limiting their economic growth. Institutional and regulatory constraints, such as complex legal frameworks, bureaucratic challenges, and institutional biases, can delay development projects and hinder sustainable growth. Cultural and social factors, such as deep-seated mistrust of financial institutions and unique economic practices, also impact their ability to integrate into mainstream financial systems. Internal leadership and governance challenges also impact their ability to engage with external financial actors and manage development projects (Sakapaji et al., 2024).

Indigenous communities have historical, institutional, and cultural obstacles that need for creative solutions, inclusive financial products, enabling legislative frameworks, and solid collaborations. Indigenous communities will be able to fully engage in economic growth as a result. Researchers are looking at novel financial models including trust funds, community-based lending circles, and Indigenous financial institutions that aim to improve inclusion. These models improve the application and acceptance of financial practices by bringing them into line with Indigenous worldviews (Sullivan & Hill, 2019).

The effectiveness of Indigenous-led financial institutions, which frequently offer specialized services including microloans, financial literacy training, and mentorship, is highlighted in the literature (Smith, 2021). By emphasizing community values and Indigenous economic empowerment, these institutions have demonstrated greater success rates (Foley & Wheeler, 2018). In order to reduce investment risks in Indigenous businesses, other study recommends implementing "blended finance" models, which combine funding from the public and private sectors. This concept is becoming more and more popular as a way to grow infrastructure projects and Indigenous commercial endeavors (Jackson, 2020).

Indigenous communities confront several obstacles to financial access, many of which have their roots in structural, systemic, and historical problems. The financial marginalization of Indigenous peoples is caused by a number of factors, including prejudice, cultural disconnection, financial illiteracy, restricted access to traditional financial services, insecure land tenure, and insufficient government policies. Financial institutions, governments, and Indigenous communities themselves must work together to develop solutions that are culturally appropriate, community-driven, and considerate of Indigenous rights and governance in order to remove these obstacles. Unlocking the potential of Indigenous communities and making sure they have the means, opportunity, and resources to prosper in the global economy depend on addressing these issues.

3. INNOVATIVE FINANCIAL SOLUTIONS FOR INDIGENOUS ECONOMIC DEVELOPMENT

Enhancing financial inclusion for Indigenous communities is a multifaceted challenge that requires a comprehensive and culturally sensitive approach. Effective strategies must address the unique barriers faced by these communities while leveraging their strengths and fostering sustainable economic development. The following strategies outline actionable steps to improve financial inclusion for Indigenous peoples.

The text proposes tailored financial products and services for Indigenous communities, including culturally relevant banking services, microfinance, cooperative models, flexible lending criteria, alternative credit assessments, and reduced collateral requirements. It emphasizes the need for culturally appropriate financial education programs, business development services, innovation hubs, and business incubators to support Indigenous entrepreneurs. The text also suggests leveraging technology, such as mobile banking and digital financial services, to overcome geographical barriers and provide accessible financial solutions. It advocates for inclusive policies that promote financial inclusion and protect Indigenous peoples' rights, advocating for legislation supporting microfinance, cooperative banking, and alternative credit assessments (Irfan, Elmogy, Majid, & El-Sappagh, 2023).. The text also highlights the importance of public-private partnerships, international cooperation, community-driven approaches, and capacity building for local Indigenous financial institutions to improve financial inclusion. It also highlights the need for green financing, social impact investment, and cultural sensitivity training in sustainable development. The text also highlights the importance of respecting traditional practices and enhancing engagement with Indigenous communities through financial inclusion strategies.

Enhancing financial inclusion for Indigenous communities requires a comprehensive, culturally sensitive approach that considers barriers rooted in geography, history, institutions, structure, culture, and society. By implementing tailored financial products and services, boosting financial literacy and capacity, leveraging technology, promoting inclusive policies and regulatory frameworks, promoting multi-stakeholder partnerships, and accounting for social and environmental factors, we can create a more sustainable and equitable financial system. These strategies give Indigenous communities economic power while also promoting their long-term development and overall well-being (Irfan, Elmogy, Majid, & El-Sappagh, 2023, Gumbo, 2023).

The obstacles to economic participation and development are being addressed in part by creative financial solutions that are adapted to the particular requirements and values of Indigenous communities. These strategies, which range from digital and blended finance to community-based lending models and Indigenous-led financial institutions, provide new avenues for Indigenous peoples to get financing, launch enterprises, and become financially independent over the long run. These solutions can open the door to a more fair, sustainable, and inclusive future for Indigenous communities throughout the world by utilizing financial innovation while honoring Indigenous traditional values and governance structures.

4. THE ROLE OF STAKEHOLDERS

The cooperation of all parties is essential to the future of Indigenous inclusion and the release of funds for economic growth. In order to address the particular difficulties that Indigenous communities experience and to create an atmosphere that supports sustainability and economic development, each stakeholder is essential. The responsibilities of important stakeholders and the contributions they may make to accomplishing these objectives are covered in detail in this section.

Indigenous communities play a crucial role in promoting financial inclusion and self-determination, requiring skill development and advocacy for sustainable development. Governments must develop inclusive policies, regulatory frameworks, infrastructure investment, and public services to protect Indigenous peoples' rights. Financial institutions should develop tailored products and services for Indigenous communities, including culturally relevant savings accounts, loans, insurance, and investment products. Corporate social responsibility initiatives can support local development projects and capacity-building efforts. Inclusive practices, such as employing Indigenous staff and involving community representatives, enhance trust and collaboration. Non-Governmental Organizations (NGOs) play a vital role in advocating for Indigenous communities' rights, influencing policy changes, and raising awareness about their challenges. They provide support services like legal assistance, financial education, and business development training, helping Indigenous communities build economic empowerment capacity.

International organizations can support Indigenous communities' development projects and capacity-building initiatives, promoting sustainable economic development. They can also offer technical assistance in areas like financial inclusion, sustainable development, and governance. They can influence global policy frameworks to prioritize Indigenous rights and financial inclusion and facilitate knowledge sharing among countries and communities. The private sector can invest in businesses and projects that benefit Indigenous communities through impact investing, technological innovation, and corporate partnerships, enhancing financial inclusion, supporting sustainable development, and creating jobs. Universities can develop educational programs on financial literacy, entrepreneurship, and sustainable development for Indigenous students and communities, and engage with communities through outreach programs and collaborative projects (Kajiita, 2024).

Current research emphasizes how important government regulations are in determining Indigenous peoples' access to financing. The funding gap can be filled in part by government grants, tax breaks, and incentives aimed toward Indigenous companies (Hunt & Gray, 2021). Nonetheless, policy framework analysis frequently shows a discrepancy between goals and actual results. Many programs have little effect because they either don't effectively incorporate Indigenous people in their creation or don't address underlying structural impediments (Jones, 2019).

Some governments are increasingly adopting more inclusive strategies, making sure that programs acknowledge Indigenous governance institutions, and integrating feedback from Indigenous communities in the creation of policies (King & Brown, 2020). There is proof that these kinds of cooperative activities may increase the efficacy of policies and promote Indigenous confidence in government programs.

For Indigenous communities to achieve financial inclusion and sustainable development, a wide range of stakeholders must actively engage in and work together. By working together, these parties can solve the unique challenges faced by Indigenous peoples and create an environment that supports their economic development. From developing specialized financial services and products to promoting inclusive policies and laws, each stakeholder has a crucial role to play. By collaborating and demonstrating our dedication to this objective, we can support Indigenous communities in realizing their full potential and making a positive impact on a more equitable and sustainable global economy.

A wide range of stakeholders must actively work together to unlock finance for Indigenous communities, each of whom must make a distinctive contribution to removing the obstacles to financial inclusion. With the help of governments, financial institutions, development organizations, investors, and academic institutions, indigenous communities themselves must assume a leading role in determining their economic destiny. These stakeholders can build a more prosperous, sustainable, and inclusive future for Indigenous communities around the world by establishing partnerships that uphold Indigenous rights, cultures, and governance structures and by creating financial solutions that are suited to the unique needs of Indigenous peoples.

5. INDIGENOUS LAND RIGHTS AND FINANCIAL LEVERAGE

Indigenous land rights serve as a basis for economic empowerment in addition to cultural heritage preservation. Indigenous communities may unleash the economic potential of their lands by resolving the historical issues around land tenure, establishing financial structures that support them, and guaranteeing legal legitimacy. Land may be used as a potent asset for sustainable economic growth as well as a symbol of identity through creative finance models, regulatory change, and capacity-building initiatives. To guarantee that Indigenous peoples have equitable access to the resources they need to prosper, this approach necessitates striking a delicate balance between upholding traditional governance structures and incorporating them into the global financial system.

Indigenous economic development is based on the rights to own and utilize land. According to research, Indigenous people are unable to utilize land as collateral due to restricted land-use rules or a lack of land tenure, which restricts their access to financial resources (Smith & Hill, 2020).

Indigenous land may be utilized as financial leverage without giving up control thanks to certain creative approaches that incorporate collaborations between financial institutions and Indigenous communities (Davidson, 2019). Indigenous communities have the ability to raise money while preserving their cultural identity, according to research on "land-backed" financing approaches (Johnson & Peters, 2021). Additionally, research highlights the necessity of legislative changes that uphold Indigenous land rights, since this would improve financial inclusion and facilitate long-term economic planning (Anderson & Hoxie, 2018).

The cornerstone for obtaining funding for the economic development of Indigenous peoples is their land rights. The legal framework required to access money, leverage land as collateral, and create land-based ventures that promote sustainable economic growth is provided by secure land tenure. Financial leverage, however, necessitates removing structural and historical obstacles to land recognition, establishing legal frameworks that honor Indigenous governance, and building creative financial structures that are consistent with Indigenous values. To establish solutions that acknowledge the special significance of land for Indigenous peoples and empower them to use it for sustainable development and economic empowerment, governments, financial institutions, and Indigenous communities must collaborate. Indigenous communities may achieve their economic potential while preserving their cultural identity and environmental stewardship via these cooperative endeavors.

5. CASE STUDIES ON SUCCESSFUL INDIGENOUS FINANCE INITIATIVES

Number of case studies demonstrate how Indigenous people are overcome financial disadvantage globally. Prominent of these case studies are presented below.

A government agency called Indigenous Business Australia (IBA) helps Indigenous Australians build money, acquire assets, and become economically independent. It provides a variety of financial services and products, such as home loans, business loans, and investment options. Customized company loans, capacity building services, and collaborations with other financial institutions, governmental bodies, and neighborhood associations are some of IBA's main projects. Increased house and company ownership as well as the development of Indigenous entrepreneurs' capabilities are the results. Many Indigenous families have been able to become homeowners because to IBA's house lending programs, which has increased their wealth and financial security (Yap & Yu, 2006, Peredo & McLean, 2020).

By providing culturally appropriate financial products and services, First Nations Bank of Canada (FNBC), a Canadian financial institution, hopes to become the preferred bank for Indigenous people. To address the unique requirements of Indigenous communities, FNBC provides a variety of banking products, including as commercial and personal accounts, loans, and investment services. In order to promote the development and prosperity of Indigenous communities, the bank also makes investments in community development initiatives including housing and infrastructure. Furthermore, FNBC offers financial literacy initiatives to assist Indigenous communities and people in developing better money management practices (Parmenter, 2016).

In New Zealand, the Tahoe Trust is a tribal organization that looks after resources and assets for the Tahoe people. It emphasizes economic empowerment and sustainable development through business and financial practices that are suitable for the local culture. Ecotourism, sustainable agriculture, and sustainable investment in renewable energy are important projects. Additionally, the trust provides training and education programs to increase the leadership, financial management, and entrepreneurial skills of Tahoe people. To generate economic possibilities, it works with other Maori organizations, business sector partners, and government agencies. In order to ensure sustained growth and capacity building, the trust's investments have generated employment and economic possibilities (Campbell, 2023).

Indigenous communities and people in Canada can access financial services from the non-profit Aboriginal Savings Corporation of Canada (ABSCAN). Through loans, savings plans, and financial education, it seeks to enhance Indigenous peoples' financial well-being. To assist Indigenous people in accumulating money and reaching financial objectives including retirement, education, and property, ABSCAN provides savings plans. Additionally, it offers lending options with adjustable terms and conditions. In order to enhance Indigenous people's financial literacy and management abilities, the group also conducts financial education programs. Financial literacy, capital access, and wealth accumulation are among the results (Anderson et al., 2006, Sayers & Steele, 2020).

These case studies illustrate the many tactics and significant outcomes of initiatives aimed at providing funds for Indigenous communities' sustainable development. These initiatives, which range from cooperative partnerships and sustainable investment to capacity-building exercises and customized financial products, demonstrate the importance of community-driven and culturally relevant strategies. By incorporating these examples, stakeholders may develop and implement effective plans to enhance Native American financial inclusion and promote sustainable economic development.

6. FUTURE DIRECTIONS FOR INDIGENOUS FINANCE AND ECONOMIC DEVELOPMENT

There is a lot of promise for the future of Indigenous inclusiveness and the release of funds for economic growth. Stakeholders must adopt new technology, investigate creative solutions, and create all-encompassing plans that take into account the particular difficulties that Indigenous people experience in order to fulfill this potential. In order to achieve financial inclusion and sustainable development for Indigenous peoples, this section suggests a number of potential approaches.

Indigenous populations, especially those in rural places, can benefit from improved financial inclusion through digital financial services. Secure access is offered via digital payment systems, online banking platforms, and mobile banking apps. Blockchain technology can allow Indigenous communities to control their own financial resources by increasing transaction efficiency, security, and transparency (Irfan, Kadry, Sharif, & Ullah Khan, 2023). While community centers with internet connection and digital training materials can offer a supportive atmosphere, digital literacy training programs can give Indigenous people the skills they need to utilize digital financial services (Jackson & Martin, 2021).

Supporting Indigenous communities requires the development of financial solutions that are culturally appropriate. The cultural and economic circumstances of micro-finance and micro-insurance products should be taken into account (Irfan, Elmogy, Gupta, Khalifa, & Dias, 2024). Indigenous values and long-term objectives should be reflected in savings and investment products. Financial solutions that are more universally accepted and successful might result from collaborative design approaches. By including Indigenous people in the design process, these goods are guaranteed to satisfy their unique requirements and tastes.

To encourage financial inclusion and safeguard the rights of Indigenous peoples, governments should implement inclusive policies. Through pilot projects and sandboxes, regulatory innovation and adaptable frameworks may promote financial inclusion. By fostering best practices and information sharing, international collaboration on the creation of global standards for Indigenous financial inclusion may guarantee uniformity and efficacy across geographical boundaries.

The significance of strengthening multi-stakeholder partnerships—such as impact investing, cross-sector cooperation, and joint ventures involving governments, financial institutions, and Indigenous organizations—is emphasized throughout the book. Impact investing promotes private sector investment in Indigenous communities, promoting sustainable economic development, while joint ventures can pool resources and expertise for financial inclusion programs. For comprehensive and long-lasting results, holistic methods combine financial inclusion with other development objectives.

Green finance, sustainable agriculture, and renewable energy initiatives led by Indigenous peoples may all help to advance both environmental sustainability and economic progress. For Indigenous communities, renewable energy projects may promote energy independence, lower energy costs, and provide revenue. Green financing tools, such climate funds and green bonds, can supply funding for sustainable development initiatives. Agro-ecology and permaculture are two examples of sustainable agricultural techniques that can improve food security and economic resilience (Irfan, Hussainey, Chan Bukhari, & Nam, 2024). Economic growth may be increased by combining financial technologies with agricultural activities.

The significance of supporting education and capacity building in Indigenous communities is emphasized throughout the chapter. It implies that entrepreneurial training, financial literacy instruction, youth involvement, and scholarships may all support economic growth and well-being. While entrepreneurship training encourages creativity and business growth, financial literacy programs enable people to make wise financial decisions. Youth initiatives that emphasize leadership training, skill development, and cultural preservation can support the long-term success of a community.

Indigenous companies are increasingly seen as possible collaborators in accomplishing environmental and social impact objectives as interest in ethical and sustainable investing rises globally. With an emphasis on sustainable development and cultural preservation, recent studies support frameworks that integrate Indigenous engagement in impact investment (Smith, 2021). Furthermore, research points to blockchain, fintech, and digital platforms as possible disruptors that may expand Indigenous peoples' access to financing by lessening their reliance on conventional banking models (Watson & Green, 2020).

Diverse stakeholders must work together to embrace innovation, create culturally appropriate solutions, and promote cooperation if Indigenous inclusiveness and the unlocking of funds for economic growth are to continue. We can establish a supportive atmosphere for Indigenous economic empowerment by utilizing digital technology, fortifying policy frameworks, and encouraging education and capacity building. It is imperative that we give Indigenous communities' voices and leadership top priority going ahead in order to make sure that their beliefs, wisdom, and goals direct the course toward a more just and sustainable future(Jones, 2019).

7. CONCLUSION

Adopting inclusive finance as a means of achieving self-determination is essential to the future of Indigenous economic growth. Indigenous communities may realize their full potential in the global economy by removing obstacles, promoting collaborations with cultural respect and economic justice, and supporting financial models headed by Indigenous peoples. Indigenous inclusion in finance has the potential to establish a global standard for sustainable development through governmental interventions and community-driven financial innovation, guaranteeing that Indigenous economies and voices flourish in an era of fair prosperity. To fully realize the economic potential of Indigenous communities and support a more sustainable and inclusive global economy, we must keep up our efforts and innovations in the future. The significance of Indigenous engagement in financial decision-making processes is continuously emphasized in the studied literature.It is recommended that future research look more closely at how culture, money, and economic development interact in Indigenous environments(King, 2020). Comprehensive policies, culturally relevant financial products, and partnerships between governments, private investors, and Indigenous people are also recommended by research. A revolutionary financial environment where Indigenous people may exercise complete economic self-determination would be made possible by these advancements.

7.1 Implications for Practice and Policy

When it comes to allocating monies for sustainable development in Indigenous communities, there are many intricate implications for policy and practice. Practical measures including skill training, access to specialized financial services, and supportive settings are essential for the economic empowerment of Indigenous communities. At the same time, creating an atmosphere that promotes sustainable growth requires regulatory backing, international collaboration, and inclusive policy frameworks. By addressing these concerns, stakeholders may promote financial inclusion, bolster economic resilience, and aid in the long-term prosperity of Indigenous communities.

REFERENCES

Akinmolayan, E. S., Hingston, C. A., Akpan, U. J., & Arise, O. A. (2024). Towards decolonisation of primary school education in south africa. [SAJCE]. *South African Journal of Childhood Education*, 14(1). Advance online publication. DOI: 10.4102/sajce.v14i1.1440

Altman, J. C. (2016). Indigenous Policy: Economic Development and Indigenous Australia: Contestations over Property, Institutions and Rights. *The Australian Journal of Agricultural and Resource Economics*, 60(3), 460–470. DOI: 10.1111/1467-8489.12156

Anderson, R. B., Dana, L. P., & Dana, T. E. (2006). Indigenous Land Rights, Entrepreneurship, and Economic Development in Canada: "Opting-in" to the Global Economy. *Journal of World Business*, 41(1), 45–55. DOI: 10.1016/j.jwb.2005.10.005

Anderson, R. B., Kayseas, B., Dana, L. P., & Hindle, K. (2004). Indigenous Land Claims and Economic Development: The Canadian Experience. *American Indian Quarterly*, 28(3), 634–648. DOI: 10.1353/aiq.2004.0089

Bargh, M. (Ed.). (2014). *A Hidden Economy: Māori in the Contemporary Economy*. Huia Publishers.

Campbell, T., & Bourbonnais, V. (2023). From Compliance To Inclusion: Implementing An Equity, Diversity And Inclusion Action Plan For A Federal Funding Program In CANADA. [R]. *The Journal of Research Administration*, 54(2), 37–53.

Cornell, S., & Kalt, J. P. (2000). Where's the Glue? Institutional and Cultural Foundations of American Indian Economic Development. *Journal of Socio-Economics*, 29(5), 443–470. DOI: 10.1016/S1053-5357(00)00080-9

Cornell, S., & Kalt, J. P. (2010). *American Indian self-determination: The political economy of a successful policy*. Harvard Project on American Indian Economic Development.

Datta, R., & Kairy, B. (2024). Decolonizing climate change adaptations from indigenous perspectives: Learning reflections from munda indigenous communities, coastal areas in bangladesh. *Sustainability (Basel)*, 16(2), 769. DOI: 10.3390/su16020769

De-Gol, A., Le Quéré, C., Smith, A. J. P., & Aubin Le Quéré, M. (2023). Broadening scientific engagement and inclusivity in IPCC reports through collaborative technology platforms. *Npj Climate Action*, 2(1), 49. DOI: 10.1038/s44168-023-00072-3

First Nations Development Institute. (2018). *Investing in Native Communities: Philanthropic Funding for Native American Communities and Causes*. First Nations Development Institute.

Foley, B. (2019). Intersectionality: A Marxist Critique. *New Labor Forum*, 28(3), 10–13. DOI: 10.1177/1095796019867944

Foley, D., & Wheeler, J. (2018). Empowering Indigenous communities through economic development: Successes in Indigenous-led financial institutions. *Journal of Indigenous Economic Studies*, 11(4), 203–219.

Freeborn, C., Mardhani-Bayne, A., & Soetaert, C. (2023). Quality and educator dispositions for indigenous families in the urban early learning and child care context: A scoping review. *International Journal of Child Care and Education Policy*, 17(1), 6. DOI: 10.1186/s40723-023-00108-5

Gumbo, M. (2023). Digitisation of higher education and research: Raising inclusivity and equity issues for indigenous students. *South African Computer Journal = Suid-Afrikaanse Rekenaartydskrif*, 35(1). Advance online publication. DOI: 10.18489/sacj.v35i1.1107

Hunt, J., & Gray, M. (2021). The impact of government incentives and tax relief on Indigenous business financing: Policy implications. *Journal of Indigenous Policy and Development*, 19(2), 88–104.

Indigenous Business Australia (IBA). (2021). Annual Report 2020-21. Retrieved from https://www.iba.gov.au/reports/annual-report/2020-21

International Labour Organization (ILO). (2019). *Indigenous Peoples and Climate Change: From Victims to Change Agents through Decent Work*. ILO.

Irfan, M. (2021). Do Shariah Indices converge? Evidence from Gulf Cooperation Council countries. *International Journal of Business Excellence*, 23(2), 251–269. DOI: 10.1504/IJBEX.2021.113448

Irfan, M., Elhoseny, M., Kassim, S., & Metawa, N. (2023). *Advanced Machine Learning Algorithms for Complex Financial Applications*. IGI Global., DOI: 10.4018/978-1-6684-4483-2

Irfan, M., Elmogy, M., Gupta, S., Khalifa, F., & Dias, R. (2024). *AI-Driven Decentralized Finance and the Future of Finance*. IGI Global., DOI: 10.4018/979-8-3693-6321-8

Irfan, M., Elmogy, M., Majid, M. S., & El-Sappagh, S. (2023). *The Impact of AI Innovation on Financial Sectors in the Era of Industry 5.0*. IGI Global., DOI: 10.4018/979-8-3693-0082-4

Irfan, M., Hussainey, K., Chan Bukhari, S. A., & Nam, Y. (Eds.). (2024). *Issues of Sustainability in AI and New-Age Thematic Investing*. IGI Global Publisher., DOI: 10.4018/979-8-3693-3282-5

Irfan, M., Kadry, S., Sharif, M., & Ullah Khan, H. (2023). *Fintech Applications in Islamic Finance: AI, Machine Learning, and Blockchain Techniques*. IGI Global., DOI: 10.4018/979-8-3693-1038-0

Jackson, R. (2020). Blended finance for Indigenous business ventures: Public-private partnerships in Indigenous economic development. *International Journal of Economic Development and Indigenous Studies*, 15(1), 33–50.

Jackson, R., & Martin, L. (2021). Training programs in digital literacy and their role in enhancing Indigenous access to digital financial services. *Journal of Digital Inclusion and Economic Development*, 12(4), 145–160.

Jackson, S., & Yarwood, R. (2021). Financial accessibility and systemic barriers among Indigenous populations: Addressing inequalities in economic resources. *Indigenous Economic Studies Journal*, 15(3), 101–119.

Jones, L. (2019). Policy frameworks and Indigenous financial inclusion: An analysis of gaps between intention and outcome. *Journal of Economic and Social Policy*, 27(3), 112–130.

Kajiita, R. M., & Kang'ethe, S. M. (2024). Socio-economic dynamics inhibiting inclusive urban economic development: Implications for sustainable urban development in south african cities. *Sustainability (Basel)*, 16(7), 2803. DOI: 10.3390/su16072803

Khub, A. A., Saeudy, M., & Ali, M. G. (2024). Digital financial inclusion in emerging economies: Evidence from jordan. *Journal of Risk and Financial Management*, 17(2), 66. DOI: 10.3390/jrfm17020066

King, R. (2020). Exploring the interplay between culture, finance, and economic development in Indigenous contexts. *Journal of Indigenous Economic Studies*, 21(3), 112–130.

King, R., & Brown, T. (2020). Inclusive policy formation for Indigenous economic development: Recognizing Indigenous governance in program design. *Indigenous Policy Journal*, 22(1), 41–58.

Kingsbury, R. (2018). Challenges in financial models for Indigenous communities: Communal landholding and governance structures. *Journal of Indigenous Governance and Economics*, 10(1), 75–92.

Mabela, M. L., & Ditsele, T. (2024). Exploring intellectualisation of south african indigenous languages for academic purposes. *Literator*, 45(1). Advance online publication. DOI: 10.4102/lit.v45i1.1980

Maddison, S. (2019). *The Colonial Fantasy: Why White Australia Can't Solve Black Problems*. Allen & Unwin.

Maina, P., & Parádi-Dolgos, A. (2024). The effectiveness of climate adaptation finance and readiness on vulnerability in african economies. *Climate (Basel)*, 12(5), 59. DOI: 10.3390/cli12050059

Parmenter, J. (2015). The Experience of Aboriginal Financial Institutions in Canada: Alternative Approaches to Development Finance. *Canadian Journal of Development Studies*, 36(3), 315–331. DOI: 10.1080/02255189.2015.1065283

Peredo, A. M., & Chrisman, J. J. (2019). Socio-economic barriers to credit access in Indigenous communities: The impact of income levels and credit history. *Journal of Entrepreneurship and Economic Development*, 22(3), 201–217.

Peredo, A. M., & McLean, M. (2020). Indigenous entrepreneurship and economic resilience: Exploring models of community-based business. *Journal of Indigenous Business and Economic Development*, 15(1), 37–52.

Peters, E. (2020). Culturally sensitive financial products and the exclusion of Indigenous communities from mainstream finance. *Journal of Indigenous Economic Development*, 12(2), 45–63.

Sakapaji, S. C., García Molinos, J., Parilova, V., Gavrilyeva, T., & Yakovleva, N. (2024). Navigating legal and regulatory frameworks to achieve the resilience and sustainability of indigenous socioecological systems. *Resources*, 13(4), 56. DOI: 10.3390/resources13040056

Sayers, J., & Steele, M. (2020). Financial models for Indigenous infrastructure: The role of First Nations Finance Authority in Canada. *Journal of Indigenous Economic Development*, 16(2), 89–105.

Smith, L. (2021). Indigenous-led financial institutions: A pathway to economic empowerment through micro-loans and financial literacy. *Indigenous Economic Empowerment Journal*, 18(2), 45–61.

Smith, L. (2021). Incorporating Indigenous participation in impact investing: Sustainable development and cultural preservation. *Journal of Indigenous Business and Sustainable Finance*, 18(2), 75–91.

Smith, L. T. (2012). *Decolonizing Methodologies: Research and Indigenous Peoples* (2nd ed.). Zed Books.

Sullivan, M., & Hill, J. (2019). Innovative financial models for Indigenous inclusivity: Financial institutions, trust funds, and community lending circles. *Journal of Indigenous Finance and Economic Development*, 14(3), 123–140.

Venkateswaran, R. (2023). Indigenous indian management. *Decision (Washington, D.C.)*, 50(3), 363–366. DOI: 10.1007/s40622-023-00353-0

Walker, S., Kannan, P., Bhawra, J., & Tarun, R. K. (2023). Evaluation of a longitudinal digital citizen science initiative to understand the impact of culture on indigenous youth mental health: Findings from a quasi-experimental qualitative study. *PLoS One*, 18(12), e0294234. Advance online publication. DOI: 10.1371/journal.pone.0294234 PMID: 38127846

Washington, S. A. (2023). Reflecting on an Indigenist Methodology in Indigenous Family and Community Engagement Research. *The Qualitative Report*, 28(4), 1210–1229. DOI: 10.46743/2160-3715/2023.5899

Watson, J., & Green, A. (2020). The role of digital platforms, fintech, and blockchain in increasing Indigenous access to finance. *International Journal of Financial Innovation*, 14(1), 33–48.

Yap, M., & Yu, E. (2016). Operationalising the Capability Approach: Developing Culturally Relevant Indicators of Indigenous Well-being - An Australian Example. *Oxford Development Studies*, 44(3), 315–331. DOI: 10.1080/13600818.2016.1178223

Chapter 10
Alternative Financing Mechanisms:
Increase Access to Finance for MSMEs in India

Nidhi Upendra Argade
https://orcid.org/0000-0002-5692-1306
The Maharaja Sayajirao University of Baroda, India

Priya Chandak
https://orcid.org/0000-0002-0419-846X
The Maharaja Sayajirao University of Baroda, India

Nidhi Bansal
Upgrad Education Pvt Limited, India

Suchi Dubey
Symbiosis International University, Dubai, UAE

ABSTRACT

This study is aimed at bridging finance gap of Micro Small and Medium Enterprises (MSMEs) in India despite their large contribution to GDP and employment, by studying alternative financing mechanisms. It also looks at new instruments of the like- crowdfunding, fintech solutions, supply chain financing, and venture capital. The paper examines how alternative credit evaluation techniques and digital lending, along with public private collaborations are transforming MSME financing. The paper examines the challenges of putting these mechanisms in place and the potential they have to spur financial inclusion and economic growth. An overview of these financing options is provided through a conceptual framework and descriptive analysis of their concepts, uses and descriptive levels. Finally, the paper presents a study of the potential strategies that can enhance MSMEs' access to finance in India by providing innovative financial products to fill the huge financing gap for such firms.

DOI: 10.4018/979-8-3693-7924-0.ch010

1. INTRODUCTION

MSME sector has indeed come out as one of the most important segments of the Indian economy that has been contributing a large share of the country's GDP, exports and employment. According to the estimates made in March 2024 there were 4 crores registered MSMEs in India and according to the growth rate the estimated MSMEs may reach 7.5 crore in the future with a CAGR of 2.5%. This growth trajectory shows the continuous development of the sector and the possibility of its future growth. MSMEs contribute to approximately 30% of India's GDP and as much as 45.56% of the total exports up to September of year 2023 therefore showing the importance of MSMEs in the Indian economy. MSMEs form the largest sector of the economy and one of their biggest contributions is in the employment creation. These enterprises generate employment to more than 110 million people with an emphasis on employment generation in rural and semi urban regions. There are schemes like Prime Minister's Employment Generation Programme (PMEGP), it has assisted around 9.29 lakh micro enterprises and created about 78.36 lakh jobs. The MSME sector has been identified to be the backbone of the economy in the promotion of business, innovation and contribution to the growth of the economy across all sectors. In the manufacturing sector alone, MSMEs contribute about one third of the total output as important suppliers and sub-contractors to large scale industries. This contribution is important for India's intended transformation into a global manufacturing hub. Nevertheless, MSMEs have remained enormous in the economy due to the following challenges that affect their growth and development. The most significant problem is the access to finance. Of the 6.3 crore MSMEs the country boasts of, only 2.5 crores have ever accessed credit from formal institutions which shows that there is a great funding deficit. Due to lack of collateral MSMEs face difficulties in getting loans, which is why schemes like the Credit Guarantee Fund Trust for Micro and Small Enterprise (CGTMSE) has been introduced to provide collateral free credit. The problem of high cost of credit has been another issue, the revamped CGTMSE scheme is expected to help in reducing the cost of credit by about 1%. Lack of venture capital is another problem; the government has put in place venture capital funds such as the Self-Reliant India (SRI) Fund to address the problem of lack of growth capital for the MSMEs. Till November 30, 2023, the SRI Fund had invested Rs. 7,593 crores in 425 MSMEs manufacturing products including agricultural, pharma, automobile, chemical segments etc. The payment problems from government departments and large corporations persist, thus the development of the MSME Samadhaan portal. The government has put in place several measures to support the sector as follows. Interim budget 2024-2025 also approved the creation of a corpus of Rs. 1 lakh crore for providing 50 years interest free loans to encourage private sector research and innovation. Other important measures are the establishment of the Udyam Assist Platform (UAP) for the formalization of Informal Micro Enterprises IMEs into formal, whereby 1.11 crore informal micro enterprises got registered by December 31, 2023. But still, MSME sector has not been an exception to the challenges such as access to credit, skilled personnel, technology upgrade and even on government schemes. In order to increase the performance of the sector in the future years, the government focus on increasing the access to credit, digitalization, and skill development is crucial which is expected to help (IBEF Report, May 2024; MSME Annual Report, 2023-24; Figure 1).

Figure 1. Growth of MSME units over the years.

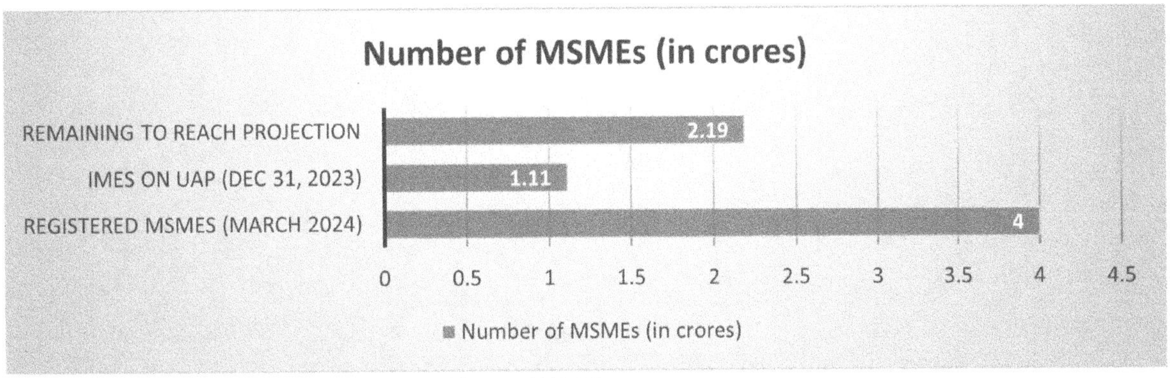

(Source: IBEF Report, May 2024; MSME Annual Report, 2023-24).

As per Avendus: MSME Lending Report (2023) (Figure 2), India's sector induction of formal loans falls significantly short of global practice, and this is a major hurdle for India's economic growth and development. It's shocking that we have a credit shortfall of $530 billion for MSMEs, which form the backbone of our economy and are struggling with substantial obstacles. In spite of its crucial economic part in India, only 14 percent of India's 64 million MSMEs are able to get the formal financing. However, this alarming statistic highlights the huge gap between what the sector requires in terms of resources and what is really available. This requires a large inflow of finance into the MSME sector and the demand for the same is increasing to $1,955 billion with a debt-to-equity ratio of 3.8x. Further, breaking this down, the demand for debt finance alone is totaling $1,544 billion. The truth, however, is that more than 47% of the credit needs are unmet for MSMEs, providing an obvious gap in the market. There are several factors that contribute to this substantial amount of credit shortfall, such as a significant percentage of these businesses are not making profits or choosing to go in search of funding via forms of non-transparent informal channels that charge huge interest rates. Formal credit providers, private banks have been able to fulfill only $289 billion of the $819 billion total loan demand. At the end of the day, this creates a massive market opportunity of $530 billion that other FinTech companies and Non-Banking Financial Companies (NBFCs) like CredAble have a clear path to monetizing. These are innovative financial institutions endowed with the potential of bridging the gap between the financial needs of MSMEs and the constraints of traditional banking systems. To enable such access of MSMEs to formal credit, MSMEs have to prioritize digitalization.

Figure 2. Unmet credit demand of MSMEs.

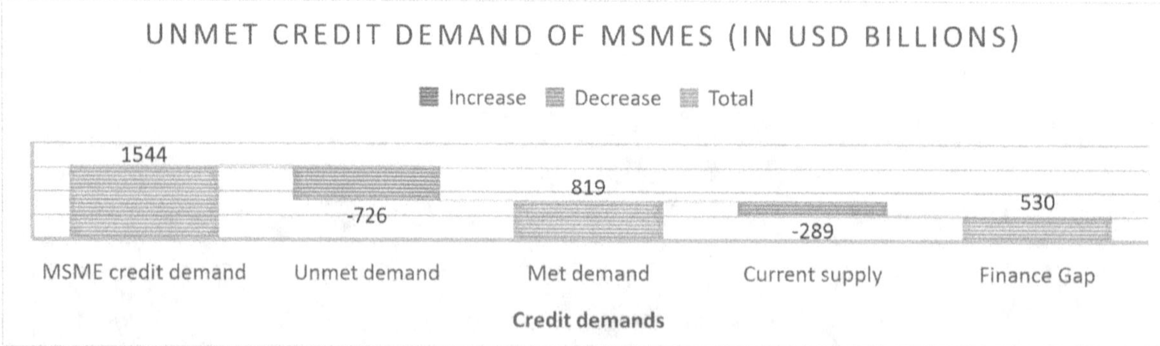

(Source: Avendus: MSME Lending Report, 2023).

A RedSeer investigation (Mohan, 2023) reveals it turns out that India's 64 million MSMEs boast only 7.7 million that have achieved high levels of digital maturity, whereas the rest of the MSMEs adopt digital technologies at different stages. There are many reasons why this needs to be a digital transformation: financial transparency, access to alternative lending platforms, operational efficiency, adjusted for leaders in scaled businesses. With MSMEs increasingly turning to digitalization, formal credit, in turn, may become more accessible to them as it could unleash the potential of the sector to its full extent, and this could help India reach the targeted growth rate. Digital adoption can keep MSMEs better in terms of financial records, and this makes them attractive for digitized Fintech solutions and online lending platforms. With technological advancements, MSMEs will be able to bypass conventional barriers, and get comfortable with new possibilities for growth and success in the changing business landscape.

Despite these efforts, MSMEs are facing large challenges on their way to becoming more digitized and financial inclusion. The impact of implementation of the India Stack, Unite Payments Interface (UPI) and Goods and Services Tax (GST) on digital infrastructure and financial access on the MSME has been limited. Sure enough, the mature India Stack and API based data availability have metamorphosed the MSME credit value chain, but still a majority of these businesses perpetuate in the informal sector, suffering from the digital inflexibility. While digital payments are being rapidly accelerated by the COVID-19 pandemic, many MSMEs are left behind while they are ill equipped to adapt to this pace of change. However, despite the ever-growing level of digital skills, resources and awareness, there is still a seeming digital divide between those that have the knowledge and those that don't. In particular, this gap is glaringly visible in rural and semi-urban areas, where traditional cash-based transactions are overwhelming. Indian MSMEs seem to receive a good chance for digital financing, however there has not been wide acceptance of digital loans into the sector. There are end to end digital MSME financing solutions, but that is only feasible for a small fraction of businesses, generally those that already have a certain level of digital sophistication. A large number of these MSMEs have remained highly constrained in their efforts at obtaining formal credit facilities, and they are forced to seek credit from informal sources at very high interest rates. MSME is still a long way from digital formalization, and the process is still in its infancy. But understanding digital compliance, record keeping, and navigating a changing regulatory landscape can be tricky – and its no easy feat for a lot of companies. Alongside these challenges, the lack of digital literacy among MSME owners and employees only worsens the problem, consequently constraining their capacity to optimally harness the full capability of digital tools and platforms. Overall, while India's MSME sector has been digitized, reality on ground shows a long way to go. However, this digital divide needs to be bridged and digital financial services need to be accessible far and wide to really empower India's vast MSME landscape, and this will continue to be a difficult challenge for all the public and private sectors to accomplish (Mohan, 2023).

Figure 3: Future integrated framework for MSME growth and financial inclusion.

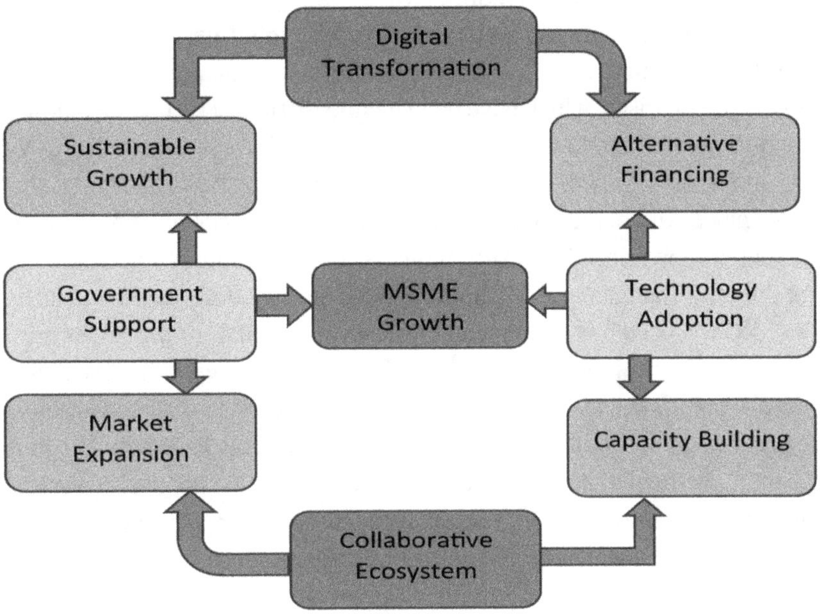

(Source: Author).

Figure 3 shows a conceptual model of the development of MSMEs based on the digital transformation and the collaborative ecosystem. It also describes how the various components interact to drive the growth of MSMEs and why tech and support from the government are important components. The significance of a synergistic environment that synchronizes market-oriented opportunities for growth to capacities development is highlighted. The framework shows how positive growth can be achieved under the right financial model and how digital transformation is a unifying factor that ties in all elements and presents a model for future growth and inclusion of MSMEs.

It is an undisputed fact that MSMEs are of great importance for Indian economy as it is generating number of employments, industrial output and also growing of country's economy. On the other hand, however vital they are, MSMEs are yet to shake off their chronicle financial constraints that limit their growth and sustainability. It is a persistent challenge for adequate financing for the simple fact that most of the MSMEs are informal and do not have proper financial records together with the bank's reluctance to provide an extension of credit since it is deemed as high risky. A large percentage of MSMEs are trapped in a vicious cycle where they experience low profitability, poor growth and very high operating costs. These pressing challenges demand an immediate focus on exploring and implementing innovative alternate financing modalities, which have been found to respond to the specific MSME requirements. A new crop of digital lending platforms has come into view as faster processing time and more flexible eligibility criteria compared to traditional banks. Some of these platforms use technology to rate credit-worthiness based off alternative data which could potentially create more opportunities for MSMEs that were excluded from formal credit systems. Supply chain finance is another emerging area and another approach to working capital structures where MSMEs can access working capital by financing their invoices, or their relationship with larger buyers, over a sustained period of time. The advantage of this type of financing is that it allows businesses to have immediate liquidity to help with cash flow gaps and meet operational expenses, eliminating the responsibility of existing loan repayments. Additionally, other alternative financing solutions including crowdfunding, peer to peer lending and cash flow-based lending are demonstrating potential in satisfying diverse capital needs of MSMEs. Offering a greater degree of flexibility and often requiring fewer rigid criteria than that of standard bank loans, they appeal especially to smaller enterprises, which have been having difficulty fitting the lending bill. But there's no way to get around these alternative financing mechanisms. However, most of the MSMEs are unaware of these options and have difficulty in maneuvering digital space. Furthermore, the regulatory regime of certain of these newer financing models is also subject to further scrutiny. Unlocking growth potential of MSMEs and empowering them truly requires a multi-pronged approach. Access to alternative financing is not the only change required, but problems such as delayed payments from buyers must be fixed, owners of MSMEs need better financial literacy, and regulatory processes need to be streamlined. The Trade Receivables Discounting System (TReDS) is a government initiative that intends to overcome some of these issues but uptake is limited. Finally, the MSMEs financial constraints appear formidable, however, there is some ray of hope from alternative financing mechanisms. The present study focusses by developing a total overhaul of present conceptual framework by integrating various financing options and then conducting a thorough descriptive analysis on their efficacy for policymakers and financial institutions to create a more inclusive and supporting ecosystem toward the growth of MSME. Thus, it will not only be helpful for the MSMEs, but play a supportive role in strengthening economic resilience and growth of the nation.

An Introduction is to the chapter to set out the background to the study, its objectives and significance. Then follows Review of Literature in which theories relevant to this study, previous studies, and research gaps are highlighted. In the Methodology and Analysis, the research design is described, and the findings are presented. The main results are recapitulated, research questions answered, implications discussed in a Summary and Conclusion section. Last, the Suggestions and Recommendations section presents practical applications of results from the study, suggests future lines of research, and outlines potential policy implications of results.

Objectives of the Study:

1. To analyze the development and trends of alternative financing mechanisms for MSMEs in India.
2. To evaluate MSMEs' utilization of alternative financing mechanisms.
3. To depict the scenario of alternative financing mechanisms for MSMEs in India.

2. REVIEW OF LITERATURE

A review of the MSME literature on financing shows that the problems and opportunities facing small businesses are complex with a particular reference to the Indian context. The various studies used in this review to explain the financial challenges MSMEs face and the measures taken to address them are discussed in detail in this paper.

The Emerge of MSME Finance Research

The initial studies in the area aimed at identifying the core financial problems of MSMEs. Gill *et al.* (2012) conducted a considerable work on the financial leverage concerns of small Indian companies and identified various factors that affect the financial leverage of small businesses such as growth, performance, total assets, sales, taxes, and family involvement. This study adds to the literature to help the financial managers and investors attempting to decipher the financing choices of SMEs in India. The analysis of the MSME financing challenges made researchers turn to the various supporting structures and other financing options. Sonne (2012) Villgro, an inclusive business incubator in India was the subject of a study that revealed that the success of MSMEs is not limited to financial support. Villgro's approach is based on the high touch portfolio management, unique financing solutions and market and growth opportunities. This holistic model points to the fact that MSMEs require support in various forms such as mentoring, technical support and development of an ecosystem. At the same time, government schemes such as the Credit Guarantee Fund Trust for Micro and Small Enterprises (CGTMSE) and the Prime Minister's Employment Generation Programme (PMEGP) were also discussed to show an emerging trend of comprehensive intervention for the promotion of MSMEs in India. Venkatesh and Kumari (2012) have described SIDBI's Multi-agency MSME Financing and Development Project (MSMEFDP) which focused on improving the attractiveness of MSME loans and feasibility of the project and enhancing the turnover and employment opportunities. This initiative was both supply and demand-side targeted at loan flow, new financial products, capacity development, policy, and business development services for MSMEs. When conventional sources of funding failed to sustain, researchers started searching for other sources of funding. OECD report by Cusmano and Thompson (2013) commissioned by the OECD on mezzanine financing for SMEs recommended it for upper tier SMEs with good cash flows and moderate growth prospects. They are subordinated loans, convertible loans and preference shares. This research provided a way out of the conventional bank loans. The analysis proceeded to investigate crowdfunding, which appeared as a potential source for initial financing of MSMEs. Digital credit scoring and P2P lending have emerged as new ways through which MSMEs can access financing and therefore new opportunities for growth.

The Rise of Alternative Finance

Ibrahim (2018) explored crowdsourcing as an innovative source of funding for Small and Medium Enterprises (SMEs) to determine how the crowdfunding platforms may assist SMEs to secure capital to replace traditional banking institutions. This research underlined the possibility of overcoming capital constraints and enhancing growth sustainability through cooperation that is carried out through the Internet. The study defined the various crowdfunding models which are reward-based, equity-based, and debt-based, and determined which model is best suited for an SME. It also analyzed elements of campaign success, including how to engage the crowd, what goals and objectives should be set for a project, and being transparent with the crowd. The study showed that crowdfunding holds potential and sustainability for SMEs in raising capital, particularly innovative and specialized firms that struggle to access conventional bank finance. Maiti (2018) suggested that the following ways can be used to address the financing of India's MSMEs; Crowdsourcing; E-commerce; Mobile financial services; Specialty banks. Crowdfunding sites were identified as a source through which MSMEs can mobilize capital from online investor networks. In addition, E-commerce was seen as a transformative model that helped MSMEs to extend their marketing portfolios and enhance their business processes. They were applauded for enhancing financial access especially in the remote regions. The specialty banks are to offer specific services to MSMEs through extending the right kind of services to the MSMEs. The study also revealed that government should support MSMEs through various measures and schemes and programmes. Finally, this study recommended an option of a technological supplement coupled with the policy intervention in order to enhance the sustainable development of MSMEs in India. Rupeika-Apoga and Saksonova (2018) considers the ways of Latvian SMEs to obtain alternative finance. Venture capital, business angels, and crowdfunding are also developing together with bank-based financing. Alternative financial service providers are gradually competing with banks for funding of startups and early-stage companies, the survey suggests. The survey of the bank board members and the SME management showed that Friends and Family, governmental assistance programmes, venture capital, and business angels are the most accessible non-bank funding options. Thus, for SME development in Latvia, the alternative sources of financing should be more popular and easily available. The OECD report by Thompson et al. (2018) describes private equity as the current forms of SME financing options that include debt and collective investment vehicles. More and more private equity is being invested in the US and Europe to finance expansion and ownership shifts. Since the 2008 financial crisis, private debt has expanded across Europe and is a source of flexible financing. Both the US Business Development Companies (BDCs) and the UK Venture Capital Trusts (VCTs) mobilize retail capital for the fostering of SMEs and provide tax incentives, and diversification opportunities. These tools are crucial for high risks, high returns SMEs. As the field evolved further, the researchers started comparing various forms of the alternative financing. Irfan (2021) analyzes the interactions between the Domestic Shariah Indices of GCC nations and finds unidirectional and bidirectional Granger causality between them. For this reason, this information is beneficial to Muslim and non-Muslim investors in rebalancing their portfolios and for market regulators to avoid future financial crises.

The New Age of MSME Finance

Block *et al.* (2020) have done a study between the ICO market and the crowdfunding market. In such environments, this study has analyzed investor conduct, contractual terms, storytelling, and the use of blockchain. Besides, there are some more detailed discussions of MSME financing, including the role of digital platforms, the use of the new credit scoring methods, and the impact of regulations on giving small businesses access to venture capital using these innovative forms of financing. According to Kanojia *et al.* (2020) financing trends among listed Indian SMEs reveal severe credit constraints and substantial reliance on short term loans. The study also focused on the obstacles these businesses face in securing long term capital and beyond funding. Limitations of short-term financing can potentially limit small and medium enterprise's (SMEs) ability to invest or bankroll growth and innovation. Seeing funding alternatives for small businesses during the COVID-19 crisis, Hyde (2021) have looked at capital access beyond the traditional bank loans. This latest research analyzes the intersection of the technologies and MSME financing by looking at how digital lending platforms, peer to peer lending and alternative credit scoring can be innovative solutions. The study of these highlights the potential of fintech in providing an MSME funding solution and enhance financial inclusion in the post pandemic world. The research by Chikwira and Rawjee (2022) examined new financing options for SMEs to remove financial barriers and prosper. These results indicate that SMEs start by using personal resources and family assistance, and as their business expands, they require financial institutions. Research suggests that technology and social media could enable project and trade trust finance. The report stresses through the need to assist SME owners with economic development and sustainability through accessible capital and financial literacy, as well as the need for government and private sector assistance. In Beltrame *et al.* (2023) entrepreneurial orientation (EO) is analyzed as affecting SMEs' credit access. The research surveys Austrian and Italian SMEs to uncover how proactiveness, autonomy as well as competitive aggressiveness relates to finance availability, particularly relationship financing. These EO characteristics reduce opaqueness, and further improve SME access to bank finance, especially through relationship lending. Credit rejection rates increased as innovation increased. During COVID-19 epidemic, supply chain financing (SCF) implementation hurdles faced by Indian MSMEs are focused on the report as the implementation hurdles for SMEs' financial success through use of EO, Sahoo and Thakur (2023) using intuitionistic fuzzy-analytic hierarchy process (IF-AHP), the study puts in priority these hurdles and its revealed that inadequate cash flow and working capital management are the greatest. The least critical challenge is cultural. The findings can assist managers and policymakers to improve the application of the SCF in MSMEs to avoid financial problems and sector growth. In the context of Industry 5.0, the work of Irfan *et al.* (2023) focuses on analyzing the impact of artificial intelligence on the financial industry. This explores how, in the field of finance, AI is influencing reshaping financial processes, risk management and decision backed by resilience, human centric approach and sustainable development. It helps researchers, academia, and industry folk realize the potential possibilities that AI can play in things like algorithmic trading, secure transactions, customer data management and others that help contribute to the ongoing conversation on the role AI is playing in finance. Irfan *et al.* (2024) digs at the idea of migrating to a low carbon economy and insertion of the AI/ML in the financial system. It provides researchers, policymakers and industry experts insight and solutions on renewable energy, blockchain and data science, in order to unlock private investment for sustainable initiatives. Sharma *et al.* (2024) explored the relationship between small businesses and financial technology, identifying four key themes: FinTech service usage, Effect, Opportunities and Threats, and Future Research Direction. FinTech was the focal area of research and how the Fintech industry can support the growth of MSMEs and financial inclusion. Through it, digital financial services can transform small businesses, which can get access to capital and the right financial tools to set up and start growing, as well as enter new markets. Irfan *et al.* (2024) the authors give a description on how to optimize the smart contracts, improve the security and provide personalized financial experiences while considering the legal and moral concerns. In response, Bridging the Gap: To achieve this, the book AI & Finance: From Technology to Application focuses on the translation of new technologies into application, the advancement of financial inclusion, and the attainment of sustainable development through sharing the practical way of applying the latest AI strategies in the ever-changing financial environment.

However, these studies generally offer important insights about particular aspects of MSME financing, but do not fully fill a lacuna in the literature on MSME financing. While most of the studies are concerned with certain financing methods or challenges, yet there is no comprehensive research work that organizes all these channels of financing as one framework for Indian MSMEs. Also, a number of studies point to the alternatives of financial methods; however, there is very little work done on its practicality and long-term impact in the Indian context. In conclusion, the existing literature provides a rich foundation for understanding MSME financing challenges and potential solutions with a general call for more integrated, context specific research on the complex interplay of traditional and alternative MSME financing methods in Indian context. Future studies should aim to develop syntheses of insights from the various methods of financing into comprehensive frameworks that are informed by the unique challenges faced by the Indian MSMEs. Such research would give a more holistic view about the MSMEs financing landscape including practical policy recommendations to policymakers, financial institutions and MSMEs owners. Longitudinal studies exploring long term impacts of alternative financing methods on MSME growth and sustainability would be especially useful furthering policy and practice in this vital sector of the Indian economy. To fill the gap in the literature, the present research constructs a conceptual framework examining the current use and difficulties of alternative financing instruments, and the potential of such instruments to bridge the financial gap and promote sustainable development for Indian MSMEs.

3. METHODOLOGY AND ANALYSIS

With the aim of contributing towards the identification and analysis of the Various Mechanisms of Financing MSMEs in India, an attempt has been made in this research to build a conceptual model. The purpose of this work is to focus on the existing finance deficit problem in the MSMEs and design new financial products convenient for the sector. In order to meet this aim, the research uses a range of analysis. The empirical material for the paper has been gathered from a wide variety of secondary sources, such as government documents, financial institutions' publications, and academic journals. This literature review has been rather comprehensive to build the foundation for the current state of MSME financing in India. Thus, drawing from these different sources of information, the research seeks to establish trends, challenges and opportunities in the MSME finance sector. In attempt to identify new ways to foster MSMEs' access to credit, the research investigates the combination between conventional and novel financing approaches. The overall objective of this study is to produce practical recommendations that can help improve the financial situation of MSMEs in India. The following recommendations will therefore be made based on the findings of this study and the real-life situation of MSMEs, financial institutions and the governmental bodies. With the view of adding value to the current initiatives being taken to enhance the growth of the MSME sector in India, this work presents an understanding of the current situation and recommendations for improvement. This way, the study aims at contributing to the practice by linking academic literature with policymaking and the creation of financial products.

3.1 Fintech Innovations

Fintech which is short for financial technology has been picked as a disruptor in the financial services sector. It consists of a vast number of advanced technologies and products that are created with the aim of enhancing, optimizing and revolutionizing regular financial activities and products. In its simplest form, fintech is the use of advanced technologies to design new financial products, enhance the existing ones and come up with new ways of doing business that compete with conventional banks. The four big technological drivers of this revolution are Artificial Intelligence, Blockchain, Cloud computing, and Big Data. The use of Artificial Intelligence is to analyze data and provide financial advice and make decisions. Application of the blockchain includes secure and an efficient means of conducting and recording transactions through cryptocurrencies and smart contracts. Among the advantages of cloud computing, there are flexibility and efficiency in delivering infrastructure for fintech services, and with big data analytics, it is possible to get lots of insights from the financial information. FinTech's have leveraged the smartphone as the primary delivery channel for mobile banking, investing and borrowing apps that provide financial services to customers' fingertips. This does mean that more people are able to engage with their finances in a way that is convenient, because it is mobile. Furthermore, the emergence of cryptocurrencies and other digital assets has provided new ways of value transfer and investment that exist beyond conventional finance. The application of Fintech Innovation is not confined to the front end but has actually changed the back-end processes, risk management, regulation, and business model of the whole financial services industry. With the help of AI, machine learning, and analytics, Fintech firms can develop better credit scoring, automated underwriting and fraud detection. The efficiency and cost effectiveness of these innovations, along with the ability to offer services to unbankable population, make these innovations compelling. The financial services market is changing and fintech is advancing that change, making traditional players change too. This evolution is going to continue to improve delivery, availability of and relevance for financial services so as to reduce the cost of doing business and enhance consumers' experience (Puschmann, 2017). Islamic financial systems have been explored in intersection of financial technology and Islamic Finance by Irfan *et al.* (2023) like the applications of advanced technologies like artificial intelligence, machine learning, and blockchain, in the context of Islamic financial systems. The objective of this comprehensive work is to present the potential ways Islamic financial practices can be enhanced and modernized using these innovative technologies and also to comply with the Sharia principle.

Fintech technologies are increasing access to financing for MSMEs by providing:

a) Digital lending platforms that facilitate quicker, more convenient loans.
b) Alternative credit scoring Using non-traditional data.
c) Enabling direct connection between MSMEs and the investors through peer-to-peer financing.
d) Product offerings include invoice financing and supply chain financing products.
e) APIs that enable data exchange by way of open banking to improve credit evaluation enable quicker and more convenient loans.

All these technologies are the most innovative and revolutionizing the financial operations of SMEs and their use is highly beneficial for SMEs. Fintech solutions are also increasing access to operating cash, which allows for the running of daily operations and short-term needs. Through the use of advanced algorithms, alternative data sources, and this allows small businesses to access much faster periods when it comes to borrowing than what they'd get with traditional methods. In addition, these technologies are making notable subtractions in the operational costs of SMEs. Financial process automation, including invoicing, bookkeeping, payment processes help minimize the manual labor and human errors by redirecting the resource in a better manner. This cost efficiency is an extremely important issue when smaller businesses must compete in markets where larger firms are strongest. The use of technology has also fast tracks financial procedures. The automation of systems allows for instant transactions and real time data analysis supporting SMEs to make fast decisions and make fast changes to meet market demands. This is the speed that dictates how fast you can seize opportunities, and retain your competitive edge. Fintech is providing SMEs easier access to bank loans, significantly. These platforms are tearing down the financial barriers traditionally in place by using advanced credit assessment methods, and simple application processes. By implementing this innovative method, SMEs get faster approvals and more flexible lending criteria, which leads to the more supportive SME development environment. These technologies are allowing SMEs to get operating cash, cut costs, speed up processes and easier financing. Technology-enabled fintech is helping SMEs to get loans from the bank.

Digital Lending Platforms

Digital lending platforms offer efficiency in SME loan application than conventional lending because of its fast and straightforward process. The main features include online application, quick approval, using data other than credit history to analyze the borrower's creditworthiness, and improved customer interface. These platforms enhance the access of credit for SMEs that have challenges in acquiring bank loans especially the expansion capital. The advantages include; quick loan processing, low charges, financial inclusion, and availability of services at all times. Digital lenders rely on automation, algorithms and alternative data to determine the creditworthiness of a loan applicant. The study identified that SME owners have compliance, cybersecurity, and digital literacy concerns. This paper explains how digital lending platforms ease access to capital and thereby aid SME development through quicker and better financial services (Basha *et al.*, 2021).

Figure 4. Indian digital lending platform growth over the years 2012-2023.

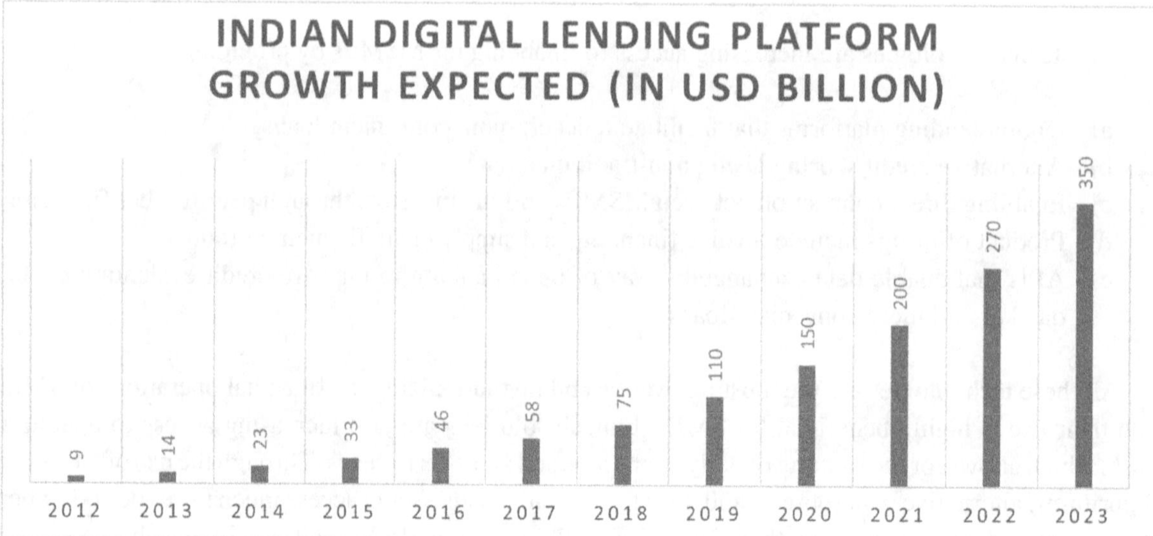

(Source: FICCI reports, 2019).

The digital lending market in India (Figure 4) has also shown a fast growth rate and is expected to grow to USD 350 billion by the year 2023 as per FICCI Reports (2019). MSMEs have been the major drivers of this expansion given that they form about one third of India's GDP. The growth of digital financing in India is on the rise, and expected to increase to USD 75 billion by 2023 according to Statista Research Department (2024) and $515 billion by 2030 at a CAGR of 22%.

This is a rapid expansion powered by a number of drivers including rising Internet penetration in the country, rising smartphone adoption rates and growing consumption of online financial services by consumers as well as businesses. Despite this impressive growth trajectory, the digital lending market has failed to reach the levels of previous projections, as stated by the Statista Research Department (2024). Yet the projected versus actual growth difference points to the many challenges of the digital lending ecosystem, especially for the MSME sector. Digital lending has given MSMEs access to credit in new areas, but there are still a lot of hurdles. MSME owners in rural and semi-urban area are constrained by limited digital literacy skills, that preclude them from truly unlocking the potential of online lending platforms. In addition, poor documentation and concerns of cybersecurity have also guarded some MSME from fully embracing digital lending solutions. Regulatory uncertainties further complicate both lenders and borrowers in their ability to evolve the digital lending landscape at a rapid pace. There is also trust deficit with some other MSMEs who still guard against going to traditional banking relationships owing to fear of data privacy and security. Informal nature of many MSME businesses makes it difficult for digital lenders to assess financial health and creditworthiness of the businesses accurately.

Alternative Credit Scoring Using Non-Traditional Data_(Ahmed, 2020; Saraswat, 2023)

One of these involving alternative credit scoring algorithms seems to be a promising tool to assess MSMEs creditworthiness without traditional credit history or collateral (Table 1). These models use non-traditional data sources such as social media activities, telecommunications data, and online behavior to assess borrowers that are often outside the scope of conventional credit assessments. This method has great promise to expand financial inclusion and access to credit for underserved MSMEs in emerging economies.

But alternative data and complex algorithms also raise questions about privacy and discrimination, and transparency. Vast amounts of personal data may be collected and analyzed for lending decisions which could in the future infringe on someone's rights to privacy and introduce unintended bias into lending decisions. Furthermore, many machine learning algorithms, which are usually opaque, make it difficult to detect and remedy such discriminations.

These new issues cannot be dealt with by the Indian judicial system. The Personal Data Protection Bill proposed might not stop discrimination totally. To answer these, policymakers and industry stakeholders are suggested to regulate algorithmic impact assessments, audits and certification processes. In order to create innovation without sacrificing involvement of consumer interests, possibly a combination of government oversight and industry self-regulation at balance may be necessary. Yet alternative credit scoring can lead to MSME financing transformation and boost financial inclusion, if safeguards are put in place to curtail risks and make for fair lending.

Table 1. Difference between alternative credit scoring and traditional credit scoring

Aspect	Alternative Credit Scoring	Traditional Credit Scoring
Data Sources	Transactions on e-commerce sites, social media, electronic transactions, cellular data, utility payments, rent payments, online behavior	Credit history, payment history, income statements, loan trails
Applicability	Suitable for underbanked or those with no credit history	Requires established credit history
Flexibility	More adaptable to different business models and situations	Rigid, based on standardized criteria
Processing Speed	Faster, often automated	Can be slower, may require manual review
Data Privacy Concerns	Higher, due to use of personal and non-financial data	Lower, focuses on established financial data
Customization	Allows for more personalized credit offerings	Generally, offers standardized products

Source: Author.

Peer-to-Peer Lending Connecting SMEs Directly with Investors

Digital P2P lending platforms provide MSMEs with better financing solutions by providing higher speed and cheaper financing by eliminating many intermediaries through the use of technology. These platforms usually have shorter turnaround times and better rates compared to conventional banks, besides which they use non-conventional data and less stringent underwriting criteria. These include exposure limits and maximum tenor which may negatively influence P2P lending in supporting MSMEs. The repayment of P2P loans also depends on the financial status of the business, performance of the business, the loan terms, and the general economic conditions. In order to strengthen support, most P2P platforms have added such services as financial workshop, tutoring, and business solutions. However, these platforms are slowly integrating the use of AI and other forms of data in credit scoring and trying to enhance the credit risk assessment to include more unserved MSMEs (Dsouza 2019; Purwanto *et al.*, 2023).

P2P lending which is one of the youngest financial industries that enables to get credit directly online is expected to grow up to $10.5 billion by 2026. This growth is projected to have a compound annual growth rate (CAGR) of 21.6% in the years between 2021 and 2026 as indicated in Figure 5. This revolutionary financial system allows people of all classes to get relatively small amounts of money online and target the underbanked population that lacks enough financial history to be approved for a loan by conventional banks. P2P platforms employ a mechanized and electronic system of underwriting borrowers and extending credit to the entire nation. Therefore, P2P financing will be of great value to the SME sector due to the fact that such platforms provide better solutions than the conventional financial institutions. Through innovative use of technology and other forms of data, P2P lenders can provide a better assessment of SMEs, and provide credit facilities to businesses that can create employment and help stimulate economic growth that they might not have been able to access otherwise (Gandhi, 2022).

Figure 5. Projected Peer 2 Peer lending in India over the years-2021-2026.

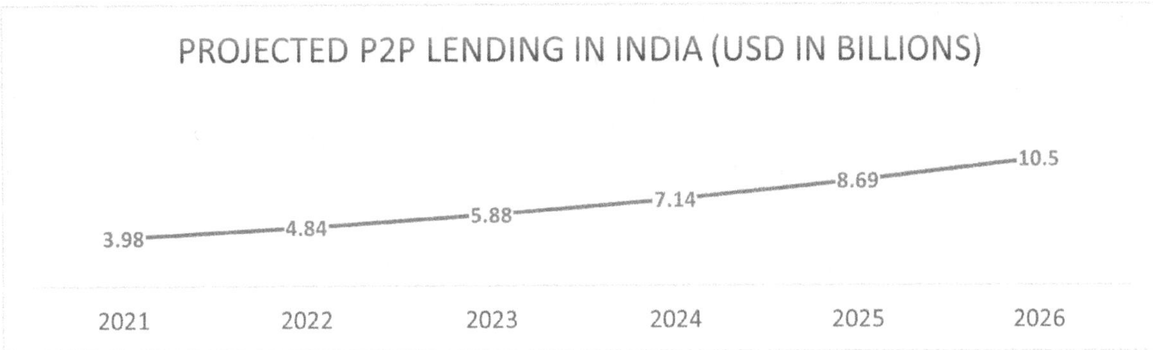

(Source: Gandhi, 2022)

The growth of peer to peer (P2P) lending in India has tremendous opportunities to help MSMEs, yet there remain many gaps and opportunities to improve financing MSMEs. Additionally, at present, the P2P lending market concentrates predominantly on individuals and SMEs as borrowers and does not extend to mid-sized enterprises, which require higher loans. P2P platforms have to augment their capacity to cater larger loan sizes and work towards more tailored products across business stages and sectors, to better serve MSMEs. At the same time, P2P lenders rely on alternative data for credit assessment, however, there is a lot of room for further improvement in the development of more sophisticated risk assessment models for MSMEs by considering industry trends, cash flow patterns and the growth prospects. Moreover, trust and awareness on P2P lending among MSME are still low and further a significant number of MSMEs are located in semi urban and rural areas. P2P platforms must invest in the education and outreach programs in order to truly bridge the funding gap through the adoption of P2P by MSMEs from all regions. Finally, regulatory frameworks for P2P lending in India continue to evolve and greater supportive policies which balance innovation with investor protection are needed in order to fully realize the potential of P2P lending for MSME financing.

Invoice Financing and Supply Chain Finance Solutions

One of the ways to help MSMEs plug their credit gap cost effectively is through supply chain finance (SCF). Its most important benefit is the credit without collateral, so MSMEs don't have to take advantage of their assets. Typically, SCF solutions finance suppliers using invoices and receivables as interims collateral, bringing working capital without seizin dome fixed assets. The two important SCF techniques are factoring and reverse factoring (Figure 6). Factoring in fact refers to selling accounts receivable to a bank or FinTech company for a discounted price, this way suppliers get instant payment and improved cash flow. Buyer initiated reverse factoring is where a financial institution will offer early payment to suppliers based on their ability to lean on the buyer's credit rating. This enables their larger customers to leverage in their stronger credit profiles. Besides, these SCF solutions not only increase provision of funding to MSMEs but they also boost their financial health as a whole. SCF can improve supplier buyer relationships and accelerate payment cycles and working capital resulting in efficiency in operations. With the transformation to digital, SCF platforms have further improved accessibility and efficiency, such as many providers that have made accessible user-friendly online interfaces to simplify the financing process. In addition, modern SCF solutions are data driven and more accurately assess risks and more dynamically price the risks, which may present financing possibilities for businesses that may have been too risky under traditional credit assessment methods. SCF helps in general by ensuring that the smaller suppliers can get the working capital that is so important as supply chains are built and strengthened amid the economic pressures and market shocks (PWC report, 2019). The market size of the reverse factoring market globally was $536.4 billion in 2022 and is expected to grow at a CAGR of 11.4% from 2023-2030 (IFC report, 2023).

Figure 6. Invoicing and supply chain mechanisms for buyers and suppliers.

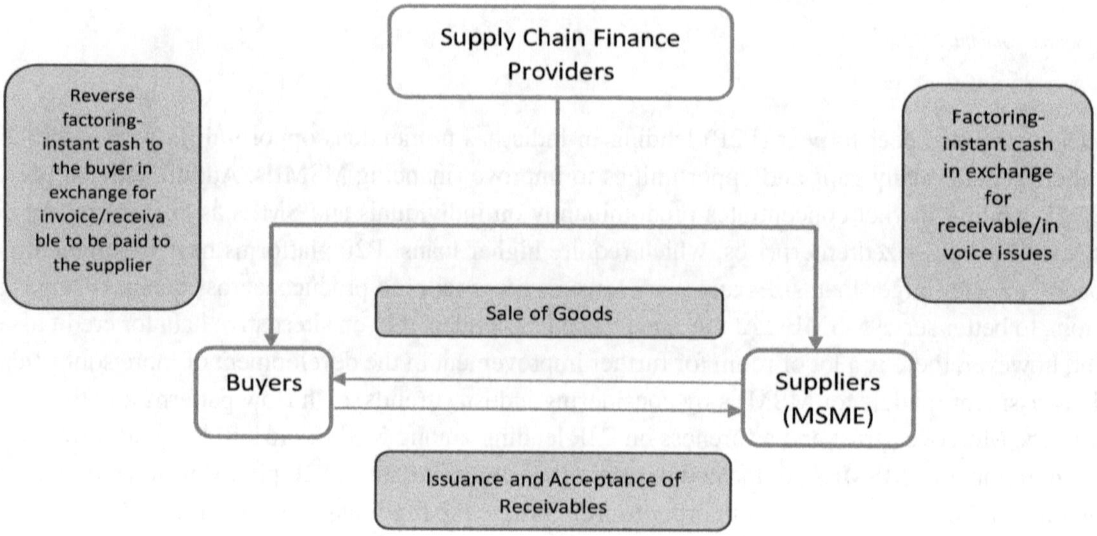

(Source: Author)

Open Banking APIs Enabling Data Sharing for Better Credit Assessment

Established by the Reserve Bank of India (RBI) in 2016, India's Account Aggregator (AA) framework has changed the game for Open Banking in the country, being the juncture for secure and consent-based sharing of financial data across institutions. This system has made it possible to create an open and connected financial system which has brought considerable benefit to micro, small and medium enterprises (MSMEs). The advanced machine learning algorithms also extend credit assessment by using the Open Banking data. All these algorithms are capable of looking at vast amounts of data that is related to finance, for instance, transaction histories, and spending patterns to name but a few in order to identify relations and patterns that are invisible to the naked eye. Consequently, enhanced risk profiling, tailored credit products, and enhanced fraud control can be achieved, which will enhance the capacity of lenders to make quicker and more informed decisions to extend financial services to the unserved or underserved markets (Irfan *et al.*, 2023). The AA system permits MSMEs to freely share their financial information with lenders, enabling a more efficient credit assessment, and bridging the traditional gap of financing for MSMEs. Through aggregated data from multiple sources, lenders can now have a larger picture of an MSME's financial health, making credit decisions richer and potentially more favorable. Safely sharing financial data across borders further expedites funding MSMEs across borders, which could create additional avenues for the funding for MSMEs. Further, through AA, loan processing is faster and there are efforts at the development of personalized financial products, which are in line with the needs of MSMEs. Meanwhile, as these developments continue, the global digital payment market is growing at 11 percent per annum over the next five years, and many G20 countries can expect the trend to be even more explosive within this space. Until December 2023, a total of 1.94 billion accounts on India's AA system have been activated for sharing data. This exercise also validates the extent to which the AA framework can leverage the disruption of financial services provision beyond the MSMEs segment. This paper also shows that, India's AA framework and Open Banking initiatives will also work in conjuncture to increase the transparency in the financial sector, improve efficiency through data driven decision making and reduce the cost of lending for the bank; The efforts made by India are expected to help in growing the financial inclusion and support the growth of MSME business in the coming years (ADBI, 2024; IFC report, 2023).

3.2 Embedded Finance

Digital lending has seen great strides in integrating financial products into non-financial channels, a development that provides new opportunities for small business to access credit. Through partnerships large e commerce platforms and big tech companies can now utilize vast sets of information they have on small business customers to facilitate lending. These platforms analyze inventory levels, accounts receivable and sales patterns, and can thus provide tailored financing solutions to the small businesses operating within their ecosystem. The impact of this embedded finance model on SME banking, as projected here, is likely to be significant; embedded banking services for small and medium enterprises could come to represent up to 26 per cent of global SME banking revenue by 2025. These financial services are perfect for MSMEs as they can help them to manage their cash flow, get more capital or buy big order/ inventory when opportunity comes. It may lead to increased sales and more income for small businesses as well as propel growth for the platforms that the small businesses utilize (Kumar, 2024).

In 2017 to 2025 India internet penetration shows a major growth of internet users: 384 million internet users in 2017, and an estimated 900 million users by 2025. The rapid growth is another reflection of the high adoption of digital services in the country, particularly across the lines of the fast expansion of smartphones and improving internet infrastructure. Figure 7 provides a graph of steady increase of internet users but in a noticeable drop in the growth rate around 2019. This declivity indicates that although adoption of the internet has manufactured a well-known thing, there have been times in which growth has been slow. These are variations that would indicate there may be potential in the future for environmental challenges in regards to maintaining consistent growth in some areas that potentially locate to them or grow into them because of limitations of infrastructure or because other areas market saturation may saturate before there is opportunity for continued growth. Even though these fluctuations took place we see a positive trend, with a very strong upward trajectory in internet penetration. As a result, connectivity has increased and has important implications in financial services. Having increased internet users has helped more people to access digital financial services and make it convenient to do transactions. However, figure 7 also reveals potential gaps between Micro, Small, and Medium Enterprises (MSMEs) which may not be fully availing of these digital benefits. To close these gaps, alongside targeted investments in digital literacy, investments in digital infrastructure, and particularly in underserved areas, may be needed. With this, it will help India ensure that the digital transformation is well distributed thereby addressing the challenge of financial inclusion as well as the economic development across all sectors (Mulye, 2021).

Figure 7. Internet penetration of Indian users over the years- 2017-2025.

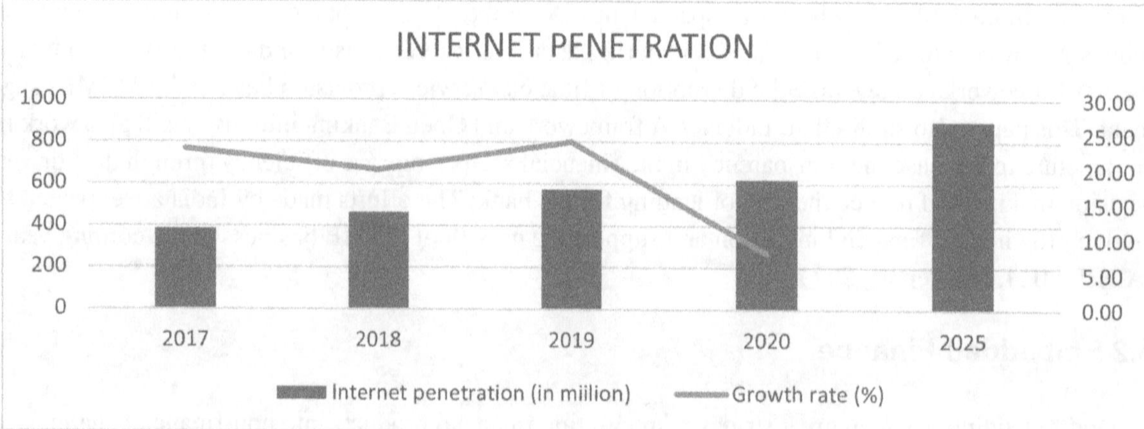

(Source: Mulye, 2021)

3.3 Venture Capital

Venture capital funding (VC) is one of the many types of private equity financing. Venture capitalists put money in exchange for equity, putting their money at significant risk in the hopes of significantly high returns. The dynamic of high risk and high reward is at the heart of venture capital, to find the companies that will deliver big growth and profitability. Venture Capital in India is picking up steam, particularly for Micro, Small, and Medium Enterprises (MSMEs). Generally, MSMEs were dependent on bank loans, but with the growing NPA (Non-Performing Assets) worries of bank, they have now become more careful. Venture capital has therefore become a critical source of startup funding, providing money and, just as important, strategic counsel and mentoring. The reason this is important for MSMEs, which account for about 30% of the GDP and generate millions of employments in India, is that their position in the market is shifting in many ways.

The venture capital space in India has remarkable growth. From 2014 – 2021, VC investments grew 49% CAGR (compared to 12% for China's). Meanwhile, VC funding in India declined to $25.7 billion in 2022 from $38.5 billion in 2021 but still surpassed the pre pandemic levels. However, according to the India Venture Capital Report (2024) by Sheth et al. the Indian venture capital system became developed in 2023 even with the challenges.es. It appears that the world is hunkering down for the long haul, at least as far as venture capital financing is concerned; it decreased from $25.7 billion in 2022 to $9.6 billion in 2023 (Figure 8). They, however, continued to be the second largest recipient of venture capital financing in the Asia-Pacific region. This ongoing trend in the market by Indian shows that there is a strong startup culture and the right digital environment for that (Jain, 2024).

Figure 8. Venture capital funding in India over the years- 2021-2023.

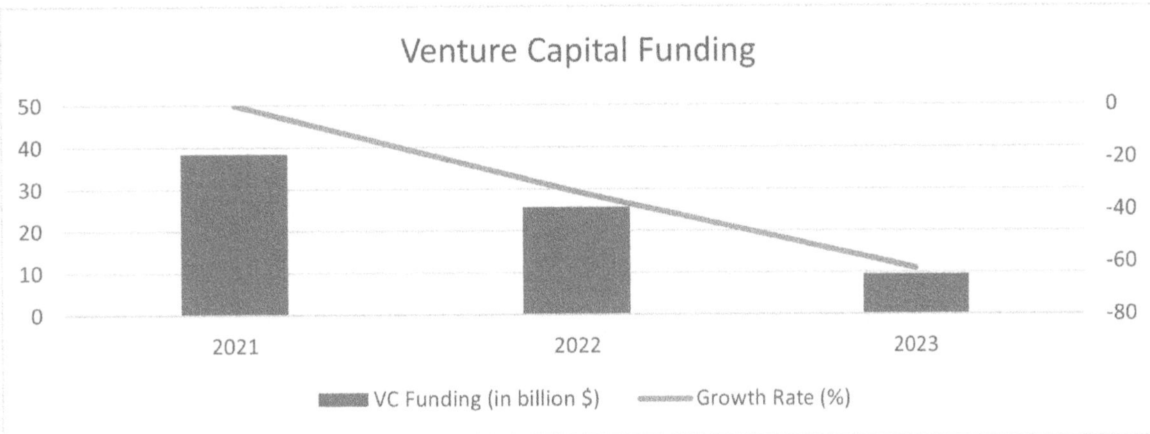

Source: Sheth et al., 2024; Jain, 2024.

As VC investments are made in stages (Seed, Early stage, and late-stage funding). These are the phases that the startups pass through from the time innovation is conceived to the time they grow to be organizations. VCs give more than money at each stage, they engage the business, give access to networks and other professionals and act more as the business's advisor. Venture capital in India is expanding into new areas of the economy beyond its usual focus areas of IT to healthcare, clean energy and retail. MSMEs diversification provides competitiveness through access to new markets as well as new technologies which provides for innovation and growth. Venture capitalists help support MSMEs and help the country grow towards the dream of becoming a $5 trillion economy by 2026-27 (Jain, 2024).

3.4 Equity Crowdfunding

Conventional modes of financing, particularly bank loans, are out of reach because of the many conditions that must be met and the high costs of borrowing. This has led to the research on other ways of financing like the newly emerging one – crowdfunding. Crowdfunding allows MSMEs to seek capital directly from investors and not through other financial institutions. These are donations-based crowdfunding, reward-based crowdfunding, equity-based crowdfunding and debt-based crowdfunding. These platforms do not only offer the financial support to the MSMEs but also, they help them to pilot business ideas, conduct pre-launch market research and do marketing. By going for a large audience, MSMEs can be able to get convictions of their ideas and the feedback that they require to make a change in their business. But, using crowdfunding presents a problem for MSMEs. It is still possible that many enterprises have not changed their operational approaches and may be quite reluctant to introduce innovations. Language constraints including low English literacy, and the use of informal funding rails can also pose a challenge to the move to digital channels. Nonetheless, the opportunities that can be gained from the application of crowdfunding, such as access to capital, and increased business exposure, imply that this is an area of opportunity for the MSMEs in overcoming financial barriers and driving growth (Rani & Katoch, 2022).

Figure 9: Indian crowdfunding over the years- 2017-2027.

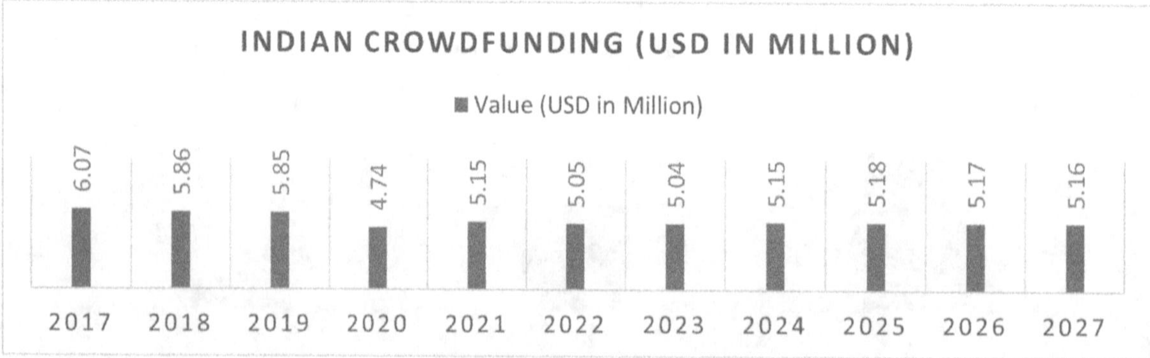

(Source: Vodolazhska, 2023)

Transaction volume in the Indian crowdfunding industry is estimated to grow at a CAGR of 0.59% (Figure 9) (Vodolazhska, 2023).

In India, crowdfunding is becoming an alternative to conventional fundraising options for startups and small and medium sized companies. Crowdfunding platforms also use the internet and social networks to channel a large potential funding force towards businesses. By offering financial resources, this approach not only validates business ideas and gathers potential customers but does so at the very early stages of developing a startup. Although the prospects are clear, the growth of Crowdfunding in India has been met by a number of legislative roadblocks. Expansion of this funding model depends on an enabling regulatory environment. Existing regulations are very clamp down and make it difficult for platforms to operate freely and capital to flow freely to those innovative projects. Leveraging these regulations through the process of streamlining them can actually provide a much-needed boost to the ecosystem of entrepreneurs in India. In research from September 2016, it was found that around 200 firms in India raised between 35,057,840 INR to 45,074,366 INR over an 18-month period on a crowdfunding platform. This is an encouraging sign of growing interest, but with maximum transaction values far behind markets such as China, which achieved $5,572 million. The gap highlights that crowdfunding in India is still very nascent. The United States, United Kingdom and China lead the way globally in crowdfunded investments, with an astonishing 96% of total investments. To catch up, India also has to create an environment, that will support both domestic and international investors. Moreover, this has to go beyond regulatory reform and involve awareness–building and trust–creation in crowdfunding as a legitimate and effective way of financing. In conclusion, it is possible to note that India's crowdfunding is relatively new but has high opportunities for SMEs and start-ups financing. For Instance, the country needs to remove legal hurdles and foster a culture of innovation and new business creation in order to enhance its market share of the global crowdfunding (Ritika & Khanna, 2024).

4. SUMMARY AND CONCLUSIONS

Micro, Small, and Medium Enterprises (MSME) sector has come out as a cornerstone of the Indian economy and has been instrumental in promoting economic growth, growth of innovation and creation of jobs. As of March 2024, India had around 4 crores registered MSMEs and by the end of the next five years, the registered MSMEs are anticipated to reach 7.5 crores with CAGR of 2.5%. This is the growth story of the sector, the story of a sector that has the potential to grow even more. In addition, it has been established that these small and medium-sized enterprises, MSMEs, contribute more than 30% of India's GDP and 45.56% of total exports as of September 2023. These enterprises are indeed a lifeline for more than 110 million people and notably create jobs in rural and semi urban areas. But it's Government initiatives such as the Prime Minister's Employment Generation Programme (PMEGP) that have given this sector a strong support, with more than 9.29 lakh micro units set up under this Programme that are estimated to have generated around 78.36 lakh jobs. However, for all their value to the economy, MSMEs have a mountain to climb in realizing their full growth and sustainability potential. The major issue is the large financing gap as only 2.5 cr. out of 6.3 cr. MSMEs have ever accessed credit from the formal source. That equates to an almost unimaginable credit shortfall of $530 billion and speaks to the urgency of supporting financial inclusion. The other challenges involve poor or limited access of skilled labor, reluctance to adopt technology, and the lack of ability to benefit from government schemes.

However, in order to achieve these potential solutions and unlock full potential of the MSME sector there is an emerging need for alternative financing mechanisms as potential solutions. Using technology to enable acquisition of SME bank loans is fintech. When it comes to digital lending, SME owners have the challenges of regulatory compliance, cyber security and digital literacy. The FICCI 2019 has estimated that the digital lending industry in India is expected to touch USD 350 billion by 2023. This has been good for the MSME sector especially since MSMEs account for 30% of India's GDP. The size of India's economy is, however, US$ 75 billion in 2023 and is projected to grow to US$ 515 billion by 2030 at a CAGR of 22%. Current Fintech trends such as Digital financing platforms, Alternate credit scoring techniques, Peer to Peer (P2P) financing, Invoice financing, Open banking APIs have become innovative in MSME lending. In particular, P2P lending has started to emerge, and it is expected to reach $10.5 billion by 2026 with a CAGR of 21.6%. Using this innovative model, anyone with a computer can apply for small loans directly online and the company is now deep into providing this service to the underserved that traditional banks tend to ignore. However, today's P2P lending still serves individual customers and small businesses, while ignoring the medium-sized enterprises which need more money. To achieve the most potential out of alternative credit scoring, combined with a minimum risk, a balancing act between innovation and consumer safety can be possible through government industry co regulation. Social media, telecommunications and online behavior data are all alternative forms of credit scoring algorithms. The proposed Personal Data Protection Bill may not be able to eliminate prejudice completely. Keeping all this in mind, and despite the challenges, alternative credit scoring could transform MSME finance, and its potential to increase financial inclusion. Small and medium sized enterprises (MSMEs) may use supply chain financing (SCF) efficiently to deal with their shortage of credit. The reverse factoring market is expected to reach a value of US$ 536.4 billion in 2022. The market is projected to increase by 11.4% from 2023 to 2030. Annual growth over the next five years is projected to be 11% in global digital payment transactions, and many G20 countries should see faster expansion. By December 2023, total number of active accounts for sharing data in the AA system was 1.94 billion. The quickly developing digital lending business has another significant benefit that you can apply financial products within non-financial applications. Global revenue share of embedded banking services for SMEs stands to reach approximately 26% of the total SME banking market by 2025. Similarly, the venture capital industry has expanded dramatically in India at a CAGR of 49 percent between 2014 and 2021. Although it fell in 2023, India remained the second largest recipient of venture capital funding in the Asia Pacific Asia; one could contend that there is still extent of interest in the Indian market. MSMEs are able to use this diversification of funding sources to explore new markets and technology and innovate and grow. Though in its infancy in India, crowdfunding does have the potential to grow, but it faces regulatory hurdles. Yet despite having good ideas for absorbing the enthusiasm of local entrepreneurs, the transaction volume of India's crowdfunding industry is expected to grow at a modest CAGR (0.59%) against global leaders like United States, United Kingdom and China in the industry. The possible uptake of digital technologies and the predicted growth in the number of internet users in India to 900 million within the year 2025 is a chance and challenge for MSMEs. Successful trends include: more access to people's financial services through the use of technology. It also shows possible shortcomings in the digital literacy and availability that exist in areas that are not effectively incorporated into the digital environment.

However, to enhance the effectiveness of alternate financing mechanisms in addressing MSME financing gap in India, multi-dimensional approach may be required to address existing challenges. Accordingly, opportunities can be identified by enhancing the level of digitalization literacy, tackling legal ambiguity, enhancing the confidence of digital platforms' consumers, and developing a new range of MSME targeted financial products for various stages of their development and for different sectors.

5. SUGGESTIONS AND RECOMMENDATIONS

The current model to build Indian Micro, Small and Medium Enterprises (MSMEs) has lacking in terms of financing and digitization. To achieve these goals this MSMEs has to entail by increasing awareness of the current digital products and services, offering affordable technology products and enhancing the delivery of financial services and interfaces in the local languages is important through the finance providers. In place of traditional methods, the following should be embraced by MSMEs; peer to peer lending, supply chain financing and linking up with Fintech firms for innovative financing. Recommendations for MSME financing also includes, the laws should be strengthened so that they can foster innovation the same way they regulate firms in a way that will have least adverse effects to consumers; there should be adequate protection of data and regular reviews of algorithms. In addition, the potential of the MSMEs can be enhanced through training in some areas, awareness creation, and through the identification of peer roles so as to enable the MSMEs to harness the new financial instruments.

Also, there should be a promotion of the adoption of new technologies in credit operations including cloud computing and AI, and development of fintech solutions for the industry. The financing of MSMEs can be enhanced through the combined effort of banks and fintech's as well as the academia. Further the implementations needed are credit guarantee schemes, and the registration of a central credit reference bureau. Further to boost their growth, digital platforms have to be exposed for MSMEs to international markets and compliance advice can help firms that are ready to export. Promoting green financing options and developing specific measures for women entrepreneurs and rural MSMEs will foster sustainable development of the economy.

Hence, instrumenting these recommendations within an integrated framework will help Indian MSMEs to be in a position to overcome current challenges and efficiently exploit other sources of financing and thrive in the context of a highly digitalized economy and grow sustainably. This approach addresses including key areas like digital adoption, regulatory delivery, capacity building and ecosystem development to pave the way for MSMEs to operate effectively within a rapidly digitalizing and interconnected economy.

REFERENCES

Ahmed, S. (2020). Alternative credit scoring – a double-edged sword. In *Journal of Indian Law And Society* (Vols. 2–2).

Annual Report, M. S. M. E. 23-24). *Ministry of MSME, India*. https://www.msme.gov.in/sites/default/files/FINALMSMEANNUALREPORT2023-24ENGLISH.pdf

Avendus. (2023). MSME Lending, unlocking potential realizing dreams. In *Avendus*. https://www.avendus.com/crypted_pdf_path/msme-lending-report-formattedvf-img-642a719b97ccc-.pdf

Basha, M. J., Gupta, A., Raphael, P. D., Rajeev, V., & Rao, R. (2021). The Role of Digital Platforms in Revolutionizing the Lending Sector. *International Journal of Innovative Research*, 10(6), 6529–6536. DOI: 10.15680/IJIRSET.2021.1006354

Beltrame, F., Grassetti, L., Bertinetti, G. S., & Sclip, A. (2023). Relationship lending, access to credit and entrepreneurial orientation as cornerstones of venture financing. *Journal of Small Business and Enterprise Development*, 30(1), 4–29. DOI: 10.1108/JSBED-07-2021-0281

Block, J. H., Groh, A. P., Hornuf, L., Vanacker, T. R., & Vismara, S. (2020). The entrepreneurial finance markets of the future: A comparison of crowdfunding and initial coin offerings. *Small Business Economics*, 57(2), 865–882. DOI: 10.1007/s11187-020-00330-2

Chikwira, C., & Rawjee, V. P. (2022). Innovative Financing Strategies in the Small and Medium Business Sector, Tapping the Right Sources. *Journal of Accounting and Management*, 12(3), 7–17.

Cusmano, L., & Thompson, J. (2013). *Alternative financing instruments for SMEs and entrepreneurs*. OECD SME and Entrepreneurship Papers., DOI: 10.1787/3709429e-

D'Souza, V. (2019, April 1). *P2P lenders to the rescue of MSMEs*. Entrepreneur.

Digital lending industry in India. (2024, May 6). Statista Research Department.

G20 Global Partnership for Financial Inclusion. (2023). Innovations in financial services for Micro, Small and Medium-Sized Enterprises. In *G20 Global Partnership for Financial Inclusion*. International Finance Corporation.

Gandhi, R. (2022, July 31). Role of P2P lending in empowering SMEs in India. *ETBFSI.com*.

Gill, A. S., Mand, H. S., Sharma, S. P., & Mathur, N. (2012). Factors that Influence Financial Leverage of Small Business Firms in India. *International Journal of Economics and Finance*, 4(3). Advance online publication. DOI: 10.5539/ijef.v4n3p33

Hyde, K. R. (2021). *Alternative Finance Strategies for small business Sustainability and Growth*. Walden University.

IBEF. Indian Brand Equity foundation. (2024). Registered MSMEs in India in FY24. In *IBEF Re-imagining India's M&E Sector* [Report]. https://www.ibef.org/download/1720513075_MSME_May_2024.pdf

Ibrahim, P. A. (2018). Innovations in Financing SMEs: A Study on the Growth of Crowdfunding in India. *Wealth: International Journal of Money. Banking & Finance*, 7(3), 66.

Irfan, M. (2021, January). Do Shariah Indices converge? Evidence from Gulf Cooperation Council countries. *International Journal of Business Excellence*, 23(2), 251–269. DOI: 10.1504/IJBEX.2021.113448

Irfan, M., Elhoseny, M., Kassim, S., & Metawa, N. (2023). *Advanced Machine Learning Algorithms for Complex Financial Applications*. IGI Global., DOI: 10.4018/978-1-6684-4483-2

Irfan, M., Elmogy, M., Gupta, S., Khalifa, F., & Dias, R. (2024). *AI-Driven Decentralized Finance and the Future of Finance*. IGI Global., DOI: 10.4018/979-8-3693-6321-8

Irfan, M., Elmogy, M., Majid, M. S., & El-Sappagh, S. (2023). *The Impact of AI Innovation on Financial Sectors in the Era of Industry 5.0*. IGI Global., DOI: 10.4018/979-8-3693-0082-4

Irfan, M., Hussainey, K., Chan Bukhari, S. A., & Nam, Y. (Eds.). (2024). *Issues of Sustainability in AI and New-Age Thematic Investing*. IGI Global Publisher., DOI: 10.4018/979-8-3693-3282-5

Irfan, M., Kadry, S., Sharif, M., & Ullah Khan, H. (2023). *Fintech Applications in Islamic Finance: AI, Machine Learning, and Blockchain Techniques*. IGI Global., DOI: 10.4018/979-8-3693-1038-0

Jain, A. (2024). Role And Growth of Venture Capital in India with Availability of Funds for Small and Medium Enterprises and Start-Up for Bringing Sustainability in Economic Development. *Vidhyayana, An International Multidisciplinary Peer-Reviewed E-Journal, 9*(2), 138–161. https://vidhyayanaejournal.org/journal/article/view/1630/1747

Kanojia, S., Aggarwal, V., & Bhargava, A. (2020). Descendants of Financing Decision with Reference to Capital Structure: An Empirical Analysis of Indian SMEs. *Small Enterprises Development, Management & Extension Journal (SEDME)/SEDME. Small Enterprises Development. Management and Extension Journal*, 47(1), 33–42. DOI: 10.1177/0970846420930449

Kapoor, R., Indian Council for Research on International Economic Relations (ICRIER), & Goyal, T. M. (2024). Open banking systems for enhancing financial access for Micro, Small, and Medium-Sized Enterprises: the case of India. *ADBI Policy Brief*, 2024–13.

Kumar, P. (2024, June 27). Backbone of India: Empowering MSMEs through financial inclusion. *Business Today (Norwich)*.

Maiti, M. (2018). Scope for alternative avenues to promote financial access to MSMEs in developing nation evidence from India. *International Journal of Law and Management.International Journal of Law and Management*, 60(5), 1210–1222. DOI: 10.1108/IJLMA-06-2017-0141

Mohan, K. (2023b, March 18). *MSME Credit Capital Deficit – How much of a difference can Alternate Finance make?* Redseer Strategy Consultants. https://redseer.com/newsletters/msme-credit-capital-deficit/

Mulye, D. (2021, April 8). Challenges with MSME lending and how Embedded Finance solves them? *Finbox*.

Purwanto, I., Isnanto, R. R., & Widodo, A. P. (2023). Investigation of the impact of the Peer-To-Peer lending market on the membership motivation of the MSME. *E3S Web of Conferences, 448*, 02037. DOI: 10.1051/e3sconf/202344802037

Puschmann, T. (2017). Fintech. *Business & Information Systems Engineering*, 59(1), 69–76. DOI: 10.1007/s12599-017-0464-6

Ramasubramanian, S., & Belgavi, V. (2019). *A wider circle: Digital lending and the changing landscape of financial inclusion*.

Rani, P., & Katoch, R. (2022). Contribution of crowdfunding in the growth of MSMEs. *Journal of Applied Development Economics, 1–1*, 1–10.

Ritika, & Khanna, A. (2024,). *Crowdfunding: Exploring its Role as an Alternative Financial Avenue in the Indian Context*. In 14th International Conference on Industrial Engineering and Operations Management, .DOI: 10.46254/AN14.20240457

Rupeika Apoga, R., & Saksonova, S. (2018). SMEs' alternative financing : The case of Latvia. *European Research Studies Journal*, 21(3), 43–52.

Sahoo, P. B. B., & Thakur, V. (2023). Enhancing the performance of Indian micro, small and medium enterprises by implementing supply chain finance: Challenges emerging from COVID-19 pandemic. *Benchmarking*, 30(6), 2110–2138. DOI: 10.1108/BIJ-11-2021-0668

Saraswat, R. (2023, August 19). *Alternative credit scoring model for MSME*.

Sharma, S. K., Ilavarasan, P. V., & Karanasios, S. (2024). Small businesses and FinTech: A systematic review and future directions. *Electronic Commerce Research*, 24(1), 535–575. DOI: 10.1007/s10660-023-09705-5

Sheth, A., Krishnan, S., Kashyap, P., Deo, S., & Muralidhar. (2024, March 13). *India Venture Capital Report 2024*. Bain. https://www.bain.com/insights/india-venture-capital-report-2024/

Sonne, L. (2012). Innovative initiatives supporting inclusive innovation in India: Social business incubation and micro venture capital. *Technological Forecasting and Social Change*, 79(4), 638–647. DOI: 10.1016/j.techfore.2011.06.008

Thompson, J., Boschmans, K., & Pissareva, L. (2018). *Alternative financing instruments for SMEs and entrepreneurs*. OECD SME and Entrepreneurship Papers., DOI: 10.1787/dbdda9b6-

Unlocking credit for MSMEs: Innovations in supply chain finance. (2019). PwC.

Venkatesh, J., & Kumari, R. L. (2012). Enhancing SMEs Access to Green Finance. *International Journal of Marketing. Financial Services & Management Research*, 1(7), 22–35.

Vodolazhska, A. (2023, July 11). *Crowdfunding in India: Market Overview*. LenderKit.

Chapter 11
Understanding the Intellectual Contribution on Sustainable Development Goals:
A Scientometric and Thematic Assessment of Scientific Database

Santosh Satyanarayan Baheti
Christ University, India

Debora Dhanya Amarnath
Christ University, India

Aishwarya Satish Joshi
Independent Researcher, India

Gilney Figueira Zebende
State University of Feira de Santana, Brazil

ABSTRACT

The present study investigates the intellectual contribution of researchers, academicians, and industry experts on sustainable development goals. In the era of cut-throat competition companies across the globe wants to occupy top most position in the competition and have their dominance across the globe. This quench of profit and dominance resulting in exploitation of resources and affecting global environment across the globe. The gap between rich and poor is increasing day by day. The world is divided between rich and poor economies where the access and privileges of resources is concentrated in the hand of few. From 1972 till today different initiatives are taken at global level in order to address such global challenges, the formation of SDG is made by United Nations in the year 2016 is one of the breakthroughs in this process.

DOI: 10.4018/979-8-3693-7924-0.ch011

1. INTRODUCTION

The United Nations has published its first report in 1972 defining the importance of sustainability adoptions and its necessity. Since then, different commission committees and reports have been published in public domain to spread awareness about sustainability across the globe. One of the promising efforts was the formation of *Millennium Development Goals* in 2008. Most of the economies across the globe realized the importance of MDG's and showed positive response in its implementation. Despite formation of MDG's different challenges like poverty alleviation, equality at workplace, infrastructure development, responsible consumption and production, quality of education, good working conditions, quality of life, sustainable living place and so on remains a matter of prime attention. In order to address the above challenges and provide a broader framework in 2016 United Nations' (UN) has provided a framework of 17 sustainable development goals (SDGs), a global roadmap towards achieving a more sustainable and promising future for all. These goals were designed as a universal political agenda that call for an action to achieve socio, environmental and economic wellbeing for all by 2030 (United Nations 2015). The UN General Assembly has approved 17 interconnected SDGs with 169 specific targets and 213 indicators for the action plan "Transforming our world: the 2030 Agenda for Sustainable Development" (United Nations, 2017). Some of the most essential objectives on the list include those designed to eradicate poverty, end malnutrition, promote wellness and health, offer high-quality schooling, improve gender equality, give easy access to clean water and sanitation, move forward affordable and clean energy, present decent work and boost the economy, deal with infrastructure, creativity, minimize disparities, foster environmentally friendly towns and cities, motivate ethical consumption and manufacturing, tackle the effects of climate change, foster life below the water, enable life on land, and strive towards justice, peace, and resilient institutions (United Nations, 2020). Since achieving these objectives would require significant and transdisciplinary efforts, the scientific community's intellectual contributions have become crucial for advancing towards these ambitious goals. Analysing and understanding these scientific contributions from various fields necessitates an intricate review of relevant studies that emphasizes important themes, concepts, frameworks, behaviour, developments and gaps in the scientific database.

The quantity and quality of related research has increased significantly since the SDGs were adopted. A bibliometric assessment of the Web of Science database was carried out by Zhou et al. (2022), who found a notable increase in publications addressing the Sustainable Development Goals (SDGs), particularly in domains such as clean water and sanitation (SDG 6) and climate action (SDG 13). According to Zhou and Leidesdorff (2020), their investigation illustrates a growing academic interest as well as financial support for sustainability studies. Based on earlier studies on geographic analysis, the most prominent three countries contributing to SDG-related research are China, the United States, and Europe (Bormann and Mutz (2015).

Because of their strong research infrastructure and dedication to sustainability challenges, organisations like the Chinese Academy of Sciences and the University of California have a significant impact (Bornmann & Mutz, 2015). Although wealthy nations such as the US and Europe are at the forefront of SDG research, countries that are developing noticeably contribute very little to the field. The global relevance and inclusivity of study results are limited because of the disparity. To assure equitable distribution of resources and knowledge, efforts should be carried out to foster and support research in developing regions. After a comprehensive thematic analysis, Salvia et al. (2019) revealed that issues revolving around climate change, renewable energy, and sustainable urban development are prevalent.

Additionally, some of the researchers focused on interdisciplinary SDG research in the context of public health, engineering, and economics (Salvia et al., 2019; Le Blanc, 2015). and suggested to further explore the impact of SDG through impact assessments and citation analysis. Applying altmetrics to assess publications' societal impact, Haunschild et al. (2016) found that research on health (SDG 3) and education (SDG 4) substantially engages and influences society. This demonstrates the significance that research is for influencing policies and practices as well as educational institutions (Haunschild et al., 2016; Fuso Nerini et al., 2018). The study identified important gaps based on the literature review and made an effort to fill those gaps with the current investigation. Many literature studies have mentioned that there is a significant disparity towards scientific research and its real-world applications in business and public policy. Effective scientometric and thematic analyses depend on the readily accessible and availability of high-quality data. On the other hand, inconsistent data standards and limited access to the datasets provide significant challenges. It is essential to conduct Scientometric and Thematic Assessment of Scientific Database on the resilience and sustainability of growth strategies can be strengthened by the use of such studies. The multifaceted scope of the SDGs warrants further examination of various industries as the current state of research at times demonstrates silos within particular disciplines, which limits the solutions that simultaneously address multiple Sustainable Development Goals.

The objective of this book chapter is to provide a comprehensive thematic and scientometric review of the scientific contributions to the SDGs. By utilising bibliometric tools and methodologies, we will map out the landscape of SDG-related research. We would like to delineate the terrain of SDG-related research studies, emphasizing current domains, major studies, and widely recognized investigators and institutions, by applying bibliometric methodology. Our investigation relies on a broad spectrum of scholarly academic publications that investigated the scientific pursuits of sustainable development. In order to attain shared and sustainable prosperity the various stakeholders such as companies, sectors, community organisations, governments, nonprofit groups, research, and other stakeholders must work together to implement the Sustainable Development Goals (SDGs) advancement of technology (Khaled et al. 2021). Thus, this study was intended to shed light on assessing the existing literature and research trends of scientific publications on SDGs over the previous 5 years (2015–2019). Traditional bibliometric technique (Broadus, 1987), which has been widely applied to analyse and evaluate a wide range of scientific and medical topics (Sweileh, 2018; 2019; 2020) provided the base for the analysis. Through this chapter, we aim to not only quantify the scholarly output related to the SDGs but also to understand the thematic orientations and interdisciplinary collaborations that are driving this research. By providing a scientometric and thematic assessment, we seek to illuminate the intellectual landscape of SDG-related research, offering insights into its evolution, current state, and future directions. This comprehensive analysis will serve as a valuable resource for researchers, policymakers, and practitioners committed to advancing sustainable development worldwide.

1.1 Research Objectives

Research objectives provide directions for conducting research. In order to understand broader perspectives on sustainable development goals and contribution from academicians, researchers and corporations, the study has framed following research objectives.

RO1: To understand evolution, development and dominance of intellectual contribution on sustainable development goals.

RO2: To conduct quantitative assessment of published research work on different aspects of sustainable development goals
RO3: To conduct impact assessment through thematic analysis and analysis of influential studies on sustainable development goals
RO4: To understand influential authors, countries, organizations and journals defining the domain of sustainable development goals.

1.2 Framing of Research Questions

RQ1: What are the prominent themes emerging in SDG domain?
RQ2: What is the impact of literature published on SDG to the knowledge domain?
RQ3: What is the co-citation analysis structure of literature published on SDG?
RQ4: What is the network and collaborative tendency of literature published on SDG?
RQ5: What is the bibliographic coupling analysis of literature published on SDG?

1.3 Execution Strategy to Address Research Questions

RQ1 Strategy: Co-occurrence analysis of all keywords through Vos-viewer
RQ2 Strategy: Citation analysis of authors, institutions, countries, and journals through Vos-viewer
RQ3 Strategy: Co-citation analysis of authors, institutions, countries, and journals through Vos-viewer
RQ4 Strategy: Co-authorship analysis of authors, institutions, countries, and journals through Vos-viewer
RQ5 Strategy: Bibliographic coupling analysis of authors, institutions, countries, and journals through Vos-viewer

2. RESEARCH METHODOLOGY

'Scopus' database is used for the present analysis. It is one of the exhaustive and broadest databases which consists of more than 22000 journals (Baheti and Lenka, 2021). It is a reliable database as journals and books under Scopus has to go through double blind peer review process. Under keyword criteria selection 'sustainable development goals or 'SDG' was the only keyword which is used in the filtration process. Language as English only and articles published in journals only considered for the final analysis. (Baheti and Lenka, 2023). The top twenty-five journals from Q1, Q2, and Q3 category are considered in the further evaluation process. Under the exclusion criteria Books, Chapters, Note and Editorial excluded from the analysis. Through the filteration process we have 828 papers for the final analysis. Time span covered for the analysis is from 2016 to 2024. Forthcoming articles are excluded from the study.

3. RESULTS OF STUDY

3.1 Analysis of Different Themes Through Keyword Analysis

Keyword analysis helps in understanding development of the domain and prominent areas where most of the research work is being conducted (Donthu et al. 2021). Occurrence of keywords for number of times also highlights the most recurrent theme discussed by the academicians and researchers. Through VOS Viewer keyword analysis is performed, keywords with minimum 25 occurrences are considered, out of 5436 keywords 26 match the threshold. For each of these keywords total strength link is calculated and keywords with greatest strength links are selected. All these 26 items are divided into three clusters.

Cluster One: Cluster one is depicted in red color with ten items namely carbon, climate change, developing countries, economic and social effects, economics, energy utilization, environmental protection, greenhouse gases, investments, and planning. Most of the keywords under cluster one are environmental impact assessments.

Cluster Two: Cluster two is depicted in green color and it consists of eight items, corporate social responsibility, environmental economics, innovation, sustainability, sustainable development goals and united nations. Cluster two primarily emphasizes the role of corporate social responsibility and sustainability in innovation of environmental economics.

Cluster Three: Cluster three is depicted in blue color and it consists of eight items, circular economy, decision making, environmental impact, environmental sustainability, life cycle, supply chain management, supply chain and sustainable development. Cluster three emphasis on most of the research studies pertaining to supply chain management, circular economy and environmental sustainability.

Table 1. Co-occurrence analysis of all keywords

Sr	Keyword	O	TLS	Sr	Keyword	O	TLS
1	Sustainable Development	461	1033	11	Investments	39	133
2	Sustainability	173	409	12	Circular Economy	45	132
3	Sustainable Development Goal	144	315	13	United Nations	41	124
4	Planning	96	276	14	Greenhouse Gases	36	120
5	Decision-making	67	223	15	Supply Chain	37	117
6	Economic and Social Effects	58	218	16	Environmental Sustainability	35	112
7	Climate Change	58	187	17	SDG	57	111
8	Economics	53	173	18	Environmental Protection	27	105
9	Environmental Impact	48	163	19	Carbon	27	102
10	Life Cycle	54	160	20	Developing Countries	28	99

Note: Data derived from Scopus Database and VOS Viewer Software

Note: Data analysis conducted as on 11 July 2024

Figure 1. Co-occurrence analysis of all keywords

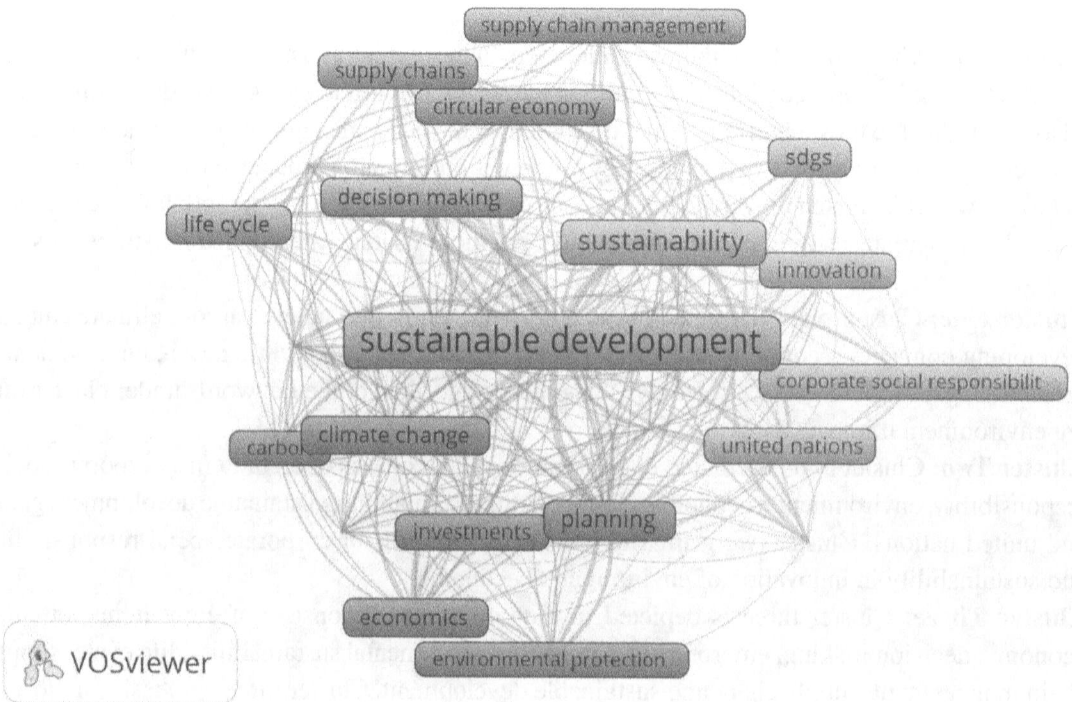

Source: VOS Viewer Software

3.2 Citation Analysis

Citation analysis helps in understanding to examine the documents that have generated highest documents and created their impact through among research community. Through VOS Viewer citation analysis of documents, authors, countries, institutions and journals is conducted (Van Eck and Waltman, 2017; Baker et al. 2020).

3.2.1 Citation Analysis of Documents

Documents with minimum 100 citations considered for the analysis. Of the 828 documents 80 meet the threshold. For each of the 80 documents total strength link is calculated and documents with maximum strength lin k are considered for the final analysis. Highly cited documents are considered as influential and impactful document among the research community. Bai et al. 2020 has received highest 695 citations, followed by Demato et al. 2017 with 647 citations. A study conducted by Demato et al.2017 has focused comparative assessment of green, circular and bio economy. A study conducted by Bai et al. 2020 has focused on technological assessment of Industry 4.0. Both the studies are published in Journal of Cleaner Production which is a Q1 category and ABDC 'A' category journal. A study conducted by

Shahbaz, Balsalobre-lorente and Sinha in 2017 has generated 437 citations and focused on the nexus between foreign direct investment and CO2 emission.

Figure 2. Citation analysis of document

Source: VOS Viewer Software

3.2.2 Citation Analysis of Journals

Sources with minimum 5 documents and 25 citations considered for the analysis. Out of the 28 sources 24 meet the threshold criteria. Journal of Cleaner Production has published 310 documents with 17357 citations. Technology Forecasting and Social Change has 1969 citations from 45 documents. Journal of Sustainable Tourism has received 1968 citations from 40 documents. Journal of Production Economics has received 1645 citations from 12 documents. Business Strategy and The Environment has received 1715 citations from 51 documents. Journal of Business Research has received 1432 citations from 23 documents. All these journals are Q1 category and ABDC 'A' category listed.

Figure 3. Citation analysis of journals

Source: VOS Viewer Software

3.2.3 Citation Analysis of Organization

Organization with minimum 3 documents and 25 citations considered for the analysis. Of the total 2326 organization 22 match the threshold criteria. For each of these 22 organizations total strength link is calculated and the organisations with greatest strength link are selected for further analysis. These 22 items are divided into 22 different clusters. Figure 4 indicates organization-wise citation analysis. *'Goa Institute of Management, Centre for Excellence in Sustainable Development, India'* has published 7 documents and received 1147 citations. *'Shanghai Maritime University, China'* has published 9 documents and received 1107 citations. *'Centre for Supply Chain Engineering, Department of Technology and Innovation, Danish Institute'* has published 5 documents and generated 630 citations. School of Business and *'Economics, Linnaeus University'*, Sweden has generated 472 citations and *'Lund University, Sweden'* has generated 395 citations.

Figure 4. Citation analysis of organizations

Source: VOS Viewer Software

3.2.4 Citation Analysis of Authors

Authors with minimum 2 documents and 25 citations considered for the analysis. Of the total 819 authors 9 authors meet the threshold criteria. For each of the 9 authors total strength link is calculated and authors with greatest strength links are selected. Rosati and Farai has published two documents in collaboration and generated 619 citations. Gossling has generated 167 citations from 2 documents. Van Zanten and Van Tadler has generated 143 citations from 2 documents. Muff, Kapalka and Dyllick has generated 112 citations from 2 documents. Khan, Zohal and Akhtar has produced 85 citations from 2 documents. These 9 items are divided into 9 clusters as depicted in Figure 5.

Figure 5. Citation analysis of authors

Source: VOS Viewer Software

3.2.5 Citation Analysis Country-Wise

Countries with 5 documents and 100 citations considered for the analysis. Of the total 102 countries 45 countries meet the threshold criteria. For each of these 45 items total strength link is calculated and items with greatest strength links are selected.UK has generated 9551 citations from 173 documents. China has generated 4762 citations from 89 documents. Italy has generated 4444 citations. India has generated 3961 citations and USA has generated 3456 citations. All these 44 items are divided into 44 cluster depicted in the Figure 6 as follows. Average citations received by the UK is 55.28, China 52.49, Italy 45.81, USA 41.61 and Spain 36.36.

Figure 6. Citation analysis of countries

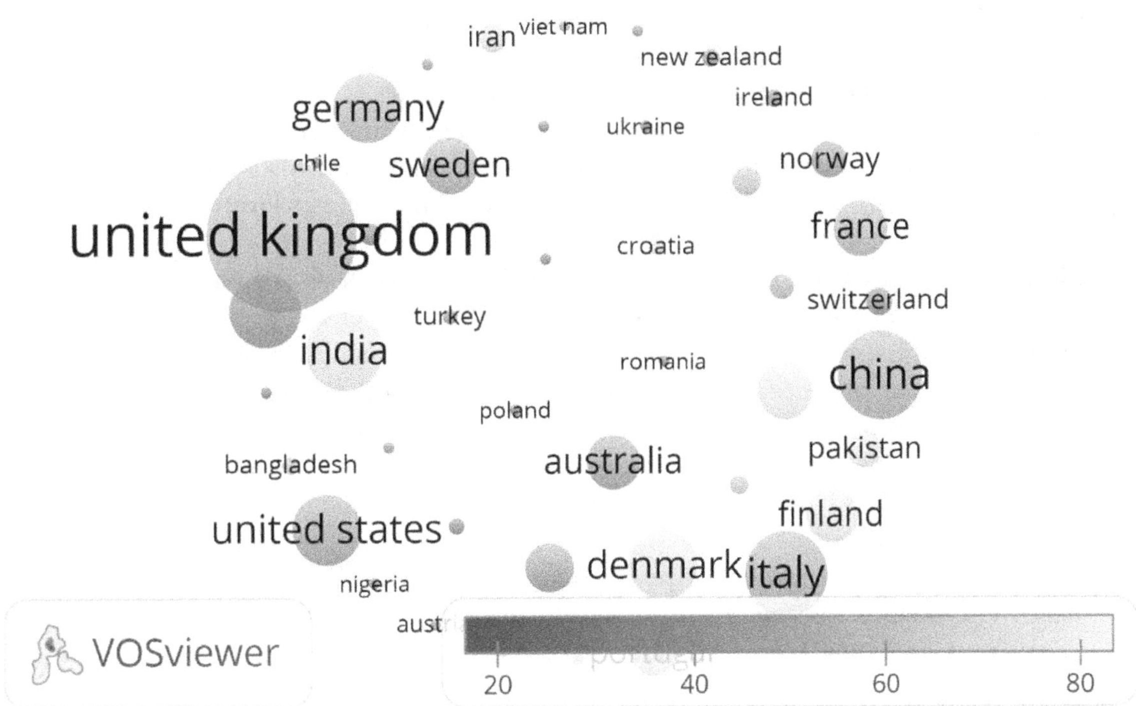

Source: VOS Viewer Software

3.3 Co-Citation Analysis

Co-citation analysis helps in understanding the relationship between the two documents (Small, 1973). It reflects the frequency in which two research studies are cited together. (Small, 1973).

3.3.1 Co-Citation Analysis of Cited References

Minimum number of 5 citations of cited references considered for the analysis. Of the total 58531 references 106 match the threshold criteria. For each of the 106 items total strength link is calculated and items with greatest strength links are considered for the further analysis. These 106 items are divided into 7 different clusters. These 7 clusters are connected with 758 links and 1121 total strength links.

Cluster One: Cluster one is depicted in red color and it consists of 22 items. A study by Ghissilini et al. on review of circular economy has received 11 citations with total link strength of 22 and 13 links connected. Most common theme discussed in cluster one is circular economy. Two prominent theories are also discussed in cluster on Resource Based View and Stakeholders Theory.

Cluster Two: Cluster two is depicted in green color and it consists of 18 items. Most prominent theme discussed in cluster two is stakeholders approach, institutional theory, stakeholder's theory, agency theory, sustainability reporting and social and ethical consideration.
Cluster Three: Cluster three is depicted in blue color and it consists of 15 items. Most common themes discussed in cluster three are sustainability for tourism, tourism policy, sustainable tourism development, tourism labor and sustainable development goals.
Cluster Four: Cluster four is depicted in yellow color and it consists of 15 items. Most common themes discussed cluster four are sustainable development goals, SDG reporting, sustainable development agenda, SDG and private sector participation, corporate involvement for SDG and SDG challenges.
Cluster Five: Cluster five is depicted in purple color and it consists of 15 items. Most common themes discussed cluster renewable energy consumption, corporate involvement in sustainable development goals, renewable energy policies, technological innovation and environment quality and advancing the role of education for implementing corporate sustainability.
Cluster Six: Cluster six is depicted in sky color and it consists of 12 items. Most common themes discussed are business models for sustainable innovations, corporate social responsibility, transforming sustainability challenges and sustainability reporting. Dynamic Capability Theory is also discussed in this cluster.
Cluster Seven: Cluster seven is depicted in orange color and it consists of 9 items. Most common themes discussed partnership to address social issues, sustainable urbanization, MNC and SDG compliances, transitioning from MDG to SDG.

Figure 7. Co-citation analysis of cited references

Source: VOS Viewer Software

3.3.2 Co-Citation Analysis of Cited Authors

Authors with minimum 50 citations considered for the analysis. Of the total 81893 authors 17 meet the threshold criteria. For each of these 17 authors total strength link is calculated and authors with greatest strength links are selected. These 17 items are divided into 4 clusters. Cluster 1 consist of 9 items, cluster 2 consists of 4 items, cluster 3 and cluster 4 consists of 2 items respectively. All the clusters are connected with 134 links and total link strength of 7,309. Table indicates all 17 authors citations, links, and total link strength. Figure represent cluster wise graphical analysis.

Table 2. Co-citation analysis of cited authors

Sr.	Author Name	Citations	Links	TLS
1	Shahbaz, M.	141	16	1544
2	Sinha, A.	144	14	1540
3	Liu,Y.	163	16	1334
4	Wang,Y.	175	16	1261
5	Zhang, Y.	161	16	1129
6	Sarkis, J.	169	16	1005

continued on following page

Table 2. Continued

Sr.	Author Name	Citations	Links	TLS
7	Govindan, K.	167	16	992
8	Li, Y.	137	16	989
9	Li, J.	113	16	838
10	Wang, S.	101	15	796
11	Liu,J.	106	16	781
12	Zhang,X.	102	16	767
13	Wang,X.	105	16	747
14	Rockstorm,J.	111	16	282
15	Schaltegger, S.	134	16	253
16	Leal Fillho.W.	137	16	240
17	Hall,C.M.	118	16	120

Note: Interpretation taken from Scopus Generated CSV file and VOS Viewer Software

Figure 8. Co-citation analysis of cited authors

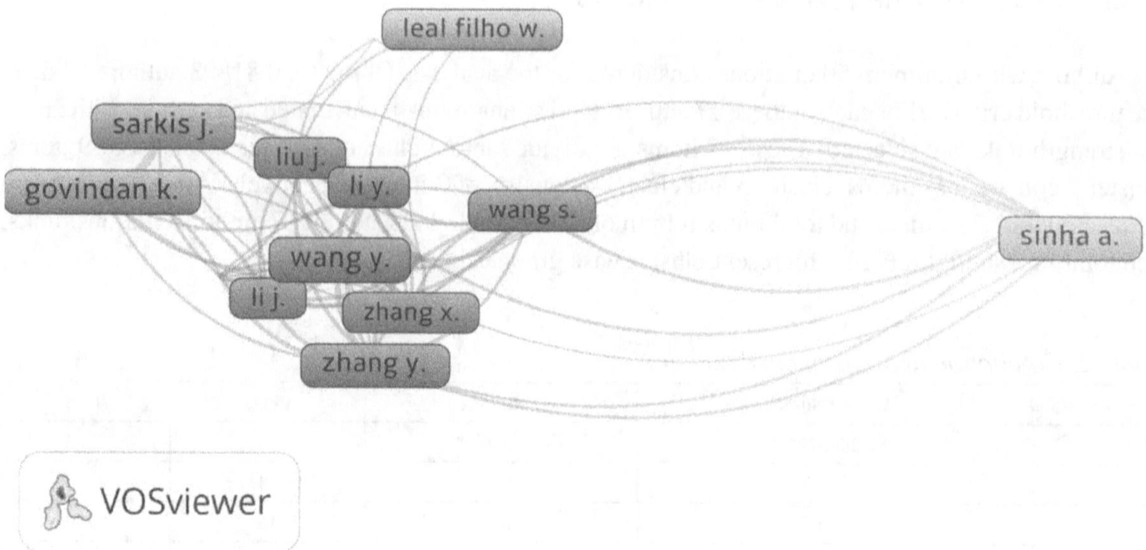

Source: VOS Viewer Software

3.4 Co-Authorship Analysis

3.4.1 Co-Authorship Analysis Author-wise

Authors with minimum 2 documents and 10 citations considered for the analysis. Of the total 819 authors only 9 authors match the threshold criteria. For each of the 9 authors total strength link is calculated and authors with greatest strength links are considered for the further analysis. All these 9 items are divided into 9 clusters'. Density visualization all the clusters is depicted in the figure. Rosati and Faria has generated 619 citations from 2 documents. Gossling through 2 collaborations has generated 167 citations. Van Zanten and Van Tudler has received 143 citations from 2 documents.

Figure 9. Co-authorship analysis of cited authors

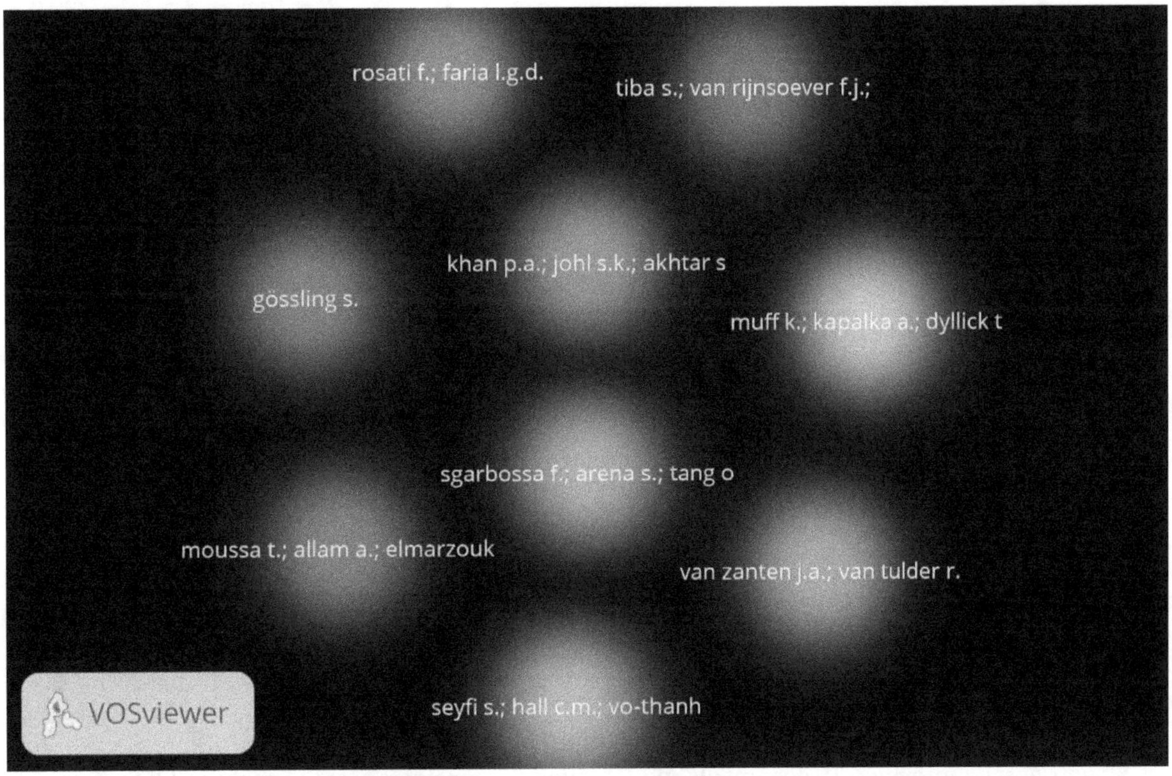

Source: VOS Viewer Software

3.4.2 Co-Authorship Analysis of Organization

Organization with minimum 3 documents and 30 citations considered for the analysis. Of the total 2326 organizations 22 match the threshold criteria. For these 22 items total strength link is calculated and organizations with greatest strength links are considered for the further analysis. These 22 items are divided into 12 clusters. Goa Institute of Management, India, has produced 7 documents and generated

1147 citations. Shanghai Maritime University, China, has produced 9 documents and generated 1107 citations through collaboration. Cluster 1 consists of 6 items, cluster 2 consists of 4 items, cluster 3 to cluster 4 consists of 2 items respectively. All these clusters are connected with 20 links with total link strength of 57.

Figure 10: Co-authorship analysis of organization-wise

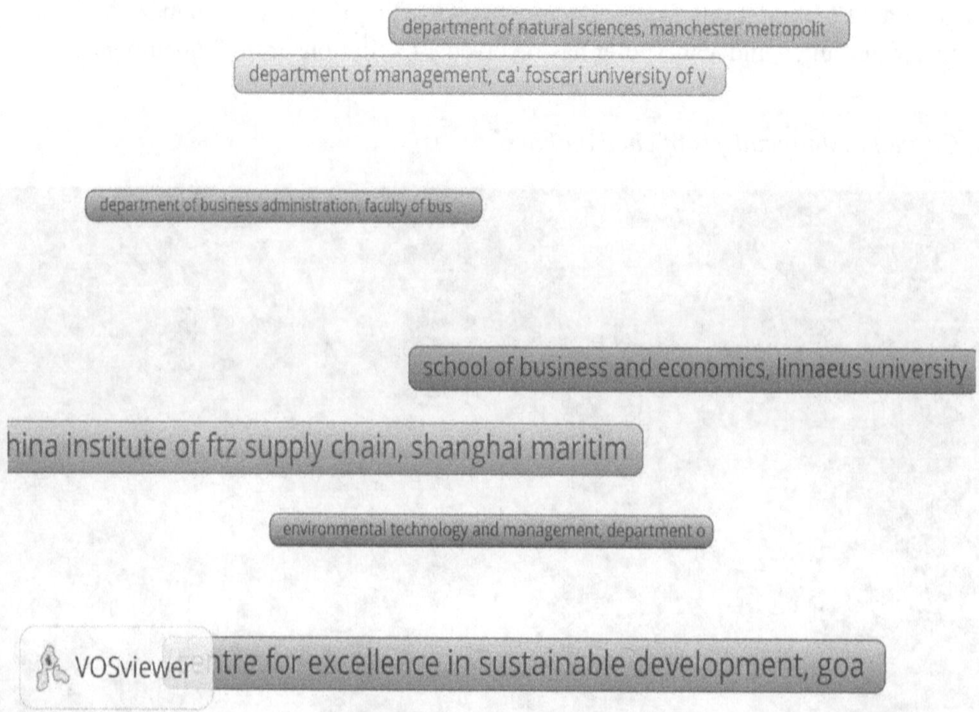

Source: VOS Viewer Software

3.4.3 Co-Authorship Analysis Country-Wise

Countries with minimum 10 documents and 100 citations considered for the analysis. Of the total 102 countries 34 match the threshold criteria. For each of the 34 items total strength link is calculated and items with greatest strength links are selected for further analysis. These 34 items are spread among 9 different clusters shown in the below figure. UK has generated 173 documents and 9551 citations, China 89 documents and4672 citations, USA 83 documents and 3456 citations, Germany 60 documents and 3391 citations. UK is connected with 31 links and total link strength of 216. Spain is connected with 25 links and total link strength of 83. China is connected with 25 links with total link strength of 125.

Figure 11. Co-authorship analysis of country-wise

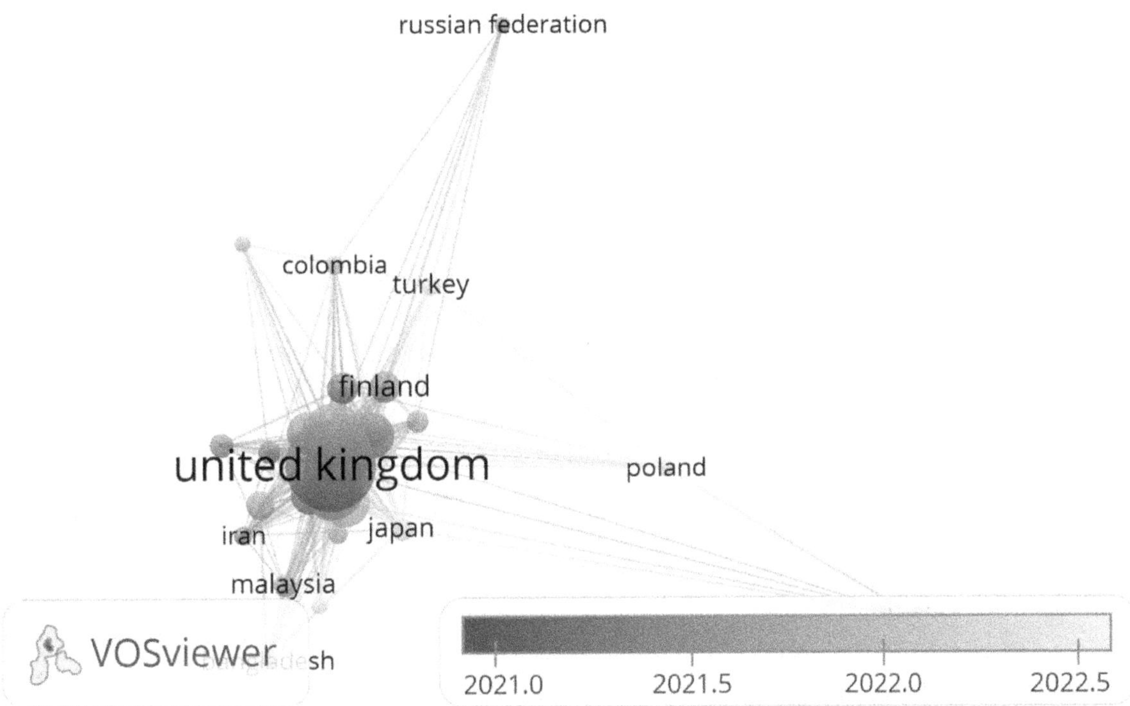

Source: VOS Viewer Software

3.5 Bibliographic Coupling

3.5.1 Bibliographic Coupling Document wise

Documents with minimum 100 citations considered for the analysis. Of the total 828 documents 80 documents match the threshold criteria. For each of the 80 documents total strength link is calculated and documents with highest strength links are considered for the further analysis. A document by Sinha, Sengupta and Saha (2020) has generated 109 citations with total link strength of 69. Another document by Sinha, Sengupta, and Alvarado (2020) has generated 313 citations with total link strength of 62. Of the total 80 documents the largest connected 59 documents are considered for the final analysis.

Figure 12. Bibliographic coupling document wise

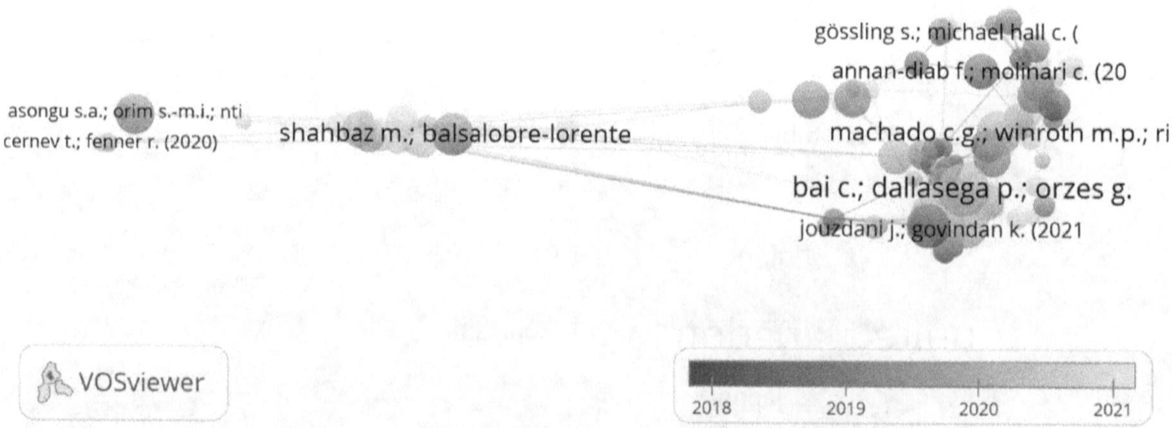

Source: VOS Viewer Software

3.5.2 Bibliographic Coupling Source Wise

Sources with minimum 10 documents and 100 citations considered for the analysis. Of the 28 sources 19 meet the threshold criteria. For each of these 19 sources total strength link is calculated and sources with highest strength link are considered for the further analysis. '*Journal of Cleaner Production*' has produced 310 documents with 17537 citations and total link strength of 1528. '*Business Strategy and The Environment*' has produced 51 documents with 1715 citations and total link strength of 1120. '*Corporate Social Responsibility and Environmental Management*' has produced 24 documents and generated 959 citations with total link strength of 1023. '*Journal of Business Ethics*' has produced 17 documents and generated 607 citations with total link strength of 627. These 19 items are divided into 3 different clusters, cluster 1 consists of 7 items and cluster 2 and cluster 3 consists of 6 items each respectively.

Table 3. Bibliographic coupling of source

Cluster	Color	Cluster Items	ND	Links	TLS	C	NC
Cluster One	Red	Administrative Sciences	27	16	247	315	10.36
		Cities	33	16	204	898	32.11
		International Journal of Management Education	12	15	145	803	10.39
		Journal of Risk and Financial Management	32	15	108	333	11.84
		Journal of Sustainable Tourism	40	16	443	1968	45.62
		Problems and Perspectives in Management	32	15	191	228	6.65
		Statistical Journal of IAOS	27	14	205	116	2.41
Cluster Two	Green Color	Business Strategy and Development	16	16	343	142	7.64
		Business Strategy and The Environment	51	17	1081	1715	65.47
		Corporate Social Responsibility and Environment Management	24	15	980	959	39.91
		Journal of Business Ethics	17	17	625	607	14.23
		Journal of Business Research	23	16	377	1432	42.62
		Sustainability Accounting and Policy Journal	15	17	581	199	7.24
Cluster Three	Blue Color	International Journal of Production Economics	12	9	251	1645	34.78
		Futures	15	10	39	323	9.88
		Journal of Cleaner Production	310	17	1406	17537	350.29
		Technological Forecasting and Social Change	45	17	502	1969	56.42

Figure 13. Bibliographic coupling source wise

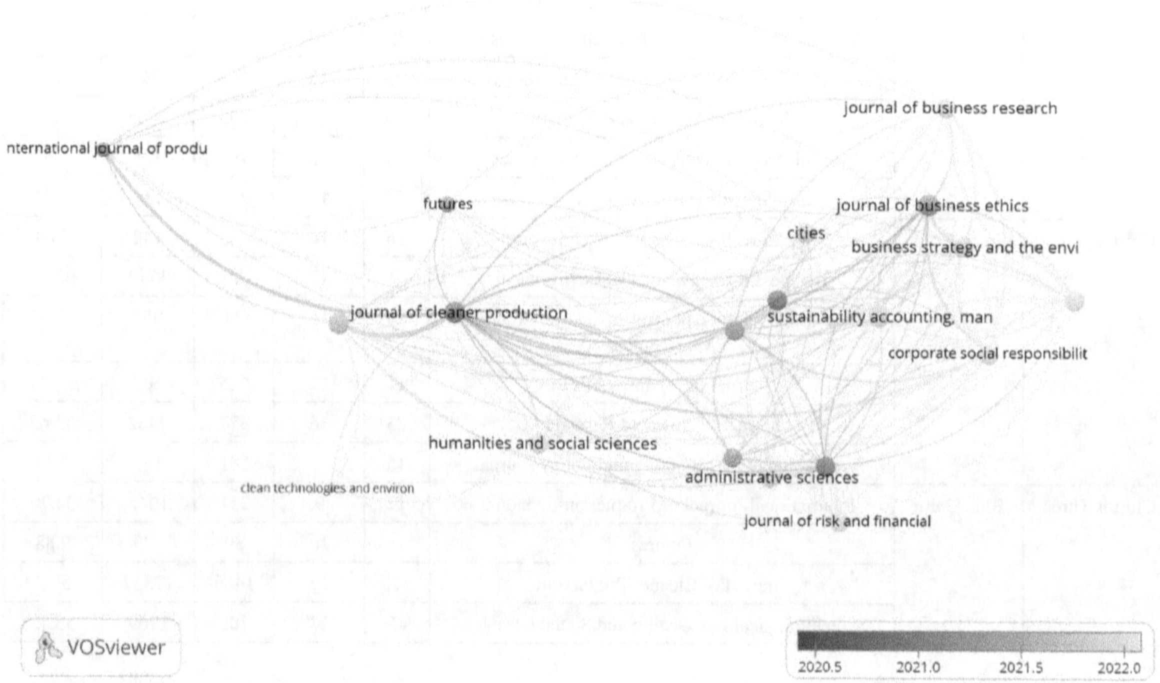

Source: VOS Viewer Software

3.5.3 Bibliographic Coupling Organization Wise

Organization with minimum 2 documents and 20 citations are considered for the analysis. Of the total 2326 organizations 71 meet the threshold criteria. The largest set of 68 items are considered for the final analysis. These 68 items are further divided into 8 different clusters. Cluster 1 consists of 17 items, clusters 2 and cluster 3 consists of 12 items, cluster 4 consists of 11 items, cluster 5 consists of 9 items, cluster 6 consist of 3 items and cluster 7 and cluster 8 consists of 2 items respectively. All the clusters are connected with 439 links with total link strength of 13611.

Figure 14. Bibliographic coupling organization wise

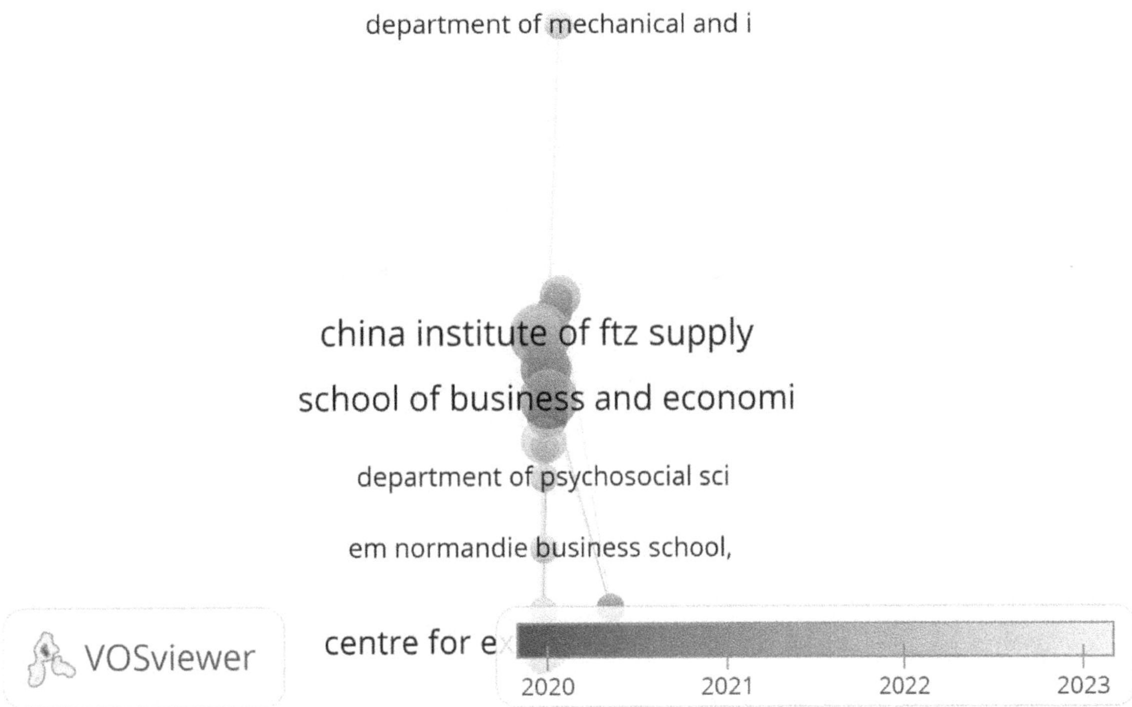

Source: VOS Viewer Software

3.5.4 Bibliographic Coupling Country Wise

Countries with minimum 5 documents and 50 citations are considered for the analysis. Of the 102 countries 51 meet the threshold criteria. For each of these 51 items total strength link is calculated and items with greatest strength links are selected. All these 51 items are divided into 6 different clusters. *UK* is the largest thread among all the clusters with 173 documents, 25569 TLS, and 50 links, which indicates it is connected with all threads of clusters. *Spain* has produced 89 documents with 99 documents and 11246 citations. *USA* has produced 83 documents 83 documents and 11590 citations.

Figure 15. Bibliographic coupling country wise

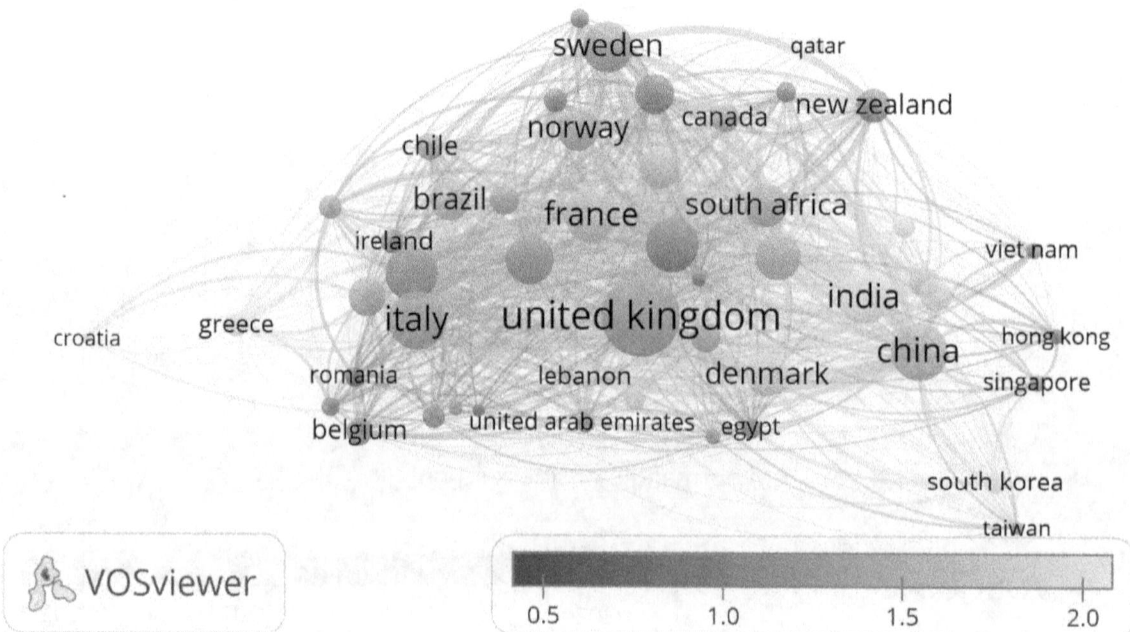

Source: VOS Viewer Software

4. CONCLUSIVE REMARKS, LIMITATIONS AND FUTURE IMPLICATIONS OF STUDY

4.1 Findings of Study

- More than 70 percent of the research output is the result of collaborative research tendency between two or more authors
- Single author contribution is found to be lesser in number.
- *'Goa Institute of Management, Centre for Excellence in Sustainable Development, India'*, *'Shanghai Maritime University, China'*, *'Centre for Supply Chain Engineering, Department of Technology and Innovation, Danish Institute'*, *'Economics, Linnaeus University'*, Sweden are the published maximum research output on sustainable development goals.
- *UK* has generated 9551 citations; *China* has generated 4762 citations. *Italy* has generated 4,444 citations. India has generated 3961 citations and *USA* has generated 3456 citations. Average citations received by the *UK* is 55.28, *China* 52.49, *Italy* 45.81, *USA* 41.61 and *Spain* 36.36.
- *Journal of Cleaner Production* has published 310 documents with 17357 citations. *Technology Forecasting and Social Change* has 1969 citations from 45 documents. *Journal of Sustainable*

Tourism has received 1968 citations from 40 documents. *Journal of Production Economics* has received 1645 citations from 12 documents. *Business Strategy and The Environment* has received 1715 citations from 51 documents. *Journal of Business Research* has received 1432 citations from 23 documents.

- *Rosati and Farai* has published generated 619 citations through collaborative research work. *Gossling* has generated 167 citations from 2 research studies. *Van Zanten and Van Tadler* has generated 143 citations from 2 documents. *Muff, Kapalka and Dyllick* has generated 112 citations from 2 research studies. *Khan, Zohal and Akhtar* has produced 85 citations from 2 research studies.
- Most of the keywords under cluster one are *environmental impact assessment.* Cluster two primarily emphasis on the *role of corporate social responsibility and sustainability in innovation of environmental economics.* Cluster three emphasis on most of the research studies pertaining to *supply chain management, circular economy and environmental sustainability.*

4.2 Limitation of Study

- The present study is quantitative assessment of data on sustainable development goals. It lacks empirical investigations.
- The literature published only Scopus database is considered for the analysis other prominent database like web of science is excluded while filtering the data to get the relevant results.
- The present study has not emphasized on the development of conceptual framework.

4.3 Future Implications of Study

- In future the study intends to develop a conceptual framework defining the different dimensions of sustainable development goals and its impact of on all the stakeholders.
- In future the study also intends to conduct empirical relationship between the constructs identified in the conceptual framework.
- Industry comparison will be conducted in order to check applicability of SDG among all the industries.

REFERENCES

Baheti, S. S., & Lenka, U. (2021). Sustainable innovation for sustainable business performance-a systematic review of recent literature (2008-2018). *International Journal of Business Excellence*, 23(4), 517–545. DOI: 10.1504/IJBEX.2021.114733

Baheti, S. S., & Lenka, U. (2023). A scientometric evaluation of International Journal of Business Innovation and Research:(2006-2019). *International Journal of Business Innovation and Research*, 30(3), 283–322. DOI: 10.1504/IJBIR.2023.129362

Bai, C., Dallasega, P., Orzes, G., & Sarkis, J. (2020). Industry 4.0 technologies assessment: A sustainability perspective. *International Journal of Production Economics*, 229, 107776. DOI: 10.1016/j.ijpe.2020.107776

Baker, H. K., Kumar, S., & Pandey, N. (2020). A bibliometric analysis of managerial finance: A retrospective. *Managerial Finance*, 46(11), 1495–1517. DOI: 10.1108/MF-06-2019-0277

Bornmann, L., & Mutz, R. (2015). Growth rates of modern science: A bibliometric analysis based on the number of publications and cited references. *Journal of the Association for Information Science and Technology*, 66(11), 2215–2222. DOI: 10.1002/asi.23329

Broadus, R. N. (1987). Toward a definition of "bibliometrics". *Scientometrics*, 12(5-6), 373–379. DOI: 10.1007/BF02016680

Donthu, N., Kumar, S., Mukherjee, D., Pandey, N., & Lim, W. M. (2021). How to conduct a bibliometric analysis: An overview and guidelines? *Journal of Business Research*, 133, 285–296. DOI: 10.1016/j.jbusres.2021.04.070

Fuso Nerini, F., Henriksson, G., & Vennström, E. (2018). A comprehensive review of climate change adaptation in the built environment: Assessing scientific knowledge and policy instruments. *Energy Procedia*, 153, 44–49.

Haunschild, R., Bornmann, L., & Marx, W. (2016). Climate change research in view of bibliometrics. *PLoS One*, 11(7), e0160393. DOI: 10.1371/journal.pone.0160393 PMID: 27472663

Khaled, R., Ali, H., & Mohamed, E. K. A. (2021). The Sustainable Development Goals and corporate sustainability performance: Mapping, extent and determinants. *Journal of Cleaner Production*, 311, 127599. DOI: 10.1016/j.jclepro.2021.127599

Le Blanc, D. (2015). Towards integration at last? The sustainable development goals as a network of targets. *Sustainable Development (Bradford)*, 23(3), 176–187. DOI: 10.1002/sd.1582

Salvia, A. L., Leal Filho, W., Brandli, L. L., & Griebeler, J. S. (2019). Assessing research trends related to Sustainable Development Goals: Local and global issues. *Journal of Cleaner Production*, 208, 841–849. DOI: 10.1016/j.jclepro.2018.09.242

Shahbaz, M., Balsalobre-Lorente, D., & Sinha, A. (2019). Foreign direct Investment–CO2 emissions nexus in Middle East and North African countries: Importance of biomass energy consumption. *Journal of Cleaner Production*, 217, 603–614. DOI: 10.1016/j.jclepro.2019.01.282

Small, H. (1973). Co-citation in the scientific literature: A new measure of the relationship between two documents. *Journal of the American Society for Information Science*, 24(4), 265–269. DOI: 10.1002/asi.4630240406

Sweileh, W. M. (2018). Global output of research on the health of international migrant workers from 2000 to 2017. *Globalization and Health*, 14(1), 1–12. DOI: 10.1186/s12992-018-0419-9 PMID: 30409221

Sweileh, W. M. (2018). Global research output on HIV/AIDS–related medication adherence from 1980 to 2017. *BMC Health Services Research*, 18(1), 1–13. DOI: 10.1186/s12913-018-3568-x PMID: 30305093

Sweileh, W. M. (2019). A bibliometric analysis of health-related literature on natural disasters from 1900 to 2017. *Health Research Policy and Systems*, 17(1), 1–11. DOI: 10.1186/s12961-019-0418-1 PMID: 30744641

United Nations. (2015) A/RES/70/1 - Transforming our world: the 2030 agenda for sustainable development. Resolution adopted by the General Assembly on 25 September 2015, p 35. https://docum ents-dds -ny.un.org/doc/UNDOC/GEN/N15/291/89/PDF/N1529 189.pdf?OpenElement United Nations (2017) A/RES/71/313 - Work of the Statistical Commission pertainingto the 2030 Agenda for Sustainable Development. Resolution adopted by the General Assembly on 6 July 2017, p 25. https://documents-dds -ny.un.org/doc/UNDOC/GEN/ 17/207/63/PDF/N1720763.pdf?OpenElement

United Nations:Sustainable development goals [(https://www.un.org/sustainabledevelopment/sustainable -development-goals/]. Accessed 10 July 2020

Van Eck, N. J., & Waltman, L. (2017). Citation-based clustering of publications using CitNetExplorer and VOSviewer. *Scientometrics*, 111(2), 1053–1070. DOI: 10.1007/s11192-017-2300-7 PMID: 28490825

Verma, D., Kalra, R., & Baheti, S. S. (2023). Examining the Domain of Green Finance Through Bibliometric Research Analysis of 22 Years (2000–2022): An Analytical Retrospective. *Vision (Basel)*, •••, 09722629231157470. DOI: 10.1177/09722629231157470

Zhou, P., & Leydesdorff, L. (2020). The emergence of China as a leading nation in science. *Research Policy*, 49(6), 1039–1056.

Zou, D., Huang, X., Kohnke, L., Chen, X., Cheng, G., & Xie, H. (2022). A bibliometric analysis of the trends and research topics of empirical research on TPACK. *Education and Information Technologies*, 27(8), 10585–10609. DOI: 10.1007/s10639-022-10991-z

Chapter 12
Indigenous Empowerment as a Catalyst for Sustainable Development

Anand Soni
https://orcid.org/0009-0001-4896-0639
Bahrain Polytechnic, Bahrain

Zakir Hossen Shaikh
https://orcid.org/0000-0003-4733-4166
Kingdom University, Bahraian

Mohammad Irfan
https://orcid.org/0000-0002-4956-1170
Chirst University, India

Vishwanath Bijja
https://orcid.org/0009-0009-7828-6460
UTAS-Ibri, Oman

ABSTRACT

Indigenous empowerment is a process of recognizing and supporting the rights, knowledge, and self-determination of indigenous communities. It acknowledges their unique perspectives, cultural heritage, and sustainable practices that have sustained their communities for generations. This chapter explores the challenges and importance of indigenous empowerment for achieving sustainable development and fostering a more inclusive and equitable society. This empowerment is not just about justice and rights but a strategic path to sustainable development. Collaborative partnerships among indigenous groups, governments, civil societies, and stakeholders are vital for promoting empowerment and addressing indigenous peoples' interconnected challenges. This chapter highlighted successful initiatives led by indigenous communities with significant progress in advancing the SDGs and fostering genuine partnerships that respect indigenous knowledge and promote cultural diversity is crucial for sustainable development that leaves no one behind.

DOI: 10.4018/979-8-3693-7924-0.ch012

1. INTRODUCTION

Today, when the world started really getting behind the 2030 Sustainable Development Goals, it was an important issue that we make sure Indigenous communities weren't left out. These people have been pushed aside for too long--but they've got a lot to say and do when it comes to goals regarding making the world a better location. It seems that including Indigenous people isn't simply good undercurrents - it's intelligent and informed, especially for a country's wallet/ economy (Scheyvens & van der Watt, 2021). By bringing their knowledge, customs, and manner of ruling themselves into the amalgam, we can grow economies, cut down on poverty, and keep the environment from going under. Indigenous people have a clever way of doing things, especially with farming, taking care of woods, bringing in tourists, and making handcrafted goods, that is a surprise to many. They understand how to use what the earth gives without destroying it, which is essentially the special power we need to fix several environmental messes, and even break the ice for new kinds of businesses to bloom. In 2015, the UN came up with 17 important goals called the Sustainable Development Goals (SDGs) to fix several worldwide problems (Murveit et al. 2023). Indigenous people are really helping out with two of these goals: SDG 15 (Life on Land) and SDG 13 (Climate Action), by doing things such as using land wisely, farming in a manner that's good for the earth, and living in a way that doesn't hurt the planet (Newman Carroll et al. 2021). They don't only stop there, though. They also make things better by supporting everyone in the local area, promoting men and women being treated the same, and helping everyone stay healthy. In this chapter the author points out how important it is to make the most out of what Indigenous communities offer economically. To really help Indigenous communities get ahead, it's key for governments, major decision-makers, and groups to agree on respecting Indigenous rights. They must make plans that everyone's quite accepting of and help by building skills, making it easier to access resources, and sharing knowledge. All these can create a comfortable area for Indigenous people to do well financially and help with those important goals. This chapter further goes into how we can better support Indigenous people, looking at new ways, such as having them run their own businesses; tourism that's okay for the planet; and working together with others from outside their groups. these methods draw on what Indigenous people know—their cultural characteristics and how they live in tune with nature—to push for a better economy, keep their culture strong, and fight for a cleaner planet (Scheyvens & van der Watt, 2021). But, specifically finding new ways for Indigenous people to make money and save their cultures was delayed a bit. It's found in many studies that right environment for Indigenous people to make it a key piece in the economy and they play a major part in reaching those global goals. But unfortunately, these people are trying to overcome some very difficult problems. Indigenous communities have gone through a lot: such as having their land taken; facing unfair treatment; being left out; and not having the same chances or access to items, such as schools, hospitals, or jobs. It may seem unfathomable, but to make things better, we must sort out issues with owning land, keeping their cultures alive, making fully sure everyone's included, and giving equal chances for education, health care, and jobs. In addition, the author has also highlighted the different challenges for native communities to gain more control over their lives. Few of these can be in the form of sometime dealing with the scenario of losing their land, being discriminated against, left out, and not having enough resources or options. As per the report food and agriculture organization of united nation (FAO, 2022), "Indigenous: In other literature, the word "indigenous" as an adjective often refers to the native, traditional or ancestral nature of an entity in a geographic location".

Figure 1. Criteria for Indigenous

Source: (FAO, 2022)

Table 1.Criteria for indigenous

Feature	Explanation
Historical Territory	Emphasizing the historical significance and relevance of activities to the territory.
Cultural Uniqueness Preservation	Safeguarding cultural distinctiveness including language, social structures, and spiritual beliefs.
Group Identity Recognition	Confirming self-identity and recognition as a distinct group by others.
Acknowledging Community Struggles	Recognizing past and present instances of oppression, marginalization, or discrimination within and beyond the community.

Source: (FAO, 2022)

1.1 Background of the Study

The combination of indigenous methodologies for environmental sustainability into the Sustainable Development Goals (SDGs) extremely shapes sustainable improvements. Empowerment, a pivotal aspect within development dialogues, challenges inequitable systems for community well-being (Scheyvens & van der Watt, 2021). Indigenous identity, recognized within communities, shapes a combined awareness (Magni, 2017). Gender equality initiatives in SDG projects across sectors are gaining traction (Leal Filho et al., 2022). SDGs focusing on economic growth, innovation, and sustainable production are attracting substantial industry interest (Saxena et al., 2021). Indigenous businesses prioritize essential policies and the preferential hiring of indigenous individuals (Eva et al., 2023). Corporate Social Responsibility (CSR) practices in indigenous firms integrate cultural assets for sustainable development, acknowledging indigenous wisdom (Abeysekera, 2023).

Swapping from the Millennium Development Goals to Sustainable Development Goals was a strikingly large change for how the world looks at making things better. (Cummings et al., 2019). When you mix Artificial Intelligence and Machine Learning into financial material, it could make things different by making things better or more complicated, which is an idea we find interesting.

(Irfan et al., 2024) The old manner of dealing with money isn't proving sufficient anymore when we're trying to be more eco-friendly -- it's stopping private cash from going into green projects (Irfan et al., 2024). Trying to repair the environment while also making some value is the goal for green innovation (Khurana et al., 2022). It's vitally important to successfully deal with climate change and different cultures if we're going to make any real progress (Khan & Rahman, 2010). By bringing in what indigenous people know into the SDGs, we're making fully sure everyone's included in improving (Murveit et al., 2023). The relationship indigenous people have with the planet and their green ways are key for all of us making progress (Buergelt et al., 2022).

1.2 Need and Scope

Examining the perspectives and actions of indigenous communities is vital for a more empowered world. A study would show the hurdles, shared goals, and what's important, making completely certain our steps forward respect everyone's culture and include everybody. Also, identifying and tackling what's holding back the empowerment of indigenous people is a must--ending up with special actions and rules to clear these obstacles. And it's crucial to see where we can fit well together and come up with plans to connect old wisdom with new sustainable practices.

1.3 Objectives

The primary objective of this chapter is to investigate how indigenous enablement influences the progression of sustainable development objectives. The study aims to:

To explore how indigenous empowerment influences facilitating the attainment of the SDGs through acknowledging and utilizing the distinctive viewpoints, traditional wisdom, and sustainable methodologies of indigenous societies.

To pinpoint and tackle obstacles that delay indigenous empowerment, such as concerns related to land rights and the accessibility of fundamental services.

To underscore the importance of collaborative partnerships in addressing the obstacles encountered by indigenous communities and advancing towards the SDGs.

1.4 Research Question

RO1: How does indigenous empowerment leverage distinctive viewpoints and traditional knowledge to propel Sustainable Development Goals forward?

RO2: What barriers need to be identified and resolved to promote indigenous empowerment?

RO3: How does the significance of collaborative partnerships in addressing challenges faced by indigenous communities and advancing towards the SDGs stand out?

2. LITERATURE REVIEW

The incorporation of indigenous practices for environmental sustainability into the implementation of SDGs has a profound impact on various facets of sustainable development. The notion of empowerment, which confronts unjust systems to improve the welfare of individuals or communities, is widely acknowledged in development dialogues (Scheyvens & van der Watt, 2021) An indigenous individual is characterized by self-identification with indigenous populations (group consciousness) and acknowledgment and acceptance by these communities as one of their own (acceptance by the group) (Magni, 2017) There is a growing emphasis on gender equality in projects related to SDGs across all sectors

(Leal Filho et al., 2022). SDGs linked to economic growth, sustainable industrialization, innovation, and sustainable production have garnered attention and investment from various major industries (Saxena et al., 2021). Indigenous businesses uphold specific policies deemed essential, cautioning against implementing strategies without a strong knowledge foundation (Eva et al., 2023). Businesses owned by Indigenous groups are significantly more inclined to employ Indigenous individuals compared to those owned by non-Indigenous entities. The mounting multiplicity within the Indigenous self-employed population necessitates nuanced analysis for effective policy formulation (Hunter, 2014).

The major change from old global goals or Millennium development Goals (MDGs) to the new ones called sustainable development goals (SDGs) was a strikingly large shift in the world's plan for the future (Cummings et al., 2019). A switch is primarily focused on coming up with ways to do things better and in ways that don't destroy the environment or people's lives. It means thinking about the planet and people when creating new items, hoping to cut down awful conditions, such as pollution, and make a better, tougher future for both businesses and people (Khurana et al., 2022). It turned the spotlight on how important it is to really delve into different goals for different places, based on what they can handle and what they're dealing with (Sarvajayakesavalu, 2015): to actually hit these targets, it's crucial that we find intelligent and informed ways to fit pieces together and fix conflicts by shaking up how we do things before (Pradhan et al., 2017). While it's abundantly clear that there are major problems, like losing cultural material, beginning people their land, making some people poor, and ruining the environment, these things make it hard to keep old ways alive (Khan & Rahman, 2010). When we discuss Corporate Social Responsibility (CSR), it's not only moving around; it's really hooked into where businesses come from, the people there, and what they've always done (Amaeshi et al., 2006).

By mixing old notably positive characteristics and items with ways to keep the planet going, we can build things that really work well and respect where they came from. This combo honors who Indigenous people are and the movements of their heads they can bring to save the planet (Abeysekera, 2023). I engage in an intense examination thinking regarding many things, it starts to make sense. This matters because doing things this way not only respects people's old and special ways--but also shows how key their knowledge is in beginning projects that actually take care of the earth. Indigenous knowledge isn't only something people pass around for fun; it's actually a deep pool of wisdom that shows people how to act—similar to how your grandma knows exactly what to do when you're feeling sick (Beckett & O'Loughlin, 2024).When it comes to making fully sure both the rules of the government and the rights of Indigenous people are quite accepting of each other, speaking things out is key. An apt simile, similar to a seesaw--but instead of young ones, it regards balancing power, as Anaya and Puig explained in 2017. Making things normal isn't only about getting items to blend in.

It's also a crafty way to push Indigenous creativity and smarts into the spotlight (Ernst, 2011). For several Indigenous enterprises out there, it regards a lot more than just making money. They're fond of keeping their traditions alive, doing really well in their communities, and yes, earning some cash along the way (Tripathy & Dastrala, 2023). Now, the reader is encouraged to contemplate the real intelligent and informed people from Indigenous backgrounds who find themselves in special schools. They're not only dealing with homework and exams. They're often wrestling with feeling out of location, which is why working together to create a welcoming sensation is extremely important (Smith et al., 2023).If we start valuing Indigenous knowledge and thinking through the complexities of how to work it into our major plans for making the world a better spot—those Sustainable Development Goals that everyone discusses—we could, basically, enhance on making progress that counts for everyone (Murveit et al., 2023). Colleges and universities need to keep going with Indigenous communities, putting Indigenous leaders at the front, and really dive into making changes that heal old wounds, and mix new ways of learning with traditional ones (Raffoul et al., 2022). Indigenous communities share a profound connection with nature and often possess valuable insights on environmental preservation, biodiversity conservation, and sustainable resource management (Newman Carroll et al., 2021). Acknowledging and respecting Indigenous resilience is crucial in promoting mental health, well-being, and empowerment within Indigenous communities, facilitating healing, progress, and sustainable development (Burack et al., 2024).

Empowerment and Representation Indigenous methodologies focus on empowering Indigenous voices, perspectives, and communities, aiming to represent their interests authentically (Woodroffe, 2020). The right to Indigenous self-determination is a core human right that enables Indigenous peoples to uphold and reinforce their unique political, legal, economic, social, and cultural institutions (O'Sullivan, 2023). Indigenous communities demonstrate profound reverence for the environment and embrace sustainable living in balance with nature (Buergelt et al., 2022). Businesses owned by Indigenous peoples, characterized by at least 50% Indigenous ownership, have been observed to sustain superior rates of Indigenous employment contrasted to non-Indigenous businesses (Eva, Bodle, et al., 2023). Indigenous social enterprises are increasingly recognized as pivotal players in fostering economic development within Indigenous communities worldwide (Evans et al.,2024). Increasing Indigenous employment rates not only gains individuals and communities but also adds to the overall development of the economy. Addressing the employment gap through targeted policies and interventions can lead to a range of positive economic and social outcomes (Director & caepradmin.cass@anu.edu.au, 2014). AI has unique use cases that are available to all big enterprises, making it a valuable ally in this era of digital acceleration. Artificial intelligence (AI) is transforming traditional paradigms in every sector of the economy, including supply chain management, robotics, healthcare, public safety, retail, HR services, financial services, and financial inclusion and governance.(Shaikh, et al, 2022, 2024, Sheela, P et al, 2024, Selwin et al, 2024, Gupta et al, 2024, Kusuma, K., et al,2024, Panigrahi, Rashmi Ranjan, et al,2023 and Sarea, A.et al, 2021).

3. RESEARCH METHODOLOGY

The researchers employed descriptive research methodology in this study, utilizing a design that delves into the role of indigenous empowerment in advancing sustainable development. The aim is to comprehensively depict and assess the existing knowledge, viewpoints, and experiences concerning indigenous empowerment and its influence on sustainable development. Primarily drawing on secondary data from academic journals, industry reports, case studies, and relevant publications, the study gathers a wide array of information on indigenous empowerment and sustainable development. Furthermore, it conducts a reasonable examination of intuitions from diverse sources to identify commonalities, discrepancies, and gaps in the literature, facilitating the synthesis of information and the cultivation of a complete understanding of the subject matter.

4. THE RALLYING CALL: SDGS AND INDIGENOUS EMPOWERMENT: SUSTAINABLE DEVELOPMENT GOALS

In 2015, the United Nations decided to pay close attention to some major problems around the world by creating what they named the Sustainable Development Goals, or SDGs for short. They came up with 17 goals they want to reach by 2030. These goals are noticeably focused on fixing all sorts of different, yet connected, issues, such as eliminating poverty; ensuring universal access to education; promoting gender equality; guaranteeing access to clean water and sanitation; utilizing sustainable energy; constructing environmentally friendly cities; actively addressing climate change; and fostering responsible consumption. They're aiming for a future where everything is equal for everyone, everyone learns and improves at the same time. Ordinarily, it appears like such a strikingly large thing to aim for. Achieving these important goals isn't something just one person or one country can do on their own. It's more similar to a team effort where governments, businesses, regular people, and groups working for a good cause all have to help each other. (2030 Agenda and Indigenous Peoples | Division for Inclusive Social Development (DISD)).

Framework of SDGs and Indigenous

The worldwide monitoring framework for tracking the advancement of the 17 SDGs includes two distinct indicators (2.3.2 and 4.5.1) aimed at assessing the welfare of Indigenous Peoples, along with indicators such as 1.4.2 and 5.a.1, which center on land rights, particularly significant for Indigenous Peoples. These indicators are associated with goals such as zero hunger, eradicating poverty, ensuring inclusive education, and promoting gender equality (2030 Agenda and Indigenous Peoples | Division for Inclusive Social Development (DISD)). With reference to (*Sustainable Development High-Level Political Forum on Sustainable Development, convened under the Auspices of the Economic and Social Council Progress towards the Sustainable Development Goals Report of the Secretary-General Summary*, 2023) target review of some SDGs which are directly/ indirectly linked to indigenous.

Table 2. Framework of SDGs

SDG #	Target review
1	The percentage of the global employed population existing in poverty has consistently declined, dropping from 8.4% in 2015 to 6.9% in 2023, contributing partially to Goal 1 of the Sustainable Development Goals - End poverty.
2	2.2: Globally, in 2022, around 22.3% of children under the age of 5 (equivalent to 148 million children) suffered from stunting, marking a decline from 24.6% in 2015 and 26.3% in 2012 (the baseline year for WHO sustenance targets). Based on current trends, it is expected that 1 in 5 (19.5%) children under 5 will be affected by stunting by 2030, partially contributing to Goal 2 of the SDGs - End Hunger.
4	4.5: Half of primary schools lack the essential infrastructure and resources required to create a suitable learning environment for students with disabilities. Additionally, one out of 5 primary schools worldwide does not have gender-segregated hygiene facilities. In 2022, on average, 44% of primary schools, 56% of lower secondary schools, and 69% of higher secondary schools had Internet access, showing a nearly twofold increase from the previous year. At the upper secondary level, 91% of schools have access to electricity, 81% are equipped with educational computers, and 69% are connected to the internet. partially contributing to Goal 4 of the SDGs – Ensure quality education.
5	5.1: According to information gathered in 2022 from 120 countries, 55% of these nations did not possess legislation against discrimination that specifically bans direct and indirect forms of discrimination in contradiction of women. Moreover, half of the countries still did not have mandates for female representation in their national parliaments. 5.a: In thirty-three percent of the 49 countries surveyed, less than half of both women and men possess secure rights to agricultural land. Partially contributing to goal 5 of SDG s to achieve gender equality,

Source: SDG Progress Report 2023 (fao.org)

Echoing Resilience: Indigenous Voices at the HLPF

The Indigenous Peoples Major Group for Sustainable Development (IPMG) and the Permanent Forum on Indigenous Issues (PFII) have led efforts to coordinate indigenous engagement in the annual High-Level Political Forum (HLPF) and its associated activities. During the 2019 HLPF, which centered on encouragement, inclusivity, and equality, 28 indigenous delegates from 11 nations delivered their viewpoints. The Indigenous Peoples' Major Group made a heartfelt statement regarding how often indigenous rights are ignored. This leads to more unfairness, people getting criminalized, and really awful violations of human rights against their leaders and the people living in their communities. They discussed how serious it is to make sure Indigenous peoples are recognized, are protected, and have fair chances to obtain justice.

They brought attention to the standing tasks of prejudice, marginalization, and exclusion within their groups, while also highlighting the significant contributions and endeavors they have undertaken towards sustainable development. A touching declaration from the IPMG stressed the recurring infringements on indigenous rights, subsequent in reinforced inequality, criminalization, and severe human rights violations against their leaders and communities. This emphasized the pressing necessity for concrete actions to promise the recognition, protection, and equitable access to justice for Indigenous peoples, including the defense of their territories and the cessation of the persecution they meet (Permanent Forum on Indigenous Issues (PFII) | High-Level Political Forum 2016).

Indigenous knowledge: When it comes to what Indigenous peoples know and how they live, their wisdom is deeply rooted in traditions and ways of doing things that have been around for hundreds of years. The entire system is built by these communities to deal with nature and social challenges.

This unique knowledge, specific to each group, encompasses traditional wisdom, beliefs, and practical knowledge vital for their sustainability and works. Transmitted across generations, indigenous knowledge intricately intertwines with the social, economic, and environmental facets of indigenous life. It not only bolsters their resilience in the face of change but also provides invaluable perspectives for tackling contemporary global challenges like climate change, sustainable resource management, and social equity. Embracing and incorporating indigenous knowledge systems into broader developmental strategies can pave the way for more comprehensive and efficient approaches towards a sustainable future (Magni, 2017).

Means of Indigenous Knowledge Transfer

Following are few displayed means of indigenous knowledge transfer are deeply rooted in cultural traditions, community values, and the interconnectedness between individuals, their environment, and their heritage (Magni, 2017)

Figure 2. Means of Indigenous knowledge transfer

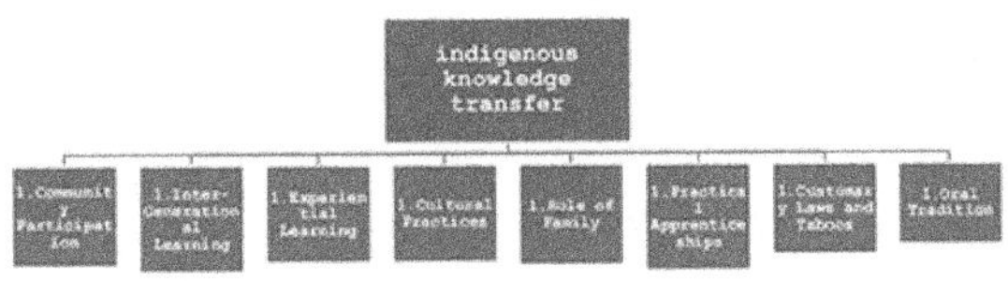

Source: (Imoro et al., 2022)

a. **Community Participation**: its widely accepted that in indigenous communities, knowledge transfer occurs through engagement in rituals, communal activities, and hands-on experiences, embedding teachings into daily practices.
b. **Cultural Practices**: The transmission of Indigenous knowledge integrates cultural customs and rituals to not just convey information but also strengthen values, beliefs, and the community's deep bond with nature.
c. **Customary Laws and Taboos**: The transfer of Indigenous knowledge is closely linked with traditional laws and taboos, governing conduct, relationships, and resource utilization to sustain the longevity of customary practices.
d. **Experiential Learning**: Indigenous education highlights the use of more practice on experiential learning, focusing on individuals acquiring knowledge through direct engagement with the environment and hands-on experiences.
e. **Inter-Generational Learning**: Knowledge sharing starts at a young age, relying heavily on the elders: they are the most important people for learning important material regarding life, in a way you could say, an inter-generational learning setup. Next, there's the spoken stories. Stories, songs, and ceremonies are key for passing down what they know from one generation to the next.
f. **Practical Apprenticeships**: It is not just talking, however. They believe in learning through practice; there's a lot of practical apprenticeships where the younger ones do hands-on work under the watchful eyes of those who are very knowledgeable in the field.

5. RESULTS AND DISCUSSIONS

RO1: How does indigenous empowerment leverage distinctive viewpoints and traditional knowledge to propel Sustainable Development Goals forward?

Ordinarily, it seems, when indigenous communities understand the power to use their own special insights and age-old smarts, they can really push the Sustainable Development Goals (SDGs) along. They bring to the table disparate manners of seeing things and old wisdom that helps the world get closer to hitting those SDG targets. Indigenous empowerment means letting these communities use what they know regarding nature and their cultural stories to help the planet.

It's primarily focused on getting them involved in making decisions that respect their traditions, help the environment, and ensure their knowledge keeps being passed down. The entire idea supports building ways to meet those important global goals that the reader is encouraged to contemplate: all people should be kind to the Earth, and remember our past.By really listening to what indigenous people have to say; making fully sure their rights are protected; and integrating their traditional practices into today's plans, we find a stronger, smarter direction to move toward those SDGs. This makes sure the future is fairer and greener for everyone.

Figure 3. Indigenous perspectives and practices

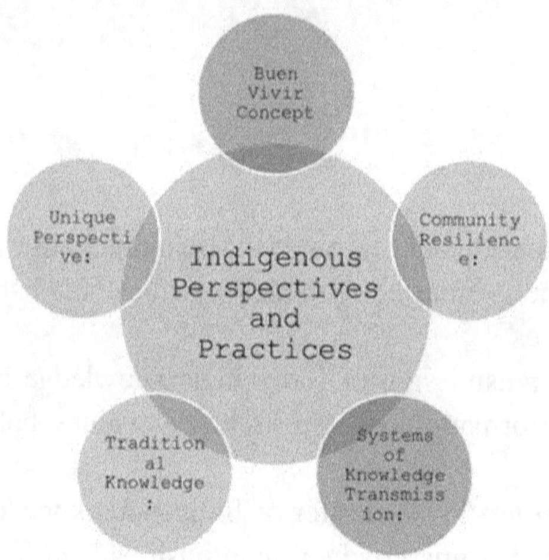

Source: (Buergelt et al., 2022)

Table 3. Indigenous perspectives and practices in sustainability and knowledge preservation

#	Indigenous perspectives	Practice
a	Buen Vivir	Indigenous communities present different viewpoints on advancement, exemplified by the notion of buen vivir, which emphasizes thriving in balance with nature and society. It is noticeably focused on living well by maintaining a harmonious relationship with nature and with one another; they're fond of keeping their land, holding onto their culture—and making their own rules, which gets them a lot of praise for not letting bad building ideas change them.
	Community Resilience	Believing in values, such as being part of a community, being fair to everyone, helping each other out, and looking after the planet, is what makes their manner of living keep going strong; these important ideas are what keep Indigenous peoples healthy and tough. When it's time to teach what they know, Indigenous communities involve everyone - young ones, adults, everyone; they prefer learning through activities rather than just discussing it.
	Traditional Knowledge:	The wisdom possessed by indigenous, traditional, or local communities is deeply rooted in cultural customs, values, beliefs, and unique worldviews. This knowledge structure is flexible and practical, providing essential tools for survival and enduring ways of life. It reflects a legacy of inventive thought and adaptive practices honed over generations in response to changing conditions. (Magni, 2017)
	Unique Perspective:	In addition, the manner they figure things out and adapt to new changes is outright intelligent and informed, and it's been working for them for years; to top it all off, when it comes to standing strong, Indigenous people know how to take the lead; they are focused on recognizing who they are, leading themselves—and ensuring they are heard, both at home and on the world stage. By interjecting their wisdom and fighting for their rights, they make sure they're not simply a footnote in today's fast-moving world.

Source: (Buergelt et al., 2022)

Effective Instances of Incorporating Indigenous Knowledge Into Scientific Research Endeavors

Agricultural Sustainability: Indigenous agricultural techniques like agroforestry, diversified cropping, and soil preservation methods have influenced sustainable agriculture studies. Researchers have advanced agricultural sustainability, food security, and resilience to climate change by amalgamating indigenous land management wisdom and traditional seed varieties.

Indigenous groups have really tried hard to introduce some innovative ideas for clean energy, even in remote places. They set up items such as solar panels and small water-power systems, making fully sure more people can use clean energy without tinkering with their traditions or the environment. This is vitally important for reaching Sustainable Development Goal 7, which is focused on renewable energy solutions. (Francis, 2024)

Biodiversity Conservation: Indigenous wisdom regarding ecosystems and animal behavior plays a pivotal role in global biodiversity conservation endeavors. Initiatives merging indigenous views on land care, customary hunting methods, and habitat safeguarding have aided in protecting endangered species, rejuvenating deteriorated habitats, and advancing sustainable resource supervision. (Sobrevila, 2008)

Climate Change Adaptation: Indigenous groups in areas such as the Arctic and Pacific Islands engage in climate change adaptation research. By merging traditional ecological insights with scientific information, novel resilience tactics like community-led environmental monitoring and adaptation strategies are formulated. (UNDP, 2024).

Medicinal Plant Research: Joint research endeavors involving indigenous healers and scientific researchers have resulted in the discovery of bioactive compounds in traditional medicinal plants. This fusion of indigenous wisdom has paved the way for the creation of novel pharmaceuticals and alternative therapies rooted in traditional healing methods. (Francis, 2024)

Water Resource Management: Incorporating indigenous water management methods like rainwater harvesting, aquifer replenishment, and sustainable irrigation practices into contemporary water resource initiatives has enhanced water conservation, quality, and accessibility across various regions through the amalgamation of traditional wisdom and scientific knowledge. (admin, 2024)

RO2: What barriers need to be identified and resolved to promote indigenous empowerment?

Interconnected Challenges: Poverty, Education, and Decent Work

Tackling the complex hurdles confronting indigenous groups demands a comprehensive strategy. The IPMG's declarations at the HLPF highlighted obstacles hindering SDG advancements in poverty alleviation, education quality, and job availability. Within talks on economic expansion and decent work (SDG 8), indigenous representatives stressed the importance of recognizing and protecting their longstanding customary livelihoods, such as agriculture, seed conservation, rotational farming, hunting, and fishing. These practices are essential for their survival, dietary well-being, cultural diversity, and the conservation of indigenous knowledge. (*Permanent Forum on Indigenous Issues (PFII) | High-Level Political Forum 2016*, 2016)

Financing for Inclusion: Addressing Land and Resource Grabs

The IPMG highlighted a concerning trend in which public-private partnerships (PPPs) prioritize economic progress at the expense of extensive land and resource seizures. These alliances often neglect indigenous rights, exacerbating inequalities and limiting access to vital services like renewable energy, particularly for isolated indigenous communities. (*Permanent Forum on Indigenous Issues (PFII) | High-Level Political Forum 2016*, 2016)

Voluntary National Reviews: A Call for Meaningful Participation

At the 2019 HLPF session focusing on Voluntary National Reviews (VNRs), which involve countries reporting on their progress in achieving the SDGs, just one indigenous delegate was allocated the chance to speak on behalf of all major groups and stakeholders. Although numerous VNRs recognized "marginalized groups" as those disadvantaged, few nations established systems that would allow indigenous communities to participate meaningfully or outlined detailed strategies, objectives, and financial allocations to tackle their distinct obstacles.

Four Years of SDG Implementation: Progress and Persisting Gaps

As per the 2019 Global Sustainable Development Report (GSDR), progress towards fulfilling the 17 SDGs and their 169 targets is inadequate. Escalating inequalities, climate change, biodiversity decline, and the growing waste generated by human actions are alarming developments that jeopardize the vision of universal human welfare outlined in the SDGs.

The GSDR explicitly acknowledged the persistent discrimination and marginalization experienced by indigenous communities, underscoring the obstacles related to the loss of ancestral territories, risks to traditional languages and cultures, and disproportionately elevated levels of poverty, health issues, and limited educational opportunities.

SOLUTIONS

Indigenous Knowledge: A Catalyst for Sustainable Solutions

Understanding the problems, the report praised indigenous peoples for their roles as guardians of vital ecosystems and bearers of traditional intelligence in sustainable resource stewardship. Their knowledge stands to impact global health, food security, and climate change solutions. (Sarvajayakesavalu, 2015)

The Decade of Action: Transformational Change on the Ground

With the United Nations designating 2020-2030 as the Decade of Action for SDG attainment, pivotal shifts at grassroots levels are essential. This entails withdrawing detrimental trends such as rising disparities, climate change consequences, biodiversity loss, and excessive waste production, all profoundly impacting the well-being and rights of indigenous populations. (*The Indigenous World 2024: Sustainable Development Goals (SDGs) and Indigenous Peoples - IWGIA - International Work Group for Indigenous Affairs*, 2024)

UNDRIP and the SDGs

The United Nations Declaration on the Rights of Indigenous Peoples (UNDRIP) is a key document highlighting the link between indigenous rights and the SDGs. It recognizes the natural rights of indigenous groups, including self-governance, control over their lands and resources, and preservation of their traditions and residues.

Collective Rights

Collective rights are foundational to indigenous cultures, determining their attitudes and customs across land tenure, resource management, and cultural heritage. Although not explicitly mentioned in the SDGs, objectives such as SDG 1.4 seek to secure equitable economic resource access, reflecting the significance of communal land rights for indigenous communities' ties to their lands and resources. (FAO, 2022).

Customary Law

Indigenous governance approaches are rooted in customary law, embodying inherited practices, norms, and regulations. Progress has been made globally in recognizing the importance of engaging indigenous communities in decision-making through these traditional justice frameworks. For example, in Ecuador and Colombia, the entitlement of indigenous peoples to administer legal functions in accordance with their traditional laws is acknowledged in the Constitution, provided that these laws align with constitutional or globally acknowledged human rights principles. (FAO, 2022).

Accelerating Action: The HLPF 2020 and Beyond

2020 HLPF, "Accelerated action and transformative trails: realizing the decade of action and delivery for sustainable development," underscores the pressing need to speed up advancements. Conversations will center around the connections among the SDGs and pivotal catalysts for change, including well-being and human potential, sustainable economies, food networks, energy sustainability, urban growth, and environmental resources.

Among the 50 nations delivering their VNRs in 2020, 24 encompass indigenous communities, such as Kenya, Bangladesh, Finland, Nepal, and Peru, which are providing their reports for the second time. This offers a significant chance for indigenous groups in these countries to interact with their governments, request discussions, and engage in decision-making procedures linked to the execution of the SDGs.

Empowering Indigenous Voices: A Pathway to Sustainable Progress

As the world handles with complex development challenges, the empowerment of indigenous peoples and their envoy organizations emerges as a critical pathway to achieving the SDGs. Acknowledging and upholding their rights, wisdom, and autonomy unleashes their priceless input into sustainable development endeavors. (FAO, 2022).

RO3: How does the significance of collaborative partnerships in addressing challenges faced by indigenous communities and advancing towards the SDGs stand out?

Collaborative Partnerships: Fostering Inclusive Development

Realizing inclusive sustainable development necessitates cooperative alliances among indigenous groups, governments, NGOs, and stakeholders, founded on mutual respect, trust, and a genuine dedication to enhancing indigenous empowerment.

a. **Capacity Building and Knowledge Sharing:** Allocating resources to capacity-building programs that enable indigenous communities and organizations to champion their rights, oversee their resources, and drive their development projects can promote self-determination and enduring advancement.
b. **Culturally Sensitive Approaches:** Incorporating culturally respectful methods that honor and merge indigenous knowledge, values, and traditions can amplify the efficacy and longevity of development interventions.

c. **Inclusive Policy and Legal Frameworks:** Creating inclusive policy and legal frameworks that recognize and protect the rights of indigenous peoples, including their right to free, prior, and informed consent (FPIC), can cultivate a conducive environment for their empowerment and involvement.
d. **Meaningful Consultation and Engagement:** Creating vigorous systems for meaningful discussion and engagement with indigenous groups across project phases is crucial to amplify their voices and integrate their partialities into development endeavors.
e. **Monitoring and Evaluation:** Fetching indigenous communities in overseeing and assessing development projects can guarantee accountability, pinpoint areas for development, and bolster the successful deployment of culturally suitable and sustainable strategies.

PARTNERSHIPS FOR INDIGENOUS-LED SUSTAINABLE DEVELOPMENT

Indigenous-to-Indigenous Cooperation

Shared efforts among indigenous groups have proven effective in driving sustainable development objectives. This strategy values the marked insights and histories of indigenous communities, promoting partnerships that respect customary methods while confronting contemporary issues. The Assembly of First Nations (AFN), representing 634 member nations, exemplifies this synergy. Particularly, the AFN's Infrastructure and Safe Drinking Water Sector has played a pivotal role in urging the Canadian government to strive for SDG 6, guaranteeing that every First Nation has access to the UN-recognized human rights of clean drinking water and sanitation. (*Advancing Progress to Achieve UN SDG 6 for First Nations through Advocacy with the Canadian Government | Department of Economic and Social Affairs*, 2024)

Government-Indigenous Collaboration

Vital for sustainable development goals, partnerships between governments and indigenous groups must uphold indigenous rights and autonomy. Guided by the UN Declaration on the Rights of Indigenous Peoples (UNDRIP) and ILO Convention No. 169, sustainable energy projects should ensure human rights are preserved. Collaborative efforts should prioritize recognizing First Nations' water rights and self-determination, a commitment championed by the AFN, fostering effective collaborations. International mechanisms for the protection of the rights of people of Indigenous Peoples (FAO, 2022).

- Convention on Biological Diversity, UN (1992)
- Expert Mechanism on the Rights of Indigenous Peoples – UN (2007)
- Foro Permanente de las Naciones Unidas para las Cuestiones Indígenas (2000)
- Indigenous and Tribal Peoples Convention, ILO (No. 169) (1989)
- Special Rapporteur on the rights of indigenous peoples – UN (2001)
- UN Declaration of the Rights of Indigenous Peoples (2007)
- American Declaration on the Rights of Indigenous Peoples – IACHR (2016)

Private Sector Rendezvous

Within indigenous-led sustainable advancement, the private sector holds a pivotal position. Company sustainability teams are vital in averting and coping societal risks, crafting approaches that benefit indigenous communities. In Latin America and the Caribbean, where indigenous peoples constitute 9.8% of the population, private sector experts must grasp the importance of incorporating indigenous perspectives into their operations. (World Bank, 2023)

Different tools and strategies:

a. **Free, Prior, and Informed Consent (FPIC):** This principle ensures the rights of indigenous peoples are respected and safeguarded throughout the entirety of the engagement process. (*OHCHR | Consultation and Free, Prior and Informed Consent (FPIC)*, n.d.)
b. **Identification of Local Markets:** Expanding value chains through indigenous supplier partnerships fosters economically, culturally, and socially sustainable development within companies. (How, 2023)
c. **Participatory Business Plans:** Employing tools such as the Canvas model, businesses can collaboratively design business strategies with indigenous groups, ensuring economic ventures resonate with cultural values and aspirations. (How, 2023)
d. **Participatory Mapping:** This approach enables indigenous communities to document and share their knowledge on land, resources, and cultural sites, allowing sustainability teams to better understand community preferences and values. (Smith et al., 2023)
e. By adopting these approaches, private sector organizations can create reciprocal value that benefits both businesses and indigenous groups, fostering lasting, sustainable partnerships that go beyond mere regulatory compliance. (How, 2023)

Indigenous-Led Initiatives Advancing the SDGs

Worldwide, indigenous communities spearhead sustainable projects supporting SDG achievement, showcasing the impact of encouragement and community-driven solutions in advancing goals. (*2025 ECOSOC Partnership Forum | Department of Economic and Social Affairs*, 2024)

a. **Community-Based Conservation (SDG 14 and 15):** Indigenous communities are instrumental in community-led conservation endeavors, safeguarding marine and land ecosystems sustainably to preserve biodiversity for the benefit of future generations.
b. **Cultural Tourism and Entrepreneurship (SDG 8):** Drawing on their cultural heritage and traditional wisdom, indigenous groups have created sustainable tourism ventures and entrepreneurial pathways, fostered economic growth while safeguarding their cultural identities.
c. **Renewable Energy Solutions (SDG 7):** Indigenous groups have really tried hard to introduce some innovative ideas for clean energy, even in remote places. They set up items such as solar panels and small water-power systems, making fully sure more people can use clean energy without tinkering with their traditions or the environment. This is vitally important for reaching Sustainable Development Goal 7, which is focused on renewable energy solutions

d. **Sustainable Agriculture and Food Security (SDG 2):** when it comes to farming sustainably—and making fully sure everyone has enough to eat (which hits Sustainable Development Goal 2)—these Indigenous farming communities are leading the charge. They're using intelligent and informed farming techniques, such as mixing different kinds of crops together—holding to agroforestry—and saving seeds to help with food security and taking care of the planet at the same time.
e. **Sustainable Forest Management (SDG 15):** it's important to note regarding the Amazon rainforest. The local groups there are really good at managing the forest in a sustainable manner for Sustainable Development Goal 15. They're mixing antiquated knowledge with modern ways to protect all kinds of plant and animal life, and they're doing it all to fight against climate change

6. LIMITATIONS

The study explores the connection between indigenous empowerment and sustainable development in a particular context, highlighting the importance of not generalizing across diverse indigenous groups with distinct backgrounds. Access to reliable data on indigenous empowerment and its roles in sustainable development may be limited, relying on scarce literature and data that could impact the depth and scope of the analysis. Time limitations might restrict the thoroughness of the investigation, resulting in incomplete coverage and highlighting the necessity for additional exploration in specific domains. Consequently, it's crucial to interpret the study's findings and recommendations cautiously, taking into account the unique attributes of each indigenous community and the inherent limitations of available data and research methods.

7. CONCLUSION

Indigenous sustainability methods play a pivotal role in advancing the Sustainable Development Goals. Engrained in traditional knowledge and environmental respect, these enduring practices provide vital guidance for addressing global environmental tasks and shaping sustainable development across diverse areas, from upholding indigenous rights to promoting economic growth within ecological boundaries.

Recognizing and applying indigenous wisdom is revolutionary for building, from the ground up, a better tomorrow, mixing respect for the old ways with new solutions to today's serious issues. Just remember, though, when looking at what a study tells us, be a little doubtful. Every community's different, and there's only so much you can say definitively with the data and time we've got.

As we dive into the Decade of Action for the SDGs, it's vitally important to make sure Indigenous peoples are understood very well. We have to team up with them, really listening and working together, so they can take part in making important decisions. This is not only simply regarding being fair and respecting human rights—it's key for a future where everyone can thrive.

Their knowledge and leadership are important factors when it comes to tackling strikingly large problems our planet faces, such as warming climates, disappearing animals and plants, and not having enough food for everyone. By putting a premium on what they offer—and making fully sure they're in the mix—we're not simply avoiding leaving anyone out—we're setting up a world that's good for all of us.

REFERENCES

Abeysekera, I. (2023). Integrating First Nations peoples' cultural capital for sustainable development. *Sustainable Development (Bradford)*, 32(1), 43–56. DOI: 10.1002/sd.2643

Admin. (2024, April 16). Indigenous Water Conservation Methods: Unraveling the Role of Traditional Knowledge in Sustainable Resource Management - Welcome to Areness Foundation. Welcome to Areness Foundation. https://www.arenessfoundation.com/indigenous-water-conservation-methods-unraveling-the-role-of-traditional-knowledge-in-sustainable-resource-management/

Advancing progress to achieve UN SDG 6 for First Nations through advocacy with the Canadian Government | Department of Economic and Social Affairs. (2024, February 7). Un.org. https://sdgs.un.org/partnerships/advancing-progress-achieve-un-sdg-6-first-nations-through-advocacy-canadian-government

2030. Agenda and Indigenous Peoples | Division for Inclusive Social Development (DISD). (n.d.). Social.desa.un.org. https://social.desa.un.org/issues/indigenous-peoples/2030-agenda-and-indigenous-peoples/2030-agenda-and-indigenous-peoples

Akin, I., & Akin, M. (2024). Promoting sustainable practices through green investments in the United Kingdom real estate industry. *Sustainable Development (Bradford)*, sd.3194. Advance online publication. DOI: 10.1002/sd.3194

Amaeshi, K. M., Adi, A. B. C., Ogbechie, C., & Amao, O. O. (2006). Corporate Social Responsibility in Nigeria: Western Mimicry or Indigenous Influences? SSRN Electronic Journal. DOI: 10.2139/ssrn.896500

Anaya, S. J., & Puig, S. (2017). MITIGATING STATE SOVEREIGNTY: THE DUTY TO CONSULT WITH INDIGENOUS PEOPLES. *University of Toronto Law Journal*, 67(4), 435–464. DOI: 10.3138/utlj.67.1

Beckett, R. C., & O'Loughlin, A. (2024). The utility of indigenous knowledge in the pursuit of a UN sustainable development goal. *Collective Intelligence*, 3(2), 26339137241241295. Advance online publication. DOI: 10.1177/26339137241241295

Briefing Note Indigenous Peoples' Rights and the 2030 Agenda. (2017). Office of the High Commission for Human Rights.

Buergelt, P. T., Mahypilama, L. E., & Paton, D. (2022). The Value of Sophisticated Indigenous Ways of Being-Knowing-Doing Towards Transforming Human Resource Development in Ways that Contribute to Organizations Thriving and Addressing Our Existential Crises.

Buergelt, P. T., Mahypilama, L. E., & Paton, D. (2022, December). The Value of Sophisticated Indigenous Ways of Being-Knowing-Doing Towards Transforming Human Resource Development in Ways that Contribute to Organizations Thriving and Addressing Our Existential Crises. *Human Resource Development Review*, 21(4), 391–409. DOI: 10.1177/15344843221134351

Burack, J. A., Bombay, A., & Kirmayer, L. J. (2024). Cultural continuity, identity, and resilience among indigenous youth: Honoring the legacies of Michael Chandler and Christopher Lalonde. *Transcultural Psychiatry*, 61(3), 301–312. Advance online publication. DOI: 10.1177/13634615241257349 PMID: 39056364

Cummings, S., Seferiadis, A., & de Haan, L. (2019). Getting down to business? Critical discourse analysis of perspectives on the private sector in sustainable development. *Sustainable Development (Bradford)*, 28(4), 759–771. DOI: 10.1002/sd.2026

Director, C., & caepradmin.cass@anu.edu.au. (2014, October 21). The Economic and Social Benefits of Increasing Indigenous Employment -. Centre for Aboriginal Economic Policy Research. https://caepr.cass.anu.edu.au/research/publications/economic-and-social-benefits-increasing-indigenous-employment

2025. ECOSOC Partnership Forum | Department of Economic and Social Affairs. (2024). Un.org. https://sdgs.un.org/2025ECOSOCPartnershipForum

Ernst, D. (2011). IndIgenous InnovatIon and globalIzatIon the Challenge for China's standardization strategy Dieter Ernst A joint publication of the UC Institute on Global Conflict and Cooperation and the East-West Center.

Eva, C., Bodle, K., Foley, D., Harris, J., & Hunter, B. (2023). The importance of understanding Indigenous employment in the Indigenous business sector. *The Australian Journal of Social Issues*, 58(3), 494–522. DOI: 10.1002/ajs4.271

Eva, C., Harris, J., Bodle, K., Foley, D., Hunter, B., & Nichols, N. (2023). "It's Self-Determination. Blackfullas Making Right Decisions for Blackfullas": Why Indigenous-owned businesses create better Indigenous employment outcomes. *The Australian Journal of Social Issues*, 59(1), 29–56. DOI: 10.1002/ajs4.292

Evans, M., Robinson, J., & Williamson, I. (n.d.). The Effect of HRM Practices on Employment Outcomes in Indigenous Social Enterprises Short title: AQ0 Title: The Effect of HRM Practices on Employment Outcomes in Indigenous. https://doi.org/DOI: 10.13039/501100000923This

FAO. (2022). FAO regional strategy for collaboration with Indigenous Peoples and people of African descent in Latin America and the Caribbean Revised edition (p. 67). FAO. https://openknowledge.fao.org/handle/20.500.14283/cb7823en

Francis, O. (2024, June 21). The Role Of Indigenous Knowledge In Environmental Conservation. Medium; Medium. https://olamidefrancis.medium.com/the-role-of-indigenous-knowledge-in-environmental-conservation-f16db06e5a83

Gupta, S., Srivastava, R., Shaikh, Z. H., & Irfan, M. (2024). Revolutionizing Rural Finance: Exploring the Impact of FinTech on Financial Inclusion in India. In Irfan, M., Muhammad, K., Naifar, N., & Khan, M. A. (Eds.), *Applications of Block Chain technology and Artificial Intelligence. Financial Mathematics and Fintech*. Springer., DOI: 10.1007/978-3-031-47324-1_3

How. (2023). How Can Sustainability Teams Co-Create Shared Value with Indigenous Peoples? Idbinvest.org. https://www.idbinvest.org/en/blog/development-impact/how-can-sustainability-teams-co-create-shared-value-indigenous-peoples

Hunter, B. (2014). Reflecting on the Growth of Indigenous Self-employment. Agenda - a Journal of Policy Analysis and Reform, 21(1). https://doi.org/DOI: 10.22459/AG.21.01.2014.03

Imoro, A. Z., Boaka Hlordze, R. G., Duwiejuah, B. A., Abukari, A., Alidu, S. M., Acheampong, N. A., & Imoro, Z. A. (2022). Indigenous technologies: knowledge and practices for sustainable development. Indigenous People and Nature, 593–612. DOI: 10.1016/B978-0-323-91603-5.00013-0

Irfan, M. (2021, January). Do Shariah Indices converge? Evidence from Gulf Cooperation Council countries. *International Journal of Business Excellence*, 23(2), 251–269. DOI: 10.1504/IJBEX.2021.113448

Irfan, M., Elhoseny, M., Kassim, S., & Metawa, N. (2023). *Advanced Machine Learning Algorithms for Complex Financial Applications*. IGI Global., DOI: 10.4018/978-1-6684-4483-2

Irfan, M., Elmogy, M., Gupta, S., Khalifa, F., & Dias, R. (2024). *AI-Driven Decentralized Finance and the Future of Finance*. IGI Global., DOI: 10.4018/979-8-3693-6321-8

Irfan, M., Elmogy, M., Majid, M. S., & El-Sappagh, S. (2023). *The Impact of AI Innovation on Financial Sectors in the Era of Industry 5.0*. IGI Global., DOI: 10.4018/979-8-3693-0082-4

Irfan, M., Hussainey, K., Chan Bukhari, S. A., & Nam, Y. (Eds.). (2024). *Issues of Sustainability in AI and New-Age Thematic Investing*. IGI Global Publisher., DOI: 10.4018/979-8-3693-3282-5

Irfan, M., Kadry, S., Sharif, M., & Ullah Khan, H. (2023). *Fintech Applications in Islamic Finance: AI, Machine Learning, and Blockchain Techniques*. IGI Global., DOI: 10.4018/979-8-3693-1038-0

Khan, A., & Rahman. (2010). Development of small and medium scale enterprise in Bangladesh: prospects and constraints.

Khurana, S., Luthra, S., Haleem, A., Kumar, A., & Mannan, B. (2022). Can sustainability be achieved through sustainable oriented innovation practices? Empirical evidence of micro, small and medium scale manufacturing enterprises. *Sustainable Development (Bradford)*, 30(6), 1591–1615. DOI: 10.1002/sd.2330

Kusuma, K., Sheela, P., Panigrahi, R. R., & Shaikh, Z. H. (2024). Blockchain Technology and Islamic Finance: A Decade of Growth Trends. In Irfan, M., Kadry, S., Sharif, M., & Khan, H. (Eds.), *Fintech Applications in Islamic Finance: AI, Machine Learning, and Blockchain Techniques* (pp. 59–79). IGI Global., DOI: 10.4018/979-8-3693-1038-0.ch004

Leal Filho, W., Kovaleva, M., Tsani, S., îrcă, D.-M., Shiel, C., Dinis, M. A. P., Nicolau, M., Sima, M., Fritzen, B., Lange Salvia, A., Minhas, A., Kozlova, V., Doni, F., Spiteri, J., Gupta, T., Wakunuma, K., Sharma, M., Barbir, J., Shulla, K., & Tripathi, S. (2022). Promoting gender equality across the sustainable development goals. *Environment, Development and Sustainability*, 25(12), 14177–14198. DOI: 10.1007/s10668-022-02656-1 PMID: 36124160

Magni, G. (2017). Indigenous knowledge and implications for the sustainable development agenda. *European Journal of Education*, 52(4), 437–447. DOI: 10.1111/ejed.12238

Newman Carroll, S., Mombourquette, A., Boxer, M., Williams, R., & Brewer, S. (2021). Indigenous Empowerment Through Community-Engaged Health Education Curriculum: Health Promotion in a Commercial Tobacco Cessation Campaign. *Pedagogy in Health Promotion*, 7(4), 237337992110061. DOI: 10.1177/23733799211006130

O'Sullivan, D. (2023). The UN Sustainable Development Goals, national values, and Indigenous self-determination: Australian perspectives. AlterNative. *Alternative*, 19(4), 741–749. DOI: 10.1177/11771801231196924

OHCHR | Consultation and free, prior and informed consent (FPIC). (n.d.). OHCHR. https://www.ohchr.org/en/indigenous-peoples/consultation-and-free-prior-and-informed-consent-fpic

Panigrahi, R. R., Dash, M., Shaikh, Z. H., & Irfan, M. (2023). Review of Machine Learning Techniques in the Supply Chain Management of Indian Industry: A Future Research Agenda. In Irfan, M., Elhoseny, M., Kassim, S., & Metawa, N. (Eds.), *Advanced Machine Learning Algorithms for Complex Financial Applications* (pp. 199–219). IGI Global., DOI: 10.4018/978-1-6684-4483-2.ch013

Permanent Forum on Indigenous Issues (PFII) | High-Level Political Forum 2016. (2016). Un.org. https://hlpf.un.org/inputs/permanent-forum-on-indigenous-issues-pfii

Pradhan, P., Costa, L., Rybski, D., Lucht, W., & Kropp, J. P. (2017). A Systematic Study of Sustainable Development Goal (SDG) Interactions. *Earth's Future*, 5(11), 1169–1179. DOI: 10.1002/2017EF000632

Raffoul, J., Ward, J., Calvez, S., Kartolo, A., Haque, A., Holmes, T., Attas, R., Kechego, J., Kustra, E., & Mooney, J. (2022). Institutional structures and individual stories: Experiences from the front lines of Indigenous educational development in higher education. AlterNative. *Alternative*, 18(1), 163–172. DOI: 10.1177/11771801211062617

Sarea, A., Subramanian, S., Alareeni, B., Shaikh, Z. H., Hawaldar, I. T., & Elshaker, A. H. (2021). Financial Disclosures by Using Machine Learning Analysis. In Alareeni, B., Hamdan, A., & Elgedawy, I. (Eds.), *The Importance of New Technologies and Entrepreneurship in Business Development: In The Context of Economic Diversity in Developing Countries. ICBT 2020. Lecture Notes in Networks and Systems* (Vol. 194). Springer., DOI: 10.1007/978-3-030-69221-6_5

Sarvajayakesavalu, S. (2015). Addressing challenges of developing countries in implementing five priorities for sustainable development goals. *Ecosystem Health and Sustainability*, 1(7), 1–4. DOI: 10.1890/EHS15-0028.1

Saxena, A., Ramaswamy, M., Beale, J., Marciniuk, D., & Smith, P. (2021). Striving for the United Nations (UN) Sustainable Development Goals (SDGs): What will it take? *Discover Sustainability*, 2(1), 20. Advance online publication. DOI: 10.1007/s43621-021-00029-8

Scheyvens, R., & van der Watt, H. (2021). Tourism, Empowerment and Sustainable Development: A New Framework for Analysis. *Sustainability (Basel)*, 13(22), 12606. DOI: 10.3390/su132212606

Selwin, S., Saseendran, H., Vemavarapu, K. R., Shaikh, I., Shaikh, Z. H., & Harris, S. B. (2024). AI-Driven Employee Engagement: Transforming Banking Workforce Dynamics Using the BEULA Model. In Awwad, B. (Ed.), *The AI Revolution: Driving Business Innovation and Research. Studies in Systems, Decision and Control* (Vol. 525). Springer., DOI: 10.1007/978-3-031-54383-8_32

Shaikh, Z., Irfan, M., Sarea, A., & Panigrahi, R. R. (2024). *The Emergence of Islamic Fintech and Bahrain: Prospect for Global Financial Sectors* (Vol. 503). Springer., DOI: 10.1007/978-3-031-43490-7_52

Shaikh, Z. H., Irfan, M., Nomran, N. M., & Lawin, M. L. (2024). The Effect of Strategic Partnership on Innovation and Business: Performance of the Fintech Industry in Bahrain. In Irfan, M., Kadry, S., Sharif, M., & Khan, H. (Eds.), *Fintech Applications in Islamic Finance: AI, Machine Learning, and Blockchain Techniques* (pp. 236–254). IGI Global., DOI: 10.4018/979-8-3693-1038-0.ch016

Shaikh, Z. H., Irfan, M., Nomran, N. M., & Ratnakaram, S. P. (2024). Unlocking the Potential of AI for Efficient Governance: Innovative Approaches of Bahrain. In Irfan, M., Elmogy, M., Gupta, S., Khalifa, F., & Dias, R. (Eds.), *AI-Driven Decentralized Finance and the Future of Finance* (pp. 115–142). IGI Global., DOI: 10.4018/979-8-3693-6321-8.ch005

Shaikh, Z. H., Sarea, A., & Irfan, M. (2022). *Islamic Banking Strategies in the World of Fintech: Success Story of Bahrain* (Vol. 423). Springer., DOI: 10.1007/978-3-030-93464-4_10

Sheela, P., Kusuma, K., Panigrahi, R. R., & Shaikh, Z. H. (2024). Fintech and Islamic Banking: A Systematic View and Future Research Agenda. In Irfan, M., Kadry, S., Sharif, M., & Khan, H. (Eds.), *Fintech Applications in Islamic Finance: AI, Machine Learning, and Blockchain Techniques* (pp. 1–23). IGI Global., DOI: 10.4018/979-8-3693-1038-0.ch001

Smith, C., Diver, S., & Reed, R. (2023). Advancing Indigenous futures with two-eyed seeing: Strategies for restoration and repair through collaborative research. *Environment and Planning. F, Philosophy, Theory, Models, Methods and Practice*, 2(1-2), 121–143. DOI: 10.1177/26349825221142292

Sobrevila, C. (2008). The Role of Indigenous Peoples in Biodiversity Conservation. In https://documents1.worldbank.org/curated/pt/995271468177530126/pdf/443000WP0BOX321onservation01PUBLIC1.pdf. The International Bank for Reconstruction and Development / THE WORLD BANK.

The Indigenous World 2024: Sustainable Development Goals (SDGs) and Indigenous Peoples - IWGIA - International Work Group for Indigenous Affairs. (2024, March 26). Www.iwgia.org. https://www.iwgia.org/en/the-sustainable-development-goals-sdgs-and-indigenous-peoples/5413-iw-2024-sdg.html

Tripathy, A., & Dastrala, S. M. (2023). Make in India: So Far and Going Ahead. SSRN Electronic Journal. https://doi.org/DOI: 10.2139/ssrn.4384039

UNDP. (2024). Indigenous knowledge is crucial in the fight against climate change – here's why | UNDP Climate Promise. UNDP Climate Promise. https://climatepromise.undp.org/news-and-stories/indigenous-knowledge-crucial-fight-against-climate-change-heres-why

Woodroffe, T. (2020). Presentation Feedback as an Indigenous methodology. *Australian Journal of Education*, 65(1), 73–83. DOI: 10.1177/0004944120969987

Chapter 13
Fostering Indigenous Inclusivity Financial Pathways to Economic Development and Sustainability

Rishikaysh Marotrao Kaakandikar
https://orcid.org/0000-0003-0349-6788
SaiBalaji International Institute of Management Sciences, India

Vani Raghuwanshi
https://orcid.org/0009-0002-1590-323X
SaiBalaji International Institute of Management Sciences, India

Supriya Pathak
https://orcid.org/0009-0004-3602-3172
Oriental University, Indore, India

Mohammad Irfan
https://orcid.org/0000-0002-4956-1170
Christ University, India

ABSTRACT

This book chapter explores and analyses two important areas that have been postulated as central to economic development and sustainable economic growth: local participation and access to finance. Regardless of having a wealthy background and the physical capital developed over thousands of years of living in Australia, Aboriginal people still encounter great hurdles when trying to obtain financial capital, and therefore face great constraints on finding ways to improve their status and living conditions. In this paper, the current financial accounting systems are reviewed and other new financial models for Indigenous people are discussed, including social capital and enterprise. Understanding the measures in the Government policy, cooperation and partnership with the private sector, we develop concept of open Finance where hopeful and important people are. 'When there is a problem,' this paper also indicates how this research is promoting independent lives while also taking care of the environment and society in Aboriginal communities.

DOI: 10.4018/979-8-3693-7924-0.ch013

INTRODUCTION

Indigenizing the future will reshape the process of building an economy and, consequently, the discourse on sustainable development, while authoritatively elucidating its meaning through finance and partnerships with Indigenous agencies. When we allocate dedicated financial resources to these communities, we invest in and support businesses. However, our primary goal is to integrate knowledge and culture into modern business practices. In the case of culture, we employ cultural assets and implement changes to achieve specific results, thereby adding value to the area's environment and economy. We are then able to develop a relationship between the First Nations, government, and business where First Nations rights and title, investment needs, and Indigenous peoples are met. Technology and the implementation of friendly policies will aid in generating capital, thereby enabling local business owners to participate in the current economy. However, where commitment to participation is evidenced, this option not only reinforces the power of Indigenous people but also provides the linkage between justice and sustainable development goals to ensure the conditions for human flourishing and interstellar harmony for future generations.

We must take the lead in creating an economy that respects heritage and invest in Indigenous peoples as our sponsors and partners. Therefore, the cultural Old Way and New Way, which means innovation has to be adopted, will be the way forward to enhance our standard of living.

Indigenous peoples encounter significant obstacles in obtaining funds for economic development and growth, regardless of their location in the world. Some of these concerns have been raised in prior works exploring usable finance for Indigenous people. Bhattacharya (2019) has stated that it becomes important to mention here that Indigenous economic mobilization largely relies on the availability of those qualified service types to the Indigenous consumer base. Similarly, Bressers and De Groot (2019) mentioned impediments related to Indigenous Peoples in banking, and according to the authors, they argue that existing standards established in banking do not take into account the culture and socio-economic attributes of the Indigenous Peoples. Furthermore, Doyle (2017) provides an elaborate list of the financial interventions that shall enhance the sustainable development of these regions; the author posits that it is naive to seek development solutions that would not harness Indigenous knowledge.

The text also covers such aspects as otherwise about a dozen rights and Indigenous people's self-governance, deepening the sporadic financial dilemma for the Indigenous people. Banerjee (2019) for decolonizing management theory entails a renewed examination of Indigenous management models that can be favourable for more desirable financial modalities. LaDuke (1999) presented a health-contextual perspective that emphasizes the need to view land, culture, and economy as a continuum in Indian Country. As Cornell (2007) did, it is argued the tools of governance have to be re-envisioned since it is ridden with colonialism that hampers the Indigenous economy. That is, aware of the mentioned above considerations, it is possible to contribute to the formation of the above-mentioned frameworks, which in turn will contribute to the development of further, sustainable, and equitable financial opportunities for the Indigenous peoples.

Indigenous inclusion is the future, not a fantasy: it is the key to leveraging the world's intense multicultural potential for economic revival and stable development in this era of global crisis. The position of indigenous persons assumes a very important responsibility in terms of running social systems within the twenty-first-century world since the world is becoming more challenging. Such societies adopt positive cultural attributes offering promising solutions to current issues like climate change, degradation of the biophysical environment, and injustices among people.

The concept of inclusivity holds significant value in enabling access to funding for bolstering indigenous economies. Economic discourses have marginalized indigenous people, preventing them from participating in processes that could improve their economic status and well-being. But as the global community becomes more sensitized to indigenous rights and ways, there is an emerging realization that they constructively support the framework for the economy's informing by looking for how to birth sustainable solutions for the common good. Based on the above discussion, this paper shall focus on one liberal space of possibility: the relationship between finance and Indigenous inclusion. By investing in indigenous-led endeavors, there will also be the likelihood of providing for the indigenous people while at the same time nurturing the economic, cultural, and environmentally sensitive value system among those peoples. It is not about putting money into projects; it is about supporting programs and projects that affirm the existence of Indigenous peoples, things we as Indigenous peoples stand for—self-determination.

The Economic Development (ED) with Indigenous Inclusion flowchart outlines how incorporating Indigenous people into financial systems leads to economic growth:

1. **Indigenous Inclusion**: Start by recognizing and integrating Indigenous communities into economic frameworks.
2. **Access to Financial Services**: Provide targeted financial resources tailored to their needs.
3. **Investment in Indigenous Businesses**: Support Indigenous-led enterprises through funding and partnerships.
4. **Development of Local Economy**: Boost the economy by fostering local industries and markets.
5. **Job Creation and Wealth Generation**: Create employment opportunities and improve income distribution.
6. **Improved Infrastructure and Living Standards**: Enhance community well-being through better facilities.
7. **Equitable Economic Growth**: Achieve inclusive growth that benefits both Indigenous and broader populations.

This pathway emphasizes the transformative potential of Indigenous participation in economic systems.

Flowchart 1: Economic Development (ED) with Indigenous Inclusion

Figure 1. Economic Development (ED) with Indigenous Inclusion

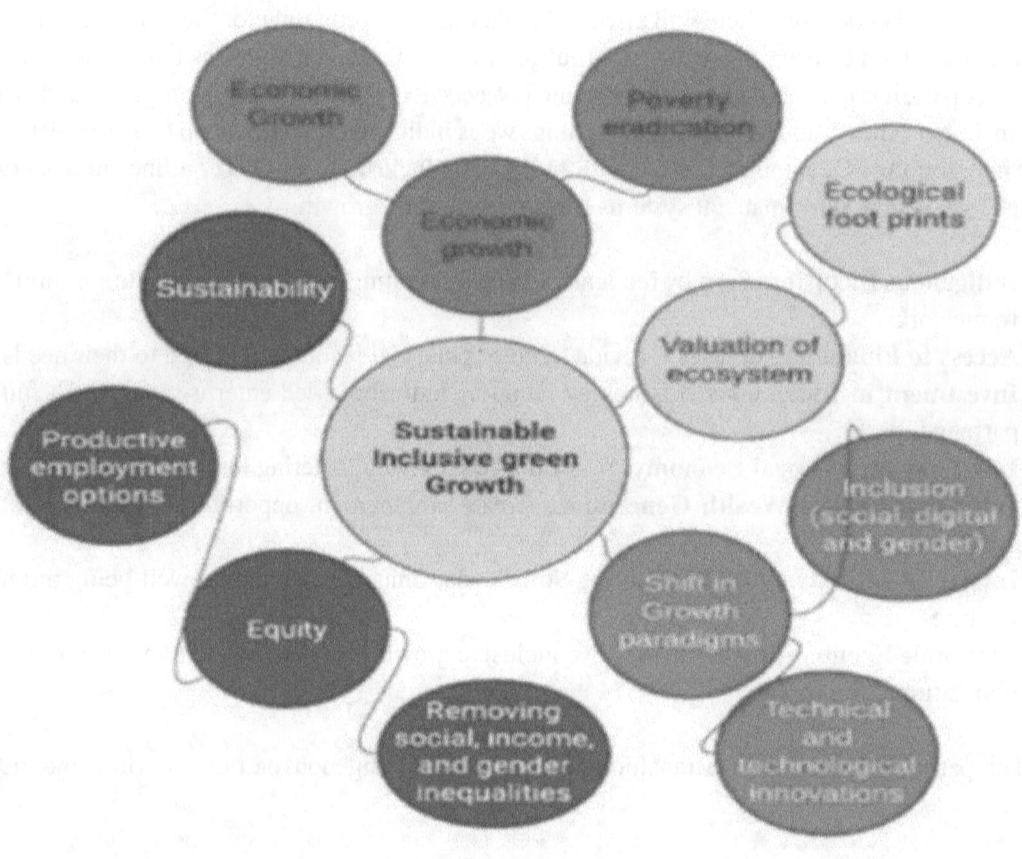

The Sustainable Development (SD) with Indigenous Inclusion flowchart highlights how Indigenous participation supports long-term sustainability:

1. **Integration of Indigenous Knowledge**: Incorporate traditional practices and wisdom into sustainability initiatives.
2. **Environmentally Conscious Practices**: Use Indigenous approaches to balance ecological preservation with resource use.
3. **Preservation of Cultural Heritage**: Protect and promote Indigenous cultural values alongside development.
4. **Policy Support and Partnerships**: Establish supportive policies and partnerships among governments, businesses, and Indigenous communities.

5. **Balanced Resource Utilization**: Ensure resources are used efficiently and equitably, considering environmental and social impacts.
6. **Strengthened Community Well-being**: Improve Indigenous communities' health, education, and living standards.
7. **Long-Term Sustainability Goals Achieved**: Create a future that balances economic growth, cultural preservation, and environmental stewardship.

This flowchart emphasizes the synergy between Indigenous knowledge and modern sustainability efforts, driving inclusive and lasting development.

Figure 2. Sustainable Development (SD) with Indigenous Inclusion

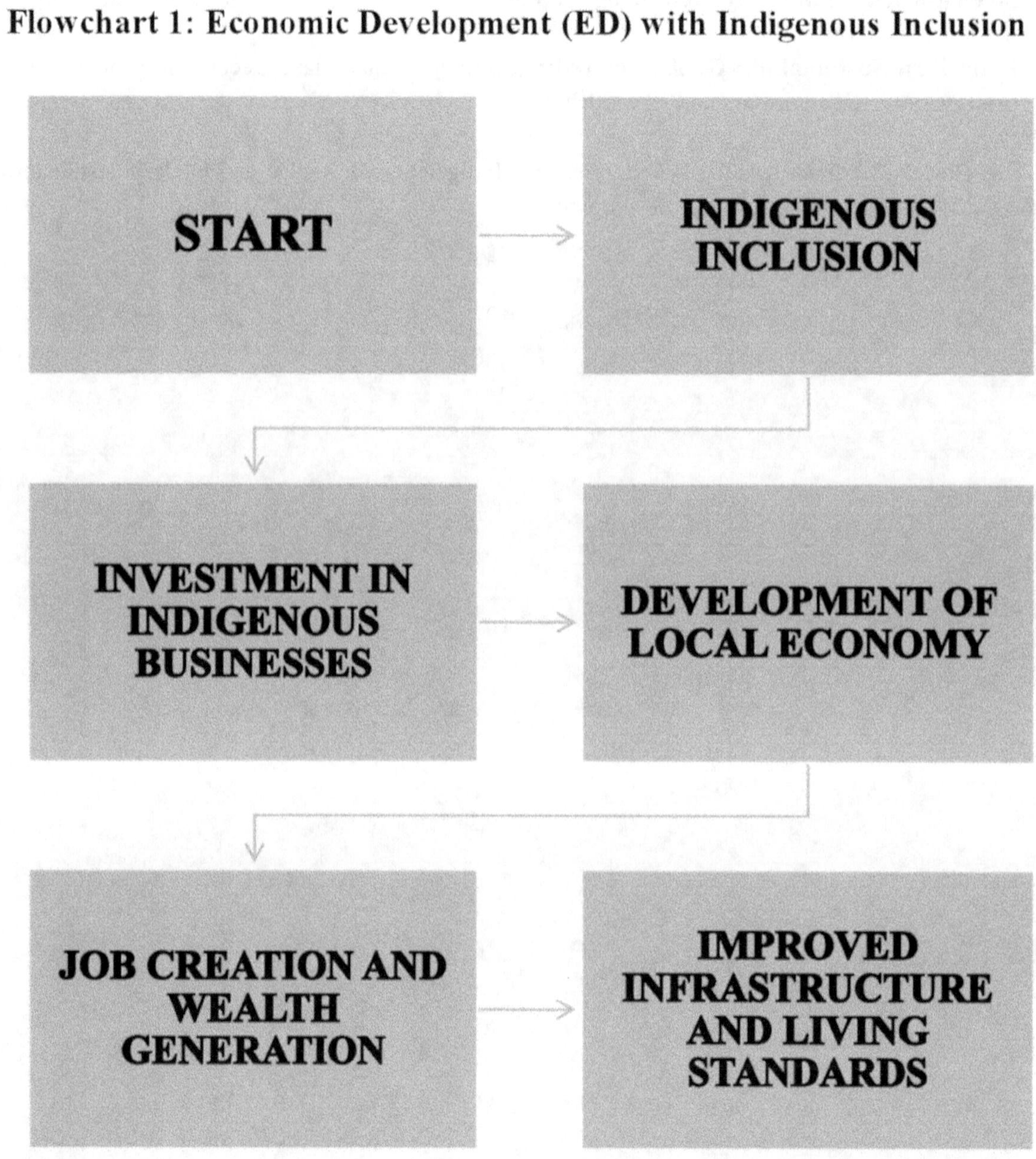

THE CONCEPT OF INDIGENOUS INCLUSIVITY AND ITS IMPORTANCE TO ECONOMIC GROWTH ON THE INTERNATIONAL DEVILMENT

Aboriginal inclusion means that aboriginal people should have an active role in economic development focusing on their rights, opinions and beliefs, and their involvement in the decision making. This is an important idea in the concept of international trade because it acknowledges the special place of Indigenous people who usually are well endowed with information about their people and the natural endowment. Let Aboriginal people participate in financial planning to show that it brings good and noticeable results that bring value to their native people as well as benefit society collectively. Their knowledge can help with the management of the environment and the promotion of the more robust concept of biodiversity, a core factor for the modern economy. Also, the local agriculture can play the role in correction of the historical mistakes and provide more qualitative generation of the businessman representatives of other nation. This would mean that instead of considering local thinking as a problem that hinders global thinking, local thinking can be embraced as an opportunity that can open the way to possibilities that allow all parties to engage in efficient, innovative thinking that leads to a sustainable global economy. These are important things. Indigenous entrepreneurship and sustainability have increasingly been recognized as vital areas of research, emphasizing the integration of traditional knowledge and contemporary practices. Anderson and Dana (2006) identify Indigenous entrepreneurship as an emerging field that highlights unique cultural and economic contexts, while Banerjee (2019) calls for decolonizing management theories to incorporate Indigenous perspectives in business practices. Ansell and Clapham (2023) underscore the importance of Indigenous climate leadership, where traditional ecological knowledge drives innovative adaptation strategies. Bartlett and Green (2024) discuss renewable energy governance as a pathway to resilience and self-determination for Indigenous communities. Similarly, Aragon and Kessler (2020) focus on leveraging resource windfalls for public investments that directly benefit Indigenous populations, reinforcing the importance of equitable resource allocation.

Concept and its Impact on Global Development

Here are some key points about the concept of Indigenous participation and its impact on global economic development:

1. **Definition:** Working especially with the First Nation people and ensuring their participation, especially in matters of decision-making as well as economic development matters.
2. **Traditional Knowledge:** Indigenous population possesses culturally specific information on how to manage resources and run organizations for the betterment of the current methodologies of the existing business".
3. **Economic Empowerment:** Aboriginal people should participate in business formation and development, entrepreneurship, and innovations to grow the local and national economies.
4. **Speaking of Inequality:** Public Service Management can assist in remedying past wrongs and social imparity and offering reasonable and affordable resource capability.
5. **Corporate Social Responsibility:** Employers who handle both aspects at the same time in a different place.

6. **Cultural Protection:** Aboriginal support encompasses assisting the maintenance of the Indigenous cultural sites and assets, enhancing the identification of Aboriginal people and boosting the spirit of Aborigines.

7. **Sustainability:** Interacting with indigenous knowledge assists in prospecting sustainable solutions, which are necessary when considering global issues like climate change and the loss of species diversity.

8. **Social Cohesion:** It makes social cohesion and integrity since everyone's voices are heard whenever issues affecting the development of business empowerment is being addressed. Speaking about the value and the need to build a stable and stable life.

Figure 3. Global economic development by Indigenous inclusivity

Flowchart 2: Sustainable Development (SD) with Indigenous Inclusion

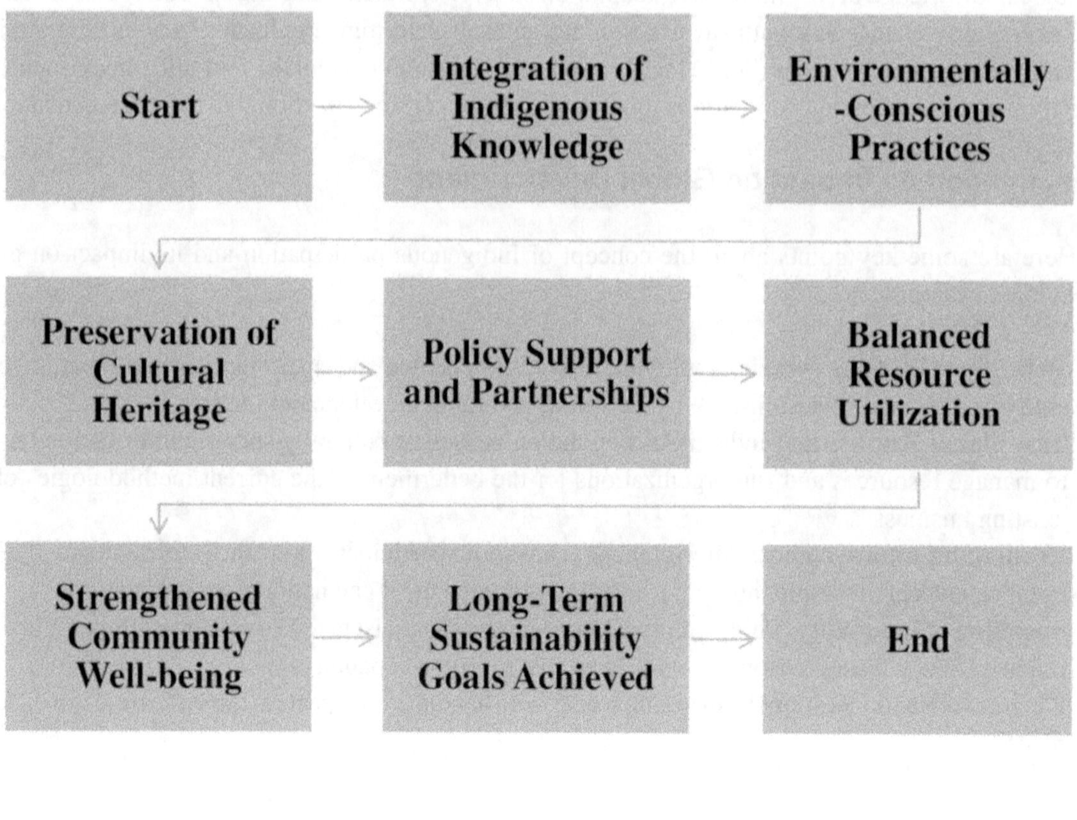

THE HISTORICAL BARRIERS WITNESSED BY INDIGENOUS POPULATIONS IN PROCURING CASH WEALTH

The economic development that is labelled Aboriginal inclusion entails acknowledging and embracing the Aboriginal rights and submissions, along with their assorted cultures, whilst also incorporating these people within the economic improvement programs. This concept is useful in the development of international trade as it respects Indigenous contribution, the majority of whom have adequate knowledge about their traditions and product endowment. Aboriginal engagement in financial planning results in forming more positive and tangible impacts that involve their own people but the society at large or all humanity. This research argues that it is valuable to learn from locals as their knowledge can enhance environmental management and boost concerns about Biodiversity within the current economy. Furthermore, local agriculture is useful to increment overall uneven equity and make fairer world by responding to historical injustices. They suggest that recognizing and incorporating local ways of thinking help create innovation and smarter development for the worldwide economy and its inhabitants. Aboriginal participation means not just participation but a consistent focus on interaction processes between the Aboriginal people as well as other parties, such as government and business. This approach promotes participation, recognition and reciprocity and results in more satisfactory solutions because they are consistent with the needs and desires of Aboriginal people. If Indigenous people's voices are involved in policy formulation and building business models for development, possibly such policies and models will contain Indigenous-appropriate development paradigms and are, therefore, likely to be effective in the implementation of sustainable development goals. These are important things. When Australia's first people on the air, water, and ground as native proprietors, they are in a position to run proper economic activities that are environmentally sensitive and get health facilities that are proper for them. It should be noted that the rights may result in the restoration of preindustrial methods of agriculture and plant cultivation, as well as fishing and forest management that embrace food supply and maintain diverse living species. An important factor has also emerged: ethical and sustainable business practices into their awareness. Purchasers, as well as investors, expect goods and services that are responsive to their ethical and social concerns, such as Indigenous people's rights and environmental conservation. The role of inclusive finance and governance in supporting Indigenous communities has been widely explored. Bhattacharya (2019) highlights how financial inclusion fosters Indigenous economic empowerment, while Besser and De Groot (2019) examine the challenges and opportunities of extending financial services to Indigenous populations. Doyle (2017) delves into sustainable financial strategies tailored to Indigenous contexts, emphasizing long-term developmental goals. Friedland and Harris (2021) advocate for Indigenous inclusion in global economic governance, promoting policies that address systemic inequalities. Furthermore, Smith and James (2024) argue for the establishment of decolonial financial systems as the future of Indigenous banking models, ensuring greater autonomy and equity.

Integrating Indigenous Communities

The basic economic functionality of Aboriginal peoples in tourism and preserving and popularizing their knowledge and practice. It is worthy of note also, that due to our extensive knowledge of sustainable management practices, many aboriginal people can lead to Environmental and Biodiversity Conservation. This means that if we are to incorporate their opinions into achieving the goals of a sustainable profit-margined and rightfully responsible business we can. But, extending Integrative moves to incorporate

Indigenous communities will be in the best interest of the theory of social justice because it would provide them with the hitherto unavailable tools of mainly resources which will be of benefit to them. whose implementation will also facilitate addressing problems related to social inequality, international trade and business from multiple viewpoints. Thus, development of economic growth in Indigenous regions will mean better future built by Indigenous people themselves. Culture-based practices on the land and other resources would better the condition of the environment and hence is feasible for all people, making it hard to get. There are increased risks to the business, and it means higher costs. The plan is inadequate in addressing the distinctive features and needs of the Aboriginal Groups.

The success of Aboriginal people and communities in accessing financial resources with regard to their economic development and welfare continues to be a major contentious issue that has its roots in the past. These problems originate from colonial history, racism and poverty that other races have inflicted on Indigenous people for decades.

Such ignorance can hamper their financial literacy, credit, and investment all in one package. Nevertheless, if they receive no training and guidance, it becomes difficult for First Nations to obtain the necessary finances for economic development. Sustainable development in Indigenous communities often intersects with environmental stewardship and governance innovations. Yazzie and Johnston (2024) discuss sustainable initiatives within the Navajo Nation as models for global Indigenous economies. LaDuke (1999) emphasizes the struggles of Native communities to maintain their land and resources amidst external pressures. Goodland and Daly (1996) advocate for universal environmental sustainability principles, which are integral to Indigenous approaches to resource management. Torres and Cruz (2024) explore the use of blockchain to enhance transparency in managing Indigenous resources, presenting a modern technological approach to traditional governance challenges. Similarly, Wilson and Thomas (2024) highlight blockchain's potential to ensure fair and transparent Indigenous land agreements, aligning technological advances with Indigenous needs.

The Global Economic Fabric, Focusing on Sustainability and Equitable Growth

Aboriginal participation with Aboriginal people in the development of economic ventures so that their ways of knowing and doing are respected. First nation people more often than not have a wealth of knowledge in the management for sustainable yield resulting in conservation. This could basically entail giving the customers an opportunity to express their opinion and in so doing building sustainable, profitable and responsible business. At the same time, integration of indigenous communities may contribute to social justice because it can provide the people of these communities with resources and services that were previously inaccessible for them. It will further assist in fixing social injustice and also international trade from various perspectives and practices. Finally, the paper demonstrates why the economic growth that integrates Indigenous people's voice will result in the formation of coherent and well-developed communities that affect people positively. The use of indigenous knowledge in management of land and resource can increase ecological fitness and hence enhance ecosystem and species diversity. valued. Aboriginal people often have a deep understanding of sustainable management leading to environmental and biodiversity conservation. By acknowledging their views, we can create a sustainable, profitable and responsible business. In addition, integrating Indigenous communities can promote social justice by providing resources and opportunities that were not previously available to them. This will not only help to address social injustice but will also encourage international trade from a range of perspectives and practices. Ultimately, inclusive economic growth that includes Indigenous voices will lead to stronger, more sustainable communities that benefit people.

1. **Sustainable Practices:** Indigenous knowledge for land and resource management can improve ecological sustainability and biodiversity conservation.
2. **Equity and Justice:** They mean that due to participation it is possible to counteract historical discrimination and provide Indigenous people with the same chances as everyone else to take part in the economic process.
3. **Cultural Diversity:** Through Indigenous integration, there is enhanced creation of interfaces of several stances as well as; modification of the practices thus enhancing International business commerce.
4. **Resilience:** Segment integrating the indigenous knowledge raises the ability to change, and to address change as well as the challenges it brings, which makes the system sustainable.
5. **Community Empowerment:** The remaining affirmative joint venture initiatives that are still exercised benefit indigenous peoples and enhance their quality of life as well as their culture.

Development of indigenous peoples into the global economy does not only concern the ideal of equity but appropriation and equal growth.

Indigenous people's integration in the global economy is vital in many ways especially while fulfilling the need that addresses sustainable and sustainable development needs. This integration satisfies the Aboriginal right and cultural requirements while at the same time adds to sustainable and inclusive economy. Here are some main issues to be taken into account.

INDIGENOUS INCLUSIVE FUTURES

The intersection of renewable energy and Indigenous rights has emerged as a significant area of research. Finley-Brook and Thomas (2011) highlight the human rights violations faced by Indigenous communities due to hydroelectric projects in Panama, emphasizing the need for equitable solutions. Bartlett and Green (2024) present renewable energy governance as a tool for fostering Indigenous resilience. Yazzie and Johnston (2024) reinforce this by showcasing sustainable energy initiatives within the Navajo Nation as a global example. Goodland and Daly (1996) advocate for non-negotiable sustainability principles, aligning with Indigenous values of environmental stewardship. These studies collectively underline the critical role of renewable energy in supporting Indigenous communities.

Paralyzed by the idea that economic development means development for some and sustenance for others, people are missing a key aspect of empowering Indigenous communities: for the release of funds for pillar I and for funding sustainable economic development of Indigenous peoples. In the recent past, scholars accepted the need to capture the Aboriginal approaches into economics and especially in financial and investment economies. For instance, there is still citizenship question, which has continued to be argued as a form of injustice, there is land issue, and there are cultural encampments, which are remnants of historical form of injustice. Moreover, aboriginal six concerning higher poverty, unemployment, and low services are expected to be relevant to communities of aboriginal people. From the above it is clear that, to address such issues one should have an attitude to save money in order to put in place measures that enhance the economy for the focus to be inclusive. Financial access therefore the opportunity and chance of individuals and communities to engage in and use the demand side of financial services such as banking, credit and capital. Aboriginal people for the most part of do not get what they require from the traditional economy. Among the aboriginal industries, there are dissimilarities of credit histories, geographical restrictions or/and cultural differences to address in order to obtain the capital needed for their businesses the main difficulties. This covers savings and other financial services accounts and linkages with other Aboriginal-owned financial services. Decolonization remains a central theme in Indigenous economic and governance models. Banerjee (2019) critiques traditional management theories, urging for decolonized approaches rooted in Indigenous practices. Smith and James (2024) propose decolonial financial systems as a transformative solution for Indigenous banking. Cornell (2007) emphasizes the importance of reclaiming governance tools and promoting Indigenous solutions over colonial legacies. Lopez and Vargas (2024) explore Indigenous-led financial models in Latin America, offering lessons for broader decolonial efforts. Escobar (2011) further critiques conventional development paradigms, advocating for integrating Indigenous perspectives to ensure inclusivity and equity.

Also, understanding Aboriginal rights and the sovereignty of their lands is essential to financing economic development. All governments and financial institutions must recognize Aboriginal native title rights and undertake no activities on Aboriginal land without obtaining the free, prior, and informed consent of the Aboriginal peoples. That way, it is also a fair approach, producing better outcomes that are more efficient and have greater economic gain. Kristin said that PPPs can invest in Indigenous leadership and support capacity building. At its core, stakeholder collaboration is the process of building the social architecture needed to promote and protect innovation and sustainable enterprise. Assistance in business development can help Aboriginal businesspersons enhance their work experience, thus enhancing their competency in a strict financial world. Moreover, raising Indigenous voices on the economic impact involves allowing Indigenous people to have leadership in these assessments so that their views would be valued. It means that we can eliminate prejudices that prevent Indigenous people from getting credit, support Indigenous sustainability, and recognize their rights to Indigenous economization for sustainable growth and for the sustainable economic development of Indigenous communities. In addition, recognition of Aboriginal rights and land sovereignty is crucial to funding economic development. Governments and financial institutions must respect Aboriginal land rights and ensure that any development involving Aboriginal lands has their free, prior, and informed consent. This approach not only promotes fairness but also leads to greater efficiency and economic value. Public-private partnerships can facilitate investment in Indigenous leadership and support capacity building. Working together, stakeholders can create an ecosystem that supports innovation, entrepreneurship, and sustainable growth. Providing training and support to Aboriginal entrepreneurs can improve their business skills and financial literacy, enabling them to thrive in a challenging financial environment. Furthermore, promoting Indigenous leadership in economic assessments ensures that Indigenous voices are heard and respected in decision-making processes. Growth unlocks capital. We can create economic equity for Indigenous communities by removing barriers to accessing finance, promoting sustainable practices, and respecting Indigenous rights and economic development.

Indigenous Communities Face Due to Limited Access to Financial Services

Currently, Aboriginal people are disadvantaged by socioeconomic disparities occasioned by poor access to banking services. Most indigenous communities have still been poorer and had fewer jobs than non-indigenous communities. This is compounded by a problem of non-connectivity to banking, which can complicate an ability to borrow or get credit. Lack of financial capital means that it is almost impossible to bootstrap a business, and this has left many Aboriginal people either working low-wage jobs or struggling to find work. Such problems as lack of education and poor financial literacy thereby make many of these people in these community's lack understanding on how to use this money or even how to source for capital or investment. This, in turn, results in a vicious cycle that is quite hard to come by. That is, discrimination and historical injustice are resulting in distrust of formal financial institutions and returning some First Nations to costly and usurious credit. All in all, these economic contention issues produce severe threats to the status of economic security and development, which efficiently reduces the possibilities of Indigenous peoples to become wealthy. Financial inclusion is vital for Indigenous economic empowerment. Bhattacharya (2019) and Doyle (2017) discuss inclusive financial strategies tailored to Indigenous needs, highlighting their role in sustainable development. Besser and De Groot (2019) explore the challenges Indigenous communities face in accessing financial services and identifying opportunities to bridge gaps. Friedland and Harris (2021) call for systemic changes in global economic governance to include Indigenous voices. Hulme and Arun (2009) emphasize microfinance as a tool for empowering marginalized groups, aligning with Indigenous economic aspirations. Together, these studies provide a comprehensive view of financial inclusion's potential to transform Indigenous economies.

Lack of access to finances is a key determinant of health for aboriginal contexts, hence a significant mechanism that leads to health inequalities among the identified population. These disparities manifest themselves in a few ways:

1. **Poverty and Unemployment:** Reports show that many Aboriginal communities suffer from poverty, and the unemployment rate is high and above that of people who are non-Aboriginal. This weak Economy makes it very hard for Them to invest in Education, health and other services.
2. **Limited Access to Financial Services:** Unfortunately, the number of Aboriginal people without local banks or financial institutions is vast, and many travel a long distance just to attain basic financial services. Because of this, they shy away from credit or account facilities, hence being discriminated against and locked out of the legitimate market.
3. **Business Challenges:** In the absence of credit or loans, starting or even expanding a business is often a herculean task. Indigenous business owners encounter constraints that limit innovative and growth prospects, including credit constraints, collateral, and support.
4. **Low Financial Literacy:** Cognitive loss and lack of formal education resulted in poor financial management and poor knowledge about money or going to the bank and asking for a loan among the First Nations people. Lack of knowledge denied them an opportunity to access the available resources.
5. **Dependence on Informal Loans:** Because of mistrust in established financial organizations, some of these First Nations people resort to borrowing informal money that is relative in terms of quality but high and expensive in terms of interest rates. This can lead to an unending cycle of indebtedness that is difficult to come out of.
6. **Systemic Discrimination:** Prejudice arising from past events along with current racism means that Indigenous persons cannot obtain services of the sort offered by a bank. It results in the shunning of operations with traditional financial institutions.

7. **Impacts on Community Development:** It is something that does not affect people alone but also hampers community development projects. One thing that is almost synonymous with lack of access to financial resources. Proposals that attempt to grow the organization of building, schooling, and health in the Aboriginal community's fight for achievement with no money are needed.
8. **Long-Term Consequences:** These economic battles will have future generational repercussions. They will limit children's chances of a good education and better job prospects because children from poor economic backgrounds will not have a chance at a good education. This is important.

Historical Barriers, Including Colonization, Exclusion from Financial Institutions, and Lack of Representation in Decision-Making Processes

Historical factors are issues that concern the Aboriginal group by denying them funding and financial progression. European colonization disturbed their way of life by removing them from their ancestral territories and wiping out their indigenous values. Here, the missing is not merely in terms of material resources but in terms of representation within society. Aboriginal people are also locked out of the formal financial sector, suffer discrimination, and struggle to obtain credit and banking. The further result is that the policies regulating their lives are adopted regardless of the patient's needs and concerns because the latter have no seats in the decision-making process. Indigenous Peoples of Australia continue to suffer from the effects of history and can never be freed economically to be empowered to contribute to society. Dealing with these challenges is crucial to increasing work opportunities and supporting social justice for current employees. The role of Indigenous knowledge in sustainable development continues to gain recognition in global conservation efforts. Park and Choi (2024) explore the application of Indigenous knowledge systems for biodiversity conservation in Asia, emphasizing the importance of integrating traditional practices in modern environmental strategies. Howitt (2011) highlights the challenges of implementing sustainable futures in remote Indigenous areas, highlighting the failed state approaches that often overlook Indigenous perspectives. Bargh (2007) critiques the impact of neoliberalism on Maori development in New Zealand, advocating for Indigenous-led development models that prioritize cultural and ecological sustainability. Similarly, LaDuke (1999) discusses the ongoing struggles for land and life within Native communities, stressing the importance of Indigenous environmental stewardship. These studies collectively advocate for the inclusion of Indigenous knowledge in both local and global sustainability practices.

1. **Colonization:** Cultures were eliminated, and the population was removed from their homelands.
2. **Exclusion from Financial Institutions:** Prejudice that results in exclusion from the banking services.
3. **Lack of Representation in Decision-Making:** Despite the policies that touch on the indigenous communities have lost the voice of the Indigenes.
4. **Historical Injustices:** Over the years, people of color have learned not to trust the government and established financial channels.
5. **Impact on Economic Independence:** Resource acquisition constraints hamper business entry and expansion.

It should, however, be noted that a table illustrates some of the past challenges Indigenous people had, including integration, or lack thereof, in mainstream society, and particularly exclusion from financial systems and lack of representation in decision-making processes.

Review Current Literature that Addresses Such Barriers and Try to Identify the Current Policies and Frameworks That Seek to Eliminate Such Barriers, such as the United Nations Sustainable Development Goals that Focus on the Indigenous People. Recent research has explored diverse aspects of AI, machine learning, and blockchain within the financial sector, emphasizing their role in advancing fintech, sustainability, and thematic investing. For example, Irfan (2021) investigated the convergence of Shariah indices within Gulf Cooperation Council (GCC) countries, revealing key insights into the regional financial alignment. Additionally, Irfan, Elhoseny, Kassim, and Metawa (2023) addressed the potential of advanced machine learning algorithms to manage complex financial applications, signifying a substantial technological evolution. Exploring the impact of Industry 5.0, Irfan, Elmogy, Majid, and El-Sappagh (2023) examined AI innovation's transformative effects on financial sectors, highlighting industry-specific advancements. Complementary studies by Irfan, Kadry, Sharif, and Khan (2023) further demonstrated the integration of fintech applications within Islamic finance, focusing on AI and blockchain. Expanding on these themes, Irfan et al. (2024) curated works on sustainability challenges in AI and thematic investing, while Irfan, Elmogy, Gupta, Khalifa, and Dias (2024) examined AI's role in decentralized finance, discussing future financial landscapes. Together, these studies provide a robust framework for understanding the role of emerging technologies in reshaping finance across regions and sectors.

Economic Development Through Financial Inclusion

Like any other society, economic development is crucial for Indigenous people, but its achievement is slightly more problematic due to a range of historically rooted disparities. Education and financial literacy (the process of enabling individuals and communities to gain access to financial services) are important in solving those problems. Indigenous people and a few other communities would greatly benefit from financing to help their businesses grow and gain a level of autonomy and re-employment. To mean it, financial products and services are needed by each person and all groups within the societies. They include Savings, loans, insurance, and payments. A roadmap: For Indigenous people, financial inclusion can make or mar their economic future. There is no question that financial inclusion for Indigenous peoples is the key to capital unlocking the ages of Indigenous communities for economic enfranchisement and inclusive development. Thus, through financial services with necessary products like loans and savings and basic financial literacy, these communities that eventually closed in the past can now go out and invest in businesses, education institutions, and healthcare facilities within the communities. In turn, this empowers entrepreneurship, enables the preservation of a culture, and fosters social cohesion. Positive examples illustrate the change in financial services: Mirroring the trends demonstrates that having enough capital for the Aboriginal groups ensures their economic viability without a negative impact on their heritage. Finally, without financial inclusion, it is almost impossible for Indigenous peoples to be able to determine their own future and achieve sustainable livelihoods. Governance structures and financial systems in Indigenous communities are undergoing significant transformations. Torres and Cruz (2024) explore how blockchain technology can improve transparency and accountability in Indigenous resource management, enabling fairer distribution of resources. Wilson and Thomas (2024) further discuss blockchain's potential in ensuring transparency in Indigenous land agreements, offering new tools for managing land and resource rights. Lopez and Vargas (2024) examine Indigenous-led financial models in Latin America, providing insights into how decolonizing economic policies can enhance Indigenous governance. Gibson (2020) advocates for incorporating Indigenous models of sustainable development into mainstream economic frameworks, promoting equity and environmental justice. Finally, Daly (1996) underscores the importance of sustainable growth principles that align with Indigenous values, suggesting a shift towards more inclusive, resource-conscious governance.

The Gap Between Mainstream Financial Services and The Needs of Indigenous Communities

This research identified the difference between simple transaction banking services and the complex needs of Indigenous populations as one of the fundamental issues in a history of oppression, marginalization, and lack of recognition by traditional financial organizations. This means there is an economic imbalance, constant poverty, and limited Indigenous people's capacity for autonomy in their affairs. To fill this gap, the realities of the cultural, social, and economic nature of Aboriginal communities must be spelled out, and financial products have to be designed to successfully answer these realities. There are a lot of issues with Indigenous people being unable to access basic financial services: this is due to historical and present injustice, inequality, and exclusion from the formal financial sector. This inequality retards economic development and perpetuates poverty, and erodes Aboriginal people's sovereignty. To address this gap, one must comprehend the cultural, social, and economic demographics of Aboriginal people and design financial services solutions that address these demographics. Currently, Indigenous people have experienced colonialism, displacement, and assimilation policies, which, therefore, result in immense socio-economic inequity. He said that for many Latinos, historical injustices have led to scepticism when it comes to banking and other mainstream organizations. Most Indigenous peoples are completely financially marginalized, with no access to deposit accounts, credit, and limited investment. This exclusion not only affects the economic aspects but also sustains unjust social systems that prevent wards' development.

Sustainable Growth: Integrating Indigenous Perspectives in Economic Policies Fosters Sustainable Growth

> "Integrating Aboriginal perspectives into economic policy is not about respecting the past; it is about creating a future where all communities live in harmony with the land."

Sustainable development is now a significant achievement people seek worldwide, especially now that the world has so many problems. To this effect, it is important that an Aboriginal perspective is embraced as part of business policy since Aboriginal people may have a more profound insight into the advanced work of permaculture throughout generations. By incorporating these views, policymakers should be in a better position to foster more proper business strategies that enhance the stewardship of the environment and equity and support culturally bearish traditions.

Integrating Indigenous financial models in global governance has become a key focus in recent studies. Cornell (2007) argues for remaking governance tools to reflect Indigenous solutions rather than colonial legacies, highlighting the importance of autonomy for Indigenous communities. Aragon and Kessler (2020) examine the role of resource windfalls and public investment in benefiting Indigenous communities, stressing the need for equitable distribution. Similarly, Irfan et al. (2023) explores the role of advanced machine learning algorithms and fintech in enhancing financial strategies, which can also benefit Indigenous populations by providing more inclusive financial services. Gibson (2020) further supports this by illustrating how Indigenous financial models can contribute to sustainable development and social equity. These contributions highlight the growing recognition of Indigenous communities as active participants in shaping global economic and governance frameworks.

Aboriginal Perspectives for Sustainable Environment: Aboriginal people have used sustainable environmental relationships with land, water, and resources for thousands of years. This knowledge also includes sustainable land use and management of biological and ecological resources for diverse sustainability-based approaches. As an example, Traditional Ecological Knowledge (TEK) is a phenomenon that captures relations between ecosystems, and it operates under a framework that encourages healthy ecosystems for people.

In its wider sense, Aboriginal knowledge refers to knowledge specific to Indigenous people of a certain race or nationality. It is generally implemented along with language, stories, traditions, and practices. This knowledge is not fixed but constantly underpaid as the community changes regarding environmental and social constructs.

Indigenous knowledge systems benefit the communities that practice them and social and environmental sustainability. Sustainable Resource Management: IKS contains information concerning best practices that involve generations. Such information can help to develop today's resource management approaches to health and conservation. Culture has several ways to conserve animals and their environment within society. Therefore, meaningful climate change adaptation strategies can be achieved by improving the understanding of the Aboriginal communities' traditional knowledge of local environmental and historical predictors for current climate change challenges. A tradition that is on the verge of extinction.

Paths and transmission: Education is a central reality and is mainly found in indigenous knowledge through storytelling, singing and dancing, and communal games. This allows sharing learning through experiences and knowledge base within environments that encourage communal learning. Education and Training: Older people ensure that young people embrace cultural and ecological knowledge and their heritage. Education fosters an appreciation of traditional knowledge and the use of conventional knowledge in different situations. They are practices that enrich knowledge and bring up social, interpersonal, and teamwork aspects.

With the help of the table, we also differentiate it; to know about it:

Table 1. Indigenous knowledge system and conventional practices

Aspect	Indigenous Knowledge Systems	Conventional Practices
Perspective on Nature	Holistic and interconnected	Ecosystems are viewed as interdependent
Resource Management	Long-term pleasing dominion	Emphasis on sustainability and balance
Cultural Integration	Profound cultural practices and customs	A deep respect for traditions
Decision-Making	Community-driven and inclusive	Engages local stakeholders
Adaptability	Low sensitivity to environmental change	Resilience and flexibility in practices
Biodiversity Approach	Promotes conservation and variety	Focus on protecting diverse species
Innovation	Integrates traditional and modern practices	Fosters creative solutions for challenges

THE IMPORTANCE OF ABORIGINAL KNOWLEDGE SYSTEMS AND SUSTAINABILITY

A Holistic View of Ecosystems: Aboriginal knowledge systems promote a better understanding of ecosystems and recognize species sharing and their habitats. Stewardship: Traditional practices are often linked to sustainability and ensure resources are ready for the future.

Cultural Preservation: Integrating Aboriginal knowledge into sustainable development can help preserve cultural heritage and strengthen communities. It can also create effective environmental policies. Innovation in Practice: Indigenous knowledge systems provide sustainable development opportunities for new practices that can complement and enhance existing practices.

Table 2. Aboriginal knowledge system and sustainability

Aspect	Description	Key Characteristics
Perspective on Nature	Holistic and interconnected	Emphasizes the independence of ecosystem.
Resource Management	Sustainable, long-term stewardship	Focus on balance and sustainability
Cultural Integration	Deeply embedded in cultural practices and traditions	Respect and integrate traditional knowledge
Decision-Making	Community-driven, inclusive	Involves local stakeholders in processes
Adaptability	Highly adaptive to environmental changes	Resilient and flexible practices

Indigenous-Led Businesses and Projects Support Environmental Sustainability Alongside Economic Development

This system bases the ownership of the land to the aboriginal people all over the world this is by acknowledging the country with that culture. Such linkage generally results in implementing activities that can foster environmental conservationism and economic growth. Indigenous business ventures and initiatives have emerged as strong examples for these two purposes. In this discussion, I ask what is an Indigenous business, how they contribute to development, and what economic value they bring to the community. These industries can be very diverse, ranging from arts and crafts to traditions and customs, renewable energy, and permaculture. One characteristic of this business is that it incorporates Aboriginal values, knowledge, and frameworks. This means that selection must be made kindly to the environment and culture and consider people's health. For instance, the Aboriginal tourism business may provide eco-tours enabling the guests to master systems together with Aboriginal histories and cultures. Likewise, fishing companies can address fish and marine water supply issues, knowing that there are resources ready for use in the future by adopting methodologies promoting sustainable fishing.

Environmental Sustainability Through Aboriginal Practices: aborigines who inhabit these regions have been tending to their areas for thousands of years. Such knowledge entails awareness of ecosystems, wildlife, and culture of the traditional domain of the people concerned. Protector of the environment and the economy can be seen to be used by the indigenous people in the management of businesses.

Cultural and Social Inclusivity

Cultural care and community participation will inform the future of a more just and equitable society. These are especially relevant for Indigenous people who have experienced prejudice and oppression in the past. Hearing and celebrating the origins of voices is equally relevant when approaching grand global matters such as climate change, economic warfare, and social inequality. In this session, the participants will understand the place of cultural conservationism in the assessment of stocks and flows and how policy creation can benefit from indigenous people's direction.

Offering New Financial Instruments

1. Engaging Communities

In general, any efforts towards the creation of tailored financial services should start with the processes of inclusion of Indigenous peoples. This involves:

Needs Analysis: Carrying out questionnaires and focus group discussions to determine the debt, savings, investment, or credit requirements and goals of community members.

Cultural Sensitivity: Addressing how concerns of Indigenous culture and traditions are considered in the processes of developing products.

2. Improving Financial Literacy

Lack of knowledge about financial products is one of the primary reasons why it is nearly impossible for the Aboriginal communities to make proper financial choices. Education sessions can increase the confidence of the members of the community in the knowledge and experience of members.

Public-Private Partnerships (PPP): To develop sustainable and effective financial systems, more attention should be paid to promoting partnerships between governments, financial institutions, and Indigenous organizations.

PPPs have become one of the greatest approaches for finding solutions amidst hard societal challenges that involve both the public and private domains. With a constantly increasing consciousness of social and environmental problems worldwide, the importance of an open and sound fiscal system also increases. An especially significant development area is to improve cooperation with the governments, financial institutions and Aboriginal organizations. In this approach, disruption of the economy is sought to achieve participation of Aboriginal peoples in the decision-making that shapes their lives. Public-Private Partnerships (PPPs) are partnership structures that seek to optimize resources, experience and creativity between the public and private domain. Incorporating Indigenous organizations enhances the partnerships and could enhance the impact on the disadvantaged populace. Further below, we look at why these partnerships and the financial ecosystem must be sustained.

CONCLUSION

In addition, Indigenous peoples should be provided with support concerning financial and economic procedures. At the heart of this vision is the recognition that Aboriginal groups hold epistemologies unlike those of the Anglo-European colonial capitalistic society, and they are capable of developing a better way of life and organizing relationships between peoples. This vision is, however, achieved through many activities, including financial enlightenment, leadership mentoring, and the generation of culture-sensitive new businesses, particularly among the First Nations.

In conclusion, this means one of power, power and possibility. Merely recognizing Indigenous people, accumulating human capital, aspiring to enable Indigenous leaders, enhancing the culture of innovativeness, and forming collaborative partnerships are how to guarantee the future. This vision is not just an idea; it calls on all stakeholders to come together to respect Indigenous rights and work together to achieve a sustainable and balanced economy: rights, equal treatment, and obligations with the Indigenous people as holding the power of economic power to make the change and a superior future. Therefore, the future of the Aboriginal population is not only a dream but also a challenge for everyone. However, if the country's authorities decide to accept the Indigenous peoples, to develop education empowering Indigenous leaders and leaders, stimulating innovations and Indigenous cooperation, the future of the Indigenous people's businesses and cultures will be great. As for the future, is it possible to respect the Indigenous Outlook as one of the foundational parts that can ensure the construction of a moral and fair business perspective? This transformation will not be easy, but together, we can realize this vision and effect this change for the future of all. Aboriginal groups possess different ways of knowing, which, if utilized, have the potential for advancing a more sustainable way of life and interacting with other groups. The journey towards this vision involves numerous strategies involving financial literacy, leadership apprenticeship, and contextual new business solutions, especially among First Nations.

REFERENCES

Anderson, R. B., & Dana, L. P. (2006). Indigenous entrepreneurship: An emerging field of research. *Journal of Small Business and Entrepreneurship*, 19(1), 1–17.

Ansell, M., & Clapham, K. (2023). Indigenous climate leadership: Advancing adaptation strategies through traditional ecological knowledge. *Environmental Policy and Practice*, 15(3), 56–78.

Aragon, F. M., & Kessler, A. S. (2020). Resource windfalls, public investment, and Indigenous communities. *Journal of Development Economics*, 144, 102450.

Banerjee, S. B. (2019). Decolonizing management theory: A critical perspective on Indigenous management practices. *Journal of Business Ethics*, 161(1), 27–44.

Bargh, M. (2007). Maori development and neoliberalism in Aotearoa/New Zealand. *Alternatives*, 32(3), 297–314.

Bartlett, C., & Green, L. (2024). Empowering Indigenous resilience: Innovations in renewable energy governance. *Renewable Energy and Society*, 10(2), 113–131.

Besser, N., & De Groot, G. (2019). Financial inclusion for Indigenous communities: Challenges and opportunities. *Journal of Social Inclusion*, 10(2), 34–50.

Bhattacharya, S. (2019). Indigenous economic empowerment: Role of inclusive finance. *International Journal of Business and Economic Research*, 8(2), 56–65.

Carroll, W. K., & Ratner, R. S. (2001). Sustaining oppositional cultures in 'post-socialist' times: A comparative study of three social movements. *Sociology*, 35(3), 655–672.

Chambers, R. (1997). *Whose reality counts? Putting the first last*. Intermediate Technology Publications. DOI: 10.3362/9781780440453

Cornell, S. (2007). *Remaking the tools of governance: Colonial legacies, Indigenous solutions*. National Centre for First Nations Governance.

Daly, H. E. (1996). *Beyond growth: The economics of sustainable development*. Beacon Press.

De la Cadena, M., & Starn, O. (2007). *Indigenous experience today*. Berg Publishers.

Doyle, J. (2017). Financial strategies for sustainable development in Indigenous communities. *Journal of Indigenous Studies*, 4(3), 45–60.

Escobar, A. (2011). *Encountering development: The making and unmaking of the Third World*. Princeton University Press.

Finley-Brook, M., & Thomas, C. (2011). Renewable energy and human rights violations: Indigenous people's experiences with hydroelectric projects in Panama. *Latin American Perspectives*, 38(4), 28–33.

Friedland, H., & Harris, J. (2021). Indigenous inclusion in global economic governance. *International Journal of Inclusive Finance*, 12(1), 15–26.

Gibson, K. (2020). Inclusive economies: Indigenous models for sustainable development. *Sustainability*, 12(14), 5678.

Goodland, R., & Daly, H. E. (1996). Environmental sustainability: Universal and non-negotiable. *Ecological Applications*, 6(4), 1002–1017. DOI: 10.2307/2269583

Government of Canada. (2023). Indigenous-led climate change adaptation: A path to self-determined resilience. *Canadian Climate Reports*, 12(1), 45–62.

Howitt, R. (2011). Sustainable Indigenous futures in remote Indigenous areas: Relationships, processes and failed state approaches. *GeoJournal*, 74(5), 391–405.

Hulme, D., & Arun, T. (2009). *Microfinance: A reader*. Routledge. DOI: 10.4324/9780203882764

Irfan, M. (2021, January). Do Shariah indices converge? Evidence from Gulf Cooperation Council countries. *International Journal of Business Excellence*, 23(2), 251–269. DOI: 10.1504/IJBEX.2021.113448

Irfan, M., Elhoseny, M., Kassim, S., & Metawa, N. (2023). *Advanced machine learning algorithms for complex financial applications*. IGI Global., DOI: 10.4018/978-1-6684-4483-2

Irfan, M., Elmogy, M., Gupta, S., Khalifa, F., & Dias, R. (2024). *AI-driven decentralized finance and the future of finance*. IGI Global., DOI: 10.4018/979-8-3693-6321-8

Irfan, M., Elmogy, M., Majid, M. S., & El-Sappagh, S. (2023). *The impact of AI innovation on financial sectors in the era of Industry 5.0*. IGI Global., DOI: 10.4018/979-8-3693-0082-4

Irfan, M., Hussainey, K., Chan Bukhari, S. A., & Nam, Y. (Eds.). (2024). *Issues of sustainability in AI and new-age thematic investing*. IGI Global., DOI: 10.4018/979-8-3693-3282-5

Irfan, M., Kadry, S., Sharif, M., & Ullah Khan, H. (2023). *Fintech applications in Islamic finance: AI, machine learning, and blockchain techniques*. IGI Global., DOI: 10.4018/979-8-3693-1038-0

LaDuke, W. (1999). *All our relations: Native struggles for land and life*. South End Press.

Lopez, J. R., & Vargas, H. (2024). Decolonizing economic policies: Lessons from Indigenous-led financial models in Latin America. *Development Policy Review*, 42(1), 78–94.

Park, J., & Choi, M. (2024). Indigenous knowledge systems as catalysts for biodiversity conservation in Asia. *Global Ecology and Conservation*, 31, 210–229.

Smith, L., & James, K. (2024). Decolonial financial systems: The future of Indigenous banking models. *Journal of Development Alternatives*, 18(3), 99–120.

Torres, A., & Cruz, R. (2024). Blockchain-based transparency frameworks for Indigenous resource management. *Technological Innovations for Indigenous Economies*, 22(1), 50–67.

Wilson, R., & Thomas, C. (2024). Leveraging blockchain for transparency in Indigenous land agreements. *Journal of Emerging Technologies in Social Equity*, 9(1), 12–28.

Yazzie, C., & Johnston, T. (2024). Sustainable development initiatives in Navajo Nation: Lessons for global Indigenous economies. *International Journal of Sustainability and Indigenous Affairs*, 7(2), 145–162.

Chapter 14
The Technology Disruptor Artificial Intelligence in Finance Domain:
A Bibliometric Analysis

Varun Kesavan
https://orcid.org/0000-0002-2373-2613
VIT Business School, VIT University, India

Aruna Polisetty
https://orcid.org/0000-0002-9391-6442
VIT Business School, VIT University, India

Viana Imad Hassan
https://orcid.org/0000-0002-7372-5059
American University of Malta, Malta

ABSTRACT

In the last two decades, there has been a continuous innovation in the field of AI and it has been adopted in different fields inclusive of finance. At the same time, numerous works have been published exploring the use of AI in the sphere of financial services. The objective of this work is to review the available literature and discuss gaps in the body of knowledge on this subject. For this purpose, bibliometric and content analysis techniques were used on a number of articles available from 1990 to July 2024. The bibliometric technique was employed to classify core fields and productivity in FinTech research, though using VosViewer and Biblioshiny to offer maps regarding top authors, sources, countries, scientific developments, and concepts.

1. INTRODUCTION

Due to the development of top-notch digital technologies and applications in artificial intelligence AI, technological advancement has been boosted in the first two decades of the twenty-first century. The artificial intelligence area in the field of computer science involves designing smart machines for

DOI: 10.4018/979-8-3693-7924-0.ch014

humans, like thinking since cognitive tasks such as reasoning, learning, action, and speech recognition, are intelligence tasks that are otherwise done by humans (Team, 2024). Bresnahan & Trajtenberg (1995) defined AI itself as a rapidly growing field of technology incorporating multiple specific technologies and creating a framework for many different kinds of new technologies and industries, implying that AI is a generalized technology, similar to those that they classified as general-purpose technologies that spread, develop, and spur complementary innovation. Thus, it is fully justified that at present, there is confusion about the definition of AI (Van Roy et al., 2020). A novel and accurate definition has been given by Acemoglu and Restrepo in 2019 are AI as, "the study and development of intelligent or intellectual (machine) agents, which are machines, software, or algorithms that function intelligently, and can process and understand their environment". Although it is challenging to determine demarcation lines sharply, some of the innovative and budding sectors include machine learning, deep learning, NLP.

The practice of the term "artificial intelligence" was made by John McCarthy at Dartmouth College Conference meant on "thinking machines" in 1956 (Buchanan & The Alan Turing Institute, 2019). Still until 2000, no advance can be made in this field due to commercial databases' low storage capacity and computers' low processing power. Thus, it is for this reason, the governments and the stakeholders mislaid their attention and the monetary provision and backing of AI in 1974–1980 and further in 1987–1993. We also name such phases the AI winters' (Bahoo et al., 2024).

Though, the most important developments as well as expansion of AI-based technologies are significantly younger and have been resultant to the capacity of large unformatted databases, enhanced computer power and venture capital meant for technological-related developments (Ernst et al., 2019). To the best of my knowledge, the term that can be referred to as AI winter is traceable to 2019 only. The second characteristic is that while industrial robots must be given precise commands to proceed, which are usually from software most of the time, AI technologies may 'teach' themselves how to translate data about the setting obtained from an android's devices, for instance visual and tactile information, into signals to the machine's actuators that would cause a response (Raj & Seamans, 2019). According to Ernst et al., (2019) pointed out that while industrial robots are mainly used to perform physical responsibilities, artificial intelligence knowledges are capable of undertaking chiefly human activities, or what Ernst and co-authors categorise as 'mental tasks,' (Bahoo et al., 2024).

Thus, the subjects introducing AI may encounter quite significant effects, in the broad sense, the impacts can be on the economy and society. In particular, an examination led by (PWC) in 2017 and is expecting a 14% rise of the international GDP by 2030. Also, when using AI technologies, various organizations experience enhanced performance (Van Roy, Lievens, Butler, & Verbeke, 2020). Thus, gaining the most benefit from the economic returns of AI belong to North America and China, which are the most active investors in this area. Europe and the emerging markets of Asia and South America will also follow, yet moderate profits await them due to lesser and delayed investments (PricewaterhouseCoopers, 2017). AI will also permeate labour markets; and the solutions to these challenges can be found in the nation's response to the 4th Manufacturing Revolution. There is projected to be a high requirement for highly skilled workforces in relation to low skill demand resulting to automation. The corresponding increase in unemployment, though, is working to be compensated for by the new employment options made possible by artificial intelligence (Ernst et al., 2019; Acemoglu & Restrepo, 2019; Bahoo et al., 2024).

All departments of economy have already implemented AI solutions, but the financial department has changed significantly because of the continuing technological advance. Monetary establishments, which rely deeply on giant information and development mechanization, are indeed in a "unique position to lead the adoption of AI" (PwC, 2020), which produces numerous merits: for instance, it promotes automation of production procedures which in turn increases the level of efficiency and output. Subsequently, since machines do not get influenced by human errors or psychological problems, there is accurate and bias free predictive analysis and also trading plans. With the support of AI, the business model evolves, and customer relationships are revolutionized due to personalized digital finance; along with such processes as automation of services, it contributes to the improvement of service quality and cost reduction (Cucculelli & Recanatini, 2021). More so, it is expected that AI will impact monetary conduct and prudential administrators and aid supervisors to discover such violations and assist in anticipating the effects of alterations in the regulation (Wall, 2018). Also, complex algorithms of AI and ML enable Fintech lenders to provide almost immediate credit decisions which in that regard and also in terms of enhancing borrowers' credit access, is beneficial for both the lenders and the borrowers (Jagtiani and John 2018). Diverse regions and operations within the finance field use smart devices like fraud detection, trading through algorithms, fast trading, portfolio control, credit decisions using credit scoring or support replicas, insolvency forecast, risk control, sentiment analysis used in behavioural analysis, and compliance with the law (Bahoo et al., 2024).

Artificial intelligence and machine learning have significantly impacted financial services, making investment decisions, macroeconomic analysis, and credit evaluation more complex. Their success and unprecedented accuracies have made them progressively significant in the money ecosphere, making them crucial tools for decision-making and analysis. (Irfan, Elhoseny, et al., 2023) Traditional finance institutions face challenges like outdated processes and limited accessibility, hindering their ability to meet the diverse needs of a digital-first society. As DeFi and AI technologies become more prevalent, bridging the gap between innovation and traditional financial systems is critical for monetary inclusion and sustainable growth, preventing progress. (Irfan, Elmogy, et al., 2024)

The amalgamation of AI and ML in the banking and finance business presents significant challenges, particularly in Industry 5.0. Financial institutions must navigate complex decisions regarding investments, macroeconomic examination, and credit assessment. The increasing volume of financial transactions necessitates efficient data processing and analysis. Scholars and practitioners are exploring the part of AI and ML in enhancing resilience, sustainable development, and adopting human-centric approaches in the financial sector. (Irfan, Elmogy, et al., 2023)

In numerous nations, the Islamic financial system has evolved considerably, with the Islamic stock market emerging as a key element within their financial frameworks (Irfan, 2021; (Shaikh et al., 2024). The finance sector is facing challenges in adapting to climate change and sustainable development, with traditional models struggling to tackle the transition to a low-carbon economy. The amalgamation of AI and ML into financial systems presents both opportunities and challenges, with the potential to reshape the industry while posing unprecedented challenges. (Irfan, Hussainey, et al., 2024). The intricacy of asset choices, macroeconomic studies, and credit assessments is a significant challenge in Islamic finance. (Irfan, Kadry, et al., 2023)

While, over the past scarce years, interest of scholars in the part of artificial intelligence knowledges in a vast number of monetary requests has risen significantly, the literature under scrutiny is very extensive and diverse in terms of the study queries posed, countries and industries examined, close of examination, and technique pursued, which hampers the identification of the more promising areas of AI research. On the basis of such reflections, we therefore look at AI applied to finance carrying out a detailed analysis of scientific literature in order to present a thorough mapping of what has been done to date, but also, and mainly, to highlight some broader research questions that still remain (partially) unexplored. This survey may help the guide the researchers who do not have intensive knowledge in this field and may face difficulties when choosing the materials and the approaches to analyze the composite and rather vast literature on this topic. Thus, it can represent a useful guideline for upcoming experimental contributions, as it gives information about the state-run of the art and of the themes that need further development. In doing so, this examination matches some preceding systematic appraisals on the theme, such as the ones lately showed by Henzen et al. (2021) and Biju et al. (2023; (Bahoo et al., 2024), which vary from our effort in the subsequent main compliments: While Hentzen and co-authors' work focuses on front-office financial services, thus presenting a real-life perspective, their paper provides a valuable perspective on the technical aspects of implementing the proposed solutions as well as a tendential valuation of the efficiency and potential predictive capacity of ML, AI, and deep learning tools and strategies in the financial markets, thus addressing an important issue that, however, lies outside of the possibility of this work.

RQ1: What is the specific yearly rise in the rate of publication of scientific papers related to AI in money sector?
RQ2: Which authors contribute to the publications regarding the theme, and which journals are most relevant to AI in the finance context?
RQ3: What trends and shifts can be identified in the choice of topics for research in the sphere of AI in the finance business?

Figure 1. PRISMA chart representing the collection of AI related papers in the finance sector derived from Scopus database.

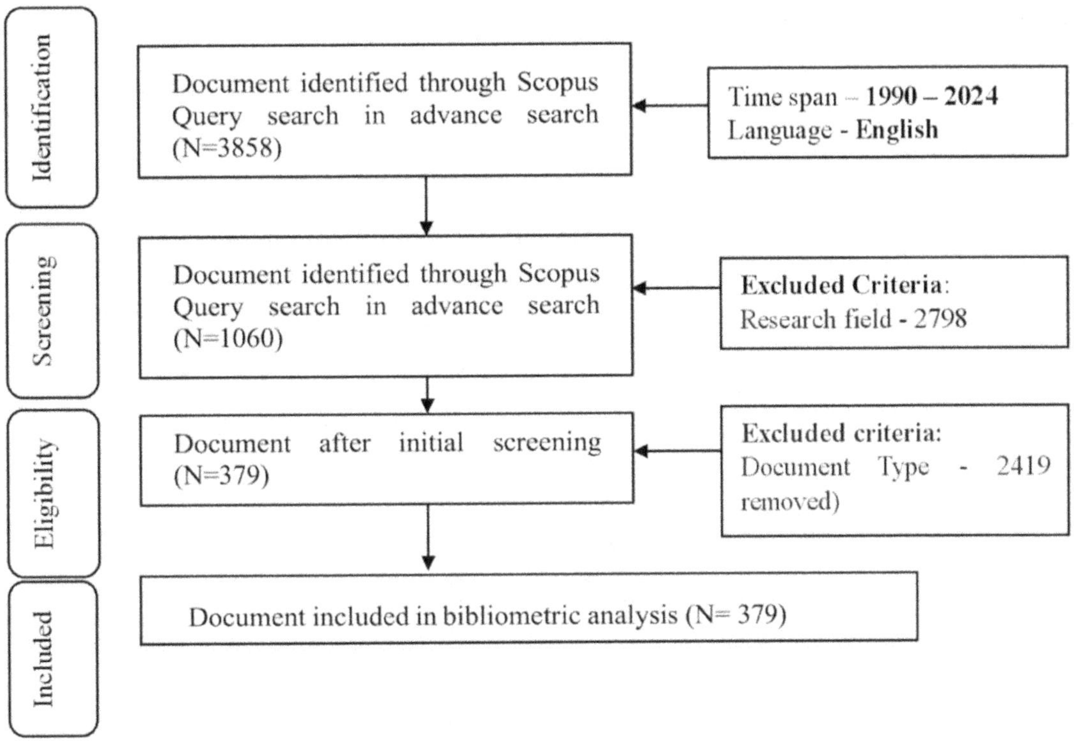

2. METHODOLOGY

In reports of study design in figure - 1, this study applied a bibliometric methodology to respond to the posed research questions whereas in relation to data collection procedures, the study applied a retrospective and descriptive survey. Coe bibliometric and citation analysis (Broadus, 1967; Pritchard, 1969) are a group of methods that can be applied to bibliographic data in quantitative data analysis. Its major advantage is in providing the information concerning the research patterns which enable the researchers to evaluate the literature, review the advancement of knowledge, and outline new research strategies (Albort-Morant et al., 2017; Madhan et al., 2023).

The bibliometric analysis was done in Biblioshiny R and VOSviewer which are useful in manipulating data established on countries, institutions, journals, and authors. These tools also give information concerning the history of the AI in the setting of finance. Regarding the observation of research interest and activity, we did keyword analysis. It is the review of such keywords that is considered one of the most significant stages of bibliometric and scientometric research. Author and index keywords of the papers represent mainly clusters; the densities in the relation of the most regularly used words are investigated regarding other variables, including keywords characterizing essential research themes and trends. Bibliometric maps are regarded as effects of new evolution of scientometrics aim for visualizing and analyzing the networking of objects that can be articles, authors, keywords, or research domains exist in the document.

2.1 Refined Search Query

Table 1. Search query description

Description	Conditions
Search query	TITLE-ABS-KEY (artificial AND intelligence AND finance) **No of documents – 3858**
Search query after refining	TITLE-ABS-KEY (artificial AND intelligence AND finance) AND (LIMIT TO (SUBJAREA, "BUSI") OR LIMIT TO (SUBJAREA, "ECON") OR LIMIT-TO (SUBJAREA, "SOCI")) **No of documents – 1060**
Search query after final refining	TITLE-ABS-KEY (artificial AND intelligence AND finance) AND (LIMIT-TO (SUBJAREA, "BUSI") OR LIMIT-TO (SUBJAREA, "ECON") OR LIMIT-TO (SUBJAREA, "SOCI")) AND (LIMIT-TO (DOCTYPE, "ar")) AND (LIMIT-TO (SRCTYPE, "j")) AND (LIMIT-TO (LANGUAGE, "English")) AND (LIMIT-TO (PUBSTAGE, "final")) **No of documents - 379**
Query search date	July 11th, 2024
Years	1990 – 2024
Subject area	Business, Management and Accounting, Social Sciences, Economics, Econometrics and Finance
Source type	The search was limited to Journals.
Document type	Journal articles
Publication stage	Final publication
Language	The search was limited to the English language.

Source: Author Compilation of data based on Scopus query search.

For collecting the data for this analysis, data was gathered from Scopus database as referred in Table 1. We used Scopus as the database because it is a source for finding academic research articles and papers that focus on technical areas and scholarly journals from different fields across the globe. It could extend such an effort and offer the potential to learn many similar articles in the money part of AI. Last but not the least, Scopus only entails a spiffy reviewing process and journals to be included hence defining a quality and standardized highly rated papers with reference to score. While conducting this present research, it became possible to categorise the papers systematically based on set criteria according to their relevance and significance to AI and financial fields respectively. Having decided to examine the subject, we could only start a rather basic preliminary search with the aid of Scopus search engine utilising the following words 'artificial intelligence and finance' of which the exact search terms provided around 3858 documents. This ensured me that the recovered papers had some linkage to the finance area as well as AI. The keywords entered were then subjected to subject filter using such subjects as business, management and accounting and other sciences such as social sciences business economics econometrics & finance. This narrowed down the search results from 3858 documents to 1060 papers as it allowed for a much more specific filter of the citation databases. This filter helped to filter the articles which stated both these concepts in the title or keywords to be comprised in the analysis. In the present study though, the criteria used for counting the number of articles included research articles only and only those that were fully published in English written journals amounting to 379. With comprehensive process, the first and foremost step was to guarantee the validity of sampling in order to identify the best papers. To ensure a non-biased process, the above sampling procedure was followed rigorously irrespective of the type of documents being used.

Each paper that met the inclusion criteria underwent examination, which established the overall relationship between AI and the finance segment in the sample. Therefore, by strictly adhering to these selection criteria and exerting significant effort in the review process, we minimized bias effects to enhance the credibility of the study's results. Thus, the literature search using the Scopus database provided 379 publications containing the specified topics.

We collected the data (records and references) using an a.csv file, which we then uploaded to the Biblioshiny R and VOSviewer software for further analysis. Using the bibliometric analysis as a guide, we conducted a performance analysis to identify the top journals, authors, top nations, and conceptual structure. Using a tree chart, we conducted a keyword analysis, specifically focusing on author keywords. Additionally, we conducted a co-word analysis to pinpoint the key research areas and themes related to artificial intelligence in the finance area. Co-word analysis is based on the principle that "the occurrence of two terms defines the conceptual and thematic space of the scientific field" (Callon et al., 1983). Co-word analysis can identify the relationships between topics in a research field by analysing the co-occurrences of word or phrase pairs; this makes it possible for researchers to track the progress of science (He, 1999).

3. RESULTS

The bibliometric analysis comprises two main components: It embraces 1) performance analysis; and 2) conceptual structure. Performance analysis can involve evaluating the contribution of research stakeholders in a given area (Donthu et al., 2021). Forliano et al., 2021; Sadeqi-Arani & Kadkhodaie, 2023, examined examples of performance analysis and science mapping to determine the most important documents, authors, journals, and countries employing various criteria.

In this research, it will be the designers' intent to provide information sourced from literature which is the actual year of publication of most of the research. It also presents authors who wrote about the influence of AI on finance, indicates in which countries the analyzed co-authors have cooperated, and illustrates the research trends of this field by means of tree diagram. Finally, this feature presents additional papers and top-listed journals with a higher number of publications. Therefore, in accordance with our established objectives, we begin the literature review suggests the following main questions: "What is the extent of exploration into the relationship between AI and finance over the years?" ism has been explored over the years?" "Who are the scholars researching the relationship between the following is a summary of the articles, based on data from the Scopus database and the findings of the bibliometric analysis is a summary of the articles:

- Performance Analysis
- Science Mapping
- The conceptual structure employs co-word analysis, Tree map, and author keyword analysis

3.1 Performance Analysis

3.1.1 Descriptive Statistics of Data Frame

Table 2. Summary statistics of the data used in this study

Sl. No.	Description	Results
1.	"Timespan"	1990:2024
2.	"Sources (Journals, Books, etc.)"	230
3.	"Documents"	379
4.	"Annual Growth Rate %"	12.45
5.	"Document Average Age"	4.77
6.	"Average citations per documents"	29.14
7.	"References"	22581
8.	"Author's Keywords (DE)"	1335
9.	"Authors"	1037
10.	"Authors of single-authored documents"	83
11.	"Single-authored documents"	88
12.	"Co-Authors per Documents"	2.91
13.	"International co-authorships %"	24.8

Source: Author Compilation of data from Bibilioshiny R program.

Table – 2 depicts about the summary statistics of the data frame. In Scopus database, the articles and review articles published from 1990 July to 2024 are indexed. These documents are on average citing, 29 sources. For four categories, the authors provided 14 citations for each of them, and the entire number of citation sources was up by 14 percent. On balance, the higher numbers per document are indicative of higher growth in the research papers related to the usage of AI in the finance domain. Further, this study found out that out of the scholars who have contributed to the works on the practice of AI in this finance arena, 1037 have contributed towards the development of most of the research. This shows that there are 83 documents authored by a single author and the average number of authors documented in the 83 documents was 2. Occasionally, an average number of co-authors per document is 91 percent, which indicates collaboration typical in research within this area of science. A very small and thin measure of international co-authorship of 24.

Figure 2. Annual scientific production of AI in finance sector (1990 -2024).

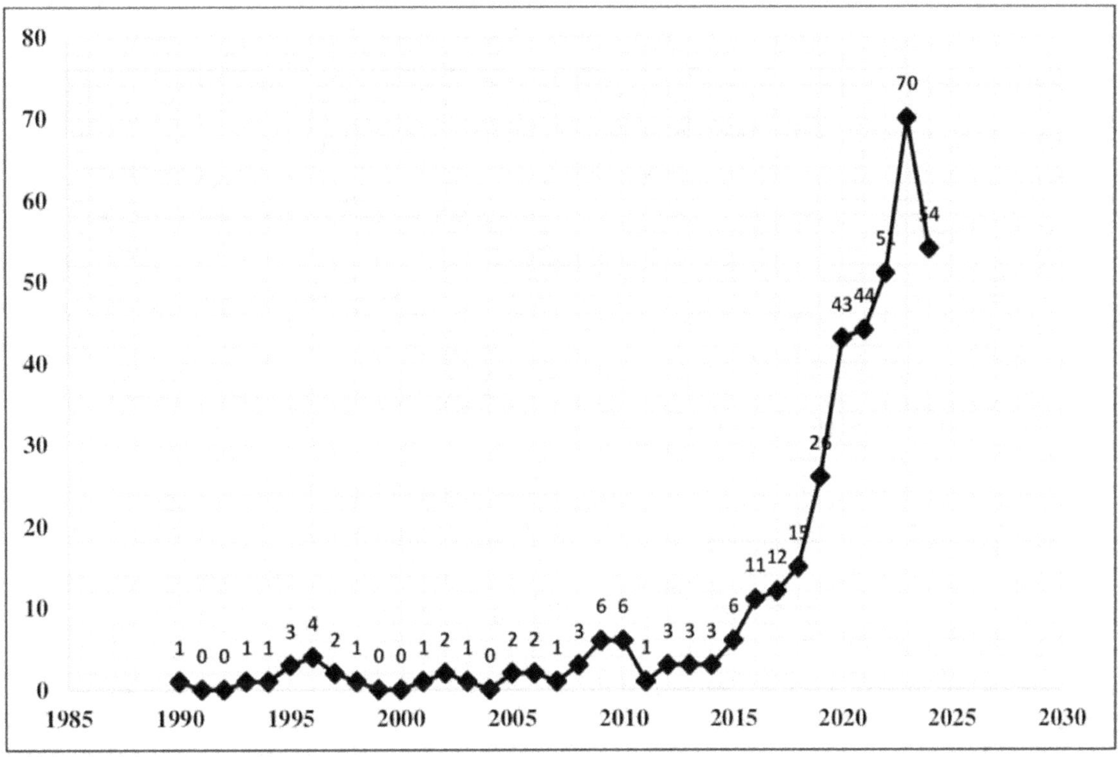

The figure – 2 illustrates, the annual growth rate in the technical works on AI for finance from the Scopus 1990–2024 database was 12.45 percent. It was clear from the figure above that the number of documents has increased since 2016. The growth can be attributed to the fact that the majority of the articles in the current study were published within the last nine years, at 86 percent.

3.1.2 Performance Analysis of Most Influential Journals

Table 3. Top 15 most relevant journals

Rank	Journal names	Count	%	Q	ABDC/Scopus	Publisher	
1	Decision Support Systems	13	3%	Q1	A*	Elsevier	
2	Sustainability (Switzerland)	12	3%	Q1	Scopus	MDPI	
3	Journal of The Operational Research Society	9	2%	Q1	A	T&F	
4	Knowledge-Based Systems	8	2%	Q1	A	Elsevier	
5	Technological Forecasting and Social Change	8	2%	Q1	A	Elsevier	
6	Artificial Intelligence Review	7	2%	Q1	Scopus	Springer	

continued on following page

Table 3. Continued

Rank	Journal names	Count	%	Q	ABDC/Scopus	Publisher
7	Resources Policy	7	2%	Q1	B	Elsevier
8	Finance Research Letters	6	2%	Q1	A	Elsevier
9	Electronic Commerce Research and Applications	5	1%	Q1	C	Elsevier
10	Intelligent Systems in Accounting, Finance and Management	5	1%	Q1	B	Wiley
11	Journal of Risk and Financial Management	5	1%	Q1	B	MDPI
12	International Journal of Financial Studies	4	1%	Q2	B	MDPI
13	Journal of Behavioral and Experimental Finance	4	1%	Q1	A	Elsevier
14	Journal of Cleaner Production	4	1%	Q1	A	Elsevier
15	Journal of Forecasting	4	1%	Q1	A	Wiley

Source: Author Compilation of data from Bibilioshiny R program Q – Quartiles based upon Scopus Classification, MDPI – Multidisciplinary Digital Publishing Institute, Taylor & Francis (T&F).

As revealed in Table 3 and figure – 3, "Decision Support Systems" has contributed the most with 13 articles, followed by "Sustainability (Switzerland)" with 12 articles, and "The Journal of the Operational Research Society" has contributed nine articles to this area of artificial intelligence in the finance research domain. "Knowledge-Based Systems" and "Technological Forecasting and Social Change" have each contributed eight articles, while "Artificial Intelligence Review" and "Resources Policy" have each published seven articles. Furthermore, "Finance Research Letters" has contributed six articles on AI in finance. "Electronic Commerce Research and Applications," "Intelligent Systems in Accounting, Finance, and Management," and "Journal of Risk and Financial Management" have each published five articles, while "International Journal of Financial Studies," "Journal of Behavioural and Experimental Finance," "Journal of Cleaner Production," and "Journal of Forecasting" have each contributed four articles. Together, the top three journals have contributed nine percent of articles in the domain of artificial intelligence in the finance segment.

Figure 3. The top 15 journals

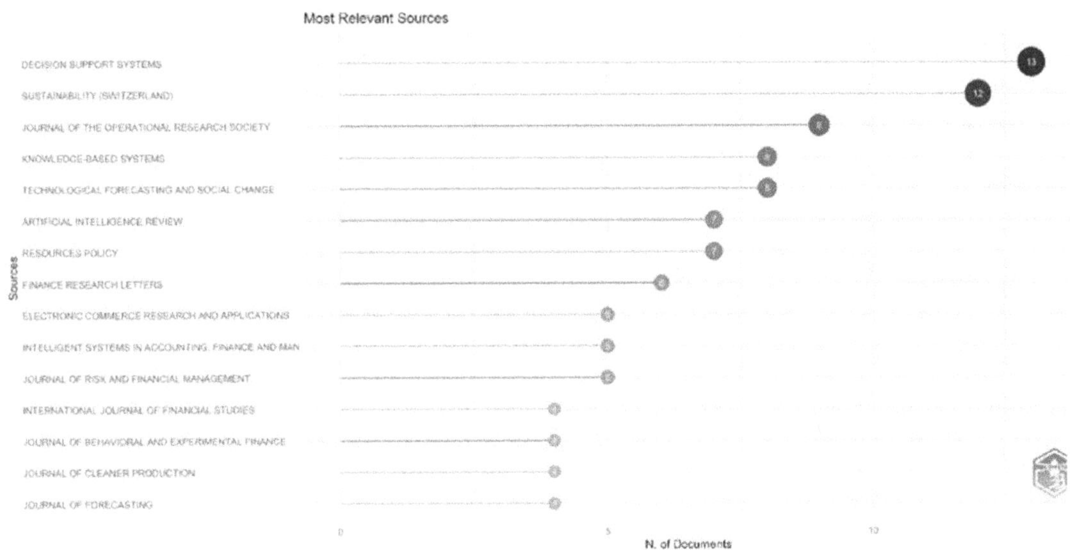

Figure 4: Bradford's Law As revealed in Figure 4, 230 journals published around 253 articles in the inter-collection, whereas 23 core journals contributed 126 articles in the AI in finance domain. Bradford's Law, which allows you to search for the core journals within a given discipline and is known for both the principle of diminishing returns and scattering (Sadeqi-Arani and Kadkhodaie, 2023), Therefore, Bradford's Law divides each field into three areas. “The topmost third (Zone 1 or core), according to the author, refers to the frequency of citations of the journals in the literature on that subject that are likely of most interest to the researchers in that field. The journals in the middle third, or zone 2, have a moderate citation rate, while the journals in the bottom third, or zone 3, have a low citation rate and are often considered peripheral for the subject area or field (K. Singh, 2014). According to Bradford's Law, the number of periodicals in the second zone will be 'n', and the third zone will be 'n^2' times as large as the first zone (Nash-Stewart et al., 2012).

Figure 4. Bradford's Law of core sources of journals

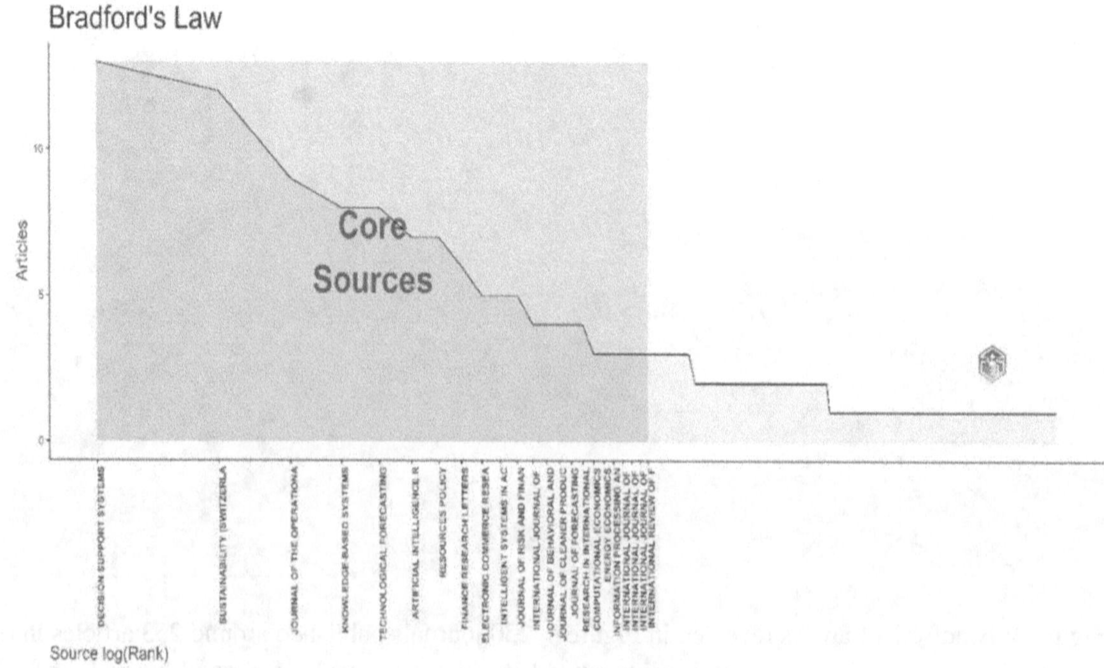

3.1.3 Performance Analysis of Top Prolific Authors, Affiliations, and Countries

Table 4. Top 15 authors, affiliations, and countries

Top Authors	TP	TC	Top Affiliations	Articles	Top Countries	TP	TC
Li X	5	36	Swansea University	12	China	161	997
Mhlanga D	4	444	University of Michigan	10	USA	151	1408
Ghosh I	3	17	Qatar University	8	UK	108	2022
Gupta S	3	102	Queensland University of Technology	8	India	93	431
Lee J	3	50	Wuhan University	8	Spain	41	507
Li J	3	09	Dublin City University	7	Australia	38	472
Li W	3	05	Taras Shevchenko National University of Kyiv	7	Germany	35	113
Rabbani MR	3	94	Yonsei University	7	South Korea	30	148
Zheng Z	3	125	Beijing University of Technology	6	Italy	22	294
Alfaro-Cort S E	2	17	Democritus University of Thrace	6	Brazil	21	95
Arner DW	2	28	Rise Research Institutes of Sweden	6	Malaysia	21	17

continued on following page

Table 4. Continued

Top Authors	TP	TC	Top Affiliations	Articles	Top Countries	TP	TC
Buckley RP	2	28	Satbayev University	6	Lithuania	18	44
Chan SWK	2	162	Seoul National University	6	France	16	32
Chen Y	2	01	Symbiosis International (Deemed University)	6	Canada	15	49
Dong K	2	14	Ufla Â€“ Universidade Federal De Lavras	6	Sweden	14	22

Source: Author Compilation of data from Bibilioshiny R program.

Table – 4 and figure – 5 showcases the publication in the arena of AI in the finance domain was contributed by 1037 researchers. Taken together, these authors are affiliated with 465 organisations in 68 different countries. The following scholars are among the most prolific contributors, as measured by the number of articles: In the following representation in table 4, the authors who have written just one documents are Li X, Mhlanga D and Ghosh I, whereas the authors having three documents each are Lee J, Li J, Li W, Rabbani MR, and Zheng Z. Similarly, Table 4 presents top institutions that have contributed to the production of AI finance research. On this research, Swansea University contributed the most with a total of 12 publications followed by the University of Michigan with 10 publications and Qatari University with 8 publications. Number of publications is also seen to be useful when comparing a country and its power in relation to the study of AI finance. Among them, 68 countries and regions participated in this field between 1990 and 2024. As depicted in figure 4, majority of the top-ranking countries are from Europe, while two from North & South America respectively; and four from Asia. China has the uppermost number of AI publications with a total of 161, USA ranked second with 151 and UK ranked third with 101.

Figure 5. Country scientific production

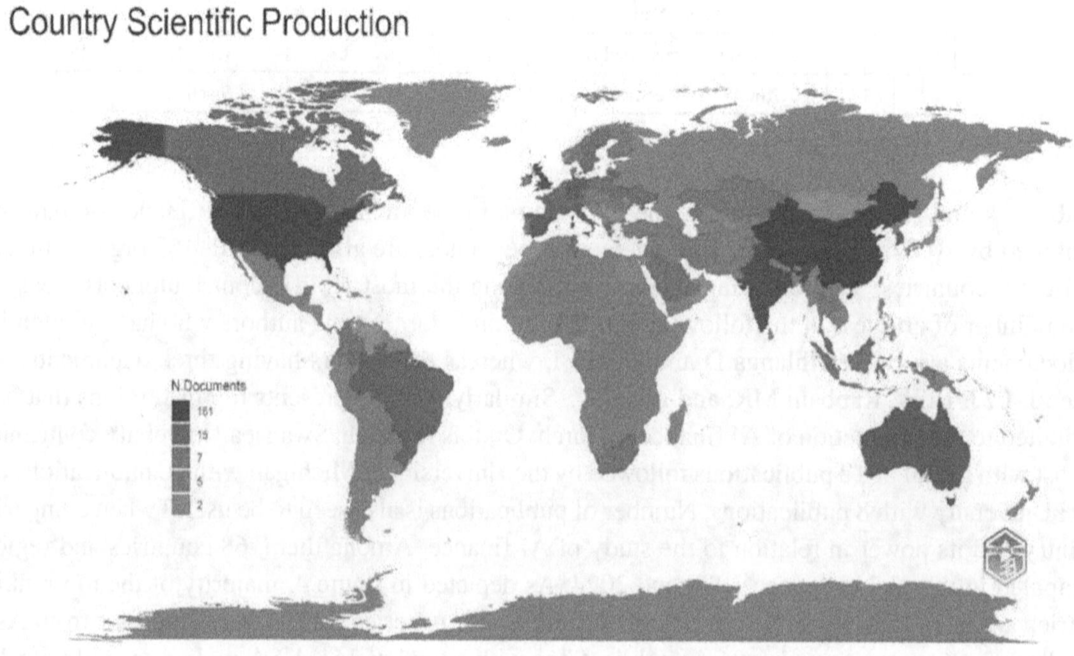

3.1.4 Performance of Authors Based Upon Lokta's Law

Table 5. Frequency of author publications

Documents written	No. of Authors	Proportion of Authors
1	984	0.949
2	44	0.042
3	7	0.007
4	1	0.001
5	1	0.001

Source: Author Compilation of data from Bibilioshiny R program.

The results presented in the table – 5 show that more than 95% agreed on varying levels with all of Table 5's assertions. This study also showed that 95% of the authors are occasional authors, having written only one document that supports Lotka's law. Lotka subsequently postulated an inverse square law, stating that the sum of writers who publish a given sum of articles is inversely proportional to the sum of writers who publish a single article. This principle suggests that the theoretical beta coefficient of Lotka's law, which measures the authors' frequency of publication (scientific productivity) across any given topic or field, should be 2. Nevertheless, Li X contributed to a total of five articles, which makes him one of the furthermost prominent authors in the AI in finance domain.

3.1.5 The Performance Analysis of Top Nations

Table 6. The top 20 corresponding countries

Country	Articles	SCP	MCP	Freq	MCP _ Ratio
China	52	30	22	0.137	0.423
USA	39	33	6	0.103	0.154
India	22	19	3	0.058	0.136
United Kingdom	21	16	5	0.055	0.238
Spain	14	10	4	0.037	0.286
Australia	9	4	5	0.024	0.556
Germany	8	8	0	0.021	0
Korea	8	6	2	0.021	0.25
Italy	7	5	2	0.018	0.286
Canada	6	4	2	0.016	0.333
South Africa	6	6	0	0.016	0
Hong Kong	5	3	2	0.013	0.4
Ireland	5	2	3	0.013	0.6
France	4	1	3	0.011	0.75
Greece	4	4	0	0.011	0
Indonesia	4	2	2	0.011	0.5
Lithuania	4	4	0	0.011	0
Malaysia	4	2	2	0.011	0.5
Poland	4	4	0	0.011	0
Brazil	3	3	0	0.008	0

Source: Author Compilation of data from Bibilioshiny R program.

From Table 6 and figure – 6, China has published 52 papers associated to the AI in Finance theme followed by USA 39 articles and India 22 articles which contributed more than 29% of the total articles. Articles typically fall into two groups grounded on author collaboration: The two categories that they have pointed out are "single country publications" (SCP) and "multiple country publications" (MCP). SCP assures that the research was done by researchers from the same country, referred to as intra-country collaboration. On the other hand, MCP has an author. On the other hand, MCP hosts authors from different countries, a situation termed as inter-country or international contribution (China is in the 42. 3% MCP ratio category in the 20 nations; see table 6).

Figure 6. Major corresponding countries

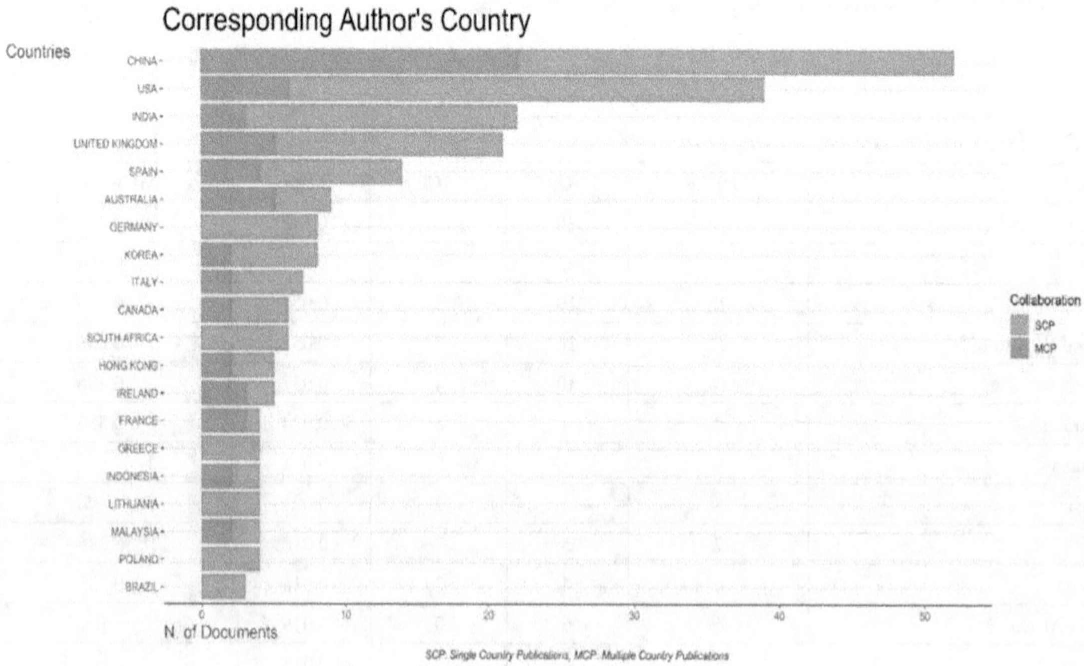

3.1.6 Major Collaborated Countries

Table 7. Top world collaborated countries

From	To	Frequency
China	USA	9
Australia	Hong Kong	5
China	Hong Kong	5
China	United Kingdom	5
United Kingdom	India	5
United Kingdom	France	4
China	Australia	3
China	France	3
China	Malaysia	3
China	Saudi Arabia	3

continued on following page

Table 7. Continued

From	To	Frequency
USA	Australia	3
Australia	France	2
Australia	Germany	2
Australia	New Zealand	2
China	Singapore	2
France	Tunisia	2
Germany	Hong Kong	2
India	France	2
India	Malaysia	2
India	Netherlands	2

Source: Author Compilation of data from Bibilioshiny R program.

Table 7 presents an overview of the level of internationalisation of the AI/Finance literature surveyed worldwide, is shown in Table 7. Therefore, in relation to the sum of published articles in the area of AI and finance, China and USA have nine, Australia and Hong Kong with five, and China and Australia with the similar number of five.

3.1.7 Performance Analysis of Documents

Table 8. The top documents

Rank	Paper	DOI	Total Citations	TC per Year	Normalized TC
1	DWIVEDI YK, 2021, INT J INF MANAGE	10.1016/j.ijinfomgt.2019.08.002	1267	316.75	22.02
2	DAS SR, 2007, MANAGE SCI	10.1287/mnsc.1070.0704	867	48.17	1
3	BELANCHE D, 2019, IND MANAGE DATA SYS	10.1108/IMDS-08-2018-0368	336	56	6.98
4	MA X, 2018, ELECT COMMER RES APPL	10.1016/j.elerap.2018.08.002	293	41.86	8.83
5	ANDROUTSOPOULOU A, 2019, GOV INF Q	10.1016/j.giq.2018.10.001	280	46.67	5.81
6	MHLANGA D, 2020, INTERN J FINANCIAL STUD	10.3390/ijfs8030045	203	40.6	5.05
7	DOWLING M, 2023, FINAN RES LETT	10.1016/j.frl.2023.103662	197	98.5	21.48
8	YOON Y, 1993, JOPERRESSOC	10.1057/jors.1993.6	187	5.84	1
9	KUSHWAHA AK, 2021, INT J INF MANAG DATA INSIGHTS	10.1016/j.jjimei.2021.100017	180	45	3.13
10	HAJEK P, 2017, KNOWL BASED SYST	10.1016/j.knosys.2017.05.001	173	21.63	4.16

Source: Author Compilation of data from Bibilioshiny R program.

Based on the citation frequency, Table 8, and figure - 7 depicts the top papers on artificial intelligence in the finance doamin. “Multidisciplinary perspectives on emerging challenges, opportunities, and agenda for research, practice, and policy” is the title of the top-cited paper. Authored by Dwivedi et al. and printed in the International Journal of Information Management in 2021, it has received 1267 citations, all inclusive. The second position goes to the paper titled “Yahoo! for Amazon: Sentiment Extraction from Small Talk on the Web,” authored by Das and Chen in 2007 and published in Management Science, which attains 867 citations. The third place goes to the paper titled “Artificial Intelligence in FinTech: Understanding robo-advisors adoption among customers.” Belanche et al.'s 2019 publication, “Industrial Management & Data Systems,” has received 336 citations. Dwivedi et al. published the most significant research paper in the 'International Journal of Information Management' in 2021, titled 'Multidisciplinary perspectives on emerging challenges, opportunities, and agenda for research, practice, and policy.' The paper focuses on the multidisciplinary opportunities, challenges, and implications of generative conversational AI for research practice and policy.

Figure 7. The most cited journals

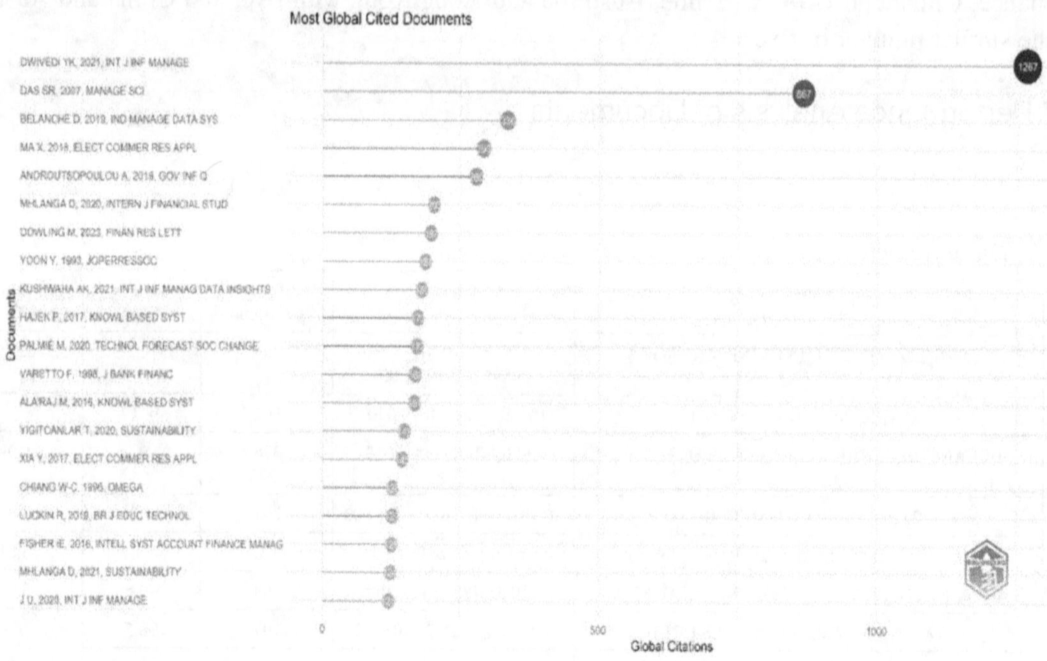

3.1.8 Multiple Correspondence Analysis

Figure – 8 and figure – 9 shows the (MCA) feature in Bibliometrix Biblioshiny enables the creation of a theoretical building of a given field while utilizing k-means clustering to identify documents that have similar concepts. MCA is a statistical technique which is used commonly in the medical field due to its capability to transform the data into figures of two dimensions thus illustrating the similarities in the data. In this study, terms closer to the map center are more popular than others and have received more attention in recent years; more evenly distributed terms are related to less discussed topics in research. This study, using Matute & Linsen (2022) and Ejaz et al. (2022) as its source, also presents the conceptual structure map for the frequently used terms in bibliometrics research papers. This is done by partitioning of words on the foundation of their interactions and these are shown by area mapping. The words are plotted based on Dim 1 and Dim 2, demonstrating how close the words are (Srisusilawati et al., 2021). It focuses on two regions, red and blue, with all the terms from each region connected. In the red area there are more and different connected words, which means that many research papers have explored the connection between the terms in this area (Sofik et al., 2021). The factorial analysis was also similar (Figures 8 and 9). When the research used multiple correspondence analysis with 'plus' as the field, two clusters emerged (Figure 8). The first cluster (red) was on artificial intelligence for finance and the second cluster (blue) was on the innovation of AI implementation in decision-making in banking and marketing research. Topic dendrogram highlighted the clustering order and interrelationship of keywords as presented in Figure 11, which gave an approximation of the number of clusters for further study (Andrews, 2003; Shekhar, S., 2023). In the dendrogram, the same two clusters were observed as in the circumstance of multiple correspondence analysis. On the first cluster, labeled as red, the top key terms tagged pertinent Information to data analysis involved implementation of Al in banking as well as its application in decision making processes in marketing.

Figure 8. Multiple correspondence analysis

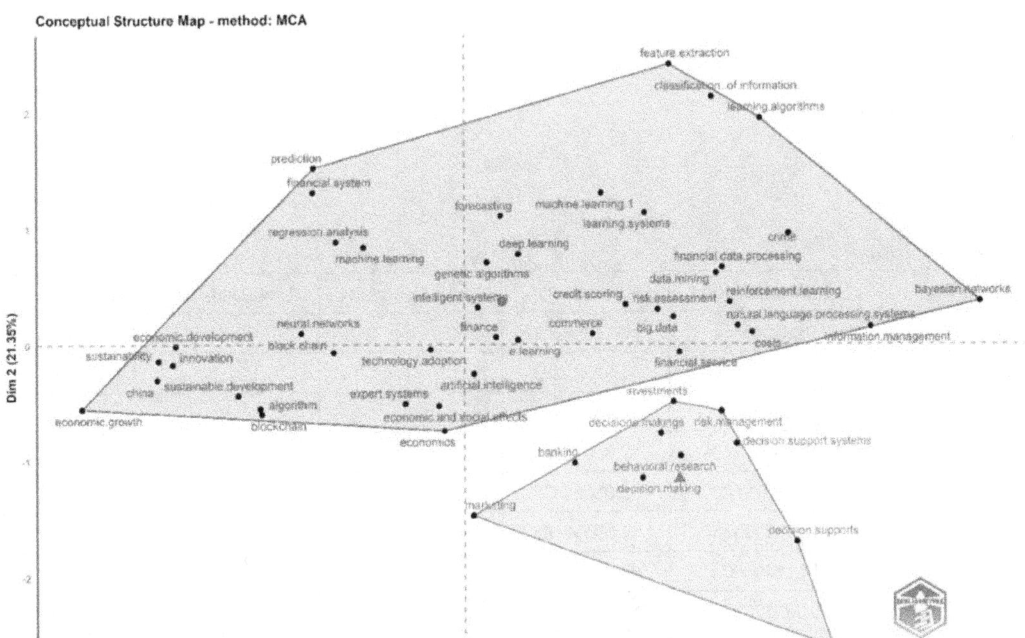

Figure 9. Dendogram

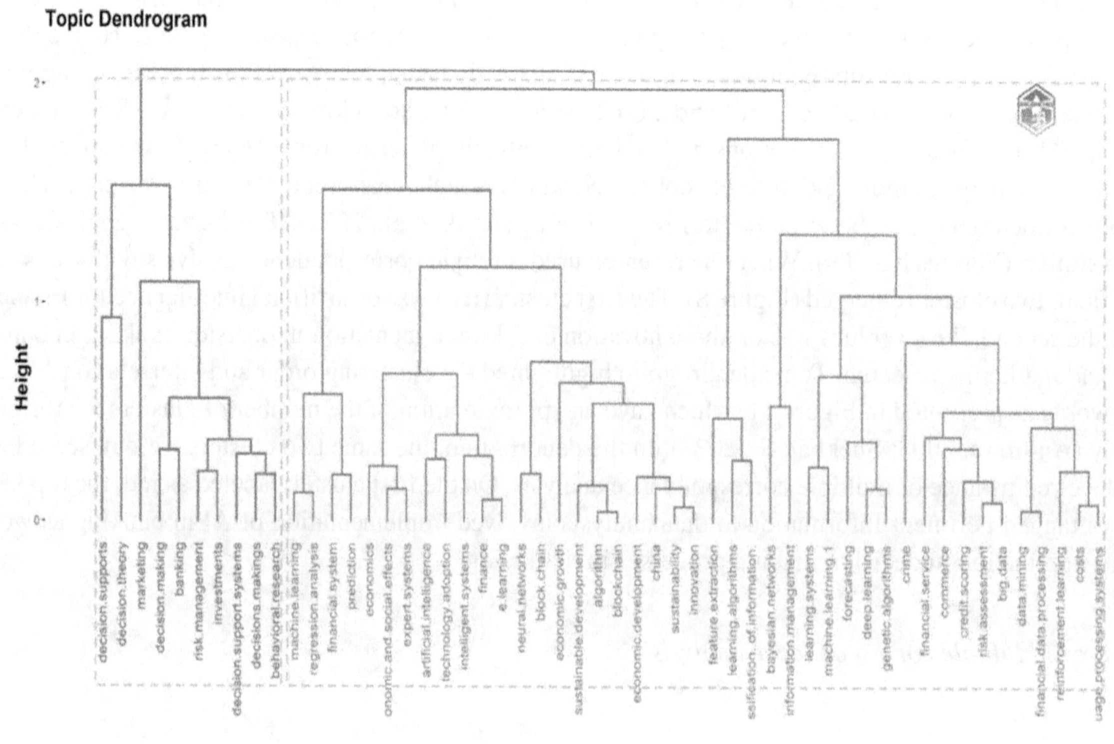

3.1.9 Thematic Map

Table 9. Thematic map

Cluster	Callon Centrality	Callon Density	Rank Centrality	Rank Density	Cluster Frequency
Sustainability	10.21645816	100.0329301	9	9	124
Neural Networks	2.306944444	67.92929293	4	3	38
Decision Support Systems	8.69609515	54.15794307	8	1	134
Innovation	5.898307753	82.80032468	7	7	94
Artificial Intelligence	21.78979126	62.08655434	12	2	414
Learning Systems	12.21272335	71.09599188	10	5	202
Forecasting	14.00406002	68.00246466	11	4	143
Article	0.277777778	134.7222222	3	11	22
Reinforcement Learning	2.408333333	114.0530303	5	10	32

continued on following page

Table 9. Continued

Cluster	Callon Centrality	Callon Density	Rank Centrality	Rank Density	Cluster Frequency
Crowdfunding	0	93.75	1.5	8	8
Financial Services	2.9375	76.78571429	6	6	19
Application Domains	0	225	1.5	12	16

Source: Author Compilation of data from Bibilioshiny R program

Table 9 and figure 10 illustrate the density and centrality of themes, represented by keyword groupings, can be organized into a single circle, and visualized as a two-dimensional image. Figure 10 displays a thematic map that categorizes themes based on their quadrant: motor themes in the upper-right quadrant, fundamental or basic themes in the lower-right quadrant, emerging or declining themes in the lower-left quadrant, and highly specialized or niche topics in the upper-left quadrant.

Table 9 and figure 10 provides the data about keywords in the publications related to AI and finance for the examination of thematic clusters based on the values of Callon's centrality, Callon's density, rank centrality, and rank density. All these statistics, together with the thematic map in Table 9 and Figure 10, expose the genetic relationships, developmental stages, paths, and shifts of the thematic material in the field. The first purpose was to determine themes from publications of the decade 1990-2000s up to 2024 with an understanding of the changes in the AI and finance themes over the years.

The thematic map analysis categorizes 12 clusters into four themes: The thematic map analysis categorizes 12 clusters into four themes:

Cluster 1: They are all connected with the topic of sustainability and include such keywords as 'sustainable development' and 'algorithm'

Cluster 2: Introduces the concept of neural networks and how they can be applied to plan the industries.

Cluster 3: directly focuses on decision making support, considering decision making in economic operations.

Cluster 4: Focused on the objective related to innovation aspects of China's growth.

Cluster 5: Concerns artificial intelligence with a special reference to finance and risk management.

Cluster 6: Attentions on the learning systems and their uses in the mining and learning of data.

Cluster 7: Excavates the forecast of such aspects while laying emphasis on the incorporation of machine learning and the classification of information.

Cluster 8: Involves articles which cover the social and the accounting angle of things.

Cluster 9: Searches for the research topic in the arena of reinforcement learning in the financial markets.

Cluster 10: Concerned with crowdfunding, which is a rather narrow field; conducts research on crowdsourcing and face recognition.

Cluster 11: Focuses SE only on financials and gives an emphasis on digitization and Fintech aspects.

Cluster 12: focuses on different application areas among them decision performance and decision support systems.

As a result of this extensive literature review, one acquires knowledge on the growth of themes in AI & finance papers, including areas of focus and recent innovations.

Figure 10. Thematic map based upon keyword plus

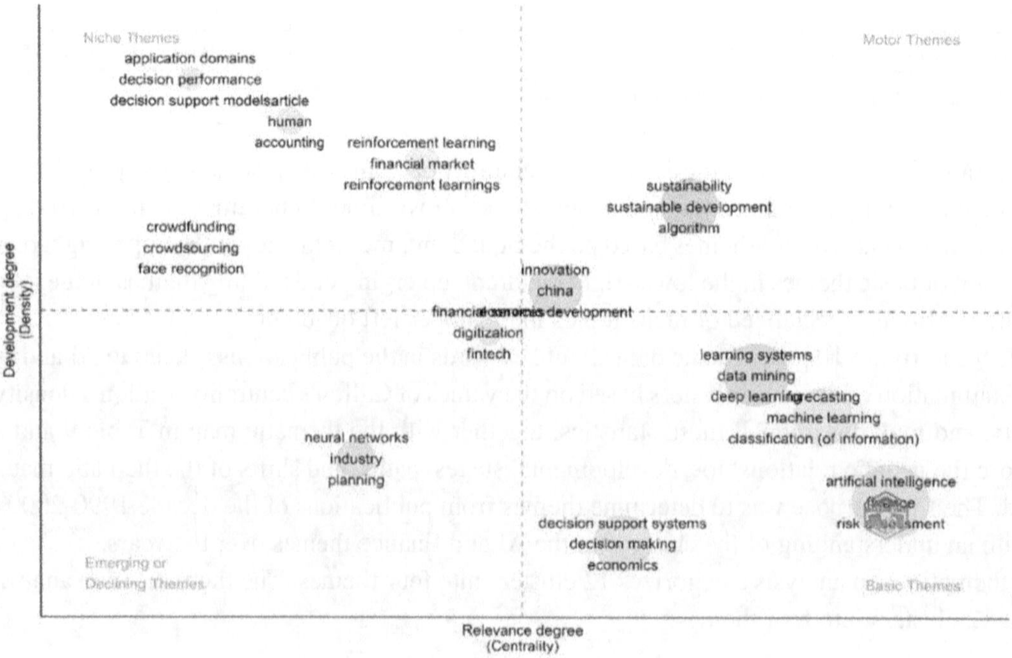

3.2 Science Plotting

Science mapping involves studying the connection between different scientific components, which include elements of research (Baker et al., 2021). The kind of analysis performed on such elements deals with the pattern of structural relationships coupled with the interaction of ideas in the formation of the artistic work. The final section of the paper employs the science mapping analysis method to present the results, namely the key primary authors and journals (Madhan et al., 2023).

3.2.1 The Greatest Regularly Quoted Writers

Figure – 11 shows the identification process performed by the authors revealed a total of 32,723 authors involved in 379 different publications. In order to address the issue of validity we thereby also filtered the articles according to authors who were cited not less than 20 times, which resulted a list of 109 articles. The proposed authors' co-citation is depicted in the enlarged nodes in Figure 11 indicating the most cited authors. These are the most published authors in the global research base: Liu Y. with 92 citations; Zhang Y. with 90 citations; Wang Y. with 85 citations; Li Y. with 81 citations; Li X. with 71 citations. In that regard, all the highly cited scholars have contributed significantly to the development of the fintech literature.

Figure 11. The top cited writers based upon co-citation analysis

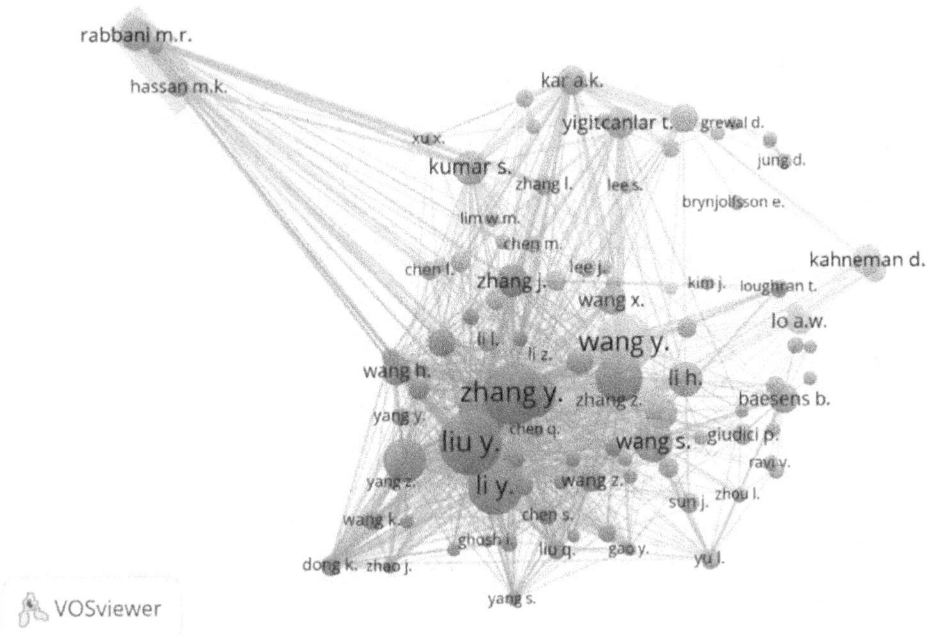

3.2.2 The Concurrence of Writer Keywords

Figure – 12 depicts the article's list of key words encapsulates its primary topics. Thus, the keyword analysis gives a concise and detailed view of the article's theme and its additional growth in the AI and finance arenas. This study employed a biblioshiny software package for data mining and statistical examination of the high-frequency keywords from the research articles. We selected keywords that appeared ten or more times and generated word tree maps and network maps (Figure 12). Keywords frequently used in AI and finance research are artificial intelligence (25%), machine learning (8%), finance (6%), fintech (5%), big data (3%), blockchain, and deep learning, each with 3% and 3%, respectively.

Figure 12. Word cloud of author keywords

3.2.3 The Linkages Between Authors, Themes, and Nations

The three-field diagram in Figure 13 places authors in the first field, keywords in the additional, and countries in the third. The majority of authors used 'artificial intelligence' as a keyword. Furthermore, research articles frequently include terms such as 'machine learning', 'finance', 'fintech', 'big data', and other AI and finance-related terms. In summary, research in AI and finance literature is most active in the United Kingdom, India, the USA, and China.

Figure 13. Three - fold chart

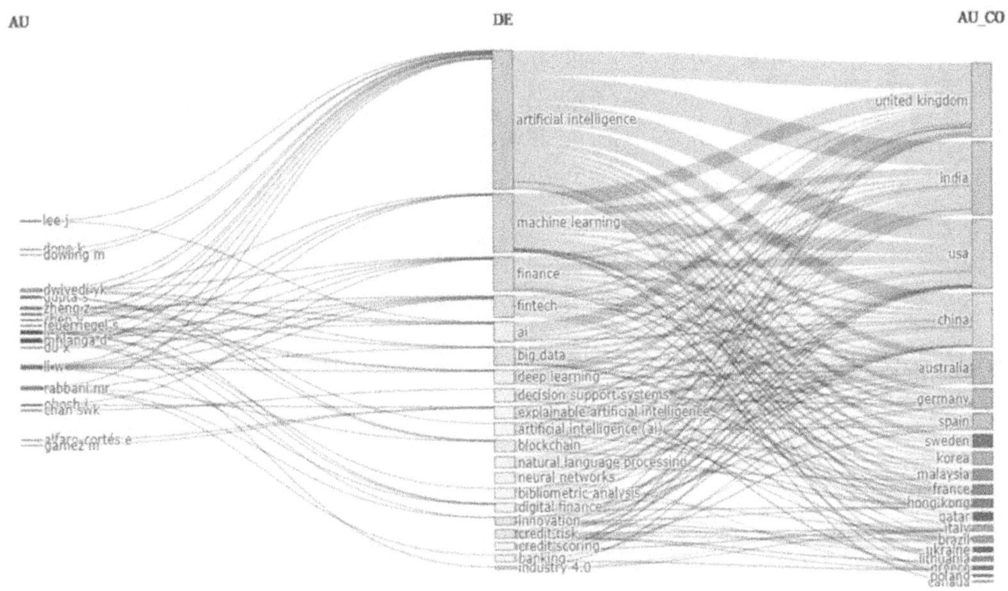

Figure 14, there has been a modification in the orientation of the research fields. There seems to have been a significant shift in the research trends in AI and finance from the period 1990–2010 to 2011–2022. In the beginning, AI progress was slow, and more emphasis was placed on inventing and using technologies for sustainable development, such as regression analysis. Likewise, slowly from the period 1990–2010 to 2011–2022, neural networks began to accentuate on the industrial faces. Likewise, the learning systems were majorly aligned with fields such as AI, risk management, and sustainable development research prior to the period of 2011–2022. Within the machine learning domain, financial systems have established much consideration. Comparing the research trend from 2011-2022 to 2023-2024, there was a shift in trend. Since 2011, AI has received a lot of attention and there has been a focus on risk assessment, big data, class imbalance, and forecasting, deep learning Further, machine learning has begun to be applied in the forecasting and risk assessment fields.

Figure 14. Thematic evolution

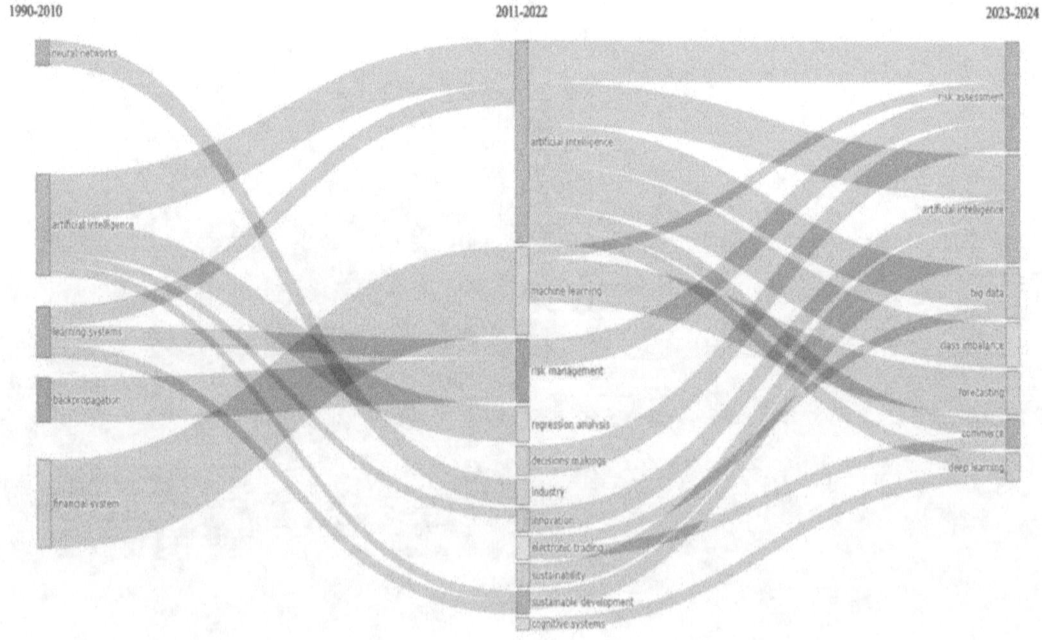

3.3 Conceptual Structure

Co-word analysis is founded on the opinion that "the occurrence of two terms defines the conceptual and thematic space of the scientific field" (Callon et al., 1983). This method can define co-occurrence quantitatively through rates of occurrence, such as correlation or mutual information. Co-word analysis can identify the relationships between topics in a study arena by analysing the co-occurrences of word or phrase pairs; this makes it possible for researchers to track the progress of science (He, 1999). It is a tool that assists in recognising and documenting all the connections between keywords in a scientific field, as well as mapping and illustrating them (Del Barrio-García et al., 2020).

Figure 15. Author keyword analysis

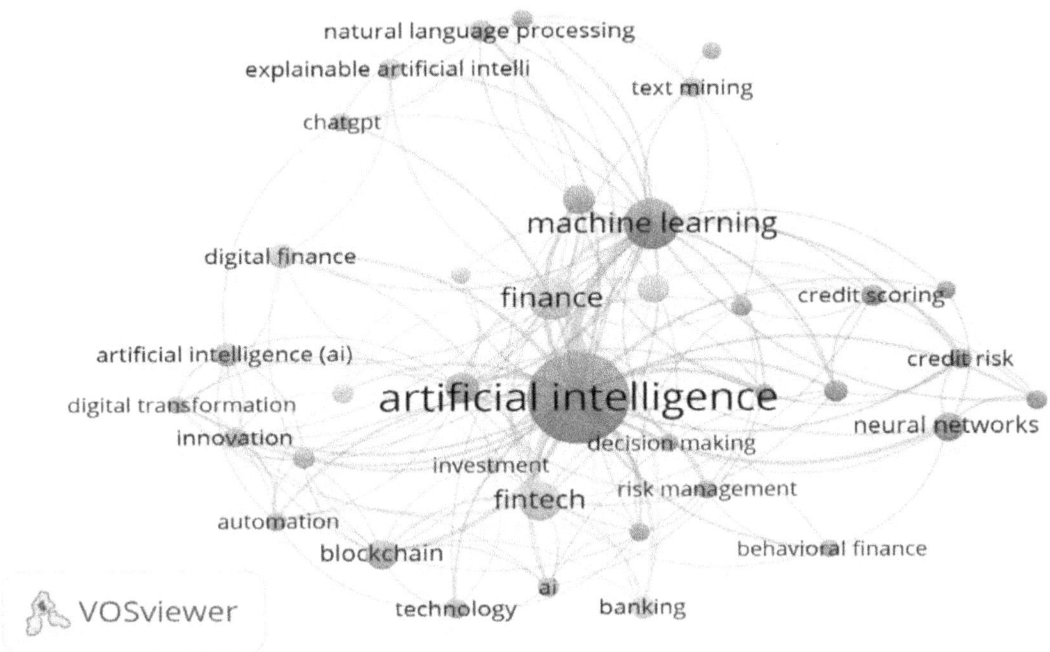

Figure 15 illustrates the network of co-word appearances. Determining the minimal co-occurrence frequency of 5 and considering 1335 keywords in general, there are six clusters, which are the utmost prevalent themes in the analysed research on the AI and finance domain. Each circle's size directly correlates with the frequency of the keyword's occurrence. A different colour distinguishes each cluster, and all the words within a cluster share the same colour.

Figure 16. Temporal outlay of author keywords

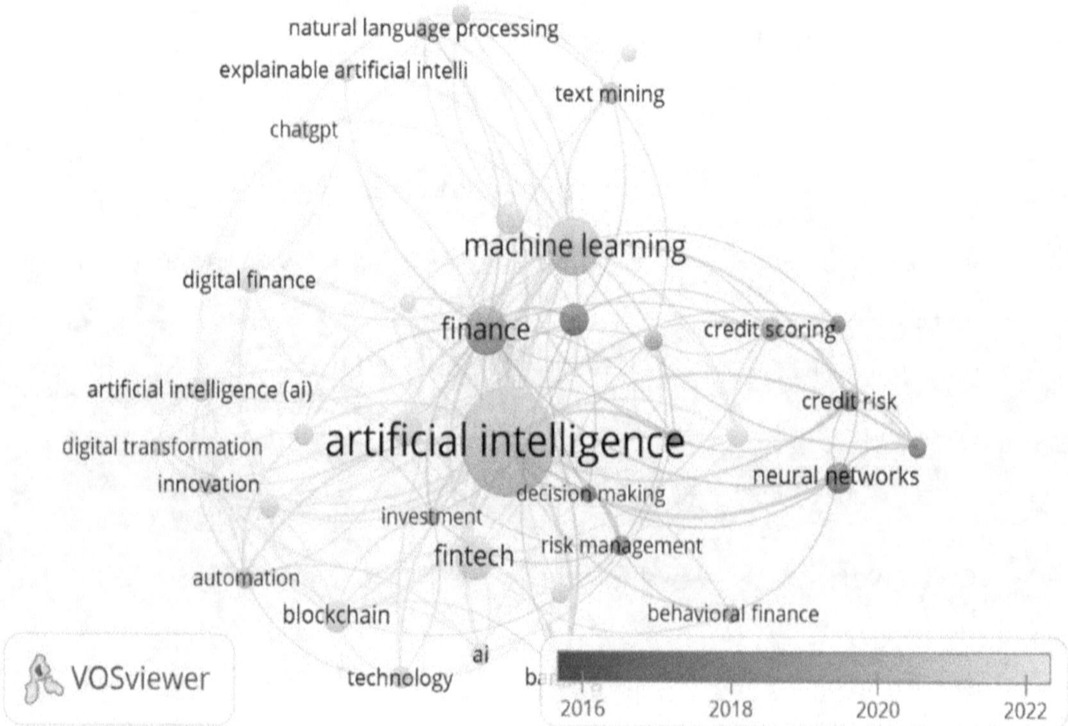

Figure – 16 illustrates the Article frequencies chart in the work above as shows the use of criteria that requires the minimum frequency of 5. When extracting the keyword, the author got 1335 themes. The part of the circle corresponds to the quantity of associations as regards to the keyword in the current or utilized system. The sums in the rounds isolating the letters g depict the years that the two keywords appeared together and it has the legend at the lower right corner of the figure. For example, application areas such as neural networks, risk management, decision making, credit scoring/credit risk have been used and discussed in the past whereas 'explainable artificial intelligence' is popular in the present. Such keywords as 'chatgpt,' 'blockchain,' 'digital finance,' 'digital transformation,' 'artificial intelligence in finance,' 'big data,' 'deep learning.'

4. DISCUSSION AND CONCLUSION

AI is relatively new to the world but has seemingly disrupted the financial system due to computer science improvements, increased output of large data to analyze, and data from consumers, investors, businesses, and governments. Therefore, the amount of study papers that discuss specific applications of

AI in the domain of finance as well as benefits that can be obtained from AI solutions has only increased. The scope of this work is to look at AI in the background of finance, and to include a literature review spanning both years and months, ending in 2020. The information for the examination comes from the 379 articles identified in 230 peer-reviewed journals in English from all over the world between 1990 and July 26, 2024. In order to answer the research questions posed for this study, bibliometric analysis methods such as citation, co-citation, and keyword co-occurrence in author names were used. The results of bibliometric analysis also provide information on the circumstance that the number of papers on the theme of AI and finance has been gradually growing over the past eight years. The first period from 1990 to 2016 indicate that the topic of study generated comparatively little number of articles. After 2016, the literature on fintech was ushered in, and there was an increasing number of articles. Based on the citation count, the most prominent work in this area is the article titled "Multidisciplinary perspectives on emerging challenges, opportunities, and agenda for research, practice, and policy" in the International Journal of Information Management in 2021 written by Dwivedi et al. and having 1267scitation. Li X has the most overall publications with five articles; however, most citations pertain to Mhlanga D with 444 citations and three articles. The total amount of periodicals is as follows: Swansea University with 12 publications is the most productive institution out of all those involved in the study followed by the University of Michigan with 10 and Qatar University with 8.

While the current publication leaders are China with 161, the USA with 151, and the UK with 101 in AI and finance. Finally, China, the USA and the UK are commented to be producing the largest shares of single and multi-country publications and exhibit the highest degree of international collaboration among shame researchers. The authors have published in 81 articles in 54 different journals out of which the most productive journals include the following; Decision Support Systems 13, Sustainability-Switzerland 12, and Journal of the Operational Research Society 9. Among the journals, Management Science has been cited most frequently with 867; followed by International Journal of Information Management with 1388, Sustainability with 571 and Knowledge-Based Systems with 566.

From the list of co-citation analysis, Liu Y., Zhang Y., Wang Y. are recognized as frequently cited authors in the arenas of AI and finance. Other frequently employed terms and expressions in the AI finance literature comprise neural networks, risk management, decision making, credit scoring, credit risk, and so much more, pointing to certain active subfields in the discipline. In this paper about author keywords, CSA shows that neural networks, risk management, decision making, credit scoring, and credit risk stand out in conceptual structure while the frequency of words such as AI, ChatGPT, blockchain, digital finance, digital transformation, big data, and deep learning has been on the rise recently.

The thematic map displays specific tendencies of AI within the finance field, application of the AI in various aspects of finance, AI usage contributing to decision making, decision support models, and possibility to use AI in crowfunding/crowsourcing, and face recognition. AI is developed as a strong tool, helping to predict markets to make them more stable due to the reduction of information asymmetry and fluctuations increasing profitability of investment systems and performance measurement. Thus, AI is used in insolvency and credit risk forecast, in fraud and early caution replicas which means that the expectations towards forthcoming artificial marketplace scrutiny and prevention of global financial crisis are raised.

Considering that the choice of AI solutions increases in the financial industry, the development of applications in other areas and countries, and the general technological progress, further advancement is expected. Those organizations that are struggling to operate in an environment of technological changes should acknowledge this as a weakness with an aim of embracing AI change in a bid to gain on the development of the business and sustain its operation. The government should support firms by offering capital or undertaking the task of skills acquisition to enable such firms to manage advanced AI systems.

5. LIMITATIONS AND FUTURE DIRECTION OF THE RESEARCH

The results of the present study can be beneficial for the AI and finance sectors. Furthermore, future studies could delve into how AI applications can aid companies and the financial sector in preventing fraudulent activities, as well as how AI can contribute to societal sustainability, ultimately leading to sustainable goals. However, due to its bibliometric nature, this research is subject to certain limitations. However, it only encompasses information gained from the Scopus database and indicates that further studies might focus on the other databases, like Google Scholar, WOS, and Dimension. Furthermore, this study focuses on 379 journal articles in business, management and accounting, social sciences, economics, econometrics, and finance. It will be possible to continue the study on other subjects to get a comprehensive view of the publication trends. For data analysis and visualization, the current study utilized Biblioshiny R-programming version 4.2.2 and VOS viewer version 1.6.0. To achieve this, future researchers who want to replicate the same or similar analyses should use other ad hoc apt tools that are currently available, such as Jamovi, N-vivo, Gephi, HistCite, Bib-Excel, or Publish or Perish.

REFERENCES

Acemoglu, D., & Restrepo, P. (2019). The wrong kind of AI? Artificial intelligence and the future of labour demand. *Cambridge Journal of Regions, Economy and Society*, 13(1), 25–35. DOI: 10.1093/cjres/rsz022

Albort-Morant, G., Henseler, J., Leal-Millán, A., & Cepeda-Carrión, G. (2017). Mapping the Field: A Bibliometric Analysis of Green Innovation. *Sustainability (Basel)*, 9(6), 1011. DOI: 10.3390/su9061011

Andrews, J. E. (2003, January 1). *An author co-citation analysis of medical informatics*. PubMed. Retrieved November 11, 2024, from https://pubmed.ncbi.nlm.nih.gov/12568157

Bahoo, S., Cucculelli, M., Goga, X., & Mondolo, J. (2024). Artificial intelligence in Finance: A comprehensive review through bibliometric and content analysis. *SN Business & Economics*, 4(2), 23. Advance online publication. DOI: 10.1007/s43546-023-00618-x

Baker, H. K., Kumar, S., Goyal, K., & Sharma, A. (2021). International review of financial analysis: A retrospective evaluation between 1992 and 2020. *International Review of Financial Analysis*, 78, 101946. DOI: 10.1016/j.irfa.2021.101946

Belanche, D., Casaló, L. V., & Flavián, C. (2019). Artificial Intelligence in FinTech: Understanding robo-advisors adoption among customers. *Industrial Management & Data Systems*, 119(7), 1411–1430. DOI: 10.1108/IMDS-08-2018-0368

Biju, A. K. V. N., Thomas, A. S., & Thasneem, J. (2023). Examining the research taxonomy of artificial intelligence, deep learning & machine learning in the financial sphere—A bibliometric analysis. *Quality & Quantity*, 58(1), 849–878. DOI: 10.1007/s11135-023-01673-0 PMID: 37359968

Bresnahan, T. F., & Trajtenberg, M. (1995). General purpose technologies 'Engines of growth'? *Journal of Econometrics*, 65(1), 83–108. DOI: 10.1016/0304-4076(94)01598-T

Buchanan, B. G. PhD, FRSA & The Alan Turing Institute. (2019). *Artificial intelligence in finance*. https://www.turing.ac.uk/sites/default/files/2019-04/artificial_intelligence_in_finance_-_turing_report_0.pdf

Callon, M., Courtial, J., Turner, W. A., & Bauin, S. (1983). From translations to problematic networks: An introduction to co-word analysis. *Social Sciences Information. Information Sur les Sciences Sociales*, 22(2), 191–235. DOI: 10.1177/053901883022002003

Das, S. R., & Chen, M. Y. (2007). Yahoo! for Amazon: Sentiment Extraction from Small Talk on the Web. *Management Science*, 53(9), 1375–1388. DOI: 10.1287/mnsc.1070.0704

Del Barrio-García, S., Muñoz-Leiva, F., & Golden, L. (2020). A review of comparative advertising research 1975–2018: Thematic and citation analyses. *Journal of Business Research*, 121, 73–84. DOI: 10.1016/j.jbusres.2020.08.023

Donthu, N., Kumar, S., Mukherjee, D., Pandey, N., & Lim, W. M. (2021). How to conduct a bibliometric analysis: An overview and guidelines. *Journal of Business Research*, 133, 285–296. DOI: 10.1016/j.jbusres.2021.04.070

Dwivedi, Y. K., Hughes, L., Ismagilova, E., Aarts, G., Coombs, C., Crick, T., Duan, Y., Dwivedi, R., Edwards, J., Eirug, A., Galanos, V., Ilavarasan, P. V., Janssen, M., Jones, P., Kar, A. K., Kizgin, H., Kronemann, B., Lal, B., Lucini, B., & Williams, M. D. (2019). Artificial Intelligence (AI): Multidisciplinary perspectives on emerging challenges, opportunities, and agenda for research, practice and policy. *International Journal of Information Management*, 57, 101994. DOI: 10.1016/j.ijinfomgt.2019.08.002

Ejaz, H., Zeeshan, H. M., Ahmad, F., Bukhari, S. N. A., Anwar, N., Alanazi, A., Sadiq, A., Junaid, K., Atif, M., Abosalif, K. O. A., Iqbal, A., Hamza, M. A., & Younas, S. (2022). Bibliometric Analysis of Publications on the Omicron Variant from 2020 to 2022 in the Scopus Database Using R and VOSviewer. *International Journal of Environmental Research and Public Health*, 19(19), 12407. DOI: 10.3390/ijerph191912407 PMID: 36231710

Ernst, E., Merola, R., & Samaan, D. (2019). Economics of Artificial Intelligence: Implications for the future of work. *IZA Journal of Labor Policy*, 9(1), 20190004. Advance online publication. DOI: 10.2478/izajolp-2019-0004

Forliano, C., De Bernardi, P., & Yahiaoui, D. (2020). Entrepreneurial universities: A bibliometric analysis within the business and management domains. *Technological Forecasting and Social Change*, 165, 120522. DOI: 10.1016/j.techfore.2020.120522

He, Q. (1999). Knowledge Discovery through Co-Word Analysis. *Library Trends*, 48(1), 133–159. https://dblp.uni-trier.de/db/journals/libt/libt48.html#He99

Hentzen, J. K., Hoffmann, A. O. I., & Dolan, R. M. (2021). Which consumers are more likely to adopt a retirement app and how does it explain mobile technology-enabled retirement engagement? *International Journal of Consumer Studies*, 46(2), 368–390. DOI: 10.1111/ijcs.12685

Irfan, M. (2021). Do Shariah Indices converge Evidence from Gulf Cooperation Council countries. *International Journal of Business Excellence*, 23(2), 251. DOI: 10.1504/IJBEX.2021.113448

Irfan, M. Elhoseny, Kassim, S., & Metawa, N. (2023). Advanced machine learning algorithms for complex financial applications. In *Advances in finance, accounting, and economics book series*. IGI Global. https://doi.org/DOI: 10.4018/978-1-6684-4483-2

Irfan, M., Elmogy, M., Gupta, S., Khalifa, F., & Dias, R. (2024). AI-Driven decentralized Finance and the future of Finance. In *Advances in finance, accounting, and economics book series*. IGI Global Publisher., DOI: 10.4018/979-8-3693-6321-8

Irfan, M., Elmogy, M., & Majid, M. S. (2023). The Impact of AI Innovation on Financial Sectors in the era of Industry 5.0. In *Advances in finance, accounting, and economics book series*. IGI Global., DOI: 10.4018/979-8-3693-0082-4

Irfan, M., Hussainey, K., Bukhari, S., & Nam, Y. (2024). Issues of sustainability in AI and New-Age thematic investing. In *Advances in finance, accounting, and economics book series*. IGI Global Publisher., DOI: 10.4018/979-8-3693-3282-5

Irfan, M., Kadry, S., Sharif, M., & Khan, H. (2023). Fintech applications in Islamic Finance. In *Advances in finance, accounting, and economics book series*. IGI Global., DOI: 10.4018/979-8-3693-1038-0

Jagtiani, J., & John, K. (2018). Fintech: The impact on consumers and regulatory responses. *Journal of Economics and Business*, 100, 1–6. DOI: 10.1016/j.jeconbus.2018.11.002

Madhan, K., Shagirbasha, S., Mishra, T. K., & Iqbal, J. (2023). Adoption of service robots: Exploring the emerging trends through the lens of bibliometric analysis. *International Hospitality Review*, 38(2), 239–257. DOI: 10.1108/IHR-12-2022-0058

Martinelli, A., Mina, A., & Moggi, M. (2020). The enabling technologies of industry 4.0: Examining the seeds of the fourth industrial revolution. *Industrial and Corporate Change*, 30(1), 161–188. DOI: 10.1093/icc/dtaa060

Matute, J., & Linsen, L. (2022). Evaluating Data-type Heterogeneity in Interactive Visual Analyses with Parallel Axes. *Computer Graphics Forum*, 41(1), 335–349. DOI: 10.1111/cgf.14438

Nash-Stewart, C. E., Kruesi, L. M., & Del Mar, C. B. (2012). Does Bradford's Law of Scattering predict the size of the literature in Cochrane Reviews? *Journal of the Medical Library Association: JMLA*, 100(2), 135–138. DOI: 10.3163/1536-5050.100.2.013 PMID: 22514511

PricewaterhouseCoopers. (2017). *PwC's Global Artificial Intelligence Study: Sizing the prize*. PwC. Retrieved July 16, 2024, from https://www.pwc.com/gx/en/issues/data-and-analytics/publications/artificial-intelligence-study.html

PwC. (2020). How mature is AI adoption in financial services? In *A PwC Study Across the DACH Region*. Retrieved July 16, 2024, from https://www.pwc.de/de/future-of-finance/how-mature-is-ai-adoption-in-financial-services.pdf

Raj, M., & Seamans, R. (2019). Primer on artificial intelligence and robotics. *Journal of Organization Design*, 8(1), 11. Advance online publication. DOI: 10.1186/s41469-019-0050-0

Sadeqi-Arani, Z., & Kadkhodaie, A. (2023). A bibliometric analysis of the application of machine learning methods in the petroleum industry. *Results in Engineering*, 20, 101518. DOI: 10.1016/j.rineng.2023.101518

Shaikh, Z. H., Irfan, M., Nomran, N. M., & Abey, J. (2024). Does COVID-19 affect shariah compliant stock? Evidence from selected oic countries. *Jurnal Ilmiah Ilmu Terapan Universitas Jambi*, 8(2), 720–731. DOI: 10.22437/jiituj.v8i2.33159

Shekhar, S. (2023). Covid-19 and Destination Marketing: A Science Mapping and Descriptive Analysis. [Formerly known as Iranian Journal of Management Studies]. *Interdisciplinary Journal of Management Studies*, 16(4), 989–1010. DOI: 10.22059/ijms.2023.348750.675381

Singh, K. (2014). *Application of Bradford's Law on Journal Citations: A Study of Ph*. D. Theses. [Doctoral dissertation]

Sofik, S., Dr, Z. R., & Dr, S. N. (2021). Productivity Trends and Pattern of Scientific Collaboration of Bibliometric Research: An Exploratory Analysis. *Library Philosophy and Practice (E-journal)*. https://digitalcommons.unl.edu/cgi/viewcontent.cgi?article=10984&context=libphilprac

Srisusilawati, P., Rusydiana, A. S., Sanrego, Y. D., & Tubastuvi, N. (2021). Biblioshiny R Application on Islamic Microfinance Research. *Library Philosophy and Practice*. https://digitalcommons.unl.edu/cgi/viewcontent.cgi?article=9428&context=libphilprac

Team, I. (2024, April 9). *What is artificial intelligence (AI)?* Investopedia. Retrieved July 16, 2024, from https://www.investopedia.com/terms/a/artificial-intelligence-ai.asp

Van Roy, V., Vertesy, D., & Damioli, G. (2020). AI and Robotics Innovation. In *Springer eBooks* (pp. 1–35). https://doi.org/DOI: 10.1007/978-3-319-57365-6_12-2

Wall, L. D. (2018). Some financial regulatory implications of artificial intelligence. *Journal of Economics and Business*, 100, 55–63. DOI: 10.1016/j.jeconbus.2018.05.003

Chapter 15
Natural Resources and Climate Change in Resource Rich African Countries:
The Role of Inclusive Finance

Ayobola Olufolake Charles
https://orcid.org/0000-0002-0172-1075
Trinity University, Nigeria

Oluyemi Theophilus Adeosun
http://orcid.org/0000-0003-1683-4053
Pan Atlantic University, Nigeria

ABSTRACT

The research investigates the effect of natural resources on climate change and the role inclusive finance plays in the natural resource-climate change nexus among thirty-two resource-rich African countries from 2004-2022. Data acquired from World Development Indicator Database and International Monetary Fund Database are analyzed using the heterogeneous dynamic Pooled Mean Group estimation technique. The research demonstrates that natural resources negatively but insignificantly impact climate change. Also, inclusive finance negatively but significantly impacts climate change in the long run. Finally, the interactive effect of natural resource and climate change have a negative and significant effect on climate change among the selected resource-rich African nations. The findings show that inclusive finance is very key in enabling resource-rich African countries to adapt sufficiently to and fight climate change. From these findings, the study recommends priority toward the development of inclusive financial systems by policymakers in resource-rich countries in Africa.

INTRODUCTION

Africa has abundant natural resources, including 30 per cent of the world's mineral reserves and 65 percent of its uncultivated arable land. These resources encompass fertile agricultural land and highly productive forests crucial for timber and carbon sequestration. Additionally, the continent benefits from

DOI: 10.4018/979-8-3693-7924-0.ch015

extensive solar, wind, and hydropower potential. However, the exploitation and management of these resources come with complex challenges, especially in the face of climate change. Natural resources have complex effects on a country's financial landscape.

On the one hand, resource-rich nations can leverage these assets to generate revenue, attract foreign investments, and build financial infrastructure (Li et al., 2024). On the other hand, abundant natural resources can lead to economic distortions, rent-seeking behaviour, and a concentration of wealth, which may hinder financial inclusion. The quality of a country's institutions, including governance, rule of law, and regulatory frameworks, is crucial in determining whether natural resources contribute positively or negatively to inclusive finance and overall economic development.

In resource-rich African countries, the adverse effects of climate change are particularly pronounced. These nations face the dual challenge of managing their natural resources sustainably while mitigating the impacts of climate change. Climate-related phenomena such as rising temperatures, changing precipitation patterns, and extreme weather events threaten the stability and productivity of these countries, making effective resource management even more crucial. Climate change and environmental sustainability have emerged as critical concerns, particularly in the rapid industrial growth observed since the Industrial Revolution (Pu et al., 2024). The global community has recognized the urgent need to address these issues, leading to the establishment of various international agreements aimed at mitigating climate change and promoting sustainable development. In resource-rich African countries, the challenges posed by climate change are particularly acute. These nations, endowed with abundant natural resources, face the dual pressure of managing these resources sustainably while combating the adverse effects of climate change. (Pu et al., 2024)

Promoting inclusive finance is essential for governments globally to foster inclusive economic growth and development. Inclusive finance involves providing loans and other essential financial services, often through microfinance institutions, and its macroeconomic impacts are diverse. (Corrado & Corrado, 2017). An inclusive financial system reduces socio-economic inequality and contributes to a more prosperous economy and higher economic growth. Additionally, inclusive finance plays a crucial role in mitigating the effects of macroeconomic shocks on households and small and medium-sized enterprises. Inclusive finance refers to the accessibility of a wide range of financial services for individuals and businesses at affordable terms. This has emerged as a crucial global driver of inclusive economic growth and development (Li et al., 2024; Corrado & Corrado, 2017). It aligns with the United Nations Sustainable Development Goals Framework for 2030, aiming to promote financial inclusion and ensure that everyone, significantly the most disadvantaged and marginalized, can benefit from development. Lee (2020) described financial inclusion as providing affordable banking services to a large population of low-income and disadvantaged groups. Similarly, Hallegatte, Rentschler, & Rozenberg (2020) defined *financial inclusion* as the process through which institutions ensure the availability of formal financial services to underserved populations. Financial inclusion can also be understood as the art of offering banking services to a broad segment of low-income and disadvantaged individuals at reduced costs.

The relationship between natural resources and a country's financial capability is complex. Natural resources provide opportunities for resource-rich nations to generate revenue, attract foreign investments, and build financial infrastructure. However, the mismanagement of these resources can lead to economic distortions, rent-seeking behaviour, and a concentration of wealth, ultimately hindering financial inclusion and exacerbating socio-economic inequalities. The quality of a country's institutions, including governance, rule of law, and regulatory frameworks, is critical in shaping the outcomes of natural resource management and ensuring that the benefits of these resources are equitably distributed. The research seeks to investigate the impact of natural resources on climate change. Also, it will analyze the effect of natural resources on climate change and investigate the interactive effect of natural resources and inclusive finance on climate change. Previous studies are discussed in section 2, and a review of theory, methodology and estimation technique is discussed in section 3. The results and discussion are shown in section 4, while section 5 entails conclusion and policy recommendations.

2. EMPIRICAL REVIEW

Pu et al. (2023) investigated the asymmetric impacts of natural resources, fintech, and digital banking on climate change and environmental sustainability in BRICS countries from 1995 to 2022. Using Methods of Moments Quantile Regression (MMQR), their study found that while natural resources and banking sector development exacerbate environmental issues, financial technologies have a significant negative impact, suggesting they may improve environmental outcomes. The study recommended directing finance towards eco-friendly projects. However, it did not address how inclusive finance, which targets underserved populations, affects resource management in resource-rich African countries. This research aims to fill this gap by exploring whether inclusive financial services enhance resource management and contribute to sustainability.

Xixi et al. (2023) explored the relationship between natural resource rent and inclusive finance through an institutional perspective. A panel data set of 109 countries was utilized in the study, from 1996 to 2020, highlighting the crucial role of inclusive finance in fostering inclusive economic growth and development. The fixed-effects and two-stage least squares regression analyses reveal that natural resource rent negatively impacts inclusive finance, aligning with the resource curse theory. Notably, the study finds that the effect of natural resource rent on inclusive finance varies with institutional quality. In contexts with strong institutions, natural resource rent is positively associated with inclusive finance, whereas in weaker institutional settings, the relationship is negative. These findings pass robustness tests, emphasizing reliability and offering valuable insights for policymakers and stakeholders. Despite these insights, the study must address how inclusive finance explicitly impacts natural resources and climate change in resource-rich countries.

Sun (2024) investigates the impact of fiscal pressures on natural resources policy and green recovery techniques, focusing on how inclusive finance affects oil resource production targets in Gulf countries. The study explores the relationship between financial inclusion, oil production goals, and fiscal constraints in economies heavily reliant on oil revenues. The study finds that fiscal pressures, driven by fluctuations in global oil prices and changing environmental regulations, significantly influence natural resources policy and green recovery efforts. These pressures necessitate the development of green initiatives and diversification strategies to mitigate vulnerabilities associated with oil market volatility. The study explained that inclusive finance is crucial in supporting oil production targets by providing access to financial resources for investments in green technologies and sustainable practices. The study emphasizes that financial inclusion helps balance the need for oil revenue with adopting environmental sustainability measures. The study clarifies the importance of policy frameworks integrating financial inclusion with oil production and environmental sustainability through empirical data and case studies. It highlights the necessity of circular economy models, enhanced energy efficiency, and investments in renewable energy to achieve balanced and sustainable development. The study recommends several strategies for achieving sustainability, including implementing circular economy principles to reduce waste and enhance resource efficiency. While the study offers valuable insights, Sun (2024) focuses on oil production and green recovery but only covers the broader impacts of climate change on resource management.

3. METHODOLOGY

3.1 Succinct Review of Theory

This study theoretically hinges on the Resource curse theory, inclusive finance, and climate change mitigation theory. According to the resource curse theory, over-reliance on natural resources has led to slower growth, poor institutions, accelerated instability of the polity and poor governance outcomes in countries with abundant natural resources compared to resource-poor countries. The exploitation of natural resources, especially fossil fuels, can have a detrimental impact on the environment and cause climate change by way of greenhouse gas emissions. (Sachs & Warner, 1995; Cai et al, 2024; Zheng et al, 2023). The theory posits that over-dependence on these natural resources may result in the neglect of other sectors, such as renewable energy, and overall, leading to the inability of the countries to ameliorate climate change (Caglar et al., 2024; Auty, 1993). The inclusive finance and climate change mitigation theory postulates that the ease and availability of low-cost financial services to everyone, especially the poor and the underserved in society, can serve as a tool for mitigating climate change through investments in clean energy and climate-resilient activities (Owusu, 2024; Demirgüç-Kunt et al., 2018).

3.2 Model Estimation

The empirical model will be specified following works such as Pu et al, (2024) and Sadiq et al (2024). Model (1) involves the analyses of natural resources and climate change, and is shown thus:

$$CES_{it} = NRN_{it} + STIN_{it} + GDP_{it} + TOPSS_{it} + URBS_{it} + u_{it} \tag{1}$$

Where CES (Carbon emissions) captures climate change, and NRN (Natural resource rent) proxies' natural resources. Control variables used in the study are Structure of Industry (STIN), Gross domestic per capita (GDP), Trade openness (TOPSS) and Urbanization (URBS) as shown in Table 1.

Model 2 involves investigating inclusive finance and climate change and is presented thus:

$$CES_{it} = INCF_{it} + STIN_{it} + GDP_{it} + TOPSS_{it} + URBS_{it} + u_{it} \tag{2}$$

Where CES (carbon emissions) captures climate change, and INCF measures inclusive finance. All other moderating regressors are as explained earlier.

Model 3 involves analysing the interactive effect of natural resources and inclusive finance on climate change, and is shown thus:

$$CES_{it} = NRN_{it} + INCF_{it} + STIN_{it} + GDP_{it} + TOPSS_{it} + URBS_{it} + NRNINCF_{it} + u_{it} \tag{3}$$

Where CES (carbon emissions) captures climate change and NRNINCF captures the interactive effect of natural resources and climate change. All other moderating variables remain as earlier explained. The data utilized in the study were obtained for the period 2004-2022 from the World Development Indicators (WDI, 2023), and International Financial Statistic (IFS), an IMF database. The inclusive finance index is calculated via the principal component analysis using some financial indicators such as Number of commercial bank branches per 100,000 adults, institutions of commercial banks, Number of ATMS per 100,000 adults, outstanding deposits with commercial banks (% of GDP), and outstanding loans from commercial banks (% of GDP), utilized in accord with extant literature (Nchofoung et al, 2024; Avom et al, 2022). These variables were normalized using the minimum-maximum method as shown in equation 4.

$$M_{ij}^{KL} = \frac{N_{ij}^{t} - Min(N_{ij})}{Max(N_{ij}) - Min(N_{ij})} \quad (4)$$

The rescaled variable is M_{ij}^{KL}, N_{ij} is the country, and t represents the period considered. The minimum value of each variable and the corresponding maximum value is denoted by $Min(N_{ij})$ and $Max(N_{ij})$ respectively. The rescaled variable takes values between 0 and 1, with 0 being the lowest score, while 1 is the highest score. The rescaled variable then undergoes principal component analysis to obtain the inclusive finance index. In the principal component analysis, the distribution of each indicator is considered and the weights to the sub-indexes based on their importance in the aggregate index is also attributed. This is a unique advantage of the principal component analysis and why it is preferred rather than other methods of aggregation such as simple arithmetic mean (Nchofoung et al, 2024). Also, thirty-two (32) resource-rich African countries were selected, and they include: Zambia, Uganda, Togo, South Africa, Sierra Leone, Senegal, Rwanda, Nigeria, Niger, Namibia, Morocco, Mozambique, Mali, Malawi, Madagascar, Kenya, Guinea, Ghana, Gabon, Ethiopia, Equatorial Guinea, Egypt, Arab Rep., Cote d'ivoire, Congo Dem. Rep., Chad, Central African Republic, Cameroon, Burundi, Burkina Faso, Botswana, Angola, Algeria. Lastly, the availability of total data for all the variables and cross-section utilized is the basis of the choice of countries.

3.3. Estimation Technique

The Pooled Mean Group (PMG) based on Pesaran et al (1999) is the technique f estimation utilized in this study. The PMG has a dynamic heterogeneous framework that makes it easier for panel studies analysis and its ability to accommodate heterogeneous panels. Its consistency and efficiency give it an advantage over the mean Group (MG) and the dynamic fixed effect (DFE) models. Its appropriateness for panel data analysis with large time series (T) and cross-section (N) gives it an advantage over the generalized method of moments (GMM). Finally, it gives allowance for different dynamic specification from one country to another in the short-run, while in the long-run, it gives allowance for same specification (Bangake & Eggoh, 2012).

Therefore, the PMG model is given thus:

$$c_i(K)n_{it} = b_i(K)l_{it} + p_i x_{it} + \mu_{it} \quad (5)$$

Where $c_i(K)n_{it}$ depicts the vector of dependent regressors, $b_i(K)l_{it}$ shows auto regressive indicators, p_i x_{it} depicts the vector and coefficient of explanatory variables, and μ_{it} depicts the residual term., I represents the cross-sections, which ranges from 1 to N, while t is time series. The estimate for country I in the long-run is shown as

$\Theta_i \frac{b_i(1)}{p_i(1)}$ while $\Theta = N^{-1}\sum_{i=1}^{N}\widehat{\Theta}_i$ is the panel mean group estimate.

Due to the long-run and the short-run parameters constraints of the PMG, the unrestricted PMG model for countries I, periods t, vector of the independent variables l and dependent variable n is given thus:

$$n_{it} = \sum_{g=1}^{h} \infty_{ik} n_{i,j-k} + \sum_{i=0}^{q} \lambda_{ik}^{i} l_{i,j-k} + \varepsilon_i + \mu_{it} \quad (6)$$

Where l_{ik} represents jx1 vector of explanatory variables for cross-section I, while ε_i represents the fixed effects (Pesaran & Smith, 1995; Pesaran et al., 1999).

Table 1. Variables' identification and data source

Variable	Identification	Description	Source
CES	Climate change	CO2 emissions (metric tons per capita)	WDI 2023
NRN	Natural Resources	Total natural resources rents (% of GDP)	WDI 2023
STIN	Structure of Industry	Industrial Output/GDP	WDI 2023
GDP	Growth	GDP per capita (Constant 2015 US$)	WDI 2023
TOPSS	Trade Openness	Trade (% of GDP)	WDI 2023
INCF	Inclusive finance	Principal component analysis using five financial Indicators	IMF DATA 2023
URBS	Urbanization	Urban population growth (annual %)	WDI 2023

Source: Author's Compilation

4. RESULTS OF EMPIRICAL ANALYSIS AND DISCUSSION

The findings of this study are presented in this section. Firstly, we show the result of the descriptive statistics, then the correlation, the panel unit root tests (PURTS) and cointegration. Finally, the empirical result and discussion is shown.

4.1 Panel Data Summary Statistics of the Main Variables

A snapshot of the variables used is shown in Table 2. Climate change measured with C02 emissions has an average of 1.02 metric tons per capita among the thirty-two resource-rich countries in Africa is 1.02. The minimum C02 emissions is 0.02 metric tons per capita, while the maximum C02 emissions is 8.45 metric tons per capita. Natural resources as measured by total natural resource rents (% of GDP), has an average of 12.06 per cent of GDP, while the maximum and the minimum values are 56.29 per cent of GDP and 0.3 per cent of GDP respectively.

Table 2. Summary statistics for the panel variables

Variables	Description	Minm	Maxm	STND	Mean
CES	CO2 emissions (metric tons per capita)	0.02	8.45	1.67	1.02
NRN	Total natural resources rents (% of GDP)	0.3	56.29	9.69	12.06
STIN	Industrial Output/GDP	0.04	0.71	0.12	0.27
GDP	GDP per capita (Constant 2015 US$)	262.18	14222.55	2345.06	2086.7
TOPSS	Trade (% of GDP)	22.24	144.67	22.65	62.91
INCF	Principal component analysis using five financial Indicators	-3.03	7.57	1.74	-1.75e-08
URBS	Urban population growth (annual %)	-0.01	7.69	1.22	3.84

Source: Author's compilation; Number of Observation: 608; STND-Standard Deviation; Maxm. -Maximum; Minm. – Minimum

4.2. Unit Root Tests

Table 3. PURTS result

Variables	Level			1st Difference		
	LLC	Breit	IPS	LLC	Breit	IPS
CES	3.1899[k]	2.2858	1.5700	23.8231[k]	12.2999[k]	10.7383[k]
NRN	4.2571[k]	2.8543[k]	2.7469[k]	16.0463[k]	9.7496[k]	12.0369[k]
STIN	3.9054[k]	2.3301	0.5636	9.5941[k]	10.8721[k]	10.1606[k]
GDP	0.1786	6.4498	4.7091	6.0174[k]	9.8970[k]	9.3991[k]
TOPSS	3.2368[k]	1.9815[j]	1.9656[j]	10.8856[k]	12.2530[k]	11.7250[k]
URBS	2.5261[k]	3.1041	2.4916	18.0481[k]	8.3902[k]	7.2203[k]
INCF	5.8634[k]	6.0197	0.0488	5.5663[k]	8.5223[k]	8.8590[k]

NB: LLC denotes Levin, Lin & Chu (2002), Breit denotes Breitung (2001), IPS denotes Im-Pesaran-Shin; [k] means 1% level of significance, [j] means 5% level of significance.

The result of the PURTS is shown in Table 3. confirming that climate change, and inclusive finance, are not stationary at level. However, after all the variables became stationary after first differencing. This indicates the absence of unit root among the variables.

4.3. Panel Cointegration

Table 4. Pedroni test for cointegration

	Statistic	P-value
Modified Phillips-Perron t	6.1072	0.0000[k]
Phillips-Perron t	-5.7505	0.0000[k]
Augmented Dickey-Fuller t	-6.0018	0.0000[k]

Source: Authors' compilation. [k], represent 1% significant level respectively

The existence of long-run relationship among the regressors is being established by the Pedroni test as shown in Table 4. Therefore, the null hypothesis of no cointegration is rejected at the 1 per cent significant level, showing that there is a long run association among the regressors used in the study.

4.4 Panel Correlation Analysis

Table 5. Panel Correlation analysis

	CES	NRN	STIN	GDP	TOPSS	URBS	INCF
CES	1.000						
NRN	0.214	1.000					
STIN	0.484	0.551	1.000				
GDP	0.844	0.305	0.709	1.000			
TOPSS	0.272	0.317	0.538	0.9215	1.000		
URBS	-0.244	0.063	0.063	-0.0647	0.0487	1.000	
INCF	0.122	0.115	0.115	0.1669	0.0618	-0.162	1.000

Source: Author's Compilation

Table 5 depicts the panel correlation analysis which shows that none of the variables are perfectly correlated. It means that our panel estimates are in order. This is an indication that all our estimated models exhibit no multi-collinearity problems.

4.5 Empirical Results

Table 6. Natural resources and Climate change nexus

Dependent Variable: CES					
	Long run			**Short run**	
Variable	**Coefficient**	**Standard errors**	**Variable**	**Coefficient**	**Standard errors**
NRN	-0.0001	0.0007	NRN	-0.0021	0.0023
STIN	-0.2796[k]	0.0637	STIN	0.6036	0.4928
GDP	0.0003[k]	0.0000	GDP	0.0002[j]	0.0001
TOPSS	0.0004	0.0004	TOPSS	-0,0005	0.0004
URBS	-0.0258[k]	0.0059	URBS	0.1183	0.0365
			ECT (-1)	-0.1769[k]	0.0441

Source: Authors' compilation. [k], represent 1% significant level respectively

Table 6 shows the short-run and the long-run pooled mean group results of the natural resources and the climate change nexus. In the short run and the long run, natural resources negatively but insignificantly impact climate change among the resource-rich African countries. This result shows that the vast natural resources of African nations have the potential to reduce greenhouse gas emissions, through their vast forests and vegetation, clean energy resources such as solar, wind, hydro and geothermal. However, this potential may not have been fully utilized. The results of the control variables show that Structure of the industry and urbanization negatively and significantly impacts climate change among the resource-rich African nations in the long-run. Trade openness significantly and positively impacts climate change in the long run. Likewise, economic growth positively and significantly impacts climate change.

Table 7. Inclusive finance and climate change nexus

Dependent Variable: CES					
	Long run			**Short run**	
Variable	**Coefficient**	**Standard errors**	**Variable**	**Coefficient**	**Standard errors**
INCF	-0.0065[k]	0.0850	**INCF**	-0.0132	0.0142
STIN	-0.6202[k]	0.085	**STIN**	0.2607	0.4136
GDP	0.0004[k]	0.0000	**GDP**	0.0002[k]	0.0001
TOPSS	0.0006[i]	0.0003	**TOPSS**	-0.0002	0.0005
URBS	-0.0221[k]	0.0043	**URBS**	-0.0132	0.0142
			ECT (-1)	-0.1980[k]	0.0542

Source: Authors' compilation. [k], represent 1% significant level respectively

The PMG result in Table 7 shows the short-run and long-run results of the inclusive finance and the climate change nexus. In the short-run, inclusive finance has a negative but insignificant effect on climate change. However, in the long run, inclusive finance negatively and significantly impacts climate change.

The insignificant effect may be adduced to the fact that inclusive finance, which is the availability of low-cost and low-priced financial services to businesses and households especially the underserved and the minority, which has a great potential to reduce greenhouse gas emissions, may have limited scale and reach among the resource-rich African nations. The long-run results show that inclusive finance negatively and significantly impacts climate change. This infers that among the resource-rich African nations inclusive finance has the potential to reduce greenhouse gas emissions.

Table 8. Interactive role of inclusive finance in the natural resource-climate change nexus

Dependent Variable: CES					
	Long run			**Short run**	
Variable	**Coefficient**	**Standard errors**	**Variable**	**Coefficient**	**Standard errors**
NRN	-0.0023^{k}	0.0007	**NRN**	-0.0026	0.0048
STIN	-3.4305^{k}	0.1926	**STIN**	0.6338	0.4141
GDP	0.0006^{k}	0.00002	**GDP**	0.0002^{j}	0.0001
TOPSS	-0.001^{k}	0.0002	**TOPSS**	0.0005	0.0007
URBS	0.1904^{k}	0.0101	**URBS**	-0.0742	0.1208
INCF	-0.039^{k}	0.0093	**INCF**	-0.0002	0.0031
NRNINCF	-0.0008^{k}	-0.0003	**NRNINCF**	-0.0002	0.0031
			ECT (-1)	-0.0804^{i}	0.0478

Source: Authors' compilation. ^{k}, ^{j}, ^{i} represent 1%, 5% and 10% significant level respectively

Table 8 shows the long-run and short-run results of the interactive effect of inclusive finance on the natural resource-climate change nexus. The results show that the interaction of natural resources and inclusive finance has a negative impact on climate change, although it was insignificant in the short-run, it was significant in the long-run. This result infers that when there are available low-priced and low-cost financial services to individuals and businesses especially among the marginalized and minority groups in the resource-rich African nations, they can embark on clean energy projects such as solar, wind power or geothermal, and other climate-smart technologies which have a great potential of reducing emissions and improving the environment.

4.6 Discussion of Results

The PMG shows the empirical analysis of natural resources and inclusive finance on climate change. The findings show that natural resources negatively impact climate change in the short-run and the long-run, albeit insignificant. This can be attributed to the fact that the sustainable management of natural resources among the resource-rich African nations plays a critical role in climate change reduction through the following ways: The abundance of vegetation and forests in African nations serve as a natural carbon sink, whereby carbon dioxide is absorbed by plants and trees, enhancing carbon sequestration and reducing greenhouse gas emissions. Also, many African nations are abundantly blessed with renewable natural resources such as solar and wind energy, which, if sustainably utilized, can help reduce dependence on fossil fuels, which contribute primarily to the depletion of the ozone layer. The insignificance of the results can be attributed to the unsustainable use of natural resources in many African countries

(Iyiola et al., 2023). These findings, however, do not align with those of Pu et al. (2024), Ahmad et al. (2023), Ulucak & Ozcan (2020) and Cen & Yin (2024).

Also, the findings of this study show that inclusive finance negatively and significantly impacts inclusive finance in the long run. As low-priced and low-cost financial services are made available and accessible to individuals, small-scale farmers, entrepreneurs and businesses, most especially the underserved and the marginalized in the rural and undeveloped areas of the resource-rich African nations, they can transition to the use of sustainable and clean energy, thereby mitigating climate change. Inclusive finance can help fight climate change by enabling the underserved and marginalized with funds to invest in cleaner energy sources such as solar panels, wind turbines, etc, which can help to displace the fossil fuel, wood or charcoal, which can emit greenhouse gases. Furthermore, the availability of climate finance helps small businesses in rural communities invest in infrastructure that is resilient to climate, such as flood-resistant housing and climate-proof irrigation methods. The affordability of loans can also help rural households purchase clean energy cookware, reduce reliance on traditional cookware, and reduce the felling of trees and carbon emissions (Mchkulu, 2019; Mahoro, 2015). This study aligns with the findings of Cen & Yin (2024), who posited that green finance, fintech, and financial inclusion enhanced environmental quality in China. It also corresponds to the findings of Zhoe et al. (2020) and Kwilinski et al. (2023).

The interactive effect of inclusive finance on natural resources and climate change nexus reveals that the interaction of natural resources and inclusive finance negatively impacts climate change. This finding reveals that inclusive finance is crucial in ensuring natural resources do not exacerbate climate change among the resource-rich African nations. This is because when structures are put in place so that the underserved can access financial services easily, they can invest in clean energy and sustainable technologies. Also, inclusive finance ensures that small-scale rural dwellers in weak communities have access to loans, enabling them to adapt to the impact of climate change (Adegbite & Machete, 2020; Paul et al., 2016). Miners and small-scale farmers can be given funds to adopt cleaner technologies and climate-resistant practices, thereby reducing their dependence on the over-exploitation of natural resources (Jhariya et al., 2022; Nyakuwanika et al., 2022).

5.0. CONCLUSION AND POLICY RECOMMENDATION

From 2004 to 2022, this study analyzed the effect of natural resources on climate change and the role of inclusive finance in the natural resources-climate change nexus in thirty-two resource-rich African countries. The relationship among the regressors was presented using the dynamic heterogeneous framework of the Pooled Mean Group. The main findings are that natural resources have a negative but insignificant effect on climate change in the long run and short run. Furthermore, inclusive finance harms climate change. Although it was insignificant in the short run, it became significant in the long run. Finally, the interactive effect of natural resources and inclusive finance on climate change has a negative and significant effect.

These results show that the sustainable use of natural resources in resource-rich African countries significantly mitigates the adverse effect of climate change. Resource-rich African economies should ensure the sustainability and proper management of their forest and ecosystems by educating their citizens about the dangers of deforestation and over-exploitation of natural resources. Additionally, since many African nations are rich in renewable natural resources such as Solar, hydro, wind and geothermal energy sources, government agencies should ensure that these clean energy resources are optimally harnessed to reduce carbon dioxide emissions significantly. Resource-rich African countries must implement programs and schemes that foster inclusive finance, such as green financing, as these help to mitigate climate change and increase the adaptation of the underserved and rural poor to climate change tendencies. Therefore, governments and financial institutions can embark on climate-resilient projects by organizing microfinance programs that help support rural communities in adopting eco-friendly technologies that help reduce emissions and protect the environment. Finally, resource-rich African governments should ensure the establishment of environmental regulations such as the Environment Impact Assessments (EIA) and Resource management policies, which foster and promote sustainable use of natural resources.

Although this study significantly contributes to the literature, it has limitations. Firstly, the study looked at the impact of total natural resource rents on climate change. Future research can look at the impact of different types of natural resources, such as oil and solid mineral resources. Also, inclusive finance was computed using the principal component analysis on five financial indicators. Subsequent research can expand the number of financial indicators beyond the ones used in this study.

REFERENCES

Abbass, K., Qasim, M. Z., Song, H., Murshed, M., Mahmood, H., & Younis, I. (2022). A review of the global climate change impacts, adaptation, and sustainable mitigation measures. *Environmental Science and Pollution Research International*, 29(28), 42539–42559. DOI: 10.1007/s11356-022-19718-6 PMID: 35378646

Adegbite, O. O., & Machethe, C. L. (2020). Bridging the financial inclusion gender gap in smallholder agriculture in Nigeria: An untapped potential for sustainable development. *World Development*, 127, 104755. DOI: 10.1016/j.worlddev.2019.104755

African Development Bank Group. (2016). African Natural Resources Center: Catalyzing growth and development through effective natural resources management. African Natural Resources Center. https://www.afdb.org/fileadmin/uploads/afdb/Documents/Generic-Documents/AfDB_ANRC_BROCHURE_en.pdf

African Union. (n.d.). Sustainable environment. African Union. Retrieved August 2, 2024, from https://au.int/en/directorates/sustainable-environment

Ahmad, M., Ahmed, Z., Khan, S. A., & Alvarado, R. (2023). Towards environmental sustainability in E− 7 countries: Assessing the roles of natural resources, economic growth, country risk, and energy transition. *Resources Policy*, 82, 103486. DOI: 10.1016/j.resourpol.2023.103486

Auty, R. M. (1993). *Sustaining Development in Mineral Economies: The Resource Curse Thesis*. Routledge.

Avom, D., Bangake, C., & Ndoya, H. (2022). Does bank concentration stem from financial inclusion in Africa? *Applied Economics*, 54(28), 3261–3278. DOI: 10.1080/00036846.2021.2006134

Bangake, C., & Eggoh, J. C. (2012). Pooled Mean Group estimation on international capital mobility in African countries. *Research in Economics*, 66(1), 7–17. DOI: 10.1016/j.rie.2011.06.001

Caglar, A. E., Avci, S. B., Daştan, M., & Destek, M. A. (2024). Investigation of the effect of natural resource dependence on environmental sustainability under the novel load capacity curve hypothesis. *International Journal of Sustainable Development and World Ecology*, 31(4), 431–446. DOI: 10.1080/13504509.2023.2296495

Cai, H. H., Lee, H. F., Khan, N. U., & Yuan, Q. (2024). Are natural resources a curse, a blessing, or a double-edged sword? Implications for environmental sustainability. *Journal of Environmental Management*, 367, 122008. DOI: 10.1016/j.jenvman.2024.122008 PMID: 39079490

Cen, Y., & Yin, J. (2024). Navigating climate challenges: Focusing on the effectiveness of natural resource rents, fintech, green finance, environmental quality, and digitalisation. *Resources Policy*, 95, 105102. DOI: 10.1016/j.resourpol.2024.105102

Chitadze, N. (2023). World Natural Resources and Their Impact on the Environmental Conditions of Our Planet. Www.igi-Global.com. https://www.igi-global.com/chapter/world-natural-resources-and-their-impact-on-the-environmental-conditions-of-our-planet/327102. IGI Global.

Corrado, G., & Corrado, L. (2017). Inclusive finance for inclusive growth and development. *Current Opinion in Environmental Sustainability*, 24, 19–23. DOI: 10.1016/j.cosust.2017.01.013

Corrado, G., & Corrado, L. (2017). Inclusive finance for inclusive growth and development. *Current Opinion in Environmental Sustainability*, 24, 19–23. DOI: 10.1016/j.cosust.2017.01.013

Demirgüç-Kunt, A., Klapper, L., Singer, D., & Ansar, S. (2018). *The Global Findex Database 2017*. World Bank.

Godde, C., Mason-D'Croz, D., Mayberry, D., Thornton, P., & Herrero, M. (2021). Impacts of climate change on the livestock food supply chain; a review of the evidence. *Global Food Security*, 28, 100488. DOI: 10.1016/j.gfs.2020.100488 PMID: 33738188

Hallegatte, S., Rentschler, J., Rozenberg, J., (2020). Adaptation Principles: a Guide for Designing Strategies for Climate Change Adaptation and Resilience.

IPCC. 2014 https://www.ipcc.ch/report/ar5/wg3/

Iyiola, A. O., Akinsorotan, O. A., Ojeleye, A. E., & Fajimolu, A. O. (2023). An overview of environmental resources in Africa: emerging issues and sustainable exploitation. *Sustainable Utilization and Conservation of Africa's Biological Resources and Environment*, 543-570.

Jhariya, M. K., Banerjee, A., & Meena, R. S. (2022). Importance of natural resources conservation: Moving toward the sustainable world. In *Natural resources conservation and advances for sustainability* (pp. 3–27). Elsevier. DOI: 10.1016/B978-0-12-822976-7.00027-2

Kushawaha, J., Borra, S., Kushawaha, A., Singh, G & Singh, P. (2021). Climate change and its impact on natural resources. .DOI: 10.1016/B978-0-12-820200-5.00002-6

Kwilinski, A., Lyulyov, O., & Pimonenko, T. (2023). Spillover effects of green finance on attaining sustainable development: Spatial Durbin model. *Computation (Basel, Switzerland)*, 11(10), 199. DOI: 10.3390/computation11100199

Lee, J. W. (2020). Green finance and sustainable development goals: the case of China. Lee, Jung Wan (2020). Green Finance and Sustainable Dev. Goals: The Case of China. *J. Asian Finance Eco. Business*, 7(7), 577–586. DOI: 10.13106/jafeb.2020.vol7.no7.577

Li, X., Yang, J., & Zeng, N. (2024). Natural resource rent and inclusive finance: An institutional perspective. *Economic Change and Restructuring*, 57(1), 45. DOI: 10.1007/s10644-024-09593-1

Mahoro, G. (2015). *Organic matter fuel briquettes as an alternative to charcoal: an initiative for forest conservation* (Doctoral dissertation, Kampala International University, School of Natural and Applied Sciences).

Malhi, G. S., Kaur, M., & Kaushik, P. (2020). Impact of Climate Change on Agriculture and Its Mitigation Strategies: A Review. *Sustainability (Basel)*, 13(3), 1318. DOI: 10.3390/su13031318

Mchakulu, M. G. (2019). *Rural Malawi Households' Environmental Concern and Consciousness About Appropriate Energy Consumption Practices Amidst Prevailing Socio-Economic Conditions*. University of Pretoria.

Nchofoung, T. N., Asongu, S. A., & Tchamyou, V. S. (2024). Gender political inclusion and inclusive finance in Africa. *Economic Systems*, 48(2), 101187. DOI: 10.1016/j.ecosys.2024.101187

Nyakuwanika, M., van der Poll, H. M., & van der Poll, J. A. (2021). A conceptual framework for greener goldmining through environmental management accounting practices (Emaps): The case of zimbabwe. *Sustainability (Basel)*, 13(18), 10466. DOI: 10.3390/su131810466

Oeurng, C., Cochrane, T. A., Chung, S., Kondolf, M. G., Piman, T., & Arias, M. E. (2019). Assessing climate change impacts on river flows in the Tonle Sap Lake Basin, Cambodia. *Water (Basel)*, 11(3), 618. DOI: 10.3390/w11030618

Owusu, E. A. (2024). Financial inclusion and economic growth the moderating role of financial stability in Sub-Saharan Africa.

Paul, C. J., Weinthal, E. S., Bellemare, M. F., & Jeuland, M. A. (2016). Social capital, trust, and adaptation to climate change: Evidence from rural Ethiopia. *Global Environmental Change*, 36, 124–138. DOI: 10.1016/j.gloenvcha.2015.12.003

Pesaran, M. H., Shin, Y., & Smith, R. P. (1999). Pooled mean group estimation of dynamic heterogeneous panels. *Journal of the American Statistical Association*, 94(446), 621–634. DOI: 10.1080/01621459.1999.10474156

Pesaran, M. H., & Smith, R. (1995). Estimating long-run relationships from dynamic heterogeneous panels. *Journal of Econometrics*, 68(1), 79–113. DOI: 10.1016/0304-4076(94)01644-F

Pu, G., Wong, W., Du, Q., Al Shraah, A., Alromaihi, A., & Muda, I. (2024). Asymmetric impact of natural resources, fintech, and digital banking on climate change and environmental sustainability in BRICS countries. *Resources Policy*, 91, 104872. DOI: 10.1016/j.resourpol.2024.104872

Sadiq, M., Paramaiah, C., Dong, Z., Nawaz, M. A., & Shukurullaevich, N. K. (2024). Role of fintech, green finance, and natural resource rents in sustainable climate change in China. Mediating role of environmental regulations and government interventions in the pre-post COVID eras. *Resources Policy*, 88, 104494. DOI: 10.1016/j.resourpol.2023.104494

Shammin, M. R., Haque, A. K. E., & Faisal, I. M. (2022). A Framework for Climate Resilient Community-Based Adaptation. In Haque, A. K. E., Mukhopadhyay, P., Nepal, M., & Shammin, M. R. (Eds.), *Climate Change and Community Resilience*. Springer., DOI: 10.1007/978-981-16-0680-9_2

Singh, N. P., Bantilan, C., & Byjesh, K. (2014). Vulnerability and policy relevance to drought in the semi-arid tropics of Asia – A retrospective analysis. *Weather and Climate Extremes*, 3, 54–61. DOI: 10.1016/j.wace.2014.02.002

Sun, T. (2024). Role of inclusive finance on oil resource production targets: How fiscal pressures influence natural resources policy and green recovery in Gulf countries. *Resources Policy*, 88, 104337. DOI: 10.1016/j.resourpol.2023.104337

Tadesse, B., & Ahmed, M. (2023). Impact of adoption of climate smart agricultural practices to minimize production risk in Ethiopia: A systematic review. *Journal of Agriculture and Food Research*, 13, 100655. DOI: 10.1016/j.jafr.2023.100655

Tiony, O. (2023). The Impact of Digital Financial Services on Financial Inclusion in Kenya. *American Journal of Industrial and Business Management*, 13(6), 593–628. DOI: 10.4236/ajibm.2023.136035

Ulucak, R., & Ozcan, B. (2020). Relationship between energy consumption and environmental sustainability in OECD countries: The role of natural resources rents. *Resources Policy*, 69, 101803. DOI: 10.1016/j.resourpol.2020.101803

World Bank. (n.d.). Financial inclusion. World Bank. Retrieved August 2, 2024, from https://www.worldbank.org/en/topic/financialinclusion

Zheng, Z., Lisovskiy, A., Vasa, L., Strielkowski, W., & Yang, Y. (2023). Resources curse and sustainable development perspective: Fresh evidence from oil rich countries. *Resources Policy*, 85, 103698. DOI: 10.1016/j.resourpol.2023.103698

Zhou, X., Tang, X., & Zhang, R. (2020). Impact of green finance on economic development and environmental quality: A study based on provincial panel data from China. *Environmental Science and Pollution Research International*, 27(16), 19915–19932. DOI: 10.1007/s11356-020-08383-2 PMID: 32232752

Compilation of References

Abate, G., Basile, I., & Ferrari, P. (2024). The integration of environmental, social and governance criteria in portfolio optimization: An empirical analysis. *Corporate Social Responsibility and Environmental Management, 31*(3), 2054–2065. *Scopus.* Advance online publication. DOI: 10.1002/csr.2682

Abbass, K., Qasim, M. Z., Song, H., Murshed, M., Mahmood, H., & Younis, I. (2022). A review of the global climate change impacts, adaptation, and sustainable mitigation measures. *Environmental Science and Pollution Research International*, 29(28), 42539–42559. DOI: 10.1007/s11356-022-19718-6 PMID: 35378646

Abeysekera, I. (2023). Integrating First Nations peoples' cultural capital for sustainable development. *Sustainable Development (Bradford)*, 32(1), 43–56. DOI: 10.1002/sd.2643

Abgaz, Y., Rocha Souza, R., Methuku, J., Koch, G., & Dorn, A. (2021). A Methodology for Semantic Enrichment of Cultural Heritage Images Using Artificial Intelligence Technologies. *Journal of Imaging*, 7(8), 121. Advance online publication. DOI: 10.3390/jimaging7080121 PMID: 34460757

Abhilash, S., Shenoy, S. S., Shetty, D. K., Lobo, L. S., & N, S. K. (2023). Green Bond as an Innovative Financial Instrument in the Indian Financial Market: Insights from Systematic Literature Review Approach. *SAGE Open*, 13(2), 21582440231178783. DOI: 10.1177/21582440231178783

ABSA. (2023). *Indices exchange rates.* Retrieved January 29, 2022, from https://www.absa.co.za/indices/exchange-rates/

Acemoglu, D., & Restrepo, P. (2019). The wrong kind of AI? Artificial intelligence and the future of labour demand. *Cambridge Journal of Regions, Economy and Society*, 13(1), 25–35. DOI: 10.1093/cjres/rsz022

Achugamonu, U. B., Adetiloye, K. A., Adegbite, E. O., Babajide, A. A., & Akintola, F. A. (2020). Financial exclusion of bankable adults: Implication on financial inclusive growth among twenty-seven SSA countries. *Cogent Social Sciences*, 6(1), 1–15. DOI: 10.1080/23311886.2020.1730046

Adegbite, O. O., & Machethe, C. L. (2020). Bridging the financial inclusion gender gap in smallholder agriculture in Nigeria: An untapped potential for sustainable development. *World Development*, 127, 104755. DOI: 10.1016/j.worlddev.2019.104755

Adeoti, O. O. (2013). Challenges to the efficient use of Point of Sale (PoS) terminals in Nigeria. *African Journal of Business Management*, 7(28), 2801–2806. DOI: 10.5897/AJBM12.1129

Adil Rasheed, Omer San, and Trond Kvamsdal. (2020) Digital twin: Values, challenges and enablers from a modeling perspective. *IEEE Access 8*, 21980–22012. DOI: 10.1109/ACCESS.2020.2970143

Admin. (2024, April 16). Indigenous Water Conservation Methods: Unraveling the Role of Traditional Knowledge in Sustainable Resource Management - Welcome to Areness Foundation. Welcome to Areness Foundation. https://www.arenessfoundation.com/indigenous-water-conservation-methods-unraveling-the-role-of-traditional-knowledge-in-sustainable-resource-management/

Advancing progress to achieve UN SDG 6 for First Nations through advocacy with the Canadian Government | Department of Economic and Social Affairs. (2024, February 7). Un.org. https://sdgs.un.org/partnerships/advancing-progress-achieve-un-sdg-6-first-nations-through-advocacy-canadian-government

Afolabi, A. O., Ojelabi, R. A., Oyeyipo, O., Tunji-Olayeni, P. F., Omuh, I. O., & Amusan, L. M. (2017). Integrating software development courses in the construction curriculum. *The Turkish Online Journal of Educational Technology*, •••, 215–225.

African Development Bank Group. (2016). African Natural Resources Center: Catalyzing growth and development through effective natural resources management. African Natural Resources Center. https://www.afdb.org/fileadmin/uploads/afdb/Documents/Generic-Documents/AfDB_ANRC_BROCHURE_en.pdf

African Union. (n.d.). Sustainable environment. African Union. Retrieved August 2, 2024, from https://au.int/en/directorates/sustainable-environment

Agarwal, K., & Nandram, S. S. (2021). Domestic products in Swadeshi-Global entrepreneurship for sustainable socioeconomic growth. *World Review of Entrepreneurship, Management and Sustainable Development*, 17(5), 624–646. DOI: 10.1504/WREMSD.2021.117445

Agarwal, R., & Basu, S. (2021). Policy frameworks for blockchain adoption in rural economies: Lessons for India. *Journal of Public Policy & Marketing*, 40(3), 388–403.

Ahmad, D., Lutfiani, N., Ahmad, A. D. A. R., & Rahardja, U. (2021). Blockchain Technology Immutability Framework Design in E-Government. [Public Administration Journal]. *Jurnal Administrasi Publik*, 11(1), 32–41.

Ahmad, M., Ahmed, Z., Khan, S. A., & Alvarado, R. (2023). Towards environmental sustainability in E– 7 countries: Assessing the roles of natural resources, economic growth, country risk, and energy transition. *Resources Policy*, 82, 103486. DOI: 10.1016/j.resourpol.2023.103486

Ahmed, S. (2020). Alternative credit scoring – a double-edged sword. In *Journal of Indian Law And Society* (Vols. 2–2).

Ahn, S. (2021). Digital finance and the future of financial inclusion. *Journal of Financial Innovation*, 7(3), 445–463.

Ahunov, M. (2018). *Financial inclusion, regulation, and literacy in Uzbekistan, ADBI Working Paper*, No. 858, Asian Development Bank Institute (ADBI), Tokyo. Accessed on March. 28. 2023. https://hdl.handle.net/10419/19027

Ajaps, S., & Mbah, M. F. (2022). Deconstructing Community-Based Research for Sustainable Development: The Role of Indigenous Knowledge Holders. *World Sustainability Series*, 65–76. DOI: 10.1007/s11160-021-09661-z

Akin-Adetoro, A., & Kabanda, S. (2021). Factors affecting the adoption of BYOD in South African small and medium enterprises. *The Electronic Journal on Information Systems in Developing Countries*, 87(6), 1–14. DOI: 10.1002/isd2.12185

Akin, I., & Akin, M. (2024). Promoting sustainable practices through green investments in the United Kingdom real estate industry. *Sustainable Development (Bradford)*, sd.3194. Advance online publication. DOI: 10.1002/sd.3194

Akinmolayan, E. S., Hingston, C. A., Akpan, U. J., & Arise, O. A. (2024). Towards decolonisation of primary school education in south africa. [SAJCE]. *South African Journal of Childhood Education*, 14(1). Advance online publication. DOI: 10.4102/sajce.v14i1.1440

Albort-Morant, G., Henseler, J., Leal-Millán, A., & Cepeda-Carrión, G. (2017). Mapping the Field: A Bibliometric Analysis of Green Innovation. *Sustainability (Basel)*, 9(6), 1011. DOI: 10.3390/su9061011

Ali Dorri, Salil S Kanhere, Raja Jurdak, and Praveen Gauravaram. (2019) LSB: A Lightweight Scalable Blockchain for IoT security and anonymity. *J. Parallel and Distrib. Comput.* 134, 180–197. DOI: 10.1016/j.jpdc.2019.08.005

Ali, O., Momin, M., Shrestha, A., Das, R., Alhajj, F., & Dwivedi, Y. K. (2023). A review of the key challenges of non-fungible tokens. *Technological Forecasting and Social Change*, 187, 122248. DOI: 10.1016/j.techfore.2022.122248

Ali, S. H., & Grewal, A. S. (2006). The ecology and economy of indigenous resistance: Divergent perspectives on mining in New Caledonia. *The Contemporary Pacific*, 18(2), 361–392. DOI: 10.1353/cp.2006.0001

Allen, D. W. (2022). DeFi and the promise of decentralized finance. *Journal of Financial Technology*, 14(1), 102–118.

Allied Market Research. (2023). Robo Advisory Market Outlook–2027. DOI: 10.2139/ssrn.2238

Almansoori A.NobaneeH.NobaneeH. (2019). *How Sustainability Contributes to Shared Value Creation and Firms' Value*. SSRN. https://ssrn.com/abstract=3472411 or http://dx.doi.org/ doi:10.2139/ssrn.3472411

Alonso, M. P., Gargallo, P., López-Escolano, C., Miguel, J., & Salvador, M. (2023). Financial exclusion, depopulation, and ageing: An analysis based on panel data. *Journal of Rural Studies*, 103, 1–15. DOI: 10.1016/j.jrurstud.2023.103105

Alshater, M. M., Atayah, O. F., & Hamdan, A. (2023). Journal of Sustainable Finance and Investment: A bibliometric analysis. *Journal of Sustainable Finance and Investment, 13*(3), 1131–1152. *Scopus*. Advance online publication. DOI: 10.1080/20430795.2021.1947116

Altman, J. C. (2016). Indigenous Policy: Economic Development and Indigenous Australia: Contestations over Property, Institutions and Rights. *The Australian Journal of Agricultural and Resource Economics*, 60(3), 460–470. DOI: 10.1111/1467-8489.12156

Alzamel, H. A., Alshabanah, M., & Alsmadi, M. (2019). Point of Sale (PoS) Network with embedded fingerprint biometric authentication. [IJSRST]. *International Journal of Scientific Research in Science and Technology*, 6(5), 95–223. https://papers.ssrn.com/sol3/papers.cfm?abstract_id=3464825. DOI: 10.32628/IJSRST119659

Amaeshi, K. M., Adi, A. B. C., Ogbechie, C., & Amao, O. O. (2006). Corporate Social Responsibility in Nigeria: Western Mimicry or Indigenous Influences? SSRN Electronic Journal. DOI: 10.2139/ssrn.896500

Anaya, S. J., & Puig, S. (2017). MITIGATING STATE SOVEREIGNTY: THE DUTY TO CONSULT WITH INDIGENOUS PEOPLES. *University of Toronto Law Journal*, 67(4), 435–464. DOI: 10.3138/utlj.67.1

Anderson, R. B., & Dana, L. P. (2006). Indigenous entrepreneurship: An emerging field of research. *Journal of Small Business and Entrepreneurship*, 19(1), 1–17.

Anderson, R. B., Dana, L. P., & Dana, T. E. (2006). Indigenous Land Rights, Entrepreneurship, and Economic Development in Canada: "Opting-in" to the Global Economy. *Journal of World Business*, 41(1), 45–55. DOI: 10.1016/j.jwb.2005.10.005

Anderson, R. B., Kayseas, B., Dana, L. P., & Hindle, K. (2004). Indigenous Land Claims and Economic Development: The Canadian Experience. *American Indian Quarterly*, 28(3), 634–648. DOI: 10.1353/aiq.2004.0089

Andrea Castellani, Sebastian Schmitt, and Stefano Squartini. (2020) Real-World Anomaly Detection by using Digital Twin Systems and Weakly-Supervised Learning. *IEEE Transactions on Industrial Informatics*, 1–1. https://doi.org/DOI: 10.1109/TII.2020.3019788

Andrews, J. E. (2003, January 1). *An author co-citation analysis of medical informatics*. PubMed. Retrieved November 11, 2024, from https://pubmed.ncbi.nlm.nih.gov/12568157

Annual Report, M. S. M. E. 23-24). *Ministry of MSME, India*. https://www.msme.gov.in/sites/default/files/FINALMSMEANNUALREPORT2023-24ENGLISH.pdf

Ansell, M., & Clapham, K. (2023). Indigenous climate leadership: Advancing adaptation strategies through traditional ecological knowledge. *Environmental Policy and Practice*, 15(3), 56–78.

Aoki, N. (2021). The importance of the assurance that "humans are still in the decision loop" for public trust in artificial intelligence: Evidence from an online experiment. *Computers in Human Behavior*, 114, 106572. DOI: 10.1016/j.chb.2020.106572

Apostolakis, G., Kraanen, F., & van Dijk, G. (2016). Pension beneficiaries' and fund managers' perceptions of responsible investment: A focus group study. *Corporate Governance (Bingley), 16*(1), 1–20. *Scopus*. Advance online publication. DOI: 10.1108/CG-05-2015-0070

Aragon, F. M., & Kessler, A. S. (2020). Resource windfalls, public investment, and Indigenous communities. *Journal of Development Economics*, 144, 102450.

Aravind Ramachandran, Dr Kantarcioglu, et al. (2017) *Using blockchain and smart contracts for secure data provenance management*. arXiv:1709.10000

Argent, N. M., & Rolley, F. (2000). Financial exclusion in rural and remote New South Wales, Australia: A geography of bank branch rationalisation, 1981–98. *Australian Geographical Studies*, 38(2), 182–203. DOI: 10.1111/1467-8470.00110

Arias Fogliano de Souza Cunha, F., & Samanez, C. P. (2013). Performance Analysis of Sustainable Investments in the Brazilian Stock Market: A Study About the Corporate Sustainability Index (ISE). *Journal of Business Ethics, 117*(1), 19–36. *Scopus.* Advance online publication. DOI: 10.1007/s10551-012-1484-2

Aristei, D., & Gallo, M. (2024). Gender-related effects of financial knowledge and confidence on preferences for ethical intermediaries and sustainable investments. *International Journal of Bank Marketing, 42*(3), 486–512. *Scopus.* Advance online publication. DOI: 10.1108/IJBM-06-2023-0355

Arner, D. W., Zetzsche, D. A., Buckley, R. P., & Barberis, J. N. (2017). FinTech and RegTech Financial Stability. *Georgetown Journal of International Affairs*, 18(3), 47–58. DOI: 10.1353/gia.2017.0036

Arora, J., & Chakraborty, M. (2023). Role of financial literacy in investment choices of financial consumers: An insight from India. *International Journal of Social Economics*, 50(3), 377–397. DOI: 10.1108/IJSE-12-2021-0764

Arribas, I., Espinós-Vañó, M. D., García, F., & Tamosiuniene, R. (2019). Negative screening and sustainable portfolio diversification. *Entrepreneurship and Sustainability Issues, 6*(4), 1566–1586. *Scopus.* Advance online publication. DOI: 10.9770/jesi.2019.6.4(2)

Arruda, G. M. (2018). Arctic resource development: A sustainable prosperity project of co-management. In *Renewable Energy for the Arctic* (pp. 106–117). Routledge. DOI: 10.4324/9781351173322-6

Ashta, A., & Herrmann, H. (2021). Artificial intelligence and fintech: An overview of opportunities and risks for banking, investments, and microfinance. *Strategic Change*, 30(3), 211–222. https://doi.org/ https://doi.org/10.1002/jsc.2404. DOI: 10.1002/jsc.2404

Atana, R., Razali, F. A., Said, J., & Zainun, S. (2016). Environmental, Social, and Governance (ESG) Disclosure and Its Effect on Firm's Performance: A Comparative Study. *IJEM*, 10(S2), 355–375.

Attoukou, M., & Nchare, K. (2022). Financial exclusion and poverty reduction in Benin. *Asian Journal of Economics and Empirical Research*, 9(2), 121–131. DOI: 10.20448/ajeer.v9i2.4146

Auer, R., Cornelli, G., & Frost, J. (2020). Rise of the central bank digital currencies: Drivers, approaches, and technologies. BIS Working Papers, 880.

Auty, R. M. (1993). *Sustaining Development in Mineral Economies: The Resource Curse Thesis*. Routledge.

Avendus. (2023). MSME Lending, unlocking potential realizing dreams. In *Avendus*. https://www.avendus .com/crypted_pdf_path/msme-lending-report-formattedvf-img-642a719b97ccc-.pdf

Avom, D., Bangake, C., & Ndoya, H. (2022). Does bank concentration stem from financial inclusion in Africa? *Applied Economics*, 54(28), 3261–3278. DOI: 10.1080/00036846.2021.2006134

Baheti, S. S., & Lenka, U. (2021). Sustainable innovation for sustainable business performance-a systematic review of recent literature (2008-2018). *International Journal of Business Excellence*, 23(4), 517–545. DOI: 10.1504/IJBEX.2021.114733

Baheti, S. S., & Lenka, U. (2023). A scientometric evaluation of International Journal of Business Innovation and Research:(2006-2019). *International Journal of Business Innovation and Research*, 30(3), 283–322. DOI: 10.1504/IJBIR.2023.129362

Bahoo, S., Cucculelli, M., Goga, X., & Mondolo, J. (2024). Artificial intelligence in Finance: A comprehensive review through bibliometric and content analysis. *SN Business & Economics*, 4(2), 23. Advance online publication. DOI: 10.1007/s43546-023-00618-x

Bai, C., Dallasega, P., Orzes, G., & Sarkis, J. (2020). Industry 4.0 technologies assessment: A sustainability perspective. *International Journal of Production Economics*, 229, 107776. DOI: 10.1016/j.ijpe.2020.107776

Baker, T. (2018). Regulating Robo Advice Across the Financial Services Industry Regulating Robo Advice Across the. Penn Law: Legal Scholarship Repository. DOI: 10.4337/9781849809108

Baker, H. K., Kumar, S., Goyal, K., & Sharma, A. (2021). International review of financial analysis: A retrospective evaluation between 1992 and 2020. *International Review of Financial Analysis*, 78, 101946. DOI: 10.1016/j.irfa.2021.101946

Baker, H. K., Kumar, S., & Pandey, N. (2020). A bibliometric analysis of managerial finance: A retrospective. *Managerial Finance*, 46(11), 1495–1517. DOI: 10.1108/MF-06-2019-0277

Balachandran, G. (2023). Debasing indigenous statehood: Sovereign monies, markets and imperial power in the Indian subcontinent, c. 1893–1905. *Past & Present*, 259(1), 117–154. DOI: 10.1093/pastj/gtac017

Banerjee, S. B. (2019). Decolonizing management theory: A critical perspective on Indigenous management practices. *Journal of Business Ethics*, 161(1), 27–44.

Bangake, C., & Eggoh, J. C. (2012). Pooled Mean Group estimation on international capital mobility in African countries. *Research in Economics*, 66(1), 7–17. DOI: 10.1016/j.rie.2011.06.001

Bansal, S., Rathi, P., Agarwal, R., & Ahluwalia, R. (2024). Leveraging AI to Enhance the Global Mobility Experience: Trends in Indian Higher Education. In Transforming the Financial Landscape With ICTs (pp. 108-133). IGI Global.

Barbara Rita Barricelli, Elena Casiraghi, and Daniela Fogli. (2019) A Survey on Digital Twin: Definitions, Characteristics, Applications, and Design Implications. *IEEE Access 7*, 167653–167671. DOI: 10.1109/ACCESS.2019.2953499

Barber, B. M., Morse, A., & Yasuda, A. (2021). Impact investing. *Journal of Financial Economics, 139*(1), 162–185. *Scopus.* Advance online publication. DOI: 10.1016/j.jfineco.2020.07.008

Bargh, M. (2007). Maori development and neoliberalism in Aotearoa/New Zealand. *Alternatives*, 32(3), 297–314.

Bargh, M. (Ed.). (2014). *A Hidden Economy: Māori in the Contemporary Economy*. Huia Publishers.

Barraclough, A. D., Sakiyama, M., Schultz, L., & Måren, I. E. (2021). *"Stewards of the future: accompanying the rising tide of young voices by setting youth-inclusive research agendas in sustainability research"*. *Sustainable Earth* (Vol. 4). Springer., DOI: 10.1186/s42055-021-00041-w

Bartlett, C., & Green, L. (2024). Empowering Indigenous resilience: Innovations in renewable energy governance. *Renewable Energy and Society*, 10(2), 113–131.

Basak, S., Basu, P., Avittathur, B., & Sikdar, S. (2024). Corrigendum: Manufacturer driven strategic coordination as a response to "showrooming.". *Decision Support Systems*, 178, 114120. DOI: 10.1016/j.dss.2023.114120

Basha, M. J., Gupta, A., Raphael, P. D., Rajeev, V., & Rao, R. (2021). The Role of Digital Platforms in Revolutionizing the Lending Sector. *International Journal of Innovative Research*, 10(6), 6529–6536. DOI: 10.15680/IJIRSET.2021.1006354

Becker, M., Beketov, M., & Wittke, M. (2021). Machine Learning in Automated Asset Management Processes 4.1. *Die Unternehmung*, 75(3), 411–431. DOI: 10.5771/0042-059X-2021-3-411

Beckett, R. C., & O'Loughlin, A. (2024). The utility of indigenous knowledge in the pursuit of a UN sustainable development goal. *Collective Intelligence*, 3(2), 26339137241241295. Advance online publication. DOI: 10.1177/26339137241241295

Beketov, M., Lehmann, K., & Wittke, M. (2018). Robo Advisors: Quantitative methods inside the robots. *Journal of Asset Management*, 19(6), 363–370. DOI: 10.1057/s41260-018-0092-9

Belanche, D., Casaló, L. V., & Flavián, C. (2019). Artificial Intelligence in FinTech: Understanding robo-advisors adoption among customers. *Industrial Management & Data Systems*, 119(7), 1411–1430. DOI: 10.1108/IMDS-08-2018-0368

Belfer, E., Ford, J. D., Maillet, M., Araos, M., & Flynn, M. (2019). Pursuing an indigenous platform: Exploring opportunities and constraints for indigenous participation in the UNFCCC. *Global Environmental Politics*, 19(1), 12–33. DOI: 10.1162/glep_a_00489

Bell, K. (2017). 'Living well' as a path to social, ecological and economic sustainability. *Urban Planning*, 2(4), 19–33. DOI: 10.17645/up.v2i4.1006

Beltrame, F., Grassetti, L., Bertinetti, G. S., & Sclip, A. (2023). Relationship lending, access to credit and entrepreneurial orientation as cornerstones of venture financing. *Journal of Small Business and Enterprise Development*, 30(1), 4–29. DOI: 10.1108/JSBED-07-2021-0281

Belu, M. G. (2019). Application of blockchain in international trade: An overview. *The Romanian Economic Journal*, 22(71), 2–15.

Benedikt Putz, Marietheres Dietz, Philip Empl, and Günther Pernul. (2021) EtherTwin: Blockchain-based Secure Digital Twin Information Management. *Information Processing & Management* 58, 1, 102425. DOI: 10.1016/j.ipm.2020.102425

Bertelli, B., & Torricelli, C. (2024). The trade-off between ESG screening and portfolio diversification in the short and in the long run. *Journal of Economics and Finance.Journal of Economics and Finance*, 48(2), 298–322. Advance online publication. DOI: 10.1007/s12197-023-09652-9

Besser, N., & De Groot, G. (2019). Financial inclusion for Indigenous communities: Challenges and opportunities. *Journal of Social Inclusion*, 10(2), 34–50.

Bhagat, R., & Raju, B. (2022). Digital literacy and financial inclusion: A study on the impact of digital literacy on financial inclusion in rural India. *Journal of Digital and Social Media Marketing*, 10(2), 155–166.

Bhatia, A., Chandani, A., Atiq, R., Mehta, M., & Divekar, R. (2021). Artificial intelligence in financial services: A qualitative research to discover robo-advisory services. *Qualitative Research in Financial Markets*, 13(5), 632–654. DOI: 10.1108/QRFM-10-2020-0199

Bhatore, S., Mohan, L., & Reddy, Y. R. (2020). Machine learning techniques for credit risk evaluation: A systematic literature review. *Journal of Banking and Financial Technology*, 4(1), 111–138. DOI: 10.1007/s42786-020-00020-3

Bhattacharya, S. (2019). Indigenous economic empowerment: Role of inclusive finance. *International Journal of Business and Economic Research*, 8(2), 56–65.

Bhattacharya, S., & Singh, A. (2023). Understanding the digital divide: Implications for financial inclusion in India. *Journal of Rural Studies*, 50, 110–125.

Bhuvaneskumar, A., Sivakumar, V. J., & Pushparaj, N. (2023). Performance assessment and ranking of socially responsible companies in India using FAHP, TOPSIS and Altman Z-score. *Benchmarking, 30*(3), 736–765. *Scopus.* Advance online publication. DOI: 10.1108/BIJ-09-2021-0512

Bianchi, R. J., & Drew, M. E. (2012). Sustainable stock indices and long-term portfolio decisions. *Journal of Sustainable Finance and Investment, 2*(3–4), 303–317. *Scopus.* Advance online publication. DOI: 10.1080/20430795.2012.715577

Biju, A. K. V. N., Thomas, A. S., & Thasneem, J. (2023). Examining the research taxonomy of artificial intelligence, deep learning & machine learning in the financial sphere—A bibliometric analysis. *Quality & Quantity*, 58(1), 849–878. DOI: 10.1007/s11135-023-01673-0 PMID: 37359968

Bilbao-Terol, A., Arenas-Parra, M., & Bilbao-Terol, C. (2023). Measuring the overall efficiency of SRI and conventional mutual funds by a diversification-consistent DEA model. *International Transactions in Operational Research, 30*(5), 2224–2256. *Scopus.* Advance online publication. DOI: 10.1111/itor.12974

Bilbao-Terol, A., Arenas-Parra, M., Cañal-Fernández, V., & Obam-Eyang, P. N. (2018). Multi-criteria analysis of the GRI sustainability reports: An application to Socially Responsible Investment. *Journal of the Operational Research Society, 69*(10), 1576–1598. *Scopus.* Advance online publication. DOI: 10.1057/s41274-017-0229-0

Biswas, S., & Nair, P. R. (2021). Integrating blockchain technology with traditional economic systems: A framework for rural development. *Journal of Rural Studies*, 58, 82–90.

Blakely, E. J. (2014). The future of sustainable economic development in cities. In *Elgar Companion to Sustainable Cities* (pp. 397–412). Edward Elgar Publishing. DOI: 10.4337/9780857939999.00027

Block, J. H., Groh, A. P., Hornuf, L., Vanacker, T. R., & Vismara, S. (2020). The entrepreneurial finance markets of the future: A comparison of crowdfunding and initial coin offerings. *Small Business Economics*, 57(2), 865–882. DOI: 10.1007/s11187-020-00330-2

Bodlani, L. L. (2021). *The impact of spatial inequality on financial inclusion in South Africa*. Masters Dissertation, University of the Western Cape.

Bornmann, L., & Mutz, R. (2015). Growth rates of modern science: A bibliometric analysis based on the number of publications and cited references. *Journal of the Association for Information Science and Technology*, 66(11), 2215–2222. DOI: 10.1002/asi.23329

Brenner, L., & Meyll, T. (2020). Robo-advisors: A substitute for human financial advice? *Journal of Behavioral and Experimental Finance*, 25, 100275. Advance online publication. DOI: 10.1016/j.jbef.2020.100275

Bresnahan, T. F., & Trajtenberg, M. (1995). General purpose technologies 'Engines of growth'? *Journal of Econometrics*, 65(1), 83–108. DOI: 10.1016/0304-4076(94)01598-T

Briefing Note Indigenous Peoples' Rights and the 2030 Agenda. (2017). Office of the High Commission for Human Rights.

Brito-Ramos, S., Cortez, M. C., & Silva, F. (2024). Do Sustainability Signals Diverge? An Analysis of Labeling Schemes for Socially Responsible Investments. *Business and Society, 63*(6), 1380–1425. *Scopus*. Advance online publication. DOI: 10.1177/00076503231204613

Broadus, R. N. (1987). Toward a definition of "bibliometrics". *Scientometrics*, 12(5-6), 373–379. DOI: 10.1007/BF02016680

Brodmann, J., Wuthisatian, P., & Malladi, R. K. (2023). The liquidity, performance and investor preference of socially responsible investments. *Review of Behavioral Finance, 15*(2), 224–239. *Scopus*. Advance online publication. DOI: 10.1108/RBF-09-2021-0191

Brondízio, E. S., Aumeeruddy-Thomas, Y., Bates, P., Carino, J., Fernández-Llamazares, Á., Ferrari, M. F., Galvin, K., Reyes-García, V., McElwee, P., Molnár, Z., Samakov, A., & Shrestha, U. B. (2021). Locally Based, Regionally Manifested, and Globally Relevant: Indigenous and Local Knowledge, Values, and Practices for Nature. *Annual Review of Environment and Resources, 46*(Volume 46, 2021), 481–509. https://doi.org/https://doi.org/10.1146/annurev-environ-012220-012127

Brookes, B. C. (1969). Bradford's Law and the Bibliography of Science. *Nature*, 224(5223), 953–956. DOI: 10.1038/224953a0 PMID: 4902657

Brown, J. A., Lewans, M., Menon, D., & Nykiforuk, C. I. (2024). Advancing socio-ecological considerations in impact assessment of extractive industries: A realist interview study in the Canadian context. *Environmental Science & Policy*, 153, 103677. DOI: 10.1016/j.envsci.2024.103677

Brunen, A.-C., & Laubach, O. (2022). Do sustainable consumers prefer socially responsible investments? A study among the users of robo advisors. *Journal of Banking and Finance, 136.Journal of Banking & Finance*, 136, 106314. Advance online publication. DOI: 10.1016/j.jbankfin.2021.106314

Buchanan, B. G. PhD, FRSA & The Alan Turing Institute. (2019). *Artificial intelligence in finance*. https://www.turing.ac.uk/sites/default/files/2019-04/artificial_intelligence_in_finance_-_turing_report_0.pdf

Buergelt, P. T., Mahypilama, L. E., & Paton, D. (2022). The Value of Sophisticated Indigenous Ways of Being-Knowing-Doing Towards Transforming Human Resource Development in Ways that Contribute to Organizations Thriving and Addressing Our Existential Crises.

Buergelt, P. T., Mahypilama, L. E., & Paton, D. (2022, December). The Value of Sophisticated Indigenous Ways of Being-Knowing-Doing Towards Transforming Human Resource Development in Ways that Contribute to Organizations Thriving and Addressing Our Existential Crises. *Human Resource Development Review*, 21(4), 391–409. DOI: 10.1177/15344843221134351

Burack, J. A., Bombay, A., & Kirmayer, L. J. (2024). Cultural continuity, identity, and resilience among indigenous youth: Honoring the legacies of Michael Chandler and Christopher Lalonde. *Transcultural Psychiatry*, 61(3), 301–312. Advance online publication. DOI: 10.1177/13634615241257349 PMID: 39056364

Buthelezi, M. M., Zulu, Z. P., & Nkalanga, D. S. (2024). The impacts of social exclusion and inequality in rural communities: A qualitative study in Limpopo Province, South Africa. *International Journal of Development and Sustainability*, 13(5), 330–345.

Bvuma, S., & Marnewick, C. (2020). An information and communication technology adoption framework for small, medium and micro-enterprises operating in townships South Africa. *The Southern African Journal of Entrepreneurship and Small Business Management*, 12(1). Advance online publication. DOI: 10.4102/sajesbm.v12i1.318

Caferra, R., & Falcone, P. M. (2023). From the "age of instability" to the "age of responsibility": Economic uncertainty and sustainable investments. *Journal of Economic Studies, 50*(6), 1297–1316. *Scopus.* Advance online publication. DOI: 10.1108/JES-06-2022-0353

Caglar, A. E., Avci, S. B., Daştan, M., & Destek, M. A. (2024). Investigation of the effect of natural resource dependence on environmental sustainability under the novel load capacity curve hypothesis. *International Journal of Sustainable Development and World Ecology*, 31(4), 431–446. DOI: 10.1080/13504509.2023.2296495

Cai, H. H., Lee, H. F., Khan, N. U., & Yuan, Q. (2024). Are natural resources a curse, a blessing, or a double-edged sword? Implications for environmental sustainability. *Journal of Environmental Management*, 367, 122008. DOI: 10.1016/j.jenvman.2024.122008 PMID: 39079490

Callon, M., Courtial, J., Turner, W. A., & Bauin, S. (1983). From translations to problematic networks: An introduction to co-word analysis. *Social Sciences Information. Information Sur les Sciences Sociales*, 22(2), 191–235. DOI: 10.1177/053901883022002003

Campbell, T., & Bourbonnais, V. (2023). From Compliance To Inclusion: Implementing An Equity, Diversity And Inclusion Action Plan For A Federal Funding Program In CANADA. [R]. *The Journal of Research Administration*, 54(2), 37–53.

Capelle-Blancard, G., & Monjon, S. (2014). The Performance of Socially Responsible Funds: Does the Screening Process Matter? *European Financial Management, 20*(3), 494–520. *Scopus.* Advance online publication. DOI: 10.1111/j.1468-036X.2012.00643.x

Carbone, V., Moatti, V., & Vinzi, V. E. (2012). Mapping Corporate Responsibility and Sustainable Supply Chains: An Exploratory Perspective. *Business Strategy and the Environment, 21*(7), 475–494. *Scopus.* Advance online publication. DOI: 10.1002/bse.1736

Carlsson Hauff, J., & Nilsson, J. (2023). Is ESG mutual fund quality in the eye of the beholder? An experimental study of investor responses to ESG fund strategies. *Business Strategy and the Environment, 32*(4), 1189–1202. *Scopus.* Advance online publication. DOI: 10.1002/bse.3181

Carroll, W. K., & Ratner, R. S. (2001). Sustaining oppositional cultures in 'post-socialist' times: A comparative study of three social movements. *Sociology*, 35(3), 655–672.

Carvalho, L., Mota, C., & Ramos, P. (2024). Socially Responsible Investment Funds—An Analysis Applied to Funds Domiciled in the Portuguese and Spanish Markets. *Risks, 12*(1). *Scopus.*, 12(1), 9. Advance online publication. DOI: 10.3390/risks12010009

Catalano, F., Nasello, L., & Guterding, D. (2024). Quantum Computing Approach to Realistic ESG-Friendly Stock Portfolios. *Risks, 12*(4). *Scopus.*, 12(4), 66. Advance online publication. DOI: 10.3390/risks12040066

Catalini, C., & Gans, J. S. (2019). Some simple economics of the blockchain. *Communications of the ACM*, 63(7), 80–91. DOI: 10.1145/3359552

Cen, Y., & Yin, J. (2024). Navigating climate challenges: Focusing on the effectiveness of natural resource rents, fintech, green finance, environmental quality, and digitalisation. *Resources Policy*, 95, 105102. DOI: 10.1016/j.resourpol.2024.105102

Chakraborty, R., & Basu, S. (2022). Digital finance adoption in rural India: Overcoming barriers through strategic management. *Journal of Rural Management*, 16(2), 176–189.

Chambers, R. (1997). *Whose reality counts? Putting the first last.* Intermediate Technology Publications. DOI: 10.3362/9781780440453

Chanco, A. J., Albia, B., & Blanza, M. (2023). From Icons to AI: Evolution of Imagery in Religious Communication. *Religion and Social Communication*, 21(2), 270–293. Advance online publication. DOI: 10.62461/BMA112923

Chang, C. E., Krueger, T. M., & Witte, H. D. (2020). Relative importance of sustainability measures and costs in mutual fund selection. *Journal of Wealth Management, 23*(1), 32–46. *Scopus.* Advance online publication. DOI: 10.3905/jwm.2020.1.103

Chang, X., Fu, K., Jin, Y., & Liem, P. F. (2022). Sustainable Finance: ESG/CSR, Firm Value, and Investment Returns*. *Asia-Pacific Journal of Financial Studies, 51*(3), 325–371. *Scopus.* Advance online publication. DOI: 10.1111/ajfs.12379

Chan, K. M. A., Boyd, D. R., Gould, R. K., Jetzkowitz, J., Liu, J., Muraca, B., Naidoo, R., Olmsted, P., Satterfield, T., Selomane, O., Singh, G. G., Sumaila, R., Ngo, H. T., Boedhihartono, A. K., Agard, J., de Aguiar, A. P. D., Armenteras, D., Balint, L., Barrington-Leigh, C., & Brondízio, E. S. (2020). Levers and leverage points for pathways to sustainability. *People and Nature*, 2(3), 693–717. DOI: 10.1002/pan3.10124

Chanza, N., & De Wit, A. (2016). Enhancing climate governance through indigenous knowledge: Case in sustainability science. *South African Journal of Science*, 112(3/4), 7. Advance online publication. scielo.org.za. DOI: 10.17159/sajs.2016/20140286

Chen, Y., & Volz, U. (2021). Scaling up sustainable investment through blockchainbased project bonds. *Development Policy Review*, 40(3), e12582. DOI: 10.1111/dpr.12582

Chen, L. Y., Wu, Z., & Yang, H. (2019). How valuable is FinTech innovation? *Review of Financial Studies*, 32(5), 2062–2106. DOI: 10.1093/rfs/hhy130

Chen, X., Dong, X., & Ma, C. (2024). Investing with Purpose: The Role of CSR in Enhancing Chinese Firms' Performance in Japan. *Journal of the Knowledge Economy.Journal of the Knowledge Economy*. Advance online publication. DOI: 10.1007/s13132-024-01875-3

Chhabra, A. B. (2005). Beyond Markowitz : THEORY AND REALITY A Comprehensive Wealth Allocation Framework for Individual Investors. *The Journal of Wealth Management*, 8(1), 8–34. DOI: 10.3905/jwm.2005.470606

Chhatwani, M. (2022). Does robo-advisory increase retirement worry? A causal explanation. *Managerial Finance*, 48(4), 611–628. DOI: 10.1108/MF-05-2021-0195

Chikwira, C., & Rawjee, V. P. (2022). Innovative Financing Strategies in the Small and Medium Business Sector, Tapping the Right Sources. *Journal of Accounting and Management*, 12(3), 7–17.

Chitadze, N. (2023). World Natural Resources and Their Impact on the Environmental Conditions of Our Planet. Www.igi-Global.com. https://www.igi-global.com/chapter/world-natural-resources-and-their-impact-on-the-environmental-conditions-of-our-planet/327102. IGI Global.

Chitimira, H., & Magau, P. (2022). A Legal Conspectus of Some Role-Players in the Development of Financial Education in South Africa. *EIRP Proceedings, 17*(1), 360-375.

Chiu, A. S., & Yong, G. (2004). On the industrial ecology potential in Asian developing countries. *Journal of Cleaner Production*, 12(8-10), 1037–1045. DOI: 10.1016/j.jclepro.2004.02.013

Chiu, J., & Koeppl, T. V. (2019). Blockchain-based settlement for asset trading. *Review of Financial Studies*, 32(5), 1716–1753. DOI: 10.1093/rfs/hhy122

Chohan, U. W. (2021). Non-Fungible Tokens: Blockchains, Scarcity, and Value. *Critical Blockchain Research Initiative*, Notes on the 21st Century.

Choudhary, A., & Saxena, P. (2023). Digital inclusion through decentralized finance: Pathways for India's rural economy. *Journal of Digital Economy*, 15(1), 112–127.

Christopher Santi Götz, Patrik Karlsson, and Ibrahim Yitmen. (2020) Exploring applicability, interoperability and integrability of Blockchain-based digital twins for asset life cycle management. *Smart and Sustainable Built Environment* DOI: 10.1108/SASBE-08-2020-0115

Ciplet, D., & Harrison, J. L. (2020). Transition tensions: Mapping conflicts in movements for a just and sustainable transition. *Environmental Politics*, 29(3), 435–456. DOI: 10.1080/09644016.2019.1595883

Cocca, T. (2018). Potential and Limitations of Virtual Advice in Wealth Management. *Operational*, 1(1), 45–57.

Colbourne, R. (2017). Indigenous entrepreneurship and hybrid ventures. In *Hybrid ventures* (pp. 93–149). Emerald Publishing Limited. DOI: 10.1108/S1074-754020170000019004

Collomb, A., & Sok, K. (2016). Blockchain/distributed ledger technology (DLT): What impact on the financial sector? *Digiworld Economic Journal*, (103).

Colnar, S., Dimovski, V., & Bogataj, D. (2019). Knowledge management and the sustainable development of social work. *Sustainability (Basel)*, 11(22), 6374. DOI: 10.3390/su11226374

Consolandi, C., Phadke, H., Hawley, J., & Eccles, R. G. (2020). Material ESG Outcomes and SDG Externalities: Evaluating the Health Care Sector's Contribution to the SDGs. *Organization and Environment, 33*(4), 511–533. *Scopus.* Advance online publication. DOI: 10.1177/1086026619899795

Cordes, A. (2024). Storying Indigenous cryptocurrency: Reckoning with the ghosts of US settler colonialism in the cultural economy. *Journal of Cultural Economics*, 17(4), 434–451. DOI: 10.1080/17530350.2022.2110924

Cornell, S. (2007). *Remaking the tools of governance: Colonial legacies, Indigenous solutions*. National Centre for First Nations Governance.

Cornell, S., & Kalt, J. P. (2000). Where's the Glue? Institutional and Cultural Foundations of American Indian Economic Development. *Journal of Socio-Economics*, 29(5), 443–470. DOI: 10.1016/S1053-5357(00)00080-9

Cornell, S., & Kalt, J. P. (2010). *American Indian self-determination: The political economy of a successful policy*. Harvard Project on American Indian Economic Development.

Corntassel, J. (2012). Re-envisioning resurgence: Indigenous pathways to decolonization and sustainable self-determination. In *Decolonization: Indigeneity, Education & Society* (Vol. 1). dspace.library.uvic.ca. Retrieved from https://dspace.library.uvic.ca/handle/1828/12471

Corrado, G., & Corrado, L. (2017). Inclusive finance for inclusive growth and development. *Current Opinion in Environmental Sustainability*, 24, 19–23. DOI: 10.1016/j.cosust.2017.01.013

Crifo, P., Durand, R., & Gond, J.-P. (2019). Encouraging Investors to Enable Corporate Sustainability Transitions: The Case of Responsible Investment in France. *Organization and Environment, 32*(2), 125–144. *Scopus.* Advance online publication. DOI: 10.1177/1086026619848145

Cummings, S., Seferiadis, A., & de Haan, L. (2019). Getting down to business? Critical discourse analysis of perspectives on the private sector in sustainable development. *Sustainable Development (Bradford)*, 28(4), 759–771. DOI: 10.1002/sd.2026

Curry, G. N., & Koczberski, G. (2013). Development implications of the engagement with capitalism: Improving the social returns of development. In *Engaging with capitalism: Cases from Oceania* (pp. 335-352). Emerald Group Publishing Limited.

Cusmano, L., & Thompson, J. (2013). *Alternative financing instruments for SMEs and entrepreneurs.* OECD SME and Entrepreneurship Papers., DOI: 10.1787/3709429e-

D'Hondt, C., De Winne, R., Ghysels, E., & Raymond, S. (2020a). Artificial Intelligence Alter Egos: Who might benefit from robo-investing? *Journal of Empirical Finance*, 59, 278–299. DOI: 10.1016/j.jempfin.2020.10.002

D'Souza, V. (2019, April 1). *P2P lenders to the rescue of MSMEs*. Entrepreneur.

da Silva, R. G., & Marques, F. P. (2022). Blockchain technology and indigenous economies: A case study from Brazil. *Journal of Development Economics*, 108(4), 345–362.

Dahiya, S., & Kumar, M. (2020). Linkage between financial inclusion and economic growth: An empirical study of the emerging Indian economy. *Vision (Basel)*, 24(2), 184–193. DOI: 10.1177/0972262920923891

Daly, H. E. (1996). *Beyond growth: The economics of sustainable development*. Beacon Press.

Das, S. R., & Chen, M. Y. (2007). Yahoo! for Amazon: Sentiment Extraction from Small Talk on the Web. *Management Science*, 53(9), 1375–1388. DOI: 10.1287/mnsc.1070.0704

Datta, R., & Kairy, B. (2024). Decolonizing climate change adaptations from indigenous perspectives: Learning reflections from munda indigenous communities, coastal areas in bangladesh. *Sustainability (Basel)*, 16(2), 769. DOI: 10.3390/su16020769

Davidson, S., De Filippi, P., & Potts, J. (2016). Economics of blockchain. SSRN Electronic Journal. DOI: 10.2139/ssrn.2744751

Davis, F. D. (1989). Perceived usefulness, perceived ease of use, and user acceptance of information technology. *Management Information Systems Quarterly*, 13(3), 319–340. DOI: 10.2307/249008

Dawkins, C. E. (2018). Elevating the Role of Divestment in Socially Responsible Investing. *Journal of Business Ethics, 153*(2), 465–478. *Scopus*. Advance online publication. DOI: 10.1007/s10551-016-3356-7

De la Cadena, M., & Starn, O. (2007). *Indigenous experience today*. Berg Publishers.

de Lange, D. E. (2017). Start-up sustainability: An insurmountable cost or a life-giving investment? *Journal of Cleaner Production, 156*, 838–854. *Scopus*. Advance online publication. DOI: 10.1016/j.jclepro.2017.04.108

De-Gol, A., Le Quéré, C., Smith, A. J. P., & Aubin Le Quéré, M. (2023). Broadening scientific engagement and inclusivity in IPCC reports through collaborative technology platforms. *Npj Climate Action*, 2(1), 49. DOI: 10.1038/s44168-023-00072-3

Dei, D. G. J. (2024). *Sustainability and development of EWE communities in Ghana through indigenous knowledge management practices*. Collection and Curation. DOI: 10.1108/CC-11-2023-0035

Del Barrio-García, S., Muñoz-Leiva, F., & Golden, L. (2020). A review of comparative advertising research 1975–2018: Thematic and citation analyses. *Journal of Business Research*, 121, 73–84. DOI: 10.1016/j.jbusres.2020.08.023

Demirgüç-Kunt, A., Klapper, L., Singer, D., & Ansar, S. (2018). *The Global Findex Database 2017*. World Bank.

Demirgüç-Kunt, A., Klapper, L., Singer, D., Ansar, S., & Hess, J. (2017). *The Global Findex Database 2017: Measuring Financial Inclusion and the Fintech Revolution*. World Bank.

Desai, R., & Kumar, V. (2023). Digital transformation in rural India: Bridging the gap through decentralized finance. *Journal of Technological Innovation in Finance*, 5(1), 91–110.

Deshpande, A. (2020). AI/ML applications and the potential transformation of Fintech and Finserv sectors. *2020 13th CMI Conference on Cybersecurity and Privacy (CMI) - Digital Transformation - Potentials and Challenges(51275)*, 1–6. DOI: 10.1109/CMI51275.2020.9322734

Dessus, S. C., & Hanusch, M. (2018). South Africa economic update: Jobs and inequality. The International Bank for Reconstruction and Development/World Bank., https://documents.worldbank.org/en/publication/documents-reports/documentdetail/368961522944196494/south-africa-economic-update-jobs-and-inequality, Retrieved March 12, 2024, from.

Devi, A. (2023). What is Financial Exclusion? A Review. *Review on Islamic Accounting*, 3(2). Advance online publication. DOI: 10.58968/ria.v3i2.365

Devie, D., Liman, L. P., Tarigan, J., & Jie, F. (2020). Corporate social responsibility, financial performance and risk in Indonesian natural resources industry. *Social Responsibility Journal, 16*(1), 73–90. *Scopus*. Advance online publication. DOI: 10.1108/SRJ-06-2018-0155

Dietzmann, C., Jaeggi, T., & Alt, R. (2023). Implications of AI-based robo-advisory for private banking investment advisory. *Journal of Electronic Business & Digital Economics*, 2(1), 3–23. DOI: 10.1108/JEBDE-09-2022-0037

Digital lending industry in India. (2024, May 6). Statista Research Department.

Director, C., & caepradmin.cass@anu.edu.au. (2014, October 21). The Economic and Social Benefits of Increasing Indigenous Employment -. Centre for Aboriginal Economic Policy Research. https://caepr.cass.anu.edu.au/research/publications/economic-and-social-benefits-increasing-indigenous-employment

Dolata, M., & Schwabe, G. (2017). Tuning in to More Interactivity – Learning from IT Support for Advisory Service Encounters. *I-Com*, 16(1), 23–33. DOI: 10.1515/icom-2016-0042

Donthu, N., Kumar, S., Mukherjee, D., Pandey, N., & Lim, W. M. (2021). How to conduct a bibliometric analysis: An overview and guidelines. *Journal of Business Research*, 133, 285–296. DOI: 10.1016/j.jbusres.2021.04.070

Dowling, M. (2021). Is non-fungible token pricing driven by cryptocurrencies? *Finance Research Letters*, 44, 102097. DOI: 10.1016/j.frl.2021.102097

Doyle, J. (2017). Financial strategies for sustainable development in Indigenous communities. *Journal of Indigenous Studies*, 4(3), 45–60.

Doyon, A., Boron, J., & Williams, S. (2021). Unsettling transitions: Representing Indigenous peoples and knowledge in transitions research. *Energy Research & Social Science*, 81, 102255. Advance online publication. DOI: 10.1016/j.erss.2021.102255

Dwivedi, Y. K., Hughes, L., Ismagilova, E., Aarts, G., Coombs, C., Crick, T., Duan, Y., Dwivedi, R., Edwards, J., Eirug, A., Galanos, V., Ilavarasan, P. V., Janssen, M., Jones, P., Kar, A. K., Kizgin, H., Kronemann, B., Lal, B., Lucini, B., & Williams, M. D. (2019). Artificial Intelligence (AI): Multidisciplinary perspectives on emerging challenges, opportunities, and agenda for research, practice and policy. *International Journal of Information Management*, 57, 101994. DOI: 10.1016/j.ijinfomgt.2019.08.002

Ediagbonya, V., & Tioluwani, C. (2023). The role of fintech in driving financial inclusion in developing and emerging markets: Issues, challenges and prospects. *Technological Sustainability*, 2(1), 100–119. DOI: 10.1108/TECHS-10-2021-0017

Edward Glaessgen and David Stargel. (2012) *The digital twin paradigm for future NASA and US Air Force vehicles*. In 53rd AIAA/ASME/ASCE/AHS/ASC structures, structural dynamics and materials conference 20th AIAA/ASME/AHS adaptive structures conference 14th AIAA. Honolulu, Hawaii, 1818. DOI: 10.2514/6.2012-1818

Efthymiou, L., Kulshrestha, A., & Kulshrestha, S. (2023). A Study on Sustainability and ESG in the Service Sector in India: Benefits, Challenges, and Future Implications. *Administrative Sciences, 13*(7). *Administrative Sciences*, 13(7), 165. Advance online publication. DOI: 10.3390/admsci13070165

Ejaz, H., Zeeshan, H. M., Ahmad, F., Bukhari, S. N. A., Anwar, N., Alanazi, A., Sadiq, A., Junaid, K., Atif, M., Abosalif, K. O. A., Iqbal, A., Hamza, M. A., & Younas, S. (2022). Bibliometric Analysis of Publications on the Omicron Variant from 2020 to 2022 in the Scopus Database Using R and VOSviewer. *International Journal of Environmental Research and Public Health*, 19(19), 12407. DOI: 10.3390/ijerph191912407 PMID: 36231710

El Baz, H. (2020). Financial Inclusion in Egypt: Challengers and Recommendations. *L'Egypte Contemporaine*, 111(538), 520–577. DOI: 10.21608/espesl.2020.214263

Elia, G., Stefanelli, V., & Ferilli, G. B. (2023). Investigating the role of Fintech in the banking industry: What do we know? *European Journal of Innovation Management*, 26(5), 1365–1393. DOI: 10.1108/EJIM-12-2021-0608

Ernst, D. (2011). IndIgenous InnovatIon and globalIzatIon the Challenge for China's standardization strategy Dieter Ernst A joint publication of the UC Institute on Global Conflict and Cooperation and the East-West Center.

Ernst, E., Merola, R., & Samaan, D. (2019). Economics of Artificial Intelligence: Implications for the future of work. *IZA Journal of Labor Policy*, 9(1), 20190004. Advance online publication. DOI: 10.2478/izajolp-2019-0004

Escobar, A. (2011). *Encountering development: The making and unmaking of the Third World*. Princeton University Press.

Escrig-Olmedo, E., Rivera-Lirio, J. M., Muñoz-Torres, M. J., & Fernández-Izquierdo, M. Á. (2017). Integrating multiple ESG investors' preferences into sustainable investment: A fuzzy multicriteria methodological approach. *Journal of Cleaner Production, 162*, 1334–1345. *Scopus*. Advance online publication. DOI: 10.1016/j.jclepro.2017.06.143

Eva, C., Bodle, K., Foley, D., Harris, J., & Hunter, B. (2023). The importance of understanding Indigenous employment in the Indigenous business sector. *The Australian Journal of Social Issues*, 58(3), 494–522. DOI: 10.1002/ajs4.271

Eva, C., Harris, J., Bodle, K., Foley, D., Hunter, B., & Nichols, N. (2023). "It's Self-Determination. Blackfullas Making Right Decisions for Blackfullas": Why Indigenous-owned businesses create better Indigenous employment outcomes. *The Australian Journal of Social Issues*, 59(1), 29–56. DOI: 10.1002/ajs4.292

Evans, M., Robinson, J., & Williamson, I. (n.d.). The Effect of HRM Practices on Employment Outcomes in Indigenous Social Enterprises Short title: AQ0 Title: The Effect of HRM Practices on Employment Outcomes in Indigenous. https://doi.org/DOI: 10.13039/501100000923This

Evans, T. M. (2019). Cryptokitties, cryptography, and copyright. *AIPLA Quarterly Journal*, 47, 219.

Fanning, K., & Centers, D. P. (2016). Blockchain and its coming impact on financial services. *Journal of Corporate Accounting & Finance*, 27(5), 53–57. DOI: 10.1002/jcaf.22179

FAO. (2022). FAO regional strategy for collaboration with Indigenous Peoples and people of African descent in Latin America and the Caribbean Revised edition (p. 67). FAO. https://openknowledge.fao.org/handle/20.500.14283/cb7823en

Farnaghia, M., & Mansouriana, A. (2022). Blockchain, an enabling technology for transparent and accountable decentralized public participatory GIS. *Cities*, 105.

Fei Tao and Qinglin Qi. (2019) Make more digital twins. *Nature 573*, 490-491. DOI: 10.1038/d41586-019-02849-1

Fei Tao, He Zhang, Ang Liu, and Andrew YC Nee. (2018) Digital twin in industry: State-of-the-art. *IEEE Transactions on Industrial Informatics* 15, 4, 2405–2415. DOI: 10.1109/TII.2018.2873186

Fei Tao, Jiangfeng Cheng, Qinglin Qi, Meng Zhang, He Zhang, and Fangyuan Sui. (2018) Digital twin-driven product design, manufacturing and service with big data. *The International Journal of Advanced Manufacturing Technology* 94, 9-12, 3563–3576. DOI: 10.1007/s00170-017-0233-1

Fei Tao, Meng Zhang, Yushan Liu, and AYC Nee. (2018) Digital twin driven prognostics and health management for complex equipment. *Cirp Annals* 67, 1, 169–172. DOI: 10.1016/j.cirp.2018.04.055

Fenwick, M., & Mv, E. P. (2020). BANKING AND REGULATORY RESPONSES TO FINTECH REVISITED — BUILDING THE SUSTAINABLE FINANCIAL SERVICE ' ECOSYSTEMS ' OF TOMORROW Author (s): Mark Fenwick and Erik P M Vermeulen Source : Singapore Journal of Legal Studies, March 2020, (March 2020), pp. *Singapore Journal of Legal Studies*, (March), 165–189.

Ferrario, F., Araújo, C. A. S., Bélanger, S., Bourgault, D., Carrière, J., Carrier-Belleau, C., Dreujou, E., Johnson, L. E., Juniper, S. K., Mabit, R., McKindsey, C. W., Ogston, L., Picard, M. M. M., Saint-Louis, R., Saulnier-Talbot, É., Shaw, J.-L., Templeman, N., Therriault, T. W., Tremblay, J.-E., & Archambault, P. (2022). Holistic environmental monitoring in ports as an opportunity to advance sustainable development, marine science, and social inclusiveness. *Elementa*, 10(1), 00061. Advance online publication. DOI: 10.1525/elementa.2021.00061

Ferrat, Y., Daty, F., & Burlacu, R. (2023). The role of size effects in moderating the benefits of sustainable investing. *BRQ Business Research Quarterly.Business Research Quarterly*. Advance online publication. DOI: 10.1177/23409444231162872

Filippini, M., Leippold, M., & Wekhof, T. (2024). Sustainable finance literacy and the determinants of sustainable investing. *Journal of Banking & Finance*, 163, 107167. DOI: 10.1016/j.jbankfin.2024.107167

Finance, B. (2020). Robo-Advice: Can Consumers Trust Robots? *Journal of Chemical Information and Modeling*.

Finley-Brook, M., & Thomas, C. (2011). Renewable energy and human rights violations: Indigenous people's experiences with hydroelectric projects in Panama. *Latin American Perspectives*, 38(4), 28–33.

Firdaus Khan, M. R. (2021). Socially Responsible Investing and Sustainable Indices: A Sustainability Agenda. *Indian Journal of Corporate Governance, 14*(2), 209–225. *Scopus.* Advance online publication. DOI: 10.1177/09746862211045757

First Nations Development Institute. (2018). *Investing in Native Communities: Philanthropic Funding for Native American Communities and Causes*. First Nations Development Institute.

Flavián, C., Pérez-Rueda, A., Belanche, D., & Casaló, L. V. (2022). Intention to use analytical artificial intelligence (AI) in services – the effect of technology readiness and awareness. *Journal of Service Management*, 33(2), 293–320. DOI: 10.1108/JOSM-10-2020-0378

Foley, B. (2019). Intersectionality: A Marxist Critique. *New Labor Forum*, 28(3), 10–13. DOI: 10.1177/1095796019867944

Foley, D., & Wheeler, J. (2018). Empowering Indigenous communities through economic development: Successes in Indigenous-led financial institutions. *Journal of Indigenous Economic Studies*, 11(4), 203–219.

Folger-Laronde, Z., Pashang, S., Feor, L., & ElAlfy, A. (2022). ESG ratings and financial performance of exchange-traded funds during the COVID-19 pandemic. *Journal of Sustainable Finance and Investment, 12*(2), 490–496. *Scopus.* Advance online publication. DOI: 10.1080/20430795.2020.1782814

Fomba, E. M. (2009). Reinforcing experiential learning with training culture as an innovative governance strategy in informal microfinance institutions. *International Journal of Technology Management*, 45(1-2), 141–155. DOI: 10.1504/IJTM.2009.021525

Fonchingong Che, C. (2024). Reframing social justice through indigenous know-how: Implications for social development, policy and practice. *Global Social Policy*, 24(1), 5–24. DOI: 10.1177/14680181231170532

Forliano, C., De Bernardi, P., & Yahiaoui, D. (2020). Entrepreneurial universities: A bibliometric analysis within the business and management domains. *Technological Forecasting and Social Change*, 165, 120522. DOI: 10.1016/j.techfore.2020.120522

Fourchard., & Azeez., A. K. (2023). The 2023 cashless election in Nigeria: The politics of withdrawing money. *African Affairs,* (00/00), 1-17. https://doi.org/.DOI: 10.1093/afraf/adad019

Francis, O. (2024, June 21). The Role Of Indigenous Knowledge In Environmental Conservation. Medium; Medium. https://olamidefrancis.medium.com/the-role-of-indigenous-knowledge-in-environmental-conservation-f16db06e5a83

Frank, E. (2024). *Balancing Innovation and Compliance in Fintech AI.* DOI: 10.1007/s10676-022-09631-4

Freeborn, C., Mardhani-Bayne, A., & Soetaert, C. (2023). Quality and educator dispositions for indigenous families in the urban early learning and child care context: A scoping review. *International Journal of Child Care and Education Policy*, 17(1), 6. DOI: 10.1186/s40723-023-00108-5

Freeman, M. C., & Groom, B. (2013). Biodiversity valuation and the discount rate problem. *Accounting, Auditing and Accountability Journal, 26*(5), 715–745. *Scopus.* Advance online publication. DOI: 10.1108/AAAJ-02-2013-1226

Freitas, C. E., Kahn, J. R., & Rivas, A. A. (2004). Indigenous people and sustainable development in Amazonas. *International Journal of Sustainable Development and World Ecology*, 11(3), 312–325. DOI: 10.1080/13504500409469834

Friedland, H., & Harris, J. (2021). Indigenous inclusion in global economic governance. *International Journal of Inclusive Finance*, 12(1), 15–26.

Fukuda, K., & Watanabe, C. (2012). Hybrid management of technology in innovation ecosystem.

Fuso Nerini, F., Henriksson, G., & Vennström, E. (2018). A comprehensive review of climate change adaptation in the built environment: Assessing scientific knowledge and policy instruments. *Energy Procedia*, 153, 44–49.

G20 Global Partnership for Financial Inclusion. (2023). Innovations in financial services for Micro, Small and Medium-Sized Enterprises. In *G20 Global Partnership for Financial Inclusion*. International Finance Corporation.

Gajendran, T., Tucker, C., Ware, S., & Tose, H. S. (2022). Integrating Indigenous, Western and inclusive pedagogies for work-integrated learning partnerships in architecture and design disciplines. *International Journal of Work-Integrated Learning*, 23(2), 259–277. https://eric.ed.gov/?id=EJ1346569

Galán-Guevara, C. (2024). Understanding change in traditional sustainable livelihoods: A complex socio-ecological system in an indigenous community in Mexico. *Community Development Journal: An International Forum*, 59(3), 495–513. DOI: 10.1093/cdj/bsad010

Galeone, G., Ranaldo, S., Shini, M., & Dicuonzo, G. (2023). SUSTAINABILITY REPORTING: EVIDENCE FROM GLOBAL SYSTEMICALLY IMPORTANT BANKS (G-SIBs). *Journal of Financial Management, Markets and Institutions, 11*(2). *Scopus.*, 11(2), 2350011. Advance online publication. DOI: 10.1142/S2282717X23500111

Gallego-Losada, R., Montero-Navarro, A., Rodríguez-Sánchez, J.-L., & González-Torres, T. (2022). Retirement planning and financial literacy, at the crossroads. A bibliometric analysis. In *Finance Research Letters* (Vol. 44). Elsevier Ltd., DOI: 10.1016/j.frl.2021.102109

Gandhi, R. (2022, July 31). Role of P2P lending in empowering SMEs in India. *ETBFSI.com*.

Gandullia, L., & Piserà, S. (2020). Do income taxes affect corporate social responsibility? Evidence from European-listed companies. *Corporate Social Responsibility and Environmental Management, 27*(2), 1017–1027. *Scopus.* Advance online publication. DOI: 10.1002/csr.1862

Gangi, F., & Varrone, N. (2018). Screening activities by socially responsible funds: A matter of agency? *Journal of Cleaner Production, 197*, 842–855. *Scopus.* Advance online publication. DOI: 10.1016/j.jclepro.2018.06.228

Gaur, A., & Potnis, D. D. (2022). Service innovations in mobile banking for creating value for the poor in developing countries. *The Electronic Journal on Information Systems in Developing Countries*, 88(4), e12209. https://doi.org/https://doi.org/10.1002/isd2.12209. DOI: 10.1002/isd2.12209

Gawusu, S., Zhang, X., Ahmed, A., Jamatutu, S. A., Miensah, E. D., Amadu, A. A., & Osei, F. A. J. (2022). Renewable energy sources from the perspective of blockchain integration: From theory to application. [Part B]. *Sustainable Energy Technologies and Assessments*, 52, 52. DOI: 10.1016/j.seta.2022.102108

Geczy, C. C., Stambaugh, R. F., & Levin, D. (2021). Investing in Socially Responsible Mutual Funds. *Review of Asset Pricing Studies, 11*(2), 309–351. *Scopus.* Advance online publication. DOI: 10.1093/rapstu/raab004

Gefen, D., Karahanna, E., & Straub, D. W. (2003). Trust and TAM in online shopping: An integrated model. *Management Information Systems Quarterly*, 27(1), 51–90. DOI: 10.2307/30036519

George, A. S. (2024). Finance 4.0. *The Transformation of Financial Services in the Digital Age.*, 02, 104–125. DOI: 10.5281/zenodo.11666694

Ghosh, A.K.; Ullah, A.S.; Kubo, A. (2019) Hidden Markov model-based digital twin construction for futuristic manufacturing systems. *Artif. Intell. Eng. Des. Anal. Manuf.* 33, 317–331. [CrossRef]

Gibson, K. (2020). Inclusive economies: Indigenous models for sustainable development. *Sustainability*, 12(14), 5678.

Gill, A. S., Mand, H. S., Sharma, S. P., & Mathur, N. (2012). Factors that Influence Financial Leverage of Small Business Firms in India. *International Journal of Economics and Finance*, 4(3). Advance online publication. DOI: 10.5539/ijef.v4n3p33

Godde, C., Mason-D'Croz, D., Mayberry, D., Thornton, P., & Herrero, M. (2021). Impacts of climate change on the livestock food supply chain; a review of the evidence. *Global Food Security*, 28, 100488. DOI: 10.1016/j.gfs.2020.100488 PMID: 33738188

Gok, I. Y., Duranay, S., & Uzunoglu Unlu, H. (2020). Co-movement dynamics of sustainability indices: Investigating the diversification opportunities through FTSE4Good index family and Borsa Istanbul sustainability index. *Social Responsibility Journal, 16*(8), 1475–1487. *Scopus.* Advance online publication. DOI: 10.1108/SRJ-02-2019-0073

Gomber, P., Kauffman, R. J., Parker, C., & Weber, B. W. (2018). On the Fintech Revolution: Interpreting the Forces of Innovation, Disruption, and Transformation in Financial Services. *Journal of Management Information Systems*, 35(1), 220–265. DOI: 10.1080/07421222.2018.1440766

Gomber, P., Koch, J. A., & Siering, M. (2017). Digital finance and FinTech: Current research and future research directions. *Journal of Business Economics*, 87(5), 537–580. DOI: 10.1007/s11573-017-0852-x

Gómez-Villegas, M. (2021). Towards an accounting of socio-environmental conflicts in South America. In *Routledge handbook of environmental accounting* (pp. 339–349). Routledge. DOI: 10.4324/9780367152369-29

Goodell, J. W., Kumar, S., Lim, W. M., & Pattnaik, D. (2021). Artificial intelligence and machine learning in finance: Identifying foundations, themes, and research clusters from bibliometric analysis. *Journal of Behavioral and Experimental Finance*, 32, 100577. DOI: 10.1016/j.jbef.2021.100577

Goodland, R., & Daly, H. E. (1996). Environmental sustainability: Universal and non-negotiable. *Ecological Applications*, 6(4), 1002–1017. DOI: 10.2307/2269583

Government of Canada. (2023). Indigenous-led climate change adaptation: A path to self-determined resilience. *Canadian Climate Reports*, 12(1), 45–62.

Gozman, D., Liebenau, J., & Mangan, J. (2018). The Innovation Mechanisms of Fintech Start-Ups: Insights from SWIFT's Innotribe Competition. *Journal of Management Information Systems*, 35(1), 145–179. DOI: 10.1080/07421222.2018.1440768

Grable, A. C. L. J. (2018). An Introduction to Big Data. *Journal of Financial Service Professionals*, (September), 17–20. DOI: 10.1515/9781474463546-002

Granger, R. C. (2012). Enterprise zone policy: Developing sustainable economies through area-based fiscal incentives. *Urban Research & Practice*, 5(3), 335–341. DOI: 10.1080/17535069.2012.727554

Gumbo, M. (2023). Digitisation of higher education and research: Raising inclusivity and equity issues for indigenous students. *South African Computer Journal = Suid-Afrikaanse Rekenaartydskrif*, 35(1). Advance online publication. DOI: 10.18489/sacj.v35i1.1107

Gupta, A., & Sharma, R. (2022). Blockchain technology adoption in India: Current trends and future prospects. *Journal of Technology Management & Innovation*, 17(4), 65–75.

Gupta, S., & Khurana, N. (2023). Evaluating the impact of digital finance on indigenous communities: Challenges and future directions. *Journal of Digital Finance and Development*, 12(2), 150–168.

Gupta, S., Srivastava, R., Shaikh, Z. H., & Irfan, M. (2024). Revolutionizing Rural Finance: Exploring the Impact of FinTech on Financial Inclusion in India. In Irfan, M., Muhammad, K., Naifar, N., & Khan, M. A. (Eds.), *Applications of Block Chain technology and Artificial Intelligence. Financial Mathematics and Fintech*. Springer., DOI: 10.1007/978-3-031-47324-1_3

Gutsche, G., Nakai, M., & Arimura, T. H. (2021). Revisiting the determinants of individual sustainable investment—The case of Japan. *Journal of Behavioral and Experimental Finance*, 30, 100497. DOI: 10.1016/j.jbef.2021.100497

Gutsche, G., Wetzel, H., & Ziegler, A. (2023). Determinants of individual sustainable investment behavior—A framed field experiment. *Journal of Economic Behavior & Organization*, 209, 491–508. DOI: 10.1016/j.jebo.2023.03.016

Haddaway, N. R., Page, M. J., Pritchard, C. C., & McGuinness, L. A. (2022). *PRISMA2020*: An R package and Shiny app for producing PRISMA 2020-compliant flow diagrams, with interactivity for optimised digital transparency and Open Synthesis. *Campbell Systematic Reviews*, 18(2), e1230. DOI: 10.1002/cl2.1230 PMID: 36911350

Hadfield-Hill, S. (2014). CSR in India: Reflections from the banking sector. *Social Responsibility Journal*, 10(1), 21–37. DOI: 10.1108/SRJ-11-2012-0145

Haffke, M., Fromberger, M., & Zimmermann, P. (2020). The regulation of blockchain technology: Perspectives and challenges for the financial sector. *Journal of Banking Regulation*, 21(3), 224–234.

Hallegatte, S., Rentschler, J., Rozenberg, J., (2020). Adaptation Principles: a Guide for Designing Strategies for Climate Change Adaptation and Resilience.

Haq, I. U. (2023). Time-frequency comovement among green financial assets and cryptocurrency uncertainties. *Economic Notes, 52*(1). *Economic Notes*, 52(1), e12216. Advance online publication. DOI: 10.1111/ecno.12216

Harrison, H., Birks, M., Franklin, R., & Mills, J. (2017). Case study research: Foundations and methodological orientations. In Forum qualitative Sozialforschung. *Forum Qualitative Social Research*, 18(1), •••.

Harvey, C. R., Ramachandran, A., & Santoro, J. (2021). DeFi and the future of finance. Research Paper.

Hassan Al-Tamimi, H. A., & Anood Bin Kalli, A. (2009). Financial literacy and investment decisions of UAE investors. *The Journal of Risk Finance*, 10(5), 500–516. DOI: 10.1108/15265940911001402

Haunschild, R., Bornmann, L., & Marx, W. (2016). Climate change research in view of bibliometrics. *PLoS One*, 11(7), e0160393. DOI: 10.1371/journal.pone.0160393 PMID: 27472663

Hawashin, D., Salah, K., Jayaraman, R., & Musamih, A. (2023). Using Composable NFTs for Trading and Managing Expensive Packaged Products in the Food Industry. *IEEE Access: Practical Innovations, Open Solutions*, 11, 10587–10603. DOI: 10.1109/ACCESS.2023.3241226

Hayward, A., Sjoblom, E., Sinclair, S., & Cidro, J. (2021). A New Era of Indigenous Research: Community-based Indigenous Research Ethics Protocols in Canada. Https://Doi.Org/10.1177/15562646211023705, *16*(4), 403–417. DOI: 10.1177/15562646211023705

Heines, R., Dick, C., Pohle, C., & Jung, R. (2021). The Tokenization of Everything: Towards a Framework for Understanding the Potentials of Tokenized Assets. *PACIS 2021 Proceedings*, 40. Research Gate.

Hentzen, J. K., Hoffmann, A. O. I., & Dolan, R. M. (2021). Which consumers are more likely to adopt a retirement app and how does it explain mobile technology-enabled retirement engagement? *International Journal of Consumer Studies*, 46(2), 368–390. DOI: 10.1111/ijcs.12685

He, Q. (1999). Knowledge Discovery through Co-Word Analysis. *Library Trends*, 48(1), 133–159. https://dblp.uni-trier.de/db/journals/libt/libt48.html#He99

Higgins-Desbiolles, F., Blanchard, L. A., & Urbain, Y. (2022). Peace through tourism: Critical reflections on the intersections between peace, justice, sustainable development and tourism. *Journal of Sustainable Tourism*, 30(2–3), 335–351. DOI: 10.1080/09669582.2021.1952420

Hill, R., Grant, C., George, M., Robinson, C. J., Jackson, S., & Abel, N. (2012). A typology of indigenous engagement in Australian environmental management: Implications for knowledge integration and social-ecological system sustainability. *Ecology and Society*, 17(1), art23. Advance online publication. DOI: 10.5751/ES-04587-170123

Hlophe, S. L., & Ellis, D. (2024). Changing consumer attitudes to make the Corporate Social Responsibility investment in sustainable fish production, a worthwhile investment to corporates. *Corporate Social Responsibility and Environmental Management, 31*(1), 344–356. *Scopus*. Advance online publication. DOI: 10.1002/csr.2573

Holden, E., Linnerud, K., Banister, D., Jana Schwanitz, V., & Wierling, A. (2017). The Imperatives of Sustainable Development. In *The Imperatives of Sustainable Development*. taylorfrancis.com. DOI: 10.4324/9780203022177

Ho, S., Choudhury, P. R., Haran, N., & Leshinsky, R. (2021). Decentralization as a Strategy to Scale Fit-for-Purpose Land Administration: An Indian Perspective on Institutional Challenges. *Land (Basel)*, 10(2), 199. DOI: 10.3390/land10020199

How. (2023). How Can Sustainability Teams Co-Create Shared Value with Indigenous Peoples? Idbinvest.org. https://www.idbinvest.org/en/blog/development-impact/how-can-sustainability-teams-co-create-shared-value-indigenous-peoples

Howitt, R. (2011). Sustainable Indigenous futures in remote Indigenous areas: Relationships, processes and failed state approaches. *GeoJournal*, 74(5), 391–405.

Howitt, R. (2012). Sustainable indigenous futures in remote Indigenous areas: Relationships, processes and failed state approaches. *GeoJournal*, 77(6), 817–828. DOI: 10.1007/s10708-010-9377-3

Hulme, D., & Arun, T. (2009). *Microfinance: A reader*. Routledge. DOI: 10.4324/9780203882764

Hunter, B. (2014). Reflecting on the Growth of Indigenous Self-employment. Agenda - a Journal of Policy Analysis and Reform, 21(1). https://doi.org/DOI: 10.22459/AG.21.01.2014.03

Hunt, J., & Gray, M. (2021). The impact of government incentives and tax relief on Indigenous business financing: Policy implications. *Journal of Indigenous Policy and Development*, 19(2), 88–104.

Hunt, S. C., & Young, N. L. (2021). Blending Indigenous Sharing Circle and Western Focus Group Methodologies for the Study of Indigenous Children's Health: A Systematic Review. *International Journal of Qualitative Methods*, 20, 16094069211015112. DOI: 10.1177/16094069211015112

Hyde, K. R. (2021). *Alternative Finance Strategies for small business Sustainability and Growth*. Walden University.

Hysa, E., Imeraj, E., Feruni, N., Panait, M., & Vasile, V. (2022). COVID-19—A Black Swan for Foreign Direct Investment: Evidence from European Countries. *Journal of Risk and Financial Management, 15*(4). *Journal of Risk and Financial Management*, 15(4), 156. Advance online publication. DOI: 10.3390/jrfm15040156

I. Yaqoob, K. Salah, M. Uddin, R. Jayaraman, M. Omar, and M. Imran. (2020) Blockchain for Digital Twins: Recent Advances and Future Research Challenges. *IEEE Network* 34, 5, 290–298. DOI: 10.1109/MNET.001.1900661

IBEF. Indian Brand Equity foundation. (2024). Registered MSMEs in India in FY24. In *IBEF Re-imagining India's M&E Sector* [Report]. https://www.ibef.org/download/1720513075_MSME_May_2024.pdf

Ibrahim, P. A. (2018). Innovations in Financing SMEs: A Study on the Growth of Crowdfunding in India. *Wealth: International Journal of Money. Banking & Finance*, 7(3), 66.

Ikdal, A. (2017). *6 challenges to financial inclusion in South Africa*. World Economic Forum, Apr 27. Accessed on March. 21. 2024. https://www.weforum.org/agenda/2017/04/financial-inclusion-south-africa/

Imoro, A. Z., Boaka Hlordze, R. G., Duwiejuah, B. A., Abukari, A., Alidu, S. M., Acheampong, N. A., & Imoro, Z. A. (2022). Indigenous technologies: knowledge and practices for sustainable development. Indigenous People and Nature, 593–612. DOI: 10.1016/B978-0-323-91603-5.00013-0

Indigenous Business Australia (IBA). (2021). Annual Report 2020-21. Retrieved from https://www.iba.gov.au/reports/annual-report/2020-21

Ingale, K. K., & Paluri, R. A. (2022). Financial literacy and financial behaviour: A bibliometric analysis. *Review of Behavioral Finance*, 14(1), 130–154. DOI: 10.1108/RBF-06-2020-0141

International Labour Organization (ILO). (2019). *Indigenous Peoples and Climate Change: From Victims to Change Agents through Decent Work*. ILO.

International Monetary Fund. (2020). *Six Charts Explain South Africa's Inequality*. Accessed on March. 23. 2024. https://www.imf.org/en/News/Articles/2020/01/29/na012820six-charts-on-south-africas-persistent-and-multi-faceted-inequality

IPCC. 2014 https://www.ipcc.ch/report/ar5/wg3/

Irfan, M. (2021, Jan). Do Shariah Indices converge? Evidence from Gulf Cooperation Council countries. *International Journal of Business Excellence*, 23(2), 251-269.

Irfan, M., Hussainey, K., & Bukhari, S. A. C. Nam, Y. (2024). Issues of sustainability in artificial intelligence and new-age thematic investing (Y. Irfan, Mohammad; Hussainey, Khaled; Bukhari, Syed Ahmad Chan; Nam (ed.)). IGI-Global.

Irfan, M. (2021, January). Do Shariah Indices converge? Evidence from Gulf Cooperation Council countries. *International Journal of Business Excellence*, 23(2), 251–269. DOI: 10.1504/IJBEX.2021.113448

Irfan, M., Elhoseny, M., Kassim, S., & Metawa, N. (2023). *Advanced Machine Learning Algorithms for Complex Financial Applications*. IGI Global., DOI: 10.4018/978-1-6684-4483-2

Irfan, M., Elmogy, M., Gupta, S., Khalifa, F., & Dias, R. (2024). *AI-Driven Decentralized Finance and the Future of Finance*. IGI Global., DOI: 10.4018/979-8-3693-6321-8

Irfan, M., Elmogy, M., Majid, M. S., & El-Sappagh, S. (2023). *The Impact of AI Innovation on Financial Sectors in the Era of Industry 5.0*. IGI Global., DOI: 10.4018/979-8-3693-0082-4

Irfan, M., Hussainey, K., Chan Bukhari, S. A., & Nam, Y. (Eds.). (2024). *Issues of Sustainability in AI and New-Age Thematic Investing*. IGI Global Publisher., DOI: 10.4018/979-8-3693-3282-5

Irfan, M., Kadry, S., Sharif, M., & Ullah Khan, H. (2023). *Fintech Applications in Islamic Finance: AI, Machine Learning, and Blockchain Techniques*. IGI Global., DOI: 10.4018/979-8-3693-1038-0

Iwara, I.O., 2024. Catalysing Financial Inclusion in South Africa's Rural Landscape: A Theoretical Discourse of PoS Business Model. *e-BANGI Journal, 21*(2).

Iyer, V., & Swaminathan, K. (2022). Blockchain adoption in traditional economic frameworks: A comparative analysis. *Journal of Blockchain Research*, 11(3), 203–218.

Iyiola, A. O., Akinsorotan, O. A., Ojeleye, A. E., & Fajimolu, A. O. (2023). An overview of environmental resources in Africa: emerging issues and sustainable exploitation. *Sustainable Utilization and Conservation of Africa's Biological Resources and Environment*, 543-570.

Jackson, R. (2020). Blended finance for Indigenous business ventures: Public-private partnerships in Indigenous economic development. *International Journal of Economic Development and Indigenous Studies*, 15(1), 33–50.

Jackson, R., & Martin, L. (2021). Training programs in digital literacy and their role in enhancing Indigenous access to digital financial services. *Journal of Digital Inclusion and Economic Development*, 12(4), 145–160.

Jackson, S., & Yarwood, R. (2021). Financial accessibility and systemic barriers among Indigenous populations: Addressing inequalities in economic resources. *Indigenous Economic Studies Journal*, 15(3), 101–119.

Jadhav, A., & Mehta, D. (2022). Enhancing digital infrastructure for economic inclusivity: A policy perspective. *Journal of Rural Development and Administration*, 39(2), 201–218.

Jagtiani, J., & John, K. (2018). Fintech: The impact on consumers and regulatory responses. *Journal of Economics and Business*, 100, 1–6. DOI: 10.1016/j.jeconbus.2018.11.002

Jain, A. (2024). Role And Growth of Venture Capital in India with Availability of Funds for Small and Medium Enterprises and Start-Up for Bringing Sustainability in Economic Development. *Vidhyayana, An International Multidisciplinary Peer-Reviewed E-Journal, 9*(2), 138–161. https://vidhyayanaejournal.org/journal/article/view/1630/1747

Jangra, G., Irfan, M., Jangra, M., Verma, C., Jangra, G., Irfan, M., Jangra, M., & Verma, C. (2024). Artificial Intelligence Approach to Portfolio Management. In https://services.igi-global.com/resolvedoi/resolve.aspx?doi=10.4018/979-8-3693-3282-5.ch004 (pp. 59–73). IGI Global. DOI: 10.4018/979-8-3693-3282-5.ch004

Jangra, G., & Jangra, M. (2022). Role of Artificial Intelligence in Online Shopping and its Impact on Consumer purchasing behaviour and Decision. *2022 Second International Conference on Computer Science, Engineering and Applications (ICCSEA)*, 1–7. DOI: 10.1109/ICCSEA54677.2022.9936374

Jang, T. S., & Oh, S. (2023). Transition to sustainable growth in South Korea: Investment and trade under uncertainty. *Millennial Asia*, 14(3), 360–378. DOI: 10.1177/09763996211065139

Janicka, M. (2016). Financial markets and the challenges of sustainable growth. *Comparative Economic Research, 19*(2), 27–41. *Scopus*. Advance online publication. DOI: 10.1515/cer-2016-0011

Janssen, R., Kramer, B., & Boender, G. (2013). Life cycle investing: From target-date to goal-based investing. *The Journal of Wealth Management*, 16(1), 23–32. DOI: 10.3905/jwm.2013.16.1.023

Jhariya, M. K., Banerjee, A., & Meena, R. S. (2022). Importance of natural resources conservation: Moving toward the sustainable world. In *Natural resources conservation and advances for sustainability* (pp. 3–27). Elsevier. DOI: 10.1016/B978-0-12-822976-7.00027-2

Jing, Y., Chen, C., Dong, J., & He, Z. (2023). Blockchain-Embedded Strategic Options for Satellite Operators: Sell, SataaS, or Dual [MDPI AG.]. *Systems*, 11(11), 550. DOI: 10.3390/systems11110550

Jones, L. (2019). Policy frameworks and Indigenous financial inclusion: An analysis of gaps between intention and outcome. *Journal of Economic and Social Policy*, 27(3), 112–130.

Joshi, M., & Das, P. (2022). Building an inclusive digital economy: The role of decentralized finance in rural India. *Journal of Financial Inclusion*, 10(3), 134–149.

Juddoo, K., Malki, I., Mathew, S., & Sivaprasad, S. (2023). An impact investment strategy. *Review of Quantitative Finance and Accounting, 61*(1), 177–211. *Scopus*. Advance online publication. DOI: 10.1007/s11156-023-01149-0

Jung, D., Dorner, V., Glaser, F., & Morana, S. (2018). Robo-Advisory: Digitalization and Automation of Financial Advisory. *Business & Information Systems Engineering*, 60(1), 81–86. DOI: 10.1007/s12599-018-0521-9

Jutel, O. (2022). Blockchain humanitarianism and crypto-colonialism. *Patterns (New York, N.Y.)*, 3(1), 100422. https://doi.org/https://doi.org/10.1016/j.patter.2021.100422. DOI: 10.1016/j.patter.2021.100422 PMID: 35079720

Kajiita, R. M., & Kang'ethe, S. M. (2024). Socio-economic dynamics inhibiting inclusive urban economic development: Implications for sustainable urban development in south african cities. *Sustainability (Basel)*, 16(7), 2803. DOI: 10.3390/su16072803

Kakoty, S. (2018). Ecology, sustainability and traditional wisdom. *Journal of Cleaner Production*, 172, 3215–3224. DOI: 10.1016/j.jclepro.2017.11.036

Kang'ethe, S. M., & Serima, J. (2014). Locating the Niche of the Informal Sector as a Driver of Social and Economic Development in Selected African Countries. *Mediterranean Journal of Social Sciences*, 5(27), 3. DOI: 10.5901/mjss.2014.v5n27p1293

Kanojia, S., Aggarwal, V., & Bhargava, A. (2020). Descendants of Financing Decision with Reference to Capital Structure: An Empirical Analysis of Indian SMEs. *Small Enterprises Development, Management & Extension Journal (SEDME)/SEDME. Small Enterprises Development. Management and Extension Journal*, 47(1), 33–42. DOI: 10.1177/0970846420930449

Kapoor, R., Indian Council for Research on International Economic Relations (ICRIER), & Goyal, T. M. (2024). Open banking systems for enhancing financial access for Micro, Small, and Medium-Sized Enterprises: the case of India. *ADBI Policy Brief*, 2024–13.

Kar, D., & Patro, B. (2024). Unravelling the Impact of Financial Literacy on the Intention of Indian Retail Investors to Adopt Socially Responsible Investments: The Interplay of Social Self-Efficacy as a Mediating Mechanism. *Global Business Review.Global Business Review*, 09721509231223571. Advance online publication. DOI: 10.1177/09721509231223571

Kasprzak, P. (2021). Blockchain to the Rescue Tokenization of Residential Real Estate in the Emerging Token Economy. In H. T.A., & D. J.J., Digitalization, Digital Transformation and Sustainability in the Global Economy (pp. 21–35). *Springer*. DOI: 10.1007/978-3-030-77340-3_3

Kaur, J., & Mehta, S. (2023). Blockchain technology for financial inclusion: A roadmap for India. *Journal of Digital Banking and Finance*, 9(1), 58–72.

Khaled, R., Ali, H., & Mohamed, E. K. A. (2021). The Sustainable Development Goals and corporate sustainability performance: Mapping, extent and determinants. *Journal of Cleaner Production*, 311, 127599. DOI: 10.1016/j.jclepro.2021.127599

Khan, A., & Rahman. (2010). Development of small and medium scale enterprise in Bangladesh: prospects and constraints.

Khan, K. M., Fahim, A., Saleem, D. M., & Jokhio, M. (2022). Empirical Investigation on Blockchain Interoperability. *VFAST Transactions on Software Engineering*, 11(1), 25–36. DOI: 10.21015/vtse.v10i4.1315

Khan, I. M. (2014). Indigenous entrepreneurship among the Kalash. *International Journal of Entrepreneurship and Small Business*, 22(1), 115–134. DOI: 10.1504/IJESB.2014.062134

Khongwir, C. M., & Sharmiladevi, J. C. (2023). A Bibliometric Analysis on Financial Inclusion and Financial Literacy – Analyzing the Current Research Trends. In *Indian Journal of Finance* (Vol. 17, Issue 2, pp. 27–53). Associated Management Consultants Pvt. Ltd. DOI: 10.17010/ijf/2023/v17i2/172638

Khub, A. A., Saeudy, M., & Ali, M. G. (2024). Digital financial inclusion in emerging economies: Evidence from jordan. *Journal of Risk and Financial Management*, 17(2), 66. DOI: 10.3390/jrfm17020066

Khurana, D., & Mohanty, S. (2021). Regulatory perspectives on cryptocurrency adoption in rural India. *Journal of Financial Regulation and Compliance*, 29(4), 320–336.

Khurana, S., Luthra, S., Haleem, A., Kumar, A., & Mannan, B. (2022). Can sustainability be achieved through sustainable oriented innovation practices? Empirical evidence of micro, small and medium scale manufacturing enterprises. *Sustainable Development (Bradford)*, 30(6), 1591–1615. DOI: 10.1002/sd.2330

Kietzmann, J., Lee, L. W., McCarthy, I. P., & Kietzmann, T. C. (2020). Deepfakes: Trick or treat? *Business Horizons*, 63(2), 135e146.

King, R. (2020). Exploring the interplay between culture, finance, and economic development in Indigenous contexts. *Journal of Indigenous Economic Studies*, 21(3), 112–130.

King, R., & Brown, T. (2020). Inclusive policy formation for Indigenous economic development: Recognizing Indigenous governance in program design. *Indigenous Policy Journal*, 22(1), 41–58.

Kingsbury, R. (2018). Challenges in financial models for Indigenous communities: Communal landholding and governance structures. *Journal of Indigenous Governance and Economics*, 10(1), 75–92.

Kobo, K. L., & Ngwakwe, C. C. (2017). Relating corporate social investment with financial performance. *Investment Management and Financial Innovations, 14*(2), 367–375. *Scopus.* Advance online publication. DOI: 10.21511/imfi.14(2-2).2017.08

Koech, M. K., Munene, K. J., Kinoti, M. K., & Situma, D. K. (2023). Circular Economy Policies and Innovations in Africa: Pillars for Achieving Sustainable Development. In *Circular Economy Adoption: Catalysing Decarbonisation Through Policy Instruments* (pp. 99–130). Springer Nature Singapore. DOI: 10.1007/978-981-99-4803-1_4

Kong, L. (2009). Making sustainable creative/cultural space in Shanghai and Singapore. *Geographical Review*, 99(1), 1–22. DOI: 10.1111/j.1931-0846.2009.tb00415.x

Kopp, A., Barber, D., Cottet, R., & Susinno, G. (2022). How to improve the ESG profile of portfolios while keeping a similar risk-adjusted return. [Scopus.]. *Journal of Risk Management in Financial Institutions*, 15(1), 51–71. DOI: 10.69554/JISS7490

Krosinsky, C. (2012). Sustainable investing: The art of long-term performance. *Routledge*. DOI: 10.4324/9781849773959

Kumar, N. M., & Mallick, P. K. (2018). Blockchain technology for security issues and challenges in IoT. *Procedia Computer Science*, 132, 1815–1823. doi:. procs.2018.05.140DOI: 10.1016/j

Kumar, T., & Kaur, S. (2023). Ethical Aspects of Cybersecurity in E-Commerce. In Cybersecurity for Decision Makers (1st ed.). CRC Press. DOI: 10.1201/9781003319887

Kumar, A., & Das, S. (2022). Digital infrastructure and its impact on financial inclusion: Evidence from rural India. *International Journal of Financial Studies*, 10(2), 121–138.

Kumar, H. S., & Sharma, P. (2014). Capitalism, globalisation, cultural landscape, and rural tourism. *The International Journal of Interdisciplinary Global Studies*, 7(4), 1–12. DOI: 10.18848/2324-755X/CGP/v07i04/53354

Kumar, N., & Rao, S. (2023). Challenges and opportunities for decentralized finance adoption in rural India. *Journal of Economic Policy and Technology*, 7(2), 101–115.

Kumar, P. (2024, June 27). Backbone of India: Empowering MSMEs through financial inclusion. *Business Today (Norwich)*.

Kumar, T., & Kaur, S. (2022). Blockchain Technology: Present and Future Perspectives. In Gupta, S., Kansra, P., & Kukreja, G. (Eds.), *Applications, Challenges, and Opportunities of Blockchain Technology in Banking and Insurance* (pp. 258–265). IGI Global., DOI: 10.4018/978-1-6684-4133-6.ch016

Kuokkanen, R. (2011). From indigenous economies to market-based self-governance: A feminist political economy analysis. *Canadian Journal of Political Science/Revue canadienne de science politique, 44*(2), 275-297.

Kushawaha, J., Borra, S., Kushawaha, A., Singh, G & Singh, P. (2021). Climate change and its impact on natural resources. .DOI: 10.1016/B978-0-12-820200-5.00002-6

Kwilinski, A., Lyulyov, O., & Pimonenko, T. (2023). Spillover effects of green finance on attaining sustainable development: Spatial Durbin model. *Computation (Basel, Switzerland)*, 11(10), 199. DOI: 10.3390/computation11100199

LaDuke, W. (1999). *All our relations: Native struggles for land and life*. South End Press.

Lakshmypriya, K., & Varghese, B. (2024). Indigenous Tribes and Inclusive Engagement: An Integrated Approach for Sustainable Livelihood Into the Future. In *Future Tourism Trends Volume 1: Tourism in the Changing World* (pp. 99-114). Emerald Publishing Limited.

Lam, J. W. (2016). Robo-Advisors: A Portfolio Management Perspective Jonathan Walter Lam Advised. In These.

Latiff, N., & Marimuthu, F. (2021). Water-related sustainability reporting practices amongst South African mining and non-mining corporations. *Environmental Economics, 12*(1), 112–123. *Scopus*. Advance online publication. DOI: 10.21511/ee.12(1).2021.10

Le Blanc, D. (2015). Towards integration at last? The sustainable development goals as a network of targets. *Sustainable Development (Bradford)*, 23(3), 176–187. DOI: 10.1002/sd.1582

Leach, M. (2015). Gender equality and sustainable development. *Gender Equality and Sustainable Development*, pp. 1–209. unwomen.org. DOI: 10.4324/9781315686455

Leach, M., Reyers, B., Bai, X., Brondizio, E. S., Cook, C., Díaz, S., Espindola, G., Scobie, M., Stafford-Smith, M., & Subramanian, S. M. (2018). Equity and sustainability in the anthropocene: A social-ecological systems perspective on their intertwined futures. *Global Sustainability*, 1, e13. Advance online publication. DOI: 10.1017/sus.2018.12

Leal Filho, W., Kovaleva, M., Tsani, S., îrcă, D.-M., Shiel, C., Dinis, M. A. P., Nicolau, M., Sima, M., Fritzen, B., Lange Salvia, A., Minhas, A., Kozlova, V., Doni, F., Spiteri, J., Gupta, T., Wakunuma, K., Sharma, M., Barbir, J., Shulla, K., & Tripathi, S. (2022). Promoting gender equality across the sustainable development goals. *Environment, Development and Sustainability*, 25(12), 14177–14198. DOI: 10.1007/s10668-022-02656-1 PMID: 36124160

Lee, H. Y., Kanthawala, S., Choi, E. Y., & Kim, Y. S. (2021). Rural and non-rural digital divide persists in older adults: Internet access, usage, and attitudes toward technology. *Gerontechnology (Valkenswaard)*, 20(2), 1–9. Advance online publication. DOI: 10.4017/gt.2021.20.2.32-472.12

Lee, J. W. (2020). Green finance and sustainable development goals: the case of China. Lee, Jung Wan (2020). Green Finance and Sustainable Dev. Goals: The Case of China. *J. Asian Finance Eco. Business*, 7(7), 577–586. DOI: 10.13106/jafeb.2020.vol7.no7.577

Leins, S. (2022). Blockchain, governance, and the future of finance. *Journal of Digital Banking*, 6(1), 22–35.

Lestariningati, S. I. (2018, August). Mobile point of sale design and implementation. [). IOP Publishing.]. *IOP Conference Series. Materials Science and Engineering*, 407(1), 012094. DOI: 10.1088/1757-899X/407/1/012094

Letsatsi, M. T., Agarwal, A., & Seretse, O. M. (2019). The Battle towards Skill Based Competency Integration to Knowledge Based Competency in the Sustainable Development of Growing Economy. *Int. J. Recent Technol. Eng*, 8(1).

Lin, J. Y., & Zhou, J. (2021). China's Industrial Development Strategies and Policies. *The Oxford Handbook of China Innovation*, 56.

Lin, C. (2007). A new vision of the knowledge economy. *Journal of Economic Surveys*, 21(3), 553–584. DOI: 10.1111/j.1467-6419.2007.00514.x

Liu, W., & Jing, K. (2024). ESG portfolio for TDFs with time-varying higher moments and cardinality constraint. *International Transactions in Operational Research, 31*(6), 4270–4295. *Scopus.* Advance online publication. DOI: 10.1111/itor.13364

Li, X., Yang, J., & Zeng, N. (2024). Natural resource rent and inclusive finance: An institutional perspective. *Economic Change and Restructuring*, 57(1), 45. DOI: 10.1007/s10644-024-09593-1

Lizarazo-Rodríguez, L., De Lombaerde, P., Lizarazo Carrera, M. A., & Londono-Escudero, C. (2024). Investment projects and the protection of indigenous peoples and territories in Colombia. *Latin American Policy*, 15(2), 288–319. DOI: 10.1111/lamp.12339

Lopez, J. R., & Vargas, H. (2024). Decolonizing economic policies: Lessons from Indigenous-led financial models in Latin America. *Development Policy Review*, 42(1), 78–94.

Louis, L., & Chartier, F. (2017). Financial inclusion in South Africa: An integrated framework for financial inclusion of vulnerable communities in South Africa's regulatory system reform. *Journal of comparative urban law and policy, 1*(1), 170-196. https://readingroom.law.gsu.edu/jculp/vol1/iss1/13

Low, L. (2005). Entrepreneurship development in Ireland and Singapore. *Journal of the Asia Pacific Economy*, 10(1), 116–138. DOI: 10.1080/1354786042000309107

Lusardi, A., & Tufano, P. (2015). Debt literacy, financial experiences, and overindebtedness. *Journal of Pension Economics and Finance*, 14(4), 332–368. DOI: 10.1017/S1474747215000232

Mabela, M. L., & Ditsele, T. (2024). Exploring intellectualisation of south african indigenous languages for academic purposes. *Literator*, 45(1). Advance online publication. DOI: 10.4102/lit.v45i1.1980

Maclean, K., Rist, P., Rassip, W., & Prudames, N. (2024). A practical tool to enable Indigenous enterprise planning and development grounded in culture. *Sustainability Science*, 19(4), 1205–1220. DOI: 10.1007/s11625-023-01459-1

Maddison, S. (2019). *The Colonial Fantasy: Why White Australia Can't Solve Black Problems*. Allen & Unwin.

Madhan, K., Shagirbasha, S., Mishra, T. K., & Iqbal, J. (2023). Adoption of service robots: Exploring the emerging trends through the lens of bibliometric analysis. *International Hospitality Review*, 38(2), 239–257. DOI: 10.1108/IHR-12-2022-0058

Madudova, E., Čorejova, T., & Valica, M. (2018). Economic sustainability in a wider context: Case study of considerable ICT sector sub-divisions. *Sustainability (Basel)*, 10(7), 2511. DOI: 10.3390/su10072511

Magni, G. (2017). Indigenous knowledge and implications for the sustainable development agenda. *European Journal of Education*, 52(4), 437–447. DOI: 10.1111/ejed.12238

Mahmudnia, D., Arashpour, M., Bai, Y., & Feng, H. (2022). Drones and Blockchain Integration to Manage Forest Fires in Remote Regions. *Drones (Basel)*, 6(11), 331. DOI: 10.3390/drones6110331

Mahoro, G. (2015). *Organic matter fuel briquettes as an alternative to charcoal: an initiative for forest conservation* (Doctoral dissertation, Kampala International University, School of Natural and Applied Sciences).

Maina, P., & Parádi-Dolgos, A. (2024). The effectiveness of climate adaptation finance and readiness on vulnerability in african economies. *Climate (Basel)*, 12(5), 59. DOI: 10.3390/cli12050059

Maiti, M. (2018). Scope for alternative avenues to promote financial access to MSMEs in developing nation evidence from India. *International Journal of Law and Management.International Journal of Law and Management*, 60(5), 1210–1222. DOI: 10.1108/IJLMA-06-2017-0141

Makoni, P. L. (2014). From financial exclusion to financial inclusion through microfinance: The case of rural Zimbabwe. *Journal of Corporate Ownership and Control*, 11(4), 447–455. DOI: 10.22495/cocv11i4c5p2

Malatji, M. T. (2020). *Rural Development Outcomes and Policies in South Africa's Limpopo Province*. Doctoral Thesis, University of South Africa.

Malchyk, M. V., Popko, O. V., Oplachko, I. O., Martyniuk, O. V., & Hontarenko, N. A. (2020). Tools for marketing management of industrial enterprises in Ukraine based on the principles of sustainable development. *International Journal of Management, 11*(4), 385–394. *Scopus*. Advance online publication. DOI: 10.34218/IJM.11.4.2020.038

Malhi, G. S., Kaur, M., & Kaushik, P. (2020). Impact of Climate Change on Agriculture and Its Mitigation Strategies: A Review. *Sustainability (Basel)*, 13(3), 1318. DOI: 10.3390/su13031318

Malhotra, A., O'Neill, H., & Stowell, P. (2021). Thinking strategically about blockchain adoption risks and risk mitigation. *Business Horizons*, 65(2), 159e171

Malpani, R., Baral, M. M., Panigrahi, R. R., & Chittipaka, V. (2024). Unveiling the dynamic nexus between corporate social responsibility, innovations and financial performances in 21st-century Indian start-ups. *The International Journal of Organizational Analysis*. Advance online publication. DOI: 10.1108/IJOA-01-2024-4239

Manga, S. J. T. (2023). When digital technology innovation enhances Indigenous Peoples' e-participation in climate change resilience-building: Perspectives under the "e-GIS Smart, Inclusive, and, Climate-resilient Indigenous Peoples Landscape and Community Clearing-House Mechanism Solution.". *Journal of Environmental Planning and Management*, 66(12), 2467–2486. DOI: 10.1080/09640568.2022.2078690

Mani, M., & Agarwal, R. (2022). Payment Banks in India: Insights From the Customers' Perception. [IJABIM]. *International Journal of Asian Business and Information Management*, 13(1), 1–15. DOI: 10.4018/IJABIM.297851

Marietheres Dietz and Günther Pernul. (2020) Unleashing the Digital Twin's Potential for ICS Security. *IEEE Security & Privacy* 18, 4, 20–27. https://doi.org/DOI: 10.1109/MSEC.2019.2961650

Marietheres Dietz, Benedikt Putz, and Günther Pernul. (2019) A Distributed Ledger approach to Digital Twin secure data sharing. In IFIP Annual Conference on Data and Applications Security and Privacy, Vol. 11559. *Springer, Cham*, 281–300. https://doi.org/DOI: 10.1007/978-3-030-22479-0_15

Martenson, R. (2008). Are men better investors than women? Gender differences in mutual fund and pension investments. *Journal of Financial Services Marketing*, 13(1), 72–81. DOI: 10.1057/fsm.2008.7

Martinelli, A., Mina, A., & Moggi, M. (2020). The enabling technologies of industry 4.0: Examining the seeds of the fourth industrial revolution. *Industrial and Corporate Change*, 30(1), 161–188. DOI: 10.1093/icc/dtaa060

Marzuki, A., Nor, F. M., Ramli, N. A., Basah, M. Y. A., & Aziz, M. R. A. (2023). The Influence of ESG, SRI, Ethical, and Impact Investing Activities on Portfolio and Financial Performance—Bibliometric Analysis/Mapping and Clustering Analysis. *Journal of Risk and Financial Management, 16*(7). *Journal of Risk and Financial Management*, 16(7), 321. Advance online publication. DOI: 10.3390/jrfm16070321

Masferrer-Dodas, E., Rico-Garcia, L., Huanca, T., & Reyes-García, V. (2012). Consumption of market goods and wellbeing in small-scale societies: An empirical test among the Tsimane'in the Bolivian Amazon. *Ecological Economics*, 84, 213–220. DOI: 10.1016/j.ecolecon.2011.08.009

Matallín-Sáez, J. C., Soler-Domínguez, A., Tortosa-Ausina, E., & de Mingo-López, D. V. (2019). Ethical strategy focus and mutual fund management: Performance and persistence. *Journal of Cleaner Production, 213*, 618–633. *Scopus.* Advance online publication. DOI: 10.1016/j.jclepro.2018.12.130

Matsebula, V., & Yu, D. (2020). *South African banks need to do more to ensure financial inclusion.* The Conversation, 2, p.2020. Accessed on May. 28. 2023. https://theconversation.com/south-african-banks-need-to-do-more-to-ensure-financial-inclusion-141139

Matthias Eckhart and Andreas Ekelhart. (2018) Towards Security-Aware Virtual Environments for Digital Twins. In Proceedings of the 4th ACM Workshop on Cyber-Physical System Security (Incheon, Republic of Korea) (CPSS '18). *Association for Computing Machinery, New York, NY, USA*, 61–72. DOI: 10.1145/3198458.3198464

Matute, J., & Linsen, L. (2022). Evaluating Data-type Heterogeneity in Interactive Visual Analyses with Parallel Axes. *Computer Graphics Forum*, 41(1), 335–349. DOI: 10.1111/cgf.14438

Maume, P. (2021). Robo-advisors - How do they fit in the existing EU regulatory framework, in particular with regard to nvestor protection? Publication for the Committee on Economic and Monetary Affairs, Policy Department for Economic, Scientific and Quality of Life Policies, European Parliament, Luxembourg, June.

Mchakulu, M. G. (2019). *Rural Malawi Households' Environmental Concern and Consciousness About Appropriate Energy Consumption Practices Amidst Prevailing Socio-Economic Conditions*. University of Pretoria.

Meek, D. E. (2021). Sustainable AI Development (SAID): On the Road to More Access to Justice Chapter. In Technology, Innovation and Access to Justice (pp. 112–130). Edinburgh University Press. https://doi .org/DOI: 10.3366/j.ctv1c29sj0.15

Meena, K., & Gupta, R. (2023). Enabling financial inclusion through decentralized technologies: Managerial perspectives. *International Journal of Financial Management*, 14(1), 77–89.

Mehta, P., & Saini, S. (2021). Bridging the digital divide in rural India: The role of decentralized financial technologies. *International Journal of Rural Development and Planning*, 7(3), 301–316.

Mende, M., Scott, M. L., van Doorn, J., Grewal, D., & Shanks, I. (2019). Service Robots Rising: How Humanoid Robots Influence Service Experiences and Elicit Compensatory Consumer Responses. *JMR, Journal of Marketing Research*, 56(4), 535–556. DOI: 10.1177/0022243718822827

Miglietta, F., Di Martino, G., & Fanelli, V. (2023). The environmental policy of the Norwegian Government Pension Fund-Global and investors' reaction over time. *Business Strategy and the Environment, 32*(6), 3721–3736. *Scopus*. Advance online publication. DOI: 10.1002/bse.3324

Mika, J. P., Fahey, N., & Bensemann, J. (2019). What counts as an indigenous enterprise? Evidence from Aotearoa New Zealand. *Journal of Enterprising Communities: People and Places in the Global Economy*, 13(3), 372–390. DOI: 10.1108/JEC-12-2018-0102

Milani, F., García-Bañuelos, L., & Dumas, M. (2016). Blockchain and business process improvement. *BP Trends newsletter (October 2016)*.

Minerva, R., & Crespi, N. (2021). ● R. Minerva and N. Crespi. (2021) Digital Twins: Properties, Software Frameworks, and Application Scenarios. *IT Professional*, 23(1), 51–55. DOI: 10.1109/MITP.2020.2982896

Mishra, V., & Verma, R. (2021). Socio-cultural factors influencing the adoption of blockchain technologies in India. *Journal of Technology and Society*, 15(3), 95–110.

Miya, Z. (2022). *Overcoming Financial Exclusion In South Africa*. FinTech Financials. October 13, 2020. Accessed on April. 12. 2024. https://techfinancials.co.za/2022/10/13/overcoming-financial-exclusion -in-south-africa/

Mohan, K. (2023b, March 18). *MSME Credit Capital Deficit – How much of a difference can Alternate Finance make?* Redseer Strategy Consultants. https://redseer.com/newsletters/msme-credit-capital-deficit/

Mohanty, S., & Chakraborty, A. (2023). The role of smart contracts in enhancing traditional economic practices: A case study of rural India. *Journal of Financial Innovation and Digital Transformation*, 9(2), 132–150.

Mokobongo, F. J. J. Y., Mballa, N. U. C., Koyongozo, A. D., Dacko, G., & Gonessa, M. E. (2022). *Financial exclusion in Central African Republic*. AERC Policy Brief. Accessed on March. 28. 2023. https://publication.aercafricalibrary.org/server/api/core/bitstreams/1c2f0e81-a5a2-4a84-b2dc-1eedcbb74efa/content

Momparler, A., Carmona, P., & Climent, F. (2024). Catalyzing Sustainable Investment: Revealing ESG Power in Predicting Fund Performance with Machine Learning. *Computational Economics.Computational Economics*. Advance online publication. DOI: 10.1007/s10614-024-10618-0

Mosquera-Guerrero, A., Rodríguez Martínez, J., Ordóñez Abril, D. Y., & Calderón Sotero, J. H. (2023). Project design and development in indigenous communities: A literature review. *Gestão & Produção*, 30, e6022. DOI: 10.1590/1806-9649-2022v29e6022

Mtyapi, S. (2021). *Investigating financial inclusion in rural households: A South African case*. PhD Thesis, University of the Western Cape.

Muhammad Habib ur Rehman, Khaled Salah, Ernesto Damiani, and Davor Svetinovic. (2020) Towards Blockchain-Based Reputation-Aware Federated Learning. *IEEE INFOCOM 2020 - IEEE Conference on Computer Communications Workshops (INFOCOM WKSHPS)*. 183–188. DOI: 10.1109/INFOCOM-WKSHPS50562.2020.9163027

Mujinga, M., Eloff, M. M., & Kroeze, J. H. (2018). System usability scale evaluation of online banking services: A South African study. *South African Journal of Science*, 114(3-4), 1–8. DOI: 10.17159/sajs.2018/20170065

Mukerjee, K. (2024). A study on lender participation in peer to peer lending. *Marketing Intelligence & Planning*, 42(1), 40–58. DOI: 10.1108/MIP-05-2023-0195

Mukherjee, P., & Jain, S. (2022). Bridging the digital literacy gap in rural India: Strategies for decentralized finance adoption. *Journal of Information Technology for Development*, 28(3), 295–310.

Mulye, D. (2021, April 8). Challenges with MSME lending and how Embedded Finance solves them? *Finbox*.

Munck, R. (2021). Globalisation and Development. In *Rethinking Development: Marxist Perspectives* (pp. 189–208). Springer International Publishing. DOI: 10.1007/978-3-030-73811-2_10

Mustapha, Z., Kunhibava, S. B., & Muneeza, A. (2020). Legal and Sharī'ah noncompliance risks in Nigerian Islamic finance industry: A review of the literature. *International Journal of Law and Management*, 63(02), 275–299. DOI: 10.1108/IJLMA-03-2020-0075

Nadkarni, A., & Gupta, R. (2022). Barriers to blockchain adoption in indigenous communities: The Indian perspective. *Journal of Technology in Society*, 18(2), 150–165.

Naeem, M. A., Karim, S., Rabbani, M. R., Bashar, A., & Kumar, S. (2023). Current state and future directions of green and sustainable finance: A bibliometric analysis. *Qualitative Research in Financial Markets, 15*(4), 608–629. *Scopus.* Advance online publication. DOI: 10.1108/QRFM-10-2021-0174

Nain, I., & Rajan, S. (2023). Algorithms for better decision-making: A qualitative study exploring the landscape of robo-advisors in India. *Managerial Finance*, 49(11), 1750–1761. DOI: 10.1108/MF-01-2023-0055

Nair, M., & Prasad, P. (2022). Policy implications for scaling decentralized finance in rural India. *Journal of Public Policy and Administration*, 29(2), 112–129.

Nakamoto, S. (2019). Bitcoin: A peer-to-peer electronic cash system. *Manubot.*

Náñez Alonso, S. L., Jorge-Vazquez, J., Echarte Fernández, M. Á., Kolegowicz, K., & Szymla, W. (2022). Financial exclusion in rural and urban contexts in Poland: A threat to achieving SDG eight? *Land (Basel)*, 11(4), 539. DOI: 10.3390/land11040539

Narayan, R., & Verma, P. (2021). Challenges and opportunities for blockchain technology adoption in India's indigenous economies. *Journal of Innovation and Entrepreneurship*, 10(1), 45–60.

Narayan, V., & Bhattacharya, P. (2023). Integrating decentralized finance with indigenous economic practices: A managerial framework. *Journal of Financial Innovation and Technology Management*, 21(1), 111–126.

Nash-Stewart, C. E., Kruesi, L. M., & Del Mar, C. B. (2012). Does Bradford's Law of Scattering predict the size of the literature in Cochrane Reviews? *Journal of the Medical Library Association: JMLA*, 100(2), 135–138. DOI: 10.3163/1536-5050.100.2.013 PMID: 22514511

Nchofoung, T. N., Asongu, S. A., & Tchamyou, V. S. (2024). Gender political inclusion and inclusive finance in Africa. *Economic Systems*, 48(2), 101187. DOI: 10.1016/j.ecosys.2024.101187

Ndlovu, G. 2018. *Access to financial services: Towards an understanding of the role and impact of financial exclusion in Sub-Saharan Africa.* Doctoral Thesis, University of Cape Town.

Newman Carroll, S., Mombourquette, A., Boxer, M., Williams, R., & Brewer, S. (2021). Indigenous Empowerment Through Community-Engaged Health Education Curriculum: Health Promotion in a Commercial Tobacco Cessation Campaign. *Pedagogy in Health Promotion*, 7(4), 237337992110061. DOI: 10.1177/23733799211006130

Ng, T.-H., Lye, C.-T., Chan, K.-H., Lim, Y.-Z., & Lim, Y.-S. (2020). Sustainability in Asia: The Roles of Financial Development in Environmental, Social, and Governance (ESG) *Performance. Social Indicators Research*, 150(1), 17–44. DOI: 10.1007/s11205-020-02288-w

Ngo-ye, T., & Cummings, M. (2018). Modeling the Robo-Advisor Ecosystem: Insights From a Simulation Study. *Issues in Information Systems*, (September). Advance online publication. DOI: 10.48009/1_iis_2018_128-138

Nicholas, G. (2022). Protecting Indigenous heritage objects, places, and values: Challenges, responses, and responsibilities. *International Journal of Heritage Studies*, 28(3), 400–422. DOI: 10.1080/13527258.2021.2009539

Nikolakis, W., Cohen, D. H., & Nelson, H. W. (2012). What matters for socially responsible investment (SRI) in the natural resources sectors? SRI mutual funds and forestry in North America. *Journal of Sustainable Finance and Investment, 2*(2), 136–151. *Scopus.* Advance online publication. DOI: 10.1080/20430795.2012.690724

Nikolakis, W., Nelson, H. W., & Cohen, D. H. (2014). Who Pays Attention to Indigenous Peoples in Sustainable Development and Why? Evidence From Socially Responsible Investment Mutual Funds in North America. *Organization and Environment, 27*(4), 368–382. *Scopus.* Advance online publication. DOI: 10.1177/1086026614546812

Niszczota, P., & Błaszczyński, J. (2024). Hard to digest investments: People oppose investment in both conventional and cultured meat producers. *Ecological Economics, 218.Ecological Economics*, 218, 108094. Advance online publication. DOI: 10.1016/j.ecolecon.2023.108094

Njoku, J. (2022). *The ultimate guide on how to start a PoS business in Nigeria.* Accessed on March. 28. 2023. https://www.dockaysworld.com.ng/how-to-start-a-pos-business-in-nigeria/

Nofsinger, J. R., & Varma, A. (2023). Keeping Promises? Mutual Funds' Investment Objectives and Impact of Carbon Risk Disclosures. *Journal of Business Ethics, 187*(3), 493–516. *Scopus.* Advance online publication. DOI: 10.1007/s10551-022-05264-1

Ny, B. (2022). *Blockchain in Impact Investing: The Potential of Impact Tokens on SDGs. Medium.*https://medium.com/@Godswisdomtoday/blockchain-in-impactinvesting-the-potential-of-impact-tokens-on-sdgs-767ad67b4f3

Nyakuwanika, M., van der Poll, H. M., & van der Poll, J. A. (2021). A conceptual framework for greener goldmining through environmental management accounting practices (Emaps): The case of zimbabwe. *Sustainability (Basel)*, 13(18), 10466. DOI: 10.3390/su131810466

O'Sullivan, D. (2023). The UN Sustainable Development Goals, national values, and Indigenous self-determination: Australian perspectives. AlterNative. *Alternative*, 19(4), 741–749. DOI: 10.1177/11771801231196924

Oeurng, C., Cochrane, T. A., Chung, S., Kondolf, M. G., Piman, T., & Arias, M. E. (2019). Assessing climate change impacts on river flows in the Tonle Sap Lake Basin, Cambodia. *Water (Basel)*, 11(3), 618. DOI: 10.3390/w11030618

OHCHR | Consultation and free, prior and informed consent (FPIC). (n.d.). OHCHR. https://www.ohchr.org/en/indigenous-peoples/consultation-and-free-prior-and-informed-consent-fpic

Okunade, S. O., Olawumi, A. T., Adeyemi, O. J., & Amosun, O. O. (2023). Socio-economic and security effects of financial exclusion in Africa: An experts' View. *Annals of Social Sciences & Management studies (ASM), 8*(5). https://doi.org/.DOI: 10.19080/ASM

Olarewaju, B. (2023). *How to start PoS machine business in Nigeria.* Accessed on July 30. 2023. https://studentship.com.ng/start-pos-business-in-nigeria/?expand_article=1#google_vignette

Omondi, D., & Mwangi, J. (2022). Decentralized finance in Africa: Lessons from blockchain implementation in Kenya. *African Journal of Economic and Financial Research*, 9(1), 88–105.

Ortas, E., & Moneva, J. M. (2011). Sustainability stock exchange indexes and investor expectations: Multivariate evidence from DJSI-Stoxx. *Revista Espanola de Financiacion y Contabilidad, 40*(151), 395–416. *Scopus*. Advance online publication. DOI: 10.1080/02102412.2011.10779706

Owusu, E. A. (2024). Financial inclusion and economic growth the moderating role of financial stability in Sub-Saharan Africa.

Paliwal, P. (2005). Sustainable development and systems thinking: A case study of a heritage city. *International Journal of Sustainable Development and World Ecology*, 12(2), 213–220. DOI: 10.1080/13504500509469632

Pallathadka, H., Ramirez-Asis, E. H., Loli-Poma, T. P., Kaliyaperumal, K., Ventayen, R. J. M., & Naved, M. (2023). Applications of artificial intelligence in business management, e-commerce and finance. *Materials Today: Proceedings*, 80, 2610–2613. https://doi.org/https://doi.org/10.1016/j.matpr.2021.06.419. DOI: 10.1016/j.matpr.2021.06.419

Palma-Ruiz, J. M., Castillo-Apraiz, J., & Gómez-Martínez, R. (2020). Socially responsible investing as a competitive strategy for trading companies in times of upheaval amid covid-19: Evidence from spain. *International Journal of Financial Studies, 8*(3), 1–13. *Scopus*. Advance online publication. DOI: 10.3390/ijfs8030041

Pansera, M., & Owen, R. (2015). Framing resource-constrained innovation at the 'bottom of the pyramid': Insights from an ethnographic case study in rural Bangladesh. *Technological Forecasting and Social Change*, 92, 300–311. DOI: 10.1016/j.techfore.2014.10.004

Park, J., & Choi, M. (2024). Indigenous knowledge systems as catalysts for biodiversity conservation in Asia. *Global Ecology and Conservation*, 31, 210–229.

Parmenter, J. (2015). The Experience of Aboriginal Financial Institutions in Canada: Alternative Approaches to Development Finance. *Canadian Journal of Development Studies*, 36(3), 315–331. DOI: 10.1080/02255189.2015.1065283

Parsons, M., Fisher, K., & Nalau, J. (2016). Alternative approaches to co-design: Insights from indigenous/academic research collaborations. *Current Opinion in Environmental Sustainability*, 20, 99–105. DOI: 10.1016/j.cosust.2016.07.001

Patel, K., & Kumar, A. (2023). Bridging the regulatory gap: Strategies for the adoption of decentralized financial technologies in India. *Journal of Financial Regulation*, 31(4), 299–315.

Patel, R., & Shukla, A. (2023). The role of trust in the adoption of decentralized financial technologies: A study of rural India. *Journal of Financial Innovation and Technology*, 18(1), 79–94.

Patnaik, J., & Bhowmick, B. (2020). Promise of inclusive innovation: A Re-look into the opportunities at the grassroots. *Journal of Cleaner Production*, 259, 121124. Advance online publication. DOI: 10.1016/j.jclepro.2020.121124

Paul, C. J., Weinthal, E. S., Bellemare, M. F., & Jeuland, M. A. (2016). Social capital, trust, and adaptation to climate change: Evidence from rural Ethiopia. *Global Environmental Change*, 36, 124–138. DOI: 10.1016/j.gloenvcha.2015.12.003

Peña-Azcona, I., García-Barrios, R., García-Barrios, L., Ortega-Argueta, A., & Elizondo, C. (2021). The unruly complexity of conservation arrangements with Mexican rural communities: Who really funds the game? *Journal of Rural Studies*, 87, 112–123. DOI: 10.1016/j.jrurstud.2021.08.027

Peng, G. C. A. (2013). Green ICT: A strategy for sustainable development of China's electronic information industry. *China. International Journal (Toronto, Ont.)*, 11(3), 68–86.

Peredo, A. M., & Chrisman, J. J. (2019). Socio-economic barriers to credit access in Indigenous communities: The impact of income levels and credit history. *Journal of Entrepreneurship and Economic Development*, 22(3), 201–217.

Peredo, A. M., & McLean, M. (2020). Indigenous entrepreneurship and economic resilience: Exploring models of community-based business. *Journal of Indigenous Business and Economic Development*, 15(1), 37–52.

Pereira, P., Cortez, M. C., & Silva, F. (2019). Socially responsible investing and the performance of Eurozone corporate bond portfolios. *Corporate Social Responsibility and Environmental Management, 26*(6), 1407–1422. *Scopus*. Advance online publication. DOI: 10.1002/csr.1756

Permanent Forum on Indigenous Issues (PFII) | High-Level Political Forum 2016. (2016). Un.org. https://hlpf.un.org/inputs/permanent-forum-on-indigenous-issues-pfii

Pesaran, M. H., Shin, Y., & Smith, R. P. (1999). Pooled mean group estimation of dynamic heterogeneous panels. *Journal of the American Statistical Association*, 94(446), 621–634. DOI: 10.1080/01621459.1999.10474156

Pesaran, M. H., & Smith, R. (1995). Estimating long-run relationships from dynamic heterogeneous panels. *Journal of Econometrics*, 68(1), 79–113. DOI: 10.1016/0304-4076(94)01644-F

Peter, O. (2023). *Overview of the PoS business in Nigeria – Saving the Unbanked and Heralding A Cashless Economy.* Assessed on March. 22. 2023. https://www.withinnigeria.com/piece/2023/02/09/overview-of-the-pos-business-in-nigeria-saving-the-unbanked-and-heralding-a-cashless-economy/

Peters, E. (2020). Culturally sensitive financial products and the exclusion of Indigenous communities from mainstream finance. *Journal of Indigenous Economic Development*, 12(2), 45–63.

Pethuru Raj. 2021. Chapter Thirteen - Empowering digital twins with blockchain. In The Blockchain Technology for Secure and Smart Applications across Industry Verticals. *Advances in Computers*, Vol. 121. Elsevier, 267 – 283. https://doi.org/DOI: 10.1016/bs.adcom.2020.08.013

Petrova, N. I., Fedorova, A. V., Petrova, N. N., & Alekseeva, N. N. (2019). Arctic entrepreneurship and supply chain strategy integration as part of creative economy. *International Journal of Supply Chain Management*, 8(6), 999–1005.

Phoon, K. F., & Koh, F. (2018). Robo-Advisors and Wealth Management. *Journal of Alternative Investments*, 20(3), 79–94. DOI: 10.3905/jai.2018.20.3.079

Pilkington, M. (2016). Blockchain technology: principles and applications. In Research handbook on digital transformations. *Edward Elgar Publishing*. DOI: 10.4337/9781784717766.00019

Posel, D., & Casale, D. (2019). Gender and the economy in post-apartheid South Africa: Changes and challenges. *Agenda (Durban, South Africa)*, 33(4), 3–10. DOI: 10.1080/10130950.2019.1679439

Pradhan, P., Costa, L., Rybski, D., Lucht, W., & Kropp, J. P. (2017). A Systematic Study of Sustainable Development Goal (SDG) Interactions. *Earth's Future*, 5(11), 1169–1179. DOI: 10.1002/2017EF000632

Prasad, R., & Sharma, A. (2022). Decentralized financial technologies and economic inclusivity: Opportunities for indigenous populations in India. *Journal of Emerging Market Finance*, 21(2), 205–225.

Praseeda, C. (2018). Socially Responsible Investment, Microfinance and Banking: Creating Value by Synergy. *Indian Journal of Corporate Governance, 11*(1), 69–87. *Scopus*. Advance online publication. DOI: 10.1177/0974686218769200

PricewaterhouseCoopers. (2017). *PwC's Global Artificial Intelligence Study: Sizing the prize*. PwC. Retrieved July 16, 2024, from https://www.pwc.com/gx/en/issues/data-and-analytics/publications/artificial-intelligence-study.html

Pu, G., Wong, W., Du, Q., Al Shraah, A., Alromaihi, A., & Muda, I. (2024). Asymmetric impact of natural resources, fintech, and digital banking on climate change and environmental sustainability in BRICS countries. *Resources Policy*, 91, 104872. DOI: 10.1016/j.resourpol.2024.104872

Purwanto, I., Isnanto, R. R., & Widodo, A. P. (2023). Investigation of the impact of the Peer-To-Peer lending market on the membership motivation of the MSME. *E3S Web of Conferences, 448*, 02037. DOI: 10.1051/e3sconf/202344802037

Puschmann, T. (2017). Fintech. *Business & Information Systems Engineering*, 59(1), 69–76. DOI: 10.1007/s12599-017-0464-6

PwC. (2020). How mature is AI adoption in financial services? In *A PwC Study Across the DACH Region*. Retrieved July 16, 2024, from https://www.pwc.de/de/future-of-finance/how-mature-is-ai-adoption-in-financial-services.pdf

Qin, Y., Harrison, J., & Chen, L. (2019). A framework for the practice of corporate environmental responsibility in China. *Journal of Cleaner Production*, 235, 426–452. DOI: 10.1016/j.jclepro.2019.06.245

Raffoul, J., Ward, J., Calvez, S., Kartolo, A., Haque, A., Holmes, T., Attas, R., Kechego, J., Kustra, E., & Mooney, J. (2022). Institutional structures and individual stories: Experiences from the front lines of Indigenous educational development in higher education. AlterNative. *Alternative*, 18(1), 163–172. DOI: 10.1177/11771801211062617

Rahman, M., Ming, T. H., Baigh, T. A., & Sarker, M. (2023). Adoption of artificial intelligence in banking services: An empirical analysis. *International Journal of Emerging Markets*, 18(10), 4270–4300. DOI: 10.1108/IJOEM-06-2020-0724

Raj, A., & Bose, D. (2022). Expanding the scope of decentralized finance: Lessons from global case studies. *Journal of Global Financial Markets*, 14(2), 205–219.

Raj, M., & Seamans, R. (2019). Primer on artificial intelligence and robotics. *Journal of Organization Design*, 8(1), 11. Advance online publication. DOI: 10.1186/s41469-019-0050-0

Raj, R., & Patel, D. (2022). Regulatory frameworks and the growth of decentralized finance in India. *Journal of Financial Regulation and Compliance*, 30(3), 215–228.

Raju, B., Jumah, F., Ashraf, O., Narayan, V., Gupta, G., Sun, H., Hilden, P., & Nanda, A. (2020). Big data, machine learning, and artificial intelligence: A field guide for neurosurgeons. *Journal of Neurosurgery*, 135(2), 373–383. DOI: 10.3171/2020.5.JNS201288 PMID: 33007750

Ramasubramanian, S., & Belgavi, V. (2019). *A wider circle: Digital lending and the changing landscape of financial inclusion.*

Ramlall, S., Hattingh, M., & Van Deventer, P. (2020). *Baby Boomers' intention to use branch or digital banking channels in South Africa: An exploratory study.* In Conference of the South African Institute of Computer Scientists and Information Technologists 2020 (pp. 74-84). DOI: 10.1145/3410886.3410915

Rani, P., & Katoch, R. (2022). Contribution of crowdfunding in the growth of MSMEs. *Journal of Applied Development Economics, 1–1*, 1–10.

Rao, K., & Nair, M. (2023). Decentralized finance and regulatory frameworks: A roadmap for India. *Journal of Financial Regulation and Compliance*, 32(1), 122–139.

Rao, M. S., & Kumar, S. (2021). Financial inclusion through blockchain technology: Challenges and opportunities in India. *Global Journal of Emerging Market Economies*, 13(1), 56–72.

Rao, S., & Menon, V. (2023). Public-private partnerships and the future of decentralized finance in India. *International Journal of Financial Studies*, 11(2), 150–166.

Rasiwala, F., & Kohli, B. (2019). A Study on the Awareness and Perception of Robo Advisory Services Among Investors in Pune City. SSRN Electronic Journal, Sironi, 469–483. DOI: 10.2139/ssrn.3308595

Rathogwa, B. K. (2018). *SME adoption of digital banking in South Africa.* Master's degree Thesis, University of the Witwatersrand.

Raymond, C. M., Anderson, C. B., Athayde, S., Vatn, A., Amin, A. M., Arias-Arévalo, P., & Zent, E. (2023). *An inclusive typology of values for navigating transformations towards a just and sustainable future. Current Opinion in Environmental Sustainability* (Vol. 64). Elsevier., DOI: 10.1016/j.cosust.2023.101301

Reddy, V., & Kumar, S. (2021). The impact of regulatory uncertainty on decentralized finance adoption: A case study of rural India. *Journal of Financial Innovation*, 14(3), 211–227.

Regner, F., Schweizer, A., & Urbach, N. (2019). NFTs in Practice — Non-Fungible Tokens as Core Components of a Blockchain-based Event Ticketing Application. *In Fortieth International Conference on Information Systems.*

Renwick, N., Reid, D. R., Santos, J. A., & Piovezana, L. (2020). Indigenous People and The Sustainable Development Goals in Brazil: A Study of the Kaingang People. *Journal of Developing Societies*, 36(4), 390–414. DOI: 10.1177/0169796X20937583

Report, K. P. M. G. (2023). https://www.mckinsey.com/capabilities/quantumblack/our-insights/the-state-of-ai-in-2022-and-a-half-decade-in-review

Research, V., Aliaga-Díaz, R., & Ahluwalia, H. (2021). *Vanguard's Life-Cycle Investing Model (VLCM): A general portfolio framework for goals-based investing*. Vlcm.

Reserve Bank of India. (2020). *National Strategy for Financial Inclusion (NSFI): 2019-2024*. Accessed on March. 12. 2023. https://www.rbi.org.in/Scripts/PublicationReportDetails.aspx?UrlPage=&ID=1154

Richardson, B. J., & Cragg, W. (2010). Being virtuous and prosperous:Sris conflicting goals. *Journal of Business Ethics, 92*(SUPPL 1), 21–39. *Scopus.* Advance online publication. DOI: 10.1007/s10551-010-0632-9

Rijal, S., & Saranani, F. (2023). The Role of Blockchain Technology in Increasing Economic Transparency and Public Trust. [TACIT]. *Technology and Society Perspectives*, 1(2), 56–67. DOI: 10.61100/tacit.v1i2.51

Ritika, & Khanna, A. (2024,). *Crowdfunding: Exploring its Role as an Alternative Financial Avenue in the Indian Context*. In 14th International Conference on Industrial Engineering and Operations Management, .DOI: 10.46254/AN14.20240457

Rjoub, H., Adebayo, T. S., & Kirikkaleli, D. (2023). Blockchain technology-based FinTech banking sector involvement using adaptive neuro-fuzzy-based K-nearest neighbors algorithm. *Financial Innovation*, 9(1), 1–23. DOI: 10.1186/s40854-023-00469-3 PMID: 36919101

Rossetto, D. E., Bernardes, R. C., Borini, F. M., & Gattaz, C. C. (2018). Structure and evolution of innovation research in the last 60 years: Review and future trends in the field of business through the citations and co-citations analysis. *Scientometrics*, 115(3), 1329–1363. DOI: 10.1007/s11192-018-2709-7

Roy, S., & Sen, R. (2022). The role of regulatory clarity in the adoption of blockchain technologies in India: Implications for managers. *Journal of Financial Regulation and Compliance*, 34(3), 211–224.

Roy, V. D. (2022). For sustainable social impact at Mangalajodi: Change processes enabled by NatWest Bank India. *Emerald Emerging Markets Case Studies*, 12(2), 1–19. DOI: 10.1108/EEMCS-04-2021-0109

Ruiters, M. (2018). *Gender inequality and its impact on economic growth: a study of the relationship between gender inequality in employment, education and growth in South Africa*. Doctoral Thesis, University of Cape Town.

Rupeika Apoga, R., & Saksonova, S. (2018). SMEs' alternative financing : The case of Latvia. *European Research Studies Journal*, 21(3), 43–52.

Saari, A., Junnila, S., & Vimpari, J. (2022). Blockchain's Grand Promise for the Real Estate Sector: A Systematic Review. *Applied Sciences (Basel, Switzerland)*, 12(23), 11940. DOI: 10.3390/app122311940

Sabah Suhail, Raja Jurdak, Raimundas Matulevicius, and Choong Seon Hong. (2021) *Securing Cyber-Physical Systems Through Blockchain-Based Digital Twins and Threat Intelligence*. CoRR abs/2105.08886 arXiv:2105.08886 https://arxiv.org/abs/2105.08886

Sabah Suhail, Rasheed Hussain, Raja Jurdak, and Choong Seon Hong. (2021) Trustworthy Digital Twins in the Industrial Internet of Things with Blockchain. *IEEE Internet Computing*, 1–10. https://doi.org/ DOI: 10.1109/MIC.2021.3059320

Sadeqi-Arani, Z., & Kadkhodaie, A. (2023). A bibliometric analysis of the application of machine learning methods in the petroleum industry. *Results in Engineering*, 20, 101518. DOI: 10.1016/j.rineng.2023.101518

Sadiq, M., Paramaiah, C., Dong, Z., Nawaz, M. A., & Shukurullaevich, N. K. (2024). Role of fintech, green finance, and natural resource rents in sustainable climate change in China. Mediating role of environmental regulations and government interventions in the pre-post COVID eras. *Resources Policy*, 88, 104494. DOI: 10.1016/j.resourpol.2023.104494

Saha, R. (2016). Corporate Social Responsibility Practices: Pathways for Inclusive and Sustainable Future. *Training and Development Journal*, 7(2), 77. dspace.stellamariscollege.edu.in. DOI: 10.5958/2231-069X.2016.00011.1

Sahoo, P. B. B., & Thakur, V. (2023). Enhancing the performance of Indian micro, small and medium enterprises by implementing supply chain finance: Challenges emerging from COVID-19 pandemic. *Benchmarking*, 30(6), 2110–2138. DOI: 10.1108/BIJ-11-2021-0668

Said, M. T., & ElBannan, M. A. (2024). Do ESG ratings and COVID-19 severity score predict stock behavior and market perception? Evidence from emerging markets. *Review of Accounting and Finance, 23*(2), 222–255. *Scopus*. Advance online publication. DOI: 10.1108/RAF-03-2023-0083

Saini, M. (2023). Surviving crisis: The role of sustainable investments in navigating the impact of the Russia–Ukraine war. *International Journal of Diplomacy and Economy, 9*(2), 189–204. *Scopus*. Advance online publication. DOI: 10.1504/IJDIPE.2023.134637

Sairally, B. S. (2015). INTEGRATING ENVIRONMENTAL, SOCIAL AND GOVERNANCE (ESG) FACTORS IN ISLAMIC FINANCE: TOWARDS THE REALISATION OF MAQĀ ID AL-SHARĪʿAH. [Scopus.]. *ISRA International Journal of Islamic Finance*, 7(2), 145–154.

Sakapaji, S. C., García Molinos, J., Parilova, V., Gavrilyeva, T., & Yakovleva, N. (2024). Navigating legal and regulatory frameworks to achieve the resilience and sustainability of indigenous socioecological systems. *Resources*, 13(4), 56. DOI: 10.3390/resources13040056

Sakata, H., & Prideaux, B. (2013). An alternative approach to community-based ecotourism: A bottom-up locally initiated non-monetised project in Papua New Guinea. *Journal of Sustainable Tourism*, 21(6), 880–899. DOI: 10.1080/09669582.2012.756493

Salvia, A. L., Leal Filho, W., Brandli, L. L., & Griebeler, J. S. (2019). Assessing research trends related to Sustainable Development Goals: Local and global issues. *Journal of Cleaner Production*, 208, 841–849. DOI: 10.1016/j.jclepro.2018.09.242

Samunderu, E., & Murahwa, Y. T. (2021). Return Based Risk Measures for Non-Normally Distributed Returns: An Alternative Modelling Approach. *Journal of Risk and Financial Management*, 14(11), 2007–2008. DOI: 10.3390/jrfm14110540

Saraswat, R. (2023, August 19). *Alternative credit scoring model for MSME.*

Sarea, A., Subramanian, S., Alareeni, B., Shaikh, Z. H., Hawaldar, I. T., & Elshaker, A. H. (2021). Financial Disclosures by Using Machine Learning Analysis. In Alareeni, B., Hamdan, A., & Elgedawy, I. (Eds.), *The Importance of New Technologies and Entrepreneurship in Business Development: In The Context of Economic Diversity in Developing Countries. ICBT 2020. Lecture Notes in Networks and Systems* (Vol. 194). Springer., DOI: 10.1007/978-3-030-69221-6_5

Sarvajayakesavalu, S. (2015). Addressing challenges of developing countries in implementing five priorities for sustainable development goals. *Ecosystem Health and Sustainability*, 1(7), 1–4. DOI: 10.1890/EHS15-0028.1

Saxena, A., Ramaswamy, M., Beale, J., Marciniuk, D., & Smith, P. (2021). Striving for the United Nations (UN) Sustainable Development Goals (SDGs): What will it take? *Discover Sustainability*, 2(1), 20. Advance online publication. DOI: 10.1007/s43621-021-00029-8

Sayers, J., & Steele, M. (2020). Financial models for Indigenous infrastructure: The role of First Nations Finance Authority in Canada. *Journal of Indigenous Economic Development*, 16(2), 89–105.

Schaefer, H., Gromer, C., & Neligan, A. (2012). The demand of sustainable property investments in Germany: An explorative empirical study. *Journal of Property Investment & Finance, 30*(1), 5–17. *Scopus.* Advance online publication. DOI: 10.1108/14635781211194773

Schar, F. (2021). Decentralized finance: On blockchain- and smart contract-based financial markets. *Review - Federal Reserve Bank of St. Louis*, 103(2), 153–174.

Scheyvens, R., Banks, G., Vunibola, S., Steven, H., & Meo-Sewabu, L. (2020). Business serves society: Successful locally-driven development on customary land in the South Pacific. *Geoforum*, 112, 52–62. DOI: 10.1016/j.geoforum.2020.03.012

Scheyvens, R., Carr, A., Movono, A., Hughes, E., Higgins-Desbiolles, F., & Mika, J. P. (2021). *Indigenous tourism and the sustainable development goals. Annals of Tourism Research* (Vol. 90). Elsevier., DOI: 10.1016/j.annals.2021.103260

Scheyvens, R., & van der Watt, H. (2021). Tourism, Empowerment and Sustainable Development: A New Framework for Analysis. *Sustainability (Basel)*, 13(22), 12606. DOI: 10.3390/su132212606

Scholtens, B., & Willard, F. (2024). One size does not fit all: Responsible investor motivation and investment performance. *Corporate Social Responsibility and Environmental Management.Corporate Social Responsibility and Environmental Management*, 31(6), 6075–6082. Advance online publication. DOI: 10.1002/csr.2905

Schutte, D., & Van der Zwan, P. (2019). Turnover tax relief in South Africa: Evidence from the SARS-NT Panel. *Advances in Taxation*, 26, 135–148. DOI: 10.1108/S1058-749720190000026008

Scott, B. (2016). How can cryptocurrency and blockchain technology play a role in building social and solidarity finance? UNRISD Working Paper.

Selmi, R., Hammoudeh, S., Errami, Y., & Wohar, M. E. (2021). Is COVID-19 Related Anxiety an Accelerator for Responsible and Sustainable Investing? A Sentiment Analysis. *Applied Economics, 53*(13), 1528–1539. *Scopus.* Advance online publication. DOI: 10.1080/00036846.2020.1834501

Selwin, S., Saseendran, H., Vemavarapu, K. R., Shaikh, I., Shaikh, Z. H., & Harris, S. B. (2024). AI-Driven Employee Engagement: Transforming Banking Workforce Dynamics Using the BEULA Model. In Awwad, B. (Ed.), *The AI Revolution: Driving Business Innovation and Research. Studies in Systems, Decision and Control* (Vol. 525). Springer., DOI: 10.1007/978-3-031-54383-8_32

Sevdalis, N., & Harvey, N. (2007). "Investing" versus "investing for a reason": Context effects in investment decisions. *Journal of Behavioral Finance*, 8(3), 172–176. DOI: 10.1080/15427560701547487

Shackleton, S., Taylor, A., Gammage, L., Gillson, L., Sitas, N., Methner, N., Barmand, S., Thorn, J., McClure, A., Cobban, L., Jarre, A., & Odume, O. N. (2023). Fostering transdisciplinary research for equitable and sustainable development pathways across Africa: What changes are needed? *Ecosystems and People (Abingdon, England)*, 19(1), 2164798. Advance online publication. DOI: 10.1080/26395916.2022.2164798

Shahbaz, M., Balsalobre-Lorente, D., & Sinha, A. (2019). Foreign direct Investment–CO2 emissions nexus in Middle East and North African countries: Importance of biomass energy consumption. *Journal of Cleaner Production*, 217, 603–614. DOI: 10.1016/j.jclepro.2019.01.282

Shah, P. (2014). Creating intentional spaces for sustainable development in the Indian trans-Himalaya: Reconceptualizing globalization from below. *Intercultural Education*, 25(5), 362–376. DOI: 10.1080/14675986.2014.972610

Shaikh, Z. H., Irfan, M., Nomran, N. M., & Abey, J. (2024). Does COVID-19 affect shariah compliant stock? Evidence from selected oic countries. *Jurnal Ilmiah Ilmu Terapan Universitas Jambi*, 8(2), 720–731. DOI: 10.22437/jiituj.v8i2.33159

Shaikh, Z. H., Sarea, A., & Irfan, M. (2022). *Islamic Banking Strategies in the World of Fintech: Success Story of Bahrain* (Vol. 423). Springer., DOI: 10.1007/978-3-030-93464-4_10

Shaikh, Z., Irfan, M., Sarea, A., & Panigrahi, R. R. (2024). *The Emergence of Islamic Fintech and Bahrain: Prospect for Global Financial Sectors* (Vol. 503). Springer., DOI: 10.1007/978-3-031-43490-7_52

Shammin, M. R., Haque, A. K. E., & Faisal, I. M. (2022). A Framework for Climate Resilient Community-Based Adaptation. In Haque, A. K. E., Mukhopadhyay, P., Nepal, M., & Shammin, M. R. (Eds.), *Climate Change and Community Resilience*. Springer., DOI: 10.1007/978-981-16-0680-9_2

Sharbek, N. (2022). How Traditional Financial Institutions have adapted to Artificial Intelligence, Machine Learning and FinTech? *Proceedings of the International Conference on Business Excellence, 16*(1), 837–848. DOI: 10.2478/picbe-2022-0078

Sharma, L., & Aggarwal, R. (2021). Bridging the digital divide: Decentralized finance for inclusive growth. *Journal of Emerging Financial Technologies*, 14(2), 89–104.

Sharma, N., & Iyer, R. (2022). Regulatory challenges in the adoption of blockchain technology in India: A focus on rural inclusion. *Journal of Emerging Technologies in Financial Sector*, 14(1), 87–102.

Sharma, S. K., Ilavarasan, P. V., & Karanasios, S. (2024). Small businesses and FinTech: A systematic review and future directions. *Electronic Commerce Research*, 24(1), 535–575. DOI: 10.1007/s10660-023-09705-5

Shehzad, A., & Khan, K. I. (2024). Impediments of social responsibility investment adoption system: A post-pandemic qualitative analysis. *Qualitative Research in Financial Markets.Scopus.* Advance online publication. DOI: 10.1108/QRFM-04-2023-0089

Shekhar, S. (2023). Covid-19 and Destination Marketing: A Science Mapping and Descriptive Analysis. [Formerly known as Iranian Journal of Management Studies]. *Interdisciplinary Journal of Management Studies*, 16(4), 989–1010. DOI: 10.22059/ijms.2023.348750.675381

Shen, H., Ng, A. W., Zhang, J., & Wang, L. (2020). Sustainability accounting, management and policy in China: Recent developments and future avenues. *Sustainability Accounting. Management and Policy Journal*, 11(5), 825–839.

Sheth, A., Krishnan, S., Kashyap, P., Deo, S., & Muralidhar. (2024, March 13). *India Venture Capital Report 2024*. Bain. https://www.bain.com/insights/india-venture-capital-report-2024/

Shevchenko, K., McManus, R., & Haddock-Fraser, J. (2015). UK pension sustainability and fund manager governance: Agent duties to the principal. *Journal of Sustainable Finance and Investment, 5*(4), 205–209. *Scopus.* Advance online publication. DOI: 10.1080/20430795.2015.1106209

Shevchuk, A., & Takacs, A. (2022). Blockchain technology adoption: Opportunities and challenges. *Journal of FinTech*, 10(2), 85–101.

Shoetan, P. O., Oyewole, A. T., Okoye, C. C., & Ofodile, O. C.Philip Olaseni ShoetanAdedoyin Tolulope OyewoleChinwe Chinazo OkoyeOnyeka Chrisanctus Ofodile. (2024). REVIEWING THE ROLE OF BIG DATA ANALYTICS IN FINANCIAL FRAUD DETECTION. *Finance & Accounting Research Journal*, 6(3), 384–394. DOI: 10.51594/farj.v6i3.899

Shoetan, P. O.Philip Olaseni ShoetanBabajide Tolulope Familoni. (2024). TRANSFORMING FINTECH FRAUD DETECTION WITH ADVANCED ARTIFICIAL INTELLIGENCE ALGORITHMS. *Finance & Accounting Research Journal*, 6(4), 602–625. DOI: 10.51594/farj.v6i4.1036

Shrivastava, G. (2020). Cryptocurrencies and Blockchain Technology Applications. *Wiley eBooks*. DOI: 10.1002/9781119621201

Shuai Wang, Liwei Ouyang, Yong Yuan, Xiaochun Ni, Xuan Han, and Fei-Yue Wang. (2019) Blockchain-Enabled Smart Contracts: Architecture, Applications, and Future Trends. *IEEE Transactions on Systems, Man, and Cybernetics: Systems* 49, 11, 2266–2277. DOI: 10.1109/TSMC.2019.2895123

Sihan Huang, Guoxin Wang, Yan Yan, and Xiongbing Fang. (2020) Blockchain-based data management for digital twin of product. *Journal of Manufacturing Systems* 54, 361–371.

Simatele, M., & Maciko, L. (2022). Financial inclusion in rural South Africa: A qualitative approach. *Journal of Risk and Financial Management*, 15(9), 376. Advance online publication. DOI: 10.3390/jrfm15090376

Singh, A., & Mohan, D. (2021). Digital literacy and decentralized finance: Bridging the gap in rural India. *Journal of Digital Economy and Innovation*, 12(3), 95–109.

Singh, K. (2014). *Application of Bradford's Law on Journal Citations: A Study of Ph.* D. Theses. [Doctoral dissertation]

Singh, N. P., Bantilan, C., & Byjesh, K. (2014). Vulnerability and policy relevance to drought in the semi-arid tropics of Asia – A retrospective analysis. *Weather and Climate Extremes*, 3, 54–61. DOI: 10.1016/j.wace.2014.02.002

Singh, P., & Bansal, R. (2023). Addressing digital literacy in rural India: A framework for inclusive growth. *Journal of Rural and Community Development*, 18(1), 42–58.

Singh, R., & Khandelwal, P. (2022). Regulatory challenges and the future of decentralized finance in India. *Journal of Financial Regulation*, 33(4), 224–240.

Singh, S., & Kumar, A. (2024). Investing in the future: An integrated model for analysing user attitudes towards Robo-advisory services with AI integration. Vilakshan - XIMB. *Journal of Management*. Advance online publication. DOI: 10.1108/XJM-03-2024-0046

Skene, K. R. (2022). The circular economy: a critique of the concept. In *Towards a Circular Economy: Transdisciplinary Approach for Business* (pp. 99–116). Springer International Publishing. DOI: 10.1007/978-3-030-94293-9_5

Sloan, P., Legrand, W., & Simons-Kaufmann, C. (2014). A survey of social entrepreneurial community-based hospitality and tourism initiatives in developing economies: A new business approach for industry. *Worldwide Hospitality and Tourism Themes*, 6(1), 51–61. DOI: 10.1108/WHATT-11-2013-0045

Small, H. (1973). Co-citation in the scientific literature: A new measure of the relationship between two documents. *Journal of the American Society for Information Science*, 24(4), 265–269. DOI: 10.1002/asi.4630240406

Smith, C., Diver, S., & Reed, R. (2023). Advancing Indigenous futures with two-eyed seeing: Strategies for restoration and repair through collaborative research. *Environment and Planning. F, Philosophy, Theory, Models, Methods and Practice*, 2(1-2), 121–143. DOI: 10.1177/26349825221142292

Smith, L. (2021). Incorporating Indigenous participation in impact investing: Sustainable development and cultural preservation. *Journal of Indigenous Business and Sustainable Finance*, 18(2), 75–91.

Smith, L. (2021). Indigenous-led financial institutions: A pathway to economic empowerment through micro-loans and financial literacy. *Indigenous Economic Empowerment Journal*, 18(2), 45–61.

Smith, L. T. (2012). *Decolonizing Methodologies: Research and Indigenous Peoples* (2nd ed.). Zed Books.

Smith, L., & James, K. (2024). Decolonial financial systems: The future of Indigenous banking models. *Journal of Development Alternatives*, 18(3), 99–120.

Sobrevila, C. (2008). The Role of Indigenous Peoples in Biodiversity Conservation. In https://documents1.worldbank.org/curated/pt/995271468177530126/pdf/443000WP0BOX321onservation01PUBLIC1.pdf. The International Bank for Reconstruction and Development / THE WORLD BANK.

Sofik, S., Dr, Z. R., & Dr, S. N. (2021). Productivity Trends and Pattern of Scientific Collaboration of Bibliometric Research: An Exploratory Analysis. *Library Philosophy and Practice (E-journal)*. https://digitalcommons.unl.edu/cgi/viewcontent.cgi?article=10984&context=libphilprac

So, M. K. P. (2021). Robo-advising risk profiling through content analysis for sustainable development in the Hong Kong financial market. *Sustainability (Basel)*, 13(3), 1–15. DOI: 10.3390/su13031306

Soni, V., & Mishra, K. (2023). Perceptions and adoption of cryptocurrencies among marginalized communities in India. *Journal of Technology in Society*, 25(2), 85–101.

Sonne, L. (2012). Innovative initiatives supporting inclusive innovation in India: Social business incubation and micro venture capital. *Technological Forecasting and Social Change*, 79(4), 638–647. DOI: 10.1016/j.techfore.2011.06.008

Sosale, S. (2007). "Pre-Modern" online: Converging discourses of globalization and development. *Journalism & Communication Monographs*, 9(1), 1–52. DOI: 10.1177/152263790700900101

Srisusilawati, P., Rusydiana, A. S., Sanrego, Y. D., & Tubastuvi, N. (2021). Biblioshiny R Application on Islamic Microfinance Research. *Library Philosophy and Practice*. https://digitalcommons.unl.edu/cgi/viewcontent.cgi?article=9428&context=libphilprac

Stambaugh, R. F., & Taylor, L. A. (2021). Sustainable investing in equilibrium. *Journal of Financial Economics, 142*(2), 550–571. *Scopus*. Advance online publication. DOI: 10.1016/j.jfineco.2020.12.011

Statista. (2022). Statista Data. 2022. https://www.statista.com/outlook/dmo/fintech/digital-investment/robo-advisors/worldwide

Sternberg, H. S., Hofmann, E., & Roeck, D. (2021, March). ● Henrik S. Sternberg, Erik Hofmann, and Dominik Roeck. (2020) The Struggle is Real: Insights from a Supply Chain Blockchain Case. *Journal of Business Logistics*, 42(1), 71–87. Advance online publication. DOI: 10.1111/jbl.12240

Stringer, L. C., Simpson, N. P., Schipper, E. L. F., & Eriksen, S. H. (2022). *Climate Resilient Development Pathways in Global Drylands. Anthropocene Science*. Springer., DOI: 10.1007/s44177-022-00027-z

Sugiharto, M. E., Probohudono, A. N., Suhardjanto, D., & Widarjo, W. (2024). A bibliometric analysis of evolving trends in CEO characteristics and financial performance research. *Cogent Business and Management, 11*(1). *Scopus.*, 11(1), 2381089. Advance online publication. DOI: 10.1080/23311975.2024.2381089

Sullivan, M., & Hill, J. (2019). Innovative financial models for Indigenous inclusivity: Financial institutions, trust funds, and community lending circles. *Journal of Indigenous Finance and Economic Development*, 14(3), 123–140.

Sun, T. (2024). Role of inclusive finance on oil resource production targets: How fiscal pressures influence natural resources policy and green recovery in Gulf countries. *Resources Policy*, 88, 104337. DOI: 10.1016/j.resourpol.2023.104337

Sweileh, W. M. (2018). Global output of research on the health of international migrant workers from 2000 to 2017. *Globalization and Health*, 14(1), 1–12. DOI: 10.1186/s12992-018-0419-9 PMID: 30409221

Sweileh, W. M. (2018). Global research output on HIV/AIDS–related medication adherence from 1980 to 2017. *BMC Health Services Research*, 18(1), 1–13. DOI: 10.1186/s12913-018-3568-x PMID: 30305093

Sweileh, W. M. (2019). A bibliometric analysis of health-related literature on natural disasters from 1900 to 2017. *Health Research Policy and Systems*, 17(1), 1–11. DOI: 10.1186/s12961-019-0418-1 PMID: 30744641

T. N. Dinh and M. T. Thai. (2018) AI and Blockchain: A Disruptive Integration. *Computer* 51, 9, 48–53. https://doi.org/. 2018.3620971DOI: 10.1109/MC

Tadesse, B., & Ahmed, M. (2023). Impact of adoption of climate smart agricultural practices to minimize production risk in Ethiopia: A systematic review. *Journal of Agriculture and Food Research*, 13, 100655. DOI: 10.1016/j.jafr.2023.100655

Tapscott, D., & Tapscott, A. (2016). *Blockchain revolution: How the technology behind Bitcoin is changing money, business, and the world.* Penguin.

Team, I. (2024, April 9). *What is artificial intelligence (AI)?* Investopedia. Retrieved July 16, 2024, from https://www.investopedia.com/terms/a/artificial-intelligence-ai.asp

Teixeira, A. V., & Coates, K. (2024). Exploring Economic Development Strategies for Canadian Indigenous Communities Post-Pandemic. *Scientific Annals of Economics and Business*, 71(2), 285–300. DOI: 10.47743/saeb-2024-0015

The Indigenous World 2024: Sustainable Development Goals (SDGs) and Indigenous Peoples - IWGIA - International Work Group for Indigenous Affairs. (2024, March 26). Www.iwgia.org. https://www.iwgia.org/en/the-sustainable-development-goals-sdgs-and-indigenous-peoples/5413-iw-2024-sdg.html

Thompson, K.-L., Lantz, T. C., & Ban, N. C. (2020). A review of Indigenous knowledge and participation in environmental monitoring. *Ecology and Society*, 25(2), art10. Advance online publication. DOI: 10.5751/ES-11503-250210

Tian, Y., Minchin, R. E., Chung, K., Woo, J., & Adriaens, P. (2021). Towards Inclusive and Sustainable Infrastructure Development through Blockchain-enabled Asset Tokenization: An Exploratory Case Study. *IOP Conference Series: Materials Science and Engineering*, Volume 1218

Tiony, O. (2023). The Impact of Digital Financial Services on Financial Inclusion in Kenya. *American Journal of Industrial and Business Management*, 13(6), 593–628. DOI: 10.4236/ajibm.2023.136035

Tomar, S., Kumar, S., & Sureka, R. (2021). Financial Planning for Retirement: Bibliometric Analysis and Future Research Directions. In *Journal of Financial Counseling and Planning* (Vol. 32, Issue 2, pp. 344–362). Springer Publishing Company. DOI: 10.1891/JFCP-19-00062

Torres, A., & Cruz, R. (2024). Blockchain-based transparency frameworks for Indigenous resource management. *Technological Innovations for Indigenous Economies*, 22(1), 50–67.

Tran, H. T. T., & Le, H. T. T. (2021). The impact of financial inclusion on poverty reduction. *Asian Journal of Law and Economics*, 12(1), 95–119. DOI: 10.1515/ajle-2020-0055

Tripathi, V., & Kaur, A. (2020). Socially responsible investing: Performance evaluation of BRICS nations. *Journal of Advances in Management Research, 17*(4), 525–547. *Scopus.* Advance online publication. DOI: 10.1108/JAMR-02-2020-0020

Tripathi, V., & Kaur, A. (2022). Does Socially Responsible Investing Pay in Developing Countries? A Comparative Study Across Select Developed and Developing Markets. *FIIB Business Review, 11*(2), 189–205. *Scopus*. Advance online publication. DOI: 10.1177/2319714520980288

Tripathy, A., & Dastrala, S. M. (2023). Make in India: So Far and Going Ahead. SSRN Electronic Journal. https://doi.org/DOI: 10.2139/ssrn.4384039

Trivedi, S., Mehta, K., & Sharma, R. (2021). Systematic Literature Review on Application of Blockchain Technology in E-Finance and Financial Services. *Journal of Technology Management & Innovation*, 16(3), 89–102. DOI: 10.4067/S0718-27242021000300089

Truby, J. (2018). Decarbonizing Bitcoin: Law and policy choices for reducing the energy consumption of Blockchain technologies and digital currencies. *Energy Research & Social Science*, 44, 399–410. DOI: 10.1016/j.erss.2018.06.009

Tseng, M. L., Tan, P. A., Jeng, S. Y., Lin, C. W. R., Negash, Y. T., & Darsono, S. N. A. C. (2019). Sustainable investment: Interrelated among corporate governance, economic performance and market risks using investor preference approach. *Sustainability (Basel)*, 11(7), 2108. DOI: 10.3390/su11072108

Udeagha, M. C., & Muchapondwa, E. (2023). Green finance, fintech, and environmental sustainability: Fresh policy insights from the BRICS nations. *International Journal of Sustainable Development and World Ecology*, 30(6), 633–649. DOI: 10.1080/13504509.2023.2183526

Uitto, J. I. (2021). Evaluating environment in international development: An introduction. In *Evaluating Environment in International Development* (pp. 3–24). Routledge. DOI: 10.4324/9781003094821-2

Ulucak, R., & Ozcan, B. (2020). Relationship between energy consumption and environmental sustainability in OECD countries: The role of natural resources rents. *Resources Policy*, 69, 101803. DOI: 10.1016/j.resourpol.2020.101803

UNDP. (2024). Indigenous knowledge is crucial in the fight against climate change – here's why | UNDP Climate Promise. UNDP Climate Promise. https://climatepromise.undp.org/news-and-stories/indigenous-knowledge-crucial-fight-against-climate-change-heres-why

United Nations. (2015) A/RES/70/1 - Transforming our world: the 2030 agenda for sustainable development. Resolution adopted by the General Assembly on 25 September 2015, p 35. https://docum ents-dds-ny.un.org/doc/UNDOC/GEN/N15/291/89/PDF/N1529 189.pdf?OpenElement United Nations (2017) A/RES/71/313 - Work of the Statistical Commission pertainingto the 2030 Agenda for Sustainable Development. Resolution adopted by the General Assembly on 6 July 2017, p 25. https://documents-dds-ny.un.org/doc/UNDOC/GEN/ 17/207/63/PDF/N1720763.pdf?OpenElement

United Nations:Sustainable development goals [(https://www.un.org/sustainabledevelopment/sustainable-development-goals/]. Accessed 10 July 2020

Unlocking credit for MSMEs: Innovations in supply chain finance. (2019). PwC.

Uzsoki, D., & Guerdat, P. (2019). Impact Tokens: A blockchain-based solution for impact investing. *International Institute for Sustainable Development*.

Valadkhani, A., & O'Mahony, B. (2024). Sustainable investing in extreme market conditions: Doing well while doing good. *Journal of Economic Studies.Journal of Economic Studies (Glasgow, Scotland)*. Advance online publication. DOI: 10.1108/JES-11-2023-0626

van Doorn, J., Mende, M., Noble, S. M., Hulland, J., Ostrom, A. L., Grewal, D., & Petersen, J. A. (2017). Domo Arigato Mr. Roboto: Emergence of Automated Social Presence in Organizational Frontlines and Customers' Service Experiences. *Journal of Service Research*, 20(1), 43–58. DOI: 10.1177/1094670516679272

Van Eck, N. J., & Waltman, L. (2017). Citation-based clustering of publications using CitNetExplorer and VOSviewer. *Scientometrics*, 111(2), 1053–1070. DOI: 10.1007/s11192-017-2300-7 PMID: 28490825

Van Roy, V., Vertesy, D., & Damioli, G. (2020). AI and Robotics Innovation. In *Springer eBooks* (pp. 1–35). https://doi.org/DOI: 10.1007/978-3-319-57365-6_12-2

Vazquez-Maguirre, M., & Portales, L. (2018). Profits and purpose: Organizational tensions in social enterprises. *Intangible Capital*, 14(4), 604–618. DOI: 10.3926/ic.1208

Veeravatnanond, V., Nasa-arn, S., Nithimongkonchai, W., Wongpho, B., & Phookung, K. (2012). Development of risk assurance criteria to the utilization of natural resources and environment for sustainable development of life quality, economy and society in rural Thai communities. *Asian Social Science*, 8(2), 189. DOI: 10.5539/ass.v8n2p189

Venkatesh, J., & Kumari, R. L. (2012). Enhancing SMEs Access to Green Finance. *International Journal of Marketing. Financial Services & Management Research*, 1(7), 22–35.

Venkatesh, V., & Davis, F. D. (2000). A theoretical extension of the technology acceptance model: Four longitudinal field studies. *Management Science*, 46(2), 186–204. DOI: 10.1287/mnsc.46.2.186.11926

Venkatesh, V., Morris, M. G., Davis, G. B., & Davis, F. D. (2003). User acceptance of information technology: Toward a unified view. *Management Information Systems Quarterly*, 27(3), 425–478. DOI: 10.2307/30036540

Venkateswaran, R. (2023). Indigenous indian management. *Decision (Washington, D.C.)*, 50(3), 363–366. DOI: 10.1007/s40622-023-00353-0

Verma, D., Kalra, R., & Baheti, S. S. (2023). Examining the Domain of Green Finance Through Bibliometric Research Analysis of 22 Years (2000–2022): An Analytical Retrospective. *Vision (Basel)*, •••, 09722629231157470. DOI: 10.1177/09722629231157470

Verma, P., & Joshi, R. (2023). Digital literacy and its impact on DeFi adoption in Indian indigenous communities. *Journal of Digital Economy*, 17(1), 94–108.

Verma, S., & Gustafsson, A. (2020). Investigating the emerging COVID-19 research trends in the field of business and management: A bibliometric analysis approach. *Journal of Business Research*, 118, 253–261. DOI: 10.1016/j.jbusres.2020.06.057 PMID: 32834211

Verma, S., & Khanna, A. (2024). The Influence of Emotions and Social Value Orientation on Risk Tolerance and Sustainable Investment Choices. *Australasian Accounting, Business and Finance Journal, 18*(3), 331–351. *Scopus.* Advance online publication. DOI: 10.14453/aabfj.v18i3.17

Vodolazhska, A. (2023, July 11). *Crowdfunding in India: Market Overview*. LenderKit.

Vogels, E. A. (2021). Some digital divides persist between rural, urban and suburban America. Pew Research Centre, August 19. Accessed on June. 13. 2024. https://www.pewresearch.org/short-reads/2021/08/19/some-digital-divides-persist-between-rural-urban-and-suburban-america/

Volkan Dedeoglu, Raja Jurdak, Guntur D. Putra, Ali Dorri, and Salil S. Kanhere. (2019) A Trust Architecture for Blockchain in IoT. In Proceedings of the 16th EAI International Conference on Mobile and Ubiquitous Systems: Computing, Networking and Services (Houston, Texas, USA) (MobiQuitous '19). *Association for Computing Machinery, New York, NY, USA*, 190–199. DOI: 10.1145/3360774.3360822

Volodymyr Babich and Gilles Hilary. (2020) OM Forum - Distributed Ledgers and Operations: What Operations Management Researchers Should Know About Blockchain Technology. *Manufacturing & Service Operations Management* 22, 2, 223–240. https://doi.org/DOI: 10.1287/msom.2018.0752

Volodymyr Babich, Gilles Hilary, et al. (2019) Blockchain and other distributed ledger technologies in operations. *Foundations and Trends in Technology, Information and Operations Management* 12, 2-3, 152–172. https://doi.org/DOI: 10.2139/ssrn.3232977

Walker, S., Kannan, P., Bhawra, J., & Tarun, R. K. (2023). Evaluation of a longitudinal digital citizen science initiative to understand the impact of culture on indigenous youth mental health: Findings from a quasi-experimental qualitative study. *PLoS One*, 18(12), e0294234. Advance online publication. DOI: 10.1371/journal.pone.0294234 PMID: 38127846

Wall, L. D. (2018). Some financial regulatory implications of artificial intelligence. *Journal of Economics and Business*, 100, 55–63. DOI: 10.1016/j.jeconbus.2018.05.003

Walmsley, J. (2021). Artificial intelligence and the value of transparency. *AI & Society*, 36(2), 585–595. DOI: 10.1007/s00146-020-01066-z

Wang, B., Kang, X., & Zhang, L. (2022). The Path to Universal Coverage of Account Ownership in Rural China. Chinese Academy of Financial Inclusion (CAFI). Accessed on March. 18. 2024. https://en.cafi.org.cn/upload/portal/20220925/6f01f43a064fddec5fc32ed03b2a722d.pdf

Wani, V. P., Garg, T. K., & Sharma, S. K. (2003). The role of technical institutions in developing a techno-entrepreneurial workforce for sustainable development of SMEs in India. *International Journal of Management and Enterprise Development*, 1(1), 71–88. DOI: 10.1504/IJMED.2003.003510

Washington, S. A. (2023). Reflecting on an Indigenist Methodology in Indigenous Family and Community Engagement Research. *The Qualitative Report*, 28(4), 1210–1229. DOI: 10.46743/2160-3715/2023.5899

Watanabe, C., Lei, S., & Ouchi, N. (2009). Fusing indigenous technology development and market learning for greater functionality development—An empirical analysis of the growth trajectory of Canon printers. *Technovation*, 29(4), 265–283. DOI: 10.1016/j.technovation.2008.10.008

Watson, J., & Green, A. (2020). The role of digital platforms, fintech, and blockchain in increasing Indigenous access to finance. *International Journal of Financial Innovation*, 14(1), 33–48.

Wedajo, D. Y., Belissa, T. K., & Jilito, M. F. (2019). Harnessing indigenous social institutions for technology adoption: 'Afoosha'society of Ethiopia. *Development Studies Research*, 6(1), 152–162. DOI: 10.1080/21665095.2019.1678187

Weston, P., & Nnadi, M. (2023). Evaluation of strategic and financial variables of corporate sustainability and ESG policies on corporate finance performance. *Journal of Sustainable Finance and Investment, 13*(2), 1058–1074. *Scopus.* Advance online publication. DOI: 10.1080/20430795.2021.1883984

Wilkes, J. (2022). Reconnecting with Nature through Good Governance: Inclusive Policy across Scales. *Agriculture (Switzerland)*, Vol. 12. mdpi.com. DOI: 10.3390/agriculture12030382

Williams, P. A., Sikutshwa, L., & Shackleton, S. (2020). Acknowledging indigenous and local knowledge to facilitate collaboration in landscape approaches- lessons from a systematic review. *Land*, Vol. 9. mdpi.com. DOI: 10.3390/land9090331

Williams, D. H., Shipley, G. P., Williams, D. H., & Shipley, G. P. (2020). Enhancing Artificial Intelligence with Indigenous Wisdom. *Open Journal of Philosophy*, 11(1), 43–58. DOI: 10.4236/ojpp.2021.111005

Williams, T. H., Iriobe, G. O., Ayodele, T. D., Olasupo, S. F., & Aladejebi, M. O. (2023). Do illiteracy and unemployment affect financial inclusion in the rural areas of developing countries. *Investment Management and Financial Innovations*, 20(2), 89–101. DOI: 10.21511/imfi.20(2).2023.08

Wilson, K. B., Karg, A., & Ghaderi, H. (2021). Prospecting non- fungible tokens in the digital economy: Stakeholders and ecosystem, risk and opportunity. *Business Horizons*, 65(5), 657e670.

Wilson, R., & Thomas, C. (2024). Leveraging blockchain for transparency in Indigenous land agreements. *Journal of Emerging Technologies in Social Equity*, 9(1), 12–28.

Wipro. (2020). Future of in Investment and Wealth Management.

Witkowska, J. (2023). The Role of FDI in the Sustainable Development of the European Union. *Comparative Economic Research, 26*(1), 21–43. *Scopus.* Advance online publication. DOI: 10.18778/1508-2008.26.02

Wong, J. M., Chiang, Y. H., & Ng, T. S. (2008). Construction and economic development: The case of Hong Kong. *Construction Management and Economics*, 26(8), 815–826. DOI: 10.1080/01446190802189927

Woodroffe, T. (2020). Presentation Feedback as an Indigenous methodology. *Australian Journal of Education*, 65(1), 73–83. DOI: 10.1177/0004944120969987

World Bank. (n.d.). Financial inclusion. World Bank. Retrieved August 2, 2024, from https://www.worldbank.org/en/topic/financialinclusion

Wright, A., & De Filippi, P. (2015). Decentralized blockchain technology and the rise of lex cryptographia. SSRN Electronic Journal. DOI: 10.2139/ssrn.2580664

Yap, M., & Yu, E. (2016). Operationalising the Capability Approach: Developing Culturally Relevant Indicators of Indigenous Well-being - An Australian Example. *Oxford Development Studies*, 44(3), 315–331. DOI: 10.1080/13600818.2016.1178223

Yazzie, C., & Johnston, T. (2024). Sustainable development initiatives in Navajo Nation: Lessons for global Indigenous economies. *International Journal of Sustainability and Indigenous Affairs*, 7(2), 145–162.

Yende, S. J., & Yende, N. E. (2022). The Disparity between the Political Elites and Constituencies in the Quest for Democracy and Sustainable Development in South Africa. *African Renaissance (1744-2532), 19*(4).

Yoo, S., & Managi, S. (2021). Disclosure or action: Evaluating ESG behavior towards financial performance. *Finance Research Letters*, 102108.

Yumnam, G., Gyanendra, Y., & Singh, C. I. (2024). A systematic bibliometric review of the global research dynamics of United Nations Sustainable Development Goals 2030. *Sustainable Futures : An Applied Journal of Technology, Environment and Society*, 7, 100192. DOI: 10.1016/j.sftr.2024.100192

Zhang, N., Sun, C., Xu, M., Wang, X., & Deng, J. (2023). Catching Up of Latecomer Economies in ICT for Sustainable Development: An Analysis Based on Technology Life Cycle Using Patent Data. *Sustainability (Basel)*, 15(11), 9038. DOI: 10.3390/su15119038

Zheng, Z., Lisovskiy, A., Vasa, L., Strielkowski, W., & Yang, Y. (2023). Resources curse and sustainable development perspective: Fresh evidence from oil rich countries. *Resources Policy*, 85, 103698. DOI: 10.1016/j.resourpol.2023.103698

Zhou, P., & Leydesdorff, L. (2020). The emergence of China as a leading nation in science. *Research Policy*, 49(6), 1039–1056.

Zhou, X., Tang, X., & Zhang, R. (2020). Impact of green finance on economic development and environmental quality: A study based on provincial panel data from China. *Environmental Science and Pollution Research International*, 27(16), 19915–19932. DOI: 10.1007/s11356-020-08383-2 PMID: 32232752

Zidny, R., Sjöström, J., & Eilks, I. (2020). A Multi-Perspective Reflection on How Indigenous Knowledge and Related Ideas Can Improve Science Education for Sustainability. *Science & Education*, 29(1), 145–185. DOI: 10.1007/s11191-019-00100-x

Zohar, A. (2015). Bitcoin: Under the hood. *Communications of the ACM*, 58(9), 104–113. DOI: 10.1145/2701411

Zou, D., Huang, X., Kohnke, L., Chen, X., Cheng, G., & Xie, H. (2022). A bibliometric analysis of the trends and research topics of empirical research on TPACK. *Education and Information Technologies*, 27(8), 10585–10609. DOI: 10.1007/s10639-022-10991-z

Zurba, M., & Papadopoulos, A. (2023). *Indigenous Participation and the Incorporation of Indigenous Knowledge and Perspectives in Global Environmental Governance Forums: a Systematic Review. Environmental Management* (Vol. 72). Springer., DOI: 10.1007/s00267-021-01566-8

About the Contributors

Mohammad Irfan is presently working as an Associate Professor at School of Business and Management, Christ University, Bengaluru, India. Dr. Irfan has done his Ph.D. from the Central University of Haryana. He is MBA (Finance), M.Com (Account and Law), and MA (Economics). He has qualified UGC-JRF/SRF/NET in Management and Commerce. Dr. Irfan certified NSEs (NCFM) and BSEs certification. He has experience of more than sixteen years in the area of SAPM, Artificial Intelligence, Machine Learning, Blockchain, Cryptocurrency, Financial Engineering, Fintech, Green Finance, and Alternative Finance. He has to his credit more than 61+ Scopus Indexed articles, includes The Journal of Economic Cooperation and Development (Q2), International Journal of Business Excellence (IJBEX), International Journal of Economics and Management (IJEM), Montenegrin Journal of Economics (Q2), Cogent Business & Management (Taylor & Francis) (Q2), Indian Journal of Finance (IJF) and Journal of Islamic Monetary Economics and Finance (JIMF). His citations reached 404+ along with 13 H-index. Dr. Irfan has published 9 books in Springer, IGI Global Publication (Scopus indexed).

Mohammed Majeed, Tamale Technical University, Ghana, where he is currently Head of the Department for Marketing. His research interests include branding, hospitality and tourism, and social media in service organizations. He lectures part time at many Ghanaian public universities and also acts as a reviewer for many journals in management, hospitality, and marketing. Dr. Majeed has published in reputed journals such as the Journal of Hospitality and Tourism Insights and Cogent Business & Management. His citations are 269+.

Salina Kassim has a great passion in writing scholarly articles in various areas of Islamic banking and finance. She has published extensively in academic journals with nearly 200 scholarly articles in the areas of her research interests, with 5436+ citation. The editorial board team will connect the faculty and scholar from India, UAE, and Malaysia. The contribution of the paper diversifies the authors of chapters.

Kwame Simpe Ofori is currently working in University of Electronic Science and Technology of China. His research interests are in the areas of consumer behaviour, technology adoption and trust in online systems and PLS path modelling. His papers have appeared in Information Technology and People, Marketing Intelligence and Planning, International Journal of Bank Marketing, Total Quality Management and Business Excellence, and Society and Business Review.

***

Rachit Agarwal is working as an Assistant Professor at University School of Business, Chandigarh University, Mohali. He is having more than 7 years of work experience in teaching and research. His areas of interest are financial analysis, investment behavior analysis and behavioral study. He has published various papers in national and international journals including Scopus and ABDC listed journals. He has also organized many workshops and Faculty Development Programme on Research Methodology and on different statistical tools.

Nidhi Upendra Argade is Assistant Professor with Department of Accounting and Financial Management, Faculty of Commerce, The Maharaja Sayajirao University of Baroda, Vadodara. Her professional journey started with corporate experience of two years at ICICI Lombard General Insurance Company Ltd. Her strong urge to get associated with the noble profession of teaching made her join the field of academics 17 years ago. She was awarded Doctor of Philosophy on her Doctor Research in the area of Merger and Acquisition and she is recognized PhD guide too. Her teaching diverse subjects are- Financial Management, Personal Finance and Investments ,Capital Markets, Security Analysis, and Portfolio Management, Service Management and Accounting, Corporate Accounting. Dr Nidhi has published many research articles in the renowned international and national journals and published one book titled *Merger and Acquisition: A Detailed Insight into Performance Evaluation*.

Esther Asiedu serves as a Senior Lecturer in the Department of Management Studies at Ghana Communication Technology University in Accra, Ghana. Her academic expertise is evidenced by her extensive research interests, which include management and organizational behaviour, leadership, supply chain dynamics, graduate employability, entrepreneurship, procurement, corporate sustainability, small and medium-sized enterprises, AI and management, higher education, green human resource management, procurement practices, and gender-related issues. Dr. Asiedu earned her PhD in Business Administration from CASS Europe in France, an MPA, and a BA (Hons) in Sociology with Political Science from the University of Ghana. She also holds a Postgraduate Certificate in International Higher Education Practice from Coventry University. As a reviewer for several prestigious journals in the fields of management, business studies, AI in management, and corporate social responsibility, Dr. Asiedu has contributed to the academic community through her critical evaluations. Her own research has been published in notable journals, including the Journal of Higher Education, Skills and Work-Based Learning (Emerald), the Journal of Theoretical and Applied Information Technology (Little Lion Scientific), and publications by Palgrave Macmillan, IGI Global, Springer, Apple Academic Press, and Taylor & Francis.

Santosh Satyanarayan Baheti is an Assistant Professor in the School of Business and Management at Christ University, Bangalore. He has two years corporate experience. Hos area of research include corporate sustainability, ESG, sustainable business performance, sustainability reporting practices, and green HRM practices

Chaman Verma received the Ph.D. degree in informatics from the Doctoral School of Informatics, Eötvös Loránd University, Budapest, Hungary, with Stipendium Hunagricum Scholarship funded by the Tempus Public Foundation, Government of Hungary. During his Ph.D. degree, he won the EFOP Scholarship, Co-Founded by the European Union Social Fund and the Government of Hungary, as a Professional Research Assistant in a real-time system, from 2018 to 2021. He also received the Stipendium Hungaricum Dissertation Scholarship of Tempus Public Foundation, Government of Hungary, from 2021 to 2022. He is currently an Assistant Professor with the Department of Media and Educational Informatics, Faculty of Informatics, Eötvös Loránd University. He has been awarded several Erasmus

Scholarships for conducting international research and academic collaboration with European and non-European universities.,He Received The Best Scientific Publication Awards From The Faculty Of Informatics, Eotvos Lorand University, In The Years 2021, 2022, And 2023. He Has Also Been Awarded ÚNkp Scholarship For Research By The Ministry Of Innovation And Technology And The National Research, Development And Innovation (Nrdi) Fund, Government Of Hungary, In 2020-2021 and 2022-2023. He has around ten years of experience in teaching and industry. He has more than 100 scientific publications in the IEEE, Elsevier, Springer, IOP Science, MDPI, and Walter de Gruyter. His research interests include data analytics, the IoT, feature engineering, real-time systems, and educational informatics. He is a Life Member of ISTE, New Delhi, India; a member of the editorial board; and a reviewer of various international journals and scientific conferences. He was the leading Guest Editor of the Special Issue Advancement in Machine Learning and Applications in mathematics, IF-2.25, MDPI, Basel, Switzerland, in 2022. He is a co-editor in the series of conference proceedings of ICRIC-2021 and ICRIC-2022 published by Springer, Singapore. He reviews many scientific journals, including IEEE, Springer, Elsevier, Wiley, and MDPI. He has Scopus citations of 615 with an H-index of 15. He has Web of Science citations 81 with an H-index of 8.

Priya Chandak is a research scholar working with the department of Accounting & Financial Management, Faculty of Commerce, The Maharaja Sayajirao University of baroda, Vadodara, Gujarat. She has master's degree with specialisation in accounting and financial management, and pursuing doctoral degree (PhD) at present. The financial and technological challenges faced by Micro, Small, and Medium-sized Enterprises (MSME), as well as the support provided by the government in reducing these challenges, are encompassed in her area of research. In addition, she has successfully completed the company secretary course in three stages entrance, executive and final which are offered by "ICSI."

Dowluri Sudhakar is having more than 14 years of teaching experience at UG and PG level. He published 15 research papers in the journals of national and international repute, participated in conferences and presented papers, guided more than 300 post graduate students for their master thesis and is career guidance coach as well.

Debora is Assistant Professor of Marketing in Business and Management department at Christ University Bangalore. She hold four years of teaching experience. She has published research articles in numerous peer reviewed journals and books. Her area of interests consists smart tourism, digital marketing and E-commerce application.

Suchi Dubey is an Associate professor at Symbiosis International University, Dubai; Symbiosis International (Deemed) University, Pune, India. She is an Associate Professor for Finance SoB, a Member of the Research Committee, and a Member of the Conference Committee at SoB. Her area of research and expertise includes valuation, risk premium, and banking services. She has various international and national publications. She has done her doctorate in commerce. She teaches varied subjects including Research Methods in Management, Security Analysis and Portfolio Management, Service Marketing, Corporate Valuation, Portfolio Management etc.

Oindrilla Ghosh is a Research Scholar hailing from the School of Law at Christ (Deemed to be University) Bangalore, India, focuses her research on health of tribal communities. Her work includes publications on Environmental Disasters that are indexed in SCOPUS and Web of Sciences conference proceedings. She completed her early education at Loreto Day School, Bowbazar and went on to achieve distinction in her undergraduate (B.A/LL.B) and postgraduate (LL.M) studies at Calcutta University. Having served as an Assistant Professor of Law at Kingston Law College,Barasat, Kolkata, Ghosh has actively participated in numerous National Conferences, International Conferences, UN Global Summits, webinars, and seminars organized by prestigious academic institutions. Her expertise lies in health perspectives, environmental studies, human behavior, and related areas. Additionally, she has conducted various workshops, lectures in educational institutions, and is engaged with NGO's to help the needy.

Viana Hassan is actively involved in academic and research work in Tourism & Cultural Management in Lebanon and Malta. She got her Ph.D. in Tourism Management and Cultural from Saint Joseph University, Beirut. Her Thesis was entitled "Medical Tourism in Lebanon". She has more than 19 years of tourism experience in many related Travel and Tourism Fields, varying from airline sales experience (MEA), to Co-management several Lebanese Travel agencies. She is an Experienced Lecturer with more than 16 years' experience at several universities in Lebanon (Lebanese University, A.U. L, Lebanese International University, Islamic University), the Institute of Tourism Studies, STC higher education partner of Wolverhmapton University UK and University of Malta (Malta), GBS Malta, Scholars School system (UK) with a demonstrated history of working in the Higher education industry, Skilled in Tourism Management, Customer service, Branding, Event Management, Airline Business Management, Niche Tourism, Business operations management, Customer acquisition and Medical Tourism. Dr. Viana has participated in international conferences (Expo Dubai 2020, 7th Medical Tourism World Summit..) including Athens, Paris, Vienna, Dubai, Valencia, India, Turkey etc....

Ishmael Iwara, a Y-rated researcher by the South African National Research Foundation (NRF), is a distinguished development economist. His evolving research trajectory focuses on entrepreneurship modeling, entrepreneurial universities, business efficacy, rural development imperatives, and sustainability.

Gaurav Jangra working as an Associate Professor, Management, Chandigarh University, Published 10 text books, 5 book chapters, 10 research papers. Attended more than 20 seminars, conferences, workshops. The area of research is Digital Marketing and FinTech..

Monika Jangra is working as an Assistant Professor, University Institute of Computing, Chandigarh University, having 3 years of teaching experience. Published 2 books, 2 chapters, 2 research papers. Area of research is AI and Database.

Aishwarya Joshi is an independent HR professional. She has two years of industry and academia. She has two books to her credit. She has published her research work in peer reviewed journals. She hold gold medal in her masters in management.

Rishikaysh Kaakandikar boasts an exceptional academic journey, spanning over 12 years of dedicated teaching and a year of valuable industrial experience, and currently holds the esteemed position of Associate Professor at SaiBalaji Education Society's SaiBalaji International Institute of Management Sciences in Pune. His scholarly contributions shine brightly, encompassing a remarkable portfolio of over 40 research papers in prestigious journals. A sought-after intellectual resource, He has contributed substantially to academia through guest lectures, seminars, workshops, and conferences at esteemed institutions across India. His insights have enriched the academic community and stimulated engaging discussions on various facets of his field. He is a prominent finance columnist for leading newspapers in Maharashtra, including Sakal, Lokmat, Punyannagari, and Prabhat.

Varun Kesavan is a prolific and voracious researcher in the areas of financial technologies, digital payment systems, banking, corporate finance, financial management, green finance, artificial intelligence, sustainability, tourism, and quantum computing domains. He was a gold medalist at graduation and postgraduation. He authored 41 books, published 31 articles, case studies, and book reviews in leading international and national journals, published more than 300 articles on leading websites, and published more than 1000 newspaper articles in an English daily from Hyderabad, India, on various managerial domains.

Nilesh Kharche is a certified Data Analyst trainer with 25+ years of experience in academics, training and research. He holds B.E in Production Engineering, an MBA in Marketing Management, M.E in Production Engineering and Management and Ph.D in Marketing Management. His areas of expertise are diverse and include Business Statistics, Supply Chain Management, Operation Research, Quantitative Techniques, Marketing Research, Advanced Operation Research, Blockchain Technology. Dr. Nilesh is at presently associated with Balaji Institute of Technology & Management, Sri Balaji University, Pune as Faculty in Business Statistics and Quantitative Techniques. He has shown to be an excellent mentor, instructor, and corporate interaction facilitator. Dr. Nilesh loves to share his knowledge about SPSS (Statistical Package for Social Sciences), Minitab, Power BI and Excel. For his efforts in education and research field, he has been recognized with publications in peer-reviewed journals, book chapters in scopus indexed books and the best research paper award. In addition, he holds Four granted and published patents.

Beata Kilonzo is a senior lecturer in the Institute for Rural Development, University of Venda

Binod Kumar is an undergraduate student known for his academic excellence and active involvement in extracurricular activities. Hailing from Ranchi, Jharkhand in India, Binod is currently pursuing a Bachelor of Law degree at the prestigious Shri Venkateshwara University. His passion for technology and innovation along with climate changes is evident through his high academic performance and numerous projects. Binod has a keen interest in artificial intelligence, machine learning, neuropsychology, climate changes and disaster management, fields in which he has undertaken several research projects. He is particularly fascinated by the potential of AI to solve real-world problems and is dedicated to learning and applying new techniques in these areas. Binod's technical skills are complemented by his strong analytical abilities and attention to detail. In addition to his academic and technical pursuits, Binod is passionate about community service. He volunteers at local NGOs, teaching underprivileged children basic computer skills. With a strong foundation in law and a commitment to making a positive impact, Binod Kumar is poised to become a future leader in the legal industry.

Tanya Kumar works at Amity University, Mohali. She has experience in teaching and research. She completed her Ph.D. in commerce from MAU, Baddi. Her areas of interest are financial analysis, investment behavior analysis, and behavioral study. She has published various papers in national and international journals, including Scopus and ABDC-listed journals.

Ebenezer Malcalm is the Dean of School of Graduate Studies and Research at Ghana Communication Technology University (GCTU). He was the founding Pro-Vice Chancellor of Laweh Open University College, the first accredited Open University in Ghana. Prof. Ebenezer Malcalm was once Senior lecturer and Coordinator of Distance Learning School at University of Professional Studies, Accra. He is a trained Instructional Designer and Technologist and Communication and development Specilaist. Prof. Malcalm founded Rescue Mission Ghana, an international NGO that seeks to promote the concept of Sustainable Development. About his educational background, Prof. Malcalm obtained a Bachelor degree in Publishing Studies at Kwame Nkrumah University of Science and Technology Kumasi, Ghana and a Masters degree in Population Studies, from University of Ghana. He also graduated and earned Masters degree in International Affairs with a major in Communication and Development at Ohio University. He earned his Ph.D in Curriculum/ Instruction and Instructional Technology at Ohio University, USA.

Pampana Surya Prakasa Rao is a distinguished faculty member in the School of Commerce and Management at Dravidian University, Kuppam. He holds a doctorate in Entrepreneurship area from Andhra University. With a strong research background, Dr. Prakash has published numerous papers in esteemed journals, contributing significantly to the field of Management. His expertise encompasses various aspects of commerce and management, making him a valuable asset to both students and the academic community.

Supriya Tiwari Pathak is an accomplished academician with a distinguished background in management, mathematics, and computer science. She holds a Ph.D. in Management from Oriental University, Indore, and an MBA in Finance & Marketing, as well as an M.Sc. in Mathematics from Devi Ahilya University, Indore. Currently, Dr. Pathak serves as an Assistant Professor at Oriental University, Indore, where she teaches subjects ranging from Digital Marketing to Data Analytics at MBA and BBA levels. Her teaching career spans over a decade, with notable roles at various institutions . Dr. Pathak is highly engaged in international academia, serving as Director of Foreign Affairs for Witty Gossip Association and playing a key role in organizing international conferences, webinars, and symposiums. She is also an adjudicator for the World Book of Records, Africa, and has coordinated academic exchange programs globally. Her research primarily focuses on consumer behavior, social media marketing, and generational studies. She has published extensively in reputed journals and is the author of books like "Effects of Social Media Advertisements on Buying Behaviour." Her leadership in organizing four editions of the Global Peace and Sustainable Development Summit, along with numerous other international initiatives, underscores her commitment to promoting global education and sustainability. Recognized for her contributions, Dr. Pathak has received several awards, including the National Excellence Award from the ALMA group and honors from the Indo-British Cultural Forum. She continues to drive impactful initiatives that bridge education, sustainability, and international cooperation.

Aruna Polisetty is an Associate Professor at VIT University. Her research interests include Sustainability, Technology Adoption, Tourism, and Psychology. She has research contributions and publications in reputed journals and books. She is a prolific Case study developer and has build numerous case studies on a wide range of topics.

Vani Raghuvanshi is currently pursuing her MBA from SaiBalaji International Institute of Management Sciences in Pune. Known for her strong academic focus, she is actively engaged in developing her skills in management and leadership. As part of her MBA program, she is acquiring knowledge in various fields such as finance, marketing, operations, and human resources, which are integral to shaping her as a future business leader. Vani is also involved in extracurricular activities and student-led initiatives, which contribute to her well-rounded educational experience. Her participation in case study competitions, industry seminars, and management fests further strengthens her practical understanding of real-world business challenges. She shows a keen interest in applying theoretical knowledge to solve complex business problems, and her teamwork and leadership qualities have been well-recognized by her peers and professors. In addition, Vani is dedicated to personal and professional growth, continuously seeking opportunities to network with industry experts, engage in internships, and take part in hands-on projects that align with her career goals. Her determination, curiosity, and ability to adapt make her a promising management professional in the making.

Sakha Gangadhara Rama Rao is an accomplished academic and researcher with a Ph.D. in Marketing from Andhra University. With over a decade of teaching experience, he currently serves as an Assistant Professor at GITAM School of Business, specializing in financial accounting, financial management, and banking. Dr. Rao has authored two textbooks and over 20 research articles in prominent journals. His research interests include financial literacy, interactive marketing, and business processes. He has also presented numerous papers at national and international conferences.

Daniel Schutte is a professor in the School of Accounting Sciences at the North-West University, South Africa. Danie is a Chartered Accountant (South Africa) and holds a PhD in Accountancy obtained from the North-West University. Danie lectured financial accounting, management accounting and taxation and received the Institutional Teaching Excellence Award at the North-West University in 2007 and 2011. Danie was the Treasurer of the South African Accounting Association Central Region and he served on the education committee of the South African Institute of Professional Accountants. Danie provides supervision to students in accountancy, management accountancy, taxation and forensic accountancy. Eleven PhD and 32 master's students completed their studies under his supervision. In 2018, his PhD student received the South African Institute Professional Accounting Award for the best PhD in Accountancy. Danie presented 36 conference papers, and he is the author of 50 articles in peer-reviewed journals. Danie was the most productive researcher in the faculty in 2020 and the recipient of the best paper awards at the South African Accounting Association conference in 2018 and 2022. Danie is a visiting professor at Chandigarh University in India, a sectional editor at the South African Journal of Economic and Management Sciences and the chairperson of the School of Accounting Scientific Committee at the North-West University.

Vedantam Seetha Ram is an Associate Professor at Jain (Deemed-to-be University), Bangalore. With extensive experience in academia, he specializes in Accounting and Finance. His innovative teaching methods and dedication to research have earned him recognition in the academic community. His contributions to academic programs and student development make him a respected faculty at Jain Deemed to be University, in shaping the future leaders in business.

Zakir Shaikh is an Assistant Professor, Department of Accounting and Finance, School of Business Administration, Kingdom University, Bahrain. Prior to this, he worked more than 28 years in commercial and academic industry. He has published numerous articles in referred journals and presented many papers in various conferences, both local and abroad in the different area of Accounting, management and Islamic Banking and Finance. He has also participated in a variety of seminars, forums, workshops and international conferences. He obtained his Ph.D. (Islamic Banking and Finance) from India in 2018. His doctoral thesis explored the entrepreneurial phenomenon from an Islamic perspective and argued for profit and loss sharing (PLS) contracts as viable alternatives to conventional interest-based financing instruments. He holds Master degree in Commerce, Business Administration & Finance and Control. He is a member of AAA, Chartered Institute of Islamic Finance Professionals (CIIF), Malaysia; Indian Accounting Association; Orissa Commerce Association, India and associated with Accounting & Auditing Organization for Islamic Financial Institution (AAOIFI), Bahrain

Jayadatta Shreepad is an Assistant Professor at KLE's Institute of Management Studies and Research, brings over 14 years of teaching experience and expertise in Marketing, Strategic Management, HR, and General Management. He holds an MBA from Acharya Institute of Technology and two PG degrees in Commerce and English Literature from IGNOU. He has cleared the Karnataka State Eligibility Test (KSET) in Management and Commerce. Previously, he taught at Karnataka Folklore University and Anjuman Institute of Technology. With 139 research publications and 145 Google Scholar citations, he has contributed significantly to academia, including seven Scopus-indexed articles. Dr. Jayadatta has authored books on "Digital Marketing," "Work-Life Balance," and "The Convergence of Marketing and HR in Industry 4.0," and edited volumes on digital transformation and multidisciplinary research. He earned his Ph.D. in Digital Marketing and Rural Enterprise Marketing from Kousali Institute of Management Studies, Karnatak University.

Bivek Shrestha is a citizen of Nepal and is a business executive with Nepal Clearing House Limited, Bagmati, Kathmandu, Nepal. Though he is an industry person, he is interested in research in the technology domain that connects the academia. He has three years of industry experience during which he published three research papers apart from helping the company in developing new technology aided financial instruments service.

Animesh Singh is an accomplished academic with a robust background in commerce. He holds a B.Com and an M.Com (Pure), and has further demonstrated his expertise by qualifying for the UGC NET in Commerce. Dr. Singh completed his Ph.D. with a dissertation titled "A Comparative Study in the Role of Housing Finance Institutions in the Growth of Housing Sector in Uttar Pradesh." With 8 years of valuable teaching experience as an Assistant Professor in the MBA Department at USB, Chandigarh University, Mohali, Punjab, Dr. Singh has proven to be an effective educator and mentor. His dedication to advancing knowledge is evident through his significant contributions to research, including various research papers, book chapters, and patent publications. As a motivated researcher and dedicated academic, Dr. Singh continues to inspire and guide the next generation of commerce professionals, fostering an environment of academic excellence and continuous learning.

Anand Soni is a distinguished educator with a rich background in academia, research, and management. With over 19 years of teaching experience and a Ph.D. in Management, Dr. Soni has a profound expertise in areas such as business analytics, accounting, and management information systems. His dedication to student development and holistic societal progress is evident through his roles as a faculty member at Bahrain Polytechnic, where he not only teaches but also actively contributes to curriculum development and program reviews. A published author, patent holder, and active researcher.

Phani Kumar Tantravahi is a Senior Lecturer at the College of Economics and Business Administration, Muscat Branch, University of Technology and Applied Sciences, Sultanate of Oman. He holds a Ph.D. in Finance and has contributed significantly to the academic field through a substantial number of published articles and textbooks. Additionally, he has successfully completed a project funded by the University Grants Commission (UGC).

Manish Kumar Upadhyay is currently working as Assistant Professor in Rajiv Academy for Technology and Management, Mathura. He has completed his PhD. from Jiwaji University (NAAC Accredited A++ Grade), Gwalior (MP). His academic interests are business paradigms of Strategic management, Operation Management, and Research Methodology. He has published number of research papers in various reputed journals. Dr. Manish Kumar Upadhyay has also visited the academic institutions for imparting insights about emerging paradigms in education as well as motivating them for understanding the relevance of education in their career building.

Index

S

T

U

V

www.ingramcontent.com/pod-product-compliance
Lightning Source LLC
LaVergne TN
LVHW060403300926
849162LV00006B/1329